Weekend Breaks
from London

Edited and designed by
Time Out Guides Limited
Universal House
251 Tottenham Court Road
London W1T 7AB
Tel + 44 (0)20 7813 3000
Fax + 44 (0)20 7813 6001
guides@timeout.com
www.timeout.com

Editorial
Editor Andrew White
Deputy Editor Ros Sales
Copy Editor Nicholas Royle
Researcher Cathy Limb
Proofreader Marion Moisy
Indexer Jackie Brind

Editorial Director Peter Fiennes
Series Editor Sarah Guy
Guides Co-ordinator Jenny Noden

Design
Group Art Director John Oakey
Art Editor Mandy Martin
Senior Designer Scott Moore
Designers Benjamin de Lotz, Kate Vincent-Smith
Scanning/Imaging Dan Conway
Advertisement make-up Glen Impey
Picture Editor Kerri Miles
Deputy Picture Editor Olivia Duncan-Jones

Advertising
Group Commercial Director Lesley Gill
Sales Director/Sponsorship Mark Phillips
Sales Manager Alison Gray
Sales James Coulbault, Terina Rickit, Jason Trotman
Copy Controller Angie Davis
Advertising Assistant Sabrina Ancilleri

Administration
Publisher Tony Elliott
Managing Director Mike Hardwick
Group Financial Director Kevin Ellis
Group General Manager Nichola Coulthard
Marketing Director Christine Cort
Marketing Manager Mandy Martinez
Marketing Executives Sandie Tozer, Sammie Squire
Marketing Assisitant Clare Hojem
Accountants Sarah Bostock, Georgina Way
Production Manager Mark Lamond
Production Controller Samantha Furniss

**Chapters in this guide were researched and
written by...**
KENT North Kent Coast Derek Hammond; **Canterbury** Ruth Jarvis;
Sandwich to Sandgate Yves Baignères; **North Kent Downs**
Caroline Taverne; **Rye, Dungeness & Romney Marsh** Peter Fiennes;
The Heart of Kent Simon Radcliffe; **The Kent Weald** Nana Ocran.
SUSSEX & SURREY Battle & Hastings Amanda White; **The
Ashdown Forest** Sarah Jacobs; **Lewes & Around** Will Hodgkinson;
Brighton Ian Lawton; **South-west Sussex** Dorothy Boswell; **North
Surrey Downs** Janice Fuscoe; **The Three Counties** Sarah Guy.
HAMPSHIRE & ISLE OF WIGHT Around Newbury Andrew White;
Winchester & Around Matthew Ford; **The New Forest** Charlie
Godfrey-Faussett; **Isle of Wight** Dorothy Boswell; **Bournemouth
& Poole** Yves Baignères.
WILTSHIRE & BATH Salisbury & Stonehenge Patrick Marmion;
Bradford-on-Avon & Around Sophie Blacksell; **Bath** Angela
Jameson; **Chippenham to Avebury** Derek Hammond; **Malmesbury
& Around** Amanda White.
THE COTSWOLDS Cirencester to Gloucester Jonathan Cox;
Cheltenham to Stow Angela Jameson; **North Cotswolds** Sally
Davies; **Stratford & Warwick** Lesley McCave; **Oxford** Amanda White;
South Oxfordshire Patrick Butler; **Woodstock to Burford** Richard
Lines; **Chipping Norton to Banbury** Sally Davies.
THE CHILTERNS TO YORK Windsor & Around Derek Hammond;
North Chilterns Janice Fuscoe; **Hertfordshire** Melanie Dakin;
Rutland Will Fulford-Jones; **Lincoln** Sarah Guy; **York** Caroline Taverne.
EAST ANGLIA Cambridge Cath Phillips; **West Essex** Andrew
White; **Lower Stour Valley** Vanessa Raison; **Upper Stour Valley**
Ros Atkins; **Bury St Edmunds & Around** Will Fulford-Jones; **The
Suffolk Coast** Jonathan Cox.

Maps by JS Graphics, 17 Beadles Lane, Old Oxted, Surrey RH8 9JG
(01883 716387). Maps based on data supplied by Lovell Johns Ltd.

All photography by Jon Perugia except: page 19, 21, 24, 36 (top),
46, 92, 96, 114, 117, 135, 137, 141, 145, 156, 158(top), 160, 185, 187, 200,
211, 212 (right), 220, 225, 267, 269, 272, 275, 278, 292, 300, 302, 303 Paul
Avis; page 36 (bottom)Kent County Council; page 42 National Trust
Photographic Library/Eric Crichton; page 45 National Trust
Photographic Library/David Selman; page 50, 94 National Trust
Photographic Library/Ian Shaw; page 61 Gary Rogers Hamburg; page
64 National Trust Photographic Library/ Stephen Robson; page 94
National Trust Photographic Library/Andreas von Einsiedel; page 101
Anthony Hocker; page 170, 173, 306 Jonathan Cox; page 215 Nigel
Fisher; page 227 Joe Dougson; page 291National Trust Photographic
Library/Martin Charles
featured establishments 11, 16, 34, 35, 48, 51, 59, 67, 68, 104, 150,
161, 181, 189, 190, 197, 230, 236, 254, 259, 270, 276

Published by the Penguin Group
Penguin Books Ltd, 80 Strand, London, WC2R 0RL, England
Penguin Putnam Inc, 375 Hudson Street, New York, NY10014, USA
Penguin Books Australia Ltd, 250 Camberwell Road, Camberwell, Victoria 3124, Australia
Penguin Books Canada Ltd, 10 Alcorn Avenue, Toronto, Ontario, Canada M4V 3B2
Penguin Books (NZ) Ltd, 182-190 Wairau Road, Auckland 10, New Zealand

Penguin Books Ltd, Registered Offices: Harmondsworth, Middlesex, England

First published 1999
Second edition 2001
10 9 8 7 6 5 4 3 2 1

GNER

Tyne Bridge, Newcastle

Edinburgh Castle, Edinburgh

SEND YOURSELF ON A SHORT BREAK WITH GNER TRAINS

Contents

Page 4: Make the most of your weekend with our money-saving offers.

Introduction

Nowadays, as our horizons have expanded and travel has become quicker and cheaper, holidays abroad seem to be the norm. We fly off to sample the authentic food, laze in the burning sun, admire the spectacular settings and marvel at the cultural relics that earn these faraway parts such golden reputations. In fact, we all have some corner of a foreign field that is forever, well, foreign. Meanwhile, millions cross continents and oceans to come and visit these diminutive islands, to marvel at our very own spectacular settings and cultural relics, even perhaps sample our cuisine. This cultural exchange is unquestionably healthy, and yet it's amazing how little most of us know about our own country. Of course, there are patches we're familiar with, as we rush from home to favourite country boozer to relatives in town to friends by the sea, but what about all the other bits?

It's also true that most of us like to get away for the weekend (or at least dream of doing so) several times a year, but little has been published to help the weekend breaker make those difficult where-to-stay, what-to-see decisions. Those guides that are available tend to cover too wide an area (usually the whole country) and, thus, supply only sketchy information. In order to provide as full a coverage as possible, we've deliberately restricted the scope of this book to the south-east portion of England (although, with places such as Bath and York included, this is a very liberal definition).

The basic rationale behind choosing which areas to include and which to exclude is that they should be within two hours' rail or road travel from the capital. This is something of an elastic criterion, too – if you live in Epping, say, a trip up to the Stour Valley will obviously be quicker than it would be, say, from Streatham. The presence of York, Lincoln and Rutland in this book, however, is testament to the speed of the rail links to these places. Furthermore, while the breaks featured here may radiate out from London, this is by no means a book aimed only at Londoners.

For us, one of the most rewarding aspects of putting this guide together has been to learn just how much great stuff to see and do there is out there, and just how many first-rate restaurants and drinking holes are awaiting our custom. It has inspired us to want to get away and explore; we hope it'll do the same for you.

Andrew White

Legend for Town Maps

	Place of interest		Restricted road
	College or University	WC	Toilet with disabled access
	Station	WC	Toilet without disabled access
	Park	P	Car park
		✛	Church

How the book is arranged

For ease of use, we've split the guide into seven chapters, roughly corresponding to county boundaries. But, as the breaks we feature don't conveniently follow county lines, this has produced a number of anomalies. For instance, in the 'Hampshire & Isle of Wight' section, we're well aware that Newbury and Bournemouth aren't in either of these counties, but felt that such inconsistencies were preferable to using unwieldy chapter names such as 'Hampshire, West Berkshire, Dorset & the Isle of Wight'.

Accommodation rates and booking

Unless otherwise stated, breakfast is included in room prices. Where breakfast is extra, we indicate this and give prices: 'Eng' for a full English breakfast, 'cont' for a continental breakfast.

Booking accommodation in advance is always recommended; most of the places we feature in this book are very popular, and at least several weeks' (and often months') notice is required, particularly in peak season. Also, bear in mind that many establishments close for a couple of weeks during the year, so it is always risky to turn up without phoning first. If you are unable to find a room in any of the places we feature, most Tourist Information Centres we list should be able to help you find somewhere to rest your head.

Things to check when booking

We have attempted to find out most of the following accommodation information for you, but always double-check if you don't want the risk of an unwelcome surprise.

Children and dogs – It's remarkable the number of places that treat kids and pets as one and the same. We have shown where there is an age restriction on children, and indicated the places that are happy to take dogs.

Maps and directions – The maps in this book are intended (with the exception of the town plans) for general orientation and you will need

a road atlas or other detailed map to find your way around. We have included instructions of how to find your way to the hotels, guesthouses and B&B establishments we list, unless their location needs no explanation.

Minimum stay – Some hotels and B&Bs insist on a minimum stay of two nights or more (usually over a Friday and Saturday).

No-smoking policies – Many places (hotels less so than B&Bs) have strict no-smoking policies in their bedrooms and/or throughout the building.

Wedding parties – Be warned that some of the larger hotels are often taken over by wedding parties at weekends.

Sponsors and advertisers

We would like to thank our sponsor MasterCard for their involvement in this book. We would also like to thank the advertisers. However, we stress that they have no control over editorial content. No establishment has been included because it has advertised, and no payment of any kind has influenced any review. The opinions given in this book are those of *Time Out* writers and entirely impartial.

Listings

All the listings information was fully checked and correct at the time of going to press, but owners and managers can change their arrangements at any time, and prices do rise. Therefore, it is always best to check opening times, admission fees and other details before you set off. While every effort and care has been made to ensure the accuracy of the information contained in this book, the publishers cannot accept responsibility for any errors it may contain.

Credit cards

In the 'Where to stay' and 'Where to eat & drink' sections, the following abbreviations have been used – **AmEx**: American Express; **DC**: Diners Club; **MC**: MasterCard; **V**: Visa.

Let us know what you think

We hope you enjoy this book and welcome any comments or suggestions you might have. A reader's reply card is included at the back of the book. We will be entering returned cards in a draw; the winner will receive ten guides from our international city guides series. We'll also give free copies of the next edition of this book to those who send the most helpful replies.

Special offers

To make your weekend break even more of a treat, we've once again exclusively negotiated some great offers for our readers. All the hotels participating in these offers are cross-referenced in the guide and are signposted with the **Offer** symbol.

In addition, many hotels and some B&Bs offer regular special weekend package breaks, which we have indicated in our listings as 'Special Breaks'. It's well worth calling the hotel to see if any further offers are available.

As always, your comments are of great help to us. Help us to continue creating great guides by filling in our readers' survey card at the back of this guide. The first name drawn at random will win a set of ten city guides from our series, and the best suggestions win a copy of the next updated edition of *Weekend Breaks from London*.

Kent

Jarvis Marina Hotel
Ramsgate (01843 588276). *See page 14.*
Offer: £75 (normally £105).
Conditions: Minimum two nights.
Based on two sharing.
Valid until: Oct 2003.

Bishopsdale Oast
Biddenden (01580 291027). *See page 44.*
Offer: From £42 (normal price from £60) per night plus a free bottle of house wine with the £22.50 four-course dinner (normal price £89 per night).
Conditions: Minimum two nights.
Exclusions: Christmas and New Year; 1 May-31 Aug.
Valid until: Oct 2003.

Bishopsdale Oast

Sussex

The Griffin Inn,
Fletching, nr Uckfield (01825 722890). *See page 67.*
Offer: Three nights for the price of two. From £170 (with bath/shower) for three nights (normal price £255).
Conditions: Lowest rate applies as free night.
Exclusions: Christmas and New Year.
Valid until: Oct 2003.

Griffin Inn

Hampshire

Westover Hall
Milford on Sea (01590 643044). *See page 119.*
Offer: £30 off normal dinner, bed and breakfast rate per night when staying any two consecutive nights for two sharing (normal price £155-£185).
Conditions: Excludes Saturday nights.
Exclusions: Christmas and New Year.
Valid until: Oct 2003.

Westover Hall

Seaview Hotel

Isle of Wight

Seaview Hotel
Isle of Wight (01983 612711). *See page 125.*
Offer: Winter weekends only. Three nights for
               the price of two.
Conditions: Fri, Sat & Sun nights only.
Exclusions: Christmas and New Year; 16 Mar-
               30 Sept.
Valid until: Oct 2003.

Priory Bay
Isle of Wight (01983 613146). *See page 125.*
Offer: Three nights for the price of two.
Conditions: Based on two sharing. Quote *Time Out*
               offer on booking. Bed and breakfast only
Exclusions: Bank Holidays; 1 July-31 Aug.
Valid until: Oct 2003.

Wiltshire & Bath

Rudloe Hall
Rudloe (01225 810555). *See page 160.*
Offer: Two-day leisure break from £65pp/pn
               including dinner, bed and breakfast
               (normal price £89pp/pn B&B only).
               Jan/Feb/Mar offer – book three nights
               dinner, bed and breakfast and get a fourth
               night bed and breakfast free (dinner on the
               fourth night must be taken).
Conditions: Quote *Time Out* offer on booking.
               Based on two sharing.
Exclusions: Valentine's Day, Easter, Christmas and
               New Year.
Valid until: Oct 2003.

Overview

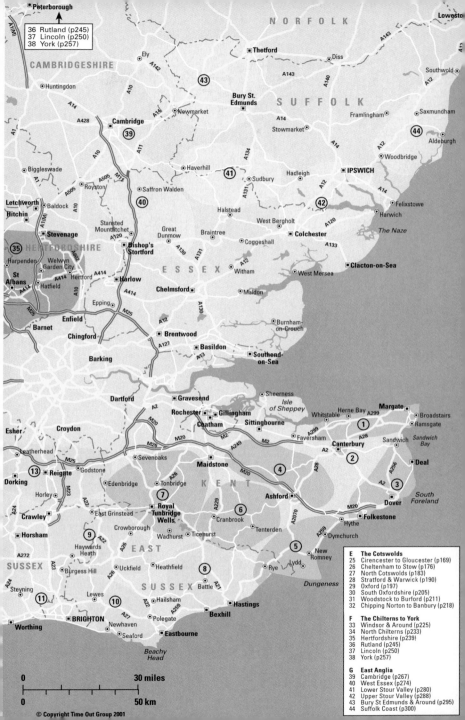

North Kent Coast

We do like to be beside the seaside.

Few regions within weekend-break range of London can offer such a startling variety of moods as this northern stretch of Kent coast, which ends at the (once upon a time) Isle of Thanet to the east. In Roman times the isle was separated from the mainland by the Wantsum Channel – then up to a mile across at its widest points – before the odd billion tons of silt washed on to the scene, reducing it to a six-foot drainage ditch that's easy to miss as you speed past in the car. Thanet is now home to the seaside resorts of Margate, Broadstairs and Ramsgate. The 26 miles or so of **Thanet Coastal Path** are one of the area's prime attractions, fabulous for walking under white cliffs, arches and stacks to quiet coves. Or just crash out behind a windbreak at one of the popular sandy beaches along its route.

Heading Londonward back along the North Kent coast leads to **Reculver**, the site of a Roman fort that once guarded the northern entrance to the Wantsum, and of the Reculver Towers, visible for miles around. Beyond quiet **Herne Bay** lies **Whitstable**, a beneficiary of the arrival of the silt, for along with it came the town's stock-in-trade of oysters (*see p14*, **'O Oysters, come and walk with us!'**). Inland from all this coastline is some gorgeous, unspoiled countryside: attractions include the famous **Wantsum Walk**, **St Augustine's Trail**, and some deeply fulfilling village pubs.

By train from London

Trains run from **Victoria** to **Ramsgate** about every 20-30mins, and take **1hr 50mins**. Most of these stop at **Whitstable**, **Margate** and **Broadstairs** on the way. Info: www.connex.co.uk.

Contemplate – as Peter Cushing did before you – the view from **Whitstable** seafront.

It's in this low-lying area that farmers have regularly unearthed Roman boats buried in their fields, now miles from the sea.

'Margate made me'

Margate has its place in history as Britain's first ever seaside resort. Back in the 1730s, Margate chalked up the first use of a beach deck-chair, the first-ever donkey rides and seaside boarding houses. Benjamin Beale, a local man, revolutionised bathing with his patented modesty hood, which allowed naked therapeutic paddling from the back of a bathing machine. Throughout the Georgian and Victorian eras and up until the 1960s, boatloads of cockneys used to pour down the Thames, offloading excitedly on Margate Pier (another famous first, sadly hit by storms in 1978 and finally demolished a couple of years ago).

Then came the Spanish tourist trade. Nowadays, a dwindling number of those holidaymakers' descendants flock here for the traditional summer delights of the beach, the theatre and the seafront Strip. But Margate still offers great value for a few hours' aimless mooching. Enjoy Grab City amusements, with its synthesised barrel-organ jingles; the white-knuckle thrills of Dreamland; the mixed aromas of seaweed from the harbour, hot doughnuts and pungent fish 'n' chips. Here, a pound in a slot will buy you an adults-only key-ring, a Lucky Lady charm or a pair of naughty undies – 'knickers for a nicker, pouches for a pound'. Yet away from the weak neon temptations of the seafront, parts of the town are visibly poor, and the place has something of the fractured air of a frontier town. 'Margate made me what I am,' declared artist Tracey Emin. But the town's most illustrious daughter won't be bringing charges… 'Because to me, Margate is beautiful, romantic, charismatic, sad, eccentric and screwed up.' Buster Bloodvessel, rotund skinhead frontman with ska stompers Bad Manners, opened a guesthouse here called Fatty Towers, for punters with a taste for 'gutbuster' breakfasts. It closed down, while many Regency hotels in the Cliftonville area are only kept open to shelter the town's newest residents, asylum seekers.

The town's surprise prize is hidden away behind a shell shop above the atmospheric yet dilapidated Old Town and Market Place. Dismally undersold, the **Shell Grotto** is in fact a 150-foot temple hewn from solid chalk by the followers of a forgotten Eurasian nature cult somewhere between 2,000 and 3,000 years ago. Millions of shells decorate this national site that's almost as old as Stonehenge – adding some historical perspective to the town's current wave of seekers from the east.

What the Dickens

Broadstairs is the maiden aunt of Thanet resorts, haughtily disapproving of its noisy neighbours. 'Our English Watering Place' is how Charles Dickens described his favourite seaside town, and precious little has changed since – except for the annual Dickens Festival (01843 865265/www.broadstairs.gov.uk) and the steady theming of place names to the likes of Dickens Walk, Dickens' Pantry, The Old Curiosity Shop, Bill Sykes' Market, the Barnaby Rudge pub, Dodger's and Quilp's restaurants, and so on, ad infinitum. For a weekend break to Thanet, Broadstairs represents the best bet for a base: there's more of a mix of accommodation, plus a decent selection of restaurants and pubs; and the sweep of dramatic coast really takes some beating. There's an inescapable retro ambience to the place, but that's no bad thing. Check out the tiny, pebble-dashed Windsor Cinema under the harbour's York Gate, and the proliferation of Formica 'milk bars', which disappeared from the rest of Britain 40 years ago. Take a step back in time along the blooming clifftop Prom, around the seven beautiful bays, and back to the bandstand in time for tea. And if you're here for Folk Week (second week of August; 01843 604080), you'll see the streets packed with jostling morris dancers, and the whole town brought to life with music, song and dance.

While **Ramsgate**, a couple of miles south, offers many of the old-style seaside attractions – a long, sandy beach sheltered by towering cliffs, a clifftop model village and putting green – it doesn't rely excessively on the tourist dollar. OK, so the prime crowd-puller of Pegwell Bay, to the west, is a Viking longboat that has somehow survived the onslaught of small children since 1949, but Ramsgate is primarily a working town, with a major continental ferry terminal and a teeming Royal Harbour. Climbing out of the harbour to the west, ramps scale the impressive brick-vaulted cliffs topped by the stately Victorian Yacht Club; to the east, Madeira Walk twists upward through a slalom of landscaped rock walls and waterfalls to the clifftop Wellington Terrace, which looks almost as impressive as Bath's Royal Crescent on the postcards, but is actually becoming rather tatty. For the visitor, there's little to see or do beyond the immediate vicinity of the seafront, shopping centre and harbour; but as is the case with the other Thanet towns, there's more than enough to happily fill a summer's day.

Whitstable's ramshackle seafront is superb – Peter Cushing was a great fan, as a viewpoint plaque attests – cluttered with toy cottages, fishermen's huts and sailmakers. Built well below the level of high spring tides, the town has survived its inevitable historical flooding tragedies and offshore pollution, and retains an atmosphere of gentle bohemianism.

What to see & do

Tourist Information Centres
6B High Street, Broadstairs, CT10 1LH (01843 862242/www.tourism.thanet.gov.uk). **Open** 9.15am-12.15pm, 1-4.45pm Mon-Fri; 10am-12.15pm, 1-4.45pm Sat, Sun.

22 High Street, Margate, CT9 1DS (01843 220241/www.tourism.thanet.gov.uk). **Open** 9.15am-1pm, 1.45-4.45pm Mon-Fri; 10am-1pm, 1.45-4.45pm Sat, Sun.

17 Albert Court, York Street, Ramsgate, CT11 9DN (01843 583333/www.tourism.thanet.gov.uk). **Open** 9.30am-4.30pm daily.

7 Oxford Street, Whitstable, CT5 1DB (01227 275482/www.canterbury.co.uk). **Open** *Sept-June* 10am-4pm Mon-Sat. *July, Aug* 10am-5pm Mon-Sat.

Bleak House
Fort Road, Broadstairs (01843 862224). **Open** 10am-6pm daily. **Admission** £3; £2-£2.60 concessions.
A museum devoted partly to Dickens, and also to maritime matters and smuggling, housed in the novelist's favourite holiday home, which dominates the harbour. The view across Viking Bay from Dickens' authentically decked-out study is quite inspirational.

Clock House Maritime Museum
Pier Yard, Royal Harbour, Ramsgate (01843 587765/www.ekmt.fsnet.co.uk). **Open** *Apr-Oct* 10am-5pm Tue-Sun. *Nov-Mar* 10am-4.30pm Tue-Fri. Last entry 30mins before closing. **Admission** £1.50; 75p concessions.
This local museum includes a bizarre section on the cricket team that plays matches out at sea on the deadly, shifting Camber Sands.

Dickens' House Museum
2 Victoria Parade, Broadstairs (01843 861232). **Open** *Apr-mid* Oct 2-5pm daily. Closed Oct-Mar. **Admission** £2; 50p-£1 concessions.
Another seafront Dickens haunt with plenty of letters and memorabilia, costume exhibits and Victoriana.

Dreamland Fun Park
Belgrave Road, Margate (01843 227011). **Open** *Mar-June, Sept* 11am-5pm daily. *July, Aug* 11am-10pm daily. Closed Oct-Feb. **Admission** free. **Credit** *rides* MC, V.
The largest seaside leisure complex in southern England features a rollercoaster from 1863, a new Wild Mouse coaster, water rides, dodgems, waltzers and amusements.

Margate Caves
1 Northdown Road, Cliftonville (01843 220139). **Open** *Easter-June, Sept, Oct* 10am-4pm daily. *July, Aug, bank hols* 10am-5pm daily. Closed Nov-Easter. **Admission** £1.80; 90p concessions.
Thousand-year-old man-made chalk caverns, variously used as a refuge from invaders, a secret church, a prison and a smugglers' store.

Margate Museum
The Old Town Hall, Market Square, Margate (01843 231213). **Open** *Apr-Sept* 10am-5pm daily. *Oct-Mar* 9.30am-4.30pm daily. Last entry 1hr before closing. **Admission** £1; 50p concessions.
An agreeable wander through Margate's back pages, housed in the historically multi-purpose old town hall – it was once a police station and courthouse.

Quex House & Gardens/ Powell-Cotton Museum
Quex Park, Birchington (01843 842168/www.powell-cottonmuseum.co.uk). **Open** *Apr-Oct* 11am-5pm Tue-Thur, Sun, bank hols. *Nov, Dec, Mar* 11am-4pm Sun. **Admission** £4; £3 concessions. *Gardens only* £1; 50p concessions.
A superb furnished Regency house, set in 17 acres of gardens and woodland. The museum includes oriental porcelain, African and Asian fine arts and 500 animal dioramas courtesy of the Victorian explorer-naturalist-ethnographer Major PHG Powell-Cotton.

Ramsgate Motor Museum
West Cliff Hall, The Paragon, Ramsgate (01843 581948). **Open** *Easter-Sept* 10.30am-5.30pm daily. Closed Oct-Easter. **Admission** £3; £1-£2.50 concessions.
A subterranean clifftop museum packed with a huge, astonishing array of vintage cars and motorcycles, all entertainingly presented in time-machine dioramas.

Hold tight at Margate's **Dreamland Fun Park**.

There's everything from a 1900 Benz to a Sinclair C5, including bizarre evolutionary dead-ends such as the bubble-car, and brilliantly obscure scooters dating from long before Vespas and Lambrettas tied up the market.

Sarre Windmill & Animal Farm

Canterbury Road, off A253, Sarre (01843 847573). **Open** 10am-5pm daily. **Admission** £2; £1 concessions.

A rare fully-functioning Edwardian windmill, which features licensed tearooms with home-made goodies from the mill's own bakery.

Shell Grotto

Grotto Hill, off Northdown Road, Margate (01843 220008/www.8thwonder.co.uk). **Open** *Easter-Oct* 10am-5pm Mon-Fri; 10am-4pm Sat, Sun. Closed Nov-Easter. **Admission** £2; £1 concessions.

The chalk walls of this hand-hewn temple are embellished with intricate shell mosaics in soot-blackened yellow, pink and blue: a three-pointed star; ram's horns and snakes; phallic icons; the sun, the moon and stars. The mysteries of this 150-foot subterranean temple are manifold and apparently insoluble. No one can accurately identify the worshippers who spent long years in its sacred decoration, and Victorian oil-lamp deposits ruin any chance of accurate carbon-dating. The discovery of turtle bones behind the main altar has recently led some experts to the opinion held by HG Wells that the temple is nearly 3,000 years old. A truly major national site – Stonehenge was only completed around 1,500 BC – and not even subject to basic preservation guidelines.

Whitstable Museum & Gallery

5A Oxford Street, Whitstable (01227 276998/ www.whitstable-museum.co.uk). **Open** *Jan-June, Sept-Dec* 10am-4pm Mon-Sat. *July, Aug* 10am-4pm Mon-Sat; 1-4pm Sun. **Admission** free.

Some impressive exhibitions from the local arty set, plus all you need to know about Whitstable's Victorian seafront rollerskating rink.

Where to stay

There's absolutely no problem finding an inexpensive family B&B or small hotel in any of the towns of Thanet and the North Kent Coast – the Esplanade at Broadstairs should prove a particularly happy hunting ground, and is a recommended base for 'doing' the area. These selections highlight some of the more unusual options.

Crown Inn

Ramsgate Road, Sarre, CT11 0LF (01843 847808/ fax 01843 847914). **Rates** £55 single occupancy; £75 double/twin; £110 four-poster; £90-£110 family room. Special breaks. **Rooms** (all en suite) 5 double; 2 twin; 1 four-poster; 3 family. **Credit** AmEx, MC, V.

The word 'quaint' could have been coined to describe the Crown halfway house on the Canterbury-Thanet road, a living antique with its four-poster luxury, snug restaurant and bar, and secret cherry brandy recipe (don't ask). Dating back to 1492 (when Sarre, long since landlocked, was a Cinque Port), the inn has a lengthy celebrity guest list including the ubiquitous Charles Dickens, as well as Douglas Fairbanks, Lloyd George, Mary Pickford... and the mob-capped ghost in Room 14. One room is specially adapted for disabled guests. Children and dogs welcome.

Sarre is 7 miles NE of Canterbury on A28 towards Margate. Crown Inn is next to mini-roundabout on right.

Fishermen's Huts

On the seafront near the harbour, Whitstable (01227 280280/fax 01227 280257/www.oysterfishery.co.uk). **Rates** £75-£115 two-person hut; £85-£125 four-person hut. Special breaks. **Rooms** (all en suite) 1 two-person hut; 5 four-person huts. **Credit** AmEx, DC, MC, V.

Renovated from a state of dilapidation six years ago, these original 1860s fishermen's net-sheds are perfect for a summer break, full of air and atmosphere, opening directly on to the beach. They're all en suite, furnished comfortably in minimalist fashion, with a sofabed, director's chairs and a plain table (laden with cups, a kettle, tea and fresh coffee) in a bright yellow downstairs room, and a plain pine bed awaiting up a ladder-like flight of stairs. The huts were brought to life by Barry Green and family, who also own the Whitstable Oyster Fishery Company (*see p16*). Prices include a full English or continental breakfast served in the Hotel Continental restaurant (*see below*). In fact, the only problem you're likely to come across is that the huts get booked up well in advance. Children welcome. All huts are no-smoking.

On A290 into Whitstable; first left before harbour.

Hanson Hotel

41 Belvedere Road, Broadstairs, CT10 1PF (01843 868936). **Rates** £20-£25 per person. **Rooms** 2 single; 2 twin (1 en suite); 3 double (2 en suite); 2 family (1 en suite, 1 shower). **No credit cards.**

A small, friendly hotel nestling behind Virginia creeper in a Georgian mansion block once owned by Nelson's contemporary and 'hero of a hundred battles', Admiral Sutherland. Good honest breakfasts are included in the price of a room, and there's the bonus of an outrageously cosy basement bar, a real swirly carpet movie-set flash-back to 1974. Children and dogs welcome.

Follow High Street from Broadstairs station towards seafront; Belvedere Road is on right.

Hotel Continental

29 Beach Walk, Whitstable, CT5 2BP (01227 280280/fax 01227 280257/www.oysterfishery.co.uk). **Rates** £45-£65 single occupancy; £65-£125 double; £75-£115 family room. **Rooms** (all en suite) 21 double; 2 family. **Credit** AmEx, DC, MC, V.

This sunny yellow art deco gem is tucked away up a cul-de-sac on the sea wall on the far side of Whitstable's industrious little harbour. Once again, it's part of the local Whitstable Oyster Fishery Company empire (*see p16*), so rest assured the food at the stylishly split-level Continental Restaurant (open to non-residents) is of top quality. There are bench seats right down on the beach, a superb spot for a tipple as the dark closes in around a warm summer's evening. Residents can then move indoors and drink till late before retiring to an angular, airy bedroom – or even a cool balcony – for a nightcap. And if you spend a little extra, you can wake up to a sea view. Children welcome. All bedrooms no-smoking.

On the Blean Road (A290); past swimming pool; hotel is first left after the Waterfront Club.

Jarvis Marina Hotel

*Harbour Parade, Ramsgate, CT11 8LZ
(01843 588276/fax 01843 586866/
www.jarvis.co.uk).* **Rates** £37.50-£90 single;
£60-£105 double/twin; £60-£105 family; £130
mini-suite. Special breaks. **Rooms** (all en suite)
4 single; 46 double/twin; 7 family; 1 mini-suite.
Credit AmEx, DC, MC, V.

This is a large, ultra-modern brick affair overlooking the
marina. It may be the priciest hotel on the Isle of Thanet,
but you get what you pay for in terms of the range of
amenities available, including an indoor heated pool,
sauna, solarium and spa. Clean, smart rooms are all en
suite, with satellite TV. Hobson's Restaurant is open to
non-guests, and the Club Bar enjoys great views over the
busy harbour. Children and dogs welcome. No-smoking
rooms available.

*A2/M2 to Ramsgate, which turns into A299; follow signs to
Ramsgate; then signs to Motor Museum; follow the hill
down; hotel is at the bottom, opposite the harbour.*

Royal Albion Hotel

*Albion Street, Broadstairs, CT10 1AN (01843
868071/fax 01843 861509/www.albion-bstairs.
demon.co.uk).* **Rates** £57-£63 single; £75-£83

double; £73 family room. Breakfast £7.95 (Eng); £5
(cont). Special breaks. **Rooms** (all en suite) 2 single;
14 double/twin; 2 family. **Credit** AmEx, DC, MC, V.

The only AA stars in Thanet are on offer at the Royal
Albion, a weighty stucco pile with unbeatable views over
Viking Bay – as enjoyed by Charles Dickens when he
should have been getting on with finishing *Nicholas
Nickleby*. The rooms are extremely comfortable and the
friendly staff are willing to act as a childminding service
while parents grab a tardy snifter in the hotel bar. The
Marchesi restaurant, the sister establishment a couple of
doors down on Albion Street, is recommended for dinner
(*see p16*). Children welcome. No-smoking rooms available.
*On corner of High Street opposite seafront in Broadstairs
town centre.*

Where to eat & drink

Located precariously close to the incoming
waves at Whitstable, the **Old Neptune** takes
the idea of a seaside pub to the absolute limit.
Take your pint outside in summer and you're
in immediate danger of getting your feet wet.

'O Oysters, come and walk with us!'

The celebrated Whitstable native oyster
is the gourmet world's gastropod of
choice. Unique in flavour, it has exerted a
pervasive influence on the Kentish coastal
town from Roman times, its message
reaching out via the pages of Charles
Dickens and Mrs Beaton. Today, there's
an agreeably modest buzz of tourist
interest about Whitstable's history, all tied
up with its ideally warm and silty coastal
waters – and those waters' biggest,
tastiest, most succulent inhabitants.

A hundred years ago the Whitstable
shoreline was packed with a continuous
line of fishermen's huts, stores and
shipyards that built the local smacks and
yawls in which oystermen gathered their
catch. The harbour, opened in 1832,
dealt in coal as well as seafood, and
the Crab and Winkle Line that linked
Whitstable's port and resort to Canterbury
was the first regular steam passenger
railway in the world.

Whitstable isn't quite as hectic today,
but it's still a pearl for visitors. Walking
along the seafront, treading on the millions
of oyster shells shucked up and spat out
by the harbour businesses, you can still
see rows of fishermen's huts (pictured,
opposite), converted only in part to holiday
accommodation. Up on the boardwalks of

the tight little harbour, have a stroll and a
nose into the oystermen's puttering boats
and galvanised cages, and hang around for
a boatful of slithering sealife to be landed.

Plenty of the old yawls are still working
local waters and are raced in an annual
regatta, part of the week-long Whitstable
Oyster Festival at the end of July. At this
time, a pre-season catch of oysters is
paraded around the town by locals doing
the Fish Slapping Dance – a kind of
maritime morris dance with seaweed and
shell costumes, traditional songs and
(inevitably) much fish slapping.

It takes five years for an oyster to reach
maturity, and conservation and breeding
seasons partly dictate the strict oyster
season of September through to the end

The best pubs in Margate are to be found around the Market Square area, also home to the **Wig & Pen Thai** and **Clementine's**, with its fine game and seafood specials. Getting into the Margate spirit, visit **Ye Olde Humbug & Honeycombe Shoppe** on Marine Drive Parade for a loose quarter of all those sweeties you haven't even thought of since Kojak sucked his last lolly.

In Broadstairs, the **Dolphin** pub on Albion Street features live music most nights; **Neptune's Hall** on Harbour Street opposite serves a super pint of Shepherd Neame, the premium North Kent bitter. The **Charles Dickens** on the clifftop prom offers the best sea views, while foodies won't be let down at **Osteria Pizzeria Posillipo** (14 Albion Street; 01843 601133).

In Ramsgate, the **Queen's Head** on Harbour Parade has a marvellous Victorian tile-and-sculpted-brick façade, a cosy period bar and boules out back. **Harvey's Crab & Oyster**

House (Harbour Parade; 01843 591110) is a popular pub with harbour views from the first-floor restaurant.

The best spot for a coffee and a snack, though, is undoubtedly the **Eagle** café, perched out on the end of the East Pier, with amazing views of the sea, the town and the puttering maritime traffic.

Broadstairs Tandoori
41 Albion Street, Broadstairs (01843 865653). **Food served** noon-2pm, 6-10pm Mon-Thur, Sun; noon-2pm, 6-10.30pm Fri, Sat. **Credit** AmEx, DC, MC, V.
Better-than-average pre-balti cuisine, deserving of a mention for its tag-line alone: 'the only Gurkha restaurant in Kent'. After a couple of days of seafood specialities, it's quite a relief to tuck into the BT's exemplary tandoori starters and a seriously hardcore garlic nan. A slight question-mark hung over a dubious-sounding Nepalese speciality, tandoori khasi (£5.30) and the seemingly 'easy-cook' pilau rice; but all doubts were eventually washed away by a pint of Cobra and the lamb pasanda (£5.90).

of April; it's true that they taste nowhere near as good in the off-season. Drop into the oldest building on the harbour and learn more at the **Oyster & Fishery Exhibition**, where kids even get to fumble with the jet-propelled little blighters. For more on oysters, pioneer divers, Stephenson's railway and local shipbuilding, the **Whitstable Museum** on Oxford Street (*see p13*) is a very good bet.

For adults, too, the oyster experience is ultimately best enjoyed hands-on. When it comes to dining out on local produce, the **Whitstable Oyster Fishery Company** (*see*

p16) is undeniably the upscale option; but **Wheeler's Oyster Bar** remains Whitstable's oldest oyster bar, as unpretentious as when it was founded in the mid-19th century by Richard 'Leggy' Wheeler.

Oyster & Fishery Exhibition
East Quay, The Harbour, Whitstable (01227 276998). **Open** phone for details.

Wheeler's Oyster Bar
8 High Street, Whitstable (01227 273311). **Open** 10.30am-9pm Mon, Tue; 10.15am-9pm Thur; 10.15am-9.30pm Fri; 10am-10pm Sat; 11.30am-9pm Sun.

Relax at the **Royal Albion Hotel**. *See p14.*

Dove Inn

Plum Pudding Lane, Dargate (01227 751360).
Food served noon-2pm, 7-9pm Tue-Sat; noon-2pm
Sun. **Credit** MC, V.
Situated in a beautifully traditional Kentish village close
to the main London-Thanet route (A299 exit west of
Whitstable), the Dove Inn is a true gastropub. Period
floorboarding, wood-panelled walls and a large open fire
set the tone; the menu may be innovative and imaginative but it's solidly grounded and in little need of gimmickry. Starters (£4-£8) range from superbly presented
pork rillettes with tomato and apple chutney to a deli-
ciously simple spread of local herring grilled to perfec-
tion with olive oil. Main courses (£10-£17) can be from
the carte or selected from daily specials – such as a noteworthy monkfish with sorrel, oysters and asparagus
with potato pea purée. Shepherd Neame ales are on tap,
although there's also a respectable, well-priced wine list.
Booking is essential.

Gate Inn

Marshside, Chislet (01227 860498). **Food served**
11am-2pm, 6-9pm Mon-Sat; noon-2pm, 7-9pm Sun.
No credit cards.
An idyllic country boozer secreted deep amid the
marshes and high-banked lanes inland from Herne Bay.
Bearded, lovably eccentric landlord Chris Smith makes
his own Dragon's Breath mustard, presides over a celebrated specials board and keeps a mean pint of Shepherd
Neame. In a textbook country pub garden, streams
tinkle into a dreamy pond while geese, ducks and doves
scrap for crumbs. Hostelry heaven.

Harbour Indian Cuisine

6-8 Westcliff Arcade, Ramsgate (01843 580290).
Food served noon-3pm, 6-10.45pm Mon-Thur, Sun;
noon-3pm, 6-11.45pm Fri, Sat. **Set meals** £22.50
for 2, 2 courses. **Credit** MC, V.
This large, smart Indian restaurant perched halfway
up the brick-vaulted cliffs on the town's western front
enjoys a gull's-eye view down over the marina. There
are few surprises on the menu, but ingredients are fresh,
spicing is spot-on, and when what you really fancy is
a succulent burnt-edged tandoori chicken or shaslik
kebab, there's nothing in the whole of Ramsgate to
beat it. Next door along the cliff is the rather more
intimate and homey Thai option of Noknoi's Thai Diner
(01843 852750).

Marchesi's Restaurant

*16-18 Albion Street, Broadstairs (01843 862481/
www.marchesi.co.uk).* **Food served** noon-2pm, 6.30-
9.30pm Tue-Sat; noon-2pm Sun. **Set lunch** £11.50

2 courses; £13.50 3 courses. **Set dinner** £17 2
courses; £19.50 3 courses. **Credit** AmEx, MC, V.
Owned and run by the same Swiss family for 111 years
– or since Charles Dickens's day, as they're most likely
to say in these parts. There's an agreeable old-school feel
to the restaurant and the solid-quality French-English
fare is especially recommended on a balmy summer
evening when it's possible to sit out back on the terrace
overlooking Pegwell Bay. Duck and prune pâté with
muscat jelly (£4.75) is an impressive starter; mains
range from classics such as rack of lamb and peppered
steak in creamy sauces to a more adventurous poached
fillet of monkfish with spinach, in saffron and orange
sauce (£12.95). *See also p14.*

Pearson's

Horsebridge, Whitstable (01227 272005). **Food
served** noon-2.30pm, 6.30-10pm Mon-Sat; noon-
10pm Sun. **Credit** MC, V.
Situated on the seafront at Whitstable, right next door
to the Oyster Fishery Company (*see below*), Pearson's
offers a more pubbish – though still good-quality – take
on local seafood. This 'Original Crab & Oyster House'
(which lays claim to smuggling credentials) belies its
exterior appearance of a fairly unremarkable hostelry.
Get inside out of the wind on a blustery night into the
cosy glow of the bar and tuck into a Pearson's Paradise
– a three-tier trawlerful of lobster, crab, oysters, prawns,
mussels, langoustines and clams.

Tartar Frigate

Harbour Street, Broadstairs (01843 862013).
Food served noon-2pm, 7-9.30pm Mon-Sat;
noon-4pm Sun. **Set lunch** (Sun) £11.95 4 courses.
Credit AmEx, MC, V.
This highly rated Mediterranean-tinged fish restaurant
overlooks Viking Bay. The floral arches, cutesy dolls
and hundreds of Jeff Koons-ish ornaments may not be
to everybody's taste; the exemplary mozzarella skate
and pan-fried monkfish certainly should be. The proof
of the local origin of much of the fish is in its ultra-fresh
taste, complemented and supported by fine sauces and
garnishes. There's a decent-value table d'hôte menu from
Monday to Friday (£9.95 two courses, £13.95 three
courses), but best push the boat out and go à la carte
(mains £11-£16).

Whitstable Oyster Fishery Company

*Horsebridge, Whitstable (01227 276856/
www.oysterfishery.co.uk).* **Food served** *Winter*
noon-1.45pm, 7-8.45pm Tue-Fri; noon-2.30pm,
6.30-9.45pm Sat; noon-3.15pm Sun. *Summer* noon-
1.45pm, 7-8.45pm Tue-Fri; noon-2.30pm, 6.30-9.45pm
Sat; 6-8.30pm Sun (phone to check). **Credit** AmEx,
DC, MC, V.
As you might expect at the premier restaurant in the
world oyster capital, seafood is treated with ultimate
respect at the WOFC shrine to fish. Garnishes are
classically simple and unnecessary sauces are frowned
upon. Obviously, prime choices change by the day and
it's always best to know what the chef is eating; but
we were pleasantly surprised at the excellence of the
mackerel we tried. Always an undervalued fish, it
was, in fact, marginally superior to the sea bass stuffed
with rosemary and garlic (which came with four small
potatoes). Pudding was chocolatey and sticky, and the
bill for three people, including several Peronis and one
bottle of Shiraz, came to £105.

Canterbury

Ancient heritage and modern comforts: pilgrims' progress.

England has many medieval cathedral cities, some better preserved, some more idyllically situated than Canterbury. But it is not fanciful to say that so signficant were the events of its early history – the coming of Christianity with St Augustine in the sixth century, and the murder of the Archbishop of Canterbury in 1170 – that they continue to reverberate in its narrow streets and landmark cathedral. And not only do tourists empathise with the past, but with the past of tourism: Geoffrey Chaucer's pilgrims must have been as ubiquitous as today's coach parties and language-school crocodiles. Pilgrims converged on Canterbury throughout the Middle Ages to pay homage to the martyred Archbishop Thomas à Becket, and continued to make the journey until his tomb was destroyed during the Reformation.

Even the least historically minded visitor can't fail to be affected by the high-drama story of the murder of Becket, in his cathedral, by knights hoping to curry favour with King Henry II. It has rags-to-riches (Becket was relatively low born, the son of a merchant), church v state (he systematically opposed reforms devolving ecclesiastical power to the crown), betrayal (one-time friend Henry charged him with treason and even his monks finally opposed him), exile (in France), a bloody climax (historical accounts don't spare the gore of amputation and scalping) and a tragic footnote (Henry claimed he never intended to order the killing and had himself scourged at Becket's tomb).

As well as ancient buildings, pretty gardens, ecclesiastical ruins and that sense of living history, the city offers the 21st-century visitor copious amounts of decent pubs and restaurants, a mix of mainstream and quirky shopping, heritage-related tourist diversions and the civic spoils of a continuously and currently prosperous county town.

The **Cathedral** dominates the city's skyline.

The main axis is St Peter's Street, which changes its name to High Street as it bisects the walled oval and exits it as George's Street. The entrance to the cathedral grounds is on the Butter Market, a little way up Mercery Lane. Wandering streets such as Palace Street, punting along the Stour or exploring the western corner around St Mildred's Church and Stour Street make peaceable escapes from the frenzy.

A point worth noting: for a city, Canterbury is surprisingly child-friendly. Extensive pedestrianisation, plentiful greenery, some fun museums and a cathedral that can't fail to impress combine to give plenty of running, learning and gawping opportunities.

By train from London

Trains to **Canterbury East** leave **Victoria** every half-hour (journey time **1hr 25mins**). Trains to **Canterbury West** leave **Charing Cross** hourly (journey time **1hr 25mins**). Info: www.connex.co.uk.

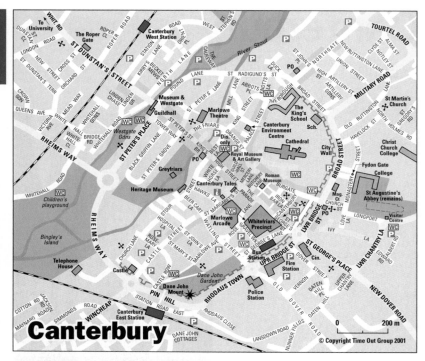

Canterbury

© Copyright Time Out Group 2001

0   200 m

What to see & do

Tourist Information Centre

34 St Margaret's Street, CT1 2TG (01227 766567/ www.canterbury.co.uk). **Open** *Apr-Oct* 9.30am-5.30pm Mon-Sat; 10am-4pm Sun. *Nov, Dec* 9.30am-5pm Mon-Sat; 10am-4pm Sun. *Jan-Mar* 9.30am-5pm Mon-Sat.

Canterbury Castle

Castle Street (tourist info 01227 766567/ www.canterbury.co.uk). **Open** 8am-dusk daily. **Admission** free.

This huge Norman stone keep, built successively by William the Conqueror and William Rufus, retains some fine brickwork, giving clues to where the various doorways, dungeons and staircases once stood. The three floors have long since gone, but the remaining edifice is evocative of the once-great castle that was attacked by Wat Tyler and his revolting peasants in 1381.

Canterbury Cathedral

The Precincts (01227 762862/www.canterbury-cathedral.org). **Open** *Cathedral* Easter-Sept 8.45am-7pm Mon-Sat; 12.30-2.30pm, 4.30-5.30pm Sun. Oct-Easter 8.45am-5pm Mon-Sat; 12.30-2.30pm, 4.30-5.30pm Sun. *Crypt* 10am-4.30pm Mon-Sat; 12.30-2.30pm, 4.30-5.30pm Sun. **Admission** £3.50; £2.50 concessions; free under-5s.

The centrepiece of the city, and justifiably so. From the splendour of the 16th-century Christ Church Gate, which serves as the entry point, the cathedral rises up before you, with Bell Harry tower soaring heavenward some 250ft. Augustine first established a cathedral here in 602; the current incarnation was begun by Archbishop Lanfranc in 1070. To see what remains, descend to the huge crypt to view the fine pillars with intricate capitals and carved columns. On reappearing in the north transept, note the Altar of the Sword's Point, the site of Becket's gruesome end. The main nave dates from around 1400; its intricate lierne vaulting (a complex form of ribbed vaulting) is its finest feature, although this is more than matched by the magnificent fan vaulting beneath Bell Harry. Other essential viewing includes the tombs of the Black Prince and Edward the Confessor in the Trinity Chapel at the eastern end, and, outside, the magnificent cloisters and Green Court overlooked by King's School. The cathedral is at its most magical just before dusk, with a recital reverberating from within, and the otherwise ubiquitous coach parties long gone.

Canterbury Tales

St Margaret's Street (01227 479227/ www.thecanterburytales.org.uk). **Open** *Mid Feb-June, Sept-mid Oct* 10am-5pm daily. *July, Aug* 9.30am-5.30pm daily. *Nov-mid Feb* 10am-4.30pm daily. **Admission** £5.90; £4.90 concessions.

Commune with the spirits on **Butter Market**.

Chaucer's tales, adapted, abridged and brought to life by waxwork models, mechanical movements and Bernard Cribbins reading through your headset as you stroll through. It's hardly state-of-the-art animatronics – the clunks are audible – but it's endearing and educational, and the content is not watered down too much. Lasts 45 minutes.

Chaucer Centre
22-23 St Peter's Street (01227 470379). **Open** 10am-4pm Tue-Sat, phone to check. **Admission** free. An interesting and concise exploration of the poet's life and works, although not the most impressively housed exhibition. Suitable for all ages.

Dane John Garden
Entrance at Watling Street.
The name of this garden and motte is a corruption of the Norman French 'donjon', meaning motte. While there is only a simple mound to testify to its earlier use, the city council has created a gentle garden with children's maze and play area. The walk along the ramparts allows commanding views of, er, the ring road.

Eastbridge Hospital
25 High Street (01227 471688).
Open 10am-4.45pm Mon-Sat. **Admission** £1; 50p concessions; free under-5s.
Founded to meet the growing kipping needs of pilgrims in the wake of Becket's murder in 1170, this small but ancient 'spital' retains the smell and damp of ages past. The display boards are a bit DIY, but the undercroft, with its tilting arches, and the chapel upstairs, with its 13th-century mural and crown-post roof, are more than worth the entrance fee.

Greyfriars
entrance on Stour Street (01227 462395).
Open *Mid May-Sept* 2-4pm Mon-Sat. Closed Oct-Apr. **Admission** free; donations welcome.
This 13th-century Franciscan building spans the River Stour on the edge of a field of wild flowers. It's small – a fraction of its size in its heyday – and simply kept. The brothers moved out in 1982 but one service a week is still held here, contributing, along with its quietness, to a sense of the spiritual not felt in the oversubscribed cathedral. There's also something magical about its isolated position – away from the throng, and close to the relaxing Westgate Gardens.

Heritage Museum
Stour Street (01227 452747/ www.canterbury.gov.uk). **Open** *Nov-May* 10.30am-5pm Mon-Sat. *June-Oct* 10.30am-5pm Mon-Sat; 1.30-5.30pm Sun. Last entry 4pm. **Admission** £1.90; £1.20 concessions; free under-5s.
The best museum devoted to the history of Canterbury. It begins with displays on the early Roman settlement through to the city's emergence as the centre of English Christianity, all clearly presented in a series of well laid-out rooms. The 30-minute video on Becket's life and death is entertaining and informative, and the huge vaulted hall in this former Poor Priests' Hospital is worth the entrance fee in itself. The Rupert Bear room, in honour of its creator, Canterbury-born Mary Tourtel, is slightly overdone – more on Joseph Conrad (who lived in Canterbury and wrote most of his books here) and Christopher Marlowe (who was born in the city), would have been more apt.

Roman Museum
Butchery Lane (01227 785575/ www.canterbury.gov.uk). **Open** *Nov-May* 10am-5pm Mon-Sat. *June-Oct* 10am-5pm Mon-Sat; 1.30-5pm Sun. Last entry 1hr before closing. **Admission** £2.50; £1.60 concessions; free under-5s.
An in-depth record of Durovernum (the Roman name for Canterbury), this carefully constructed museum focuses as much on the archaeological process as the finds themselves. Built around the undulating mosaic floor of a Roman townhouse, it features interactive computer displays, speculative reconstructions and a 'hands-on' area, where children and adults can weigh up reproduction artefacts.

St Augustine's Abbey – where it all began.

Truly Original

Time Out

LONDON'S
LIVING GUIDE
EVERY WEEK

timeout.com

PHOTOGRAPHY JONATHON FOSTER WILLIAMS

A royal friend – the **Falstaff Hotel**. *See p22.*

Royal Museum & Art Gallery
High Street (01227 452747/www.canterbury.gov.uk).
Open 10am-5pm Mon-Sat. **Admission** free.
Porcelain, silver, military memorabilia and a somewhat chaotic collection of paintings (some fine, some modern, some unremarkable) take up the first floor of this Victorian monument (below is the library). Most notable is a fine collection of Thomas Sydney Cooper's livestock portraits – the huge bull on the staircase is magnificent.

St Augustine's Abbey
Longport (01227 767345/www.english-heritage. org.uk). **Open** *Apr-Sept* 10am-6pm daily. *Oct* 10am-5pm daily. *Nov-Mar* 10am-4pm daily. **Admission** (EH) £2.60; £1.30-£2 concessions; free under-5s.
The remains of this historic abbey are laid out in a park just outside the walls (Christian tradition forbade burials within city walls). In 597 St Augustine was sent to England by Pope Gregory to reintroduce Christianity to the island and, following his conversion, King Ethelbert duly gave land to the Benedictine monk to found this abbey. Archbishop Lanfranc rebuilt the abbey in the 11th century, and it flourished until Henry VIII dissolved it in 1538 and converted the buildings into lodgings for Anne of Cleves. Subsequent uses have included a brewery and missionary college; it's now part of King's School. An audio tour takes you around the site, drawing a picture of the abbey in its prime.

St Martin's Church
North Holmes Road (01227 768072).
Open 8am-5.45pm daily, phone to check.
Admission free; donations welcome.
This beautiful small church is reputed to be the oldest parish church in continuous use in England. It is thought to have been established in the sixth century, when Bertha, the Christian wife of the Anglo-Saxon King of Kent, Ethelbert, sought a place to worship. What now remains is mainly 13th- and 14th-century – look out for the font and the replica Chrismatory (a tiny chest for holy oils, set into the north wall). In the stepped graveyard are buried Mary Tourtel (the creator of Rupert Bear; directions to the grave are pinned up in the church) and Thomas Sydney Cooper (artist).

Westgate Museum
St Peter's Street (01227 452747/ www.canterbury.gov.uk). **Open** 11am-12.30pm, 1.30-3.30pm Mon-Sat. **Admission** £1; 50p-65p concessions.

Although there's been a gate on this site since the third century, the current twin towers were erected in the late 14th century. Fear of a French invasion prompted a powerful construction, much of which still stands today. The museum of weaponry and armaments on the first floor is small but informative, and the prison cells and the view from the roof are worth a gander.

Where to stay

Despite all those medieval buildings begging to house tasteful, quirky – or just plain historic – hotels, Canterbury's accommodation options are pretty run of the mill. Staying in is not the point here. That said, it's worth paying more for a berth within or near to the walls, as neither parking nor public transport are much fun.

It's not a good idea to arrive in town without a reservation, especially at the weekend, but if you find yourself stuck, your best bet is to cruise the strip of institutional B&Bs at the town end of the New Dover Road.

Acacia Lodge & Tanglewood
39-40 London Road, CT2 8LF (01227 769955/ fax 01227 478960). **Rates** £40-£48 double/twin. **Rooms** (en suite) 2 double, 1 twin. **Credit** MC, V.
Maria Cain, affable proprietor of Tanglewood, took over the neighbouring Acacia Lodge in 2000, combining the 1880s farm cottages into a single B&B. The properties share a living area (board games provided) and dining room, where a proper breakfast (lots of choice and jams in pots) is served. Rooms are not large, but they're clean and homely; Tanglewood's are in plain country style, Acacia's Lodge's in Laura Ashley blue. It's a ten-minute walk to the centre of town, but low prices compensate, and Maria used to work as a guide, so information and recommendations come free. Children welcome. Dogs by arrangement. No smoking throughout.

Cathedral Gate Hotel
36 Burgate, CT1 2HA (01227 464381/fax 01227 462800). **Rates** £23.50-£54 single; £45-£81 double; £63-£103 triple; £93-£103 family. Breakfast £6 (Eng). **Rooms** 10 single (5 en suite); 8 double (4 en suite); 3 triple (1 en suite); 2 family (both en suite). **Credit** AmEx, DC, MC, V.
Short of taking the cloth, you won't get to sleep a lot closer to the cathedral than here. In fact if the bells are ringing, you won't get to sleep at all. You can even take breakfast on a hidden roof terrace with Harry Bell Tower orange-pip spitting distance away. But it could be argued that the Cathedral Gate is resting on its location laurels: although its maze of winding corridors and plainly decorated rooms with random original features are charming, some of the furnishings are a little scruffy, the facilities ageing, not all the bathrooms are en suite and breakfast is only continental unless you stump up an extra £6. Such quibbles pale into insignificance if you're one of the lucky ones with a cathedral view, for which there's no extra cost. Book early and ask for 'Daybreak', 'Cathedral' or, best of all, 'Joy', all of which overlook the cathedral. Another down-side: there's no private parking, and little in the area. Children and dogs are welcome. No-smoking rooms available.

Quiet contemplation in the **Westgate Gardens** provides sanctuary from the masses.

Coach House

34 Watling Street, CT1 2UD (tel/fax 01227 784324). **Rates** £30-£35 single occupancy; £40-£48 double; £65 family. **Rooms** 2 double, 4 family. **No credit cards.**

A plain, graceful Georgian building within the city walls, the Coach House is new and fresh and something of an antidote to the other institutionalised B&Bs. It has an unaffected personal touch: staying here is a bit like staying with friends, if, that is, your friends have pleasantly magpie tastes: furnishings might include a papier maché alligator, a pair of pot plants or a flea-market mirror. And not a floral in sight. Rooms are large and left intact (no en suite), and there's a sweet garden where you can have breakfast. Good value. Children welcome.

County Hotel

High Street, CT1 2RX (01227 766266/fax 01227 451512/www.macdonaldhotels.co.uk). **Rates** £82-£90 single; £92-£100 double/twin; £114-£120 four-poster/deluxe. Special breaks. Breakfast £10.50 (Eng/cont). **Rooms** (all en suite) 15 single; 30 twin; 16 double; 4 four-posters; 8 deluxe. **Credit** AmEx, DC, MC, V.

The County achieves comfort rather than greatness: with mainly Victorian origins it is neither particularly historically significant nor architecturally interesting. But the bedrooms are tastefully done in restrained rusts, ochres and woods, the dressing gowns are fluffy and Sully's restaurant, beloved of wedding groups (late-night revellers are an occupational hazard in the bar) is a comfortable place for breakfast if a little institutional for dinner. And you're smack in the centre of town. Children welcome. No-smoking rooms available.

Ebury Hotel

65-67 New Dover Road, CT1 3DX (01227 768433/ fax 01227 459187/www.ebury-hotel.co.uk). **Rates** £50 single; £75 double/twin; £85-£95 family. Special breaks. **Rooms** (all en suite) 2 single; 3 twin; 7 double; 3 family. **Credit** AmEx, DC, MC, V.

This huge 'Tudorbethan' hotel, with its sweeping pebbled drive, manages to be both grand and homely. Family-run, professional and friendly, it's a particularly good choice for families. The large garden and heated swimming pool are great for unfettered frolicking and the family rooms sleep up to five. The rooms are large, light and comfortable, if decoratively uninspired, and those at the back overlook the extensive lawn, bungalows and swimming chalet. The restaurant is a good cut or two above the hotel average. The Ebury's main disadvantage is the relatively charmless ten-minute walk to the centre. Dogs by arrangement.

Falstaff Hotel

8-10 St Dunstan's Street, CT2 8AF (01227 462138/ fax 01227 463525/www.corushotels.com/thefalstaff). **Rates** £91 single; £100 double/twin; £130 four-poster/family/suite. Special breaks. Breakfast £9.50 (Eng); £6.50 (cont). **Rooms** (all en suite) 9 single; 23 double; 3 four-poster/suite; 1 family. **Credit** AmEx, DC, MC, V.

Canterbury's loveliest historic hotel – a 15th-century coaching inn just outside Westgate – has done a fine job of reconciling its chain-hotel present with its manifold period charms. Peep through the little lead-lined windows into the tastefully countrified beamed lounge and you'd expect to find a handful of charmingly wonky oak-lined rooms off creaky corridors. As indeed you do, 25 of them (three with four-posters), and lots more at the back in two converted annexes, all furnished in modern comfortable style with some rather upbeat branding from the Corus group. All the usual hotel facilities are available – plus good-value room service of simple dishes, and if no genial innkeeper at least conspicuously well-trained staff. The main complaint is that the pleasant dining room doesn't have the seating capacity to serve the increased guest numbers, resulting in too-long waits. Children welcome. Pets allowed by arrangement. No-smoking rooms available.

Magnolia House

36 St Dunstan's Terrace, CT2 8AX (tel/fax 01227 765121/http://freespace.virgin.net/magnolia. canterbury). **Rates** £48-£65 single; £85-£110 double/twin; £125 four-poster. **Rooms** (all en suite) 1 single; 4 double; 1 twin; 1 four-poster. **Credit** AmEx, DC, MC, V.

The Magnolia is the doyenne of Canterbury B&Bs, with stars and awards aplenty, accommodating hosts who really look after you well, a picture-book garden and bristling standards of cleanliness. You get tea on arrival, shoe-cleaning on request, robes and even a laundry. The rooms are a bit '80s Laura Ashley, though, with en suites eating into the space (in the case of the larger four-postered Garden Room containing a corner bath). Magnolia House's greatest bonus is that, although it's a good ten minutes from the centre on foot, in a quiet residential area off St Dunstan's Street, the walk can take you through Westgate Gardens, past the Lord Mayor's Parlour, Greyfriars and the River Stour – a lovely, peaceful introduction to the city. Children over 12 welcome. No smoking throughout.

Where to eat & drink

Eating options in central Canterbury are plentiful and varied but the quality is rarely high. The standard offerings are all here: **Pizza Express** (5A Best Lane; 01227 766938); **Café Rouge** (Cogan House, 53 St Peter's Street; 01227 763833); **Caffé Uno** (49A St Peter's Street; 01227 479777), and **ASK** (24 High Street; 01227 767617). Some of the hotels mentioned above, such as the Falstaff and the County, have decent menus if rather bland dining rooms. In addition to our selections below, best central bets are **Beaus Crêperie** (59 Palace Street; 01227 464285), which has a wide range of snacky crêpes, sarnies and salads and a light and airy setting, and **Marlowe's** (55 St Peter's Street; 01227 462194), a beamed bistro with a warm if unexceptional atmosphere.

Canterbury seems to be particularly good at bright, modern ethnic restaurants: **Bistro Vietnam** (The Linen Store, White Horse Lane; 01227 760022) is narrow and countrified with a please-all menu strong on fish; **Bangkok House** (13 Church Street; 01227 471141) is a lovely, long room with unusual teak furnishings and an authentic menu; and **Raj Venue** (92 St Dunstan's Street; 01227 462653) serves Nepalese specialities as well as a standard Indian menu in a distinctly non-standard, brightly coloured room.

Since the opening of a bar/club on the university campus, the city centre is quieter than it used to be on weekend evenings, though you might encounter the odd stag or hen do. Unexpectedly, there are few decent characterful historic boozers, and the busiest pubs are, depressingly, the **Franklin & Firkin** outside Christ Church Gate and the **Thomas Ingoldsby**, a Wetherspoon's of unparalleled blandness on Burgate (the same chain's **West Gate Inn** is better). Even the non-chain pubs,

What lies beneath

Canterbury's latest visitor destination offers no thrill rides, no digital wizardry and no animal attractions. It doesn't even have a fixed location. The **Big Dig** is a mobile museum that provides an on-the-job introduction to archaeology by taking the public down into the trenches of one of Britain's largest urban excavations.

On 1 June 1942, in reprisal for the Allies' devastating attack on Cologne, the Germans blitzed the city. Although the cathedral was saved (firefighters desperately fielded incendiaries from its roof), 15 high-explosive bombs destroyed a quarter of the medieval city in the Whitefriars area between Burgate and Watling Street. Now that the ugly 1950s and 1960s concrete buildings that grew up in its place are to be torn down in favour of more considered development, there is the opportunity for a systematic archaeological investigation of what lies below to be carried out in advance of each new phase of building work.

After 2,000 years of virtually constant and concentrated occupation – dating from Canterbury's Roman incarnation as Durovernum – the pickings are rich.

The first phase of the dig, alongside St George's Street, uncovered Roman mosaic, a near-mint condition stretch of Saxon road and remains of the medieval Whitefriars friary. Particularly productive were the deep rubbish pits behind the houses nearby, yielding a fascinating domestic mix of pottery, coins, jewellery, animal bones, tools and personal possessions.

Many of the finds are on display in the Portakabin that fronts the public entrance to the dig, along with explanatory material about the dig. What else you'll see depends on the progress of the dig when you turn up, but on a good day a steward will guide you around the site, introduce you to the workers and explain the techniques in use.

Big Dig Visitor Centre
01227 462062/
www.canterburytrust.co.uk. **Open** 10am-4pm daily. Last admission 3.45pm. **Admission** £2; £1 concessions. **No credit cards.** The Big Dig location varies within the Whitefriars area: call the Big Dig or ask at the Tourist Information Centre (*see p18*).

with the exception of the **Thomas Becket** (*see below*), are unexceptional; best bet for a sightseeing break is probably the **Three Tuns** on Castle Street (large, be-wooded and with a spanking new pool table).

The better pubs are on the outskirts: the **Bishops Finger** on St Dunstan's Street is popular despite looking a bit newer on the inside than its 16th-century origins suggest; a bit further on is the pretty and peaceable local the **Unicorn**, with a charmingly kitsch garden; and at the opposite end of town the cream-painted cottagey **Two Sawyers** (58 Ivy Lane) is unpretentious and friendly. All serve food.

For late drinking, there's one central option, **Alberry's**, with a bistro and cellar bar. Beyond the walls, a nightlife of sorts centres on the **Churchill** and **Baa Bars** nightclubs, but the city is really more a place for silent contemplation than raucous revelry.

Café des Amis du Mexique

95 St Dunstan's Street (01227 464390). **Food served** noon-10pm Mon-Sat; noon-9.30pm Sun. **Credit** AmEx, MC, V.

Bright, light and breezy, Café des Amis is one of the most popular restaurants in Canterbury. And rightly so. With the brass beat and guitar strains of the homeland as background music, ochre walls and large windows, there's an upbeat feel to the place. Young staff serve a youngish crowd a fine collection of Mexican/Mediterranean-influenced dishes: huevos rancheros (£4.75; until 6pm only), seared tuna with chipotle veg, pato con mole (£9.45; best – though still inadequately – described as a duck burger), paella, burritos, fab fajitas and some dangerously seductive chocolate puds. Book in advance.

Ha! Ha! Bar & Canteen

7 St Margaret's Street (01277 379800/ www.hahaonline.co.uk). **Food served** 11am-10pm Mon-Fri; 10am-10pm Sat; 10am-9.30pm Sun. **Credit** AmEx, DC, MC, V.

It might have the most irritating name in Christendom and be part of an aggressively marketed chain, but Ha! Ha! is a more than OK place to take a break from pounding the heritage circuit. It aims to please: the decor's modern with lots of different seating scenarios, staff are

relaxed but efficient, food both fashionable and fun and bar drinks well made, and you can get anything from a designer coffee or a glass of wine via brunch or a snack to a full-blown three course meal at any time of day. Dishes worth a mention (take contemporary bar classics as read) are fishfinger sandwich on ciabatta (£6), mushy peas (£2) and new potato and asparagus salad with parmesan and two poached eggs. Everything was fine for the money, other than the desserts, but then they did come free owing to a lapse in the service.

Lloyds

89-90 St Dunstan's Street (01227 768222/ www.lloydsofcanterbury.com). **Food served** noon-9.45pm daily. **Set lunch** £12.50 2 courses. **Credit** MC, V.

We visited this ambitious newcomer just after it opened: we can't predict its level of success but suffice to say we caught the competition sniffing it out with some concern. In a converted (Lloyds) bank, a listed building with a beamed barn roof upstairs, it aims for high-end modern dining from a determinedly imaginative menu with international and British influences. Representative dishes include velouté of chicken with coconut and lime (£4.50), braised ox tongue in crepinette (£13.25) with sauce ravigotte, and risotto of Kentish asparagus with woodland mushrooms and mascarpone (£9.75). We had the £12.50 two-course lunch menu, which varied between OK and excellent. Sparkling settings, comfortable seats and assured staff confirmed Lloyds' upmarket pitch. If the success of the culinarily similar but decoratively more traditional Augustines (1-2 Longport; 01227 453063), also recommended, is anything to go by, it should flourish.

Thomas Becket

21 Best Lane (01227 464384). **Food served** noon-9.30pm daily. **No credit cards.**

Perhaps because its back half is a restaurant, the Becket pub is seldom stormed by packs of young drinkers, instead maintaining a sedate vibe in keeping with its ancient, beamed interior. The hop-festooned drinking area is still large enough to feel like a pub, with a long bar and a couple of decent real ales; at the back on-the-ball staff serve home-cooked pub food. There are always three roasts (£5-£5.60), one vegetarian dish, good pies (including Canterbury apple and lamb) plus your classic bangers and mash, cottage pie and so on. Starters – we had ace potted prawns – and puddings (always a seasonal crumble) are similarly traditional. Portions are unfeasibly large: we counted seven vegetables.

Tuo e Mio Restaurant

16 The Borough (01227 761471). **Food served** 7-10.45pm Tue; noon-2.30pm, 7-10.45pm Wed-Sat; noon-2.30pm, 7-10pm Sun. **Credit** AmEx, DC, MC, V.

This smart black-and-white-decorated restaurant is among the best in Canterbury. White Artexed walls, starched linen and black trimmings give the premises a smart professional feel, endorsed by the smooth and stylish service. The food itself matches the surroundings – the menu includes the likes of halibut with salsa verde (£12.50), pollo Genovese with brandy, basil and mushrooms (£7.50) and a signature dish of tender and rich filetto tuo e mio (beef with cream brandy and mushrooms, £14.50). The dessert trolley is a virtual pâtisserie. Book in advance.

Canterbury is built around and over the **Stour**.

Sandwich to Sandgate

White cliffs and castles on England's front line.

It is with good reason that Dover's white cliffs have been immortalised in song, for not many places can boast such a rich heritage as this historically significant stretch of coastline. The Classis Britannica (the Roman fleet) was stationed here to defend the Channel, and the remains of the lighthouse, fort and *vicus* (hotel) are still in evidence. In the Middle Ages, this area was the heart of the curious federation of the **Cinque Ports**, which provided England's first line of defence against the beastly continentals, in return for which they were granted a range of privileges.

Sandwich: a slice of old Kent

At the north end of this region is **Sandwich**. Sitting on the River Stour, this now-landlocked former port is still very much a small medieval town, with half-timber-framed houses lining the narrow streets – Strand Street being a particularly fine example. Overlooking the grassy banks of the Stour is the town's most celebrated building, the fine 16th-century Barbican. Not far away are the golden sands and famous Royal St George golf course of Sandwich Bay. A couple of miles north of the

By train from London

Trains for **Sandwich** leave **Charing Cross** every 30mins, passing through **Dover Priory** (journey time **1hr 40mins**). Trains to **Dover** also run from **Victoria** hourly (journey time **1hr 50mins**) and pass through Canterbury East. Info: www.connex.co.uk.

town, set in bleak Pegwell Bay, are the remains of **Richborough Roman Fort**, one-time sentinel over the southern entrance of the Wantsum Channel, which formerly cut off the Isle of Thanet from the rest of Kent.

Moving south, the contiguous low-key resort towns of **Deal** and **Walmer** are notable chiefly for their Tudor castles (Henry VIII added both to the list of Cinque Ports). It's a fine 45-minute coastal walk between the two of them. Deal's winding streets – although now lined with antique emporiums, hardware stores, an old-fashioned sweet shop and an excellent second-hand bookshop – bring to mind its reputation as a one-time smugglers' den.

Patrol the coastline on **Dover** seafront.

The white cliffs of Dover

During World War II, **Dover**'s cliffs concealed the wartime operations unit where Admiral Ramsey and Winston Churchill planned the Dunkirk evacuation. The tunnels beneath the striking Castle (*see p30* **The key to England**) can be explored and are one of the area's most worthwhile attractions. The Dover Museum (01304 201066/www.dovermuseum.co.uk) traces the history of the town from the Bronze Age to the present day with dioramas, paintings, models and artefacts. There is also a new Bronze Age boat gallery, centred around the remains of a 3,500-year-old boat. Close by, the Roman Painted House (New Street; 01304 203279) discovered in 1970, is impressively well preserved with chunks of frescoed walls, hypocaust heating system and brickwork. Also worth a visit is the Old Town Gaol (Biggin Street; 01304 242766), where they'll happily let you try out a cell and lock the door. Despite these historical attractions, the town has a decidedly down-at-heel feel and is notably lacking in charm. It does, though, at least have some decent shopping at De Bradelei Wharf (01304 226616) where designer wear is sold at huge discounts.

A few miles up the coast, **St Margaret's Bay**, with its villas clinging to the chalk cliffs, is a splendidly dramatic spot from which to watch the sea, best enjoyed off-season when the car park and the neighbouring pub are empty. Beware the precipitous drive down though. The village just above it, St Margaret's at Cliffe, is very pretty and quiet and has several venerable inns. Away from the coast, **Kearnsey Abbey** at River, on the road between Dover and Folkestone, is a great spot for walks, with its sizeable duck pond and café in the remaining part of the house (it has no ecclesiastical connections at all, having been built for a Dover banker in 1820).

Folkstone and Sandgate

Folkestone and **Sandgate** are virtually one and the same, though Sandgate, with its antique shops and rows of bright Victorian villas facing the sea, is markedly more well-to-do. After the crippling decline of its ferry crossings, and despite the proximity of the entrance to the Channel Tunnel, Folkestone is still struggling to get its economy back on track. The old town hangs in limbo, caught between trendification and recession – with old and once-charming shops closing down amid new and garish cafés and bars. With a little will and imagination much could be made of the cobbled streets and crumbling architecture. One reminder of days gone by is Rowlands Confectionery in the Old High Street, selling old-fashioned humbugs, sweet pebbles and aniseed twists, and where the rock is still rolled out and cut to the delight of sweet-toothed kiddies. A somewhat more offbeat attraction is the Russian Submarine, a fascinating leftover of the Cold War, now moored on the South Quay of the harbour (01303 240400), which can also be hired for private parties.

Otherwise, stroll along the Leas, the town's main attraction, of which it is justly proud. It's a magnificent Edwardian boardwalk, full of entertainment sites, including the Rotunda

Sandwich's history is alive in **Strand Street**.

(01303 245245), a quaintly 1950s amusement complex, and the Metropole Arts Centre, which offers brilliant children's activities and events (01303 255070). Then take the quirky water-powered chair lift down to the shingle below.

What to see & do

Dover, in spite of its historical attractions, and Folkestone (apart from the Leas), are unrewarding towns for the potential *flâneur*. Those wishing to wallow in the picturesque are better off heading for Sandwich, and following its excellent historic town trail to enjoy its many superb medieval buildings. At a pinch, Deal offers some attractive streets among the seaside Victoriana.

Tourist Information Centres
Town Hall, High Street, Deal CT14 6BB (01304 369576/www.whitecliffscountry.org.uk). **Open** *May-mid Sept* 9am-12.30pm, 1.30-5pm Mon-Fri; 10am-2pm Sat. *Mid Sept-Apr* 9am-5pm Mon-Fri.
Townwall Street, Dover, CT16 1JR (01304 205108/www.whitecliffscountry.org.uk). **Open** 9am-6pm daily.
Harbour Street, Folkestone, CT20 1QN (01303 258594). **Open** *Easter-June* 9am-5.30pm daily. *July-Aug* 9am-7pm daily. *Oct-Easter* 9am-1pm, 2-5.30pm Mon-Sat; 10am-1pm, 2-4pm Sun.
Guildhall, Sandwich, CT13 9AH (01304 613565/www.open-sandwich.co.uk). **Open** *Apr-Sept* 10am-4pm daily.

Bike hire
Deal Prams & Cycles *30 Mill Hill, Deal (01304 380680).*
One mile from the rail station.

Caesar's Camp & the Warren
These marvellous chalk downs at Folkestone were once accessible from the town on foot by passing through the golf course on to fields grazed by sheep. Now, access is via a major road, which passes straight through the hillside, somewhat lessening the ambience of Caesar's Camp and Sugarloaf Hill. Nevertheless, the rocky, craggy wilds of the Warren are still great for walking, affording spectacular views of France on a clear day and access to lesser-known beaches.

Deal Castle
Victoria Road, Deal (01304 372762/www.english-heritage.org.uk). **Open** *Apr-Sept* 10am-6pm daily. *Oct* 10am-5pm daily. *Nov-Mar* 10am-4pm Wed-Sun.
Admission (EH) £3.10; £1.60-£2.30 concessions.
Built by Henry VIII in the shape of a Tudor rose, the castle is a warren of dank, spooky corridors that seem to go on for miles. In the centre is a fine display of the castle's history and that of the other coastal fortifications.

Deal Maritime Museum
St George's Road, Deal (01304 372679/ http://home.freeuk.com/deal-museum/).
Open *Easter-Sept* 2-5pm Mon-Sat.
Admission £1.50; 50p-£1 concessions.

The main gallery depicts the life and times of local sailors on this famously treacherous stretch of coast where the Goodwin sands have claimed many a vessel. There are also displays on aspects of local history, including the naval yard and the military importance of the town.

East Kent Railway
Station Road, Sheperdswell, nr Dover (01304 832042). **Open** varies year round, phone for details.
Tickets £4; £2-£2.50 concessions.
Enjoy a round trip on a steam train. You can also eat birthday teas or Sunday roasts on some services and even hire an entire train for private parties. For the serious train nut, steam locomotive driving courses are also offered. The line has been recently extended to run all the way to Bodiam Castle and a combined train-ride and castle-visit ticket can be bought. Themed events run throughout the year.

Macfarlanes Butterfly & Garden Centre
A260 Swingfield, nr Folkestone (01303 844244). **Open** *Apr-Sept* 10am-5pm daily.
Admission £2; £1.25-£1.50 concessions.
Extensive garden centre with tropical greenhouses and many varieties of free-flying butterflies from swallowtails and heliconids to the gigantic atlas moth from South-East Asia.

Richborough Roman Fort
Richborough Road, Sandwich (01304 612013/ www.english-heritage.org.uk). **Open** *Apr-Sept* 10am-6pm daily. *Oct* 10am-5pm daily. *Nov, Mar* 10am-4pm Wed-Sun. *Dec-Feb* 10am-4pm Sat, Sun.
Admission (EH) £2.70; £1.40-£2 concessions.
Site of Britain's first Roman fortress, which marks the likely spot of the AD 43 landing. The invasion of the rest of Britain was orchestrated from here. Not much remains now, but the ruins of the massive triumphal arch built to signal the might of the Roman forces are still visible.

St Margaret's Museum & Pines Garden
Beach Road, St Margaret's Bay, Dover (01304 852764/www.pinesgardenandmuseum.co.uk). **Open** *Pines Garden* 10am-5pm daily. *Museum* Easter, May-Sept 2-5pm Wed-Sun. **Admission** *Museum* £1; children free. *Garden* £2; 50p concessions.
Just past the sleepy village of St Margaret's, on the road down to the bay, this somewhat bizarre yet imaginative six-acre garden was created in 1970, and includes a lake with waterfall, Romany caravan, wishing well and Oscar Nemon's statue of Churchill. The museum opposite is equally eclectic, with a large collection of maritime objects and local curios.

South Foreland Lighthouse
Beach Road, Langdon Cliffs, St Margaret's Bay, Dover (01304 852463/www.nationaltrust.org.uk).
Open *Mar-Oct* 11am-5.30pm Mon, Thur-Sun.
Admission (NT) £1.80; 90p concessions.
Built in 1843, the lighthouse commands the Dover Straits. It was from here that Marconi made the world's first international radio transmission to Wimereux in France. Learn about the history of the tower on the short tour and marvel at the view.

Walmer Castle & Gardens

*Kingsdown Road, Walmer, Deal (01304 364288/
www.english-heritage.org.uk).* **Open** *Apr-Sept*
10am-6pm daily. *Oct* 10am-5pm daily. *Nov, Dec*
10am-4pm daily. *Jan, Feb* 10am-4pm Sat, Sun.
Mar 10am-4pm Wed-Sun. **Admission** (EH) £4.80;
£2.40-£3.60 concessions.

The most attractive and well preserved of the Cinque
Ports fortifications. Walmer is still official home to the
Lord Warden; past incumbents include William Pitt the
Younger and the Duke of Wellington (whose life is celebrated inside). The place now looks more like a stately
home than a castle; the gardens were redeveloped a few
years ago to create a Queen Mother's Garden in celebration of the current Lord Warden's 95th birthday.

Where to stay

There are hundreds of B&Bs along the coast.
Wear Bay Road in **Folkestone** is the main
drag for comfy accommodation, while the
ship-shaped **Hotel Burstin** in the harbour
('Britain's biggest entertainment hotel' boasts
the leaflet) can be stuffed full with OAPs down
for the sea air. **Dover**'s waterfront area offers
the best sea views and standards in the town –
but be warned, there are some grotty dives if
the good ones are full. **Deal** is an attractive
alternative with several reasonably priced
waterfront inns with rooms. **Sandwich** and
Sandgate are altogether classier.

The Bell Hotel

*The Quay, Sandwich, CT13 9EF (01304 613388/
fax 01304 615308/www.princes-leisure.co.uk).*
Rates £75; £100 double/twin; £155 deluxe double;
£110 family. **Rooms** (all en suite) 8 single;
17 double/twin; 6 deluxe double/twin; 1 family.
Credit AmEx, DC, MC, V.

A large and splendidly old-fashioned hotel right on the
quay. The doorway is charming, with a stained-glass
canopy depicting golfers; the entrance hall is full of
polished wood and Chesterfields. The rooms are comfortable and more than decently furnished. Some have
lovely views across the Stour and are good value for
their size. The hotel also contains a posh and expensive
restaurant (with dress code) and a more relaxed wine
bar/bistro next to it. Children and pets welcome. No-
smoking bedrooms.

The Churchill Hotel

*The Waterfront, Dover, CT17 9BP (01304 203633/
fax 01304 216320/www.churchill-hotel.com).* **Rates**
£59 single; £79 double/twin; £95 deluxe double; £94
family. Breakfast £9 per person (Eng/cont). **Rooms**
(all en suite) 4 single; 37 double; 20 twin; 5 deluxe
double; 4 family. **Credit** AmEx, DC, MC, V.

Reminiscent of the Royal Crescent in Bath, the curving
terrace of Regency townhouses that houses the Churchill
was built in 1834 for visitors wishing to indulge in the
new craze for sea-bathing. After World War I, a number of houses here were converted into hotels, which
promptly closed at the outbreak of World War II.
Reopened in peacetime and renamed the Churchill in

recognition of the wartime leader's associations with the
town, the exterior of the building has been sympatheti-
cally restored. The interior is spotless, though largely
uninspiring. There is also a new and very well equipped
gym and a hairdressing salon in the basement. Children
welcome. No-smoking rooms available.

Dunkerley's Hotel

*19 Beach Street, Deal, CT14 7AH (01304 375016/
fax 01304 380187/www.dunkerleys.co.uk).*
Rates £55-£75 single occupancy; £45-£65 per
person double/twin/family; £60 per person four-
poster/suite. Special breaks. **Rooms** (all en suite)
5 double; 7 twin; 1 four-poster; 1 suite; 2 family.
Credit AmEx, DC, MC, V.

Right on the seafront, Dunkerley's has 16 well-sized en
suite bedrooms with satellite TV, some of which also
have four-posters and Jacuzzis. The quaint wooden furniture adds a pleasantly rustic air and the sea views are
utterly unspoilt. Ask about special break prices, which
include dinner at the hotel's excellent restaurant (*see
p29*). Children welcome.

Loddington House

*East Cliff, Marine Parade, Dover, CT16 1LX (tel/fax
01304 201947).* **Rates** £45 single occupancy; £54-
£60 double; £70-£75 family. **Rooms** 1 single (en
suite); 5 double (3 en suite). **Cards** AmEx, MC, V.

Located in an attractive, crumbling row of Victorian villas, Loddington House backs right on to the cliffs, so ask
for rooms facing away from the sea if you want to gaze
up at the chalk face. These are also quieter, because at
this far end of the Parade the road is the main thoroughfare from the ferry terminal – just 200 yards further
down – with its traffic of heavy goods lorries. Rooms
are basic and clean with small TVs and rudimentary
facilities (shower, bar of soap, shampoo sachets). Not the
romantic love nest of your dreams maybe, but an attractive and friendly option for a whistle-stop all the same.
Children welcome. No smoking throughout.

Sandgate Hotel

*The Esplanade, Sandgate, CT20 3DY (01303
220444/fax 01303 220496/www.sandgatehotel.com).*
Rates £45 single; £59-£68 double/twin; £78 deluxe
double. Special breaks. **Rooms** (all en suite) 2 single;
4 double/twin; 4 deluxe double (with balcony).
Credit AmEx, DC, MC, V.

Though all the rooms in this very elegant hotel are clean
and bright (if smallish), the best ones are those with
beflowered balconies overlooking the sea. The lounge is
lush and restful, with good views of the coastline from
the terrace, and the pebble beach is just across the road.
The French restaurant **La Terrasse** (*see p29*) is highly recommended, though there's limited space, so be sure
to reserve a table when you book a room. Note that the
hotel is closed on Sunday evenings. Children welcome.

Wallett's Court
Country House Hotel

*Westcliffe, St Margaret's at Cliffe, CT15 6EW
(01304 852424/fax 01304 853430/
www.wallettscourt.com).* **Rates** £75-£115 single
occupancy; £90-£150 double/twin/deluxe; £150
four-poster; £150 suite; £110 family room. **Rooms**
(all en suite) 9 double; 1 twin; 2 deluxe; 2 four-poster;
2 suites. **Credit** AmEx, DC, MC, V.

Get your teeth into the rock in **Folkestone**.

Former home of William Pitt the Younger, this family residence is a jewel in the East Kent countryside. The main accommodation is in the substantial whitewashed farmhouse where Queen Eleanor of Castile and Edward the Black Prince still lay claim to the rooms through plaques on the doors. Rooms have beautiful antique dressers and carved wooden four-poster beds. Outside in the grounds are a sauna, steam room, heated pools and spa, further chalet-style rooms, a wooden treehouse and a bench swing affording fine views of sheep-grazed hills. Children welcome. All bedrooms no-smoking.
A2 from Canterbury; take A258 towards Deal for half a mile; 1st right after Swing Gate pub; Wallett's Court is opposite church on right.

Where to eat & drink

Though this particular part of the East Kent coast is not exactly overflowing with high-quality eateries (or classic pubs), there's many a mid-range establishment offering good value for money in the towns. **Lemongrass Thai Restaurant** (High Street, Deal; 01304 367707) makes good use of the abundance of fresh fish and seafood in the area. In Sandwich, the **Quay Side Bar & Brasserie** (Bell Lane; 01304 619899), next to the Bell Hotel, has bistro food (including a tapas-style menu) in a cool, modern interior. The **Griffin's Head** at Chillenden (between Deal and Canterbury; 01304 840325) serves wholesome pub grub in a one-time medieval timber-frame house, complete with inglenook fireplaces and exposed beams. Even

better, in Sandgate, try the delightful **Clarendon Inn** (01303 248684), just behind the Sandgate Hotel, which doles out good, unpretentious fare in a wonderfully friendly atmosphere.

Dunkerley's
Beach Street, Deal (01304 375016/ www.dunkerleys.co.uk). **Food served** *Bistro* noon-3pm, 6-10pm daily. *Restaurant* noon-2.30pm, 6-9.30pm Tue-Sun. **Set lunch** £10.95 3 courses. **Credit** AmEx, DC, MC, V.
Specialising in seafood, Dunkerley's offers both bistro and restaurant dining. Dishes are inventive but not gimmicky, with starters including crab bisque (£3.95) and caramelised scallops (£7.95). Main dishes (from £12.95) take in monkfish, Dover sole, roasted sea bass and turbot, and seasonal game and meat dishes are also available. Meals in the bistro are simpler and can sometimes be slow to materialise; the food is as good as the restaurant's, though.

The Moonflower
32-34 High Street, Dover (01304 212198). **Food served** noon-2.30pm, 5-11.30pm Mon-Sat. **Credit** AmEx, DC, MC, V.
This friendly, family-style Chinese has plenty of choice, with retro dishes like chicken chop suey (£4.80) alongside interesting seafood dishes such as baked lobster tail with ginger and spring onion (£16). For the unadventurous, there's an English menu featuring the likes of fillet steak (£12.50) and roast chicken (£5.90), plus the odd Sino-Anglo variation – including fillet steak with black bean sauce.

Park Inn
1-2 Park Place, Ladywell, Dover (01304 203300/ www.theparkinnatdover.co.uk). **Food served** 11am-10pm Mon-Sat; noon-10pm Sun. **Credit** AmEx, MC, V.
Sister to the more remote **Crown Inn** at Finglesham (01304 612555) – an oak-beamed, 16th-century restaurant – the Park Inn offers the same kind of honest cooking, but in a Victorian setting in the centre of Dover. Starters, including fried whitebait and home-made chicken liver pâté, start at just over £3; mains are an eclectic range of dishes such as baked crab cajun style (£7.95) and beef stroganoff (£12.95). There are also five startlingly luxurious rooms upstairs, including an opulent four- poster. All rooms are en suite and prices range from £27 to £45 for a double.

La Terrasse
The Esplanade, Sandgate (01303 220444/ www.sandgatehotel.com). **Food served** 12.15-1.30pm, 7.15-9.15pm Tue-Sat; 12.15-1.30pm Sun. **Set lunch** (Tue-Fri, Sun) £22 3 courses. **Set meal** (Fri dinner, Sat, Sun lunch) £31 5 courses. **Credit** AmEx, DC, MC, V.
Small and very Gallic, La Terrasse serves up some highbrow cooking, with dishes such as pan-fried scallops with sliced potatoes and black truffles in their own jus, and roast turbot with ceps in red wine sauce. Renowned for its treatment of fish and seafood, the restaurant uses other local ingredients where possible – menus could feature 'Romney Marsh' lamb, for example. The eating experience here matches the food: there are *amuse-gueules* to begin the meal; service is formal and professional; the wine list encyclopaedic.

On balmy summer days you can eat outside on the balcony overlooking the pebble beach over the road. Expect to spend about £45 a head for three courses. Booking advised.

Wallett's Court Country House Hotel Restaurant

Westcliffe, St Margaret's at Cliffe (01304 852424/fax 01394 853430/www.walletscourt.com).
Food served noon-2pm Mon-Fri, Sun; 7-9pm

daily. **Set lunch** £17.50 3 courses. **Set dinner** £35 3 courses. **Credit** AmEx, DC, MC, V.
Posh French and oriental-influence cooking, served in oak-beamed Jacobean rooms. Meals are finely presented and not lacking in substance. Starters could include duck liver and green peppercorn parfait with a sauternes jelly, on the one hand, and a sauté of baby squid and scallops with oyster sauce and cashew nut salad on the other. Mains range from the likes of roasted seafood with coconut milk and Thai fragrant rice to Chateaubriand.

The key to England

If you wanted to choose one location that exemplified British history, you could do no better than opt for Dover Castle, the 'key to England'. This vast 70-acre site, a bastion against invasion from Europe since the year dot and a brooding reminder of past conflicts, dominates the landscape for miles around. You can even see it from France with binoculars.

The bulk of the buildings now visible date from medieval times, with various 18th- and 19th-century additions. Probably the site of an iron age hillfort, the grounds house a well-preserved Roman lighthouse and a heavily restored Saxon church. William the Conqueror then built rudimentary defences on the site, but the place came into its own during Henry II's nationwide fortification programme, when it became one of the largest and most sophisticated castles in Europe. The work was continued after his death by King John and was immediately put to the test when the French landed in Dover in 1216. The siege came to its climax with the dastardly French mining under the walls (the tunnels can still be seen) and successfully breaching them, only to be beaten off by a heroic band of 140 knights.

As a symbol of defiance, this engagement presaged the events of 1940, when the castle once again became the focal point for the defence of the country. The Georgians had already dug further tunnels into the cliffs as barracks, so engineers converted them into a command centre where the evacuation of Dunkirk and, later, the invasion of Normandy were planned. The army finally left in 1958, but returned during the Cuban missile crisis of 1962 when the tunnels were re-activated for a further 22 years as a regional seat of government in the event of nuclear attack. The castle fell only once, in 1642 during the Civil War, ironically to the British themselves – the local Parliamentarians, in an amazing feat, surprised the Royalist garrison by scaling the cliffs on the seaward side.

This is an extraordinary place and visits could easily take a whole day. Highlights include a tremendous re-enactment of the siege of 1216 and a re-creation of the Tudor court preparing for the arrival of Henry VIII. Best of all is the tour of the lovingly re-created secret wartime tunnels, complete with the sound of bombers overhead. Throughout the summer season there are also special events such as gladiator fights or demonstrations of medieval siege tactics, climaxing in a mock battle. As for your own personal assault on the castle, try to approach it from the east, taking the B road that hugs the coast from St. Margaret's – the view as you come over the hill is spectacular.

Dover Castle

Castle Hill, Dover (01304 211067/www.english-heritage.org.uk). **Open** 10am-6pm daily. **Admission** (EH) £7; £4-£5.30 concessions.

North Kent Downs

Follow the path of the pilgrims or take a muddy tour of the marshlands.

To look at a road map of North Kent and see how the M2 and M20 motorways slash through the county to the ferry terminals of Dover and Folkestone, you'd think there would be little left of the surrounding countryside to savour. Yet, surprisingly, once off the tarmacked track, a cyclist or walker can be so swallowed up by the chalky escarpments of the North Downs that the swish of fast-moving traffic feels a million miles away.

The major roads are testament to the fact that this area has been a main thoroughfare since neolithic times: tracks along the Downs enabled walking travellers to stick to higher, drier ground on their journeys between the important centres of Stonehenge and Dover. Some of this route was dubbed the 'Pilgrim's Way' in the Victorian era, and this name has stuck for the section of path that ends at Canterbury (*see p36* **On the pilgrims' trail**).

Beyond the temptation of food and beer at a country pub after the satisfaction of walking the Downs, there is little in this area of Kent to draw you indoors. Two historic highlights are just outside the county seat of Maidstone, at the foot of the North Downs: the fairytale **Leeds Castle** is one of Kent's main tourist attractions and, two miles further west, is the lesser-known **Stoneacre**, a delightful yeoman's house buried in the heart of orchard country.

Village highlights

The area may not be bursting with major visitor draws, but what it does have is plenty of lovely villages. Handily, the majority of the most appealing are stretched along an axis that follows the North Downs Way (and, to the south, the M20) between Maidstone and Ashford; a country tour, taking in a handful of them, is as enjoyable a way as any to pass a leisurely day.

Despite the heavy traffic traversing it, the centre of **Lenham** (nine miles south-east of Maidstone) has retained its village character. On its large, pretty square is the Dog and Bear Hotel (01622 858219), built in 1602 as a coaching inn, which once boasted stables for 'six pairs'. Queen Anne stayed at the hotel in 1704, a visit commemorated by the royal coat of arms above the main entrance.

A few miles further south-east is **Charing**, not so much a village as an attractive tiny town with a twisting high street lined with mellow walls and roofs. An archbishop's palace was built here in 1333, the last in a chain that started at Otford, and the final resting-place for travellers en route to Canterbury. The ivy-covered ruins of this palace can still be seen by the parish church of SS Peter and Paul. The barn to the east of these ruins was built in the 14th century as the archbishops' great hall. Henry VIII stayed overnight here on his way to the famous meeting with the French king Francis I at the Field of the Cloth of Gold near Guisnes in 1520. The block upon which St John the Baptist's head fell is said to have been kept in the church – a present from Richard the Lionheart that was later removed during the dissolution of the monasteries.

Another mile or so south-east is **Westwell**, nestling beneath the Downs in the middle of luscious, pastoral countryside. Although not far from the M20, it feels well off the beaten track and from higher on the Downs is hidden from view by towering horse chestnut trees. The one place for refreshment is the 250-year-old Wheel Inn (01233 712430), which has three cosy rooms and a huge beer garden.

About the same distance south-east again, you can walk to **Eastwell** and **Boughton Lees**. En route is the bomb-damaged, 15th-century church of St Mary's, which remains sacred ground despite being in ruins. The churchyard contains a number of impressive tombs, including that of Richard III's bastard son, who fled to Kent after his father's death at

By train from London

Trains to **Maidstone East** leave **Victoria** every half an hour (journey time approx **1hr**). Trains to **Ashford** leave **Victoria** hourly and pass through **Lenham** and **Charing** (journey time to Ashford **1hr 25mins**). Trains to **Faversham** leave from **Victoria** every 25mins and pass through **Chatham** and **Sittingbourne** (journey time to Faversham is between **1hr** and **1hr 30mins**).

Lap up the beauty of the **Saxon Shore Way**.

the Battle of Bosworth and worked as a stonemason at nearby Eastwell Manor.

Two miles to the east of here is **Wye**, probably best known nowadays for its agricultural college, affiliated with the University of London. A college was founded here in 1428 by Archbishop John Kempe as a seminary college for priests, but was surrendered to the Crown during the dissolution. On the hillside to the north of the town is a white chalk crown, carved into the hillside for the coronation of Edward VII in 1902 by students of Wye College. Wye is a charming village, though not essentially Kentish: it has a remarkably Georgian look, with many of its 17th-century houses unusually uniform and small in scale, radiating out from the 13th-century church. At the bottom end of Bridge Street opposite the station, is the Tickled Trout (*see p35*), an attractive riverside pub with plenty of seats outside – perfect for al fresco imbibing. The New Flying Horse on Upper Bridge Street (01233 812297) also has rooms.

Tiny and pretty, **Chilham** (eight miles north-east of Ashford) is probably one of the most visited villages in the entire county, with half-timbered Tudor houses leading up to a picture-perfect square framed by a church and castle on opposite sides. It's a two-pub, one-tearoom village: the Copper Kettle (01227 730303) offers cream teas and does a roaring trade on hot

days. Also on the village square is the White Horse (01227 730355), with seats outside. Bar food and more substantial meals can be had at the less picturesque Woolpack (01227 730208), at the bottom of the hill towards the station. For a good vista of the castle (actually a handsome red-brick Jacobean manor) and grounds, walk down School Hill.

The lonely sea and the sky

For those who like wide open spaces, sea birds and plenty of sky, the Swale, on the north-west Kent coast, is the place for windblown estuary walks. The modern market town of Sittingbourne (one-time maker of sailing barges) and the pretty and pedestrianised Faversham are the major borough towns of the area, but it's the **Isle of Sheppey**, the Swale estuary that divides it from the mainland, and walks along the nearby coastal Saxon Shore Way, that are the draw. Avoid the caravan horrors of Leysdown or Sheerness and head to **Harty** in the south-east of the island, and the Ferry House Inn (01795 510214) for a bite to eat before a muddy tour of the surrounding marshlands and saltings. Should you fancy a dip, then the beaches east beyond Leysdown are reasonably quiet and include naturist bathing.

Maritime Medway

In the area north of the Nort Kent Downs where the Medway, Thames and Swale rivers meet, sit the sprawling towns of **Rochester**, **Gillingham** and **Chatham**. Though there's much to be found here for lovers of castles, Charles Dickens and all things maritime, the area – sliced up by the motorway – lacks noteworthy accommodation or bijou places to eat (although Newington Manor between Rochester and Sittingbourne is pleasant and convenient; 01795 842053; doubles £42-£52). Highlights in Rochester include the castle and cathedral and a number of Dickens heritage sites – his writing chalet behind the Charles Dickens Centre on Rochester High Street (01634 844176; you can see it without visiting the disappointing centre), Restoration House (01634 843666), the model for Miss Havisham's jolly abode in *Great Expectations*, and in nearby Higham-by-Rochester, Dickens' final home at Gad's Hill Place (01474 822366).

Nautical types shouldn't miss the historic dockyards at Chatham (01634 823800/ www.chdt.org.uk), or a trip on the splendid coal-fired paddle steamer the Kingswear Castle (01634 827648/www.pskc.freeserve.co.uk); for their military counterparts, there's an award-winning museum devoted to the work of the Royal Engineers at Gillingham (01634 406397/ www.royalengineers.org.uk).

What to see & do

Kent County Council produces a catalogue containing over 100 routes to explore in the county. For a free copy phone 01622 221526, or check the South East of England Tourist Board's website: www.seetb.org.uk.

Tourist Information Centres

18 The Church Yard, Ashford, TN23 1QG (01233 629165/fax 01233 639166/www.ashford.gov.uk). **Open** *Easter-Oct* 9.30am-5.30pm Mon-Sat. *Nov-Easter* 9.30am-5pm Mon-Sat.

95 High Street, Rochester, ME1 1LX (01634 843666/www.medway.gov.uk). **Open** 9am-5pm Mon-Fri; 10am-5pm Sat, Sun.

The Gatehouse, Palace Gardens, Mill Street, Maidstone, ME15 6YE (01622 602169/fax 01622 673581). **Open** *Easter-Oct* 9.30am-5pm Mon-Sat; 10am-4pm Sun. *Nov-Easter* 9.30am-5pm Mon-Fri; 9.30-2pm Sat.

The Fleur de Lis, Preston Street, Faversham, ME13 8NS (01795 534542). **Open** *Easter-Oct* 10am-4pm Mon-Sat; 10am-1pm Sun. *Nov-Easter* 10am-4pm Mon-Sat.

Bike hire

Ken James Ltd *22A Beaver Road, Ashford (01233 634334).*
Close to the rail station.

Belmont

Belmont Park, Throwley, nr Faversham (01795 890202). **Open** *Easter Sun-Sept* (guided tours) 2-5pm Sun, bank hols. Last entry 4.30pm. **Admission** *House & gardens* £5.25; £2.50-£4.75 concessions. *Gardens only* £2.75; £1 concessions.
This beautiful 18th-century mansion, the work of Samuel Wyatt, has stunning views of Kent. It was bought by General George Harris in 1801 with the proceeds from his successful military career in India. In 1815 he was made Lord Harris for his victory at the Battle of Seringapatam, and inside are mementoes from the family's history and travels, including paintings of Trinidad by Michel Cazabon, Indian silverware and the most extensive private collection of clocks in the country.

Doddington Place Gardens

Doddington, nr Sittingbourne (01795 886101). **Open** *Easter-Sept* 10.30am-5pm Tue-Thur, bank hols; 2-5pm Sun. **Admission** £3.50; 75p concessions.
During the summer, this private Victorian mansion throws open its landscaped gardens to the public. The ten acres of grounds are surrounded by gently rolling wooded countryside, including a woodland garden, a large Edwardian sunken rock garden with pools, a formal sunken garden (best in late summer), and a flint and brick folly. Kids love to walk inside the impressive clipped yew hedges that line the extensive lawns. There's also a café. Adjacent to Doddington Place is an enchanting and well-maintained church, one of two in England dedicated to the Beheading of St John the Baptist. A reference is made to a church on this site in the 1086 Domesday Book, though it's likely there has been one here since Saxon times. Inside, the 'double squint' allows views from the lectern into both the

chancel and the south chapel. On the left, towards the front of the church, is an unusually low window, thought to have been used for administering holy communion to plague or leprosy sufferers standing outside.

Leeds Castle

Broomfield, nr Maidstone (01622 765400/www.leeds-castle.co.uk). **Open** *Mar-Oct* 10am-6pm daily. *Nov-Feb* 10am-4pm daily. Last entry 1hr before closing. **Admission** *Castle & park* £10; £6.50-£8.50 concessions. *Park only* £8.50; £5.20-£7 concessions.
Stunningly sited on two small islands in the middle of a lake, Leeds was built by the Normans shortly after 1066 on the site of a Saxon manor house, converted into a royal palace by Henry VIII and now now contains a mishmash of medieval furnishings, paintings, tapestries and, bizarrely, the world's finest collection of antique dog collars. The castle's greatest attractions, however, are external. Apart from the flower-filled gardens, there's the Culpeper Garden (an outsize cottage garden), a duckery and an aviary containing over 100 rare bird species and, best of the lot, the maze, which centres on a spectacular underground grotto adorned with stone mythical beasts and shell mosaics. Facilities for disabled visitors are good. Special events are held throughout the year, including a grand firework spectacular for Guy Fawkes' day.

Rochester Cathedral

Rochester (01634 401301). **Open** 8am-6pm daily. **Admission** free; donations welcome.
The second-oldest in England, this small cathedral has a fine collection of medieval wall paintings, charming floor tiles and some very old grafitti.

Stoneacre

Otham, nr Maidstone (01622 862871/www.nationaltrust.org.uk). **Open** *Apr-Oct* 2-6pm Wed, Sat. Last entry 5pm. **Admission** (NT) £2.60; £1.30 concessions.
At the north end of Otham village, three miles southeast of Maidstone, is this National Trust property – a half-timbered yeoman's house. It's tucked away down a narrow winding road, so if you're coming by car, walk the 100 yards or so down to the house from the village car park. Stoneacre's attractions include a great hall and crownpost dating from the late 15th century, and the delightful, recently restored cottage garden surrounding the house. There's also a children's trail.

Where to stay

See also p35 **Read's**.

Barnfield

Charing, nr Ashford, TN27 0BN (tel/fax 01233 712421). **Rates** £26-£30 single; £46-£48 double/twin. **Rooms** 2 single; 2 double; 1 twin. **No credit cards.**
Almost halfway between Charing and Egerton is this 15th-century house set in 30 acres of sheep-farming land, where Martin and Phillada Pym manage a cosy home from home. There are five bedrooms, each with its own washbasin and facilities for making hot drinks, but guests share the bathroom. They can also use the tennis court and the comfortable, book-lined lounge. Children welcome. No smoking throughout.

*Leave roundabout at Charing on the A20 exit to Lenham;
after 400 yards turn left down Hook Lane; after ½ mile go
over crossroads; another ½ mile turn left through new road
barriers; go 1 mile; house is on left with white metal fence.*

Chilston Park

*Sandway, Lenham, ME17 2BE (01622 859803/
fax 01622 858588/www.arcadianhotels.co.uk).*
Rates £105-£205 double/twin; £155-£205 four-
poster; £205 suite. Breakfast £12.95 per person
(Eng/cont). **Rooms** (all en suite) 41 double/twin;
10 four-poster; 2 suites. **Credit** AmEx, DC, MC, V.
If you can cope with the eccentricities of staff in period
fancy dress, elaborate furnishings and candlelit interiors at night, Chilston Park offers the complete country
manor house experience. It's a red-brick grade I listed
17th-century mansion set in acres of parkland overlooking a lake. Many of the bedrooms (with 'Camelot',
'Raj' and 'Gothic' themes) have four-posters, and there
are drawing rooms galore, croquet lawns, tennis courts
and a formal restaurant (main courses £17.50-£21.50).
Children and small dogs welcome.
*A20 S from J8 off M20 towards Ashford, then right into
Lenham; turn right; pass Lenham station; left into Boughton
Road; over crossroads and M20; Chilston Park is on left.*

Eastwell Manor

*Eastwell Park, Boughton Lees, TN25 4HR (01233
219955/reservations 0500 526735/fax 01233
635530/www.prideofbritainhotels.com).* **Rates**
Hotel £200-£245 double/twin; £265-£355 suite;
£215 deluxe four-poster; £265 superior four-poster.
Self-catering cottages £500-£900 per week. **Rooms**
Hotel (all en suite) 18 double/twin; 5 suites. *Cottages*
4 1-bed; 10 2-bed; 5 3-bed. **Credit** AmEx, DC, MC, V.
Despite the modern spa and conference blocks that
threaten to spoil the view, Eastwell Manor itself is a fine
Tudoresque house in an impressive setting. Sheep nib-
ble at the boundaries, while manicured croquet lawns
and clipped topiary displays give way to views over the
Downs. Inside, roaring log fires, linenfold panelling and
yards of Victorian brocade give a suitably stately home
impression and there are 23 amenity-packed bedrooms
and suites, the best with views over the garden. For those
travelling with families or on business, the self-contained
mews cottages – with kitchen, sitting room, fax and ISDN
line, offer privacy and good value. There's a new spa with
treatment rooms, as well as indoor and outdoor pools,
tennis courts and a formal restaurant (*see p35*). Children
and dogs welcome. No-smoking rooms available.
*J9 off M20; take A28 towards Canterbury, then A251
towards Faversham; hotel is on right-hand side.*

Harrow Hill Hotel

*Warren Street, nr Lenham, ME17 2ED (01622
858727/fax 01622 850026).* **Rates** £50 single; £70
double/twin. Phone for prices for children sharing
parents' room. **Rooms** 6 double (5 en suite); 3 twin (all
en suite); 5 family rooms (all en suite). **Credit** MC, V.
Once a forge and pitstop on the Pilgrim's Way, the
Harrow Hill has been converted into a labyrinthine 15-
room hotel with a bar, lounge and restaurant overlooking
a patio and garden. What it lacks in country charm (the
pub is very 'olde worlde', but elsewhere the decor is
straightforward, with all mod cons) it makes up for in con-
venience. Children welcome. No-smoking rooms available.
*J8 off M20; A20 for 6 miles; turn left into Warren Street;
first house on right.*

Ringlestone Inn
& Farmhouse Hotel

*Ringlestone Hamlet, near Harrietsham, Maidstone,
ME17 1NX (01622 859900/fax 01622 859966/
www.ringlestone.com).* **Rates** £79 single occupancy;
£89 double/twin; £89 four-poster; £10 supplement
for child sharing parents' double. Breakfast £12
(Eng); £9 (cont). **Rooms** (all en suite) 2 double/twin;
1 four-poster. **Credit** AmEx, DC, MC, V.
A former hospice for monks and Tudor ale house, the
attractive Ringlestone Inn is decked out in rustic oak,
bricks, beams, flint and inglenooks. Accommodation is
in the adjoining farmhouse: three luxurious bedrooms
(there are plans for a further 10), plainly but smartly decorated, each with a reasonably-sized en suite bathroom
as well as CD player, TV and tea- and coffee-making
facilities. The whole house – including a study with
a table that seats 14 – can be hired for parties or conferences. The menu at the inn uses local Kentish ingredients and specialises in splendid home-made pies.
Children welcome. All bedrooms no-smoking.
*J8 from M20; follow signs for Hollingbourne; go through
village up steep hill; take first turning on right signposted
Ringlestone; hotel is at the bottom of the road on the right.*

Stowting Hill House

*Stowting, nr Ashford, TN25 6BE (01303
862881/fax 01303 863433).* **Rates** £30 single
occupancy; £55 twin. **Rooms** 3 twin (2 en suite).
No credit cards.
An 18th-century family house with views over the Downs
and a garden with tennis court, Stowting Hill offers modest B&B accommodation in three twin-bedded rooms.
There's a conservatory to the rear where arrivals take tea
or coffee, and a comfortable sitting room. Children over
eight welcome. All bedrooms are no smoking.
*J11 off M20; take B2068 N towards Canterbury; after 4½
miles take left turn opposite BP garage; house is nearly 2
miles further on left.*

Wife of Bath

*4 Upper Bridge Street, Wye, TN25 5AF
(01233 812232/812540/fax 01233 813630/
www.wifeofbath.com).* **Rates** £45 single; £65-£95

Eastwell Manor promises grand designs and private mews cottages (opposite and above).

double. Breakfast £5 (Eng). Closed 1 week after Christmas. **Rooms** (all en suite) 3 double; 2 twin. **Credit** AmEx, DC, MC, V.

A red-brick 18th-century house on Wye's main street, and a few minutes' walk from the train station, the Wife of Bath draws heavily on its Chaucerian theme. Each simple bedroom is named after a different character in the *Canterbury Tales*, including the Knight's and the Miller's rooms, which are in converted stables and share a small kitchen. For the restaurant, *see p36*. Children welcome. No-smoking rooms available.
J9 off M20; take A28 towards Canterbury; 4 miles after Ashford follow signs to Wye on right.

Where to eat & drink

The **Tickled Trout** on the river at Wye (01233 812227) and the **Flying Horse** on the cricket green in Boughton Lees (01233 620914) both offer better-than-average pub lunches; the **Ringlestone Inn** (*see p34*) has an excellent menu of home-made pies, hearty casseroles and snacks.

Eastwell Manor Restaurant

Eastwell Park, Boughton Lees (01233 219955/ www.eastwellmanor.co.uk). **Food served** noon-2.30pm, 7-9.30pm Mon-Thur; noon-2.30pm, 7-10pm Fri, Sat; noon-3.30pm, 7-9.30pm Sun. **Set lunches** £10 2 courses; £15 3 courses. **Set dinner** £32 3 courses. **Credit** AmEx, DC, MC, V.

The dining room at Eastwell Manor is brocaded and panelled, with stucco ceiling, giant stone fireplace and views over the formal gardens. In keeping with the surroundings, the atmosphere and service is formal. But the well-chosen menu of modern European dishes more than compensates for the hushed tone. Salmon and scallop boudin with spring vegetables, delicate fillet of beef with a punchy beetroot and onion marmalade, or monkfish with crisped aubergine slices and pesto are all expertly turned out and beautifully presented. Puddings – perhaps a bitter orange parfait or blueberry mousse – are spectacular feats of sugared engineering and come with

recommended glasses of dessert wines. There's also a seriously priced, mostly French wine list. An average dinner for two costs £40 a head including wine.

George Inn

The Street, Newnham (01795 890237). **Food served** noon-2.30pm, 7-9.30pm Mon-Thur; noon-2.30pm, 7-10pm Fri, Sat; noon-2.30pm, 7-9pm Sun. **Credit** MC, V.

Handy for visitors to Doddington Place Gardens (*see p33*), the George has served as the village brewhouse since the 16th century and formally became an inn in 1781, before Shepherd Neame got its hands on it in 1841. The place gets packed, especially at the weekends, when locals come for the superior Sunday roasts. Book in advance for evening meals (a three-course dinner without drinks is around £25). Across the road is the charming Periwinkle Press (01795 890388) picture framers and tiny bookshop, also the local newsagent and sweetshop.

Pepperbox Inn

Fairbourne Heath, nr Ulcombe (01622 842558). **Food served** noon-2.15pm Mon, Sun; noon-2.15pm, 7-9.45pmTue-Sat. **Credit** MC, V.

A few miles south of Leeds Castle and high up on Windmill Hill, the Pepperbox Inn has wonderful views across the Downs and the Weald. On fine days you can absorb the views from tables outside beneath a pergola. The menu is a mix of pub grub and more interesting bistro classics, and daily specials (around £5 for starters, £10-£11.50 for mains) might include fresh sardines fried in garlic butter, calves' liver with sage and sautéed potatoes, or baked cod and prawn mornay.

Read's

Macknade Manor, Canterbury Road, Faversham (01795 535344/www.reads.com). **Food served** noon-2pm, 7-9pm Tue-Sat. **Set lunch** £18.50 3 courses. **Set dinner** £38 3 courses. **Credit** AmEx, DC, MC, V.

Rona and David Pitchford's long-standing Faversham restaurant has recently relocated and was about to add six smart rooms (from £150 a night) to the premises as we went to press. The new home – in a handsome red-brick Georgian mansion with gravel drive and small terrace, forms a suitably country-house backdrop for a menu that mixes classic French and modern British influences and uses local ingredients where possible. So, lamb comes from Kent (perhaps slices of roasted rump, served with ratatouille and a rosemary jus) and fish from Whitstable (in a delicate trio of smoked haddock starters, or in halibut served with asparagus and lobster cream). Puddings might be an iced honey and nougatine parfait with a sablé of Kentish apples, or the house 'chocoholics anonymous' in five different formats. The 280-strong wine list contains a range of reasonably priced bottles, as well as a good selection by the glass. Coffee and sweets are served in the adjoining drawing room. Service deserves particular praise, managing to be friendly and dedicated without being too formal.

Wife of Bath

4 Upper Bridge Street, Wye (01233 812232/ www.wifeofbath.com). **Food served** noon-2.30pm, 7-10.30pm Tue-Sat. **Set lunch** £11.50 2 courses. **Set dinner** £25.75 3 courses. **Credit** AmEx, DC, MC, V. In the centre of pretty Wye, this red-brick hotel (*see p34*) and restaurant combines heavy-duty homage to

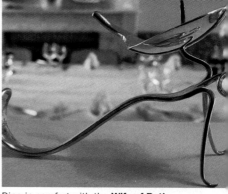

Dine in comfort with the **Wife of Bath**.

Chaucer's pilgrims with an up-to-date menu that pays tribute to local produce. Seafood comes from Hythe, fruit and asparagus from local farms, and venison from the nearby Brabourne Estate. The set dinner might include a warm chicken liver salad with baby red chard or smoked haddock and chive mousse, followed by steamed cod with cabbage and bacon or braised shank of lamb with Puy lentils and thyme. The atmosphere is relaxed.

On the pilgrims' trail

After the murder of Henry II's 'upstart priest' Thomas à Becket in Canterbury Cathedral in 1170, and his canonisation shortly afterwards, the site of his martyrdom became a shrine and the object of pilgrimage. The route taken between London and Canterbury later inspired Geoffrey Chaucer in his 14th-century tale of 'sondry folk, by aventure yfalle/In felaweshipe, and pilgrims were they alle' who set out one April day from the Tabard Inn at Southwark and embark on a story-telling contest to help pass the time on the journey. The Pilgrims' Way, as it later became known, has today been pretty much swallowed up by the well-maintained North Downs Way, a 153-mile stretch from the Surrey hills to the white cliffs of Dover. However, it does pick up the original path between the Medway towns and Canterbury.

The route – well marked with the acorn symbol of the National Trails – covers path- and bridleway and the occasional stretch of road, passing orchards and hopfields, oast houses and villages, over chalky hills and down wooded dales, and finally descends into Canterbury through the towers of the West Gate. The path between **Lenham**, **Charing**, **Westwell** and **Chilham** (pictured), overlooking the

Stour Valley, is a particularly picturesque chunk if you want to tackle a short stretch with plenty of pitstops on the way.

There are several good guides and maps devoted to the North Downs Way, details of which can be found on the excellent National Trails website (www.nationaltrails.gov.uk) which also includes information on where to stay and eat in the area. Alternatively, phone the National Trails Office (01622 696185).

Rye, Dungeness & Romney Marsh

Cobbled streets, sandy beaches and a desolate promontory.

Over the centuries it has been the threat of invasion that has defined this corner of Kent. Fear of Napoleon prompted the construction of the Royal Military Canal, the sleepy waterway that idles from Rye in the west to Hythe in the east, while to its south government concessions and paranoia launched the Cinque Ports and strewed the region with Norman and Tudor castles, Martello towers, concrete bunkers and now army rifle ranges. All this military activity has been largely irrelevant in the face of the area's real enemy, the savage storms and occasional floods that have devastated towns, changed the course of rivers and left once-thriving ports high and dry. Nowadays, the greatest influence on the area is tourism, blighting some parts of the coast but boosting the local economy and keeping its towns sleek.

Rye is a lovely place, a gorgeous jumble of Norman, Tudor and Georgian architecture, scrambling over one of the area's few hills, its narrow, cobbled streets chock-full of antique shops, tearooms and pubs, its sky filled with shrieking seagulls. Of course, it's too popular (go out of season if you can), but Rye is a living town, with real shops and a lively Thursday market. It's small enough to see most things in a day. The best antique and curio shops are on the High Street, where there's also a great old record shop in the Old Grammar School (built 1636) – pick up *Tony Blackburn Sings* for £4 – and the second-hand bookshop Chapter & Verse (01797 222692). Slightly twee pottery shops are everywhere (particularly towards the recently revamped Strand Quay), but you can at least keep the kids busy making their own at Paint Pots (01797 222033). Apart from simply wandering the streets, it is worth taking a look at **St Mary's Church** (dating originally from 1150), the pithy **Castle Museum**, the 13th-century **Ypres Tower** (both Gun Garden; 01797 226728) and the medieval Landgate gateway (built 1329). The Medieval Festival (held over a weekend in August) is a busy but fun time to visit.

Rye's prosperity was founded on its port; its fine state of preservation is partly thanks to the loss of that port when the coast retreated a couple of miles. It's worth driving to **Rye Harbour** to enjoy some windswept walks, past a bird sanctuary and the ruins of Henry VIII's Camber Castle.

Winchelsea, a couple of miles south-west of Rye, was built on a never-completed medieval grid pattern when 'Old' Winchelsea was swept into the sea in the storms of 1287. The place is proud of its status as England's smallest town, but really it's a sleepy village with a jaw-dropping wealth of medieval (and later) architecture, a pub, a shop and a tearoom. The church of St Thomas à Becket (despite the worst efforts of the pillaging French) contains some fine medieval carvings (including the head of Edward I). A further mile or so south-east of here is pebbly Winchelsea beach, which is sandy at low tide; there's a good fish shack about half way there on the left.

Heading east from Rye, along the coastal road, is popular **Camber Sands**, a vast and glittering sandy beach that's hard-pressed by the wind and caravan parks.

The desolation of Dungeness

It's hard to imagine a greater contrast to the tame pleasures of Rye than desolate **Dungeness**, only a few miles to the east. A thousand years ago Dungeness Point didn't even exist. Longshore drift has built up huge banks of flint shingle, some of them 57 feet deep, which stretch miles out into the sea in a unique promontory. There are currently over 40 square miles of this undulating giant's sandpit, making it the largest accumulation of shingle in

---

By train from London

Trains leave for **Rye** from **Charing Cross** hourly. They also pass through **Waterloo East**, **London Bridge** and **Tunbridge**. Passengers have to change at **Ashford** (journey time **1hr 45mins**) or **Hastings** (journey time **2hrs**). Info: www.connex.co.uk.

the world, with only one-third of it covered in vegetation. The light on this remote, gloriously bleak promontory is odd, reflected from the sea on both sides.

The surreal quality of the landscape is enhanced by the presence of a massive nuclear power station with a hum that's audible for miles around. The filmmaker Derek Jarman bought a small cottage here and his book *The Garden* describes his battles with the elements; the fruits of his labours can still be seen on the road to the lighthouse, although his former home is of course private property.

The power station is linked to the seaside developments straggling away to the north towards Folkestone by the dinky **Romney, Hythe & Dymchurch Railway**. Out of season (most of the year) these windswept coastal villages and towns look forlorn. Unchecked post-war development hasn't helped, but nor has the army and its rifle ranges.

The best place to stop on the coast, before you reach Hythe, is **Dymchurch**, which is proud to proclaim itself 'Children's Paradise' – the presence of MW's Amusement Park, with its dodgems and arcades, is the best explanation we can find for this. There's also a sandy beach and a fine example of a **Martello tower** (topped by a restored 26-pounder gun).

Further north, **Hythe** is the end-stop of the miniature railway and the Royal Military Canal; the latter lends most charm to a town centre of fine buildings but busy roads and random housing developments. The High Street has been pedestrianised and has some decent shops. In the summer, the hollyhock-packed little streets that meander up the steep hill to the Church of St Leonard are charming and a welcome respite from the frenetic seafront. The 11th-century church is another of the area's triumphs, complete with bone-packed crypt.

Inland is **Romney Marsh** and a score of interesting villages. Away from the Marsh, **Lympne** is worth visiting (for its castle and Wild Animal Park), as are **Warehorne**, **Stone** and **Appledore**. The latter used to be a Jute and then Norman port on the English Channel; now it's around six miles inland. It's here that you can find the best walks along the Royal Military Canal: trudge north along either bank, or drive south along the road to Rye, stopping wherever you can.

What to see & do

Tourist Information Centre

Rye Heritage Centre, Strand Quay, Rye, TN31 7AY (01797 226696/www.rye.org.uk/ryetic). **Open** *Mar-Oct* 9am-5.30pm Mon-Sat; 10am-5.30pm Sun. *Nov-Feb* 10am-4pm daily.

Winchelsea beach – pebbly at high tide, sandy at low.

As well as the tourist information centre, the Heritage Centre houses the Heritage Exhibition and the Story of Rye, a 20-minute sound and light show (£2; £1-£1.50 concessions). An audio tour of the town is available from the centre (£2; £1-£1.50 concessions).

Bike hire

Rye Hire *1 Cyprus Place, Rye (01797 223033).* A few minutes' walk from the station.

Brenzett Aeronautical Museum

Ivychurch Road, Brenzett, Romney Marsh (01233 344747). **Open** *Easter-Oct* 11am-5.30pm Sat, Sun, bank hols. *July-Oct* 1-5.30pm Wed-Fri. **Admission** £2.50; £1.50 concessions; free under-16s.

A couple of cow sheds (well, hangars) in a field don't look that inspiring, but this is a thrilling treat for World War II enthusiasts: a lovingly compiled collection of rescued aircraft and memorabilia, much of it salvaged from the region.

Dungeness Nuclear Power Station

Dungeness Point (01797 321815/www.bnfl.co.uk). **Open** *Mar-Oct* 10am-4pm daily. *Nov-Feb* by appointment only. **Admission** free.

From the eastern edge of the Weald of Kent across Romney Marsh, a huge building dominates the horizon; at night the illuminations make it look like the Pompidou Centre. This is Dungeness nuclear power station, sited almost on the tip of Dungeness Point. The hum is audible for miles, and was used as a backing soundtrack

Old Lighthouse
Dungeness Road, Dungeness (01797 321300).
Open *Mar-May, Oct* 10.45am-5pm Sat, Sun. *June-Sept* 10.30am-5pm daily, bank hols. Closed Nov-Feb. Opening times for 2002 not yet confirmed; phone to check. **Admission** phone for prices.
No longer operational, but there are fine views from the top over the power station and the Ness.

Port Lympne Wild Animal Park
Lympne, nr Hythe (01303 264647/www.howletts.net).
Open 10am-5.30pm daily. Last entry 4pm (3pm in winter). **Admission** £9.80; £7.80 concessions.
Amble round Sir Philip Sassoon's sumptous mansion (complete with a fine muralled room by Rex Whistler), then head off into the extensive grounds and get close to the wild beasts. This is the collection started and idiosyncratically run by the late John Aspinall and it's particularly good for gorillas, wolves and the big cats. The views over Romney Marsh are sensational.

Romney, Hythe & Dymchurch Railway
New Romney Station (01797 362353/www.rhdr.demon.co.uk). **Open** *Feb-end July* 10am-5pm daily. *End July-Oct* 10am-5pm daily. Closed Nov-Jan. **Tickets** phone for details.
A miniature railway barrels merrily from Dungeness Point to Hythe, stopping at the small beach towns along the coast. Along the way it passes some fine, flat scenery and seems to sweep through any number of back gardens. It was built by the millionaire racing driver Captain Howey in 1927 and everything (track, engines, the sweetest carriages) is one third standard size.

Rye Art Gallery
107 High Street, Rye (01797 222433).
Open 10.30am-1pm, 2-5pm daily. **Admission** free.
A constantly changing series of exhibitions, encompassing photography, paintings, pottery, glasswork, jewellery and crafts, mostly by locals to a consistently high standard. The fresh white walls and sympathetic lighting set off the exhibits well. Prices are reasonable.

for Derek Jarman's film *The Garden*. The slickly presented visitor centre has displays about the area and information on 'harnessing nature's forces'.

Dungeness RSPB Nature Reserve
Dungeness Road, Lydd (01797 320588/www.rspb.org.uk). **Open** *Mar-Oct* Nature Reserve 9am-dusk daily. Visitor centre 10am-5pm daily. *Nov-Feb* Both 10am-4pm daily. **Admission** £3; £1-£2 concessions.
The best place to see the fragile ecology of Dungeness Point. This reserve is built around huge gravel pits; from the hides you can see scores of wildfowl species and, in late spring, terns, reed and sedge warblers, whitethroats and yellow wagtails migrating north. There are also scores of unusual moths and butterflies. It costs just £3 for the hour-long walk around the reserve; there's no charge to look around the hide that constitutes the visitors' centre.

Lamb House
West Street, Rye (01797 890651/www.nationaltrust.org.uk). **Open** *Apr-Oct* 2-6pm Wed, Sat. Closed Nov-Mar. **Admission** (NT) £2.60; £1.30 concessions.
The novelist Henry James lived in this stately townhouse from 1898 to 1916, at which point the writer GF Benson moved in (1919-1940), closely followed by his brother, AC (1922-25). Lamb House is now a small museum. The garden house where James wrote most of his novels, including *The Ambassadors* and *The Golden Bowl*, was destroyed by bombing in 1940.

Where to stay

Most of the good accommodation is clustered around Rye and Winchelsea; the best places tend to be booked out weeks ahead. If the options below are full, try the swish **White Vine House** (01797 224748; doubles £80-£115) or the ancient **Mermaid Inn** (01797 223065; doubles £75-£90), both in Rye itself, or **Playden Cottage Guesthouse** (01797 222234; doubles £62-£66) just outside. **Wickham Manor**, a National Trust farmhouse outside Winchelsea, is also worth trying (01797 226216/07885 790597; doubles £30-£35). They'll also stable your horse.

Jeake's House
Mermaid Street, Rye, TN31 7ET (01797 222828/fax 01797 222623/www.jeakeshouse.com). **Rates** £31.50-£65 per person. **Rooms** 1 single; 10 double (9 en suite); 1 four-poster suite (en suite). **Credit** MC, V.

An very atmospheric small hotel. The look is smart (mahogany beds, heavy curtains), but light and appropriate to the house (it was built as a wool house in 1689). The rooms are lovely, have all the amenities you could want, and there is a decent selection of vegetarian dishes for breakfast. Proprietor Jenny Hadfield is the daughter of the novelist and short story writer John Burke, who was born in Rye in 1922.

Little Orchard House

West Street, Rye, TN31 7ES (tel/fax 01797 223831/www.littleorchardhouse.com). **Rates** £45-£65 single occupancy; £64-£90 double/twin/four-poster. **Rooms** (all en suite) 1 double/twin; 2 four-poster. **Credit** MC, V.
Sara Brinkhurst's appealing Georgian townhouse in the centre of Rye has retained many original features, such as a pretty walled garden and a watchtower. Open fires, antiques and a panelled bookroom enhance the period feel. There's a four-poster in the largest room. All rooms are no-smoking and breakfasts feature local organic produce. Children over 12 welcome.

Old Vicarage

66 Church Square, Rye, TN31 7HF (01797 222119/fax 01797 227466/www.oldvicaragerye.co.uk). **Rates** £54-£58 single occupancy; £70-£78 double/twin; £86 family room. **Rooms** (all en suite) 5 double/twin; 1 family. **No credit cards.**
A very pink Georgian detached house, with a small walled garden, which faces on to the lovely square surrounding St Mary's at the top of Rye. The sitting room and dining room have exposed beams, and most of the bedrooms (heavy on the Laura Ashley) have views across the rooftops of Rye. The breakfasts, making the most of excellent local produce, are stupendous. All bedrooms no-smoking. Children over five welcome.

Romney Bay House

Coast Road, Littlestone-on-Sea, New Romney, TN28 8QY (01797 364747/fax 01797 367156). **Rates** £60-£95 single occupancy; £80-£140 double/twin; £125 four-poster. **Rooms** (all en suite) 2 twin; 6 double; 2 four-poster. **Credit** MC, V.
The only really good place to stay on the Dungeness peninsula and it's bang on a pebble beach at the end of a bumpy track, enveloped by the Littlestone golf course. Helmut and Jennifer Görlich have painstakingly renovated this beach house – designed by Sir Clough Williams-Ellis, who built Portmeirion – into a ten-room hotel. Helmut is a witty host who quickly puts guests at ease; Jennifer prepares the excellent home cooking (*see below*). The rooms are spotless, the house filled with antique furniture in country-home style, and there's a lookout (with telescope) for windy days. All bedrooms no-smoking. Children over 14 welcome.
Littlestone-on-Sea is on the B2071 off the A259 at New Romney.

Where to eat & drink

Good food isn't a strong point here and a man could drown in deep-fried brie in Rye if he weren't careful. But there are some decent pubs (some quite ruined, mind you), with fantastically atmospheric interiors – and a few

good restaurants. You need to book well ahead for the area's two better places: **Landgate Bistro** and **Romney Bay House** (*see below*). If you're craving spices, Rye has **Tiger Coast** (5 High Street; 01797 224222), offering Indian fare, and Thai food at the **Lemongrass** (1-2 Tower Street; 01797 222327).

Apart from the pubs below (*and on p41* **Cathedrals of the marsh**), the cottagey **Peace & Plenty** in Playden (01797 280342) and the **Ypres Castle Inn** in Rye (with a splendid setting near the 13th-century Ypres Tower; 01797 223248) offer decent food and good beer. If you're in Winchelsea try the **New Inn** (German Street; 01797 226252) for locally caught fish, while the **Black Lion** in Appledore (15 The Street; 01233 758206) offers stronger brews than the omnipresent tearooms. And on wind-blasted Dungeness Point, the **Britannia** (01797 321959) does a fine pile of fish and chips.

Bayleaves

33-35 The Street, Appledore (01233 758208). **Food served** 10am-5.30pm Tue-Fri, Sun; 9.30am-5.30pm Sat. **No credit cards.**
With the closure of the Appledore Tea Rooms, this cluttered bistro is now the main port of call for anyone who doesn't fancy a pint or ten in the local pubs. The food is all own-made, whether it be the breakfast (from £3.95) or lunch menus (including the likes of smoked salmon salad), or the cream teas and cakes.

Landgate Bistro

5 Landgate, Rye (01797 222829/www.landgatebistro.co.uk). **Food served** 7-9.30pm Tue-Fri; 7-10pm Sat. **Set dinner** (Tue-Thur) £16.90 3 courses. **Credit** AmEx, DC, C, V.
The best restaurant in Rye occupies a small townhouse just by the Landgate gateway. The dishes are modern European in style, and London in price. Great emphasis is placed on locally produced, seasonal ingredients, so expect to find Romney Marsh lamb, fur and feathered game (wild rabbit in wine sauce, £8.90), and local seafood and salads.

Mermaid Inn

Mermaid Street, Rye (01797 223065). **Food served** noon-2.30pm, 7-9.15pm daily. **Set lunch** £17.50 3 courses. **Set dinner** £35 4 courses. **Credit** AmEx, DC, MC, V.
This ancient pub on absurdly quaint Mermaid Street was *rebuilt* in 1420 and does its best to hang on to an authentic charm, despite the ravages of mass tourism and a slight fondness for ye olde pubbe decor. There is a pricey but accomplished restaurant and a small public bar, just off the courtyard. There are also 31 rooms on site (£75 per person).

Romney Bay House

Coast Road, Littlestone-on-Sea (01797 364747). **Food served** 12.30-2.30pm Sat, Sun. **Set dinner** £29.50 4 courses; 8pm sitting, phone to check days. **Credit** MC, V.
This exemplary hotel (*see above*) also serves food to non-residents, but by prior arrangement only. Booking

Cathedrals of the marsh

The strange, low, wind-scoured area south of the Royal Military Canal is a world apart from Pop Larkin's apples-and-oasts Kent. It's at its most bleak on Dungeness Point, but the inland area north and west of Dymchurch, with its grey-stone churches, water dykes and lonely sheep, has a weird intensity. Above all, it's empty; and although there aren't many roads, there still don't seem to be enough signposts.

The area is, however, justly famous for its tiny medieval churches, of which there are 14 still standing (plus a few ruins). No one is clear why there are quite so many packed into such an impoverished region, but it seems that the local merchants (grown fat on the Romney Marsh sheep) were doing all they could to save their souls. Every one of them is worth a visit, but if you're pressed for time you could perhaps start with the grandiose **All Saints** at Lydd (known as the Cathedral of the Marsh), before heading for **St Augustine's** at Brookland, with its extraordinary detached wooden bell tower. North of here is **St Thomas à Becket** at Fairfield, which many consider to be the epitome of the isolated Romney Marsh church (just look for the sign and approach via a causeway). **St Clement** in Old Romney has a particularly lovely interior (used in the 1963 film *Dr Syn*, its aisles painted pink for the occasion), with a magnificent Georgian minstrels' gallery. And **St Mary the Virgin** (pictured) at St Mary in the Marsh carries the understated gravestone of E Nesbit, author of *The Railway Children*, who loved the area and died in the village.

If you're finding your church tour thirsty work, then rest assured that almost every one of God's houses has a public house attached. After some heroic research, we're prepared to vouch for the Shepherd & Crook in Burmarsh, the Red Lion in Snargate, the Star in St Mary in the Mead and, above all, the Woolpack Inn near Brookland (*see p41*). But there are many more, most of them stuffed to the rafters with tales of smugglers and the inevitable ghosts.

A booklet published by the Romney Marsh Historic Churches Trust should be a valuable companion on your tour and is sold at tourist offices and, we found, inside Winchelsea Church.

is essential for dinner, but you can just drop in for breakfast (£10.50), lunch (only weekends, and only snacks, from £6) or all-day coffee or afternoon tea. Dinner menus always begin with a fish starter, followed by the likes of duck breast with plum and onion compote and fresh vegetables as a main. Add a plate of cheeses, assorted fruits in season or nut meringue with cream to finish, and the reasons for its popularity become obvious.

Tea Tree
12 High Street, Winchelsea (01797 226102/ www.the-tea-tree.co.uk). **Food served** 10am-6pm Mon, Wed-Sun. **Credit** MC, V.

A low-ceilinged, whitewashed-walled Kentish tearoom done with charm and panache. Standard home-cooked food for lunch (pork and apple pie, coronation chicken, trifle) is supplemented by all-day cream teas: cottage tea (£3.10, with teacakes), meringue tea (£4.50), and so on.

Woolpack Inn
Beacon Lane, nr Brookland (01797 344321). **Food served** noon-2pm, 6-9pm daily. **Credit** MC, V.

A lovely old Romney Marsh pub, dating back to 1410 and retaining its wattle-and-daub walls and snug ceiling. Portions are huge, the fare simple but filling. Try liver and bacon, lasagne (£4.95), or grilled trout (£6.25). Or settle down to a pint – of prawns, that is (£4.95).

The Heart of Kent

An abundant rural garden that's home to the grape and the grain.

This is the very heart of the Garden of England. Here the gentle rolling hills and valleys of west Kent continue eastwards until they reach the flatlands of Romney Marsh. This enticing landscape of small towns, villages, farmland and forests has remained essentially unchanged for centuries. Countless listed buildings dot the landscape – from late medieval cottages to picture-postcard windmills.

The region began to prosper in the 14th century when Edward III invited Flemish weavers to settle in the area to teach the English a thing or two about producing good-quality cloth. It was a great success and the area became the centre for the manufacture of broadcloth, the export of which was greatly helped by the close proximity of nearby sea ports. The towns of Cranbrook and Tenterden and their surrounding villages thrived for the next 350 years until the silting up of many of the channel ports led to a decline in the industry.

Agriculture took over, especially hops and fruit, although today there are fewer hop gardens and orchards than there used to be, and many oasts, with their distinctive white cowls, have been transformed from dried hop storage to quirky homes. This part of the county also has some of the most promising vineyards in South-east England (*see p47* **Corking Kent**).

Touring country

Perhaps quieter, and attracting fewer tourists than the western Kent Weald (*see p48*), the heart of Kent is an ideal area for walking, biking or touring by car. A circular tour of the region is probably the best way to take in the sights.

The attractive town of **Cranbrook** is dominated by its array of Wealden architecture, particularly the Union Windmill. The Cranbrook Museum is an excellent way of brushing up on insider local history and knowledge. Close by are the Gardens of Gaia (01580 715289) where you will find over 20 acres of nature and sculpture. To the north-east lies the pretty white-weatherboarded village of **Sissinghurst**, known nationwide for the splendour of **Sissinghurst Castle Garden** on its outskirts. Directly north, between peaceful Frittenden and Staplehurst, is **Iden Croft Herbs**, a fascinating and unusual garden for cooking and herbal enthusiasts.

East of Staplehurst is **Headcorn**. Formerly one of the area's major cloth-making centres, today's town has little to offer visitors except the conveniences of a train station, a supermarket, a cash dispenser and a bicycle shop, which does repairs but not hire. It's a good base from which to explore, whatever mode of transport you use.

Sissinghurst Castle Gardens – a Vita Sackville-West creation.

Around here, the fabulous rolling countryside begins to flatten out, and heading south on the A274 you come to a series of beautiful villages, including the unspoilt **Biddenden**, whose village sign depicts the Chulkhurst sisters, England's first recorded Siamese twins. Kent's oldest commercial vineyard is nearby. Further east and north-east are **Smarden**, **Bethersden** and the village of **Pluckley**, which rises high above the surrounding countryside and is reputed to be the most haunted village in the South-east. Pluckley has a claim to fame as the Dering windows capital of Kent – many of the village's houses feature this arched style of window, so called because a member of the Dering family escaped from the Roundheads during the Civil War through a window of this shape. On a more familiar note, Pluckley is also known as the place where much of the *The Darling Buds of May* series was filmed. Its welcoming pub, the Black Horse (01233 840256), boasts a large peaceful beer garden where you can enjoy good pub food and cask ales.

The delightful market town of **Tenterden**, south of Biddenden, with its busy wide tree-lined thoroughfare, is filled with antique shops. The station is the main jumping-on point for the **Kent and East Sussex Railway** for all the *Thomas the Tank Engine* enthusiasts in the family. Trains now run all the way from Tenterden to the moated 13th-century **Bodiam Castle** (*see p57*), East Sussex. Younger children should also enjoy a visit to the **South of England Rare Breeds Centre** at nearby Woodchurch, where petting opportunities abound.

By train from London

Trains to **Headcorn** leave **Charing Cross** about every 30mins; the journey time is just over **1hr**.
Info: www.connex.co.uk.

Leaving Tenterden to the south, the hills gradually descend with the approaching marshlands. Arriving at the village of Small Hythe, you'll find the charming 16th-century country house, **Small Hythe Place** (*see p45* **Queen of the theatre**), once home to the actress Ellen Terry. Wine tastings, tours and tea can be had at **Tenterden Vineyards Park** across the road.

Just over the border with East Sussex at Northiam is the beautiful house and gardens of **Great Dixter** (*see p57*). Returning towards Cranbrook, **Sandhurst Vineyards** and **Rowenden Vineyards** are well worth a tasting or two, while the eccentric collection of vehicles at **CM Booth Collection of Vehicles** in **Rolvenden** is an added attraction in the pretty village.

Between Rolvenden and the tranquil village of Benenden is **Hole Park**, a fabulously peaceful garden.

What to see & do

Tourist Information Centres
Cranbrook Vestry Hall, Stone Street, Cranbrook (tel/fax 01580 712538). **Open** *Apr-Oct* 10am-5pm Mon-Sat. Closed Nov-Mar.
Tenterden Town Hall, High Street, Tenterden (01580 763572/fax 01580 766863). **Open** *Apr-Oct* 9.30am-1.30pm, 2-5pm Mon-Sat. Closed Nov-Mar.

CM Booth Collection of Historic Vehicles
63 High Street, Rolvenden (01580 241234).
Open 10am-6pm Mon-Sat. **Admission** £1.50; 75p concessions.
This small but eclectic private collection is housed in what could best be described as a Tardis-like garden shed behind the village antique shop in this attractive village. Inside, you will find three-wheeled classic Morgans, a wealth of automobile memorabilia and toy and model cars from every part of the world.

Cranbrook Museum
Carriers Road, Cranbrook (01580 715542/ www.localmuseum.freeserve.co.uk).
Open *Apr-Oct* 2-4.30pm Tue-Sat. Closed Nov-Mar. **Admission** £1.50; 50p concessions.
Housed in a building that is older than some of the exhibits, this diverting local museum features such delights as the Barking Spud, an agricultural instrument essential for keeping out intruders, and displays that recount tales of the Frittenden Forgers – a group of men

Cranbrook Union Windmill – flour power.

who made coins out of siphon tops stolen from local pubs. There is even an underwear collection of early 'drawers' and a signed photo of Elizabeth Taylor, who lived in Cranbrook as a child.

Cranbrook Union Windmill
The Hill, Cranbrook (01580 712256/712984). **Open** *mid Apr-mid July, Sept* 2.30-5pm Sat, bank hols. *Mid July-Aug* 2.30-5pm Sat, Sun. **Admission** free, donations welcome.
A local landmark, the Union Windmill is the largest and one of the best preserved smock mills in the country, so called because from a distance it was said to resemble the shape of a farmers smock. This engineering marvel is run by volunteer enthusiasts and still produces freshly milled flour that can be purchased near the entrance. More windmills can be found in nearby Rolvenden (no phone), Woodchurch (01233 860043) and Wittersham (01797 270364).

Great Maytham Hall
Off A28 in Rolvenden (01580 241346/ www.cha.org.uk). **Open** *May-Sept* 2-5pm Wed, Thur; also National Garden Scheme days. **Admission** *House & gardens* £4; £2 concessions. *Gardens only* £2; £1 concessions.
Eighteen acres of parkland back on to this Lutyens-designed mansion house. The more formal gardens include a walled garden that inspired Frances Hodgson Burnett to write the children's book *The Secret Garden.*

Headcorn Aerodrome
Shenley Farms Aviation, Shenley Road, Headcorn (01622 890226). **Open** 9am-dusk daily.
Phone for prices.
Looking at the old buildings and gardens at ground level may not appeal to the adrenaline junkie who might prefer to skydive with the Headcorn Parachute Club (01622 890862/www.headcornparachuteclub.co.uk), have flying lessons with Weald Air Services (01622 891539) or take a trip in a Tiger Moth with the Tiger Club (01622 891017/www.tigerclub.co.uk). This could be the most different and exhilarating way of exploring the heart of Kent. Book ahead for all activities.

Hole Park
Rolvenden, Cranbrook (01580 241251). **Open** *Apr-June, Oct* 2-6pm Wed; or by appointment. Also open certain Sundays as part of the National Gardens Scheme. **Admission** £3; 50p concessions.
This large, privately owned estate and garden is somewhat of a find and a beautiful and peaceful escape from the other better-known gardens in the Weald (where solitude is practically impossible). Walled and terraced areas add a certain distinction and a sunken garden is thrown in for good measure.

Iden Croft Herbs
Frittenden, Staplehurst (01580 891432/ www.herbs-uk.com). **Open** *Oct-Feb* 9am-5pm Mon-Sat. *Mar-Sept* 11am-5pm daily. **Admission** £2; £1.50 concessions.
Every herb imaginable can be found in this unique and fascinating garden set in and around an ancient walled garden. An extensive array of herbs are on sale for all your cooking and medicinal uses. One of the gardens is designed for the enjoyment of blind and disabled visitors.

Kent & East Sussex Railway
Tenterden and Northiam, East Sussex stations (01580 765155/www.kesr.org.uk). **Open** *May-Sept* daily. *Oct-Apr* Sat, Sun. Call for timetable. **Admission** *return fare* £7.50; £3.75-£6.75 concessions.
Chug back into the past with a journey on a steam train between Tenterden and Bodiam, East Sussex. Throughout the year there are special events geared for all members of the family and might include a Thomas the Tank Engine fun day or 'War on the Line', a 1940s re-enactment.

Sissinghurst Castle Garden
Sissinghurst, Cranbrook (01580 712850/ www.nationaltrust.org.uk). **Open** *Apr-mid Oct* 1-6.30pm Tue-Fri (last admission 6pm); 10am-6.30pm Sat, Sun (last admission 5.30pm). **Admission** (NT) £6.50; £3 concessions.
The most popular attraction in the area, Sissinghurst is famous not only for its wonderful, inspirational gardens but also for its celebrity creators, poet and novelist Vita Sackville-West and her husband Harold Nicholson, an historian and diplomat. There's tremendous individuality evident in the varied gardens, which have something to offer whatever the season. Visitors can also visit the 15th-century long library and tower.

South of England Rare Breeds Centre
Highlands Farm, Woodchurch (01233 861493/ www.rarebreeds.org.uk). **Open** *Apr-Sept* 10.30am-5.30pm daily. *Oct-Mar* 10.30am-4.30pm Tue-Sun. **Admission** £3.50; £2-£3 concessions.
Very much a petting farm and an ideal attraction for small children, the South of England Rare Breeds Centre has more than just a few piglets, lambs and cows. Among the more interesting fauna on view is an ancient breed of goat, brought to this country by the Crusaders, and Lincoln Longwool sheep, dating back to Roman times.

Where to stay

The area is awash with hundreds of B&Bs of varying standards; the best of them provide better and more interesting accommodation than the hotels in the region, many of which seem stuck in a 1950s time warp.

Bishopsdale Oast **Offer**
Cranbrook Road, Biddenden, TN27 8DR (01580 291027/fax 01580 292321/ www.bishopsdaleoast.co.uk). **Rates** £50-£60 double/twin. Min 2 nights at peak weekends. Special breaks. **Rooms** 5 double/twin (4 en suite, 1 with private bath). **Credit** MC, V.
Fresh ingredients from the garden are a wonderful organic touch to the optional evening meal in this comfortable converted oast house tucked down a lane in the heart of the Weald. With so many attractions nearby, this makes an ideal and relaxing base for touring. In summer you can eat outside by the wild flower garden, or in winter lounge by the roaring log fire. The decent-

Queen of the theatre

The strikingly beautiful Victorian actress Ellen Terry, known as the 'Queen of the Theatre', captivated audiences in a career that spanned 50 years. Born into an acting family in 1847, she first appeared on stage in a French comedy at the Haymarket Theatre at the age of 16, gaining good reviews. An early marriage to a much older man ended within a year and, rather than return to the family home, Ellen shocked her family and Victorian society by eloping with successful young architect Edward Godwin. After several years of domestic bliss in the country, and two children, money became scarce and the marriage began to crumble. Ellen was persuaded back to the stage and left her second husband. She then had 20 years of success at the Lyceum in London in partnership with actor-manager Henry Irving, and was recognised as the leading Shakespearean actress of the English stage.

In 1899, Ellen received a cryptic postcard saying that a house was for sale – she realised that it was Small Hythe Place, a house she had fallen in love with while touring and where she wanted to live and die. Ellen bought the property and spent the rest of her life there. An idyllic timber-framed house built in the early 1500s, it is now a fascinating theatre museum that depicts the life and times of one of the most famous board-stompers of her generation. There is a small theatre in the garden, where plays are still staged, and where Ellen's great-nephew John Geilgud once performed. Surprisingly isolated, Small Hythe Place is surrounded by wonderful walking country.

Ellen Terry Memorial Museum at Small Hythe Place

Small Hythe, nr Tenterden (01580 762334). **Open** *Apr-Oct* 1.30-6pm Mon-Wed, Sat, Sun. **Admission** £3.20; £1.60 concessions.
Opening times may change in 2002; phone to check.

---

sized rooms retain their original beams, but at the same time are kept reassuringly up to date with a TV and other mod cons. The oast room is the largest and most atmospheric. All bedrooms no-smoking.
A28 from Ashford to Tenterden; right at Cranbrook Road; after 2½ miles, follow sign for Bishopsdale Oast.

Folly Hill Cottage
Friezley Lane, Hocker Edge, Cranbrook, TN17 2LL (tel/fax 01580 714299). **Rates** £29-£31 single; £44-£48 twin. Minimum 2-night stay Fri, Sat. Special breaks. **Rooms** (1 en suite, 1 with private bathroom) 2 twin. **No credit cards.**
A great place to unwind. At the end of a narrow private lane dotted with stunning listed houses in the heart of a wooded valley, this idyllic 19th-century house has all the necessary comforts for a relaxing stay in the country. One twin room has a small balcony overlooking the outdoor (unheated) swimming pool. The rooms, though not particularly large, are modern

rather than period in style with TVs and private bathrooms (one even has its own fridge), and the owners are friendly and accommodating. Guests have the use of the small communal TV lounge. Children over ten welcome. No smoking throughout.
N of A262 between Goudhurst and Sissinghurst.

Little Hodgeham
Smarden Road, Bethersden, TN26 3HE (01233 850323/www.littlehodgeham.co.uk). **Rates** £37.50-£40 single occupancy; £60-£65 double/twin. **Rooms** (en suite) 1 four-poster, 1 twin. **No credit cards.**
Recently taken over by friendly and welcoming new owners, this picturesque Tudor cottage is surrounded by a pretty, mature garden complete with a stream, and a swimming pool for the use of guests. Inside the 16th-century house, the cosy rooms are spotless. Children welcome. No smoking throughout.
In Bethersden, take right at Bull pub; Little Hodgeham is 2 miles towards Smarden.

You can either relax in front of the fire or dine alfresco at the **Three Chimneys**. *See p47.*

Maplehurst Mill

Mill Lane, Frittenden, TN17 2DT (01580 852203/ fax 01580 852117). **Rates** £50 single occupancy; £76 double/twin; £76 four-poster. Minimum 2-night stay Fri, Sat in high season. **Rooms** (all en suite) 1 twin; 2 double/twin; 1 double; 1 four-poster. **Credit** MC, V.

An exquisite 13th-century mill oozing character; you'd be hard pressed to find a more romantic hideaway. Every antique-filled room has its own charm – whether you opt for the soothing sounds of the millstream, or prefer views over the extensive gardens and meadows beyond, or even the decadence of a four-poster bed. Kenneth and Heather Parker are welcoming hosts, and their candlelit dinners are imaginative, with an emphasis on home-grown produce and herbs. There is the bonus of a heated outdoor swimming pool in the summer months, and a grand piano in the drawing room. No smoking throughout. Children over 12 welcome. One room is wheelchair-accessible. *A229 towards Hastings; turn left at Frittenden Road after Staplehurst; after 1¼ miles, turn right down narrow lane opposite big white house, turn right at end of lane, through woods; Mill is on right.*

White Lion Inn

High Street, Tenterden TN30 6BD (01580 765077/fax 01580 764157/ www.lionheartinns.co.uk). **Rates** £59 single occupancy; £74 double; £94 four-poster. **Rooms** 13 double; 2 four-poster. **Credit** AmEx, MC, V.

This White Lion is a recently renovated 16th-century coaching inn, convenient for many of the attractions in the area from Sissinghurst to the north to Small Hythe in the south; it's also a short drive from many of Kent's best vineyards. Rooms are modern, spacious, clean and of a good standard – several make up four-poster beds. The heavily beamed bar and restaurant downstairs make up for the lack of character in the rooms. A good choice for those who prefer a more lively town location. Children and pets welcome. No-smoking rooms available.

Wittersham Court

Wittersham, Tenterden, TN30 7EA (tel/fax 01797 270425). **Rates** £55 single occupancy; £80 double. Minimum 2-night stay Fri, Sat. **Rooms** 2 double, 1 twin (1 en suite; 2 with private bathrooms). **Credit** MC, V.

This 18th-century listed house located on the Isle of Oxney has beams and comfort at every turn. Guests will enjoy extras such as towelling robes, all manner of lotions and a tennis court for the energetically inclined. In winter, log fires and electric blankets add to the warmth of this home-from-home. Guests have the run of the place from the bookish drawing room to the cosy television room with its imposing fireplace. This is great walking country and the sea and medieval Rye are only six miles away. Children over 14 welcome. No smoking throughout. *B2082 from Tenterden to Wittersham and Rye; right at war memorial in Wittersham; entrance on left before church.*

Where to eat & drink

Dining out in the area can be something of a lottery – there are some good places, but there are plenty of restaurants with pretentions that the kitchen staff can't live up to. This is, however, a fertile hunting ground for the pub lover, with some local hostelries offering seriously good food. Among the rural pubs worthy of a journey are the unpretentious and friendly **Woodcock** at Iden Green (south of Benenden; 01580 240009), the ancient and rambling 16th-century **Bell** at Smarden (01233 770283) or the **Wild Duck** in Marden Thorn (between Marden and Staplehurst; 01622 831340), popular for its interesting grub. The town pubs in this region pale by comparison but if you are staying in or near Tenterden then head down to the inviting **William Caxton** (West Cross; 01580 763142). Tenterden also has an Indian, **Badsha** (10 West Cross; 01580 765151), and a traditional Italian, **Il Classico** (75 High Street; 01580 763624); for a meze fix, try the popular Turkish restaurant **Ozgur** (126 High Street; 01580 763248). Biddenden's small, heavily beamed **West House Restaurant** (28 High Street; 01580 291341) offers Conran-influenced Med food.

Dering Arms

Station Road, Pluckley (01233 840371). **Food served** noon-2pm, 7-9.30pm daily. **Credit** MC, V.
Superb seafood can be found in this wonderfully old and atmospheric coaching inn complete with flagstones, wood floors, high ceilings and more of those Dering windows. Locals and visitors stream in to enjoy excellent dishes such as classic fish soup (£3.95), grilled John Dory with minted leeks and red wine sauce (£13.95) as well as wines from the extensive list. If you overindulge there's simple accommodation available upstairs (doubles £40). A one-hour train ride from London will deposit you 100 yards from the front door, making it an ideal starting point for cycling and walking enthusiasts.

Rankins Restaurant

High Street, Sissinghurst (01580 713964). **Food served** 7.30-9pm Wed-Sat; 12.30-2pm Sun. **Set dinner** £23.50 2 courses; £27.50 3 courses. **Credit** MC, V.
Looking out over the local chapel, the restaurant in this white wood-fronted house on the high street may be kitted out with slightly dated '60s furniture but the cooking is entirely *du jour*. The menu is short: a meal might start with roast red peppers with tomato, artichoke and basil oil followed by grilled duck breast with mustard, calvados and apple sauce. The wine list is a decent mix of French and New World, with a good selection of half bottles. This is a small, friendly place run by the husband-and-wife team of Hugh and Leonora Rankin.

Soho South

23 Stone Street, Cranbrook (01580 714666). **Food served** 11am-2.30pm, 6.30-9.30pm Wed-Sat. **Credit** MC, V.
The one-time owners of Soho's L'Epicure continue to pack them in down south with New World cuisine in an old world atmosphere. The confident and assured cooking in this charming and rustic high street restaurant will keep even the most homesick Londoner content. The stripped pine tables are left uncovered at lunch, while white tablecloths and candles appear in the evening. Ingredients are admirably fresh and the attention to detail is evident. The fusion cooking works well and might include chicken with green coconut milk curry and spicy noodles, or chargrilled swordfish with a garlic and bread sauce. Starters cost around £6, while main courses are around the £15 mark. There's also a bistro menu at lunchtime. Booking recommended.

Three Chimneys

Just off the A262, west of Biddenden (01580 291472). **Food served** noon-2pm, 6.30-9.45pm Mon-Sat; noon-2pm, 7-9pm Sun. **Credit** MC, V.
The three rooms at the front of this atmospheric and rambling country pub look as if they haven't changed in centuries. Flagstoned floors, low oak beams and big fireplaces provide a comforting background for quaffing well-kept beers straight from the cask and sampling the excellent food. Fresh marinated anchovy salad and pan-fried sea bass with tomatoes and olives are typically simple but assuredly executed dishes from the short menu. Starters are around £5, while mains hit the £13 mark. Booking recommended.

Corking Kent

If your budget won't stretch to a trip to Europe, Sydney or San Francisco and you need a wine-tasting fix, don't despair: English wine has a growing reputation and many of Britain's 400-odd vineyards are located in the South-east. The best time to visit the Kentish vineyards is September and October, when the vines are full and harvesting begins.

Biddenden Vineyards

Little Whatmans, Biddenden, Ashford (01580 291726). **Open** 10am-5pm Mon-Sat; 11am-5pm Sun. **Admission** free.
Kent's oldest commercial vineyard is also home to some CAMRA award-winning ciders. Tastings are free.

Harbourne Vineyard

Wittersham (01797 270420). **Open** 2-6pm daily. **Admission** free.
A small vineyard that even produces wine suitable for vegans and vegetarians.

Rowenden Vineyard

Sandhurst Lane, Rolvenden (01580 241255). **Open** 10am-6pm Tue-Sun. **Admission** free.
This vineyard is relatively small but it produces some excellent wines. Christopher Lindlar is considered one of the UK's best winemakers.

Sandhurst Vineyards & Hop Farm

Hoads Farm, Crouch Lane, Sandhurst (01580 850296). **Open** Apr-Dec 2-6pm Mon-Fri; 11.30am-6pm Sat; noon-3pm Sun. **Admission** free.
A friendly, family-run vineyard with some award-winning wines. The owners also run a B&B in their beautifully restored 16th-century farmhouse.

Tenterden Vineyards Park

B2082, Small Hythe, Tenterden (01580 765333/www.chapeldown wines.co.uk). **Open** 10am-5pm daily. *Tours* Easter-Oct. **Admission** free.
The second-largest winery in the UK and home to Chapel Wines. There's the added attraction of a small museum, plant centre and herb garden.

The Kent Weald

Gardens, castles and oast-houses in cosy valleys.

When the non-Kentish think of Kent, it is not the sprawling Medway towns, the superannuated resorts like Margate or the otherworldy Romney Marsh wildernesses that come to mind, but an idyllic, preserved-in-aspic, oast-house-heavy landscape of small villages tucked within the neat folds of cosy wooded valleys, of hop gardens and fruit orchards and of ancient half-timbered pubs. What these people are really thinking of is the Weald. And the Weald is actually like that.

Although the Weald is often thought of as specifically Kentish, the term does, in fact, refer to the entire basin between the North and South Downs and, thus, stretches from the South Kent coast all the way through Sussex, even spilling over into Hampshire. This chapter only covers part of the Kent Weald (for the more southerly section, *see p42* **The Heart of Kent**; for the Sussex Weald, *see p62* **The Ashdown Forest**).

The term 'weald' – meaning 'forest', from the Anglo-Saxon 'wald' – refers back to the immense swathe of oak and beech that once stretched from Hythe to Winchester. It was formidable enough that when Julius Caesar first landed on the south coast he chose to skirt around the forest rather than try to cross it. The Anglo-Saxons, searching for hog pastures, were the first to establish permanent settlements within the Weald. Anglo-Saxon terms are the most frequent suffixes on Wealden place names – '-hurst' is a wooded knoll, '-den' a clearing in a wood, '-ley' a meadow and '-ham', a small homestead.

By the early 14th century, much of the forest had been cleared and the familiar landscape of hedged, cultivated fields punctuated by small, vestigial woods had been established.

Surprisingly, perhaps, the Weald became the major manufacturing area of the country from the Middle Ages until the 18th century, and was renowned for its iron ore and sheep-rearing. Happily for us today, these industries both declined just as industrialisation got seriously ugly, leaving the Weald with an unparalleled collection of sizeable late medieval and Tudor buildings. Weather-boarded and tile-hung houses are another distinctive man-made feature of the landscape, as are the ubiquitous oast-houses that at one time were a feature of the more than 30,000 acres of Kent countryside devoted to growing hops.Once upon a time – before the mechanisation of agriculture in the 1960s – Londoners would travel to Kent to stay on the hop farms for an annual working holiday, spent picking the hops. Today, not one of Kent's oast-houses is still used for its original purpose of pressing and drying freshly harvested crops – even those of Britain's oldest brewer, Shepherd Neame in Faversham, are now redundant. At **Hop Farm Country Park** in Beltring, however, you can see how it used to be done.

So spa so good

Tunbridge Wells (more properly and pompously known, since 1909, as Royal Tunbridge Wells) exists chiefly in the public imagination as the upright, uptight home of

Anne Boleyn spent her childhood at the ivy-clad **Hever Castle**.

'disgusted' *Times* letter-writers. It's actually a rather appealing town, if a touch staid, basking in a typically Wealden wooded valley, and makes an excellent base for exploring the region. As Kentish towns go, it's something of an upstart, dating back only to the 17th century, when Lord North discovered the Chalybeate Spring in 1606, declared himself cured of consumption and set in train a development that left the town second only to Bath in the fashionable spa circuit. The spring, at the end of the Pantiles, the town's most famous street (and attraction), still draws tourists today, who come to drink a glass of the iron-bearing, apparently revolting-tasting waters. The Pantiles were once described by John Evelyn as 'a very sweet place… private and refreshing'. This colonnaded late 17th-century shopping street is still rather sweet and not yet totally overwhelmed by tacky trinket shops.

A favourite short family outing from here is to the **High Rocks**, a couple of miles south-west of the town. This series of sandstone rocks, linked by 11 bridges and set in a wooded valley, is a lovely spot for a stroll and a picnic. It isn't exactly undiscovered, though – the steam-powered **Spa Valley Railway** (01892 537715; leaving from West station close to the Pantiles irregularly from March to October; phone for details) passes by and there's a pub, restaurant and banqueting complex here.

Weald tour

The Weald is perfect country for gentle touring, either by car or bike (although parts are hilly), or walking. There are marked cycle and motoring routes and a plethora of walking trails (leaflets are available at tourist information centres). Brief highlights follow.

Between Tunbridge Wells and Sevenoaks is the workaday town of **Tonbridge** (not to be confused with its more upmarket near-namesake), with its striking ruined Norman castle. West of here is **Chiddingstone**'s much-photographed single street (entirely owned by the National Trust) – virtually an open-air museum of 15th- and 16th-century domestic architecture. Neighbouring **Penshurst** is also

exceptionally pretty and has the added attractions of **Penshurst Place & Gardens** and **Penshurst Vineyard**. Also close by is exquisite (and ultra-popular) **Hever Castle**.

South of Tunbridge Wells, on the border with East Sussex, is the equally well-patronised **Groombridge Place Gardens** (*see p51* **The pride of Groombridge**), with its award-winning kid-paradise 'Enchanted Forest'. East of here lies **Bewl Water**, the largest body of water in the South-east. It's actually a reservoir, and a popular spot for watersports, fishing, walking and horse- and bike-riding. Bikes can be hired from the visitors' centre (Granary Barn, Seven Sisters Country Park, Seaford; 01323 870310) off the A21 between Lamberhurst and Flimwell. Nearby is the evocative ruined medieval **Bayham Abbey** (01892 890381/www.english-heritage.org.uk), the extensive keyboard instruments collection at **Finchcocks** and the effortlessly romantic **Scotney Castle Gardens**.

At the point north-east of Tunbridge Wells where the High Weald tumbles down into the Low (also known as the Vale) are a clutch of stunning little villages, such as **Goudhurst**, **Horsmonden** and **Matfield**. The country gently flattens towards where the Medway flows down towards Maidstone. Nearby **Leeds Castle** (*see p33*), more remarkable for its setting than its interior, is a major draw.

On the flanks of the greensand ridge that runs from Maidstone to Sevenoaks and beyond are yet more cutesy villages (such as **Plaxtol**) and yet more fine noble piles and gardens, chief among them the medieval/Tudor manor house of **Ightham Mote** and the vast Sackville family gaff of **Knole**.

What to see & do

The phrase 'embarrassment of riches' scarcely does justice to the wealth of Wealden diversions. In addition to those listed below, other fine gardens in the area include **Marle Place Gardens and Gallery** near Brenchley (01892 722304), **Great Comp Garden** at Platt (01732 886154) near Sevenoaks, **Owl House Gardens** in Lamberhurst (01892 890230), **Stoneacre** at Otham (01622 862871) near Maidstone, **Broadview Gardens** at Hadlow (01732 850551) and the world's finest collection of conifers at the **Bedgebury National Pinetum & Forest Gardens** near Goudhurst (01580 211044/www.forestry.gov.uk).

Tourist Information Centres

Stangrove Park, Edenbridge, TN8 5LU (01732 868110/www.sevenoaks.gov.uk). **Open** 10am-4pm daily.

By train from London

Trains to **Tunbridge Wells** and **Tonbridge** leave from **Charing Cross** approximately every 15-30mins and pass through **Waterloo East** and **London Bridge** (**55mins** journey time). Trains to **Edenbridge** leave from **London Bridge** hourly and take **50mins**. Info: www.connex.co.uk.

*The Gatehouse, Palace Gardens, Mill Street, Maidstone,
ME15 6YE (01622 602169/www.heartofkent.org.uk).*
Open *Apr-Oct* 9.30am-5pm Mon-Sat; 10am-4pm Sun.
Nov-Mar 9.30am-5pm Mon-Sat.

*Buckhurst Lane, Sevenoaks, TN13 1LQ (01732
450305/www.heartofkent.org.uk).* **Open** *Apr-Sept*
9.30am-5pm Mon-Sat. *Oct-Mar* 9.30am-5pm Mon-Sat;
9.30am-4.30pm Sun.

*Old Fish Market, The Pantiles, Tunbridge Wells,
TN2 5TN (01892 515675/www.heartofkent.org.uk).*
Open *June-Sept* 9am-6pm Mon-Sat; 10am-5pm Sun.
Oct-May 9am-5pm Mon-Sat; 10am-4pm Sun.

Bike hire

Cycle-ops.co.uk *5 Bank Street, Tonbridge
(01732 500533).*
Four hundred yards from the railway station.

Finchcocks

*Riseden, nr Goudhurst (01580 211702/
www.finchcocks.co.uk).* **Open** *Easter-July, Sept*
2-6.30pm Sun, bank hol Mon. *Aug* 2-6pm Wed, Thur
(music starts at 2.45pm; also open by appointment).
Admission £7; £4-£5 concessions.

Often the venue for wedding ceremonies, this early
Georgian manor houses a collection of around 100 historical keyboard instruments, and with its high ceilings
and oak panelling, it makes a perfect setting for the
Finchcocks Festival (weekend concerts in September).
Behind the house itself are four acres of gardens with
shrub borders and also a walled garden containing a
circle of immaculately clipped flowers.

Hever Castle

*Hever, nr Edenbridge (01732 865224/
www.hevercastle.co.uk).* **Open** House &
gardens *Mar-Nov* 11am-6pm daily. Closed
Dec-Feb. **Admission** *Castle & gardens* £8;
£4.40-£6.80 concessions. *Gardens only* £6.30;
£4.20-£5.40 concessions.

The childhood home of Henry VIII's ill-fated second wife
Anne Boleyn, the 13th-century Hever Castle is surrounded by a double moat and has a splashing water
maze with water jets for visitors to negotiate. Hever
Castle was bought and restored by William Waldorf
Astor in 1903 and it was he who built the 'Tudor'
village that lies behind it and created the magnificent
gardens and lake. Other main attractions inside the

Water, woods and lawns surround the medieval and Tudor manor house at **Ightham Mote**.

The pride of Groombridge

The Manor of Groombridge has passed through many hands since its early life as a medieval pig pasture, flourishing and wilting as its owners' fortunes fluctuated on royal whims and gambling follies. Much of what we see today at Groombridge is thanks to Philip Packer, a barrister and academic, who in the mid 17th century demolished the old manor house, built Groombridge Place, and enlisted the help of diarist John Evelyn to design new gardens.

Unfortunately, by 1697, when his grandson – another Philip – inherited the estate, spiralling debts meant that even his nifty move of marrying a wealthy, much older and mentally unstable woman didn't prevent him having to sell up. A further succession of owners maintained and developed the property over the subsequent centuries, and in 1994 these magnificent gardens (but not the house), were opened to the public.

The gardens are indeed a site to behold and well worth a day's exploration. They have inspired artists and writers over the centuries – more recently Sir Arthur Conan Doyle modelled Birlstone Manor in *The Valley of Fear* on the house. In the 1980s the filmmaker Peter Greenaway shot most of *The Draughtsman's Contract*

here. Peacocks strut around the 17th-century house, and spring-fed pools and waterfalls give way to dramatic views over the Weald. Manicured hedges and strangely cut topiary in the 'Drunken Garden' lend a sense of fantasy, as does the giant chess set in the Chess Garden. Canal boat rides (£1) take you to the award-winning 'Enchanted Forest', or you could opt for a mile-long walk through the vineyard. Whichever corner takes your fancy, the possibilities for waxing lyrical are endless.

Groombridge Place Gardens
Groombridge Place, Groombridge, nr Tunbridge Wells (01892 863999/ www.groombridge.co.uk). **Open** *Easter-Oct* 9am-6pm daily. **Admission** £7.50; £6.50 concessions.

house include a miniature model houses exhibition and a fairly gruesome display of instruments of execution and torture dating back over the past few hundred years. Special events take place throughout the year and include Easter egg trails, demonstrations of jousting and archery and music festivals.

Hop Farm Country Park
Maidstone Road, Beltring, Paddock Wood (01622 872068/www.thehopfarm.co.uk). **Open** 10am-5pm daily. Last entry 1hr before closing. **Admission** £6.50; £4.50 concessions.
The largest surviving collection of Victorian oast-houses is the centrepiece of this multifaceted family attraction, which includes a children's activity centre and adventure playground, a shire horse display, the Hop Story exhibition and the Shire Pottery.

Ightham Mote
Ivy Hatch, Sevenoaks (01732 810378/ infoline 01732 811145/www.nationaltrust.org.uk). **Open** *Apr-Oct* 11am-5.30pm Mon, Wed-Fri, Sun, bank hols. Last entry 4.30pm. **Admission** (NT) £5; £2.50 concessions.

Pronounced 'eye-tam', this medieval and Tudor manor house has less of an intriguing history than the likes of Hever Castle, but it is gorgeous nevertheless. Manicured lawns and a woodland walk surround the house, which is undergoing restoration by the National Trust: its progress is charted by an exhibition within the grounds.

Knole
Sevenoaks (01732 450608/www.nationaltrust.org.uk). **Open** *House* Mar-Nov noon-4pm Wed-Sat; 11am-5pm Sun, bank hols. Closed Dec-Feb. *Garden* May-Sept noon-4pm 1st Wed of month. Closed Oct-Apr. Last entry 1hr before closing. **Admission** (NT) *House & gardens* £5; £2.50 concessions. *Gardens only* £1; 50p concessions.
Set in a magnificent deer park, this original 15th-century house was enlarged and embellished in 1603 by the first Earl of Dorset, one of Queen Elizabeth's 'favourites', and has remained unaltered ever since. Thirteen state rooms are open to the public and contain furnishings, art textiles and important portraits by Van Dyck, Gainsborough, Lely, Kneller and Reynolds.

Museum of Kent Life

Lock Lane, Sandling, nr Maidstone (01622 763936/www.museum-kentlife.co.uk). **Open** *Mar-Oct* 10am-5.30pm daily. Last entry 4.30pm. **Admission** £4.70; £3.20 concessions.

Kent's open-air museum is home to a collection of historic buildings that house both conventional and interactive exhibitions on life in Kent over the past 100 years. Visitors can explore a traditional oast-house, a thatched barn and granary as well as Ma Larkin's kitchen and lounge, re-created from the popular *Darling Buds of May* series.

Penshurst Place & Gardens

Penshurst, nr Tonbridge (01892 870307/ www.penshurst.com). **Open** *House* Apr-Oct noon-5.30pm daily. Closed Nov-Mar. *Grounds* Apr-Oct 10.30am-6pm daily. Last entry 5pm. Closed Nov-Mar. **Admission** *House & gardens* £6; £4-£5.50 concessions. *Gardens only* £4.50; £3.50-£4 concessions.

This medieval masterpiece has been the home to the Sidney family since 1552 and little has changed over the centuries. Additions to the house have seen it grow into an imposing stately home that reveals at least eight different architectural periods, with an 11 acre formal garden attached. Apart from the house, visitors can enjoy the Toy Museum, walk the new Woodland Trail or visit the area's best adventure playground. Special events take place throughout the year.

Scotney Castle Gardens

Lamberhurst, nr Tunbridge Wells (01892 891081/www.nationaltrust.org.uk). **Open** *Garden* Apr-Oct 11am-6pm Wed-Fri; 2-6pm Sat, Sun. Closed Nov-Mar. *Castle* May-mid Sept 11am-6pm Wed-Fri; 2-6pm Sat, Sun. Last entry 1 hr before closing. Closed mid Sept-Apr. **Admission** (NT) £4.40; £2.20 concessions.

One of England's most romantic gardens, designed in the picturesque style around the ruins of a 14th-century moated castle. Rhododendrons and azaleas are plentiful, with wisteria and roses rambling over the old ruins. Something of a viewing paradise with wonderful vistas, as well as lovely woodland and estate walks.

Tonbridge Castle

Castle Street, Tonbridge (01732 770929/ www.tmbc.gov.uk). **Open** 8.30am-5pm Mon-Fri; 9am-5pm Sat; 10.30am-5pm Sun, bank hols. Last entry 4pm. **Admission** £3.80; £1.90 concessions.

This 13th-century castle is surrounded by 14 acres of gardens and castle walls. Often used for weddings, it also offers seasonal tours as well as events held on the castle lawns, including summer band concerts.

Yalding Organic Gardens

Benover Road, Yalding (01622 814650/ www.hdra.org.uk). **Open** *Apr, Oct* 10am-5pm Sat, Sun. *May-Sept* 10am-5pm Wed-Sun, bank hols. Closed Nov-Mar. **Admission** £3; free under-16s.

Opened in 1995, these gardens near Maidstone allow visitors to travel through representations of ancient woodlands, medieval physic, knot and paradise gardens and a 19th-century artisan's plot, before reaching a 1940s 'Dig for Victory' allotment. The rest of the garden is devoted to a vision of the 'organic future of horticulture'.

Anven

3 Town Hill Close, West Malling, ME19 6QW (tel/fax 01732 843643/www.anven.co.uk). **Rates** £45 single occupancy; £65 twin; £69 double suite. **Rooms** (en suite) 1 twin, 1 double. **No credit cards.**

This rather stylish B&B is in a secluded location only a minute's walk from West Malling high street, making it a convenient option for scouting round the area. Some of the rooms have their own private entrance, and those who want to stick around indoors can benefit from a separate lounge with TV and video and a dining area. Children welcome (additional £10 to share double room). All bedrooms no-smoking.

Leave M20 at J4 following signposts to West Malling; on A20 heading towards London, at small roundabout signposted to West Malling turn left into Town Hill; proceed up hill for 60-70 yards and the private lane on the right is Town Hill Close.

Hoath House

Chiddingstone Hoath, nr Edenbridge, TN8 7DB (tel/fax 01342 850362). **Rates** £22.50-£25 single occupancy; £45-£50 double/twin; £25 per person family (sleeps 3-4). Min 2-night stay Fri, Sat. **Rooms** 2 double (en suite); 1 twin; 1 twin/family room. **No credit cards.**

The relaxed, friendly Streatfield family have lived in exquisite Chiddingstone village (three miles away) for 400 years and their extraordinary current home – a mishmash of architectural styles from Tudor onwards – is as far from a typical B&B as it's possible to imagine. Guests are housed in the Edwardian wing but eat breakfast in the oak-beamed and panelled Tudor dining room and can lounge in the neighbouring beamed sitting room with its wood-burning fire. Decent food is available in nearby pubs. Children welcome. All bedrooms no-smoking.

North Tonbridge exit on A21; follow signs to Penshurst Place & Vineyard; pass vineyard; right at T junction towards Edenbridge; bear left in village; house is ½ mile on left.

Hotel du Vin & Bistro

Crescent Road, Tunbridge Wells, TN1 2LY (01892 526455/fax 01892 512044/www.hotelduvin.com). **Rates** £80-£145 single occupancy/double/twin. Breakfast £11.50 (Eng); £8.50 (cont). **Rooms** (all en suite) 14 double; 18 double/twin. **Credit** AmEx, DC, MC, V.

A perfect base for visiting and exploring Tunbridge Wells and the surrounding countryside. The 32 individually decorated bedrooms feature magnificent beds, and there are CD players, minibars and satellite television for that special home from home feeling. Power showers, oversized baths, robes and fluffy towels add to the comfort, as should the well-mannered service. There's also a top-notch bistro (*see p53*). The hotel is the sister establishment to the original Hotel du Vin in Winchester (*see p111*). Children welcome.

A21 to Tunbridge Wells, A264 exit; right at traffic lights towards town centre to small roundabout; left into Crescent Road; hotel is on left.

Jordans

Sheet Hill, Plaxtol, TN15 0PU (tel/fax 01732 810379). **Rates** £44 single; £70 double. Breakfast £3 (Eng). **Rooms** 1 single (with own bathroom); 2 double (both en suite). **No credit cards.**

You'll definitely need a car to negotiate the bush-lined winding roads that lead to this lovely 15th-century cottage in the village of Plaxtol. Formerly a yeoman farmer's house, Jordans is owned by Jo Lindsay, who is also a Blue Badge guide who can help in planning your tour of the area. Nearby sights include Ightham Mote, Hever, Chartwell, Penshurst Place, Knole and Leeds Castle. Alternatively, you can stick around the house itself, enjoying the oak beams, inglenook fireplaces, leaded windows, antiques and paintings – many by Mrs Lindsay herself. Check-in is not until 6pm. No smoking throughout. Children over 12 welcome.

Take A227 off A25 towards Tonbridge; sign to Plaxtol on the left; turn left by church on to Tree Lane; after ½ mile road becomes Sheet Hill; Jordans is on the left-hand side.

The Old Parsonage

Church Lane, Frant, TN3 9DX (tel/fax 01892 750773/www.theoldparsonagehotel.co.uk). **Rates** £72-£85 four-poster/twin. **Rooms** (all en suite) 2 four-poster; 1 twin. **Credit** MC, V.

Voted the best B&B in south-east England, this pretty but grand Georgian country house, set in three acres of gardens, offers a 'deluxe' standard of accommodation. Owned by Tony and Mary Dakin, the house features antiques, chandeliers and a fine array of photographs and tapestries of local scenes and villagers. An atrium at the centre of the house provides ample natural light. Children over seven and pets welcome. All bedrooms no-smoking.

2 miles S of Tunbridge Wells off A267; Old Parsonage is next to church at Frant.

Scott House

37 High Street, West Malling, ME19 6QH (01732 841380/fax 01732 522367/www.scott-house.co.uk). **Rates** £55 single occupancy; £75 double/twin. **Rooms** (all en suite) 1 twin; 3 double. **Credit** AmEx, DC, MC, V.

Previously an antique shop, the owners of Scott House converted its upstairs floor into B&B rooms to save it from going bust during the '80s recession. The B&B does best from the weekday business trade, but the five individually styled en-suite rooms are as far from the ready-made Novotel business hotel as you could imagine. And service by the immensely likeable Ernie and Margaret Smith is attentive but low-key. No smoking throughout. *J4 off M20; West Malling is off A228.*

Where to eat & drink

There's a shortage of top-notch restaurants in this area (Tunbridge Wells represents the richest pickings), but this is compensated for by some cracking pubs, many serving decent food. Try the **Wheatsheaf Inn** (Hever Road, Bough Beech), a former hunting lodge renowned for its ales; the stereotypically picturesque **Crown Inn** (Groombridge, nr Tunbridge Wells); the rambling **Castle Inn** (Chiddingstone), which boasts the village's own-brewed Larkins Traditional; the creeper-clad **Harrow Inn** (Common Road, Ightham Common) and the **Bottle House Inn** (Coldharbour Lane, Smarts Hill; 01892 870306) in Penshurst, which offers particularly good grub. Also in Penshurst is the **Spotted Dog** (Smarts Hill), which is blessed with amazing views from its garden. In Tunbridge Wells, **Thackeray's House** (85 London Road; 01892 511921) has long been a gastronomic beacon for the Weald, but at the time of going to press it was changing hands and its future was unclear.

The Hare

Langton Road, Langton Green, Tunbridge Wells (01892 862419). **Food served** noon-9.30pm Mon-Sat; noon-9pm Sun. **Credit** AmEx, MC, V.

A two-minute drive from Groombridge Place Gardens, the Hare is a good bet for a high-quality range of food options. Containing a front bar area and a fairly refined restaurant at the back, an extensive menu is chalked up on a huge blackboard and includes decently priced starters like the deep fried coconut and chilli chicken strips with mango dressing (£4.95) and a selection of Japanese sushi and sashimi with pickled red plum and ginger (£5.50). Sturdier mains go from a simple macaroni cheese and leek bake with crusty bread (£6.50) to grilled squid piri-piri with roasted red pepper salad.

Hotel du Vin & Bistro

Crescent Road, Tunbridge Wells (01892 526455/ www.hotelduvin.com). **Food served** noon-1.30pm, 7-9.45pm Mon-Sat; 12.30-2pm, 7-9pm Sun. **Set lunch** (Sun) £23.50 3 courses. **Credit** AmEx, DC, MC, V.

You don't have to be one of this Grade II listed hotel's residents to benefit from a meal in its award-winning bistro. Burnt vanilla walls, ample wall pictures and large french windows leading to a terrace make for a very pleasant setting. The bistro's menu changes daily, but the broad range of starters could include the likes of quiche lorraine (£5.50), or confit of rabbit and foie gras terrine with tarte fine aux oignon (£8.50). Mains might be baked halibut with Welsh rarebit and roast cherry tomatoes (£16) or whole lemon sole with asparagus and hollandaise sauce. A savoury dessert of farmhouse cheeses and biscuits (£6.50), taken before a setting sun, is a fine way to cap off a first-class meal.

Old Mill Tea Room

Mill Yard, Swan Street, West Malling (01732 844311). **Open** 9.30am-4.30pm Mon-Sat. **No credit cards.**

Breakfast, light lunches and afternoon teas can all be had in this oak-beamed attic tearoom above the Malling Tourist Information Centre. Own-made cakes, cream teas and a very refreshing lemonade head the menu.

Plough at Ivy Hatch

High Cross Road, Ivy Hatch, TN15 0NL (01732 810268). **Food served** noon-2pm, 6.30-9.30pm Mon-Fri; noon-2pm, 6.30-10pm Sat; noon-2pm Sun. **Credit** MC, V.

Looking much more like a homely village pub than a restaurant, the Plough is a seafood heaven. The menu is brimming with marine life, including fresh Irish oysters (£6.50-£16), selections of fresh shellfish (£16.95) and fresh halibut with Dijon mustard and herb crust (£14.95). It's a laid-back and friendly atmosphere, with a beer garden that's a good stop-off point whether you're sampling their *poissons* or simply stopping in for a drink.

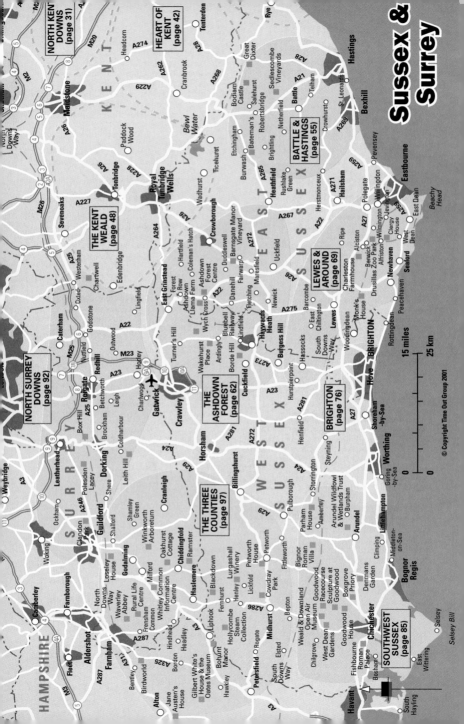

Battle & Hastings

The battle that changed English history, and a quintessential English seaside town.

East Sussex has seen its fair share of bloodshed. Most famously, it was here that the Norman hordes laid waste to thousands of Saxons on 14 October 1066. These days it is a much more peaceful place, dotted with quaint villages, genteel tea shops, lots of pubs and country house hotels set within acres of wildlife-infested countryside, and the most violence you are likely to encounter is from a blue-rinsed old lady telling you off for walking in the wrong direction in a National Trust property.

1066...

Battle should be the first port of call for anyone coming to this part of the country for the first time; there's enough history here to fire up the dullest of imaginations. The beautiful medieval town is dominated by the remains of the **Abbey** that William the Conqueror built in 1067 at the very spot where his troops defeated Harold's army. Although Battle today consists mainly of a high street filled with tea shops, pubs and retired couples taking their daily constitutionals, there's still enough here to while away a good few lazy hours. One of the most pleasant walks is around the battlefield itself, taking in the 14th-century **St Mary's Church** and ending up at the Chequers Inn on Lower Lake for a pint of the local brew. Also worth a visit is **Battle Museum of Local History**, a few minutes' walk away from the Abbey and presided over by an extremely talkative gentleman, who will make you realise how remarkably little has happened here in the 900-odd years since William took over.

By train from London

The fastest trains from **Charing Cross** (leaving approximately every half hour) take between **1hr 15mins** and **1hr 25mins** to reach **Battle** and **Hastings**. There are some additional trains from **Cannon Street**, taking **1hr 38mins**, that leave around every hour. Info: www.connex.co.uk.

... and all that

Close by are a range of villages in varying degrees of cutesyness, many with Victorian terraced houses filling tiny winding streets that look as if they haven't changed much since the last war. Five miles north of Battle is the village of **Salehurst**, worth a look after visiting the wonderfully medieval **Bodiam Castle** or the 15th-century manor house of **Great Dixter**. In the heart of the South Downs is **Netherfield**, a couple of miles north-west of Battle and home to a profusion of foxes, deer and water birds. Much of the land around this village is owned by the Forestry Commission, and there are many public bridleways. A few miles further on, just off the A265 at Burwash, is **Bateman's**, long-time home of writer Rudyard Kipling.

Hastings

Hastings could not be more different. It was once a Cinque Port, providing the Crown with naval craft before the Royal Navy existed. In the early 19th century it was a smugglers' base.

Peer out to sea or study the beached trawlers from the comfort of the Stade in **Hastings**.

The grand Victorian façades along the seafront, known as the **Stade** (from the old English for 'landing place'), suggest that Hastings was once the pride of the South-East, but it has long since fallen into decline. Despite many tatty parts – which perhaps hold a charm of their own – Hastings is having something of a revival. The pier has been done up with aspirations of creating a Covent Garden-style experience and, once you get past some tawdry amusement arcades, the old town manages to mix a wonderfully bohemian quality with kiss-me-quick seasideyness. There are intriguing little alleyways all over the old town, known locally as 'twittens'. Just a little way along the seafront is the **Rock-a-Nore** area (thought to mean 'rock of the north' or 'Black Rock'). The beach here is filled with go-kart tracks and dodgems, but walk further still and you'll find the tall, wooden, windowless fishermen's net huts that stand at the bottom of the East Hill cliff face. These sheds, first built in 1834 to house fishing gear, were only allowed to occupy eight or nine square feet each, so as the fishermen bought more nets they built their sheds upwards, resulting in multi-storey huts of differing height, many leaning dramatically to one side.

The steepest funicular railway in Britain traverses the cliff face here, and on Rock-a-Nore Road you'll find the award-winning **Shipwreck Heritage Centre** (01424 437452; admission free but donations appreciated), **Underwater World** (01424 718776/ www.underwaterworld-hastings.co.uk; admission £3.40-£5.25), and the **Fishermen's Museum** (01424 461446; admission free). You'll also find local fishermen selling their catches from the black-painted net huts – a reminder that despite the tourist tat, the Stade is still a working beach. A miniature railway can take you back along the seafront towards the centre of town.

Hastings is famed for its cluster of antique shops in the old town, along George Street and the High Street. Here you will find all kinds of oddities, ranging from 17th-century sea chests to 1960s furniture, at much lower prices than in London or Brighton. In Courthouse Mews the prices hit rock bottom, with little shacks selling second-hand records, military gear, and more often than not what looks like the contents of somebody's attic.

From George Street the West Hill Cliff Railway travels up to St Clement's Caves, home of the **Smugglers Adventure**. What is left of **Hastings Castle**, which William the Conqueror built soon after defeating the Saxons, is a short walk away. The **Hastings Museum & Art Gallery** (John's Place,

The **De La Warr Pavilion** is a modernist's dream.

Bohemia Road; 01424 781155; admission free) is worth a look for its spectacular Durbar Hall, built for the Indian and Colonial Exhibition of 1886.

Bexhill

West from Hastings lies another town of contrasts, the sedate **Bexhill**. Once notorious as the first town to permit 'risqué' mixed bathing, it is now a retirement favourite. It's a great place for rummaging through charity shops, and is also home to one of the most significant modernist buildings in England, the **De La Warr Pavilion** (01424 787949) designed by Erich Mendelsohn in 1935, recognisable as a backdrop to many period films and TV dramas, notably the *Poirot* series.

What to see & do

Tourist Information Centres

88 High Street, Battle, TN33 OAQ (01424 773721/ www.battletown.co.uk). **Open** *Mar-June, Sept, Oct* 9am-5pm daily. *July, Aug* 9.30am-5.30pm daily. *Nov-Mar* 10am-4pm daily.
Queens Square, Priory Meadow, Hastings, TN34 ITL (01424 781111/www.hastings.gov.uk). **Open** *Apr-Oct* 8.30am-6.15pm Mon-Fri; 9.30am-5pm Sat; 10am-4.30pm Sun. *Nov-Mar* 9.30am-6pm daily.

Bike hire

Hastings Cycle Hire *St Andrew's Market, St Andrew's Square (01424 444013).* A few minutes' walk from the station.

1066 Battle of Hastings – Battlefield & Abbey

High Street, Battle (01424 773792/www.english-heritage.org.uk). **Open** *Apr-Sept* 10am-6pm daily. *Oct* 10am-5pm daily. *Nov-Mar* 10am-dusk daily. (Last entry with audio guide 1hr before closing.) **Admission** (EH) £4.30; £2.20 concessions; free under-5s.

This is where it all happened – here is the field that saw the epic battle between the Normans and the Saxons. Here, too, are the remains of the Abbey that William built soon afterwards to mark his victory. English Heritage has done an excellent job with the site: the visitor is allowed to wander freely through the buildings and the grounds, and audio tours recall the events of 1066 from the perspective of a bitter Saxon foot soldier, a Norman officer and Harold's widow. In the gatehouse is an exhibition that documents the progress of the battle as well as the history of the Abbey, and there are all kinds of turrets and hidden rooms to explore that keep this from being merely an educational experience.

1066 Country Walk

Pevensey to Rye leg is 31 miles in total (Battle tourist info 01424 773721/www.battletown.co.uk/ www.1066country.com).

Duke William of Normandy and his army landed at Pevensey and marched to what is now Battle, and you can, too. Whether he continued all the way to Rye is debatable, but this country walk retraces William's route and takes in some of the most beautiful areas of the East Sussex Downs as well as marshlands that are host to herons, warblers, grebes, wagtails and other water birds. You will need an Ordnance Survey map, some stout boots and several days to undertake the entire journey; there are 17 pubs along the route and a number of guesthouses. Walkers can continue on to Bexhill or Hastings: phone the above number for details.

1066 Story in Hastings Castle

Castle Hill Road, West Hill, Hastings (01424 781112/www.hastings.gov.uk). **Open** *Apr-Sept* 10am-5pm daily. *Oct-Mar* 11am-3.30pm daily. **Admission** £3.20; £2.60 concessions.

A multimedia exploration of the events leading up to the battle within the ruins of Britain's first Norman castle. Do not miss the dungeons and 'whispering chambers'.

Bateman's

Bateman's Lane, Burwash (01435 882302). **Open** 11am-5.30pm Mon-Wed, Sat, Sun (last entry 4.30pm). **Admission** £5; £2.50 concessions.

The family home of Rudyard Kipling has been maintained as it was in his day, even down to his 1928 Rolls-Royce in the garage. The gardens and the house are very beautiful, but this is a National Trust property, which means high admission charges, much of the house cordoned off and old ladies in every room making sure your tour follows exactly the same pattern as everybody else's. Such an enquiring mind as Kipling's would surely have been outraged at such strictures.

Bodiam Castle

Bodiam, Robertsbridge (01580 830436/ www.nationaltrust.org.uk). **Open** *Mid Feb-Oct* 10am-6pm daily. *Nov-mid Feb* 10am-4pm Sat, Sun (last entry 1hr before closing). **Admission** (NT) £3.70; £1.85 concessions.

A 14th-century castle that looks as if it has risen out of a medieval fantasy, with its four round towers and ramparts reflected dramatically in the moat below. There is a museum charting the castle's history and beautiful grounds surrounding it set on the banks of the River Rother, but unfortunately your movements inside the castle are limited. Very popular with kids.

Great Dixter House & Gardens

Northiam, nr Rye (01797 252878/ www.greatdixter.co.uk/www.buzzgarden.com). **Open** 2-5pm Tue-Sun; 11am-5pm bank hols. **Admission** *House & gardens* £6. *Gardens only* £4.50.

The main part of this stunning late medieval house dates back to the 15th century, while the rest of the building is new by comparison. In 1911 the Lloyd family commissioned the soon-to-be-famous architect, Edwin Lutyens, to enlarge the property. Using materials from derelict homes, Lutyens seamlessly blended the new house into the old. The gardens are magnificent, too, with some immaculate topiary.

Herstmonceux Castle

Herstmonceux, Hailsham (01323 834444/ www.herstmonceux-castle.com). **Open** *Castle* Easter-Oct (guided tours) noon, 2.30pm Mon-Fri, Sun. *Grounds* Easter-Oct 10am-6pm daily. **Admission** *Grounds* £4; £3 concessions. *Castle tours* £2.50; £1 concessions.

This 15th-century brick-built moated castle is now used as a study centre and venue for weddings and conferences, and is only open to the public for guided tours (when there's no function taking place; phone to check). But the 500 acres of Elizabethan garden surrounding the castle are worth a visit in themselves. Open-air concerts with fireworks are held here in the summer; phone for details.

Sedlescombe Vineyards

Cripps Corner, Sedlescombe (01580 830715/ www.englishorganicwine.co.uk). **Open** 10am-6pm daily. **Admission** £3.50; free under-15s.

Visitors can taste a range of English wines and fruity drinks at this vineyard, which proudly bills itself as 'England's premier organic vineyard'. There's also a nature trail. For other vineyards in the neighbouring area, *see chapter* **Heart of Kent**.

Smugglers Adventure

St Clement's Caves, West Hill, Hastings (01424 422964). **Open** *Easter-Sept* 10am-5.30pm. *Oct-Easter* 11am-4.30pm daily. **Admission** £5.25; £3.40-£4.25 concessions.

A labyrinth of tunnels filled with menacing-looking smugglers, 'rotting corpses' chained to walls, 'skeletons' with daggers lodged between their ribs, and, on a rather different note, a tearoom.

Where to stay

The seafronts at Hastings and Bexhill are full of much-of-a-muchness seaside hotels and B&Bs, ranging from the basic to the almost grand **Royal Victoria Hotel** in Hastings, located bang on the seafront (the Marina; 01424 445544;

Relaxing hotels . . . at the end of a long drive.

The Tewkesbury Park Golf and Country Club – Regal

With around 90 hotels, locations the length and breadth of the country, Corus and Regal hotels offer you two styles to choose from.

 corus
hotels unchained

Corus hotels are fresh, bright and stylish with an enthusiastic approach to service and a commitment to getting the simple things right . . . every time. Good honest standards from people who genuinely care about making your stay special.
www.corushotels.co.uk

REGAL *Hotels*

Regal hotels are full of character and charm. Choose from country houses and historic coaching inns to town and city hotels. The warm, relaxed and comfortable surroundings make you feel at ease the moment you walk through the door.
www.regalhotels.co.uk

For a Leisure Times brochure or for further information call now on:
01905 730 370

for bookings call
0845 300 2000

for business travel call
0800 233 233

Corus and Regal hotels

Avoid the pack at **Fox Hole Farm**.

doubles £110), but the best places to stay are situated in little villages outside Battle and Hastings. If you don't have a car, the **Abbey View** (Caldbec Hill; 01424 775513; doubles £30-£35) in Battle is, logically enough, very close to the Abbey and **Parkside House** (59 Lower Park Road; 01424 433096; doubles £50-£60) in Hastings is in a quiet residential area away from the seafront, overlooking Alexandra Park.

Fox Hole Farm
Kane Hythe Road, Battle, TN33 9QU (01424 772053/fax 01424 773771).
Rates £29-£33 single occupancy; £49-£54 double.
Rooms (all en suite) 3 double. **Credit** AmEx, MC, V.
One of the best mid-range guesthouses in the area. Paul and Pauline Collins run their converted 18th-century woodcutter's cottage with a relaxed charm, and the rooms feel like they belong in someone's home rather than a hotel. Hidden away at the end of a long dirt track, this is as secluded as it gets in Sussex, with the only neighbours being foxes, deer, chickens, geese and moorhens. The Collinses have a natural way with people, and the lazy dogs usually found slumbering by the hearth add to the down-home feel. Children over ten and dogs are welcome. No smoking throughout.
Take first right on A271 west of Battle on to B2096. Farm is ¾ mile on right.

King John's Lodge
Sheepstreet Lane, Etchingham, TN19 7AZ (01580 819232/fax 01580 819562). **Rates** £45-£50 single occupancy; £60-£70 double/twin. **Rooms** (all en suite) 3 double; 1 twin. **No credit cards.**
The King John in question is the 14th-century French monarch and he didn't so much lodge here as be kept prisoner – it gives an idea of the historical pedigree of this wonderful house. Almost every architectural style from medieval to Victorian is represented somewhere, and the garden is as much of a treat. As might be expected, the bedrooms vary immensely in size and shape but all are packed with beamy character. Children are welcome (and one of the double bedrooms has an annexe for children – £20-£25 per child). All rooms no-smoking.
A21 Flimwell then B2087 to Ticehurst. In Ticehurst, take first left after church on to Sheep Street. King John's Lodge is about 1 mile along on right.

Lavender & Lace
106 All Saints Street, Old Town, Hastings TN34 3BE (tel/fax 01424 716290). **Rates** £28-£45 single occupancy; £40-£45 double/twin. Closed Jan, Feb.
Rooms 2 double (1 en suite); 1 twin. **No credit cards.**
This cutesy 16th-century guest-house is set 400 yards up from the fishing huts and is handy for all that Hastings has to offer. As the name suggests, the rooms are decorated with frills and smells and are all very clean. The tremendous breakfast sets you up perfectly for a day out and about. Children over ten welcome. All bedrooms are no-smoking. Note that Lavender and Lace is closed in January and February.
300 yards from fishing harbour on seafront.

Little Hemingfold
Telham, Battle, TN33 0TT (01424 774338).
Rates £42-£67.50 per person. Special breaks.
Rooms (all en suite) 7 double; 4 twin; 1 four-poster.
Credit AmEx, MC, V.
The setting, close to a trout lake within 40 acres of grounds, is lovely, as is the building, parts of which date back to the 17th century. Bedrooms are decorated fairly sparingly but some are of a good size and have log fires – you're unlikely to be spending too much time in them anyway with fine walks, fishing, rowing, tennis and other activities on tap. An excellent four-course dinner is available at £24.50. Children and dogs welcome.
1½ miles south of Battle on A2100; follow sign for hotel by sharp right road sign; Little Hemingfold is up short track.

Powdermills
Powdermill Lane, Battle, TN33 0SP (01424 775511/fax 01424 774540/www.powdermills.co.uk).
Rates £75 single occupancy; £90-£125 double/twin; £170 suite. **Rooms** (all en suite) 7 twin; 14 double; 6 suites. **Credit** AmEx, DC, MC, V.
This grand 18th-century country house, once a gunpowder works, sits in well-maintained grounds backing on to those of Battle Abbey. Powdermills' owners are keen antiques collectors and have decorated the house along traditional lines. The Wellington suite, where the famous Duke once stayed, is ideal for a romantic weekend, with a sunken oyster bath and four-poster bed, but the garden rooms are more basic. Staff are very attentive without being overbearing. Children and dogs are welcome. No-smoking rooms available. *See also p61.*
Powdermill Lane is opposite Battle rail station; Powdermills is 1 mile along on right.

Stone House
Rushlake Green, Heathfield, TN21 9QJ (01435 830233/fax 01435 830726/ www.stonehousesussex.co.uk). **Rates** £90-£99.95 double; £110-£135 twin; £155-£225 four-poster/suite. **Rooms** (all en suite) 3 double/twin; 1 double; 2 four-poster; 1 suite. **No credit cards.**
The jewel in the crown of East Sussex country hotels. The Dunn family, who have occupied this stately home for over five centuries, have changed little since opening it as a hotel (first in 1984; the house was destroyed in the 1987 hurricane and rebuilt thereafter): family portraits line the walls; the Elizabethan staircase is still in use; priceless antiques inhabit corners of rooms, and a library, a billiards room and a thousand acres of private land are at the guests' disposal. Guests (and guests of guests) have the chance to take dinner cooked by the

very talented Jane Dunn for £24.50, served in the pan-elled dining room decorated with family portraits. Children over nine and dogs are welcome in the hotel. *B2096 from Heathfield to Battle; take 4th turn on right to Rushlake Green. Take first left by village green (keep green on your right) to crossroads; house is on far left-hand corner and is signposted.*

Where to eat & drink

Aside from the saeside fare, the candy floss and jellied eels, Hastings has some very good cafés and bistros. **Gannets** (45 High Street; 01424 439678), offers all-day breakfasts and fabulous omelettes, and nearby the **Swedish Chef Too** (53 High Street; 01424 713674) does great Swedish cuisine and seafood. The **Mermaid** (2 Rock-a-Nore Road; 01424 438100) serves excellent fish and chips on the seafront.

Good pub food abounds across the area. The **Horse & Groom** (Rushlake Green; 01435 830320) serves up popular pub food in a homely, jolly atmosphere, and **Ye Olde Pump House** (George Street, Hastings; 01424 422016) has straightforward pub grub in a really old setting, children welcome. The **Chequers Inn** (Lower Lake, Battle; 01424 772088) specialises in trad country cooking and has an intimate atmosphere, while the **Bell** on the High Street in Burwash (01435 882304) serves a good local ale before a huge fireplace and under a bizarre range of farming implements, pots and pans and clocks. **Jack Fullers** (Robertsbridge, nr Brightling; 01424 838212) is more family oriented, with a log fire, a garden terrace and very good steak and kidney puddings. One of the best tea shops is in Battle opposite the Abbey, the **Pilgrims Rest** (1 High Street)

The music of time

One of the great successes of Hastings' promising revitalisation is **St Mary-in-the-Castle Art Centre**, standing on the seafront among the amusement arcades and opposite the crazy golf.

A castle occupied the site from pre-Conquest times, and during the Middle Ages its chapel became a foundation of some significance, but by the end of the 18th century it was in ruins. It was Thomas Pelham, Earl of Chichester, who undertook to build the new St Mary-in-the-Castle in 1824. The church built up quite a congregation, but as churchgoing in general declined, and the townsfolk of Hastings moved away from the centre, it slowly lost its flock. In 1970 the Church of England sold it, and by 1986 this elegant church was derelict and under threat of demolition. A campaign to rescue the building ensued and in October 1997 the restored building, renamed the St-Mary-in-the-Castle Arts Theatre, hosted its first concert.

The theatre has a strong and expansive emphasis on music, programming anything from blues to Mozart, techno to brass bands. There are Sunday jazz breakfasts, drawing people from London and beyond. There are poetry readings and film screenings – it recently showed Hitchcock's *Blackmail*, accompanied by live music.

The building itself is worth exploring, for it hides some quirky details. In the

19th century an immersion font was built (for the baptism of adults), fed by a natural spring emerging from the exposed rock on the church's east side. There is a crypt and catacombs, complete with creepy tombs behind a glass screen. Up above, in what was the main body of the church, is the amazing horseshoe-shaped auditorium (the acoustics here are famously good – among the finest in the South of England, they say). And then there's the pride of St Mary's, a Vulliamy clock, built by Benjamin Vulliamy, who was the third generation of the Swiss clockmakers who first arrived in London in 1730.

St Mary-in-the-Castle Art Centre
7 Pelham Crescent, Hastings, TN34 3AF (01424 781624/ www.1066.net/maryinthecastle).

Stately serenity at **Stone House**. *See p59.*

but to enjoy the sea (in all weathers) the café-bar at the **De La Warr Pavilion** (01424 787936) is a great spot for tea or a light lunch; you can eat outside on the balcony in fine weather.

Food Rooms

The Chapel, 53-55 High Street, Battle (01424 775537/www.foodrooms.co.uk). **Food served** 8.15-11am, noon-3pm Mon-Thur; 8.15-11am, noon-3pm, 6.45-9pm Fri, Sat; 10-11am, noon-3pm Sun. **Credit** MC, V.

Toby Peters, the visionary owner and driving force behind The Food Rooms, has created a 'grocery store, deli, brasserie, juice bar' that serves high quality local and seasonal food at good prices. It all looks very exclusive but the ethos is egalitarian and inclusive, and it attracts all sorts to the light and airy 'eating space' at the back of the shop. The modern European dishes are fresh, good value and inspired. Starters are around £6, mains £8.95-£17.50 and all puddings £4.95. Try the likes of smoked whiting with mascarpone and poached egg to start, Mediterranean chicken or milk-fed Sussex lamb for mains, and a divine raisin custard with poached nectarine and crème fraiche to finish. Young children have a special menu with delights such as char-grilled free-range sausages.

Maggie's

above the fish market, Rock-a-Nore Road, Hastings (01424 430205). **Food served** 5am-3pm Mon-Sat. **No credit cards**.

This is the fishermen's choice and deserves its reputation as the best fish and chip joint in town. It's an excellent location in one of the old fishermen's huts up creaky steps just up from the beach, where you'll find wonderfully light batter and super-fresh fish in the double cod and chips (£5.70) and Maggie's home-made fish pie (£4.20), all served below grainy photos of wild seas and bobbing boats.

Netherfield Arms

Netherfield Road, Netherfield, (01424 838282). **Food served** noon-2pm, 6.30-9.30pm Mon-Sat; noon-2pm Sun. **Credit** MC, V.

Fifteen minutes' stroll from Fox Hole Farm (*see p59*) is this friendly pub-restaurant, which attracts a healthy mix of villagers and visitors who come here for good staple dishes and a laid-back atmosphere. Go for the fish – tuna steak with lime and coriander sauce, or salmon fillet with cream of watercress sauce (both £10.95) or grilled whole plaice (£7.95), all served with a side salad or vegetables and, sautéed, new, or herb-diced potatoes. There is also an extensive vegetarian menu and a good wine list.

Orangery at Powdermills

Powdermill Lane, Battle (01424 775511/ www.powdermills.co.uk). **Food served** noon-2pm, 7-9pm daily. **Set lunch** £15.50 3 courses. **Set dinner** £24 2 courses, £26.50 3 courses. **Credit** AmEx, DC, MC, V.

The restaurant of this country house hotel (*see p59*) is smart but relaxed, with wicker chairs, white marble walls and a grand piano lending a rather agreeable 1920s feel. The set dinner is excellent value and might offer baked monkfish with a cherry tomato habanero salsa and pesto or seared medallions of Sussex pork with red onion confit. The extensive dessert menu includes marinated baby fig and plum tarte tartin with mandarin ice-cream and vanilla sauce or coconut and stem ginger parfait with a pear coulis and sesame tuille. Having the hotel's grounds at your disposal for an after-coffee walk round the lake is a real bonus.

Röser's

64 Eversfield Place, St Leonards, Hastings (01424 712218/www.rosers.co.uk). **Food served** noon-2pm, 7-10pm Tue-Fri; 7-10pm Sat. **Set lunch** £21.95 3 courses. **Set dinner** (Tue-Fri) £24.95 3 courses. **Credit** AmEx, DC, MC, V.

An unassuming façade and a small room with simple rows of banquette seating belie the quality of chef Gerald Röser's traditional French/European cooking. Eat from the carte and you'll have to reckon on paying £15-£25 for a main course – but don't despair, the set meals are a more affordable way to sample food that is refined yet free from pointless gimmickry. Main courses from the set menus typically might include confit of lamb with creamed savoy cabbage and rosti potatoes or Hastings cod with sun-dried tomatoes and black olives.

Sundial Restaurant

Gardner Street, Herstmonceux (01323 832217). **Food served** noon-2.30pm, 7-9.30pm Tue-Sat; noon-2.30pm Sun. **Set lunch** £15.50 2 courses, £19.50 3 courses. **Set dinner** £19.50 2 courses, £25.50 3 courses. **Credit** AmEx, DC, MC, V.

This traditional village restaurant occupying a 17th-century inn has been serving classic French cuisine for over 30 years now, and new owners Vincent and Mary Rongier are maintaining its excellent reputation. Starters might include beef carpaccio perfumed with black truffles, pan-fried scallops St Jacob and foie gras; mains could be turbot fillet roasted on a bed of French beans, rack of lamb with marjoram jus, or beef fillet steak with marrow and shallot confits with a Vigneronne sauce. For parents, there's the added bonus that children under three eat for free.

The Ashdown Forest

In which followers of Pooh can visit his heathland home.

Sussex & Surrey

If your idea of the perfect weekend away includes country walks through unspoiled, ancient heathland, the odd rejuvenating pint (or slap-up meal) in a rural pub, and playing Poohsticks off AA Milne's original Poohsticks Bridge, then you've come to the right place.

The Ashdown Forest area makes up the Sussex portion of the High Weald, a huge sweep of rolling countryside between the North and South Downs, which also spans Surrey, Hampshire and Kent (for more on the Kent Weald, *see p48*). Don't expect too much from its towns: large conurbations such as Crawley, East Grinstead and Haywards Heath principally attract commuters heading for London or Gatwick.

This part of the Weald is refreshingly tourist-free – a prime spot for getting away from it all. While serious hikers can walk all day, the less energetic can spend their time exploring the historic houses and gardens, indulging in cream teas and wandering round lost-in-time villages.

A heathy alternative

The main draw of the area is the ancient **Ashdown Forest** itself, 6,000 acres of heathland broken up by wooded valleys and copses. Originally used for deer hunting in medieval times by Edward I, the forest later became an important centre for the ship-building and iron industries, activities which contributed to considerable deforestation. Now the largest area of heathland in the South-East, the landscape is latticed by thousands of gorse-lined walks, and is also popular for cycling and horse-riding. Although the forest

Spitting image – **Ashdown Forest Llama Park.**

has no identifiable centre, the **Ashdown Forest Centre** near Wych Cross is a good place to start.

Pootle with Pooh

One of the main magnets for nostalgic visitors is the part of the forest around **Gill's Lap**, immortalised by AA Milne in his *Winnie the Pooh* stories. Milne's home was just north of the forest, which was the inspiration for the fictional Hundred Acre Wood, the setting for Pooh's many escapades. **Galleon's Lap**, the **Enchanted Place**, the **North Pole** and **Roo's Sandypit** are all within easy walking distance of Gill's Lap car park, just off the B2026, but between Marsh Green and Chuck Hatch is the real place of pilgrimage. Here, on

By train from London

Trains for **East Grinstead** leave **Victoria** about every half hour (journey time **50mins**). Trains to **Uckfield** leave **Victoria** and **London Bridge** every hour, with a change at Hurst Green or Oxted (taking **1hr 30mins**). Trains to **Haywards Heath** leave from **Farringdon, Blackfriars, Kings Cross Thameslink, London Bridge** and **Victoria** about every 15-30mins, and take between **45mins** to **1hr 10mins**. Info: www.connex.co.uk.

Poohsticks Bridge, fans queue up to race their twigs. Apart from this idle sport, most visitors seem keener to visit the Pooh-centric shop, **Pooh Corner** (01892 770456), in **Hartfield** than the forest locations themselves. Among all the gifts and Pooh-phenalia, the shop also displays directions to Poohsticks Bridge and provides free local maps.

There's plenty else to excite and exhaust children. Once they've run around in the forest, the **Ashdown Llama Park** makes for an out-of-the-ordinary afternoon. Kids aged two to 102 will also love the **Bluebell Railway**, which steams its way from Sheffield Park to East Grinstead through flower-strewn woodland, and **Wilderness Wood** has some good nature trails. Watersports are on offer all year round at the reservoir at **Ardingly** (pronounced 'Arding-lie'; 01444 892549/ www.ardinglyactivitycentre.co.uk), the village that also hosts the South of England agricultural show every June. Nearby is

Wakehurst Place, one of the many houses and gardens in the area open to the public (*see p64* **Bloomin' marvellous!**).

To escape the tourists, take a drive to a quieter part of the forest to see the **Nutley Windmill** (off the A22; 01435 873367). Another restful site is the **Airman's Grave**, a memorial marking the spot where a Wellington bomber crashed on its return from a bombing raid to Cologne in 1941. The grave is about a mile south of the village of Marlpits, which is on Danehill Road west of the B2026, just north of Duddleswell.

Tales from the past

Many of the forest's surrounding villages harbour hidden histories. The former Tiger Inn (now Church House) in the pretty village of **Lindfield**, just outside Haywards Heath, once played host to smugglers, who would sail their contraband up the River Ouse from the Cuckmere Valley to hide it in false graves in the

Piltdown Man

Many forests are shrouded in mystery and Ashdown is no exception. Detective novelist Sir Arthur Conan Doyle lived in nearby Crowborough for 23 years, but the case of the area's most infamous 'character' – the Piltdown Man – is one that may have baffled even Sherlock Holmes. Once believed to be a critical archaeological discovery, the infamous 'fossilised' figure of Piltdown Man was finally exposed as one of the most successful hoaxes in the history of science.

In 1912, amateur archaeologist Charles Dawson discovered an ape-like human skull in the Piltdown quarry east of Haywards Heath. The news caused a sensation. Following earlier findings of human fossil remains in Europe and Asia, scientists had been predicting the discovery of the Darwinian 'missing link' that would prove man had evolved from the same ancestors as modern apes. And here he was, preserved in English soil – *Eoanthropus Dawsoni* (Dawson's Dawn Man).

Although some scientists remained sceptical, it wasn't until 1953 that flouride dating proved the remains were recent. The bones had been stained with an iron solution to make them appear old, while

orang-utan jawbone molars had been filed to fit the human skull. The House of Commons was so disturbed by the announcement that it nearly passed a vote of no confidence in the British Museum (Natural History), which held the bones.

Unearthing the culprit has been far from elementary. Dawson is the most obvious suspect, yet even Conan Doyle has not escaped suspicion. Two articles, one published in 1983, the other in 1996, have accused the author (an amateur bone hunter), citing allusions in his novel *The Lost World* to the Piltdown crime.

Since Dawson died before the hoax was detected, it has been impossible to verify these claims and nobody has ever been prosecuted. Budding Sherlocks can join the impassioned debate which continues on the Internet – Tom Turrittin's reference site is a good place to start (www.tiac.net/users/cri/piltref.html). As for evidence, there isn't a whole lot to go on. The Piltdown quarry itself is on private land now belonging to Barkham Manor, and the only skull in the area is a Piltdown Man replica kept in a glass case in Dawson Hart, the Uckfield solicitors where Charles Dawson worked. The original bones remain in London's Natural History Museum, remnants of a case unsolved.

Bloomin' marvellous!

The Ashdown Forest is one area that needs no green-fingered help from Alan Titchmarsh & Co. Its crop of magnificent gardens – many of them attached to National Trust properties – yields some of the most spectacular and varied flora in England. Thanks to Sussex's temperate climate and acidic soil, rhododendrons and azaleas thrive here, and the gardens also boast impressive stocks of exotic plants and trees collected by the original owners around the end of the 18th century.

For horticultural drama, the near-theatrical landscaping of **Nymans** (pictured) is outstanding. Originally designed by Ludwig Messel in 1980, highlights include a sunken garden with a stone loggia, a laurel walk, a pinetum and beautiful herbaceous borders. A wild garden, the Rough, lies just across the road.

Two other popular venues are the beautiful **Sheffield Park Garden** and the 12th-century estate of **Wakehurst Place**, home to the Millennium Seed Bank. Wakehurst is the 'country home' of London's Kew Gardens, and once you've observed the scientists at work cleaning and preparing seeds for freezing, you can wander round grounds that include water gardens and a unique glade of species usually found in the Himalayas. Sheffield Park's 120 acres were landscaped by 'Capability Brown' in 1776, and encompass four lakes linked by cascades and waterfalls. Cleverly

planted springtime daffodils and bluebells give way to rhododendrons and the national collection of Ghent azaleas (over 40 varieties) in summer, followed by flowering shrubs in autumn.

If you're flower-gazing with children, **Borde Hill Garden** and **Leonardslee Gardens** are both fun options. Leonardslee is often described as the most beautiful garden in Europe, particularly in May. Wallabies have lived semi-wild here for 110 years, and the seven lakes are home to wild carp. Marvel at the bonsai collection and admire the Loder collection of Victorian motor cars, as well as the miniature landscape of the Behind the Dolls' House exhibition. At Borde Hill, a pirate adventure playground and holiday activities such as coarse fishing will keep impatient youngsters happy, while adults enjoy award-winning collections of azaleas, rhododendrons, magnolias and camellias.

neighbouring churchyard. The church in the delightful village of **Fletching** was where Simon de Montfort spent a night of vigil before defeating Henry III in the Battle of Lewes, while fairies have reputedly been spotted in **Tom Tit's Lane** in the small town of Forest Row.

What to see & do

Tourist Information Centres
The first tourist office in the Ashdown Forest has recently opened at the **Ashdown Forest Llama Park**. Other nearby offices include **Burgess Hill** (01444 247726/www.burgesshill.gov.uk), **Lewes** (01273 483448/www.lewes-town.co.uk) and **Royal Tunbridge Wells** (01892 515675/www.heartofkent.org.uk). If you're looking for additional information not listed in this guide, try www.sussex-country-tourism.co.uk.

Bike hire
Future Cycles *Friends Yard, London Road, Forest Row (01342 822847).*
Two miles from East Grinstead station.

Ashdown Forest Centre
Wych Cross, Forest Row (01342 823583).
Open *Oct-Mar* 11am-5pm Sat, Sun, bank hols. *Apr-Sept* 2-5pm Mon-Fri.
This information centre is the place to pick up walk leaflets and learn about the forest's history, flora and fauna. Interactive displays and games will entertain children, and there's a temporary exhibition space used by conservation groups and local artists.

Ashdown Forest Llama Park
Wych Cross, Forest Row (01825 712040/ www.llamapark.co.uk). **Open** 10am-5pm daily.
Admission £3; £2.50 concessions.
If you've got kids, a visit to this unusual farm is a fun half-day excursion. If not, once you've seen one llama,

Other smaller sites include **High Beeches**, a 20-acre woodland and water garden that contains the national collection of *stewartia* trees, and **Orchards**, a year-round garden with a herb and vegetable area and wild flower meadow. The garden at **Standen**, a house filled with Morris's fabrics and wallpaper, reflects the Arts and Crafts period of the late 19th century.

Borde Hill Gardens
Balcombe Road, Haywards Heath (01444 450326/www.bordehill.co.uk). **Open** 10am-6pm daily, or dusk if earlier. **Admission** £5; £2.50 concessions; free under-3s.

High Beeches Gardens
Handcross, Haywards Heath (01444 400589/www.highbeeches.com). **Open** *Apr-June, Sept, Oct* 1-5pm Mon, Tue, Thur-Sun. *July, Aug* 1-5pm Mon, Tue, Sun. **Admission** £4.

Leonardslee Gardens
Lower Beeding, nr Horsham (01403 891212/www.leonardslee.com). **Open** *Apr-Oct* 9.30am-6pm daily. **Admission** £5-£7. £3 concessions; free under-5s.

Nymans Garden
Handcross, nr Haywards Heath (01444 400321). **Open** *Mar-Oct* 11am-6pm or sunset Wed-Sun. *Nov-Mar* 11am-4pm Sat, Sun. **Admission** (NT) £6; £3 concessions; free under-5s.

Orchards
off Wallage Lane, Rowfant, nr Crawley (01342 718280). **Open** *Mar-Oct* noon-4pm Wed-Sat. **Admission** £2.50; free under-16s.

Sheffield Park Garden
Sheffield Park (01825 790231/ www.nationaltrust.org.uk). **Open** *Jan, Feb* 10.30am-4pm Sat, Sun. *Mar-Oct* 10.30am-6pm Tue-Sun, bank hols. *Nov, Dec* 10.30am-4pm Tue-Sun. Last entry 1hr before closing/dusk. **Admission** (NT) £4.60; £2.30 concessions; free under-5s.

Standen
West Hoathly Road, East Grinstead (01342 323029/ www.nationaltrust.org.uk). **Open** *Shop, restaurant* Apr-Oct 11am-6pm Wed-Sun. Nov, Dec 11am-3pm Fri-Sun. *Garden* Apr-Oct 11am-6pm Wed-Sun, bank hols. Nov, Dec 11am-3pm Fri-Sun. *House* Apr-Oct 12.30-4pm Wed-Sun, bank hols. **Admission** (NT) *House & garden* £5.50; £2.75 concessions. *Garden* £3; £1.50 concessions.

Wakehurst Place
Ardingly, nr Hayards Heath (01444 894066/www.kew.org.uk). **Open** *Feb* 10am-5pm daily. *Mar, Oct* 10am-6pm daily. *Apr-Sept* 10am-7pm daily. *Nov-Jan* 10am-4pm daily. **Admission** (NT) £6.50; £4.50 concessions; free under-16s.

you've seen them all. The farm's 32 llama-dotted acres make for pleasant walking, and a new visitors' centre and café have been added to the fairly interesting World of Wool exhibition and gift shop. Don't expect a petting zoo – the 70-strong woolly herd is more interested in grazing than socialising, although the farm's cashmere and angora goats are more approachable.

Barnsgate Manor Vineyard
Herons Ghyll, nr Uckfield (01825 713366). **Open** *Vineyard, shop & tearoom* 10am-5pm daily. *Restaurant* noon-2pm daily. **Admission** free. **Credit** MC, V.

Barnsgate's three friendly donkeys greet visitors to this working vineyard, which has extensive views over the whole forest. After a walk round the grounds (watch out for the grazing llamas), choose between the airy manor house or the large patio for some hearty English refreshment – tearoom titbits include an indulgent selection of scones and cakes. Barnsgate vintages are on sale in the gift shop.

Bluebell Railway
Sheffield Park Station, on A275 between Lewes & East Grinstead (01825 720800/talking timetable 01825 722370/www.bluebell-railway.co.uk). **Operates** *May-Sept* 11am-3.45pm daily. *Oct-Apr* 11am-3.45pm Sat, Sun, school hols, bank hols. **Tickets** £8; £4-£6.40 concessions; free under-3s.

One look inside the Bluebell's packed trains and you'll see that this restored steam railway isn't just for train spotters. The track runs from Sheffield Park, via Horsted Keynes to Kingscote, each station restored according to a different era: Victorian, the 1930s and the 1950s respectively. From Kingscote you can take a bus to East Grinstead while the line link is being extended. As well as two museums and a collection of locomotives, special events run through the year, including Thomas the Tank Engine days in June and a Santa Special at Christmas. Train anoraks can join a course on how to drive a steam engine (01273 731873), while the more gastronomically minded might prefer to dine in style on the beautiful Golden Arrow Pullman.

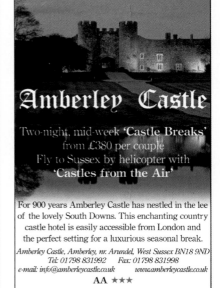

Priest House

North Lane, West Hoathley (01342 810479).
Open *March-Oct* 11am-5.30pm Mon-Sat; 2-5.30pm
Sun. **Admission** *House & garden* £2.50; £1.20-
£2.30. *Garden only* £1.

An overwhelming peacefulness pervades this delightful
15th-century farmhouse; wandering round its beautiful
cottage garden, you can really feel lost in time. The house
has been a museum since 1908; the beamed rooms contain an array of 17th- and 18th-century household items
and furniture, as well as themed temporary exhibitions.

Where to stay

Accommodation ranges from a number
of top-class hotels to a profusion of B&Bs,
with not much in between. In addition to
those listed below, luxurious but pricey
options include **Ockendon Manor** in
Cuckfield (01444 416111/www.hshotels.co.uk;
£132-£270 doubles), **Gravetye Manor**
near East Grinstead (01342 810567/
www.gravetyemanor.co.uk; £230-£320
doubles; *see p68*) and **Newick Park Hotel**
(01825 723633/www.newickpark.co.uk;
£165-£235 doubles). Cheaper choices include
Broom Cottage in Fairwarp (01825 712942;
£48 doubles) and **Bolebroke Mill** (01892
770425; £65-£78 doubles) in Hartfield.

Ashdown Park Hotel

*Wych Cross, Forest Row, RH18 5JR (01342 824988/
fax 01342 826206/www.ashdownpark.com).* **Rates**
£125-£315 single occupancy; £159-£340 double/twin;
£340 four-poster/suite. **Rooms** (all en suite) 6 single;
95 double/twin; 6 four-poster/suites. **Credit** AmEx,
DC, MC, V.

A gentle army of impeccably trained employees staffs
this grandiose 17th-century country house, set in 186
acres of landscaped gardens within the forest. The vibe
is welcoming yet formal – no jeans are allowed in the
public rooms after 7pm, and the hotel's renowned restaurant is a smart (and pricey) affair. Facilities are impressive – an 18-hole golf course, tennis courts, indoor
swimming pool, fitness studio and beauty centre are all
on site – but if it all feels a little manicured, simply cross
the road to the wilder environs of the Ashdown Forest
proper. Children welcome. No-smoking rooms available.
*From junction 6 of M25, take A22 S through East
Grinstead, then through Forest Row for a further 2 miles.
At crossroads with traffic lights, turn left (signposted
Ashdown Park Hotel and Hartfield). Hotel is three quarters
of a mile down the road on the right.*

Chillies Granary

*Chillies Lane, nr High Hurstwood, Crowborough,
TN6 3TB (tel/fax 01892 655560).* **Rates**
£35-£50 single occupancy; £52-£60 double; £55-£80
family room. **Rooms** 2 family rooms (en suite);
1 double (private bathroom); 1 twin (en suite).
No credit cards.

Owners Alan and June Peck spent seven years convert-
ing this old farm building into a homely B&B with an
imposing double minstrel gallery and mock Tudor interior. Breakfast is the main event of the stay, served up

The **Griffin Inn** – boasts both age and beauty.

with considerable aplomb by aproned Alan, who is
blessed with an amazing capacity for remembering
names. Chillies' south-facing garden has far-reaching
views over the South Downs, and if you're feeling lonely, the granary's two friendly pheasants will soon cheer
you up. Children welcome. No smoking throughout.

Copyhold Hollow

*Copyhold Hollow, Copyhold Lane, Borde Hill,
Haywards Heath, RH16 1XU (01444 413265/
www.copyholdhollow.freeserve.co.uk).* **Rates**
£35 single; £55 double. **Rooms** (all en suite) 1 single;
1 twin; 1 double. **Credit** MC, V.

This delightful 16th-century cottage, with its low,
crooked beams and cosy inglenook fireplace, sits in a
sleepy wooded hollow that is carpeted by daffodils and
bluebells in spring. The surprisingly spacious rooms are
freshly decorated and homely – just make sure you take
the 'mind your head' signs seriously if you're over six
foot. This isn't a place for airs and graces – well-behaved
dogs and cats are welcome in the house, and wellies are
advisable for stomping in the nearby woods. Copyhold
Hollow isn't licensed, so feel free to bring your own drink.
Children are welcome, and all rooms are no-smoking.
*Take M23/A23 S, following signs E to Cuckfield; then signs
for Borde Hill Gardens; over the brow of hill, turn right into
Copyhold Lane; B&B is half a mile down on the right.*

Griffin Inn Offer

*Fletching, nr Uckfield, TN22 3SS (01825 722890/
fax 01825 722810/www.thegriffininn.co.uk).*
Rates £60-£70 single occupancy (Mon-Thur, Sun);
£70-£85 twin; £85-£120 double (all four-poster).
Rooms (all en suite) 1 twin; 7 double/four-poster.
Credit AmEx, MC, V.

The village of Fletching is the idyllic setting for this boisterous establishment, the oldest continuously licensed
pub in the south of England. The Griffin promises serious food and fun, with tourists and locals mixing happily at the late-opening weekend bar. Bedrooms boast
comfort and clean lines (definitely no chintz here),
exposed beams and floaty drapes hanging from the four-
poster beds. The bathrooms, too, are a labour of love.
Guests have a choice of an evening table in the highly
regarded restaurant or in the large garden overlooking
Sheffield Park. In the summer, there is a spit roast
and jazz on the lawn on Sundays. Children and dogs
welcome. All bedrooms no-smoking.

Hooke Hall

250 High Street, Uckfield, TN22 1EN (01825 761578/fax 01825 768025). **Rates** £55 single occupancy (Mon-Thur only); £65-£85 double; £105-£120 suite. Breakfast £7.50 (Eng); £5.50 (cont.) **Rooms** (all en suite) 8 doubles; 2 suites. **Credit** MC, V.

The philosophy behind this ten-room Queen Anne townhouse is that guests should do as they would at home. The laid-back attitude is exemplified by the help-yourself honesty bar – only four beers have been stolen in 14 years of service. The house is all high ceilings and big windows, with large botanical paintings by the owner hanging on the cream walls. If you can, go for one of the spacious, airy rooms on the first floor (all named after famous lovers); the top-floor rooms are a good deal pokier. As for Uckfield itself, it was the last place Lord Lucan was spotted before his disappearance. Children welcome. No-smoking rooms available.

Where to eat & drink

The Ashdown Forest harbours a good selection of cosy, rural pubs and tearooms, as well as a number of expensive restaurants. Cuckfield's **Ockenden Manor** (01444 416111), and the **Alexander House Hotel** in Turner's Hill (01342 714914) both have notable eateries. For a relaxed meal and pint of local brew, try the **Cat** (01342 810369) in peaceful West Hoathley, the **Green Man** (01825 790656) in Horsted Keynes, or the small **Half Moon** in Friar's Gate near Hartfield (01892 661270), where on a fine day you can watch hot air balloons taking off from the field behind. For a wider choice of cuisine, drive out of the forest to one of the area's small towns. Newick is famous for its **Newick Village Tandoori** (01825 723738), and **Di Marco** in Uckfield (01825 766555) serves decent Italian grub in a loud, young atmosphere. The **Anchor Inn** (Church Street, Hatfield; 01892 770424), where seafood dominates the menu, is popular with both Pooh fans and locals.

Coach & Horses

Coach and Horses Lane, Danehill (01825 740369). **Food served** noon-2pm, 7-9pm Mon-Thur; 7-9.30pm Fri, Sat; noon-2.30pm Sun. **Credit** MC, V.

A consistently good, global menu makes this cottage-like pub a favourite, despite being off the beaten track. The varied choice of home-made dishes includes lamb and mint sausages (£7.95), stir-fried chilli beef (£8.95) and porcini mushroom carbonara (£7.95). Eating is split between a snug, candlelit upper room and a bigger and brighter main dining area, decorated with hanging baskets of flowers. The large front garden is lovely in summer, although you have to be prepared to fight for a table.

Duddleswell Tea Rooms

Duddleswell, Fairwarp (01825 712126.) **Open** Feb-Nov 10am-5pm Tue-Sun, bank hols. **No credit cards.**

These olde worlde tea rooms are positioned on the southern edge of the forest, convenient for walking off its clotted cream scone teas (£3-£5) and puddings (£3). The

Snuggle up in the candlelit **Hatch Inn**.

twee roadside cottage is suitably decorated in pink, with lace curtains, a teapot clock and a big front lawn. Lunches are becoming more and more popular, the simple menu expanding to include delicacies such as the Uckfield and Weald pie (£6.50).

Gravetye Manor

Vowels Lane, East Grinstead (01342 810567/ www.gravetyemanor.co.uk). **Food served** 12.30-1.45pm, 7-9.30pm Mon-Sat; 12.30-1.45pm, 7-9pm Sun. **Set lunch** £27 3 courses. **Set dinner** £37 3 courses. **Credit** MC, V.

With the average individual dinner bill topping the £40 mark (not including wine), eating at Gravetye isn't to be taken lightly. Nevertheless, exquisite cuisine and wine, coupled with one of the country's most famous gardens to wander round, makes for an unforgettable experience. Set in 38 acres designed by William Robinson, the Elizabethan mansion offers a seasonal, mainly British menu underpinned by vegetables from its own kitchen garden and served by a meticulously trained team of friendly staff. Delicacies include ballotine of wild Scottish salmon and sirloin of Angus beef with Rossini potatoes.

Hatch Inn

Coleman's Hatch, nr Hartfield (01342 822363/ www.hatchinn.co.uk). **Food served** noon-2.30pm Mon, Sun; noon-2.30pm, 7.30-9.15pm Tue-Sat. **Credit** AmEx, MC, V.

Dark, cosy and candlelit; you can imagine the picturesque Hatch Inn to have been an Elizabethan smuggler's haunt, as is reputed. The 15th-century pub is not far from Winnie the Pooh country and has a real country feel: fairy lights are twisted into dried flowers hanging from low beams, and two large gardens overlook the forest. The lure of the imaginative menu – featuring the likes of roast avocado filled with Mediterranean vegetables (£7.95) and fresh Scottish salmon with chargrilled pesto (£14.95) – means that nobody seems to mind waiting to eat during busy periods. Book in advance for all evening food and arrive before 12.30pm if you want Sunday lunch. But don't be put off by the crowds – it's well worth the visit.

Lewes & Around

Bonfire bonanzas, rambling walks and the smell of the sea.

In marked contrast to nearby Brighton, the East Sussex county town of **Lewes** is a genteel, refined place, with narrow cobbled streets, leaning buildings, and one second-hand bookshop after another. It's one of Britain's oldest towns, too, founded by the Saxons and then home to William the Conqueror's right-hand man William de Warenne, who constructed Lewes Castle as well as the now-demolished Priory of St Pancras. Medieval and Tudor sections of the town still survive, and despite a wealth of historical and literary moments of significance – Anne of Cleves was banished here by Henry VIII, while the Bloomsbury group were all over the surrounding countryside like a rash – it's not excessively touristy, and unlike some of the impossibly twee surrounding villages, it's a proper working town.

The **castle** and the **high street** are the focal points. Some of the shops along the high street feel as if they've been preserved in aspic: the Fifteenth Century Bookshop (100 High Street) is one, with racks of antiquarian and second-hand books filling the shelves and little to suggest that anything has changed much in the last half-century. Just off the other end of the street, at 31 Lansdowne Place, is the

The gentle rolls of the **South Downs**.

Florence Sweetshop, a Victorian child's fantasy land of aniseed twists, lemon bon-bons, and other sugar-coated treats of yore – all sold in quarters, of course. Take a walk down the phenomenally steep, cobbled **Keere Street** to see a mix of 15th-century timbered houses, Georgian façades and uneven rooftops; at the bottom of the hill are the beautiful **Southover Grange Gardens**, belonging to a house built in 1572 and later inhabited by the diarist John Evelyn. The walled gardens are open to the public, and now appear to be one of the favourite meeting places for hippyish local teenagers, who go there to do whatever they can't, presumably, do at home. Those of a more romantic persuasion wander around the ruins of nearby **Lewes Priory**, founded in 1077 by William de Warenne and destroyed by Thomas Cromwell in 1538.

Burning issues

The night that Lewes really comes alive is 5 November, when the inhabitants celebrate Bonfire Night at an almost anarchic level. Rival bonfire societies parade effigies of the Pope and Guy Fawkes, throw lit fireworks at each other, and push blazing barrels of tar over the town's cobbled streets. It's a riotous, colourful affair that everyone should witness at least once, and dates back to 1605, when Protestant Lewes celebrated the failure of the Catholic-inspired plot against King James I with almost malevolent glee. The glee's still there, but these days any straying Catholics are a lot safer than they would have been back then.

The upside of the Downs

The South Downs surrounding Lewes are very beautiful, quintessentially English in that patchwork quilt way, and great for long rambles from one pub to another. The most heavily visited of the East Sussex villages must be **Alfriston**, a Saxon village that is almost a cartoon version of what a rustic

By train from London

Direct trains from **Victoria** to **Lewes** leave approximately every half hour and the journey takes **1hr 5mins**. Info: www.connex.co.uk.

hamlet should look like. Thatched cottages, narrow lanes and the magnificent St Andrews Church draw tourist couples in matching cagoules and shorts, and while you can't find a proper shop for love or money, if it's a hand-knitted teddy bear you're after, you've come to the right place.

There are good walks from the Hindover Car Park, on the A259 just out of Alfriston, with views of the sea (particularly spectacular from **Beachy Head**) and a large expanse of hilly, gorse-strewn, windswept open land to trample over and fly kites on; on a clear day, you can see the Isle of Wight. Not far from Alfriston is the less touristy village of **Wilmington**. The draw to this fairly nondescript but pleasant little village is the nearby Windover Hill, home to a colossal chalk carving of a man carrying a couple of staffs (*see p75* **Tall stories of the Long Man**). His origins are uncertain – some believe he is a symbol of a pilgrim, others whisper of less Christian origins and suggest that he is the midsummer man of pagan folklore. Whatever he is, he's big, and it's an easy walk from the village to the hillside.

East Sussex is also Bloomsbury Group territory, and there's no better way to bore

your children than by dragging them around the former haunts of this 1920s cultural elite. The entirely restored **Charleston**, the farmhouse discovered by Virginia Woolf that became home to her sister Vanessa Bell, the artist Duncan Grant and the novelist David Garnett, is a short drive away from **Monk's House**, a small converted farmhouse that was Virginia and Leonard Woolf's country retreat. It was at the banks of the nearby River Ouse that Virginia drowned herself in 1941, wading into the water, her pockets filled with stones.

What to see & do

Tourist Information Centre

187 High Street, Lewes, BN7 2DE (01273 483448/ fax 01273 484003/www.lewes.gov.uk). **Open** *Apr-Sept* 9am-5pm Mon-Fri; 10am-5pm Sat; 10am-2pm Sun. *Oct-Mar* 9am-5pm Mon-Fri; 10am-2pm Sat, bank hols.

Anne of Cleves House

52 Southover High Street, Lewes (01273 474610/ www.sussexpast.co.uk). **Open** 10am-5pm Mon-Sat; noon-5pm Sun. **Admission** (EH) £2.60; £1.10-£2.10 concessions.

Sussex & Surrey

Alfriston (opposite and above) – can it be real?

When Henry VIII divorced his fourth wife in 1540, this timber-framed house was given to her as part of the divorce settlement (although there is no evidence of her actually staying here). Having undergone a few changes over the ensuing 400 years, the house has now been restored as near as possible to its former Tudor glory, with a Tudor kitchen, a bedroom re-created as spurned Anne's boudoir, and pieces of original furniture. The Lewes folk museum keeps its exhibits within the timbered walls, and there's a small, well-kept herb garden, too.

Charleston & Monk's House

signposted off A27 halfway between Brighton and Eastbourne, between Firle and Selmeston (01323 811265/www.charleston.org.uk). **Open** *May, June, Sept, Oct* 2-6pm Wed-Sun, bank hols. *July, Aug* 11.30am-6pm Wed-Sat; 2-6pm Sun, bank hols. Last admission 1hr before closing. **Admission** £5.50; £4 concessions.

Virginia Woolf came across this beautiful old farmhouse in 1916, and decided that it would be the perfect place for her sister Vanessa Bell to live with the artist Duncan Grant, the novelist David Garnett, and Vanessa's two sons. Bell and Grant lived there for the rest of their lives, decorating every surface with their post-Impressionist daubings and using the house as a gallery for their own paintings, those of their friends and some by Picasso, Cézanne, Sickert and Pissaro. Now the house has been restored as a testament to their work and lives. Nearby, **Monk's House**

in Rodmell (01892 890651; open Apr-Oct 2-5.30pm Wed, Sat) is the more understated home of Woolf and her husband Leonard – packed with books, and close by the site of Virginia's suicide.

Drusillas Zoo Park

Alfriston (01323 874100/www.drusillas.co.uk). **Open** *Apr-Oct* 10am-6pm daily. *Nov-Mar* 10am-5pm daily. Last admission 1hr before closing. **Admission** £7.99; £5.99-£6.99 concessions.

This small zoo and adventure park is one of the most imaginatively interactive of Britain's children's parks, with the chance to meet a meerkat, handle a snake, go on a monkey walk, and even feed a mongoose. Children and adults brave enough to follow them can climb through tunnels and over scrambling walls to come face to face with all kinds of animals, and beyond the animal adventures there's a miniature train ride, bouncy castles, a jungle adventure golf course and a re-creation of an African village. It all adds up to a frantic, exhilarating, educational day out that is guaranteed to tire out the little 'uns.

Glynde Place

Glynde, Lewes (01273 858224/www.glyndeplace. com). **Open** *House & Gardens* May-Sept 2-5pm Wed, Sun; July, Aug 2-5pm Wed, Thur, Sun, bank hols. **Admission** £5; £2.50 concessions.

A huge Elizabethan manor house built in 1589 from local flint and stone from Normandy, Glynde Place has been occupied by the same family for the last 400 years – they have been documented in numerous stern-looking oil portraits. There is also a collection of 18th-century Italian works, Elizabethan furniture, and large grounds in which to wander.

Lewes Castle & Barbican House Museum

169 High Street, Lewes (01273 486290/ www.sussexpast.co.uk). **Open** 10am-5.30pm/dusk Mon-Sat; 11am-5.30pm/dusk Sun, bank hols. **Admission** (EH) £4; £2-£3.50 concessions.

Lewes Castle was built by William de Warenne, William the Conqueror's right-hand man and a leading Norman noble, soon after the Battle of Hastings. It was extended over the next 300 years, and today the romantic outline of the castle dominates the town. It's worth a visit if only for the wonderful views of the Downs that it affords, and the price of admission includes entrance to Barbican House at the Castle Gate, which gives the story of the town and contains many remnants from the Norman conquest.

Parish Church of St Andrew & Berwick Church

St Andrew's *The Tye, Alfriston (01323 870376).* **Open** 9am-6pm/dusk daily. **Berwick Church** *off A27, halfway between Lewes and Eastbourne, Alciston (01323 870512).* **Open** 9.30am-dusk daily.

St Andrew's, known as the Cathedral of the South Downs, is a 13th-century church built in the shape of a Greek cross, with a tall and spacious interior crowned by a stunning oak-beamed ceiling. At nearby Alciston is the tiny Berwick Church, a limestone building with an exuberant interior courtesy of Bloomsbury artists Duncan Grant and Vanessa Bell.

Where to stay

Crossways Hotel

Lewes Road, Wilmington, nr Polegate, BN26 5SG (01323 482455/fax 01323 487811/ www.crosswayshotel.co.uk). **Rates** £50 single; £76-£80 double/twin. **Rooms** (all en suite) 2 single; 3 double; 2 twin. **Credit** MC, V.

On the A27, the road that connects all of the area's attractions, is this large, white house with bright blue shutters, set in a large garden that forms a small, family-run traditional hotel and restaurant. The rooms are clean, well-kept, and unlikely to upset the elderly: pot-pourri, lace curtains and little pots of fresh milk feature as standard. The restaurant sticks to time-tested favourites but uses local ingredients, and the staff are very friendly. Children over 12 welcome.
On A27, 2 miles W of Polegate.

Millers

134 High Street, Lewes, BN7 1XS (01273 475631/fax 01273 486226/www.hometown. aol.com/millers134). **Rates** £51 single occupancy; £57 double. **Rooms** (both en suite) 2 double. **No credit cards.**

This family house is an incredible find: right at the centre of town, it looks like any other Georgian townhouse from the outside, but it's actually a 16th-century building, and the low ceilings and beamed walls inside are testament to this. There are only two double bedrooms for guests (the rest of the house is used by the family who own it). One has Victorian furniture and a mahogany four-poster; the other, formerly occupied by two women artists who were friends with the Bloomsbury Group, has a more '20s feel, as well as a shower room reputed to have been used as a priest hole – a hiding place for priests during the reign of Elizabeth, when fiercely Protestant Lewes liked to do to Catholics what they do to effigies of the Pope today – burn them. No smoking throughout.

Old Parsonage

Westdean, nr Seaford, BN25 4AL (tel/fax 01323 870432). **Rates** £70-£75 double; £80 four-poster. **Rooms** (all with private bathrooms) 2 double; 1 four-poster.

Quite a way from Lewes but close to the coast, this is a secluded, ancient medieval house: it was built by monks in 1280 and they clearly intended it to last: thick stone walls, mullioned windows and huge stone fireplaces make this a wonderfully cosy place to stay – especially on cold winter nights. There are three bedrooms: the Old Hall, the Middle Room and the Solar, which has its own stone spiral staircase. Owners Raymond and Angela Woodham are friendly and welcoming, and put fresh flowers, tea and biscuits in each room when guests arrive. No babies and small children. No smoking throughout.
Off A259, about 1 mile E of Seaford.

Shelley's Hotel

137 High Street, Lewes, BN7 1XS (01273 472361/ fax 01273 483152/www.peelhotels.com). **Rates** £90 single; £130 double/twin. **Rooms** (all en suite) 1 single; 18 double/twin. **Credit** AmEx, DC, MC, V.

A little along from the castle on the High Street is the former home of the Earl Of Dorset and members of the Shelley family; a 16th-century former inn that is now home to Lewes's smartest hotel. The grandeur bestowed upon the place by its associations probably explains the rather formal atmosphere: despite the ancient beams, crooked walls, low ceilings and antiques that fill the grand hall, there isn't, for some reason, an overabundance of character about the place. What there is, however, is professionalism: staff are very efficient, standards are high, there are walk-in wardrobes, and the dinner menu is superb. The secluded garden at the rear is also a bonus, and children are welcome. No-smoking rooms available.

White Hart Hotel

55 High Street, Lewes BN7 1XE (01273 476694/ fax 01273 476695). **Rates** £62 single; £90 double/twin/family; £98 four-poster. **Rooms** (en suite) 2 single; 52 double/twin/family; 2 four-poster. **Credit** AmEx, DC, MC, V.

This looks rather like one of those hotels that had an advertisement running in the local cinema back in the '70s, but this 16th-century Tudor coaching inn in the heart of Lewes is not without its attractions. There's the large log fire, the opulent restaurant and banqueting suite with a carvery serving enormous steaks, and most importantly, an indoor swimming pool surrounded by pillars and a balcony. And with over 50 rooms at its disposal, it's a good place to keep in mind for Bonfire Night, when the smaller, more stylish places are booked up. Children and pets welcome. No-smoking rooms available.

White Lodge Country House Hotel

Sloe Lane, Alfriston, BN26 5UR (01323 870265/ fax 01323 870284/www.whitelodge-hotel.com). **Rates** £60 single; £80-£100 single occupancy; £120-£130 double/twin/family; £130 four-poster/kingsize; £150 suite. Special breaks (out of season only). **Rooms** (all en suite) 3 single; 11 double/twin; 2 four-poster/kingsize; 1 suite. **Credit** MC, V.

Very much a family hotel of old, there is much that is dated here – the flock wallpaper of the bedrooms, the formal service, the over-reliance on chintz – but the White Lodge also has a kind of slow-paced charm that few modern places have. The rooms are decorated in different styles – the best are the ones overlooking the patio at the front – and there are all kinds of places to explore, such as the games and family rooms, the two bars and the large grounds. This makes for a great place to take a baby or young children, and the staff are very accommodating. Dinner is traditional and good value (the set menu is £21.50 per head). And despite, or maybe because of, its old-fashioned feel, this makes for a romantic place to escape to for a night or two. Children and small dogs are welcome. No-smoking rooms available.
From A27 turn S at roundabout on to B2108; after one and a half miles hotel sign on right; 300 yards past sign take sharp right into narrow lane.

Where to eat & drink

Lewes itself is pretty good for restaurants and pubs. Of the smart hotel restaurants, **Shelley's** (*see above*) is probably the best, and the **Berkeley House Hotel** (01273 476057) is

Star Inn – modernised c1450. *See p75.*

also good for a treat. Lewes's pubs fall into two camps. Popular with the young crowd are the **Rainbow** on the High Street, a trendy, floorboarded, mixed-gay place, and the **Lamb** on Fisher Street (02173 470950), a smart and large bar with ciabatta melts and bowls of penne on the menu. Out of the more traditional pubs, the **Lewes Arms** on Castle Ditch Lane (at the back of the castle) is the best; it's a beautiful little inn, frequented by an older crowd. In the surrounding towns and villages a few places worth stopping at include the **Rose Cottage Inn** at the tiny village of Alciston; the **Tiger Inn** at East Dean; the **Lamb Inn** at Ripe; the **Cricketers Arms** at Berwick, which has good ales and a large garden that makes a popular stop-off for cyclists; and the **Anchor** at Barcombe, a few miles north of Lewes, is at the heart of downland walking country.

George Inn
High Street, Alfriston (01323 870319/www.the-george-alfriston.co.uk). **Food served** noon-2.30pm, 7-9pm Mon-Thur, Sun; noon-2.30pm, 7-10pm Fri, Sat. **Credit** MC, V.
Possibly the most ancient-looking building in a pretty ancient village, the George dates back to the 14th century, and is said to have once been used as a smuggler's meeting place – there's still a network of smugglers' tunnels leading from its cellars. Despite such a heinous past it is now as respectable as they come, being a popular stop-off for hikers who appreciate the hearty lunches (bangers and mash, £5.95) and real ales served here.

Dinner features good traditional dishes including whole grilled trout with oranges and pine nuts, and braised knuckle of lamb with mint and rosemary sauce (both £11.95). The large fireplace is perfect for warming your toes after a long hike, but beware: after a couple of pints of ale, those low beams become perilous.

Giant's Rest
The Street, Wilmington, nr Polegate (01323 870207/ www.giantsrest.co.uk). **Food served** noon-2pm, 7-9pm daily. **Credit** AmEx, MC, V.
A brisk stroll away from the Long Man of Wilmington is this friendly, light and spacious place, run by a cheerful couple and their children – don't be surprised if you get served by a ten-year-old – and attracting a mixed-age crowd of locals and cyclists who come here for good, simple dishes, real ales and the odd game of Connect 4 or Cluedo. Hefty wooden tables illuminated by candlelight fill the space between pots of plants, huge windows, and a blackboard that features hearty, freshly prepared dishes such as rabbit and bacon pie, salmon fishcakes (both £7.50), warm halloumi and basil salad and duck and bacon salad (both £6.50). Exactly the kind of place you want to end up at after a long walk through the downlands.

Hungry Monk
Jevington, nr Eastbourne (01323 482178/ www.hungrymonk.co.uk). **Food served** 7-9.30pm Mon-Sat; noon-2pm, 7-9.30pm Sun. **Set lunch** £24.95 3 courses. **Set dinner** £26.50 3 courses. **Credit** MC, V.
Occupying a 15th-century house in a pretty, quiet village just outside Eastbourne, the best restaurant in the South Downs is famous for two things – superb set menus and being the home of the banoffie pie, which apparently was invented here in 1972. Before trying this celebrated creation, enjoy the likes of a garlic-heavy pistou soup with scallops (made with fresh, pounded herbs), squid stuffed with spinach and pine nuts, and a daube of venison, pigeon and pheasant with horseradish dumplings. If you can move after coffee and chocolates, Jevington is a sweet village for an afternoon stroll.

Jolly Sportsman
Chapel Lane, East Chiltington (01273 890400/ www.thejollysportsman.com). **Food served** 12.30-2pm, 6-9pm Tue-Thur; 12.30-2pm, 7-10pm Fri, Sat; 12.30-3pm Sun. **Credit** MC, V.
One of the smarter country pubs in the area. The place is a salutary reminder that this is commuterland, home to well-heeled city workers who like to spend their weekend driving the Range Rover to places just like the Sportsman. As you would expect, it isn't the kind of boozer where you're going to get pub brawls: pale yellow walls are adorned with posters and prints of French scenes, there are candles everywhere, and the tables are made of unseasoned wood, meaning that they warp in ways threatening to the stability of your plate. Unsurprisingly, food is not standard pub grub – chef Bruce Wass has created a menu made up of such delicacies as nettle and asparagus soup, marinated red mullet with nuoc cham and mango salad, grilled sea bass, and crispy duck confit with plum and ginger compote. The wine list has something like 50 choices on it, too. The pub is hidden away down a dirt track, and has a beautiful garden, so it's an exclusive spot, and well worth the £40 or so a head (with wine) for a meal here.

Tall stories of the Long Man

The 226-foot-high chalk figure standing guard over the village of Wilmington is the largest of its kind in England, and second in size only to the Giant of Attacama in Chile. It was created somewhere between the neolithic and medieval periods, and is probably a fertility symbol. Beyond that, however, its origins remain a mystery, although there are innumerable theories explaining its presence.

A common explanation for the Long Man is that he was created by monks from nearby Wilmington Priory who, bored with their usual chores of gardening and beer-brewing, decided to inscribe the image of a pilgrim into the nearest hillside. The only fact backing up this theory is that England's other giant chalk man, the Cerne Abbas giant in Dorset, also had a religious house at its base. Less pedestrian theories propose that the giant was carved by a secret occult society in medieval times, and that he represents one of any number of historical or spiritual figures – Beowulf, the prophet Mohamed, Woden, Thor or Baldur – to name but a few.

Even more imaginative is the long-standing legend that the giant is the burial ground of a real giant – either a marker of where he is buried, or an outline marking the spot where he fell. His death has been explained in a variety of ways: by a shepherd throwing his dinner at the giant in a fit of pique; by the giant tripping and breaking his neck;

or that he was killed in battle with another giant (apparently they started throwing rocks at each other, and the flint mines at the top of the hill are the craters the boulders left behind).

Whatever the truth of the matter, the Long Man remains popular as a pagan symbol. Two decades ago a contemporary pagan brought several childless couples to the Long Man to have sex on the figure, in the hope that his fertile power would transmit on to the couples bouncing up and down on his outline. Votive offerings such as coins, candles and flowers are often found on the chalk figure, and in 1990 a Wiccan priest attempted to oppose the power of Saddam Hussein by performing a ritual there.

Snowdrop Inn

119 South Street, Lewes (01273 471018).
Food served noon-3pm, 6-9pm Mon-Sat; 12.30-3pm, 7-9pm Sun. **No credit cards**.
On the outskirts of Lewes, at a spot overlooked by a cliffside that avalanched and killed eight people on Christmas Day 1836, lies this wonderful, quirky place. With its courtyard filled with antiques and statues in various states of disarray, the Snowdrop Inn has a slightly hippyish feel, attracting locals of all ages who come here for the live jazz on Friday and Saturday nights, a game of pool, decent music on the stereo, a mostly vegetarian menu and a relaxed, friendly atmosphere. We enjoyed a wonderful fish stew (£6) and a pretty good pappardelle pasta with olives and pesto cream (£5), and some very good real ale. Every inch of space in the low-ceilinged rooms is filled with plastercast busts, tin adverts and nautical memorabilia,

and there's even a piano in the corner for the occasional sing-along – a feature of Lewes that most heritage seekers miss out on.

Star Inn

High Street, Alfriston (0870 400 8102/ www.heritagehotels.com). **Food served** 7-9pm Mon-Sat; 12.30-2pm, 7-9pm Sun. **Credit** AmEx, DC, MC, V. Dating back to the 14th century and developed steadily since, this is one of England's oldest pubs. Low ceilings, oak benches, a tiny bar, and animal figures carved into the timber supports all add to the atmosphere. Alfriston is a touristy village, but the locals hold their places by the bar amid the hordes who pop in for a swift half of the local ale. There's a bar menu, with everything from sandwiches to hot dishes (under £10); should the Star really catch your fancy, you can stay in one of the 37 en suite rooms (doubles £120-£140) or eat in the restaurant.

Brighton

The peerless grandeur of a Regency town and the hectic hedonism of Soho-by-the-Sea.

'Brighton looks like a town that is constantly helping the police with their enquiries,' said Keith Waterhouse, and it is as a roguish, flamboyant, even tarty city that Brighton has come to be known. Its proximity to London helps foster this – this is where the capital's hard-working sophisticates come to let their hair down, and the place is full of temptations and opportunities for you to misbehave by the sea.

From political party conference delegates to dirty weekenders (and they often overlap), Brighton looks after its visitors well. It has endless hotels, guesthouses and restaurants, a vast array of intriguing shops, and a vibrant and sophisticated cultural scene and nightlife (*see p84* **Brighton rock**) that all thrive on close connections to the capital, just an hour away by train. And with all the gaudy fun of a relatively sunny British beach town (even if the shoreline is full of pebbles rather than sand), there's a constant influx of coach parties and day-trippers here to soak up some beer, buy a stick of Brighton rock and play on the dodgems on the pier. In addition, a lot of people come down for the weekend, get bitten by the Brighton bug, and never manage to leave again.

The town is of famously liberal persuasion and greets outsiders, new agers, artists, freaks and eccentrics with open arms and a warm heart. These persecuted hipsters, along with an array of rat-race absconders, relocate to Brighton's pebbly shore to tune in, turn on and drop out. A couple of universities and a plethora of language schools help make this the most multicultural urban stew outside of the capital, and with 60 per cent of the population under the age of 44 it is quite a contrast to octogenarian Eastbourne along the coast. A thriving gay and lesbian scene has done a lot to put Brighton on the map and even the local authorities have had to acknowledge the power of the pink pound. August's **Brighton Pride** festival sees tens of thousands of revellers flamboyantly celebrating their sexual orientation without fear of harassment.

Of course, this city wasn't always a vortex of hedonism and wild abandon. Brighton began life as a village called Bristmestune, and later Brighthelmstone. It augmented its fishing income with a good deal of smuggling and remained pretty much undisturbed save for the occasional French sortie until 1750 when a Dr Richard Russell invented the seaside. Russell

Beware the frogman on **Brighton Beach**.

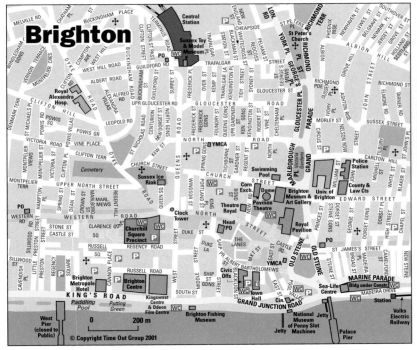

proclaimed that sea water had amazing restorative benefits, encouraging fashionable London to rush down to the coast with bucket and spade. Brighton was suddenly the cool holiday destination and there was a booming industry in hotels and bathing machines – covered wooden wagons that allowed bathers to enter the sea without having to worry about waxing their bikini line. 'Dippers' stood by, helping the gentlefolk to enjoy the salt water to the full by ducking them into it.

Things really took off in 1783 when the Prince Regent (later George IV) endorsed the delights of Brighton by renting a farmhouse

here. As time went by and his crazy old father George III refused to die, the younger George became the centre of a hip and happening court-in-waiting. Kept from the throne for so long, he filled his time not by talking to plants and pontificating about architecture, but by building a fabulous pleasure palace and inviting all the country's creative, beautiful and ambitious young things to join him there. This was the Pavilion. Thanks largely to its place at the centre of recreational Regency England, the town's population expanded from 3,500 in 1780 to 40,500 in 1831.

Victorian Brighton's greatest legacy is the two piers thrusting out into the Channel – the **Brighton Pier**, now a thriving jumble of fish and chip joints, bingo, amusement arcades and fairground rides, and the **West Pier**, a derelict hulk of a thing that hasn't been open for a quarter of a century. Not surprisingly, while the Brighton Pier is the choice of thousands of video-gaming, candyfloss-eating, rollercoaster-riding funsters, it's the latter that is far more interesting.

In December 2000 Brighton and Hove was finally granted city status following an expensively orchestrated publicity campaign.

By train from London

The fastest train to **Brighton** leaves **Victoria** every half-hour (journey time **50mins**). There are also trains from **King's Cross Thameslink** that leave about every hour and pass through **Farringdon**, **Blackfriars**, **London Bridge** and **East Croydon** (journey time **1hr 15mins**). Info: www.thameslink.co.uk.

Take in the sea view from **Alfresco**'s Milkmaid Pavilion, overlooking the West Pier. *See p83.*

Residents will probably be disappointed to find out that this actually means naff all in concrete terms, but it looks good in the tourism brochures, or so they say. Despite its new title, Brighton remains a seaside resort first and foremost (and there are seven miles of uninterrupted coastline here), but there is plenty to do away from the beach, too. For shopaholics, there's a concentrated area of clothes, records and gift shops in and around the Lanes, a tangled network of narrow cobbled alleyways just south of the Pavilion. Drinking and dining is an ever-present option, and with a brash nightlife and a constant flow of thousands of lusty arrivals, you can always be sure that in Brighton mischief awaits.

What to see & do

Tourist Information Centres
10 Bartholomew Square, Brighton, BN1 1JS (0906 711 2255/www.visitbrighton.com). **Open** *July, Aug* 9am-5.30pm Mon-Fri; 10am-6pm Sat; 10am-4pm Sun. *Sept-June* 9am-5pm Mon-Fri; 10am-5pm Sat; 10am-4pm Sun.

Bike hire
Sunrise Cycle Hire *West Pier (01273 748881).* About a mile from the station.

Booth Museum of Natural History
194 Dyke Road (01273 292777). **Open** 10am-5pm Mon-Wed, Fri, Sat; 2-5pm Sun. **Admission** free.
Its fine efforts at more modern presentation and hands-on educational involvement can't hide the fact that at heart this is a beautifully old-fashioned collection of stuffed, mounted and skeletonised flora and fauna, most of which will have spent the bulk of its life in Victorian glass-fronted boxes. Over half a million specimens are here, including a whale and the obligatory dinosaur bones, with a particularly well-stocked display of British birds shown in re-creations of their natural habitats.

Brighton Fishing Museum
201 King's Road Arches, on the lower prom between the piers (01273 723064). **Open** 10am-5pm daily. **Admission** free.
It's well worth a quick trip to this museum to get an idea of the town's maritime history. It's a small exhibit centred on a pristine example of a clinker-built Sussex beach fishing boat. There are limited displays describing the history of the local fishing industry, and one explaining the origins of 'all aboard the *Skylark*' – the name of the first pleasure boat that operated from here. This is also where the last of Brighton's traditional fishermen ply their trade, occasionally bringing home a catch for sale from one of the adjoining arches.

Brighton Marina
(01273 693636/www.brightonmarina.co.uk).
Without actually venturing out to sea, few things show off the elemental power of the ocean as much as a simple walk down the concrete breakwater arm of the Marina (although it's closed in really rough weather). Nautical types can pass hours here looking longingly at the beautiful, expensive – and occasionally historic – boats that are moored in what is the UK's largest marina. And once you've tired of imagining life on the ocean wave, you can actually attempt it by going out in one of the many sailing, fishing or diving boats to be found here. For fishing and diving trips, call Southern Marine Services (01273 693400/www.girlgray.com); for sailing trips call Marina Watersports (01273 818237). If you haven't found your sea legs yet, there are all the meretricious attractions of ten-pin bowling, an eight-screen cinema, a series of off-the-shelf bars and restaurants and shops. To find the Marina, just walk east along the beach or promenade. You'll pass some naked wrinklies (the nudist beach) and then, ahoy, thar she blows.

Brighton Museum & Art Gallery
Church Street (01273 290900/ www.museums.brighton-hove.gov.uk). **Open** phone to check after museum reopens Dec 2001. **Admission** free.
An excellent and diverse collection, taking in just about everything from Alma-Tadema's Pre-Raphaelite beauties to Salvador Dali's lips sofa. There is a particularly

strong showing of art nouveau and art deco from Gallé to Clarice Cliff, and a world art gallery with Burmese textiles, Yoruba masks and other exotic treasures; even such historic artefacts as Egyptian tomb relics (including a mummy). There are also temporary and touring exhibitions. Re-opening in Dec 2001 after a lengthy closure and a £10,000,000 facelift, there are a host of new visitor facilities and an array of interactive exhibits. Among the new additions is the Body Art gallery, devoted to tattooing, piercing, corsets and all other forms of bodily alteration. How very Brighton!

Brighton Pavilion

(01273 290900/www.royalpavilion.brighton.co.uk). **Open** *June-Sept* 10am-6pm daily. *Oct-May* 10am-5pm daily. **Admission** £5.20; £3.20-£3.75 concessions. *Guided tours* (an extra £1.25) 11.30am, 2.30pm daily.

George IV, in his days as rock 'n' roll Prince Regent, ordered the country's finest craftsmen to build him a beach-house and fill it with outrageous furniture and decor. The Pavilion was transformed between 1815 and 1822 by architect John Nash from a rather nondescript farmhouse into the oriental fantasy it is today. The result is a playful, opulent and, at times, extremely camp collection of rooms and objects, all contained in a building that would look at home next to the Taj Mahal. Even if you hate tramping around old buildings, there is plenty here to amuse and astonish. No expense was spared and acres of hand-woven carpets and fabric, amazing chandeliers and richly carved gilded furniture, predominantly in a Chinese-inspired style, were crafted for the place. Do consider a guided tour – the guides treat the exercise with a good level of tongue-in-cheek fun-poking, dropping in all manner of quirky facts about the chic world of Regency society.

British Engineerium

off Nevill Road, Hove (01273 559583/ www.britishengineerium.com). **Open** 10am-5pm daily. **Admission** £4; £3 concessions.

This, to give it its full title, is the Museum of Steam and Mechanical Antiquities, and it was originally a Victorian pumping station serving up 150,000 gallons of water an hour to the surrounding area. Big lumps of polished metal abound and, as well as the huge working beam engine that powered the pumps and its immense underground boilers, there are trim engines, locomotive models, vintage motorbikes, a horse-drawn fire engine, plus hands-on educational exhibits explaining the scientific principles at work. If you visit on the first Sunday in the month or on bank holiday Sundays and Mondays, you'll see everything fired up in full steam.

Mechanical Memories

250C King's Road Arches, Lower Esplanade, opposite the end of East Street (01273 608620). **Open** *Easter-June* noon-6pm Sat, Sun, school hols. *July-Sept* noon-6pm daily. *Oct-Easter* noon-6pm Sun (weather permitting). Last entry 5.30pm. **Admission** free.

Don't laugh. At this charming little diversion near the Fishing Museum (it was previously known ast the National Museum of Penny Slot Machines) you get to see rows of the once-raunchy hand-driven film viewers full of Edwardian 'what the butler saw' naughtiness, and several other non-electric entertainments dating from the 1890s. You buy old pennies to work them. As the motto says: 'Old-fashioned fun at old-fashioned prices.'

Preston Manor

Preston Drove (01273 290900/www.brighton-hove.gov.uk). **Open** 1-5pm Mon; 10am-5pm Tue-Sat, bank hols; 2-5pm Sun. **Admission** £3.30; £2.05-£2.80 concessions.

Compared to the off-kilter splendour of the Royal Pavilion, Preston Manor is a lesson in normality. The building itself dates back to 1250 but has been restored and furnished as it stood in Edwardian times, with sumptuous family rooms and rather more basic servants' quarters, exactly as they would have been around 1905. Twenty or so rooms are open to the public, over four floors, containing a wealth of family heirlooms from furniture and paintings to silverware and fine china. Two miles north of Brighton on the A23, the Manor is accessible by train to Preston Park station, but if you're not driving, the best way is to get a cab.

Sea-Life Centre

Marine Parade (01273 604234/recorded info 01273 604233/www.sealife.co.uk). **Open** 10am-6pm daily. Last entry 5pm. **Admission** £6.50; £4.25-£4.95 concessions.

In days gone by this was the Brighton Aquarium; now it's part of a massive Europe-wide chain of Sea-Life centres and its prime concern is supposedly environmental protection. The very best thing about it is the 60ft long undersea tunnel, which allows you to get up close and personal to sharks, rays and conger eels. But the sea horse exhibit, albeit on a much smaller scale, is equally fascinating, as you watch these rather unlikely creatures go about their sedate business. Weirder still are the life-forms to be found in the Curious Creatures tanks – wobegong sharks, nautilus, lion fish and flashlight fish being but a few of them. Kids will love the Adventures at 20,000 Leagues exhibit, a mock-up of Captain Nemo's submarine complete with animatronic attack by giant squid; children can be kept amused for far longer with the education packs that are doled out. Re-entry is allowed, so have a look at everything and return for feeding time.

Volks Electric Railway

285 Medeira Drive (01273 292718). **Open** *Easter-mid Sept* 11.15am-5pm Mon-Fri; 11.15am-6pm Sat, Sun. **Tickets** £1.30; 70p-£1 concessions.

Running along the seafront between the Marina and the Sea-Life Centre, this is the oldest electric railway in Britain, built in 1883.

West Pier

West Pier, King's Road (01273 321499/ www.westpier.co.uk). **Guided tours** *Apr-Oct* 1.30pm Mon-Fri; noon, 1.30pm, 3pm Sat, Sun. *Nov-Mar* phone for details. **Tickets** £10; £7.50 concessions. No children under 16.

Despite its neglect and slow decay since World War Two, the West Pier is a Grade I listed building. Lottery-funded restoration work has now reached the point where it's possible, provided you put on a safety harness and a hard hat, to venture on to the crumbling structure, where you get to see the elegance of the architecture, unchanged since 1916, with the magnificent theatre and concert hall at the far end, and to learn a little about the problems of restoring it. The guides will also tell you about Brighton's first pier, the 1823 Royal Suspension Chain Pier, and about the bizarre mobile pier, Brighton's 'Daddy Longlegs' railway on stilts. But

A festival float at **Brighton Pride**.

All aboard

Being the self-consciously hip place that it is, Brighton is always keen to accommodate the latest fashionable developments in human propulsion – as the number of fold-up scooters per capita attests. And, whenever the sun decides to peep through the clouds, Brighton promenade becomes Blighty's answer to Venice Beach's Oceanfront Walk.

Brighton has been the spiritual home for British skateboarding since the 1970s. The skatepark at the Level is the place where rubber-limbed ragamuffins of both sexes while away the hours with 'nollie kickflips' and 'disaster reverts'; fragile old-timers with a nostalgic yearning for the feel of red kryptonic on asphalt tend to confine themselves to cruising the seafront on gargantuan longboards, pushing and steering being the only skills required.

Compared to the real thing, sidewalk surfing remains a sensible option, as Brighton's mushy beach breaks – one by the West Pier, one by the Marina, one by Portslade power station – produce surfable waves once in a blue moon, and become overpopulated with hungry Brightonian beach bums desperately seeking a bottom turn or two.

Powder-deprived snowboarders might contemplate hiring themselves a freeboard – a contraption that looks much like a longboard but has extra wheels that allow it to also 'edge' sideways in a snowboard-like fashion.

These days, though, Rollerblading has taken over from skateboarding as the number one funky way to propel oneself up and down Brighton prom, and pedestrianism is rapidly becoming a thing of the past. It's as good a place as any to hurry – restoration work begins in 2002; when it's finished the pier will house (surprise, surprise) restaurants, bars and retail outlets. Ring the above number or visit the West Pier Trust's little kiosk at the head of the pier itself to book a tour.

Where to stay

Brighton certainly has the quantity but it's remarkably lacking in quality. Still, it's as well to book ahead even in the winter months as conferences can take up all the available hotel space. The **Tourist Information Centre** (*see p78*) operates a reservation service, so if the places mentioned below are full, it'll suggest alternatives. It also provides an accommodation guide, but the staff are obliged to refrain from passing judgement on any of the hotels included therein. Beware though: many places insist on a minimum occupancy of two nights.

There are two main seafront agglomerations of hotels. On New Steine in Kemptown there is a profusion of small three-star hotels that are much of a muchness. Then in Regency Square, close to the central shopping mall and the Grand, there is more variety, the best of which are the **Adelaide Hotel** (51 Regency Square; 01273 205286; doubles £68-£92) and the **Regency Hotel** (28 Regency Square; 01273 202690/ www.regencybrighton.co.uk; doubles £90-£95). Russell Square also has a host of houses offering accommodation. If you're

looking for somewhere clean, cheap and central, then try **Brighton Premier Lodge** (144 North Street; 0870 700 1334/www.premierlodge.com; doubles £49.95) or **Brighton Backpackers** (75-76 Middle Street; 01273 777717/ www.brightonbackpackers.com; £11 per person in dorm room; doubles £30). For a regal experience, however, then the poshest in town is the **Grand** (King's Road; 01273 321188/ www.grandbrighton.co.uk; doubles £220-£315).

Blanch House
17 Atlingworth Street, BN2 1PL (01273 603504/www.blanchhouse.co.uk). **Rates** £90 double/single occupancy; £110 deluxe double/twin; £190 suite. **Rooms** (all en suite) 3 double; 5 de luxe double/twin; 1 suite. **Credit** MC, V.
Located in the most unassuming of streets, just out of earshot from town, the great thing about this petite hotel is the seriously funky interior goings-on. A simple doorway leads into a sleekly styled bar reminiscent of a Manhattan boutique hotel, but the boudoirs are the reason this is a must-stay venue. Each room is individually themed – Rose, Renaissance, Indian, Moroccan, Boogie Nights and the Versace of bedrooms, the Perrier-Jouët Suite with a bottle of bubbly included. There's also the independently run C Restaurant attached (*see p83*). Children welcome. Dogs by arrangement.

Granville Hotel
124 Kings Road, BN1 2FA (01273 326302/ fax 01273 728294/www.granvillehotel.co.uk). **Rates** £55-£65 single; £85-£155 double/suite. **Rooms** (all en suite) 3 single; 24 double/suite. **Credit** AmEx, MC, V.

initiate yourself into the delights of inline skating, and chances are that you'll feel considerably less of a fool than you would zigzagging down Clapham High Street on a Saturday afternoon. Wrist guards, kneepads and the like are optional for that extra 'clueless novice' look, but leave your ego at home because it may end up as bruised as your butt.

If none of this sounds challenging enough for you, maybe you could try your hand at a spot of kitesurfing out on the windy wetness of the English Channel. This embryonic 'sport' is currently all the rage on the Sussex coast but is not one for the faint-hearted, requiring as it does that you be able to fly a giant kite while simultaneously riding a surfboard across the briny waves. Lessons are available at Hove Lagoon for those who feel up to it, but spectating is a safer option. Skates, scooters, longboards and freeboards can be hired or bought from the places below.

Hove Lagoon Watersports
Hove Lagoon, Kingsway, Hove (01273 424842/www.hovelagoon.co.uk). **Open** *Mar-Oct* 10am-7pm daily. *Nov-Feb* 10am-4pm Wed-Sun. A wide range of watersports courses.

Oddballs
24 Kensington Gardens (01273 696068). **Open** 10am-6pm Mon-Sat; 11am-5pm Sun. This branch is retail only.

Oddballs Hire
West Pier Upper Deck (01273 777511/www.oddballs.co.uk). **Open** noon-5pm daily (weather permitting). Hires out equipment.

Pulsestation
23-25 King's Road Arches (01273 720788). **Open** 10am-7pm daily (weather permitting). Hires out inline skates, scooters, skateboards and longboards.

If it's a sea view you're after but you'd like something with a little more personality than the Grand or the Metropole, this is the place to head for. You can opt for various degrees of splendour in this swish, entirely no-smoking modern hotel with its glorious vista of the crumbling West Pier. For sheer extravagance opt for an antique four-poster with en-suite Jacuzzi, or, for the ultimate Brighton art deco experience, grab the popular, sea-facing Noël Coward Suite (both £155). Food is served in Trogs Organic Restaurant (*see p83*) down below. Staff are friendly and helpful. Children and pets welcome. All bedrooms no-smoking.

Hotel Pelirocco

10 Regency Square, BN1 2FG (01273 327055/ fax 01273 733845/www.hotelpelirocco.co.uk). **Rates** £45-£60 single; £85-£115 double; £70-£95 twin. **Rooms** (all en suite) 5 single; 9 double; 4 twin. **Credit** MC, V.

The Pelirocco plays to a party-hard crowd and eschews bland formality in favour of extravagant kitschy decor. Each of the rooms has been kitted out by a different designer and a Playstation console comes as standard. Ageing ex-punks can take a boudoir furnished by Jamie Reid, the Sex Pistols' graphic artist; sharp-suited, non-feng-shui types can enjoy Modrophenia's target bedspread and numerous scooter-wing mirrors. The Regency Square location makes this a good base for a weekend of wild clubbing – that is if you make it out of Pelirocco's trendy chocolate-coloured bar, which is open until 2am; breakfast is served here first thing. Children welcome. No-smoking rooms available.

Hotel Twenty One

21 Charlotte Street, BN2 1AG (01273 686450/fax 01273 695560/www.s-h-systems.co.uk/hotels/21). **Rates** £35 single; £60-£95 double; £75 twin; £75 four-poster. **Rooms** (all en suite) 1 single; 2 double; 1 four-poster; 2 four-poster twin. **Credit** MC, V.

Not for nothing is this place universally recommended. Located in the quiet Kemptown conservation area, not too far from the seafront, in an early Victorian house, the Twenty One is a well-run B&B establishment that pays particular attention to detail. The finest rooms have period Victorian furniture; all of the others are designed individually with a sharp eye for cosiness and comfort, and plenty of flouncy floral fabrics to remind you you're staying in a guesthouse. Breakfast is a tour de force.

Nineteen

19 Broad Street, BN2 1TJ (01273 675529/fax 01273 675531/www.hotelnineteen.co.uk). **Rates** £95-£150 double. Min 2-night stay at weekends. **Rooms** (all en suite) 7 double. **Credit** MC, V.

Tucked away down a side road at the town end of St James Street, Nineteen manages to be right in the thick of it, and at the same time remain a tranquil hidey-hole. The over-the-top Brighton kitsch aesthetic has no place in this superbly chic, stylish and intimate little hotel. Thanks to subtle minimalist decor there is a bright, airy feel to the place. Beds are sat on bases of illuminated coloured glass bricks, the linen is crispy white, and there are CD and video facilities in all the rooms. For breakfast, perch yourself on a stool in the funky basement bar, and staff will knock you up whatever you fancy. No-smoking rooms available.

Oriental Hotel

9 Oriental Place, BN1 2LJ (01273 205050/fax 01273 821096/www.brighton.co.uk/hotels/oriental). **Rates** £25-£30 single; £55-£70 double; £100 bunk-bed room (sleeps 4). **Rooms** 4 single; 7 double (all en suite), 1 bunk-bed room. **Credit** MC, V.

If you're on a budget but looking for something laid back and a little bohemian, this is the place to head for. Located close to the sea, and a stone's throw from Regency Square and the West Pier, the Oriental has a decidedly lived-in feel about it, but is furnished tastefully throughout. The rooms are bright, many have Persian wall hangings and there is an abundance of plant life about the place – contributing to an all-round homely feel. Happily, not your bog-standard three-star Brighton affair. Children and pets welcome.

Where to eat & drink

Although Brighton has eateries galore there are very few top-notch restaurants to speak of, but there is a great deal of good mid-priced nosh to be had for diners of all persuasions – as befits a city overrun with students and chic but penniless urbanites.

Not suprisingly for a seaside town, fish and chip shops are to be found in quantity, but none of them really warrants a recommendation. Traditional no-frills seaside fare is best sampled at the **Regency** (131 Kings Road; 01273 325014), where anything with gills and scales can be had freshly cooked for a modest sum.

Vegetarians are well catered for at **Food for Friends** (18 Prince Albert Street; 01273 302310), **Infinity** (50 Gardner Street; 01273 670743), **Wai Kika Moo Kau** (11A Kensington Gardens; 01273 671117/42 Meeting House Lane; 01273 323824) and the **George** (5 Trafalgar Street; 01273 681055), a veggie/vegan pub. The **Sanctuary Café** (51-55 Brunswick Street East; 01273 770002) in Hove is a popular hangout, but pricey for what you get.

Preston Street consists entirely of restaurants, cafés and pubs, none of them particularly exciting, though **Spaghetti Junction** (60 Preston Street; 01273 737082) does excellent takeaway salads and pasta, plus the best quiche in town.

Other places worth a visit include **Moshi Moshi Sushi** (Opticon, Bartholomew Square; 01273 719195), a conveyor belt affair; the **Tamarind Tree** (48 Queens Road; 01273 298816), a chilled-out Caribbean restaurant; **Casa Don Carlos** (5 Union Street; 01273 327177) for authentic tapas; and **Saucy** (8 Church Road; 01273 324080), an increasingly popular Hove establishment. Try (but be sure to book) the popular **Gingerman Restaurant** (21A Norfolk Square, Hove; 01273 326688), a rising star for those seeking serious culinary globetrotting.

The best places for a coffee in a city full of coffee shops are **Nia Café Bar** (87-88 Trafalgar Street; 01273 671371), which has good grub too, **Café Puccinos** (35 George Street), **Alfresco** (Milkmaid Pavilion, King's Road Arches) on the beach, or try the balcony of **Kensington's Café** (1 Kensington Gardens) for people-watching in the North Lanes.

The **Hop Poles** (13 Middle Street; 01273 710444) is hands-down the cheapest and best pub grub in town; it's difficult to get a seat here, even in winter. Failing that try the **Dorset** (28 North Road; 01273 605423) or the **Basketmakers Arms** (12 Gloucester Road; 01273 689006), a favourite for cheap Sunday roast.

Pubs and bars are in abundance. Of the traditional boozers the **Cricketers** (15 Black Lion Street), **Eastern** (103 Trafalgar Street) and the **Battle of Trafalgar** (34 Guildford Road) have the most charm. For a trendier watering hole, nip along to the **St James** (16 Madeira Place) or the **Sidewinder** (65 Upper St James Street), both in Kemptown, and the **Hampton** (57 Upper North Street) or **Riki-Tik** (18A Bond Street) in town.

Of the gay bars, most fun is to be had at the **Amsterdam Hotel** (11-12 Marine Parade) and **Doctor Brighton's** (16 Kings Road) on the seafront. If you fancy camping it up large style, beeline it to the **Regency Tavern** (32-34 Russell Square).

Black Chapati

12 Circus Parade, New England Road (01273 699011). **Food served** 7-10pm Tue-Fri; 6.30-10pm Sat. **Credit** AmEx, MC, V. No cheques accepted.
We're only here for the food! Why else would you want to go and sit in a cheerless concrete box underneath Brighton Library. Despite the intimate seating arrangements, it ain't cosy, and the ultra minimalist decor does nothing to warm it. Nevertheless, the short but imaginatively co-ordinated pan-Asian menu has earned this restaurant a faithful clientele. Starters could include pan-fried Cornish scallops with glass noodles (£8.50, succulence defined), and seafood soup with rice noodles, coconut and lemongrass (£6.50) – a delicately spiced, fragrant broth that accommodated some of the plumpest mussels we'd munched in a while. Main courses on our last visit included pine nut pilaf with lentils and grilled eggplant (£11.80), the only vegetarian option, and roast cod with yellow curry and salad of dried shrimp.

C Restaurant

C at Blanch House, 17 Atlingworth Street (01273 645755/www.crestaurant.co.uk). **Food served** 7-10.30pm Tue, Wed; noon-3pm, 7-10.30pm Thur-Sat; noon-3pm, 7-9.30pm Sun. **Set lunch** £20 3 courses. **Set dinner** £30 3 courses. **Credit** MC, V.
C Restaurant is a leased dining room inside Blanch House (*see p81*), only five minutes' walk from Brighton Pavilion. The dining room is very understated, white and plain (very *Wallpaper**), and the modern European menu uses the right phrases, although not all dishes are

fluent. The simplest dishes were the most successful, such as asparagus with poached egg – simply perfect; or the main course of pan-fried sea bass with chorizo, peas, Jersey Royals and mint. Valrhona milk chocolate and cinnamon tart with a coffee and rum granita was every bit as good as it sounds. There's a very cool (and inexpensive) bar here, too, for the exclusive use of guests and diners. C-Restaurant is fun, it's very cool, but service can be slow.

La Fourchette

101 Western Road (01273 722556). **Food served** noon-3pm, 7-10.30pm Tue-Sun. **Set lunch** £7.50 2 courses; £10 3 courses. **Set dinner** £18.50 2 courses; £22.50 3 courses. **Credit** AmEx, DC, MC, V.
The almost cheesy pseudo-rustic interior of this French restaurant doesn't prepare you for the magnificent, beautifully presented food. The daily specials are heavily fish-oriented, but there is something on the menu to satisfy all palates, except veggies – well this is a French restaurant, after all. Set-price menus might include a ravioli of quail with spinach mousse starter, followed by fillet of beef grand-mère with mustard sauce, bacon, crispy potatoes and garlic confit. Fantastic.

One Paston Place

1 Paston Place (01273 606933). **Food served** 12.30-1.45pm, 7.30-10pm, Tue-Sat. **Set meals** Lunch £16.50 2 courses; £19 3 courses. **Credit** AmEx, DC, MC, V.
Up in deepest Kemptown, Mark and Nicole Emmerson's obscurely located upmarket French-biased restaurant has a reputation as the classiest joint in Brighton – you can expect dressy formality, high prices and obedient service. Get going with red mullet and aubergine mille feuille with roasted squid (£11), and for an entrée, try the likes of free range guinea fowl salsify and lemon thyme pommes paysanne with guinea foul confit (£20).

Terre à Terre

71 East Street (01273 729051). **Food served** 6-10.30pm Mon; noon-10.30pm Tue-Sun. **Credit** AmEx, DC, MC, V.
This is one of the country's most famous vegetarian restaurants, and the kitchen here cooks wildly adventurous concoctions well enough to win over seasoned carnivores. Start, maybe, with butternut and dolcelatte torta risotto (£5.75), and progress to scrumpy camembert soufflé (£11.25). Modest portions are perhaps calculated to lure you into dessert decadence. And why not? Banana and mango tatin jaggery (£4.95) might whizz you off into high-calorie hyperspace. The waiting staff are sometimes a little flustered, but there's no taking away from the food.

Trogs Organic Café & Restaurant

124 Kings Road (01273 204655). **Food served** *Café* noon-9.30pm daily. *Restaurant* 6-9.30pm daily. **Set dinner** £20 4 courses. **Credit** AmEx, MC, V.
This seafront vegetarian eatery is probably the most ideologically sound place in town. All the ingredients are organic and the eggs come from Hen Heaven (you'll have to ask!). Kick the sleepy dalmatian off the sofa and you can settle down for superb-value grub – ratatouille with basil dumplings (£6.25) or warm goat's cheese salad (£6) – in friendly, cosy surroundings. The organic restaurant next door does sophisticated global cuisine in a more formal setting at twice the price.

Brighton rock

It comes as no suprise to find that hedonism is still the *raison d'être* for many a Brightonian, given the city's historical roots as a getaway for wealthy, decadent Londoners. When the weekend visitors arrive, bringing the Prince Regent's 'lets get trolleyed by the sea' attitude with them, the fun and frolics begin.

Whatever your sexual orientation, Brighton offers plentiful opportunities for recreational overkill and has more nightclubs than you can shake a stick at. Strangely, however, given its reputation as a non-stop party place, Brighton's clubs are all over and done with by 3am (bars shut at 2am). Nevertheless, there is still plenty of fun to be had and for after-hours action you can always find out the whereabouts of the nearest free party by asking a local. Alternatively, chill out with hippies round a campfire on the beach.

To get hip with what's going down you need only take a stroll down Gardner Street and Kensington Gardens on a Saturday afternoon and you will have colourful flyers thrown at you by various grey-looking nightclub-weathered persons intent on luring you into their pleasure palaces. Or, simply arm yourself with a copy of Brighton listings mag *The Latest* (50p from newsagents), or pick up a copy of *The Brighton Source*, free from various bars and coffee shops.

The **Zap** is the grandaddy of Brighton clubs and still crams them in every weekend without necessarily needing big-name DJs to draw the crowds. The other seafront clubs play to a similar smartly dressed up-for-it crowd. Queues start early at the **Honey Club**, where there is no escape from the thud of the bass bins, and the **Beach**, where security can be quite tight. The **Escape** soldiers on but seems unable to sustain a regular night.

Discerning clubbers in search of pumpin' undergound sounds should head down to the Stompaphunk at the **Funky Buddha Lounge** on Fridays, where tech-house, electro and acid flavours combine into a heady brew.

Phonic Hoop at the **Enigma** is a Saturday institution and perhaps the most eclectic night in town, where residents and guests mix up breakbeats, funk, drum'n'bass and anything else that takes their fancy. Or try the intimate confines of the **Jazz Place**, where you can get down with the fusion flavours of Russ Dewbury – Brighton's answer to Giles Peterson.

The biggest hoe-downs are to be found at the **Concorde 2** where different nights operate in rotation. Here you will find that most famous of Brighton gigs, the **Boutique** (formerly known as Big Beat Boutique), which takes place twice a month, along with other cracking nights such as Jazz Bop, Etch and Legends of the Dark Black.

Revenge is the south coast's biggest gay club and draws a sweaty crowd every weekend. Upstairs the music is housey and hard, downstairs kitschy and campy. **Zanzibar** is also very popular, though more of a bar than a club.

Beach
171 King's Road Arches (01273 722272/www.cside.co.uk).

Concorde 2
Shelter Hall, Madeira Drive (01273 571154/www.concorde2.co.uk).

Escape Club
10 Marine Parade (01273 606906/ www.theescapeclub.co.uk).

Funky Buddha Lounge
169-170 King's Road Arches (01273 725541).

Honey Club
214 King's Road Arches (01273 202807/www.thehoneyclub.co.uk).

Jazz Place
10 Ship Street (01273 328439/www.glendola.co.uk/smugglers).

Phonic Hoop at the Enigma
10 Ship Street (01273 620712).

Revenge
32-43 Old Steine (606064).

Zanzibar
129 St James Street (01273 622100).

Zap Club
189-192 King's Road Arches (01273 202407/www.cside.co.uk).

South-west Sussex

Bird-watchers, music-lovers, horse-riders, racing enthusiasts: this area has something for everyone.

There's a lazy voluptuousness about this part of the world – in the dips and folds of the South Downs, the slow curve of the hills, in the deep forest greens and sandy yellows. Inland there is great walking in countryside that is remarkably unspoilt considering how close it is to London; although the coastline around Bognor is marred by bungalow developments, the peninsular that ends in Selsey Bill is worth exploring for the pretty villages that are scattered around.

The area's coastal location provides opportunities for watching the comings and goings of the little boats and the sun setting over Chichester Harbour. Further south, the sea off Selsey is a popular place for divers as well as sailors – under the waves here you can explore a submerged Roman road, a World War II landing craft and a jagged outcrop of limestone that is rich in marine life.

Arundel

Seen from across the river Arundel is more like a stage set than a real town; with its castle and church at the top of the hill and the river at the bottom all it needs is a clockwork soldier to appear on the battlements and sound a trumpet on the hour. Despite the tourists, Arundel has a pleasing sense of being very much at ease with itself; it's a real working town, with tiny side streets lined with antique shops, tea shops and homely places selling country jams and the like. It's hard to imagine that as late as the 1920s it was still a working port, with big ships coming up the river; although, for a small town, there is a whiff of the cosmopolitan about it with good food shops and a French affinity that lends some panâche.

Arundel Castle, built in the 11th century by Roger de Montgomery and now the seat of the Dukes of Norfolk and Earls of Arundel (the present incumbent is regularly seen pottering around the town), is well worth exploring for its fine paintings, tapestries and furniture, and the gorgeous Fitzalan Chapel. The town's other main cultural attraction is **Arundel Cathedral** – this beautiful, imposing building is the 19th-century version of French Gothic. After your fill of history, mess around in a rowing boat or take a cruise on the river – Skylark Cruises (01903 717337) runs an enjoyable trip up to Amberley.

Chichester

Chichester has all the qualities of a classic English market town but still retains a sense of being a living city, rather than one preserved in aspic. Despite being very much a country town, the mournful cry of seagulls reminds you that the sea is not far away.

It was founded in AD 70 by the Romans, who laid out the main street plan and built the original city walls, subsequently rebuilt in flint in medieval times. The main streets of the city (called logically North, South, East and West Streets) slice it neatly into four areas – the cathedral dominates the south-west sector, while the finest of the Georgian buildings are in the south-east in the streets called the Pallants. The town is at its most lively in the summer during the excellent music-oriented **Chichester Festival** in July (01243 785718/ www.chifest.org.uk).

There are two small museums: **Chichester District Museum** (29 Little London; 01243 784683/www.chichester.gov.uk) focuses on the district's geology, archaeology and social history; and the **Guildhall Museum** (Priory Park; 01243 784683), where William Blake was tried for sedition during its days as a courthouse, and which contains some medieval frescos.

The **Cathedral** is still the centre of the city. Visible from miles away and immortalised by Turner in his painting of the Chichester Canal, it is a stunning structure, best known for its soaring spire and a Marc Chagall stained-glass window. Wander around the peaceful cloisters and you get a real sense of a past age.

Rural retreats

The pretty village of **Bosham** (pronounced 'Bozzum'), two miles west of Chichester, extends right down to the water's edge (the road here is only passable at low tide) and

By train from London

Trains to **Chichester** leave **Victoria** about every 15-30mins (journey time about **1hr 40mins**). This train passes through **Arundel** (**1hr 30mins**). Info: www.connex.co.uk.

many of the houses have a high stoop at the front door, evidence of past floods. Well known as a sailing village with a history as a fishing port that dates back to Roman times (the Emperor Vespasian allegedly had a residence here), Bosham is one of the most attractive of all the villages on the shores of Chichester Harbour. The exquisitely simple Saxon church (which includes stones from the original Roman basilica) has a beautiful arched chapel in the crypt, lit only by a shaft of natural light from a small window. A stone coffin discovered in the church in the 19th century contained the body of a child, thought to be a daughter of Canute. This is, according to legend, the spot where he tried to turn back the tide. From Bosham you can walk around the coast to **Bosham Hoe** where a short ferry ride has, for centuries, saved travellers a 13-mile walk to the pretty village of **West Itchenor**.

George V wasn't overly impressed with the seaside hereabouts ('Bugger Bognor' are supposed to have been his final words), and you probably won't be either unless a monster Butlins appeals. The unspoiled stretch of coast at **Climping**, a couple of miles east of Bognor, is of the steeply shelved, pebbly variety but is a good place for a bracing walk.

Downs' sights

As the flat coastal plain rises gently into the South Downs, numerous attractions reveal themselves. There are the two important Roman sites – **Fishbourne Roman Palace** near Chichester and the smaller, but perhaps more evocative, **Bignor Roman Villa**. Other attractions include the Elizabethan **Parham House**; the gardens of **Denmans** and **West Dean**; birdlife at the **Arundel Wildfowl & Wetlands Trust**; the imaginative and educational **Weald & Downland Open Air Museum**; and **Goodwood**.

What to see & do

Tourist Information Centres

61 High Street, Arundel, BN18 9AJ (01903 882268/ fax 01903 882419/www.sussex-by-the-sea.co.uk). **Open** *Easter-Oct* 10am-6pm Mon-Sat; 10am-4pm Sun. *Nov-Easter* 10am-3pm daily.

29A South Street, Chichester, PO19 1AH (01243 775888/fax 01243 539449/www.sussexlive.com). **Open** *Apr-Oct* 9.15am-5.15pm Mon-Sat; 10am-4pm Sun. *Nov-Mar* 9.15am-5.15pm Mon-Sat.

Bike hire

Hargroves Cycles *2 Christchurch Buildings, Chichester (01243 537337).*

2XS *Rookwood Road, West Wittering, Chichester (01243 512552).* Children's mountain bikes and tag-alongs available.

Arundel Castle

Arundel (01903 882173/www.arundelcastle.org). **Open** *Apr-Oct* noon-5pm Mon-Fri, Sun. Last admission 4pm. **Admission** £7.50; £5-£6.50 concessions.

This wonderful, imposing pile has its origins in the 11th century, although the original castle was heavily damaged during the Civil War and then extensively remodelled in the 18th and 19th centuries. Inside is a fine collection of 16th-century furniture and paintings by Van Dyck, Gainsborough, Reynolds and Mytens among others. Don't miss the gem-like 14th-century Fitzalan Chapel, a Roman Catholic chapel tucked inside an Anglican church, so that the dukes and their families could worship according to Catholic rites. It is home to a clutch of tombs of Dukes of Norfolk past, and mercifully shows no signs of the time when Cromwell used it as a stable.

Arundel Cathedral

London Road, Arundel (01903 882297). **Open** 9am-6pm/dusk daily. **Admission** free.

When he wasn't designing cabs, Joseph Hansom liked to turn his hand to a spot of architecture. This Catholic cathedral, which opened in 1873, was his take on French Gothic of around 1400; its exterior is best viewed from a distance. There's a fine rose window over the west door and, inside, the shrine of St Philip Howard (the Cathedral of Our Lady & St Philip Howard is the church's full name). Howard's father, the fourth Duke of Norfolk, had been beheaded by Elizabeth I for his part in Mary Queen of Scots' intrigues. Howard converted to Catholicism and, in the anti-papist hysteria following the defeat of the Spanish Armada, was arrested and sentenced to death in 1589, although he finally died in the Tower of London six years later.

Arundel Museum & Heritage Centre

61 High Street, Arundel (01903 885708). **Open** *Apr-Sept* 10.30am-5pm Mon-Sat; 2-5pm Sun. *Oct* 10.30am-5pm Sat; 2-5pm Sun. Last entry 4.30pm. **Admission** £1; 50p concessions.

A smallish but nonetheless interesting museum that is devoted to the history of the town, with scale models and old photographs.

Arundel Wildfowl & Wetlands Trust

Mill Road, Arundel (01903 883355/ www.wwt.org.uk). **Open** *Apr-Oct* 9.30am-5.30pm daily. *Nov-Mar* 9.30am-4.30pm daily. **Admission** £5.25; £3.25-£4.25 concessions.

One of the network of nationwide wildlife centres founded by Sir Peter Scott, the Arundel WWT extends over 60 acres of beautiful parkland and lakes and is visited by thousands of migratory birds, including Bewick's swans, which can be observed from the hides dotted around the site. This is a lovely place for a wander, with good disabled access and great for kids. As this guide went to press, part of the grounds were still closed after flooding, but the centre plans to reopen completely in September 2001.

Bignor Roman Villa

Bignor, nr Pulborough (01798 869259). **Open** *Mar, Apr* 10am-5pm Tue-Sun, bank hols. *May, Oct* 10am-5pm daily. *June-Sept* 10am-6pm daily. **Admission** £3.50; £1.50-£2.50 concessions.

The harbour is just one of **Chichester**'s many different attractions.

Enjoying a lovely Downland setting, this evocative and pleasingly low-key excavated Roman villa is notable chiefly for its wonderful mosaic floors, one of which, at 80ft, is the longest stretch of mosaic on display in Britain.

The Body Shop Tour

Watersmead, Littlehampton (0800 096 0809/ www.the-body-shop.com). **Open** (guided tours) *Jan-July, Sept-Dec* 9am-5pm Mon-Sat. *Aug* 9am-5pm Mon-Sat; 10am-4pm Sun. **Admission** £4.50; £3.50 concessions.

It was in the unlikely *Dad's Army*-ish setting of Littlehampton that Body Shop founder Anita Roddick first brewed her potions on a kitchen stove. The tour, based in the incongruous Carribean-style visitors' centre, takes you through the 25-year development of this bastion of global green consumerism. Tours start every 20 minutes and last for one hour 20 minutes.

Boxgrove Priory

Church Lane, Boxgrove (01243 774045). **Open** 7.30am-dusk daily. **Admission** free; donations welcome.

This beautiful, early English church has a 16th-century painted ceiling by Lambert Barnard, a plethora of Victorian stained glass and the ruins of a Benedictine monastery nearby.

Chichester Cathedral

West Street, Chichester (01243 782595/ www.chichester-cathedral.org.uk). **Open** *Easter-Oct* 7.30am-7pm daily. *Nov-Easter* 7.30am-5pm daily (visiting restricted during services and concerts). **Admission** free; donations encouraged.

The cathedral that dominates the town was begun in the 1070s and, although modified during succeeding centuries, it has remained largely unaltered since around 1300 (although the famous slimline spire is a 19th-century addition). There's plenty of interest inside, including Chagall's powerful stained-glass window and a huge altar-screen tapestry by John Piper. Also here is the tomb of Richard Fitzalan, Earl of Arundel (d.1376), and his countess, which was the inspiration for a poem by Philip Larkin.

Denmans Garden

Fontwell, nr Arundel (01243 542808/www.denmans-gardens.co.uk). **Open** *Mar-Oct* 9am-5pm daily. **Admission** £2.95; £1.75-£2.65 concessions.

Created by author and garden designer John Brookes this unique 20th-century garden is a delightfully relaxing place to wander around. Plant sales and garden design seminars and courses available.

Fishbourne Roman Palace

Salthill Road, Fishbourne, Chichester (01243 785859/www.sussexpast.co.uk). **Open** *Jan* 10am-4pm Sat, Sun. *Nov, Dec, Feb* 10am-4pm daily. *Mar-July, Sept, Oct* 10am-5pm daily. *Aug* 10am-6pm daily. **Admission** £4.50; £2.40-£3.90 concessions.

These are the most extensive remains of a Roman palace in existence in Britain, and are particularly famed for their beautiful mosaic floors. Only the north wing of the palace has been excavated; it's likely that the original building contained around 100 rooms. There are also gardens re-created according to their Roman pattern, and a Roman gardening museum.

Goodwood House

(01243 755048/recorded info 01243 755040/ www.goodwood.co.uk). **Open** *May-July, Sept* 1-5pm Mon, Sun. *Aug* 1-5pm Mon-Thur, Sun. Closed Oct-Apr. **Admission** £6.50; £3-£6 concessions.

A beautifully restored Regency mansion that is home to Gobelin tapestries, Sevres porcelain and paintings by Canaletto, Stubbs and Van Dyck, as well as Napoleon Bonaparte's campaign chair. Goodwood also hosts interesting temporary exhibitions.

Goodwood Racecourse

(0800 018 8191/01243 755022/ www.goodwood.co.uk). **Open** phone for fixture list. **Admission** varies, phone for details.

A couple of miles north-east of Chichester lies Goodwood, famous for its horse-racing course, which must be one of the loveliest in England. The season lasts from May to September, with the five days in July, known as Glorious Goodwood, an essential part of the sporting set's social calendar.

Arundel Gothic: statues at **Arundel Cathedral**, a Victorian take on French Gothic.

Sussex & Surrey

Pallant House Gallery

9 North Pallant, Chichester (01243 774557/ www.pallanthousegallery.com). **Open** 10am-5pm Tue-Sat; 12.30-5pm Sun, bank hols. **Admission** £4; £2.50-£3 concessions.

Housed in a lovely Queen Anne townhouse, a selection of modern British art (including works by Henry Moore, Peter Blake, Bridget Riley, Lucien Freud and Hepworth) as well as interesting temporary exhibitions.

Parham House & Gardens

nr Pulborough (01903 742021/ www.parhaminsussex.co.uk). **Open** *House* Apr-Oct 2-6pm Wed, Thur, Sun, bank hols. Last admission 5pm. *Gardens* Apr-Oct noon-6pm Wed, Thur, Sun, bank hols. Last admission 5pm. **Admission** *House & gardens* £5.50; £1-£4.50 concessions. *Gardens only* £3.50; 50p concessions.

A rare example of mid 20th-century restoration ideas on a large Elizabethan manor. The result is wonderfully harmonious and includes the fine panelled Long Gallery and Great Hall plus 11 acres of exquisite gardens.

Sculpture at Goodwood

East of Goodwood House (01243 538449/ www.sculpture.org.uk). **Open** *Apr-Oct* 10.30am-4.30pm Thur-Sat. **Admission** £10; £6 concessions.

A growing collection of contemporary sculpture including works by Elizabeth Frink, Andy Goldsworthy, Anthony Caro and David Mach in an outdoor setting.

Uppark House

South Harting (01730 825415/ www.nationaltrust.org.uk). **Open** *Grounds & exhibition* 11.30am-5.30pm Mon-Thur, Sun. *House* 1-5pm Mon-Thur, Sun. **Admission** (NT) £5.50; £2.75 concessions.

Uppark House was the home of novelist HG Wells, whose mother worked here below stairs as a housekeeper. The lovely 17th-century house was gutted by fire in 1989 but has been lovingly restored by skilled craftsmen. An exhibition charts the history and restoration. Don't miss the famous doll's house, magnificent views of the sea and lovely gardens. There's an open air theatre and flower shows in the summer.

Weald & Downland Open Air Museum

Singleton, nr Chichester (01243 811348/ www.wealddown.co.uk). **Open** *Mar-Oct* 10.30am-6pm daily. Last admission 5pm. *Nov-Feb* 10.30am-4pm Wed, Sat, Sun. **Admission** £7; £4-£6.50 concessions.

One of the area's most interesting museums, this unusual collection features around 40 historic buildings that have been rescued, rebuilt and restored, and scattered over a 50-acre site to offer a fascinating historical journey through the region's architecture. They include a Tudor farmstead, a 17th-century water mill and Victorian labourers' cottages. There are regular events and plenty to amuse the kids. Phone for details.

For a full-on luxury experience, it's hard to beat a weekend at Amberley Castle. The drive up to the castle is a stunner and not a little imposing – a sign discourages visitors who haven't booked; those who remain undaunted are greeted by screeching peacocks. Inside, the bedrooms are luxurious, furnished with antiques and traditional fabrics. Many have four-poster beds and en suite jacuzzis. If you feel like playing at royalty this is the perfect location. A 'castle break' from Sunday to Thursday starts at £380. All bedrooms no-smoking. Children over 12 welcome. *See also p90.*
B2139 SW from Storrington; turning on right after Amberley turning.

Bailiffscourt Hotel
Climping Street, Climping, nr Littlehampton, BN17 5RW (01903 723511/fax 01903 723107/ www.hshotels.co.uk). **Rates** £130 single occupancy; £150 double; £190-£235 deluxe double/twin; £235-£270 four-poster; £320 suite. **Rooms** (all en suite) 8 double/twin; 11 deluxe double/twin; 13 four-poster; 7 suites. **Credit** AmEx, DC, MC, V.
Bailiffscourt is an extraordinary faux-medieval house (it was actually built in 1927) that is perfect for an indulgent summer sojourn. The place is packed with stone flagging, tapestry-hung walls, oak beams and carved doors; it also has walled gardens, and is set in 22 acres of pastureland – and it's only 200 yards from Climping beach. There are plenty of facilities, including a heated outdoor swimming pool, tennis court, croquet lawn and even a helipad. Many of the 32 bedrooms have four-poster beds. Children and dogs welcome. No-smoking rooms available.
The hotel is signposted off the A259 between Bognor and Littlehampton.

Forge Hotel
Chilgrove, Chichester, PO18 9HX (01243 535333/ fax 01243 535363/www.forgehotel.com). **Rates** £40 single; £118 double/twin. **Rooms** (all en suite) 1 single; 4 double/twin. **Credit** AmEx, DC, MC, V.
This is a gem of a B&B, with plenty of home comforts and characterful surroundings. Watch out if you're tall – the 17th-century cottage has very low ceilings, but it's worth stooping to enjoy the charming, clean and well-furnished bedrooms. Many have lovely views, and there's a garden to lounge in. Breakfast is served hot from the Aga, and dinner is available, too. One room has been equipped for wheelchair users. The Forge is very convenient if you intend to walk on the Downs – it's just a mile and a half from the South Downs Way – or for a meal in the White Horse Inn opposite (*see p91*). All bedrooms no-smoking. Dogs welcome, by arrangement.
From A286 N of Chichester, take B2141 towards Petersfield; turn right to Chilgrove; Forge Hotel is next to White Horse pub in village.

West Dean Gardens
The Edward James Foundation, West Dean, nr Chichester (01243 818210/www.westdean.org.uk). **Open** *Mar, Apr, Oct* 11am-5pm daily. *May-Sept* 10.30am-5pm daily. Last admission 4.30pm. **Admission** £4.50; £2-£4 concessions.
A fantastic place to visit, with an outstanding working kitchen garden that includes 16 Victorian glass-houses, a 300ft pergola, plus 35 acres of ornamental grounds. There's a licensed restaurant in the visitors' centre.

Where to stay

There are plenty of hotels and B&Bs in the area. Note that prices rise significantly during the Festival of Speed (June) and Glorious Goodwood races (July), so avoid these weekends if you don't want to get stung. In addition to the places listed below, the **Suffolk House Hotel** in Chichester (East Row; 01243 778899; doubles from £89) provides moderately priced accommodation.

Amberley Castle
Amberley, BN18 9ND (01798 831992/fax 01798 831998/www.amberleycastle.co.uk). **Rates** £145-£170 double/twin; £195-£325 four-poster; £275-£325 suite. Two nights min at weekends. Breakfast (Eng) £16.50. **Rooms** (all en suite) 4 double; 2 twin; 8 four-poster; 6 suites. **Credit** AmEx, DC, MC, V.

Millstream Hotel & Restaurant
Bosham, Chichester, PO18 8HL (01243 573234/ fax 01243 573459/www.millstream-hotel.co.uk). **Rates** £75 single; £120 double/twin; £120 four-poster; £160 cottage/garden suite. Children £10 per night. Special breaks. **Rooms** (all en suite) 5 single; 27 double/twin; 1 four-poster; 3 suites. **Credit** AmEx, DC, MC, V.

This hotel is set in the idyllic waterside village of Bosham within a converted 18th-century malthouse cottage. It's a warm and welcoming place, although the bedrooms in the modern extension lack character. Facilities are good, however, and the staff are notably pleasant and helpful. The place is popular, so it's best to book well in advance; request a room with a view over the gardens. Children and dogs welcome. No-smoking rooms available.

Take A259 from Chichester W to Bosham; turn left at Bosham roundabout and follow signs to Bosham church and Millstream Hotel.

St Mary's Gate Inn

London Road, Arundel, BN18 9BA (01903 883145/www.arundel-sussex.co.uk). **Rates** £55 all rooms. **Rooms** (all en suite) 3 twin; 5 double. **Credit** AmEx, MC, V.

Situated right at the top of the town, with rooms overlooking the castle keep and gardens, this friendly pub is a member of the Logis of Great Britain group and is recommended by Les Routiers. The usual facilities, including hairdryers and trouser-presses, abound. Ground floor, modern motel-style rooms have disabled access. Children welcome. All bedrooms no-smoking.

Ship Hotel

North Street, Chichester, PO19 1NH (01243 778000/fax 01243 788000/www.shiphotel.com). **Rates** £78 single; £118 double/twin; £160 four-poster; £132 suite/family room. **Rooms** (all en suite) 6 single; 26 double/twin; 1 four-poster; 3 suite/family. **Credit** AmEx, MC, V.

This small, efficiently run hotel (one-time home of Admiral Sir George Murray) is very conveniently situated if you're travelling to Chichester by train. The building's an appealing, red-brick Georgian affair, and all the clean, spacious rooms have been recently refurbished in a traditional, pleasant, if slightly generic hotel style. The larger First Sea Lord Room and those with four-posters come at a premium, but they're a nice treat. Children and dogs welcome.

Where to eat & drink

Arundel and Chichester have a decent spread of pubs and (mainly chain) restaurants. The best food, though, is out of the urban centres. In addition to the places below, it's worth journeying eight or so miles west of Chichester to sample Ramon Farthing's classically influenced yet inventive cooking at **Restaurant 36 on the Quay** (01243 375592) in the bustling harbour town of Emsworth. In Storrington the **Old Forge** (01903 743402) is worth a try.

Decent food is also available at a number of the area's pubs. The best bet in Amberley is the friendly **Bridge Inn** (01798 831619), although the pretty **Black Horse** (01798 831700) and **Sportsman's** (01798 831787), with its lovely views, are also worth a look. Other agreeable drinking holes in the area include the **Old House at Home** in Chidham

(01243 572477), Donnington's **Blacksmiths Arms** (01243 783999), the 16th-century **Woodmans Arms** in Hammerpot (01903 871240) and the thatched **Gribble Inn** in Oving (01243 786893), just east of Chichester, which brews its own ales.

Amberley Castle

Amberley, nr Arundel (01798 831992/ www.amberleycastle.co.uk). **Food served** 12.30-2pm, 7-9pm daily. **Set lunch** (Mon-Sat) £15 2 courses; (Sun) £25.50 3 courses. **Set dinner** £35-£45 3 courses. **Credit** AmEx, DC, MC, V.

The food at Amberley Castle matches the setting – grand, opulent and luxurious. Typical starters might include ballantine of fois gras and truffled green bean salad with sauterne jelly, followed by tortelloni of langoustine with buttered spinach. If you can't stretch to dinner, then Sunday lunch is a more affordable option. Jacket and tie essential for male diners. Booking is strongly advised. *See also p89.*

Comme Ça

67 Broyle Road, Chichester (01243 788724/ www.commeca.co.uk). **Food served** noon-2pm, 6-10.30pm Tue-Sun. **Set lunches** £15.25 2 courses; £17.95 3 courses. **Credit** AmEx, DC, MC, V.

This very popular restaurant is really a converted roadside pub. It's quite a way north of the city centre, but only a short stroll from the Chichester Theatre, and offers pre- and post-theatre dinners. At weekends the place gets packed to capacity and booking is essential. Its popularity is down to a combination of assured, interesting food (for example, a main of braised Sussex rabbit with shallots, white wine and pommery mustard sauce, £11.85), an extensive wine list, plus friendly and helpful service.

Fleur de Sel

Manleys Hill, Storrington (01903 742331). **Food served** noon-2pm, 7-9pm Tue-Fri; 7-9pm Sat; noon-2pm Sun. **Set lunches** (Tue-Fri) £14.50 2 courses; £18.50 3 courses. **Set dinners** (Tue-Thur) £18.50 2 courses; £22.50 3 courses. **Credit** AmEx, MC, V.

Fleur de Sel is run by the highly acclaimed, Michelin-starred Michel Perraud. Food is classical French with a modern twist – expect to experience the delights of dishes such as layers of Cornish crab and filo pastry with fresh herbs, orroast fillet of John Dory with sorrel cream sauce. The emphasis is on using the freshest of seasonal produce cooked with flair and imagination, and the place is well worth a visit.

George & Dragon

Burpham, nr Arundel (01903 883131). **Food served** *Restaurant* 7-9.30pm Mon-Sat. *Bar* noon-2.30pm, 7-9.30pm Mon-Sat; noon-2.30pm Sun. **Credit** AmEx, MC, V.

This attractive country pub is set in the lovely hamlet of Burpham, just north-east of Arundel. Its gourmet credentials are most in evidence in the evenings, when the dining room is opened for an array of well-cooked dishes such as roast guinea fowl with ragout of wild mushrooms, confit of shallots and baby leeks (£13.95) and baked quail filled with foie gras and cep farci, compote of puy lentils, juniper and game sauce (£14.95).

The South Downs Way

Britain's oldest long-distance footpath follows the escarpment of the South Downs from Winchester to Eastbourne. Veterans recommend walking in this direction; triumphantly ending the 100-mile walk at the Winchester bypass is a lot less satisfying than finishing at the dramatic white cliffs of the Seven Sisters with the sea beyond. This old trading route is in one of the warmest and driest parts of Britain and the mainly chalk and flint walking surface is good except in very wet weather. It's a perfect introduction to long-distance walking for novices and can easily be tackled in manageable sections; as most of the walk is also a bridle-way it is accessible to horse and mountain bike riders too.

As the path runs along the uninhabited peaks of the Downs it is often necessary to drop down to one of the many villages for accommodation and food – despite the wonderful sense of isolation along the route you are never more than three miles from a pub. Alternatively you could stay in one of the National Trust camping barns along the way, such as **Gumber Bothy** (01243 814484), set in an isolated spot near Bignor Hill, a mile off the footpath along the old Roman road of Stane Street.

The South Downs Way is well signposted, particularly in the Sussex section, but it's still advisable to take a map; without one you would miss some of the sites along the journey. As well as Roman roads and ancient settlements, the route passes through **Chanctonbury Ring**, the **Devil's Dyke**, the **'Jack and Jill'** windmills, and the **Beachy Head** lighthouse. Along these heights once stretched a chain of beacons, whose names are still landmarks, warning the country of the approach of the Spanish Armada.

There is talk of the Downs becoming a National Park like the Lake District and Dartmoor. Last time the idea was mooted in the 1950s it was rejected because the need for greater food production in World War II had resulted in the Downs being ploughed up for food production. Since then the Downs have reverted to their traditional agricultural use (the grazing of sheep), and they are now rich in flora and fauna: the pink and purples of common spotted and pyramidal orchids; and a variety of birdlife sufficient to delight ornithologists.

Northcommon Farm
Golf Links Lane, Selsey (01243 602725).
Horseback trekking over the Downs. Charges are £14 per hour, with a minimum two-hour ride. Full-day rides with a break for a pub lunch are also available if riders' experience and ability are up to standard.

South Downs Llama Trekking
01273 835656/www.llamatrek.co.uk.
You won't actually get to ride the llamas, but they do carry your packed lunch for you. This is included in the charge of £35 for a four-hour trek or £50 for two people sharing one llama. As this guide went to press, treks were suspended because of foot and mouth; they are planned to resume in April 2002.

South Downs Way
023 9259 7618/www.nationaltrails.gov.uk.

Platters
15 Southgate, Chichester (01243 530430). **Food served** noon-1.45pm, 7-9.30pm Tue-Sat. **Credit** MC, V. This comfy, unstuffy restaurant offers a good range of modern British dishes. There's no blow-your-socks-off originality here, but the cooking is competent, and with a duck, lamb, beef, fish, pork and veggie platter on the menu, there's a genuine choice. Portions are generous; the wine list extensive and reasonably priced.

White Horse Inn
Chilgrove (01243 535219). **Food served** noon-2pm, 6.30-9.45pm Tue-Sat; noon-2pm Sun. **Credit** AmEx, MC, V.

The White Horse looks traditional enough but once inside it is light, airy and surprisingly modern. The menus, in both the dining room and the less formal bar, make good use of fresh local ingredients such as fresh Selsey crab (£7.75) and local wild rabbit with bacon, mushroom and mustard sauce (£9.50). Daily specials include a fish of the day and dishes such as breast of guinea fowl (£10.50). Well-informed, friendly staff know their ingredients, and there's a very comprehensive selection of wines from France and the New World. The White Horse is just a mile and a half off the South Downs Way and walkers are welcome, but requested to leave their muddy boots outside – padding around in socks is quite acceptable.

North Surrey Downs

To the suburbs and beyond.

After you've trawled through the ever-burgeoning sprawl of south London, the sight of green fields on the other side of the M25 is a welcome one. Sadly, the proximity of the North Surrey Downs to London has been responsible for the area's rapid colonisation by commuters, and their desire to remain connected to the metropolis means that the Downs are now criss-crossed with major roads and two motorways. Thankfully, though, it's not all bad news. Charming villages nestle between the highways, and the National Trust has secured a number of wonderful properties within this relatively small area.

Just west of the M23 intersection is **Reigate**, essentially a thriving but rather dull commuter town. There are some reminders of its rather unexciting history, which dates back to the Norman conquest, such as the castle (of which nothing remains but an arch) and the 18th-century market hall on the high street. But you'd be advised to simply stock up here and head off south and west to sample a clutch of infinitely more rewarding villages in the Mole Valley. **Betchworth**'s claim to fame is the appearance of its church in the film *Four Weddings and a Funeral*; St Michael's is an impressively large building, parts of which date back to Saxon times. Further west, **Brockham** has won the 'Best Kept Village in Surrey' award on several occasions – it's worth checking out the village green. South-west of Reigate is the picturesque village of **Leigh** (pronounced 'Lye'). Its church dates back to about 1200 and has a fine east window designed at the end of

There are stupendous views from **Box Hill**.

the 19th century. East of Reigate, towards Redhill, **Outwood** boasts Britain's oldest working windmill. It dates from 1665 and is surrounded by acres of National Trust-owned common land – ideal for picnics and nature walks. **Godstone**, with its splendid village green, and Oxted have their attractions but are essentially commuter towns. South of Westerham, just over the border in Kent, lies Churchill's old house, **Chartwell**. **Lingfield**, the country's busiest racecourse (01342 834800/www.lingfield-racecourse.co.uk) is worth stopping at if you fancy a flutter, or visit **Epsom Downs** which has events all year round, but is particularly popular on Derby Day (June) when jellied eels, pearly kings and queens and a fair are all part of the fun.

West of Reigate lies **Dorking**, a rather uninspiring town in itself but close to some of the most beautiful parts of green belt Surrey. Nearby **Box Hill** has been a favourite spot for the people of London and the Home Counties since Victorian times, with 1,200 acres of

By train from London

Trains to **Dorking** leave **Waterloo** every half-hour (journey time **40mins**). There's an hourly service to **Reigate** from **Victoria**, with a change at Redhill (total journey time **45-50mins**). Fast trains to Guildford leave Waterloo every 15mins (journey time **35mins**); the slower service leaves every 20mins and takes **55mins**. Info: www.southwesttrains.co.uk, www.thamestrains.co.uk and www.connex.co.uk.

woodland and chalk downland and spectacular views towards the West Sussex Downs. Further west is the Regency splendour of **Polesden Lacey** (*see p94* **Edward and Mrs Greville**). Heading south of Dorking is the well-groomed village of **Coldharbour**, which is a convenient base camp for visiting nearby Leith Hill.

To the west is **Guildford**, the bustling, ancient capital of Surrey, which has an old castle, museum, gallery (dating from the 17th century) and a modern cathedral. Further east, on the A248, are manor houses, gardens and a couple of picturesque villages, including **Shere**, which is home to a 12th-century church with a Norman spire. The lychgate and other buildings in Shere were designed by Lutyens. Nearby Clandon boasts two National Trust properties: **Hatchlands Park**, and **Clandon Park**, which houses the **Queens' Royal Surrey Regiment Museum** (01483 223419). North of Clandon lies **RHS Wisley**, a 240-acre garden which includes a stunning springtime Alpine meadow, rhododendrons and azaleas in early summer and rich autumn colours.

There are plenty of cycling opportunities in Surrey. The 80-mile Cycleway follows quiet country roads and lanes, giving cyclists the chance to explore some beautiful and tranquil parts of the county.

What to see & do

Tourist Information Centres

Surrey Tourism, Room 404, County Hall, Kingston-upon-Thames, KT1 2FY (020 8541 8092/www.surreytourism.org.uk). **Open** 9am-5pm Mon-Fri.

14 Tunsgate, Guildford, GU1 3QT (01483 444333/www.guildford.gov.uk). **Open** *Mar-Sept* 9am-5.30pm Mon-Sat; 10am-4.30pm Sun. *Oct-Feb* 9am-5pm Mon-Sat.

Town Hall, Castlefield Road, Reigate, RH2 0SH (01737 276045/www.reigate-banstead.gov.uk). **Open** 9am-5pm Mon-Fri.

Clacket Lane Motorway Service Area, M25 Westbound, Westerham, TN16 2ER (01959 565615). **Open** 9am-5pm daily.

Bike hire

Box Hill Cycle Hire, Box Hill Station, Westhumble, Dorking (01306 886944/711577). Inside the station booking hall.

Box Hill

Off A24, N of Dorking (Information 01306 885502/ www.nationaltrust.org.uk). Free access, year round. The site of the traumatic picnic in Jane Austen's *Emma*, Box Hill has outstanding views in all directions. A steep, winding road leads you up to the National Trust information centre car park just below the summit, where you can strap on your walking boots, and wander off with your picnic into 1,200 acres of woodland and chalk

downland with some stunning views towards the West Sussex Downs. Trails are marked and there are also braille guides. Box Hill is home to roe deer, rare orchids, butterflies and bats.

Chartwell

nr Westerham (01732 868381/ www.nationaltrust.org.uk). **Open** *Apr-June, Sept, Oct* 11am-5pm Wed-Sun. *July, Aug* 11am-5pm Tue-Sun. Last admission 4.15pm. Closed Nov-Mar. **Admission** (NT) £5.80; £2.90 concessions. **Guided tours** *Jan-June, Sept-Dec* by arrangement Wed.
Now owned by the National Trust, Chartwell was a crumbling Victorian mansion when Winston Churchill bought it in 1922. With architect Philip Tilden, he transformed it into a light and unpretentious family home. The rooms have been preserved right down to the daily papers and his famous cigars; the garden features a lake and water garden.

Clandon Park

West Clandon, Guildford (01483 222482/ www.nationaltrust.org.uk). **Open** *House* Apr-Nov 11am-5pm Tue-Thur, Sun. Closed Dec-Mar. *Gardens* 11am-5pm Tue-Thur, Sun. **Admission** (NT) *House & gardens* £5; £2.50 concessions. Combined ticket with Hatchlands Park £7.50.
This sumptuous and elegant 18th-century Palladian mansion (located three miles east of Guildford off the A247) was built on a grand scale by the Venetian architect Leoni. The house is known for its stunning two-storey Marble Hall and the superb collection of furniture, porcelain, textiles and carpets acquired in the 1920s by the connoisseur Mrs David Gubbay. It also contains the Ivo Forde Meissen collection of Italian comedy figures and a series of Mortlake tapestries. Capability Brown designed the garden.

Denbies Wine Estate

Off A24 N of Dorking (01306 742002/ www.denbiesvineyard.co.uk). **Open** 10am-5.30pm Mon-Sat; 11.30am-5.30pm Sun. *Tours* 11am-4pm Mon-Sat; noon-4pm Sun. **Admission** free. *Tours & tastings* £7.25; £6.50 concessions. *Vineyard tours* £5; £4.50 concessions.
At 265 acres, Denbies is England's biggest wine estate ('blessed with the same chalk soil structures as the Champagne region of France') and produces 400,000 bottles of wine a year. Tours of the vineyard and winery are available, as well as tastings in the cellar. There's also a restaurant and a shop.

Guildford Cathedral

Stag Hill (01483 565287/www.guildford-cathedral. org). **Open** 8.30am-5.30pm daily. **Admission** free; donations welcome.
Guildford's Cathedral is the only one in the south of England to have been built on a new site during the 20th century. Designed by Sir Edward Maufe, its foundation stone was laid in 1936. Work stopped during World War II and its later completion was partly due to the success of the 'Buy a Brick' campaign, with Surrey locals paying for and signing 'half-crown' bricks, made from the clay of the hill. Look out for Irene Charleston's beautifully embroidered banner in memory of her brother, Lieutenant Frederick Charleston, who was killed at Ypres. The cathedral was finally consecrated in 1961.

Hatchlands Park

East Clandon, Guildford (01483 222482/ www.nationaltrust.org.uk). **Open** *House & garden* Apr-Oct 2-5.30pm Tue-Thur, Sun. Closed Nov-Mar. *Park walks* Apr-Oct 11am-6pm daily. Closed Nov-Mar. **Admission** (NT) *House & garden* £5. *Park walks & garden only* £2. Combined ticket with Clandon Park £7.50.

Heading east on the A426 from East Clandon is Hatchlands Park, built in 1758 for Admiral Edward Boscawen. The splendid interiors were designed, in an appropriately nautical style, by Robert Adam and the house also boasts a selection of Italian, Flemish and Dutch paintings as well as the world's largest group of keyboard instruments, the Cobbe Collection.

Leith Hill and Tower

Off A24 SW of Dorking, 1 mile from Coldharbour (01306 711777/www.nationaltrust.org.uk). **Open** *Tower & servery* Apr-Sept 10am-5pm Wed, Sat, Sun, bank hols. Oct-Mar 10am-3.30pm Sat, Sun. **Admission** (NT) *Tower & servery* £1.50; 75p concessions.

Leith Hill is owned by the National Trust and, at 965ft, is the highest point in the south-east of England. It is almost as popular as Box Hill with weekend walkers, who come to enjoy the view – on a clear day the panorama from the summit stretches to the English Channel. The hill is crowned by an 18th-century Gothic tower, where an exhibition depicts local archaeology and social history.

Edward and Mrs Greville

Captain the Hon Ronald Greville bought **Polesden Lacey** in 1906, but its history dates as far back as the 12th century. In the intervening years, its most famous inhabitant was the playwright and politician Richard Brinsley Sheridan. Despite Sheridan's best efforts to extend and improve the house, it was practically demolished shortly after his death in 1816. What was left of the property was bought by bookseller Joseph Bonsor in 1818, and he engaged Ambrose Poynter to design and build the Regency house that is here today.

When Captain Greville bought the house, his wife, a celebrated Edwardian hostess, insisted on having it extensively remodelled so that it would be fit for royalty. Mewès and Davis, the architects of the newly built Ritz Hotel, were commissioned, and the house was filled with Mrs Greville's fine collections of paintings, furniture, porcelain and silver, now displayed much as they would have been at the time of her celebrated house parties.

Famous for her lavish entertaining, Mrs Greville ensured that Polesden was entirely self-sufficient in meat, dairy produce and vegetables. But it is as a collector of royalty that she is best known, and a year following Ronald's premature death, his close friend King Edward VII came to stay for the first time, occupying a richly appointed suite of rooms, known as the King's Suite, which was fitted with all manner of mod cons. Edward VII sent her a number of gifts, some of which are now displayed in the 'saloon'. Their friendship was the start of Mrs Greville's lifelong devotion to the House of Windsor. Childless herself, she was later to become particularly fond of Princess Elizabeth, the present Queen Mother.

One of Mrs Greville's greatest surviving achievements was her creation of one of the country's finest Edwardian gardens, with its combination of open lawns and enclosed rose gardens, with formal terraces, Moorish pergolas and informally planted shrubs. The garden has a number of designated 'Landscape Walks'; they include the Admiral's Walk, which is a recommended route for wheelchair users (if accompanied).

Mrs Greville donated the house to the National Trust in 1942.

Polesden Lacey

Dorking Road, 5 miles NW of Dorking, 2 miles S of Great Bookham off A246 (01372 452048/ www.nationaltrust.org.uk). **Open** *House* mid Mar-Oct 11am-4.30pm Wed-Sun, bank hol Mon. *Garden, grounds & walks* 11am-6pm/dusk daily. **Admission** (NT) *House & gardens* £7; £3.50 concessions. *Garden, grounds & walks only* £4; £2 concessions.

Where to stay

This is manor-house hotel country, but there are also plenty of cosy B&Bs. If you are staying outside a town, be sure to ask for a detailed map as hotels can be way off the beaten track, without so much as a signpost.

Bulmer Farm

Holmbury St Mary, Dorking, RH5 6LG (01306 730210). **Rates** £22-£35 single occupancy; £44-£48 double/twin. **Rooms** 3 double (all en suite); 5 twin (2 en suite). Min stay 2 nights (en suite rooms). **No credit cards**.

This attractive 17th-century farmhouse B&B at the southern end of this pretty village offers peace, quiet and privacy – some of the rooms adjoin the main farmhouse, allowing guests to come and go freely. No children under 12. No-smoking rooms available.

A25 E of Dorking; turn left at Abinger Hammer on to B2126; 3 miles to Holmbury St Mary; farm is on corner opposite garage.

Herons Head Farm

Mynthurst, Leigh, RH2 8QD (01293 862475/ www.heronshead.co.uk). **Rates** £45-£50 single occupancy; £55-£60 double/twin; £75 family (sleeps 3; £15 per additional child). **Rooms** (all en suite) 4 double/twin; 1 family. **No credit cards**.

Surrounded by 1,000 acres of Surrey pastureland, this Grade II-listed 16th-century farmhouse offers great value for money: period bedrooms, some with a whirlpool, some with a dreamy view over the pretty garden and lake (with freshwater fish and ducks). The owners provide a warm welcome, and are happy to uncover the outdoor heated swimming pool for guests, who also have use of a tennis court. Children welcome. No smoking throughout.

Leigh is SW of Reigate and SE of Dorking; at crossroads in Leigh take road S towards Norwood Hill; right turn after 1 mile (after sign to Mynthurst); farm is ½ mile on right.

Langshott Manor

Ladbroke Road, Langshott, nr Horley, RH6 9LN (01293 786680/www.langshottmanor.com). **Rates** £155 single occupancy; £210 four-poster; £210-£250 suite. **Rooms** (all en suite) 10 double/twin; 3 four-poster; 2 suites. **Credit** AmEx, DC, MC, V.

For all its reconditioned 16th-century splendour, it's hard to forget that a modern 'executive' housing estate is just a few hundred yards away from the garden walls of Langshott Manor. Nevertheless, it's still a charming hotel – luxurious, with friendly, attentive staff, and surrounded by a fast-maturing walled garden. There's little, if any, noise from the nearby Gatwick-bound jets. The hotel also has a fine restaurant, the Mulberry (*see p96*).

A23 to Horley Chequers roundabout; take Ladbroke Road to Langshott; house is ¾ mile on right.

Nutfield Priory Hotel

Nutfield, Redhill, RH1 4EL (01737 824400/ www.nutfield-priory.com). **Rates** £123 single; £175 double/twin; £235 four-poster; £205 deluxe double; £295 suite. Special breaks. **Rooms** (all en suite) 8 single; 20 double; 16 deluxe double; 2 twin; 5 four-poster; 9 suites. **Credit** AmEx, DC, MC, V.

Churchill's home at **Chartwell**.

Set in 40 acres of grounds, Nutfield Priory has plenty of charm. The hotel was originally a folly, built for a Victorian MP in Gothic style and supposedly reminiscent of the Palace of Westminster. The bedrooms are spacious and elegant, and elsewhere there's stained glass, elaborate carvings, oak panelling and an impressive library. The rooms on the south side offer spectacular views of rolling Surrey countryside. There is also a health club as well as an award-winning cloistered restaurant. Children and dogs welcome (£10 per stay for dogs). No-smoking rooms available.

In Redhill take A25; follow signs E to Godstone; hotel is 1½ miles on right.

Park House Farm

Hollow Lane, Abinger Common, Dorking (01306 730101/fax 01306 730643/ www.smoothhound.co.uk/hotels/parkhous). **Rates** £45-£65 double. **Rooms** 2 double (both en suite); 1 twin (with private bath). **Credit** MC, V.

Set in 25 acres of countryside, this spacious property offers comfortable accommodation, and is an ideal base for country walks, or visits to Leith Hill and decent pubs and restaurants. No dogs allowed – the owners have enough animals of their own, including horses.

A25 towards Guildford; through Westcott, past Wooton Hatch pub; Hollow Lane is next road on the left.

Where to eat & drink

Out in the villages you will find a number of pubs offering decent ale, atmosphere, pub grub and little sign of the bored suburban youths who roam the larger towns. The **Dolphin** at Betchworth (The Street; 01737 842288) dates back to 1700 and is a popular, and usually busy, hostelry serving food and Young's beer.

William IV: real ales and panoramic views.

South-west of Dorking, the **Plough Inn** (Coldharbour Lane, Coldharbour; 01306 711793) offers nine well-kept real ales and boasts the Leigh Hill Brewery on site. It also offers accommodation (doubles £70-£95) and an extensive, reasonably priced menu.

Facing the church and the square in Shere is the striking, half-timbered **White Horse** (01483 202518), serving food and well-kept beers. The **Bull's Head** in Clandon is a friendly converted 16th-century local noted for its well-kept ales. Around Box Hill, the **King William IV** at Mickleham (Byttom Hill; 01372 372590) has attracted plaudits for its food (though it can be variable), real ales and panoramic views. West of Reigate, the **Fox & Hounds** on Tilburstow Hill (01342 893474) outside South Godstone is a warm, low-beamed affair offering expensive pub grub as well as a sit-down restaurant, with a beer garden overlooking meadowland.

La Barbe
71 Bell Street, Reigate (01737 241966/ www.labarbe.co.uk). **Food served** noon-2pm, 7.15-9.45pm Mon-Fri; 7.15-9.45pm Sat. **Set dinner** £23.95 2 courses; £27.95 3 courses. **Credit** AmEx, MC, V.
Run by a team of crack French chefs, this is a bustling, fun place to enjoy classic and provincial French food. The à la carte menu includes starters such as cold roast-ed slices of monkfish with tomato bavarois, mains of pan-fried pork fillet with a green peppercorn sauce, and desserts of the traditional crème brulée variety.

Bryce's
The Old Schoolhouse, Ockley (01306 627430). **Food served** *Summer* noon-2.30pm, 7-9pm daily. *Winter* noon-2.30pm, 7-9pm Mon-Sat. **Set lunch** £15.50 2 courses. **Set dinner** £19.50 2 courses; £24 3 courses. **Credit** MC, V.
The seafood at Bryce's has deservedly earned a number of culinary awards. The specials on the board include such treats as char-grilled halibut with auruga and cracked pepper sauce on mash (£11.95); there are also pasta and vegetarian options (£5.75-£8.50). The wine list is well-chosen and the service is friendly. Booking is essential for the restaurant, but you may be able have an impromptu meal in the bar area.

The Chapel at Hautboy
Ockham Lane, Ockham (01483 225355). **Food served** noon-2pm, 7-9pm daily. **Credit** AmEx, MC, V. The Chapel is the centrepiece of this grand, self-proclaimed 'Gothic hostelry', with its vaulted ceiling, replica Tuscan frescos and minstrel's gallery. The fish- and meat-dominated menu offers the likes of roasted sea bass on a bed of fennel purée with caviar sauce. It's a popular choice for wedding receptions, so phone to check.

The Dining Room
59A High Street, Reigate (01737 226650). **Food served** noon-2pm, 6.30-10pm Mon-Fri ; 7-10pm Sat; 12.30-2.30pm Sun. **Set lunch** £13 2 courses Mon-Fri; £25 4 courses Sun. **Set dinner** £16.95 2 courses. **Credit** AmEx, DC, MC, V.
Chef Tony Tobin's fine cooking draws gourmands from all over to experience the pleasures of the small and inti-mate Dining Room. The menu is an interesting mix of traditional English and Mediterranean – typical dishes might include roasted loin of lamb with herb couscous and red pepper chutney or grilled veal ribeye with a mustard crust and curried lentils. Dinner will set you back around £50 a head.

Kinghams Restaurant
Gomshall Lane, Shere (01483 202168/www.kinghams-restaurant.co.uk). **Food served** noon-2.15pm, 7-9.15pm Tue-Sat; noon-3pm Sun. **Set lunch** (Tue-Thur) £13.95 2 courses. **Set dinner** (Tue-Thur) £15.95 2 courses. **Credit** AmEx, DC, MC, V.
Practically the only place to eat in the tiny village of Shere, this old, squat building has tiny windows and is rather dark and cosy. There's a lot of meat: fillet of pork rolled with spinach in filo pastry (£11.95) or tronchon of calfs' liver with a wild mushroom sauce (£12.95) are typical; fishier folk will find the starters and specials board more rewarding. There's a long wine list, while post-prandial coffee can be taken out in the garden.

Mulberry Restaurant at Langshott Manor
Ladbroke Road, Langshott, nr Horley (01293 786680/ www.langshottmanor.com). **Food served** noon-2.30pm, 7-9.30pm daily. **Set lunch** £25 3 courses. **Set dinner** £37.50 3 courses. **Credit** AmEx, DC, MC, V.
This tiny, understated restaurant offers a fine mix of sophisticated English and continental cuisine in keep-ing with its luxurious hotel surroundings. Eating à la carte doesn't come cheap – a main of roast North Sea cod is £23, roast Gressingham duck breast is £26. Those strapped for cash should perhaps consider a cream tea (£6) instead. Reservations are essential. *See also p95.*

Tu Tu L'Auberge
Tilburstow Hill Road, South Godstone (01342 892318). **Food served** noon-1.45pm, 7-9.30pm Tue-Sat; noon-1.45pm Sun. **Set meals** (Tue-Fri) £13.50 3 courses; £15 3 courses. (Sat, Sun) £18.50 3 courses. **Credit** AmEx, DC, MC, V.
Set in 14 acres, this country house restaurant is a popular venue for wedding parties. If you do manage to get in, you can sample half a dozen starters (mousse of queen scallops, wilted spinach and sauce vierge, £9) and mains (tournedos of cod, grilled asparagus and crab gin-ger gratinée, £17). On a nice day you can eat al fresco.

96 Time Out Weekend Breaks

The Three Counties

Magnificent pubs and idyllic walks – yet so close to London.

Have a gander at **Petworth House.**

The area where Hampshire, Surrey and West Sussex meet – known as the Three Counties – is one of the loveliest examples of countryside near London. The combination of Downs, lushly wooded areas and pretty villages makes it an attractive prospect, and the (many) signs of commuter life are easily hidden behind the greenery. The area near Guildford and Godalming is the most developed, but even here there are wonderful pubs and villages – just ignore the A-roads and explore the byways.

Of the small towns, **Farnham**, **Petersfield**, **Midhurst** and **Haslemere** are all handsome, relatively unspoilt places, but the glory of this area is the countryside. Walkers and cyclists have a huge choice – many of the walks in the

Time Out Book of Country Walks are based in this region. The land between and around **Frensham Common** and **Hindhead** offers heath and woodland, including trails to the scenic **Devil's Punch Bowl**; sections of the **North** and **South Downs** top and tail the area; and there are wonderful gardens, ranging from the vast **Winkworth Arboretum** to the smaller **Ramster** (20 acres of woodland garden; 01428 654167) and **Bohunt Manor** (also wooded gardens, near Liphook; 01428 722208). Much of the land is owned by the National Trust; its heathland management work is explained at **Witley Common Information Centre** (01428 683207; there are also two nature trails).

Conversely, there aren't many stately homes in the Three Counties (although there's a wealth of interesting domestic architecture), but one gem is the late 17th-century mansion at **Petworth**. Also notable, especially if you have kids in tow, is **Loseley Park**, home of Loseley ice-cream. Homes worth visiting for their literary associations are Gilbert White's house at **Selborne** and Jane Austen's in **Chawton**.

The by-ways

In addition to the (well-signposted) sights, the towns and villages of the Three Counties reward investigation. The village of **Petworth**

By train from London

Trains to **Farnham** leave **Waterloo** every half an hour (journey time **50mins**). Trains to **Petersfield** also leave **Waterloo** half-hourly (journey time about **1hr**), the train also passes through **Haslemere** (journey time **45mins**). Trains to **Godalming** leave **Waterloo** every half an hour (journey time **40mins**). Info: www.southwesttrains.co.uk.

is stuffed with antique shops (parking is difficult, but persevere). The big attraction is **Petworth House**, but to see how the working classes lived, look at **Petworth Cottage Museum** (346 High Street; 01798 342100), which is based in an estate worker's cottage. Children may enjoy the **Doll's House Museum** (Station Road; 01798 344044). There's also an arts festival each summer (01798 343523 for details).

A few miles west is **Midhurst**, a picturesque town with a decent variety of cafés and restaurants (try the tiny **Rockwell Diner**, Grange Road; 01730 815678 – a full breakfast starts at £3), and the ruins of **Cowdray House** (a Tudor mansion that partly burned down in the late 18th century); it's also handy for polo at **Cowdray Park** (01730 813257). Directly north is **Haslemere**, another attractive town, with a decent bookshop, an idiosyncratic museum, a quality cheese shop, a teashop and good restaurants; the **Dolmetsch Festival of Early Music** is held here every July. Much of the surrounding countryside here, too, is owned by the National Trust; **Blackdown** (over 900 feet above sea level, the highest point in Sussex) offers wonderful views – Tennyson had a house on the slopes. Near to Haslemere is **Hindhead**, notable as the birthplace of Arthur Conan Doyle and home of **Drummonds Architectural Antiques** (25 London Road; 01428 609444/ www.drummonds-arch.co.uk), a splendid architectural salvage yard.

Further north, **Farnham** has many Georgian buildings, a castle, a museum of local history with a walled garden, a range of places to eat and some interesting shops. Just outside Farnham is **Bentley** – worth visiting for the garden and teashop at **Bury Court** (01420 23202; open Thur-Sat). Also near Farnham, on the B3001, is **Waverley Abbey**. These English Heritage-owned Cistercian monastery ruins are reached by a short lakeside walk.

West of Farnham is **Godalming**, a nice enough town worth visiting if you're interested in the Arts and Crafts movement (which was very active in Surrey). In the town museum there's a room devoted to the Gertrude Jekyll/ Edwin Lutyens collaboration and a small courtyard garden reconstructed to a Jekyll design; and behind the parish church is a memorial cloister and Jekyll garden dedicated to local man Jack Phillips, the wireless operator on the *Titanic*.

Outside Godalming, at **Hambledon**, is the National Trust-owned 16th-century **Oakhurst Cottage**, which is furnished with items from the Gertrude Jekyll collection (open by appointment only; phone 01428 684090/ www.nationaltrust.org.uk for details).

What to see & do

Tourist Information Centres

Council Offices, South Street, Farnham, GU9 7RN (01252 715109/www.waverley.gov.uk). **Open** 9.30am-5.15pm Mon-Thur; 9.30am-4.45pm Fri; 9am-noon Sat.

North Street, Midhurst, GU29 9DW (01730 817322). **Open** *Apr-Oct* 9.15am-5.15pm Mon-Sat; 11am-4pm Sun. *Nov-Mar* 10am-5pm Mon-Sat.

Market Square, Petworth, GU28 0AF (01798 343523). **Open** *Mar, Oct* 10am-4pm Mon-Sat; 11am-3pm Sun. *Apr-Sept* 10am-5pm Mon-Sat; 11am-4pm Sun. *Nov-Feb* 11am-3pm Fri, Sat.

Bike hire

Aldershot Cycle World *Alexander House, Station Road, Aldershot (01252 318790).* On the same road as the station.

Birdworld

Holt Pound, Farnham (01420 22992/ www.birdworld.co.uk). **Open** *mid Feb-Oct* 9.30am-5pm daily. *Nov-mid Feb* 9.30am-5pm Sat, Sun. **Admission** £8.50; £5.50-£6.95 concessions.
The largest bird park in the UK, apparently. There's certainly enough room to fit in birds galore, plus attractive gardens, a children's farm, an aquarium, play areas and picnic sites, a restaurant and a gift shop.

Gilbert White's House & Oates Museum

High Street, Selborne, nr Alton (01420 511275). **Open** 11am-5pm daily. **Admission** £4; £1-£3.50 concessions.
England's first ecologist, Reverend Gilbert White (1720-93), lived here for most of his life: the original manuscript of *A Natural History of Selborne* is on show. The restoration of the beautiful garden to its 18th-century form is almost complete – there are always unusual plants for sale, and once a year in June (phone for details) there's an unusual plants fair. Also here is the Oates Museum, commemorating Captain Oates (of the Scott expedition to the South Pole) and his uncle Frank Oates, a Victorian explorer. Further pluses are the superior teashop and the engaging village itself. Walk from the village on to Selborne Hill, 250 acres of which are National Trust-owned.

Hannah Peschar Sculpture Garden

Black and White Cottage, Standon Lane, Ockley (01306 627269/www.hannahpescharsculpture.com). **Open** *May-Oct* 11am-6pm Fri, Sat; 2-5pm Sun, bank hols; Tue-Thur by appointment. *Nov-Apr* by appointment only (no concessions). **Admission** £7; £4-£5 concessions.
Not as well known as Sculpture at Goodwood (*see p88*) but certainly worth a visit to see a collection of contemporary sculpture in a landscaped garden setting.

Jane Austen's House

Chawton (01420 83262). **Open** *Mar-Nov* 11am-4.30pm daily. *Dec-Feb* 11am-4.30pm Sat, Sun. **Admission** £4; 50p-£3.50 concessions; free under-8s.

The author lived here with her mother and sister, Cassandra, from 1809 until 1817. *Mansfield Park*, *Emma* and *Persuasion* were written in this red-brick 17th-century house. Looking round won't take long, though the collection of letters and memorabilia may detain you for a while. Children and steam train enthusiasts note that Alton, just north of Chawton, is the starting point for the Mid-Hants Watercress Line (*see p110*).

Loseley Park
nr Guildford (01483 304440/24hr info 01483 505501/www.loseley-park.com). **Open** *House* June-Aug 1-5pm Wed-Sun, bank hols. Closed Sept-May. *Garden, shop & tearoom/restaurant* May-Sept 11am-5pm Wed-Sun, bank hols. Closed Oct-Apr. **Admission** *House & gardens* £6; £3-£5 concessions. *Gardens only* £3; £1.50-£2.50 concessions.
An attractive Elizabethan mansion that's home to the Loseley Jersey herd (yoghurts, ice-creams and cream are all available from the gift shop). The grounds feature fountains and rose, herb and flower gardens. There's also a children's play area.

Lurgashall Winery
Windfallwood, Lurgashall (01428 707292/www.lurgashall.co.uk). **Open** 9am-5pm Mon-Sat; 11am-5pm Sun. **Admission** free.
An award-winning producer, selling fruit and flower wines, meads and liqueurs, plus honey, mead mustard and chocolates. There's also a herb garden.

Peter's Barn Gallery
Beck House, South Ambersham, nr Midhurst (01798 861388/www.petersbarngallery.co.uk). **Open** *Apr-mid Dec* 2-6pm Tue-Fri; 11am-6pm Sat, Sun, bank hols. Closed mid Dec-March. **Admission** free.
Peter's Barn is a 'garden gallery', showing work by known and up-and-coming artists. Artworks are displayed in a small barn and are also dotted around the pond, under trees and shrubs and across the lawn. Two (lovely) dogs make sure there's no funny business.

Petworth House & Park
Petworth (01798 342207/www.nationaltrust.org.uk). **Open** *House* Apr-Oct 1-5.30pm Mon-Wed, Sat, Sun. Last entry 4.30pm. Mid Nov-mid Dec 10.30am-3.30pm Wed-Sat; guided tours only Thur. Closed mid Dec-Mar. *Park* 8am-dusk daily. **Admission** (NT) £6; £3 concessions.
Run by the National Trust, Petworth is a magnificent late 17th-century pile with a notable art collection. There are works by, among others, Van Dyck, Reynolds, Titian, Blake and Turner, plus furniture, sculpture and limewood carving by Grinling Gibbons. There's also a deer park.

Rural Life Centre
Old Kiln Museum, Reeds Road, Tilford (01252 795571/www.surreyweb.org.uk/rural-life). **Open** *Apr-Sept* 11am-6pm Wed-Sun, bank hols. Closed Oct-Mar. **Admission** £4; £2-£3 concessions; free under-5s.
A social history of rural life: agricultural implements, ploughs and carts, and crafts and buildings covering aspects of farming and village life are displayed over ten acres of field, woodland and barns. There's a café and Sunday train rides.

Watts Gallery
Down Lane, Compton (01483 810235/www.wattsgallery.org.uk). **Open** *Apr-Sept* 2-6pm Mon, Tue, Fri, Sun; 11am-1pm, 2-6pm Wed, Sat. *Oct-Mar* 2-4pm Mon, Tue, Fri, Sun; 11am-1pm, 2-4pm Wed, Sat. **Admission** free.
An idiosyncratic and utterly charming gallery full of the work of George Frederick Watts (1817-1904): landscapes, social comment pieces, allegories and portraits, drawings and sculptures. His wife Mary was responsible for the nearby Watts Chapel (off Down Lane, open 9am-dusk daily), a riot of symbolism and a blend of styles that demands to be seen. A visit to the hut-like teashop (01483 811030) rounds off a trip nicely.

Winkworth Arboretum
Hascombe Road, nr Godalming (01483 208477/www.nationaltrust.org.uk). **Open** dawn-dusk daily. **Admission** (NT) £3.50; £1.75 concessions.
National Trust-owned, this is a glorious display of over 1,000 different shrubs and trees, spread over a hillside and around two lakes. In spring there are bluebell and azalea displays; in the autumn there's a fine blaze of colour. There's a lot of wildlife (dogs are welcome on leads) and a tearoom in the woods.

Where to stay

Angel Hotel
North Street, Midhurst, GU29 9DN (01730 812421/fax 01730 815928/www.hshotels.co.uk). **Rates** £80-£115 single; £110 double-twin; £130 superior double; £150 four-poster. **Rooms** (all en suite) 4 single; 9 double/twin; 10 superior double; 5 four-poster. **Credit** AmEx, DC, MC, V.
The Georgian façade hides a much older building at this townhouse hotel in the centre of Midhurst. It has the same owners as the Spread Eagle (*see p100*) but a more old-fashioned atmosphere; it also has a variety of places to eat, open fires and some four-posters. Children and dogs welcome. No-smoking rooms available.
A3 to Hindhead; A286 to Midhurst; hotel is on main street.

Crown Inn
The Green, Petworth Road, Chiddingfold, GU8 4TX (01428 682255/fax 01428 685736). **Rates** £57 single; £67 double; £90 four-poster; £110 suite. **Rooms** (all en suite) 1 single; 3 double; 3 four-poster; 1 suite. **Credit** AmEx, DC, MC, V.
A laid-back hostelry that doesn't overdo the 'olde worlde' aspect, despite having more than its fair share of wood beams, open fires, four-posters and royal visitors (right back to Edward VI in 1552). Best of all is the upholstered phone booth in the entrance hall. Bar meals are taken in an attractive, rug-strewn lounge; there's also a pleasant-looking restaurant area across several rooms. Children and pets welcome.
Chiddingfold is on A283; inn is on right.

Old Railway Station
Coultershaw Bridge, nr Petworth, GU28 0JF (tel/fax 01798 342346/www.old-station.co.uk). **Rates** £40-£65 single occupancy; £70-£116 double/twin. **Rooms** (all en suite) 5 double; 1 twin. **Credit** MC, V.
What was Petworth railway station, plus several converted Pullman carriages, is now one of the loveliest

Sleep in a converted Pullman carriage at the delightful **Old Railway Station**. *See p99.*

B&Bs we've ever seen. The rooms are simply but splendidly decorated; breakfast is served in the old waiting room or, in summer, on the platform overlooking a banked garden. The Badgers, a real ale pub, is about two minutes' walk away. Book well ahead (there's a minimum two-night stay at weekends). No children under ten years old. All bedrooms no-smoking.
On A285 1 mile S of Petworth; pull into front of Badgers pub; take slip road leading to hotel.

Park House Hotel

Bepton, nr Midhurst, GU29 0JB (01730 812880/fax 01730 815643). **Rates** £60-£90 single occupancy; £100-£150 double/twin; £150-£200 family room (sleeps 4). **Rooms** (all en suite) 15 double/twin; 4 family room. **Credit** AmEx, DC, MC, V.
This family-run country house hotel was undergoing major refurbishment work at the time of writing (although several annexe bedrooms have remained in use). It is hoped that Park House will reopen fully by the end of 2001, with the same relaxed atmosphere as before. Amusements include two grass tennis courts, a pitch and putt course, a croquet lawn and a heated outdoor swimming pool. Not a luxury venue, but a very nice one. Children welcome. Pets welcome by arrangement. No-smoking rooms available.
On B2226, 2 miles S of Midhurst.

Spread Eagle Hotel & Health Spa

South Street, Midhurst, GU29 9NH (01730 816911/fax 01730 815668/www.hshotels.co.uk). **Rates** £80-£180 single occupancy; £95-£125 double/twin; £195 four-poster/suite. Special breaks. **Rooms** (all en suite) 32 double/twin; 5 four-poster; 2 suites. **Credit** AmEx, DC, MC, V.
An ancient hotel that has been tastefully updated, and extended to include a health spa (complete with pool, gym, hot tub, sauna, steam room and beauty centre). Some of the pleasantly decorated bedrooms have four-posters, and all have satellite TV. The attractive dining room offers formal dining; lighter meals can be eaten in the conservatory, terrace or courtyard. Children and dogs welcome. No-smoking rooms available. Sister hotel to the Angel *(see p99).*

Swan Inn

Lower Street, Fittleworth, RH20 1EN (01798 865429/fax 01798 865721/www.swaninn.com). **Rates** £30 single; £60 double/twin; £75 four-poster. Special breaks. **Rooms** (all en suite) 3 single; 6 double; 4 twin; 2 four-poster. **Credit** AmEx, MC, V.
Fittleworth is a pretty village, and this 14th-century coaching inn is opposite the River Arun and is surrounded by public footpaths. There's also a decent-sized garden. The interior has several low, oak-panelled bar rooms, hung with artworks 'painted by resident artists in the late 19th century in lieu of board and lodging'. Children welcome. No-smoking rooms available.
On B2138 between Pulborough and Petworth.

Where to eat & drink

There are some very characterful pubs in these parts; the problem is that most of them can only be reached by car. The following places are just a selection. For atmosphere and a decent pint, we recommend **Noah's Ark** (The Green, Lurgashall; 01428 707346), an attractive pub serving good food – especially the sandwiches. The **Red Lion** (Shamley Green; 01483 892202) has a similarly nice mix and loads of outdoor tables. The pretty **Hollist Arms** (Lodsworth; 01798 861310) serves real ale, good food and has a beautiful garden and seats under a chestnut tree at the front; an equally lovely garden (with masses of flowers) can be found at the **Red Lion** (Fernhurst; 01428 653304), which also boasts real ale, above-average food and attractive low-slung rooms. Children will appreciate the outdoor play area at the red-brick **Prince of Wales** at Hammer Vale, just outside Haslemere; and their parents will like the Gale's ales; there's a grassy garden with a big wooden climbing frame at the **Hawkley Arms** in Hawkley, a pub with a left-of-centre feel and real ales. The **White Horse** in Hascombe is a handsome inn adorned with beautiful tiles and biblical scripts; also good-looking is the **Chequers** in Well where you can drink outside on a vine-covered terrace.

Duke of Cumberland Arms

Henley (01428 652280). **Food served** 11am-2pm, 7.30-9pm Mon-Sat; noon-2pm Sun. **Credit** MC, V.
Cosy in winter (in the wood-panelled bar) and wonderful in the summer (32 acres of steep garden with trout ponds and streams, and a view over the Weald to the North Downs), the Duke of Cumberland Arms is a one-off. Fish and seafood are the specialities: own-made tomato soup, accompanied by a whole small loaf on a breadboard, and half a lobster, made a simple but excellent meal. Children – who will love the garden – are made welcome.

King's Arms

Midhurst Road, Fernhurst (01428 652005). **Food served** noon-2.30pm, 7-9.30pm Mon-Sat; noon-2.30pm Sun. **Credit** MC, V.
A popular pub with a welcoming vibe. There are real ales and organic wines, but the focus is the food: from several excellent dishes, grilled sea bass with tapenade salad (a starter, £6.25), roast poussin with red onion tarte tatin and crispy pancetta (£11) and mango brulée stood out.

Lickfold Inn

Lickfold (01798 861285). **Food served** noon-2.30pm, 7-9.30pm daily. **Credit** AmEx, MC, V.
The charm of this old pub (notably the herringbone brick designs on floor and walls) has been enhanced by antique furniture and beautiful hangings. There's a first-floor restaurant, but at lunch we ate in the ground floor bar. Dishes run from around £6 to £15. Grilled goat's cheese salad with Mediterranean veg was much better than a slightly pedestrian Greek salad on an earlier visit, but in general dishes such as seared tuna with pawpaw salad offer a combination of style and taste.

The Swan

Petworth Road, Chiddingfold (01428 682073/ www.swaninnandrestaurant.co.uk). **Food served** noon-2.30pm, 7-10pm Mon-Sat; noon-3pm, 7-9.30pm Sun. **Set meals** £11.50 (2 courses); £14.50 (3 courses) Mon-Thur, Sun. **Credit** MC, V.
A smart bar/restaurant with rooms (three) in the same village as the **Crown Inn** (*see p99*). The menu changes regularly, but typical dinner dishes might be terrine of rabbit and chicken with garden salad, toasted brioche and balsamic reduction (£5.95), followed by roasted wood pigeon on savoy cabbage with girolles and garlic, pesto tortellini and baby veg (£14.95).

Three Horseshoes

Elsted (01730 825746). **Food served** noon-2.15pm, 6.30-9.30pm Mon-Sat; 7-8.30pm Sun. **Credit** MC, V.
The huge grassy garden, complete with roses and bantams, is set beneath the South Downs – the view is lovely. Inside, there are brick floors and bespoke oak tables. Dishes run from various ploughman's (stilton, brie, ham) or a plate of gravadlax, through to chicken breast with bacon and mushroom sauce, or prawn, salmon and avocado salad (larger dishes are around £10). The local brew, Gales, is on tap.

Full steam ahead

One of the of the best afternoons out in the Three Counties, **Hollycombe Steam Fair** is a beautiful working collection. There are steam-driven fairground rides, a steam railway and traction engine-hauled rides, plus a farm (with animals and steam-driven machinery) and woodland gardens – all run by volunteers. The fair is set in the middle of the countryside – ride the Quarry railway or the big wheel (built c1914) to get fantastic views of the Sussex Weald – with trees all around. Mechanical organs add to the festive atmosphere. We couldn't decide on a favourite attraction: contenders were the wooden helter skelter (the Lighthouse Slip); the Razzle Dazzle (a spinning, tilting device built in Hartlepool around 1908 and regarded as the world's first white-knuckle ride) or the stately roundabout. Hollycombe is occasionally open in the evenings, when an already lovely setting becomes almost

magical. Once you've paid the entrance fee, all rides are free – so you can say yes to the endless cries of 'Again! Again!'

Hollycombe Steam Fair

Hollycombe (01428 724900/ www.hollycombe.co.uk). **Open** Apr-July, Sept-mid Oct noon-5pm Sun, bank hols. *Aug* noon-5pm daily. **Admission** £6.50; £5 concessions.

Around Newbury

The heart of horse-racing country.

It's true to say that west Berkshire doesn't quite have the cosy charm of, say, Hampshire to the south or the magical mystery of Wiltshire to the west. After all, it has the misfortune of being criss-crossed by a tangle of motorways, ill-conceived bypasses and A-roads. Furthermore, **Newbury** itself – with its industrial estates and business parks – is not a particularly attractive town. Nevertheless, hidden from the hum of traffic and the bustle of business, there are patches of truly pretty, unspoilt countryside here with some beautiful villages and country houses, and plenty of opportunities for bracing walks and hearty meals in small, unassuming pubs. This is racing country – an early riser might see horses out with their trainers silhouetted against the skyline. It's rabbit country, too: the hillsides just south of the town have been immortalised in Richard Adams' *Watership Down*. West of Newbury lies **Hungerford**, a pleasant town centred around a wide high street lined with antique shops and tearooms.

Horsing around

The centre of Newbury is dominated by the Kennet shopping centre, and although some buildings from earlier eras remain, the overall effect is not compelling. Those with an interest in English history, however, might wish to visit the **West Berkshire Museum** (The Wharf; 01635 30511/www.westberks.gov.uk; it also houses the tourist office), which gives a detailed account of the area's role in the Civil War. Theatre-goers should consider a visit to the **Watermill Theatre** (Bagnor; 01635 46044), which has a well-deserved national reputation.

Newbury is home to **Newbury Racecourse**, one of the best racetracks in the country (01635 40015/ www.newbury-racecourse.co.uk). This is where the Hennessy Cognac Gold Cup is run and the racing world's community of bookmakers, stablelads, jockeys and professional gamblers can be found drowning their sorrows or celebrating their triumphs in the pubs hereabouts. Many will live in and around Lambourn to the north of Newbury. Here, stables are everywhere, white rails line the Downs, and horses trot home along the roads. Early evidence of equine

By train from London

Trains to **Newbury** leave **Paddington** hourly; journey time is about **1hr 10mins**. Info: www.thamestrains.co.uk.

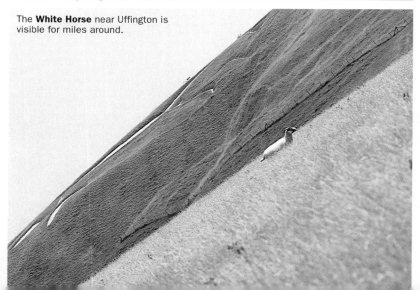

The **White Horse** near Uffington is visible for miles around.

fascination is marked by an enormous chalk **White Horse**, carved into the hillside near Uffington. Along the crest of the Lambourn Downs runs the **Ridgeway**, the ancient wayfare held by some historians to be the oldest road in Britain (*see also p208*). En route to Lambourn from Newbury, stop off in **Eastbury**. Quaint cottages line the stream that runs through the village, but it is the parish church of St James the Greater that is worth the stopover. Here you will find an enchanting window engraved by Laurence Whistler in celebration of the lives of the poet Edward Thomas, who was killed in action in Arras in 1917, and his wife Helen, who lived her last years in the village and is buried at the top of the churchyard.

Some miles to the east lies **Aldworth**, a quiet lost-in-time village with an intriguing church and a friendly pub (*see p107* **Aldworth Giants**). Further south, the wooded lanes around **Bucklebury** and **Frilsham** lead to the soaring acoustics of **Douai Abbey** (Upper Woolhampton; 01189 715300), with its gloriously light and airy modern interior.

Southern comfort

On the south side of Newbury the villages are prosperous and genteel. One of the most rewarding to visit is **Inkpen**, home to some of the most zealous ramblers in the country. These fearless defenders of the common person's right to stroll have for 25 years run the Inkpen Rights of Way Committee, which ensures not only that the area's rights of way are kept public, but also that they are clearly signposted. As a result, two of the best walks in Berkshire originate from this village; leaflets are available from the Swan and Crown & Garter pubs.

Also worth a visit for a hearty stroll is the village of **Ashmansworth**, which is made up of little more than two working farms and a church, but is imbued with a plethora of public bridleways. It is close to the stunning **Sandham Memorial Chapel**, overlooking Watership Down at Burghclere. Painter Stanley Spencer was a medical orderly during World War I and his experiences inspired the murals that fill the chapel's walls. Nearby is **Highclere Castle**, the stately family home of Lord and Lady Carnarvon, and most importantly, an excellent pub called the Yew Tree in Highclere village (*see p106*), with two log fires and a decent restaurant.

Stray further east towards Basingstoke, amid a tangle of country lanes and villages with 'Bramley' or 'Mortimer' in their names, and you will find two more fine country houses: **Stratfield Saye** (unfortunately closed until 2003; phone 01256 882882 for details of reopening) and the **Vyne**.

The highly Victorian **Highclere Castle**.

Tourist Information Centre

The Wharf, Newbury, RG14 5AS (01635 30267/fax 01635 519562/www.westberks.gov.uk). **Open** *Apr-Sept* 10am-5pm Mon-Fri; 10am-4.30pm Sat. *Oct-Mar* 10am-4pm Mon-Sat.

Barge cruising

Rose of Hungerford *from Hungerford (01488 683389).* **Tickets** £3; £2 concessions Wed, Sat, Sun.
Avon *from Newbury,* Kennet Valley *from Kintbury (both Kennet Horseboat Company; 01635 44154).* **Tickets** £4-£5.
The Kennet and Avon Canal, which fell into disuse and lay dormant until 1990, is home to some beautiful painted barges. The canal passes through Berkshire's most unspoilt countryside, so a trip on one of these boats on a summer's day is nothing short of idyllic. The *Rose of Hungerford* often has jazz bands playing on Sunday afternoons, while the *Kennet Valley* is horse-drawn from the beautiful village of Kintbury.

Highclere Castle

Highclere, Newbury (01635 253210/ www.highclerecastle.co.uk). **Open** *July, Aug* 11am-4pm Mon-Fri, Sun; 11am-2.30pm Sat. Closed Sept-June. **Admission** *Castle & grounds* £6.50; £3-£5 concessions. *Grounds only* £3; £1 concessions.
Kids looking forward to a turreted castle with a draw-bridge will be disappointed – this is more of a stately home. But those interested in Victorian architecture will be impressed; it was built by Sir Charles Barry, architect of the Houses of Parliament, and is quite similar in style. Inside, there are Egyptian relics brought over by the fifth Earl of Carnarvon in the 1920s, and the walled garden contains a Greek-style folly and a miniature temple. The grounds often host classic car rallies.

Living Rainforest

Hampstead Norreys, nr Newbury (01635 202444/ www.livingrainforest.org). **Open** 10am-5.15pm daily. Last admission 4.30pm. **Admission** £4.50; £1-£3.50 concessions; free under-3s.

A warm, wild jungle environment crammed full of plants and ponds. In among the foliage are hidden spiders, crocodiles, chameleons, fish, butterflies and birds. There's also a small shop and café. It's small, but perfect for a wet and windy day.

Sandham Memorial Chapel

Harts Lane Burghclere (01635 278394/ www.nationaltrust.org.uk). **Open** Apr-Oct 11.30am-5pm Wed-Sun. *Mar, Nov* 11.30am-4pm Sat, Sun. Closed Dec-Feb. **Admission** (NT) £2.50; £1.25 concessions.

Possibly Stanley Spencer's finest work. Painted between 1927-32, the murals are inspired by his experiences in World War I.

The Vyne

Sherborne St John (01256 881337/ www.nationaltrust.org.uk). **Open** *House* Apr-Oct 1.30-5pm Mon-Wed, Sat, Sun, bank hols. Closed Nov-Mar. *Grounds* Feb, Mar 11am-4.30pm Sat, Sun. Apr-Oct 11am-6pm Mon-Wed, Sat, Sun. Closed Nov-Jan. **Admission** (NT) *House & grounds* £5.50; £2.75 concessions. *Grounds only* £3; £1.50 concessions.

Architectural students can get their fill of styles at the Vyne. Started in the early 16th century for Henry VIII's Lord Chamberlain Lord Sandys, it was given a pioneering classical portico in the mid 17th century. The interior is in a wonderful state of preservation, with much original oak panelling and bucketloads of antiques. Don't miss the Tudor Chapel containing Renaissance stained glass or the lovely walks in the grounds.

Wilton Windmill

Wilton, nr Great Bedwyn (01672 870266). **Open** *Easter-Sept* 2-5pm Sun, bank hols. Closed Oct-Easter. **Admission** £2; 50p-£1.50 concessions.

This brick windmill, built in 1821 for local millers, has not been used since 1920, but was restored to its former state in 1980 and is now fully operational. Floodlit at night and standing on a chalk ridge 550ft above sea level, the windmill is a fun, low-key place to visit, and is within walking distance of the Kennet and Avon canal.

Where to stay

This is a well-to-do area and accommodation isn't cheap; it may also be difficult to come by at the last minute if a big race is on at Newbury. In addition to the places listed below, **Langley Hall Farm** (01635 248222; doubles £49.50) at World's End is at the heart of horse-racing country; **Rookwood Farm House** (01488 608676; doubles £60) is just outside Newbury and has a heated outdoor pool. For plain rooms in a stunning location, try the **Dundas Arms** (53 Station Road, Kintbury; 01488 658263; doubles £75). For the full five-star treatment, try the **Vineyard** (Stockcross; 01635 528770/ www.the-vineyard.co.uk; doubles £209-£499).

Esseborne Manor

Hurstbourne Tarrant, Andover, SP11 OER (01264 736444/fax 01264 736725/ www.essebornemanor.com). **Rates** £95-£105 single occupancy; £100-£150 double/twin; £150 four-poster; £180 deluxe double. **Rooms** (all en suite) 3 double; 6 deluxe double; 5 twin; 1 four-poster. **Credit** AmEx, DC, MC, V.

Relatively isolated on the crown of a hill, this country house hotel is good value. It has the trappings of a luxury hotel – tennis court, herb garden, abundance of fluffy towel robes – but its prices are not astronomical and, unlike many hotels of this size, it doesn't have a corporate approach. While the rooms inside the house are awash with silks and spa baths, the converted stable rooms are less flashy and more relaxed, with simple pine furniture and cream walls. Children and dogs welcome. No-smoking rooms available.

A343 from Newbury; turn right at Highclere; house is on left after 7 miles.

Fishers Farm

Ermin Street, Shefford Woodlands, nr Hungerford, RG17 7AB (01488 648466/fax 01488 648706/ www.fishersfarm.co.uk). **Rates** £35-£50 single occupancy; £56 double/twin. **Rooms** (all en suite) 1 double; 2 twin. **No credit cards.**

This 16th-century farmhouse is part of a working arable farm. Lying a long way down a dirt track, it offers a secluded home where you can lounge in the garden, swim in the indoor pool, or stretch out before a log fire in the sitting room. The bedrooms are kept simple, with beamed ceilings, cream walls and pine furniture. This feels like a good place to take kids: miles away from a road, awash with cats and dogs, and surrounded by fields and woodland. Children welcome. No smoking throughout.

J14 M4; A338 N for ½ mile; left to B4000; farm is on right 500 yards after Pheasant pub.

Newbury Manor Hotel

London Road, Newbury, RG14 2BY (01635 528838/ fax 01635 523406/www.newbury-manor-hotel.co.uk). **Rates** £110-£155 single occupancy; £120-£165 double/twin; £210-£270 suite. **Rooms** (all en suite) 22 double; 6 twin; 5 suites. **Credit** AmEx, MC, V.

This Georgian manor house is set in nine acres of woodland and water-meadows, with the Kennet and Lambourn rivers running through its grounds. Large and comfortable rooms have all mod cons and more (Jacuzzi spa baths, white bathrobes), and some come with river-view balconies. The idyll is somewhat spoilt by the A4 just a few hundred yards away, and the slightly corporate feel. Nevertheless, the River Bar has a pleasant setting, and the restaurant's bold decor is matched by imaginative and high-quality dishes. Children and pets welcome. No-smoking rooms available.

J13 M4; A34 and A339 towards Newbury; at Robin Hood roundabout follow A4 towards Thatcham and Reading. Hotel is on the right after the business park.

Wilton House

33 High Street, Hungerford, RG17 0NF (01488 684228/fax 01488 685037/ www.smoothhound.co.uk). **Rates** £37 single occupancy; £54 double. **Rooms** (both en suite) 2 double. **No credit cards.**

Described by Pevsner as 'the most ambitious house in Hungerford', this townhouse in the centre of Hungerford dates back to the 15th century. The front, however, is elegant 18th century, but inside everything is still creaking, sloping and bulging. The rooms, both at the front of the house, are charming – tastefully decorated in duck-egg blue or yellow, with bathrooms fit for a king. The owner, Deborah Welfare, uses local and home-grown organic produce in the fine breakfasts, and there is an elegant walled garden at the rear. A real treat. Children over eight welcome. No smoking throughout.

Where to eat & drink

The best places to eat in this area are country pub-restaurants, and a handful of very smart and very expensive destination dining spots. In addition to those below, the **Café Blue Cobra** Indian restaurant in Theale (0118 930 4040) is well worth a visit; it has now doubled up as a Thai restaurant. The restaurant at **Esseborne Manor** (*see p105*) is also good, with a reasonably priced traditional British menu. The **Swan Inn** in Lower Inkpen (Craven Road; 01488 668326) has an extensive bar and dining-room menu, and uses organic ingredients wherever possible.

The pubs are at the heart of the horse-racing community. The **Star** at Sparsholt, near Wantage, is unique: this simple, low-ceilinged inn features eccentric locals. Then there's the **Hare & Hounds** in Lambourn Woodlands, where you'll be hard-pressed to find a regular who isn't in some way connected to the racing world. Close to the Ridgeway, and not far from the Thames at Goring, the 14th-century **Bell** at Aldworth is a great place to end a walk and offers superb-value grub. The **Pot Kiln** in Frilsham, Yattendon, stands out for its location: in the middle of rambling countryside, it's a lovely place to stop for a drink.

Crown & Horns

East Ilsley (01635 281205). **Food served** noon-2.30pm, 6-10pm daily. **Credit** MC, V.
This pub, in the heart of horse-training country, is a mecca to all things equine. Copies of the *Racing Post* lie about, and horse prints line the walls. Stable lads and trainers come here to enjoy a huge range of real ales and good food including scampi Oscar Wilde and noisettes of lamb with port sauce (all £9.95). Ploughmans', sandwiches, pies and baked potatoes are also on the menu. There is a skittles alley, darts, pool, and a side bar with a television tuned to, you guessed it, the latest races. Accommodation is also available (doubles £58).

The Dew Pond Restaurant

Old Burghclere (01635 278408). **Food served** 7-10pm Tue-Sat. **Set dinner** £28 3 courses. **Credit** MC, V.
Situated somewhat bizarrely on a back road near the A34, the Dew Pond's immensely cute knocked-together 16th-century cottages are a homey setting (with some wonderful views) for simple, hearty country dishes. Yet this is not what you get. Keith and Julie Marshall's popular restaurant is more adventurous in its flavourings and ingredients and more artistic in its presentations. An excellent, fairly priced wine list adds to the appeal. Main courses from the set menu include 'today's market fish', steamed with a sauce of Noilly Prat, cream, chives and spring onions, or perhaps a pastry case with layers of wild mushrooms, asparagus and mozzarella with blue cheese and chive cream. Starters and desserts are equally extravagant. It's a no-smoking dining room.

Royal Oak

The Square, Yattendon (01635 201325). **Food served** noon-2.30pm, 7-9.30pm daily. **Credit** AmEx, DC, MC, V.
You have a choice of setting at this country pub north-east of Newbury. The bar area is low-ceilinged and pine-ridden, with tables and chairs splashed around the counter and fireplace. Pass through the smart lounge to the dining room, however, and yellow walls and gilt framed prints look down on smartly dressed couples speaking in hushed tones. In either setting you can be sure of a classy menu. On a recent visit, we enjoyed a parmesan fried brioche with caramelised cherry tomatoes and a fish delight of fried prawns, followed by plump fillet of beef on a crispy pomme rosti and a roast breast of chicken with a thick, strong tarragon sauce. Servings are generous, and food can be on the heavy side – so desserts were a course too far for us. Mind you, coffee and petit fours in the lounge after dinner provided a perfect occasion to (discreetly) loosen the belt.

The Vineyard

The Vineyard at Stockcross, Newbury (01635 528770/www.the-vineyard.co.uk). **Food served** noon-2pm, 7-10pm daily. **Set lunch** £17 2 courses; £23 3 courses. **Set dinner** £47 3 courses. **Credit** AmEx, DC, MC, V.
The Vineyard, the pet project of millionaire industrialist Sir Peter Michael, is a shrine to wealth. Flames leap up from the lake by the entrance and liveried doormen park your car. The restaurant is equally opulent, laid out on two levels with ornate ironwork and huge floor-to-ceiling windows. The Fusion menu includes such delicacies as tian of crab or spaghetti of cockles for starters; duckling or supreme of guinea fowl for mains, and cherry bakewell for dessert. Many of the wines are Californian; Sir Peter just happens to own a vineyard in the Napa Valley. Service is exemplary, and the high quality of the cuisine will surely be reflected in the bill.

Yew Tree

Hollington Cross, Andover Road, Highclere (01635 253360). **Food served** noon-2.30pm, 6.30-10pm daily. **Credit** AmEx, DC, MC, V.
A smart 350-year-old pub and restaurant on the outskirts of a very well-to-do village, the Yew Tree attracts a fair few well-heeled locals who fill the car park with shiny Mercs and BMWs. The beamed restaurant serves food that can occasionally fall into the deep-fried brie wrapped in filo pastry with a port and cranberry sauce category. Mains include a healthy mix of meat, fish and vegetarian dishes – grilled breast of chicken with a creamy coconut, pepper, garlic and pineapple sauce, or vegetable and pine nut parcelsset on a light curry sauce. Starters are around £6, mains run from £8 to £13.

Aldworth Giants

You could pass through Aldworth in the blink of an eye. Not only is it tiny, but it's not particularly remarkable either. There's a picturesque church, a small unobtrusive pub and a village shop in among the old houses spread along the small country lane. It's certainly pleasant – and some people might call it idyllic – but it's not immediately striking.

However, the unassuming façade hides some treasures and a distinguished history. Aldworth (as Elleorde) features in the Domesday Book – its population of 25 was made up of villeins, serfs and swineherd. The discovery of a Roman pottery kiln nearby and King Alfred's victory over the Danes on the Ridgeway above the village in 871 indicate even earlier activity here. Furthermore, the churchyard was originally circular, suggesting it was once a pagan burial ground, and there's a 1,000-year-old yew tree that suffered in the 1976 storm but is still managing to yield some new growth.

But it's what's inside the church that is truly fascinating: here lie the nine huge 14th-century stone effigies known as the Aldworth Giants. They represent five generations of the Norman family of de la Beche, and seem to take up most of the church. Some have lost their faces or limbs, and all have suffered the corrosive ravages of time, but they remain a spectacle nevertheless – Sir John and Isabella lie side by side, Lord Nicholas is posed as if in prayer. Perhaps the finest effigy is that of Sir Philip, who lies sideways on his tomb with a dwarf at his feet; as valet to Edward II, he was always accompanied by a dwarf to emphasise his height. A 17th-century diarist recorded that four of the figures were known locally as 'John Long, John Strong, John Ever Afraid and John Never Afraid'. (John Ever Afraid was a tenth effigy that is no longer around.)

The figures may have been renowned for centuries (Elizabeth I is said to have paid them a visit), but the village has other claims to fame. Lord Tennyson admired it, as his full title (Lord Tennyson of Freshford and Aldworth) suggests; he also married a local girl. And the 'Old

Yew, which graspest at the stones' in *In Memoriam*, may refer to the church yew. The poet Laurence Binyon lived here, too; his ashes are buried by the beech hedge in the churchyard.

The village has other attractions besides the Giants. At 372 feet, the well, opposite the tiny local pub, the Bell, is one of the deepest in the country. And the shop still sells sweets out of big glass jars.

Aldworth Shop
Church Lane, Aldworth, nr Reading (01635 578254). **Open** 8.30am-12.30pm, 1.45-5pm Mon, Tue, Thur, Fri; 8.30am-12.30pm Wed, Sat; 8.30-9.30am Sun.

Bell Inn
Aldworth, nr Reading (01635 578272). **Food served** 11am-3pm, 6-11pm Tue-Sat; noon-3pm, 7-10.30pm Sun.

St Mary's Church
Aldworth. **Open** 10am-6pm daily.

Hampshire & Isle of Wight

Winchester & Around

The ancient capital of Wessex may have lost its royal favour, but not its medieval majesty.

Winchester is a city that has seen it all before. An Iron Age settlement was established on St Catherine's Hill, just to the east, in about 450 BC. The Romans moved the town down to its present site west of the River Itchen in around AD 70, when they created their city of Venta Belgarum. After a couple of centuries it became an important centre for the newly arrived Saxons, and the first cathedral was begun in 648. In 871 Alfred the Great made Winchester capital of his kingdom of Wessex, and for a while it challenged Norwich as the country's second city. From about 1250, however, it began a steady decline. The Bishops of Winchester remained wealthy and important figures, but Winchester itself fell into being a quiet, minor country town.

As a result Winchester today can sometimes seem to have its head in the past more than just about any other city in Britain. Its medieval core is still very much the heart of town, with winding lanes of enormous, archetypically English charm – neat, compact and very easy to wander around. Within it there is a remarkable range of ancient buildings – from one of the oldest and grandest of English cathedrals to hole-in-the-wall churches, fortified gates, the great hall of a royal palace and a 15th-century watermill. In 1382 Winchester acquired the last of its great medieval institutions, when Bishop William of Wykeham founded Winchester College, and this public school remains peculiarly prominent in the life of the town, especially south of the Cathedral Close.

More recently, though, after centuries in the economic doldrums, Winchester has reached another peak of a sort. As a definitive green-field city of the 1980s it became very attractive to small, clean but prosperous high-tech industries. At the same time, the city's old-world tranquillity and the postcard-prettiness of the surrounding villages made them magnets for commuters and second-home buyers. Consequently, Winchester and the surrounding area is now frequently cited as having the highest standard of living in Britain. This is

also evidenced by the top-of-the-range four-wheel-drives and people-movers that ply the country lanes. One side effect of this affluence is that Winchester now has a notably high-standard range of restaurants.

Put to the Test

Some 16 miles to the north-west is **Andover**, under-loved ever since it was earmarked in the 1960s as a destination for 'London overspill'. Around it, though, are villages that seem lost in deep green countryside, especially in the valley of the Test, which runs due south. This is one of the most renowned trout-fishing rivers in Britain; it also has a

Winchester Cathedral – simple beauty.

beautiful long-distance footpath, the **Test Way**, running alongside, passing characterful villages with pubs, including **Wherwell**, **Longstock** and **King's Somborne**, from where another path (the Clarendon Way) leads to Winchester or Salisbury.

Shortly before the Test enters Southampton it passes through the old market town of **Romsey**, the prime attractions of which (apart from some rather twee teashops) are the 12th-century Romsey Abbey, one of the finest intact examples of Norman architecture in England, and King John's House, which, despite the name, is a non-royal but remarkably complete medieval house.

East of Winchester, beyond the barrier of the M3, the A31 road runs up to the valley of the Itchen. A turn south on to the A272 Petersfield road, around three miles from the city, will take you up to **Cheesefoot Head**, a giant ridge in the down where the road crosses the **South Downs Way**. The views are spectacular, and it makes a good jumping-off point for a shortish walk along the footpath. After seven miles the main road runs into **New Alresford**. A classically pretty old country town (the 'New' dates from the 13th century), it has a wide main street (laid out to house medieval sheep markets), a riverside walk, a quirky range of shops and a disproportionate number of pubs. Many of its visitors, though, are railway buffs, drawn by the **Watercress Line**.

South of Winchester, beyond the **Marwell Zoological Park**, the main point of interest is **Bishop's Waltham**, a likeable, unprettified, mostly Georgian town. For nearly 1,000 years it was the property of the Bishops of Winchester, who built one of their many residences there, **Bishop's Waltham Palace**. A little further south is **Wickham**, birthplace of William of Wykeham, founder of Winchester College. Although only a large village (or small town), it has a peculiarly large main square, created to fit a market fair in 1268. Surrounded by buildings dating from medieval times and the Georgian and Victorian periods, it gives Wickham an oddly grand, urban look. It's also a handy base for trips into **Portsmouth**, which apart from its naval attractions also boasts Dickens' birthplace and the Southsea Esplanade, home to a pier, fun-parks and a shingle beach.

Wickham stands at the southern end of the valley of the River Meon, another trout stream. The valley contains some of the prettiest riverbank-and-hollyhocks villages in Hampshire, such as **Droxford**, **Exton**, and **West Meon**. A long-distance path, the **Wayfarers' Walk**, runs through Exton north to New Alresford and south to the coast. Just north of Exton the A32 valley road crosses the

South Downs Way, which you can use to climb **Old Winchester Hill**, a massive down with the remains of an Iron Age fort at its top.

As well as seeking out any specific destination, though, it can be just as enjoyable to wander between villages with no particular plan. Places like **Upham**, **Owslebury**, **Beauworth** (just off the South Downs Way) and **Cheriton** make particularly pleasant spots to lose a few hours.

What to see & do

Winchester hosts several festivals, most of them in July: the **Hat Fair Street Theatre Festival** occupies the first weekend, followed by the all-the-arts **Winchester Festival**; at the end of July there is the **Southern Cathedrals Festival**, with lashings of choral music in the cathedral. In late September Winchester also hosts a **Literature Festival**.

There are plenty of enjoyable and peaceful walks within the city, and the tourist office offers guided walks and tours. Winchester is also a junction of long-distance footpaths. It is the westernmost point of the **South Downs Way**, which runs to Eastbourne, and the **Pilgrim's Way** (*see p36* **On the pilgrims' trail**), to Canterbury. The **Itchen Way** runs south to join the **Solent Way**, to Southampton and Portsmouth, and the **Clarendon Way** goes west to Salisbury. Several guides are available to these paths, and the Winchester tourist office has local guides to these and other footpaths nearby. Andover and Romsey offices have guides to the **Test Way**.

Tourist Information Centres

Town Mill House, Bridge Street, Andover, SP10 1BL (01264 324320). **Open** *Apr-June, Sept* 9.30am-5.30pm Mon-Sat. *July, Aug* 9.30am-5.30pm Mon-Sat; 1-5pm Sun. *Oct-Mar* 10am-4.30pm Mon-Sat; 11am-4pm bank hols.

Clarence Esplanade, Southsea, Portsmouth, PO5 3ST (023 9282 6722/www.visitportsmouth.co.uk). **Open** *Apr-Oct* 9.30am-5.45pm daily. *Nov-Mar* 9.30am-5.15pm daily.

13 Church Street, Romsey, SO51 8BT (01794 512987). **Open** *Apr-July, Sept* 9.30am-5pm Mon-Sat. *Aug* 9.30am-5pm Mon-Sat; 2-5pm Sun. *Oct-Mar* 10am-4pm Mon-Sat.

By train from London

Trains to **Winchester** and **Portsmouth & Southsea** leave **Waterloo** every 15mins. Journey time to **Winchester** is between **55mins** and **1hr 5mins**, and **1hr 30mins** to **Portsmouth**. Info: www.swtrains.co.uk.

*The Guildhall, The Broadway, Winchester, SO23 9LJ
(01962 840500/www.winchester.gov.uk).* **Open** *June-
mid Sept* 10am-6pm Mon-Sat; 11am-2pm Sun. *Mid
Sept-May* 10am-5pm Mon-Sat.

Bishop's Waltham Palace

*Bishop's Waltham (01489 892460/www.english-
heritage.org.uk).* **Open** *Apr-Sept* 10am-6pm daily.
Last entry 5.30pm. *Oct* 10am-5pm daily. Last entry
4.30pm. Closed Nov-Mar. **Admission** (EH) £2.10;
£1.10-£1.60 concessions.

This once-lavish residence of Winchester's medieval
bishops was begun in the 1130s, and extended many
times. It was destroyed during the Civil War in 1644,
after it had been used as a Royalist stronghold. However,
the surviving ruins, looming up in the middle of the
town, are impressively atmospheric.

Charles Dickens' Birthplace Museum

*393 Old Commercial Road, Portsmouth (023
9282 7261/www.portsmouthmuseums.co.uk).*
Open *Apr-Oct* 10am-5.30pm daily. *29 Nov-19
Dec, 7 Feb* 10am-4pm daily. **Admission** £2.50;
£1.50-£1.80 concessions; free under-13s with
full-paying adult.

One Portsmouth attraction with only a sideways
connection with the Navy, a little away from central
Portsmouth near the ferry terminal. The great novelist
actually had few memories of this house, since his
father, a Navy clerk, moved the family on not long
after Charles was born here in 1812, but it's a very
charmingly preserved example of a modest early 19th-
century house, and also has several relics of the writer's
later life. Normally closed in winter, it opens specially
on 7 February, Dickens' birthday.

Hospital of St Cross

St Cross Road, Winchester (01962 851375).
Open *Apr-Oct* 9.30am-5pm Mon-Sat. *Nov-Mar*
10.30am-3.30pm Mon-Sat. **Admission** £2; 50p-
£1.25 concessions.

The medieval almshouse of St Cross, about a mile south
of Winchester town centre, is the oldest still-functioning
house of charity in the country (founded in 1136). The
towering Norman church is 12th century; most of the
other buildings were added in the 1440s. They have a
marvellous tranquillity, and make a beautiful end to a
walk. St Cross still houses a religious community, and
hungry visitors can ask at the Porter's Lodge for the
'Wayfarer's Dole' of free bread and ale.

Marwell Zoological Park

*Colden Common, Winchester (07626 943163/
www.marwell.org.uk).* **Open** *Nov-Mar* 10am-
4pm daily. *Apr-Oct* 10am-6pm daily. Last
admission 1hr before closing. **Admission** £9;
£6.50-£8 concessions.

A family favourite, with some 1,000 animals living in
100 acres of parkland. The breeding and sustaining of
endangered species is a park speciality, but there's also
a kid's zoo, picnic areas, miniature railway and so on.
Among the most popular attractions are World of
Lemurs and Penguin World. It's off the B2177 road to
Bishop's Waltham, seven miles south of Winchester.
Phone for details of the regular special events.

Portsmouth Historic Dockyard (Flagship Portsmouth)

*Porter's Lodge, 1-7 College Road, HM Naval Base,
Portsmouth (023 9286 1512/www.flagship.org.uk).*
Open *Apr-Oct* 10am-5.30pm daily. *Nov-Mar*
10am-5pm daily. Last entry 1hr before closing.
Admission *HMS Victory & Royal Naval Museum,
HMS Warrior* £6.25; £4.75-£5.50 concessions.
Mary Rose Museum, Action Stations £6.75; £5-£6
concessions. *Royal Naval Museum* £3.50;
£2-£2.50 concessions. *Harbour Tour* £3.50; £2-£3
concessions. *Passport ticket (all attractions;
1 entry per attraction, valid for 1 year)* £17.50;
£12.50-£15.50 concessions.

Portsmouth's star historic attraction contains four main
elements: Nelson's flagship HMS *Victory*; the world's
first all-iron warship, HMS *Warrior*; the remains of
Henry VIII's *Mary Rose*, preserved in a fascinating visitor centre; and the Royal Naval Museum. The old dock-
yard buildings are of interest in themselves, and with
the 'all-ships' ticket you can return any time within a
year to catch up on parts you have missed. Fans of the
nautical and/or military naturally have many other
places to choose from around Portsmouth, such as the
D-Day Museum, the Royal Marines Museum, the Royal
Navy Submarine Museum and more (for details, contact
Portsmouth tourist office, *see p109*).

Watercress Line – Mid-Hants Railway

*The Station, New Alresford (info 01962
733810/www.watercressline.co.uk).* **Tickets**
Unlimited travel for 1 day £9; £2-£8 concessions.
Single tickets £5; £2-£4.50 concessions.
Free under-3s.

The ten-mile rural rail line between Alresford and Alton
was cast aside by British Rail in 1973, but has since been
kept going by determined local enthusiasm, with an all-
steam fleet. Trains run every Sunday and most
Saturdays from February to October, and almost daily
from June to August and during December. To appeal
to a wider public as well as the train-potty, the line also
offers special trips such as silver-service dining-car
lunches and cream teas on board, Thomas the Tank
Engine tours and so on. The line has played parts in
umpteen period TV shows.

Winchester Cathedral & Close

*The Close, Winchester (01962 857200/
www.winchester-cathedral.org.uk).* **Open** *Cathedral*
7.15am-6.30pm daily. *Triforium & library* Easter-Oct
11am-4.30pm Mon-Fri; 10.30am-4.30pm Sat. Nov,
Dec, Mar 11am-3.30pm Wed, Sat. Jan, Feb
11am-3.30pm Sat. *Visitor centre* 9.30am-5pm
daily. **Admission** *Expected donation* £3.50;
£2.50 concessions; 50p children. *Triforium &
library* £1; 50p concessions.

Winchester's majestic Norman cathedral was begun in
1079. To build it, the Norman conquerors swept aside
the Saxon old cathedral, the outline of which can still
be seen in the Close. This cathedral contained the first
tomb of Saint Swithun, Bishop of Winchester 837-61;
as every book on Winchester has to remind you, if it
rains on his day (15 July), it's due to pour down for 40
days thereafter. In the present cathedral, the beautifully
simple transepts are those of the 11th-century building;

the huge Gothic nave was added in the 14th century and is the longest in Europe. Inside, the cathedral has too many treasures to detail here, among them 12th-century wall paintings in the Chapel of the Holy Sepulcre, and the grave of Jane Austen. Don't miss the climb up to the Triforium, which gives you a spectacular view of the transepts, and contains a remarkable collection of carvings in stone and wood; in the 17th-century library the centrepiece is the Winchester Bible, a dazzling illuminated manuscript begun in 1160. Informative guided tours of the cathedral are available; ask at the information desk.

The other buildings around the Close are almost as historic. The Deanery dates from the 13th century; next to it, Dean Garnier's Garden contains the remains of a Gothic cloister. The huge half-timbered Cheyney Court, by the southern gate of the Close, was originally the Bishops' courthouse. As a change from the medieval, around the Close there is also now an interesting collection of entirely modern sculpture. Ask at cathedral information about tours of the Close buildings, most of which are not normally open to visitors.

Winchester City Mill
Bridge Street, Winchester (01962 870057/ www.nationaltrust.org.uk). **Open** *Jan-June, Sept-Dec* 11am-4.30pm Wed-Sun. *July, Aug* 11am-4.30pm daily. **Admission** (NT) £2; £1 concessions.
Established in the 15th century and last rebuilt in 1744, this grand watermill is a very impressive example of early technology, with spectacular timbering and a riverside garden behind it. Run by the National Trust, it also houses a video exhibition on the working of the mill, a shop and Winchester's youth hostel.

Winchester Great Hall & Westgate
Great Hall Castle Avenue, Winchester (01962 846476/www.winchester.gov.uk). **Open** *Mar-Oct* 10am-5pm daily. *Nov-Feb* 10am-5pm Mon-Fri; 10am-4pm Sat, Sun. **Admission** free; donations welcome.
Westgate Upper High Street, Winchester (01962 869864/www.winchester.gov.uk). **Open** *Mar-Oct* 10am-5pm Mon-Sat; noon-5pm Sun. **Admission** free; donations welcome.
One of Winchester's lesser-known gems, Henry III's spectacular Great Hall (1222-35) is the last remaining part of what was for 500 years one of England's principal royal palaces. Its most famous feature is the 'Round Table' hanging on one wall, believed to have been made in the 13th century and repainted for Henry VIII in 1522. In the small museum in the Westgate there's a 16th-century painted ceiling from Winchester College, but all eyes are drawn to the 17th-century graffiti, carved by prisoners locked up in the gate.

Winchester Military Museums
Peninsula Barracks, Romsey Road.
Winchester Gurkha Museum
(01962 828536/www.thegurkhamuseum.co.uk).
Light Infantry Museum *(01962 828550).*
King's Royal Hussars Museum *(01962 828541).*
Royal Green Jackets Museum
(01962 828549/www.royalgreenjackets.co.uk).
Royal Hampshire Regiment Museum
(01962 863658).

A sight of the Round Table in the **Great Hall**.

Military buffs can spend the whole day in Winchester going round the Peninsula Barracks, with the Gurkha Museum to add a touch of the exotic. Admission times and prices vary; phone the individual sights for details.

Wolvesey Castle
College Street, Winchester (01962 854766/ www.english-heritage.org.uk). **Open** *Apr-Sept* 10am-6pm daily. *Oct* 10am-5pm daily. **Admission** (EH) £1.90; £1-£1.40 concessions.
The 12th-century main residence of the Bishops of Winchester was one of the largest medieval palaces in England, rivalling in size the royal castle to the west. Like Bishop's Waltham it was mostly destroyed in the 1640s, and is now a rambling ruin.

Where to stay

Fortitude Cottage
51 Broad Street, Old Portsmouth, PO1 2JD (tel/fax 023 9282 3748). **Rates** £30-£35 single occupancy; £25 double/twin per person. **Rooms** 1 double (en suite); 2 twin (1 en suite). **Credit** AmEx, MC, V.
The name might suggest a hardy life before the mast, but no fortitude is really required to stay in this cosy old B&B on the main quayside street of Spice Island in Old Portsmouth. The three charming rooms have very good facilities and the one non-en suite room has its own bathroom just outside. The very pretty breakfast room and two of the bedrooms have harbour views. Children over 12 welcome. No smoking throughout.
M27 into Portsmouth; follow English Heritage and Isle of Wight signs; then follow signs for Old Portsmouth Cathedral; pass cathedral; turn right into Broad Street; house on left.

Hotel du Vin & Bistro
14 Southgate Street, Winchester, SO23 9EF (01962 841414/fax 01962 842458/www.hotelduvin.com). **Rates** £95-£99 double; £99-£110 superior double; £105-£115 deluxe double/twin; £120-£130 garden double/twin; £185 four-poster/suite. Breakfast £11.50

(Eng); £8.50 (cont). **Rooms** (all en suite) 6 double;
7 superior double/twin; 4 deluxe double/twin;
5 garden double/twin; 1 four-poster/suite.
Credit AmEx, DC, MC, V.
Robin Hutson (hotelier) and Gerard Basset (sommelier)
opened Hotel du Vin in 1994. It's a fabulous blend of
comfort and style with an egalitarian atmosphere. All
are welcome at this red-brick Georgian house, and the
young, friendly staff put guests at their ease – no whispering necessary here, and there's no dress code either.
The bedrooms (all different, each sponsored by a drinks
company or wine producer) have comfortable beds, big
baths, power showers, TVs, CD players and restrained
decor. The Bistro is equally user-friendly, and many
non-residents dine here. There's another Hotel du Vin in
Tunbridge Wells (*see p47*). Children welcome. No-smoking rooms available.
*M3 J11; follow signs to St Cross & Winchester; over 2
roundabouts; hotel is 2 miles along St Cross Road on left
approaching central Winchester.*

Malt Cottage
*Upper Clatford, nr Andover, SP11 7QL (01264
323469/fax 01264 334100/www.maltcottage.co.uk).*
Rates £35-£45 single occupancy; £60-£70
twin/double; £115 family suite. **Rooms** (all en suite)
2 double; 1 twin; 1 family suite. **No credit cards.**
Deep in the Test Valley countryside, the 250-year-old
Malt Cottage – in part a converted barn – makes a distinctive and comfortable rural B&B. Owners Patsy and
Richard Mason are garden designers, and the six-acre
garden they have created, complete with huge pond, is
truly spectacular; barbecues are cooked here (on request)
in summer. When the weather drives you inside, there's
a very attractive sitting room with log fire. Rooms are
big and well equipped, and those that are not en suite
have adjacent sole-use bathrooms of equal standard.
Many extras (a choice of fresh-produce breakfasts, airport pick-ups, car hire bookings) are also available.
Upper Clatford is well situated for fishing on the Test
(which the Masons can arrange) and walking the Test
Valley. Children welcome. No smoking throughout.
*A303; turn S on to A3057 towards Stockbridge; first right
at bend after ¼ mile; first left; right at T-junction into
Upper Clatford village; after ¼ mile Crook & Shears pub on
left; private lane opposite; house at bottom of lane.*

Old House Hotel
*The Square, Wickham, PO17 5JG (01329
833049/fax 01329 833672).* **Rates** £65-£80
single/single occupancy; £85 double/twin;
£95 family room. Breakfast £12 (Eng).
Rooms 2 single (1 ensuite); 7 double/twin/
family. **Credit** AmEx, MC, V.
An impressive Georgian brick townhouse on Wickham's
giant main square, and current haunt for chef Anthony
Gouchard (for the restaurant, *see p114*). Behind its rustic grand portico are a bar, comfortable lounges with
vaguely Regency-style sofas and huge original fireplaces, and a walled garden. The bedrooms have a similarly understated character, with assorted original
features such as beams, sloping ceilings and fireplaces
and a quirky mix of newish and slightly aged facilities.
Prices are higher than the norm, particularly since breakfast is charged separately, but the hotel has devoted
fans. Children welcome. All bedrooms no-smoking.
M27 J10; A32 to Wickham Square; hotel is on right.

Westgate Hotel – prime position, fine food.

Priory Inn
*Winchester Road, Bishop's Waltham, SO32 1BE
(01489 891313/fax 01489 896370).* **Rates**
£20 single occupancy; £20 double/twin per person;
£50 family. **Rooms** (both en suite) 1 double; 1 twin.
Credit MC, V.
An unfussy, friendly local's pub on the north-west road
out of Bishop's Waltham, the Priory has two light and
comfortable guest rooms with well-sized bathrooms (the
double more so), TVs and tea-making facilities. They're
not as striking as some B&B rooms in the area, but are
more accessibly priced. Breakfast is served in the bar;
at lunchtime and in the evenings, a big choice of pub
grub, including the odd Thai or Indian dish, is offered.
Children welcome. All bedrooms are no-smoking.
*M3 J12; follow signs to Marwell Zoological Park; turn left
on to B2117; inn is on left on way into Bishop's Waltham.*

Westgate Hotel
*2 Romsey Road, Winchester, SO23 8TP
(tel/fax 01962 820222).* **Rates** £65-£80 single
occupancy/double/twin. **Rooms** 8 double/twin
(6 en suite). **Credit** MC, V.
A highly recommended, family-run hotel located in a
prime position near both the Great Hall and the town
centre. The Westgate has six comfortable, historically
themed en suite rooms; the pleasant, airy bar (nick-
named the 'Press Gallery' as its large windows give
hacks a good view of the courts opposite) serves King
Alfred's bitter, while the cosy restaurant serves up an
interesting range of sausages (including kangaroo and
wild boar), alongside vegetarian dishes such as Mediterranean tart; desserts range from the sophisticated
(pistachio soufflé) to the traditional (spotted dick).

Wykeham Arms
*75 Kingsgate Street, Winchester, SO23 9PE (01962
853834/fax 01962 854411/www.gales.co.uk).*
Rates £45 single; £69.50-£99 single occupancy;
£79.50-£95 double/twin; £117.50 suite. **Rooms**
(all en suite) 2 single; 8 double; 3 twin; 1 suite.
Credit AmEx, DC, MC, V.

Hampshire & Isle of Wight

One of Winchester's most historic inns, open since 1755, the Wykeham Arms has so much character you could bottle it for export, with every wall of its nooks and crannies covered in sporting prints, military memorabilia and other bits of old England. It stands in an ancient lane surrounded by different parts of Winchester College. Due to the quirks of the old building some rooms are quite small, but inside them is a full range of modern comforts and extras. For more space with a little less character ask for one of the more expensive rooms (or the suite) in the St George's annexe, an 18th-century house across the street, which also has the use of a leafy garden patio with a fine view of the College buildings. The Wykeham is also one of Winchester's most popular pubs for both drinking and eating (see p114). Children over 14 and dogs welcome. No-smoking rooms available.

M3 J9; follow signs to Winchester over 3 roundabouts into Garnier Road; right at T junction into Kingsgate; pub is on left.

Where to eat & drink

Winchester has a big choice of eating places. In addition to those below, the **Hotel du Vin & Bistro** (see p111) is one of the top places in town. For good-value breakfasts, lunches or snacks, the **Cathedral Refectory** (01962 857200) in the Visitor Centre is a good bet; it's licensed, with plenty for vegetarians; the Moloko Bar (31B The Square; 01962 849236) serves light meals till 5pm, and thereafter reinvents itself as a lively bar. Of the many pubs, the tiny **Eclipse Inn** (23 The Square; 01962 865676), once the rectory of St Lawrence's church, has reliable pub nosh; the **Old Vine**, also on the Square (01962 854616), is bigger and has a wider choice. Near the river, the **Mash Tun** on Eastgate Street is a student favourite, and the **Old Monk** is a big pub with riverside garden. In the Test Valley, pubs to look out for include the **Royal Oak** in Goodworth Clatford and the **Peat Spade** in Longstock. South and east of Winchester among the most enjoyable pubs are the **White Horse** in Droxford, the historic old **Brushmakers' Arms** in Upham, the 250-year-old **Milbury's** in Beauworth (great for walkers), the **Globe** in Alresford and the **Flower Pots** in Cheriton. The last of these has the distinction of brewing its own prize-winning beer, and selling it at bargain prices. Wickham has a great local caff, the **Wickham Tea House** (01329 835017), open for breakfast and lunch every day and with tables on the Square. Portsmouth, true to form, has a clutch of high-quality (well-priced) fish and seafood restaurants.

American Bar Restaurant

58 White Hart Road, Old Portsmouth (023 9281 1585/www.americanbar.co.uk). **Food served** noon-2.30pm, 6.30-10pm Mon-Sat; noon-3.30pm, 6.30-9.30pm Sun. **Set lunch** £5.25 1 course. **Credit** AmEx, DC, MC, V.

A popular seafood restaurant/bar in Old Portsmouth, decorated in a bright mix of English nautical and American diner style. It's located right opposite the fish market, so there's no problem with the freshness of the main ingredient. The globetrotting menu combines starters like moules marinières (£4.95), with mains including char-grilled swordfish (£13.95), the 'ultimate fish and chips' (with monkfish and garlic mayonnaise, £12.95) and a catch of the day among other choices; there are also sandwiches and baguettes (£3.95-£6.95), and, for non-fish-eaters, some good meat and vegetarian options.

Chesil Rectory

1 Chesil Street, Winchester (01962 851555). **Food served** noon-2pm, 7-8.30pm Tue-Thur; noon-2pm, 7-9pm Fri, Sat. **Set lunches** £22 2 courses; £27 3 courses. **Set dinners** £32 2 courses; £37 3 courses. **Credit** AmEx, DC, MC, V.

The oldest house in Winchester – dating from 1459, with massive half-timbered gables – now contains a restaurant where chef-proprietor Philip Storey prepares sophisticated modern food with a light touch. The frequently changing menu might include char-grilled asparagus with champ potato and lemon oil, pork and black pudding with mustard mash, or beef fillet with Madeira sauce. There's also a daily choice of fresh fish dishes (pan-roast salmon with couscous, samphire and langoustine vinaigrette), and usually a vegetarian option. To follow there's a luxurious range of desserts; the wine list has been chosen with equal care.

Lemon Sole

123 High Street, Old Portsmouth (023 9281 1303/www.lemonsole.co.uk). **Food served** noon-2pm, 6-10pm Mon-Sat. **Set lunches** £5.95 1 course; £8.95 2 courses; £11.95 3 courses. **Credit** AmEx, DC, MC, V.

A seafood restaurant with a special 'pick-your-own' formula. A big range of market-fresh fish and shellfish is displayed in a big ice cabinet. You select your fish, and it's then cooked in the style of your choice, with a choice of sauces to further whet your appetite. Starters are chosen from a set list, which includes dressed crab with grain mustard mayonnaise (£5.55) and smoked mackerel and orange salad (£4.95). You similarly pick your own wine, from big racks along one wall. Non-fishophiles are catered for with a few meat and veggie choices. The basement wine bar has an interesting, well-priced bar snacks list.

Loch Fyne

18 Jewry Street, Winchester (01962 872930/ www.lochfyneoysters.co.uk). **Food served** 9am-10pm Mon-Thur; 9am-11pm Fri, Sat; 10am-10pm Sun. **Set lunch** £9.95 2 courses. **Credit** AmEx, MC, V.

A newcomer to the Winchester restaurant scene, Loch Fyne is a southern offshoot of the Argyll oyster farm and restaurant of the same name. Perhaps unsurprisingly, there's a Scottish flavour to the starters, with an excellent smoked haddock chowder and peppered mackerel pâté with oatcakes. Oysters and other shellfish are the speciality main course, but there's plenty of other tempting choices including a delicate baked seabass in a fennel butter sauce (£12.95), or a generous baked salmon (£7.95). Service is attentive, without being overbearing, and the wine list is extensive.

Old House Hotel & Brasserie

The Square, Wickham (01329 833049).
Food served 7-9.30pm Mon; noon-2pm,
7-9.30pm Tue-Sat. **Set lunches** £15 2 courses;
£18.50 3 courses. **Set dinners** £18 2 courses;
£21.50 3 courses. **Credit** AmEx, DC, MC, V.

With grand surroundings and even grander dining, the
Old House is way up among the local restaurant elite.
Chef Anthony Gouchard has a distinct individual style
taking in elements of French, contemporary British and
Mediterranean cuisine, with the emphasis on strong
flavours and excellent ingredients. A la carte dining
choices include a rich terrine of foie gras, puy lentils and
bacon with a roasted tomato vinaigrette (£8.50), and sea
bass is served with farandoles of vegetables in a shellfish velouté (£17). Booking is advisable. *See also p112.*

Wykeham Arms

*75 Kingsgate Street, Winchester (01962
853834/www.gales.co.uk).* **Food served** noon-2.30pm,
6.30-8.45pm Mon-Sat. **Credit** AmEx, DC, MC, V.

The influence of Winchester College extends inside the
Wykeham Arms: many of the bar tables are old school
desks, and College memorabilia figures heavily on the
curio-drenched walls. There's a varied, lightish lunch
menu, with good soups and sandwiches; the dinner
menu changes daily but Aberdeen Angus steaks are a
speciality. You may also find Provençale vegetable and
goat's cheese tartlet (£9.95), crispy salmon served on

Wykeham Arms – historic and labyrinthine.

couscous salad (£12.95) or rack of lamb with pesto mash
and ratatouille (£13.75). As well as local beers (Gale's)
there's a Burgundy-oriented wine list. Beyond the labyrinthine rooms you'll find a garden at the back. The
place is very popular so you'll be unlikely to get a table
without a booking. *See also p112.*

Golden years

Winchester may be a sleepy dormitory
town today, but in the Middle Ages it
was as important to royal power as
London. Back then, if you wanted to
rule the kingdom, first you had to seize
the gold at Winchester.

In medieval England the succession
was a tricky business, depending on the
support of wilful, greedy and frequently
traitorous nobles. To survive, the new
king needed gold to keep the nobility in
line through a crafty mix of intimidation
and bribery. Without the money to pay
for power you were nothing. The royal
treasure was kept at Winchester, and
so this was the first town a king and
his knights rode out to claim after being
crowned at Westminster. Barely a month
after the battle of Hastings, William the
Conqueror marched on the town to seize
control of the royal treasury; Henry I
arrived within hours of learning he was
king and Stephen and Matilda fought
viciously over the town in 1141.

Winchester first developed its royal
role when it became King Alfred's capital,
and it was probably Alfred who laid out

its new streets and rebuilt the walls.
It expanded rapidly in the tenth and
11th centuries and was soon competing
with Norwich for status as the second
city after London, while sharing the
administrative and symbolic functions
of government with Westminster.

Winchester was the birthplace for
much of modern government. It housed
many of the royal records, the ancient
palace of the Anglo-Saxon kings, royal
graves, and the royal monasteries;
the departments we now know as
the Treasury and Exchequer became
working offices within the cold walls
of Winchester Castle.

In the 12th century, however,
Winchester's symbolic status began
to fade as the economy developed
and the commercial centres of London
and Norwich became more wealthy and
influential. By the 15th century it was
little more than another provincial town,
and despite Charles II's attempts to
build an English Versailles here in 1683,
its days as a regal powerhouse were
well and truly over.

The New Forest

Woods, water and wandering nags.

Horses roam wild and free in the **New Forest**.

Neither new, nor really a forest, the New Forest is still one of the most individual stretches of countryside in the south of England, and one that Londoners have been using for R&R ever since William the Conqueror made it his personal hunting ground almost a thousand years ago. Much of the area could now more aptly be described as open heathland, although the wooded parts do contain a notable variety of trees in its 145 or so square miles, among them holly, yew, birch, Scots pine, oak and beech. Deer abound here,

but their stocky little four-legged cousins, the New Forest ponies, are the real kings of the road in these parts (*see p120* **Horse power**). Amiable enough when not with foal, these peaceable free-range grazers give the area its special character.

The historic towns and villages dotted about heave with visitors during summer, but it's always possible to get away from them all by taking a walk in the woods. Park the car and head off with a map; the **Forestry Commission** (023 8028 3141/ www.forestry.gov.uk) provides details of guided walks, camping and facilities for disabled people within the Forest. Cycling is another leisurely way to make the most of the scenery (*see p116* **Bike hire**); there are plenty of traffic-free cycling routes – and plenty of pub stop-off points to reward yourself after all that exercise.

If you want to know more about the history of the Forest, or get up to date on Forest issues, visit the **New Forest Museum & Visitor Centre** (023 8028 3914/ www.hants.gov.uk/leisure/museums) in the attractive little capital of the area, **Lyndhurst** (in the same building as the tourist information centre).

By train from London

To explore the New Forest properly you'll need your own transport, but a healthy alternative to driving is to take the train and hire bikes. Trains to **Ashurst New Forest** leave **Waterloo** every other hour (journey time **1hr 45mins** to **2hrs**). Trains to **Brockenhurst** leave **Waterloo** about every 20mins (journey time **1hr 30mins**); change here for **Lymington** (which takes an additional 9mins). Info: www.southwestrains.co.uk.

Forest flames – the **Portuguese Fireplace**.

Sailing by

Woodland isn't the area's only attraction. The nearby Solent makes it a popular sailing destination, with many boats moored on the Lymington River. **Lymington** is an ancient port, famed for its saltworkings. From the sloping main street, you can walk down the cobbled passageway to the quay to watch local fishermen landing boxes of squid. The tiny street is lined with twee little shops selling locally made ice-cream and tourist knick-knacks.

Flora and fauna

If you're looking for a little more seclusion, the village of **Sway** nestles up in the open heathland section of the Forest, where you can drive, walk or cycle through beautiful open stretches of land teeming with plant and animal life (including Disney-like foals that you will want to take home).

In fact, if flowers and furry friends are your thing, you're in the right place. Gardens are a local mania – many hotels and guesthouses take as much pride in their grounds as their rooms and there are a number of open gardens to visit (**Spinners Garden**, Boldre, Lymington, 01590 673347; **Furzey Gardens**, Minstead, nr Lyndhurst, 023 8081 2464; **Exbury Gardens**, nr Beaulieu, 023 8089 1203; **Braxton Gardens**, Lymore Lane, Milford on Sea, 01590 642008), as well as the **New Forest Otter, Owl & Wildlife Conservation Park**.

Some of us, though, are content to lie back and think of England's birds and bees buzzing away by themselves while we sun ourselves on the beach. **Milford on Sea** in Christchurch

Bay has a good beach for swimming and windsurfing, while the village is quieter and less yacht-ridden than Lymington. Georgian-fronted buildings, shops and pubs crowd around the village green.

Naval gazing

In the south-east corner of the Forest, **Beaulieu** (pronounced 'Bewley') is home to the Montagu family, who have managed to stave off selling their ancestral home by creating a popular and unpretentious museum. The village itself is gorgeous, with thatched and red-roofed dwellings clustered around the Beaulieu River. It's a lovely stroll from here along the river to **Buckler's Hard**, the single-street village where many of the ships in Nelson's fleet were cobbled together. The **Maritime Museum** (01590 616203) charts the history of this unique riverside community, and one cottage has been reconstructed to show how life would have been for those working for Nelson in 1793. Other cottages make up the Master Builder's House Hotel (*see p118*), which serves good lunches and drinks out in the garden overlooking the river.

Further east, a string of little villages known as the Waterside lines Southampton Water, the biggest being **Hythe**, from where the *Titanic* first sailed. **Fawley** and **Calshot** are also pretty and good walking and sailing areas, and **Lepe** has the best sandy beach, with views across the Solent.

What to see & do

Tourist Information Centres

New Forest Museum and Visitor Centre, Main Car Park, Lyndhurst (023 8028 2269/ www.thenewforest.co.uk). **Open** *July-Sept* 10am-6pm daily. *Oct-June* 10am-5pm daily.

Bike hire

AA Bike Hire *Fern Glen, Gosport Lane, Lyndhurst (023 8028 3349).* **Open** 9.30am-6.30pm daily.
Burley Bike Hire *Burley Village Centre, Burley (01425 403584).* **Open** 9am-5.30pm daily.
Beaulieu Cycle Hire *at the National Motor Museum, Beaulieu (01590 611029).* **Open** 9am-5pm daily.
New Forest Cycle Experience *2-4 Brookley Road, Brockenhurst (01590 624204).* **Open** 9.30am-5.30pm daily.

Hurst Castle Ferry

28 Park Road, Milford on Sea (01590 642344/ www.english-heritage.org.uk). **Times** *Apr-Oct* departs Keyhaven Quay on the hr 10am daily; returns from Hurst Castle on the half hr until 5.30pm daily. **Tickets** (EH) £3.20 return; £2-£3 concessions. You can take a boat through the salt marsh nature reserve from Keyhaven to the grim-looking Hurst Castle, which has amazing views and a warren of atmospheric rooms to explore. Built by Henry VIII as one of a chain of coastal fortresses and extended massively by the Victorians, it once held Charles I as prisoner here. Alternatively, you can walk out to the castle along the calf-stretching shingle spit.

National Motor Museum

John Montagu Building, Beaulieu (info 01590 612345/www.beaulieu.co.uk). **Open** 10am-5pm daily. Last entry 4.20pm. **Admission** £9.95; £6.75-£8.50 concessions.

Palace House at Beaulieu has been in the Montagu family since 1538 and, to keep it that way, Lord Montagu has had to come up with a few visitor-friendly ideas. The result is an odd mix of social and transport history, with lots to see and do. There are over 250 vehicles here, and you can wander down a 1930s street and motor through time in a space-age pod. In the house itself, you can chat to Victorian characters about the price of fish (literally), or check out the exhibition of monastic life at the Domus of Beaulieu Abbey, dating from 1204, before switching centuries (again) for a ride on the monorail.

New Forest Otter, Owl & Wildlife Conservation

Deerleap Lane, Longdown, Ashurst (023 8029 2408/www.ottersandowls.co.uk). **Open** *Jan, Feb* 10am-5pm Sat, Sun. *Mar-Dec* 10am-5pm daily. **Admission** £5.95; £3.95 concessions; free under-4s.

Set in 25 acres of ancient woodland on the eastern edge of the New Forest, the park is home to Europe's largest collection of otters, owls and other indigenous wildlife. The tree-lined walks make the most of the park's location, and there's a tearoom to relax in afterwards.

New Forest Water Park

Hucklesbrook Lakes, Ringwood Road, Fordingbridge (01425 656868/www.newforestwaterpark.co.uk). **Open** *Easter, Oct-mid Nov* 10am-9pm/dusk Sat, Sun, bank hols. *May* 10am-9pm Wed-Sun, bank hols. *June-Sept* 10am-9pm daily. Closed Sept-Easter. **Rates** *Waterskiing* (per tow) from £15. *Aquarides* £6. *Jet-skiing* £30. **Credit** MC, V.

Get wet 'n' wild with all sorts of activities: waterskiing gives you four laps around the lake; aquarides are on inflatable bananas or tyres and jetskis are solo stand-ups or two seater sit-downs. Tuition available; booking advisable.

Paultons Park

Ower, nr Romsey (023 8081 4442). **Open** *Mid Mar-Oct* 10am-6.30pm daily. Last admission 4.30pm. *Nov, Dec* times vary; phone to check. Closed Jan-mid Mar. **Admission** £10.50; £9.50 concessions; children under 1m in height free.

It's hardly Disneyworld, but there's plenty to keep children amused here, such as the Runaway Train, Dinosaurland and, for younger kids, Tiny Tots Town. Restaurants, shops and a picnic area complete the picture. The park is located off junction 2 of the M27.

Rockbourne Roman Villa

Rockbourne, Fordingbridge (01725 518541/ www.hants.gov.uk/museum/rockbourne). **Open** *Apr-Sept* 10.30am-6pm daily. Last admission 5.30pm. Closed Oct-Mar. **Admission** £1.75, 95p concessions.

West of Fordingbridge can be found one of the largest Roman villas ever excavated in Britain. There's an informative display on Roman life here, followed by a well-signposted look around the site itself, highlights being the exposed underfloor heating of the two bath houses built around AD 150 and the mosaic on the dining room floor.

Hampshire & Isle of Wight

Boats moored on **Lymington River** sail out to the **Solent** and return laden with squid.

Where to stay

Restaurants and pubs often have a few rooms to let in this very tourist-oriented area. The **Montagu Arms** in Beaulieu (01590 612324/ www.newforest-hotels.co.uk) and the **Nurse's Cottage** (*see p119*) are good examples.

Alderholt Mill

Sandleheath Road, Fordingbridge, SP6 1PU (01425 653130/fax 01425 652868/www.alderholtmill.co.uk). **Rates** £20 single; £22.50-£28 per person double/ twin. Special breaks. **Rooms** (all en suite) 1 single, 3 double; 1 twin. **Credit** MC, V.

A working watermill nestling in the valley of the River Allen on the western outskirts of the Forest beyond the attractive little riverside town of Fordingbridge. The Mill itself dates from the early 18th century, but Sandra and Richard Harte's delightful B&B is situated in the Victorian workers' cottages on Monkey Island next door. Here you can fall asleep to the comforting distant sound of water rushing down the race, and wake up to an excellent breakfast featuring bread freshly baked with homeground flour. The cosy rooms are mercifully free of tat and clutter, with decent showers and pleasant outlooks. In summer, barbecues are sometimes held in the sweet back garden overlooking water-meadows. The Mill is open to the public (weekends only), but Richard Harte happily gives guests a guided tour of its ancient workings and wheel. There's also a basic but comfortable self-catering flat for two (£155 per week in low season, £245 in high season). All in all, a secluded treasure and very good value. Children over eight and dogs welcome. No smoking throughout.
Follow signs to Sandleheath from Fordingbridge; beyond the post office in Sandleheath, turn left at crossroads; downhill in the direction of the brown sign for the mill.

Chewton Glen

Christchurch Road, New Milton, BH25 6QS (01425 275341/fax 01425 273310/www.chewtonglen.com). **Rates** £250-£275 double; £340-£365 superior double; £480-£695 suite. **Rooms** (all en suite) 16 double/twin; 16 superior double; 31 suites. Special breaks. Breakfast £20 (Eng); £15.50 (cont). **Credit** AmEx, DC, MC, V.

When a hotel is voted one of the top 20 in the world by numerous eminent travel publications, expectations are high. Chewton Glen is as super-luxurious as the articles and brochures make out. Rooms have either a terrace or balcony, and the views over the gardens and parklands are tremendous. There's an outdoor pool, croquet lawn and a health club with a big indoor pool and golf course. There are numerous special touches, from sherry to huge bathrobes in the rooms, but to be frank, the pervading feel is slightly corporate. Fine, if yours is the world of Eurotrash millionaires, fantastic if you need some megapampering, but, to sum it up, this is the place where Alan Partridge would come to die. Children over six welcome. No-smoking rooms available. *See also p119.*
M3/M27 towards Bournemouth; turn left (3 miles after J1) to Emery Down; at T-junction take A35 towards Christchurch; after 8 miles turn left at staggered junction; take 2nd left after Walkford into Chewton Farm Road.

Master Builder's House Hotel

Buckler's Hard, Beaulieu, SO42 7XB (01590 616253/fax 01590 616297/ www.themasterbuilders.co.uk). **Rates** £115 single occupancy; £155-£205 double/twin. **Rooms** (all en suite) 19 double; 6 superior double. Min 2-night stay Fri, Sat or Sun. £20 extra per room in August. **Credit** AmEx, MC, V.

Its location on the banks of the Beaulieu river, at the end of the single grassy street that is Buckler's Hard,

The one-street wonder of **Buckler's Hard** pays homage to 18th-century shipwrights' skills.

makes the Master Builder's House Hotel somewhere quite special. Once the daytrippers have left, guests have this peaceful 18th-century haven pretty much to themselves, give or take a few yachties and the odd resident. While the village may feel like a living museum, the hotel's interior has recently undergone extensive refurbishment in that slightly characterless but ever-so tasteful style beloved by smart country hotels. The Riverview Restaurant has a marginally more contemporary feel and the (fairly expensive) food is reliably excellent. The peaceful outside terrace can be a delightful place to dine or have a drink. There's also a little thatched self-catering or fully serviced cottage at the bottom of the garden. Children welcome. No-smoking rooms available.
M3/M27 towards Bournemouth; at Junction 1 take A337 to Lyndhurst from where the B3056 goes to Beaulieu; follow signs from here to Buckler's Hard.

Stanwell House Hotel

14 High Street, Lymington, SO41 9AA (01590 677123/fax 01590 677756/ www.stanwellhousehotel.co.uk). **Rates** £85 single occupancy; £110 double/twin; £130 four-poster; £150-£160 suites; £170 cottage (sleeps 4). **Rooms** (all en suite) 7 twin; 12 double; 6 suites, 2 four-poster. **Credit** AmEx, DC, MC, V.
This recently refurbished Georgian high street hotel is a reasonable bet if you want to stay in the centre of chi-chi old Lymington. Standard rooms are nothing special, but suites are more sumptuous, with four-posters and more than enough pillows. In fact someone here must be cushion-crazy: the bright new bar is scattered with the things in a riot of colour, making for a pleasingly informal atmosphere. The fusion food in the next-door bistro is above average. Round the back, there's an attractive conservatory and small walled garden. Children and small dogs welcome. No-smoking rooms available.
M3/M27 towards Bournemouth; at Junction 1 take A337 via Lyndhurst for Lymington.

Westover Hall `Offer`

Park Lane, Milford on Sea, SO41 0PT (01590 643044/fax 01590 644490/ www.westoverhallhotel.com). **Rates** £70 single; £125 double/twin; £160 half-tester/superior double; £160 family room. Special breaks. **Rooms** (all en suite) 1 single; 8 double/twin; 3 superior double; 1 half-tester; 1 family. **Credit** AmEx, DC, MC, V.
One of the most distinctive, laid-back and characterful small hotels on the south coast, this Victorian millionaire's coastal retreat is now owned by a couple who wanted a change from the fashion industry. And if you despair of country house hotel tweeness, Westover ('we don't do peach') Hall is for you. Built for the founder of the Siemens dynasty, most of the house's original features are intact, including the rich oak panelling, stained-glass windows and a spectacular tiled fireplace in the luxurious living room. Each bedroom is individually furnished with a mix of antique and contemporary items: one has an ornate gilt bed; another a canopied half-tester; and many have wide sea views. Guests are treated as friends and there's an unforced informality amid all the splendour. Children and pets welcome (pets at £10 per night). All bedroom no-smoking. *See also p120.*
J1 off M27; take A337 to Lymington; after Lymington follow signs to Milford on Sea and B3058; hotel is on clifftop after Milford on Sea.

Chequers

Lower Woodside, Lymington (01590 673415). **Food served** noon-2pm, 7-9.30pm Mon-Fri; noon-2pm, 7-10pm Sat; noon-9pm Sun. **Credit** MC V.
A favourite with the local yachting fraternity, this pub couldn't be more lively – there's much hearty, beer-fuelled hilarity on a regular basis. The restaurant is hugely popular at weekends, and it's best to book if you don't want to eat just before closing time. The menu makes good use of local seafood with mains such as baked seabass (£9.75) or giant geenlip mussels (£8.50), but also offers plenty for carnivores, including ostrich steak (£10.50). The back garden has recently been completely overhauled and now offers a barbecue and more room for al fresco jolliness.

Marryat Restaurant

Chewton Glen, Christchurch Road, New Milton (01425 275341/www.chewtonglen.com). **Food served** 12.30-1.45pm, 7.30-9.30pm daily. **Set dinner** £55 3 courses. **Credit** AmEx, DC, MC, V.
Even if you can't afford £250 for a bedroom at Chewton Glen, the one-Michelin-starred cooking of chef Pierre Chevillard is still available to all and the dining room of the Marryat, overlooking the hotel grounds, is just as good a way to experience a bit of luxury. Dinner could be cream of lobster soup, followed by duo of lamb 'Printanière' (pan-fried cutlets with garlic bonbons and potato mousseline), with banana and coconut tart to finish. The menu is scattered with indications of healthy or vegetarian choices – including gnocchi. *See also p118.*

Nurse's Cottage

Station Road, Sway, SO41 6BA (tel/fax 01590 683402/www.hants.gov/tourist/hotels). **Food served** 12.30-2pm Sun; 6.30-8pm daily. **Set lunch** £15.50 3 courses. **Set dinner** £20.65 3 courses. **Rates** £60 single occupancy; £100 double/twin. Special breaks. **Rooms** (all en suite) 1 single; 1 double; 1 twin. **Credit** AmEx, MC, V.
Although the building in which the award-winning Nurse's Cottage is housed isn't much to write home about, owner Tony Barnfield has certainly made the best of what he's got. The small dining room is a very popular restaurant, making use of local produce like freshly caught fish, farm eggs, English cheeses and Isle of Wight ice-cream – and there's an impressively extensive wine list, too. On the accommodation side, thoughtful details and extras are abundant – the fridges in each room have fresh milk ('No horrid UHT here'), and fruit, chocolates and sherry, afternoon tea and daily papers are all included in the price. The bedroom phones even have modem connections should urban types feel the need for some urgent downloading. Children over 10 and pets welcome. No smoking throughout.

Red Lion

Rope Hill, Boldre (01590 673177). **Food served** noon-2.30pm, 6.30-9.30pm daily. **Credit** MC, V.
A good place to stop if you're cycling through the Forest, the Red Lion is an archetypal country pub, well worth pedalling down winding lanes to get to. There are all the hallmarks of authenticity here – inglenooks, rustic whatnots on the wall, an open fire and a higgledy-piggledy

Horse power

Walking through the New Forest you could be forgiven for thinking you had stumbled on to the set of the latest TV adaptation of *Gulliver's Travels*. On the final and most satirical of his voyages, Jonathan Swift's hero finds himself in a wooded country wisely ruled over by intelligent horses, or 'houyhnhnms'. Their slaves are the disgusting ape-like creatures called 'yahoos', uncannily similar to human beings, who shit on Gulliver from a height as they clamber about in the trees. That's a fate you'll probably be able to avoid now that the yahoos have got themselves flash cars and roar along the single-track roads breaking the 40mph fast-gallop speed limit.

The feeling that the New Forest is in a world of its own doesn't stop here. This pony wonderland has its own government: the Verderer's Court in the ancient **Queen's House** (023 8028 2052/www.verderers.org.uk) in the forest capital, Lyndhurst, meets on the third Monday of every month except August and December. Proceedings can get quite lively during the adjudication of quaint anachronisms such as the commoners' rights to pasture, to 'mast' (let pigs out to eat acorns during the 'pannage' season), to 'turbary' (cut firewood) or to 'marl' (dig lime to improve the land).

The forest also has its structural peculiarities – one that is worth seeking out is the **Portuguese Fireplace**. West of the pretty village of Emery Down, off the road to Linwood (turn left at the New Forest Inn, and it's on the left 500 yards beyond Millyford Bridge car park), the Fireplace is just that: a free-standing pebble-dash chimney breast, hearth and grate in the middle of the woods beside the road, all that remains of the cookhouse built by Portuguese soldiers stationed here in World War I. It makes an excellent starting point for walks around some of the finest beech woods in the forest, most spectacular in the autumn.

Nearer the seaside, another oddity is the ruined chapel of the **Knights Templar at St Leonards Grange** on the coast road from Buckler's Hard to Lymington. It includes the impressive remains of one of the largest tithe barns in medieval England as well as a chapel used by the crusading Knights Templar in the 14th century. Although it's a private farm, there are fine views of the scale of the barn from the road (which is on the Solent Way) and anyone genuinely interested in a closer look can make arrangements through the Beaulieu estate office (01590 614621).

bar. What's more, the food is a cut above the usual ye olde lasagne and chips. Sit outside to enjoy the local Royal Oak bitter, special New Forest game pie (£10.20), dressed crab salad (£10.50) and steamed lemon sponge.

Royal Oak
Old Ringwood Road, North Gorley, Fordingbridge (01425 652244). **Food served** noon-2pm, 6-9pm daily. **Credit** MC, V.
A thatched country pub in picturesque surroundings on the western edge of the Forest, where you can sit and watch the ducks on the pond while supping your pint from the local Ringwood Brewery, then play skittles. There's also a playground for kids and a secluded garden. Food is pretty standard pub grub but very good value – the likes of faggots, mash and onion gravy (£4.95), speciality steak and kidney pie with stilton, or the New Forest mixed grill (£8.95). Sunday roasts are £5.75.

Westover Hall
Park Lane, Milford on Sea (01590 643044/ www.westoverhallhotel.com). **Food served** noon-2pm, 7-9pm daily. **Set lunch** £21.30 3 courses. **Set dinner** £29.50 3 courses. **Credit** AmEx, DC, MC, V.
During or after a day on the beach at Milford on Sea, Westover Hall is open to non-residents for lunch, drinks or afternoon tea in the pretty wood-panelled bar or outside on the garden terrace. The beautiful little dining room, which overlooks Christchurch Bay and has views of the Needles, has an excellent daily-changing dinner menu for £29.50 a head (book in advance). The three courses could consist of oak smoked duck with fruit chutney to start, followed by ragout of salmon and prawns, vegetables, herbs and white wine sauce as a main, and a lemon tart with blueberry pesto to finish. *See also p119.*

Isle of Wight

Middle England in miniature.

Looking down from the top of **Tennyson Down**, named in honour of the poet who lived nearby and described the air as being 'worth sixpence a pint', the Isle of Wight lies before you like a child's drawing of an island. Shaped like a pair of bee-stung lips, to the north-west the River Yar flows out to the Solent past the castle guarding Yarmouth harbour; at the far western tip of the island, the jagged chalk line of the **Needles**, jutting from the sea, ends with a red-and-white lighthouse; to the south is the great crumbling sweep of **Compton Bay**, while further south the sheer cliffs of **Blackgang Chine** fall dramatically (and literally) into the Channel. Often described as encompassing the whole of southern England in miniature, the island's 147 square miles contain rolling farmland, marshy estuaries, castles, cliffs, vineyards, beaches, steam trains, Roman villas, dinosaur fossils, red squirrels and a whole clutch of manor houses.

During the 1800s, visitors poured in from all over Europe to enjoy the water, the sea air and the balmy climate. As well as Tennyson, whose home, Farringford, at **Freshwater**, is now a hotel, the poet Swinburne was born (and buried) in **Bonchurch**, where Dickens wrote *David Copperfield*; and the Russian writer Turgenev conceived his most famous novel, *Fathers and Sons*, while visiting **Ventnor** for the sea-bathing. Meanwhile at **Dimbola Lodge**, Tennyson's neighbour, the Victorian photographer Julia Cameron, was taking

Yachts are a constant feature on the **Solent**.

pictures of whoever she could persuade to sit still long enough and developing the results in the coal shed. And of course, Queen Victoria herself spent her summers with her family at **Osborne House** in East Cowes.

In the 20th century, the island's star waned; in his novel *England, England* – in which the Isle of Wight has become a giant heritage theme park – Julian Barnes describes it as 'a mixture of rolling chalk downland of considerable beauty and bungaloid dystopia'. Today's grockles stick to the well-travelled coach routes from the resorts of **Sandown** and **Shanklin**, taking in the thatched tearooms of **Godshill**, **Blackgang Chine Fantasy Park**, the **Pearl Centre** (sadly not a local product harvested by nubile divers from the Channel's chilly waters) and the **Needles Pleasure Park**. All the better for the rest of us, as it leaves most of the island blissfully free of visitors even in the height of summer. There are actually far too

By train from London

Trains from **Waterloo** to **Portsmouth** leave about every 20mins (journey time approximately **1hr 30mins**), from where there's a ferry crossing to **Ryde**, and from **Waterloo** to **Lymington** (**2hrs 15mins**), with a ferry crossing to **Yarmouth**. **Wightlink** (0870 582 7744) runs car and passenger ferries from **Portsmouth Harbour** to **Fishbourne** (crossing time **35mins**) and from **Lymington** to **Yarmouth** (**30mins**), while a catamaran runs from **Portsmouth** to **Ryde** (**15mins**). Info: www.southwesttrains.co.uk and www.wightlink.co.uk.

many things to do here in a month, let alone a weekend, so unless it's raining stair rods, give the much-vaunted 'attractions' a miss and explore on foot or by bike.

The island is a paradise for walkers and cyclists, boasting more footpaths per square mile than anywhere else in Britain – all meticulously signposted and maintained. You're not going to manage the whole of the 77-mile coastal path around the island in just a weekend, but if you want to get a taste of it, skip the north-east section and take the train from **Ryde** to Shanklin. Here you can join the path as it climbs up from the sea before descending again through the beautiful ferny depths of the Landslip (so called because much of it fell into the sea in 1810). From there you can walk around Wheelers Bay to **Ventnor**, (watch out around here: sea defence work might mean there's a diversion in these parts), and if you've still got the energy, on to St Catherine's Point, the southernmost tip of the island. Above the bay in Ventnor is the newly opened **Coastal Path Visitors' Centre** where you can find extensive information about the path.

Outdoor pursuits abound along the coast. Sailors weigh anchor in the fine natural harbours of **Yarmouth**, **Cowes** and **Bembridge**, surfers brave the waves at **Compton Bay**, where fossil hunters admire the casts of dinosaurs' footprints at low tide (*see p127* **The land that time forgot?**) and paragliders hurl themselves off the cliffs. There is just one small drawback, however. The south-west of the island is disappearing into the sea, not inch by inch, but acre by acre. Every winter more cliffs collapse soufflé-like on to the beaches below, leaving fences and steps hanging suspended precariously in mid-air. In a thousand years the chalk spine that ends in the Needles could be all that remains. Better not put off your visit for too long.

What to see & do

Many attractions are closed between the end of October and Easter so always phone first when planning a visit. For information on cycling and walking, call **Rights of Way** (01983 823741/ www.iwight.com).

Tourist Information Centres
Western Esplanade, Ryde, PO33 2LW (01983 562905/www.islandbreaks.co.uk). **Open** *Mar-Oct* 9am-5.30pm daily. *Nov-Feb* 9.30am-5pm daily.
8 High Street, Sandown, PO36 ODG (01983 403886). **Open** *Mar-Oct* 9am-5.30pm Mon-Sat; 9am-5pm Sun. *Nov-Feb* 10am-4pm Mon-Sat.
67 High Street, Shanklin, PO37 6JJ (01983 862942). **Open** *Apr-Sep* 9am-5.30pm Mon-Sat; 9am-5pm Sun. *Oct-Mar* 10am-4pm Mon-Sat.

Bike hire
Autovogue *140 High Street, Ryde (01983 812989).* Ten-minute walk from the ferry terminal.
Isle Cycle *Wavells Fine Foods, The Square, Yarmouth (01983 760219).* Two-minute walk from ferry terminal.
Coastal Path Visitors' Centre *Dudley Road, Ventnor (01983 855400/www.coastalwight.gov.uk).*

Adgestone Vineyard
Upper Adgestone Road, Adgestone (01983 402503/ www.englishwine.co.uk). **Open** *Easter-Oct* 10am-5.30pm daily. *Nov-Easter* 10.30am-4.30pm Tue-Sat. **Admission** free.
Drop in for afternoon tea here and, if the mood takes her, your hostess, no mean pianist, might treat you to an impromptu concert. The vineyard makes all types of wine including fruit wines (dry white starts at £5.95).

Blackgang Chine Fantasy Park
Blackgang Chine, Chale (01983 730330/ www.blackgangchine.com). **Open** *Apr, May* 10am-5.30pm daily. *June-Oct* 10am-10pm daily. Closed Nov-Mar. Times vary during half-term; phone for details. **Admission** £6.50; £5.50 concessions.
One of the oldest of its kind in the country, it's a wonder that this low-key theme park is still clinging to the side of the cliff. Locals continue to mourn favourite rides that have long since slid into the Channel below. For many of today's children the highlight is Wild West Town, where for the price of a pistol and a few rounds of caps (on sale in the shop), they can charge around the saloon and stagecoach blasting the living daylights out of total strangers. Blissfully non-PC. The most exciting ride is the waterslide, with rubber boats hurtling down from the top of the cliff.

Brading Roman Villa
Morton Old Road, Brading (01983 406223). **Open** *Apr-Oct* 9.30am-5pm daily. **Admission** £2.75; £1.35 concessions.
There are fine mosaic floors to admire in this villa just north of Sandown. Look out for the figure representing winter, whose British hooded cloak became a wardrobe must-have for expat Romans in chilly climes.

Carisbroke Castle
Carisbroke, near Newport (01983 522107/ www.english-heritage.org.uk). **Open** *Apr-Sept* 10am-6pm daily. *Oct-Mar* 10am-4pm daily. **Admission** (EH) £4.50; £2.30-£3.40 concessions.
Charles I was held in this hilltop Norman castle before being taken back to London to be executed. The museum inside tells the story of his incarceration as well as that of other royal residents. There are wonderful views of the island from the battlements, and jousting, fayres and ghost walks in the summer months.

Dimbola Lodge
Freshwater Bay (01983 756814/www.dimbola.co.uk). **Open** 10am-5pm Tue-Sun. **Admission** £3; free under-16s.
The restored home of Victorian photographer Julia Cameron displays her work in its galleries along with contemporary exhibitions, a camera museum, antiquarian bookshop and a vegetarian café.

High Adventure Paragliding

Sandpipers, Freshwater Bay (01983 752322/
www.high-adventure.uk.com). **Open** 9am-5pm daily.
Phone details of courses and prices.

Despite its sleepy image in recent years, the island is a centre for all kinds of high excitement sports. Its climate and geography make it a particularly ideal training ground for paragliders. On a one-day course you will be introduced to the basics of handling your canopy on the ground before progressing to 'hops', moving further and further up the hill as your expertise increases. Later in the day, if the weather allows, you could make a flight in tandem with an instructor. For groups of six or more the sister company Island Activities (www.island activites.co.uk) can also arrange sailing, powerboating, jet biking, watersports, clay-pigeon shooting, horse riding, laser paintball games, gliding, falconry and mountain biking – among other energetic activities.

Isle of Wight Steam Railway

Havenstreet (01983 884343/
www.iwsteamrailway.co.uk). **Open** mid
Mar-Oct 9.30am-5pm daily. Closed Nov-mid
Mar. **Tickets** £7; £4-£6 concessions.
A five-mile line connecting with electric trains at Ryde.
Beautifully restored locos and a steam museum.

Museum of Island History

The Guildhall, High Street, Newport
(01983 823366). **Open** Easter-Oct 9am-5.30pm
Mon-Sat. Closed Nov-Easter. **Admission** £1.80;
£1 concessions.
An hands-on history of the island from dinosaurs to the present day, housed in the old town clock tower.

Museum of Smuggling History

Botanical Gardens, Ventnor (01983 853677).
Open Apr-Sept 10am-5pm daily. **Admission** £2.40;
£1.20 concessions.
Housed in the underground vaults of the lovely, informal botanical gardens, this museum recounts the ingenious methods used by smugglers over 700 years.

Needles Old Battery

West High Down, Totland Bay (01983 754772/
www.nationaltrust.org.uk). **Open** Apr-June, Sept,
Oct 10.30am-4.30pm Mon-Thur, Sun. July, Aug
10.30am-4.30pm daily. **Admission** (NT) £3;
£1.50 concessions; free under-5s.
Not to be confused with the tacky pleasure park nearby, this Victorian fort enjoys spectacular views over the Needles, the Solent and the Channel. It's best viewed at the conclusion of a bracing walk over Tennyson Down from Freshwater.

Osborne House

East Cowes (01983 200022/www.english-
heritage.org.uk). **Open** House Apr-Oct 10am-5pm
daily. Nov-mid Dec, Feb, Mar (pre-booked tours only)
10am-2.30pm Mon, Wed, Thur, Sun. Grounds
Apr-Sept 10am-6pm daily. Oct 10am-5pm daily.
Nov-mid Dec, Feb, Mar (pre-booked tours only)
10am-2.30pm Mon, Wed, Thur, Sun. **Admission**
(EH) £7.20; £3.60-£5.40 concessions.
Built in the style of an Italian villa by Thomas Cubitt, this was the much-loved country retreat of Queen Victoria and has been maintained as it was at her death

here in 1901. The Swiss Cottage, built as a playhouse in the garden for the royal children, is larger than many Londoners' flats. Pre-booking for guided tours (spring and autumn only) is essential. Note that the house will be partially scaffolded until the end of 2002.

Specialist Flying School

Embassy Way (adjacent to the airport), Sandown
(01983 402402/www.flyingschool.com). **Open** 9am-
6pm daily. Phone for details of courses and prices.
If the idea of jumping off a cliff with only a wodge of fabric above you seems a little reckless, then paragliding is probably not for you and powered flight may be more to your taste. You could take the joystick of a light aircraft with an introductory lesson flying over the island and enjoy the breathtaking views.

George Hotel

Quay Street, Yarmouth, PO41 OPE (01983 760331/
fax 01983 760425). **Rates** £115-£205 single;
£155-£205 double/twin; £205 four-poster. **Rooms**
(all en suite) 2 single; 14 double/twin; 1 four-poster.
Credit AmEx, MC, V.
The perfect hotel for a car-free weekend; disembark from the Lymington–Yarmouth ferry and the hotel is less than a minute's stroll away. The George is housed in the 17th-century former home of the island's governor, hard up against the wall of the castle, and all bedrooms are en suite, most with king-sized beds, satellite TV and phones. Situated on the old town square, the hotel has easy access to the shops and restaurants of this tiny port, and also boasts a restaurant and brasserie of its own (*see p126*). The George is also in a great position for exploring West Wight, whether walking across the spine of the island or following the coastal path to Freshwater Bay. A private motor launch is available for charter. Children and dogs welcome. No-smoking rooms available.

Kerne Farm

Alverstone, Sandown, PO36 0EY (01983 403721/
fax 01983 403908). **Rates** Rooms £30 per person.
Cottages £225-£580 per week. **Rooms** (both en suite)
1 triple; 1 four-poster; 2 cottages. Min 2 nights in
B&B. **No credit cards.**
A character-packed, higgledy-piggledy 16th-century farmhouse crammed with antiques. Guests can read in the lovely conservatory or explore the garden. Right on the Bembridge Trail, the farm is criss-crossed by a network of footpaths and bridleways (the owners will happily accommodate your horse, should you have one). Two self-catering cottages are also available for stays of a week or more. No children under 12. Pets allowed (in one cottage only). All bedrooms no-smoking.
From ferry terminal, head towards Ryde and Brading;
follow signs to Adgestone Vineyard; pass vineyard to
Alverstone village; turn right in village; Kerne Farm is
straight ahead after nearly 1 mile.

Northcourt

Shorwell, PO30 3JG (01983 740415/fax 01983
740409/www.wightfarmholidays.co.uk). **Rates**
£27.50 per person. Special breaks. **Rooms** (all en suite) 6 double/twin. **No credit cards.**

The beach at **Ventnor** conjures up all kinds of opportunities for relaxation and entanglement.

As you round the bend in the drive and see this imposing Jacobean pile you'd be forgiven for thinking you've come to the wrong place. Set in 15 acres of gardens with brooks, terraces, shady woodland, exotic flowers and an Italian garden, Northcourt seems more like a country house than a B&B. Five miles south-west of Newport, this is an ideal stopping-off point if you're walking across the island; if you're feeling really energetic you could walk the 12 miles to the Needles and catch the bus back. Enhancing the country-house feel, a full-sized snooker table has been installed in the library; table tennis, croquet and lawn tennis are also available for guests. Stroll through the gardens to the Crown Inn (*see p126*) for supper. No smoking throughout the house.

4 miles SW of Newport on Newport–Brightstone Road; B&B is in middle of Shorwell village.

Old House

Gotten Manor, Gotten Lane, Chale, PO38 2HQ (01983 551368/www.gottenmanor.co.uk). **Rates** *Rooms* £30-£35 per person. *Self-catering cottages* £300-£600 per week. *Self-catering short breaks also available.* **Rooms** (both en suite) 2 double; 2 cottages (sleep 4-6). **No credit cards.**

You'll need transport if you stay here; Gotten Manor is at the end of a long lane at the southern end of the island. The bedrooms housed in the limewashed 14th-century annexe have wooden floors, Persian rugs and antique cast-iron baths in the room. Home-made jams and local products are served at breakfast. Self-catering accommodation is available in a converted barn. No children under 12 in B&B. No smoking throughout.

On B3399 ½ mile S of Chale Green; after village, turn left at Gotten Lane; Old House is at end of lane.

Priory Bay Hotel `Offer`

Priory Drive, Seaview, PO34 5BU (01983 613146/fax 01983 616539/www.priorybay.co.uk). **Rates** £65-£99 single occupancy; £130-£198 double/twin; £98-£148 family suites/cottage suites. **Rooms** (all en suite) 9 double/twin; 7 deluxe double/twin; 2 family suites; 7 cottage suites. **Credit** AmEx, MC, V.

Opened by the genial Andrew Palmer (founder of the New Covent Garden Soup Company) in 1998, Priory Bay has established itself as the choicest and most individual of the island's luxury hotels. Yet this is a thoroughly relaxed place, boasting a nine-hole golf course and an unheated outdoor pool among its facilities. The elevated position, surrounded by trees and overlooking the sea, is stunning; walking down through the woods, past the Oyster Seafood Café to the wide sweep of sandy beach, you'd swear you were in the Mediterranean rather than on the Channel. All bedrooms are individually decorated with great panache – particularly appealing is the fresh, New Englandy Room 11 in the eaves and the Chinese-themed Room 20 with a roll-top bath in the bedroom. Self-catering accommodation, with limited room service, is available in 16 cottages in the grounds. The hotel has two restaurants: the Priory Bay restaurant and the beautifully situated Oyster Seafood Café. Children and dogs welcome. No-smoking rooms available.
From Fishbourne ferry terminal follow signs to Ryde, then Nettlestone and St Helen's; pass through Nettlestone; after ½ mile turn left at sign to Priory Bay Hotel.

Redway Farm

East Lane, Merstone, PO30 3DJ (01983 865228). **Rates** £25-£30 per person. **Rooms** 1 double; 2 twin. **No credit cards.**

This 17th-century farmhouse is set in spacious grounds with its own fishing lake. A working farm over three generations, it is situated on the walking and cycling path through the Arreton Valley. The master bedroom features an antique half tester 17th-century double bed. All rooms have tea/coffee making facilities, TV, hairdryers and radios. Children welcome by arrangement. No smoking throughout.
Turn off Newport to Sandown road for Merstone; in Merstone, turn left down Bury Lane and go over the small crossroads at the top of the lane; Redway Farm is at the end.

Royal Hotel

Belgrave Road, Ventnor, PO38 1JJ (01983 852186/fax 01983 855395/www.royalhoteliow.co.uk). **Rates** £60-£90 single occupancy; £100-£120 double/twin; family room rates on application. **Rooms** (all en suite) 5 single; 43 double/twin; 7 family. **Credit** AmEx, DC, MC, V.

A short stroll from the town centre and the beach (but not so close that it's likely to go the way of a rival establishment that slipped into the sea), this stately stone building has been refurbished to a high standard. The rooms are light and comfortable – in a grandish but not overly heavy country house style – with views over the garden, where there is a heated swimming pool. Children are catered for with early suppers, high chairs and baby listening, so parents can sit back and enjoy the excellent restaurant (*see p126*). Children welcome. No-smoking rooms available.
Follow one-way system in Ventnor; turn left at traffic lights; follow road up hill and bear left into Belgrave Road; hotel is at end of road on right.

Seaview Hotel `Offer`

High Street, Seaview, PO34 5EX (01983 612711/fax 01983 613729/www.seaviewhotel.co.uk). **Rates** £55-£75 single; £70-£130 single occupancy of double room; £95-£135 double/twin; £180-£200 family. **Rooms** (all en suite) 2 single; 13 double/twin; 1 family. **Credit** AmEx, DC, MC, V.

Described by its many regular guests as 'the perfect seaside hotel', the award-winning Seaview caters equally happily to families, romantic couples and old salts. A couple of steps from the beach, it's the social centre of the village. The hotel is very child-friendly, with high chairs and baby listening; even dogs are welcome. No-smoking rooms available. *See also p126.*

Where to eat & drink

One of the joys of the island is that it feels as if it is stuck in a time warp, but unfortunately this sometimes applies to the food as well: half-baked baguettes abound across the Solent and a decent cappuccino is like gold dust. Most pubs serve local lobster and crab in some form or another but it's sometimes let down by the limited accompaniments. Other local produce such as garlic, sweetcorn and honey rarely make their way on to menus but can be bought at farmers' markets or farm shops. **Minghella** ice-cream, still produced by the proud parents of film director Anthony, is easy to find and the tiny tomatoes grown by **Wight Salads** are superb. One weekend in August is dedicated to the **Garlic Festival**, with stalls, entertainment and the chance to sample the fragrant bulb in everything from ice-cream to honey.

For afternoon tea in peaceful surroundings visit the gardens of one of the many manor houses or vineyards. In addition to the pubs below, the **Fisherman's Cottage** (01983 863882), located at the bottom of Shanklin Chine is right on the beach, and the ultra-kid-friendly **Wight Mouse Inn** (part of the Clarendon Hotel; 01983 730431) at Chale is also worth a visit if you have very young children.

The **Bonchurch Café** (01983 856488) and the **Horseshoe Bay Café** (01983 856800), both at Bonchurch, have tables outside overlooking the Channel, which are delightful on a summer's day. If you are planning a walk or cycle ride from Yarmouth stock up with delicious cheeses, paté, bread and handraised pies from **Angela's** deli in the square. In Ryde, the **Biskra Beach Hotel** (17 St Thomas's Street; 01983 567913) adjacent to the pier is a good place for Sunday lunch in the garden overlooking the Solent.

Chequers Inn

Niton Road, Rookley (01983 840314). **Food served** noon-10pm Mon-Sat; noon-9.30pm Sun. **Credit** MC, V.
Voted the UK Family Pub of the Year in the 1999 *Good Pub Guide*, but don't let that put you off – local

farmers still drink in the flagstoned public bar. This friendly country pub combines real ale with an extensive menu, ranging from bar snacks to standard pub grub (ploughmans, sandwiches), 'catch of the day', meaty main courses and a children's menu. All this, plus views of the open country, a large adventure playground and pony rides. If you fancy a more challenging ride the Lake Farm Equitation Centre (01983 840251) is right next door.

Crown Inn
Walkers Lane, Shorwell (01983 740293). **Food served** noon-2.30pm, 6-9.30pm daily. **Credit** MC, V.
A stream with trout and ducks meanders through the garden of this pretty 17th-century inn where specials include chicken supreme (£7.95) or pan-fried tuna (£8.50). That's as grand as it gets here, with pizza, pasta, grills, salads, sandwiches and jacket potatoes – in short, classic pub grub – making up the rest of the long menu. Families are particularly welcome; there are swings, a slide and a playhouse in the garden and high chairs and children's meals are available (scampi and chips, £3.25; chicken nuggets, £2.50).

George Hotel
Quay Street, Yarmouth (01983 760331/ www.thegeorge.co.uk). **Food served** *Restaurant* 7-9.45pm Tue-Sat. *Brasserie* noon-3pm, 7-10pm daily. **Credit** AmEx, MC, V.
At the only Michelin-rated restaurant on the island, you have a choice between the restaurant and brasserie menus. The latter is more extensive, with plenty of fish (monkfish kebab, £16.25; pan-fried halibut £16.95), but also Aberdeen Angus ribeye with bacon and mushrooms (£15.50) and grilled pork cutlet £12.95 for carnivores. The three-course set meal in the restaurant (£45) is a slightly more refined affair – the ribeye here comes with braised beef, artichoke and a garlic sauce. The brasserie is also a less formal setting – in summer you can sit outside and watch the children play on the pebbly private beach adjoining the castle or watch the comings and goings of the ferry. Children under eight years old are not allowed in the restaurant but are welcome in the brasserie.

Net
Sherbourne Street, Bembridge (01983 875800/ www.bembridge.net). **Food served** noon-2.15pm, 6.30-10pm daily. **Credit** MC, V.
Bembridge is a lovely harbourn on the eastern edge of the island, popular with the DFL (Down from London) sailing set and this restaurant has become a firm favourite since it opened in 2000. The all-day menu includes light dishes such as char-grilled chicken wraps at £3.75, crab, mussels, burgers and seafood. The dinner menu changes often and might include spiced Thai fish cakes as starter, followed by blackened monkfish with curried aubergine (£12.95).

New Inn
Mill Road, Shalfleet (01983 531314). **Food served** noon-3pm, 6-11pm daily. **Credit** AmEx, DC, MC, V.
This 17th-century inn with a sunny garden has a well-deserved reputation for excellent food, which includes smoked trout with horseradish sauce (£4.95) and seafood royale (£40 for a platter for two). Shalfleet is between Newport and Yarmouth.

Red Lion
Church Place, Freshwater (01983 754925/ www.redlion-wight.co.uk). **Food served** noon-2pm, 6.30-9pm Mon-Sat; noon-2pm, 7-9pm Sun. **Credit** MC, V.
Very popular with the sailors who come down the river from Yarmouth for lunch when the tide is right, this is also a good place to stop off if you are cycling or walking along the estuary towards Freshwater. Switch off your mobile phone – if it rings you'll pay a £5 fine to the local lifeboat. Daily specials on the blackboard might include herring roes on toast (£5.25), local pork cutlets with brandy and mushroom sauce (£10.25) and steak and kidney pie. Delicious puddings (all £3.25) are also a significant draw. Booking is advisable.While you are here, check out the pretty church next door.

Royal Hotel
Belgrave Road, Ventnor (01983 852186). **Food served** *Restaurant* 7-9.15pm daily. *Bar* noon-2pm daily. **Set dinner** £27.50 3 courses. **Credit** AmEx, DC, MC, V.
A reliably classy if not ground-breaking restaurant in this hotel close to the sea (*see p125*), the Royal offers a three-course set dinner (£27.50) featuring steamed salmon and crab mousse, best end of lamb or steamed carrot and parmesan gateau and a trio of daily specials. Light lunches, including salads and omelettes (from around £8), are served in the bar and conservatory. Early suppers are also available for children, which is particularly useful if you are also staying here, allowing you the realistic possibility of being able to dine later in (relative) peace.

Salty's
Quay Street, Yarmouth (01983 761550). **Food served** *Mid July-Aug* noon-2pm, 6.30-9.30pm Mon-Sat; noon-3pm Sun. *Sept-mid July* noon-3pm, 6.30-9.30pm Thur-Sat; noon-3pm Sun. **Credit** MC, V.
A very popular local bar and restaurant right on the harbour, specialising in fish caught from the restaurant's own boats. The lively downstairs bar serves tapas, while the menu of the restaurant upstairs changes weekly; it could include such dishes as oysters (£6.75 for six) and Moroccan-style whole black bream (£15). Opening times can be erratic so phone before visiting.

Seaview Hotel
High Street, Seaview (01983 612711). **Food served** noon-1.45pm, 7.30-9.30pm Mon-Sat, bank hols. **Set lunch** (Sun) £15.95 3 courses. **Credit** AmEx, DC, MC, V.
One of the best places to eat on the island in one of the most charming and child-friendly hotels. The two relaxed and pretty dining rooms (smoking and no-smoking) use local produce wherever possible and serve imaginative modern cuisine. There's plenty to choose from (and a couple for vegetarians ,too) such as pan-fried marlin steak with exotic fruit salsa (£14.50) or Cajun chicken , fine beans and red onion (£11.95). You can have a superior bar snack, such as hot crab ramekin (£5.25), in one of the two bars or sitting under the umbrellas at the front while you watch the world make its way down to the lovely little harbour below. *See also p125.*

The land that time forgot?

Forget Jurassic Park, the Isle of Wight is a rich hunting ground for palaeontologists, whose job is made easier by the continual natural slippage of the land. Homeowners may fret over the collapse of cliffs after every storm but fossil hunters rub their hands in glee, knowing new treasures will be revealed. Most of the fossil-hunting activity takes place among the crumbling cliffs between Blackgang Chine and Compton Bay.

You can see some of the finds at the **Dinosaur Farm**, a rather scruffy collection of barns where you can chat to experts and enthusiastic amateurs as they patiently piece together the bones of the island's largest dinosaur, a brachiosaur discovered near here eight years ago. If the tides are favourable, book a place on one of Dinosaur Farm's fossil walks along the foreshore, where, at low tide, you can see the footsteps of a giant lizard and her offspring (and the bungled attempt of some idiot who attempted to steal a print, destroying it in the process).

Further down the coast along the Military Road, you can meet Martin Simpson who runs the **Fossil Shop** (next door to Blackgang Chine), where a chunk of iguanadon thigh bone sits nonchalantly in a corner. A local character well-known for his fascinating talks, in which he persuades unsuspecting members of his audience to hold fossilised dinosaur poo, Simpson isn't really a dinosaur fanatic – it's lobster fossils that are his passion.

There has been talk of housing the local finds in a purpose-built site for years, a project that has been hindered by the difficulty of getting the various interested parties to co-operate. **Dinosaur Isle**, a state-of-the-art, hands-on attraction, is

finally due to open in Sandown in August 2001. It will feature life-sized animatronic dinosaurs in their natural landscape, displays of fossils and experts at work on the latest finds. Local enthusiasts fear that by putting the new attraction on the rather tacky seafront at Sandown, away from the area where finds are made, it will be dumbed down for the coach parties; but perhaps the fact that the existing geology museum will be incorporated into the new attraction will ensure it can be both educational and entertaining.

Dinosaur Farm
Military Road, near Brightstone (01983 740401/07970 626456). **Open** *Easter-Sept* 10am-5pm Thur, Sun. *July, Aug* 10am-5pm Mon, Tue, Thur, Fri, Sun. **Admission** £1-£2.

Dinosaur Isle
Culver Parade, Sandown (01983 404344). **Open** *May-Oct* 10am-6pm daily. *Nov-Apr* 10am-4pm daily. **Admission** £2.60-£4.60.

Fossil Shop
Blackgang Chine (next to entrance to theme park), Blackgang (01983 730233/www.dinosaurisland.net). **Beach walks** £3-£4.

Spy Glass Inn
Esplanade, Ventnor (01983 855338). **Food served** *July-Aug* noon-9.30pm Mon-Sat; noon-9pm Sun. *Sept-June* noon-2.15pm,7-9.30pm Mon-Sat; noon-2.15pm, 7-9pm Sun. **Credit** MC, V.
Perched above the beach at Ventnor, this is the perfect place to have a pint of local ale and fresh seafood. It's particularly good for parents, who can have a drink while keeping an eye on children playing on the beach. It gets very crowded on summer evenings, so booking is advisable. There's often some form of live music (MOR) to lighten the mood.

Waterfront Bar & Bay View Restaurant
The Promenade, Totland Bay, Totland (01983 756969). **Food served** noon-2.30pm, 6.30-9.30pm daily. **Credit** MC, V.
Situated right on the beach of Totland Bay in West Wight, this is a wonderful place to watch the sun go down on a summer's evening. The food is mainly flame-grilled steaks, seafood (grilled lemon sole, £14.95; grilled sea bass £13.95), and a couple of chicken and vegetarian options. Live music and barbecues in the summer.

Bournemouth & Poole

A medieval trading port and a 19th-century upstart offer endless seaside sport.

Being only 200 years old is quite a stigma, especially in a country where almost every hamlet can trace its ancestry back to the Domesday Book. They feel it in America and in Australia, and, yes, they feel it down in **Bournemouth**, too – a rootless, shifting sense of everything being transitory. In short, heritage guilt. The town dates back only to the 19th century, when it was first became a summer hotel destination. In that respect, nothing has changed; in the height of summer, Bournemouth's extensive beaches are packed to capacity.

But the town is slowly making up for lost time. It will take some time to shake off that 'kiss me quick' image, but retail outlets touting surf labels and discount designer gear are becoming more common among the chip shops and amusement arcades, and there is undoubtedly a lively club scene. The pier area in particular is on the up with a brand new IMAX cinema, with both 2- and 3-D screens, plus restaurants and bars.

Poole and Brownsea Island

Neighbouring **Poole** (which virtually runs into Bournemouth), on the other hand, can reel off a long list of olde smugglers' haunts and adventures on the high seas, its narrow, winding lanes and bustling quayside having seen centuries of trade. From its inception as a borough in 1342, Poole had fishing links with Newfoundland, which brought prosperity to the area, as evidenced by the magnificent merchant houses and quayside warehouses that still stand intact. To see them properly, it's worth following the signposted Cockle Trail, a one and a half hour walk around the old town, taking in all the major sights. These days wharf buildings house the vast Poole Pottery shop. On the other side of the docks are the Sunseeker motor boat yards, whose grandiose craft are moored all over the quay.

In the heart of the harbour is **Brownsea Island**, a blissful getaway from the tourist crush of the mainland. Although about half of it remains private, there are a number of wooded nature trails and tours of the nature reserve, and it offers perfect picnicking opportunities.

Life's a beach

When the Wurzels sang 'Dorset is beautiful wherever you go', they were not lying; it's just that you'll have to put up with the fact that everyone else wants to come here, too – visitors who want a really quiet break might do better elsewhere. The best beach in the area is the award-winning **Sandbanks**, but beware the crowds; **Branksome Chine** is a nice location with a beach café and shop. On **Flaghead** and **Alum Chines** you can walk through the wooded chines to reach the sea. **Studland**, reached by car ferry, has a beautiful beach, but it gets very popular in high season.

For a taste of Old England, **Christchurch** is the nearest pretty small town, with its marketplace mostly unchanged since medieval times and its exclusive shops and ancient inns. Places to visit include the substantial Priory Church, with its array of fine medieval carvings, and the 'miraculous' beam supposedly fitted by the hand of God, which gave rise to the current name of the town. The restored watermill and Georgian Red House Museum & Gardens (Quay Road; 01202 482860), with its walled herb garden and doll's house collection, are also of note. Another church of note, Wimborne Minster in **Wimborne**, is also worth a visit.

By train from London

Trains run from **Waterloo** to **Bournemouth** about every 20mins. The fast train takes **1hr 45mins**, slow trains take **2hrs 15mins**. The station is about a mile east of the town centre, but there are frequent buses from opposite the train station into town. Trains arrive in **Poole** about 10mins after **Bournemouth**, on certain routes. Info: www.swtrains.co.uk.

Christchurch – a taste of Old England.

What to see & do

Every year from late July to the end of August the beaches in Bournemouth and Poole come alive day and night with theatre, music, jugglers and beach games (look out for the Kid Zone tagging system to make sure wandering youngsters don't get lost). Board and yacht sailing is available – contact Poole tourist office (*see below*) and if you want to hire a beach hut, call the beach hut office on 01202 708181.

Visitors to Poole Pottery (The Quay; 01202 666200) should be aware that there are plans to redevelop its premises over the next year. There will be a new Collectors Studio in the Guildhall, and a tearoom in a beautiful Georgian building in Market Street. Finally, Bournemouth is home to one of the best classical orchestras in the country; the Bournemouth Symphony. Check the local press for concerts.

Tourist Information Centres

Westover Road, Bournemouth, BH1 2BU (0906 802 0234/www.bournemouth.co.uk). **Open** *mid July-Aug* 9.30am-7pm Mon-Sat; 10.30am-5.30pm Sun. *Sept-mid July* 9.30am-5.30pm Mon-Sat.

4 High Street, Poole, BH15 1SB(01202 253253/ www.pooletourism.com). **Open** *Apr, May* 10am-5pm Mon-Fri; 10am-4.30pm Sat, Sun. *June, July, Sept* 10am-5.30pm Mon-Fri; 10am-5pm Sat, Sun. *Aug* 10am-6pm daily. *Oct-Mar* 10am-5pm Mon-Fri; 10am-3pm Sat; noon-3pm Sun.

23 High Street, Christchurch, BH23 1AB (01202 471780/ www.resort-guide.co.uk/christchurch). **Open** *July, Aug* 9.30am-5.30pm Mon-Fri; 9.30am-5pm Sat; 10am-2pm Sun. *Sept-June* 9.30am-5pm Mon-Fri; 9.30-4.30pm Sat.

Bike hire

Rent a Bike *88 Charminster Road, Bournemouth (01202 315855).* About 15 minutes' walk from the station.

Action Bikes *Link Mall, Dolphin Centre, Poole (01202 680123).* In the mall, five minutes' walk from the station.

Alice in Wonderland Family Park

Merritown Lane, Hurn, Christchurch (01202 483444/www.aliceinwonderlandpark.co.uk). **Open** 10am-6pm daily (last entry 4pm). **Admission** £5.50; free under-3s.
Themed junior rides, indoor play area, massive mazes, farmyard animals, adventure playground, theatre shows and storytelling in the summer. There's also the Mad Hatter's Restaurant, plus picnic areas.

Brownsea Island

Poole Harbour (01202 707744/ www.nationaltrust.org.uk/brownsea/). **Open** *Apr-early Oct* 10am-5/6pm daily depending on season. Check times of last boat. Closed early Oct-Mar. **Admission** (NT) £3.50; 31.50 concessions. Additional ferry charge, check price with ferry companies.
The island, now a National Trust property, has fabulous views and woodland walks ideal for picnicking. There are Smugglers', Explorers' and Historical trails and a 200-acre nature reserve, one of the last English habitats of the red squirrel (visits by prior arrangement; contact the Dorset Wildlife Trust warden on 01202 709445). There is also open-air theatre in the summer. Brownsea Castle, a holiday home for John Lewis staff, is closed to the public.

Compton Acres

Canford Cliffs Road, Canford Cliffs, Poole (01202 700778/www.comptonacres.co.uk). **Open** *Mar-Sept* 10am-6pm daily (last entry 5.15pm). Closed Oct-Feb. **Admission** £5.75; £2.95-£5.25 concessions.

Hampshire & Isle of Wight

All manner of things creepy and slithery are on view at **Poole Aquarium & Serpentarium**.

Reputed to be one of the finest gardens in Europe, with rare plant species, Italian and Japanese formal gardens, a Roman garden, tearoom, brasserie and a gift shop. New attractions include a sensory sculpture garden and a deer sanctuary with tree-top lookout.

Oceanarium

Pier Approach (next to the pier), Bournemouth (01202 311993/www.oceanarium.co.uk).
Open 10am-6pm daily. **Admission** £5.75; £3.75-£4.75 concessions.
Thousands of species of marine life, including the giant gourami from the Ganges and lionfish from the Hawaiian coral reef, plus the Ocean Eye, where you can witness undersea environments close up. Café and shop.

Poole Aquarium & Serpentarium

Hennings Wharf, The Quay, Poole (01202 686712). **Open** *July, Aug* 9am-9pm daily. *Sept-June* 10am-5.30pm daily. **Admission** *Aquarium & serpentarium* £4.50; £3.50 concessions; free under-3s. *Aquarium, serpentarium & railway* £6; £4.50 concessions. *Railway only* £3; £2 concessions.
A thrilling array of 292 terrifying swimmers, slitherers and creepy-crawlies, from rattlesnakes and crocodiles to tarantulas and sharks. There's also an animal rescue centre, coffee shop, gift shop and a 3,000ft-long model railway, with Thomas the Tank Engine and friends.

Poole Park

Close to the town centre, this pleasant park has lots of attractions for children: Cygnet Continental Café Bar (01202 742842), complete with children's play area; Gus Gorilla's Jungle Playground (a ball pool); crazy golf; boat hire; and mini-train.

Splashdown

Tower Park Leisure Complex, Poole (01202 716000). **Open** *June-mid July* 10am-9pm Mon-Fri; 10am-7pm Sat, Sun. *Mid July-Aug* 9am-10pm Mon-Fri; 9am-7pm Sat, Sun. *Sept-Dec, Feb-May* 2-9pm Mon-Fri; 10am-7pm Sat, Sun. Closed Jan.
Admission £6; £1-£2.50 concessions.
Perfect when the weather's good (though there are indoor rides as well). Have fun on the Torpedo Run, the Grand Canyon Tyre Ride, and Baron's Revenge, a near-vertical drop in total darkness. Sliders must be at least 1m tall. Although there's a paddling pool and interactive

play zone for kids, there's no swimming pool for adults. Splashdown has longer opening hours during Easter and Christmas school holidays; phone to check.

Upton Country Park

4 miles N of Poole, signposted from A3049 and A35 (01202 672625). **Open** *Park* 9am-dusk daily. *Heritage Centre* 10.30am-4.30pm daily. **Admission** free.
A perfect spot for picnics, ball games and cycling. You can ride along the bike path beside Poole harbour to reach Upton through the woods. The Heritage Centre has a range of country-related displays and exhibitions. There's a bird-watching hide looking across the estuary and you can feed the ducks and peacocks.

Vistarama Balloon

Lower Gardens, Bournemouth (01202 399939/www.vistarama.co.uk). **Rides** *Summer* 7.30am-9pm daily. *Winter* 9am-5pm daily (weather permitting). **Tickets** £9.95; £5.50-£8.50 concessions.
A tethered balloon rising up to 500ft that affords spectacular views. This is a fantastic experience – the ten or so minutes up in the clouds feel like hours.

Waterfront & Scaplen's Court Museums

4 High Street, Poole (01202 262600).
Open *Waterfront Museum* Apr-Oct 10am-5pm Mon-Sat; noon-5pm Sun. Nov-Mar 10am-3pm Mon-Sat; noon-3pm Sun. *Scaplen's Court Museum* Aug 10am-5pm Mon-Sat; noon-5pm Sun. **Admission** *Scaplen's Court & Waterfront Museums* (Aug only) £4; £2.85-£3.40 concessions. *Waterfront Museum* £3; £1.35-£1.70 concessions.
The Waterfront Museum details the history of the area from Roman times, and includes medieval cellars and plenty of smugglers' tales. Scaplen's Court Museum, currently open only in August, provides exhibitions and displays; it also has a charming walled garden.

Where to stay

Bournemouth was built as a tourist attraction so there's no shortage of hotels, guesthouses or self-catering options. The **Rockley Park Holiday Centre** in Poole (08457 753753/01202

679393) has fixed mobile homes (£147-£691 per unit per week, depending on the time of year, standard of accommodation, and number of people/pets). Facilities include indoor and outdoor swimming pools, children's play area, entertainment, cafés, bars; it's also an ideal spot for crabbing.

Bournemouth Highcliffe Marriott
St Michaels Road, West Cliff, Bournemouth, BH2 5DU (01202 557702/fax 01202 293155/ www.marriotthotels.com/bohbm). **Rates** £116-£220 per person double/twin; £220 suite. **Rooms** (all en suite) 74 standard double/twin; 59 double/twin; 17 junior suite; 2 residential suites. **Credit** AmEx, DC, MC, V.
Recently taken over by Marriott, the Highcliffe is just a stroll away from Bournemouth pier and adjacent to the lift down to a Blue Flag beach. The hotel buildings sprawl a little and the interior is labyrinthine, but the view across the bay from the front bedrooms is magnificent (sea-view supplement £10-£35). Children welcome. No-smoking rooms available.

Chine Hotel
25 Boscombe Spa Road, Bournemouth, BH5 1AX (01202 396234/fax 01202 391737/ www.chinehotel.co.uk). **Rates** £55-£80 per person. Child supplement £2.20 for each year of child's age when staying in family room. Special breaks. **Rooms** (all en suite) 6 single; 30 double; 30 twin; 15 family. **Credit** MC, V.
Sister to the equally comfortable Sandbanks and Haven Hotels (*see p133*) in Poole, the Chine is a wonderful family hotel with indoor and outdoor pools, pitch and putt and children's play equipment. It's set in three acres of grounds, with access to the lovely shady paths of Boscombe Chine that lead down to the popular Boscombe beach. Views to the rear are spectacular, looking over the tree-tops to the sea. The old Victorian lift with its open-link brass doors makes the trip worthwhile, too. Children welcome (baby listening and indoor soft play room are both available for guests). No-smoking rooms available. *See also p133.*

Expect a wet landing at **Splashdown**.

Inverness Hotel
26 Tregonwell Road, Bournemouth, BH2 5NS (01202 554968/fax 01202 294197). **Rates** £21-£36 per person. **Rooms** (all en suite) 1 single; 6 double; 1 twin; 2 family. **Credit** MC, V.
Unpretentious and set in an Edwardian-style house, close to the town centre. There are dozens of other establishments just like it, but this one is friendlier than most. There's a lounge with bar, dining area and decent rooms with en-suite showers. Some may find them a little poky, but they are reasonably priced. The optional evening meal is £11 per person if booked in advance with the room, otherwise £13. Children over five welcome.

Langtry Manor Hotel
26 Derby Road, Bournemouth, BH1 3QB (01202 553887/fax 01202 290115/www.langtrymanor.com). **Rates** (per person) £54.75 double/twin; £64.75 master double; £64.95 four-poster or Jacuzzi; £74.75 four-poster with Jacuzzi/suites; £84.75 luxury suite; £104.75 King's Room. £10 children supplement. Special breaks. **Rooms** (all en suite) 7 double/twin; 6 master double; 5 four-poster; 4 luxury suites; 2 double with Jacuzzi; 2 four-poster with Jacuzzi. **Credit** AmEx, DC, MC, V.
A gable-roofed, half-timbered house built by Lillie Langtry on land bought for her by Edward VII at the height of their affair, the Langtry wallows in their romance. Stay in Edward's suite (the King's Room) with its massive four-poster or in Lillie's room with heart-shaped corner Jacuzzi. Go the full hog and indulge in the Saturday night six-course Victorian banquet served by staff in period dress in a dining room with minstrel's gallery and stained-glass windows. Children and dogs welcome. No-smoking rooms available. Guests can also visit the local David Lloyd Sports Club for £4.50 per day. Occasional murder mystery weekends.

Mansion House
Thames Street, Poole, BH15 1JN (01202 685666/fax 01202 665709/www.themansionhouse.co.uk). **Rates** (per person) £65-£90 single; £50-£60 double or twin. **Rooms** (all en suite) 9 single; 21 double/twin; 2 deluxe double/twin; 2 family. **Credit** AmEx, DC, MC, V.
Located just behind the quayside, this stately, ivy-covered double-fronted Georgian house is easily the classiest hotel in the area. The spacious lobby opens out to a splendid, sweeping staircase leading up to rooms, which are all individually designed and named after famous Georgians and Victorians. All are immaculately furnished, often with antiques. There is also a large and excellent restaurant panelled in cherrywood and a smaller wood-beamed bistro next door (*see p133*). Understated, chic and highly recommended. Children welcome. No- smoking rooms available.

Royal Bath Hotel
Bath Road, Bournemouth, BH1 2EW (01202 555555/fax 01202 554158/www.devereonline.co.uk). **Rates** £130 single occupancy; £160-£265 double; £315-£365 suite. **Rooms** (all en suite) 22 single; 109 double; 9 suites. **Cards** AmEx, DC, MC, V.
The Royal Bath is the most imposing local example of the tourist palaces that sprang up all over the English coast in the 19th century. Once owned by the Russell-Cotes family (whose museum is next door, *see p132* **From the baronial to the parochial**), it's a vast

Hampshire & Isle of Wight

place: there are 140 rooms and three good restaurants, plus first-rate leisure facilities including a swimming pool, sauna, spa and gym. The Bistro restaurant has great sea views. Even if you can't afford to stay here, it's worth trying the Royal Tea (£9.25) with scones, clotted cream and finger sandwiches, or sampling the house champagne and strawberries (£36.50) while admiring the gardens. Children welcome.

Where to eat & drink

Among the countless hotel restaurants and fast-food joints, trendy café-bars are beginning to pop up everywhere in Bournemouth. **CH2** (Exeter Road; 01202 296296) has industrial decor and a surprisingly ambitious menu. Its sister establishment in Poole, **Custom House** (01202 676767), is a fine Georgian building on the quay with a cosy ground-floor bar and an excellent first-floor restaurant. Back in Bournemouth, the **Slam Bar** (Firvale Road) is a perfect pre-club chill zone as is the new, multi-levelled and hyper-cool **Consortium** (3 Richmond Hill; 01202 555155), which also serves delicious breakfasts and quick, Med-style lunches. Both places have DJ nights and occasional live jazz or funk. Top of the pile, though, is **Bistro on the Beach** (Solent Promenade; 01202 431473), a café by day and gourmet delight by night. As for pubs,

From the baronial to the parochial

Bournemouth's premier cultural attraction – the **Russell-Cotes Museum and Art Gallery** – has recently reopened after extensive refurbishment. The museum houses a vast collection of Victorian and Edwardian English paintings, along with oriental and European objets d'art, furnishings and porcelain.

The building, a superb example of late Victorian architecture and interior design, is worth a visit in its own right. Originally designed to be the home of Merton and Annie Russell-Cotes, owners of the next-door Royal Bath Hotel, it was completed in 1901. The exterior, combining elements of the Scottish baronial castle, French château and Italian villa, is wonderfully evocative of an opulent bygone age. The interior, reminiscent of Leighton House in London, is even more lavish, with stunning plasterwork, wallpapers and friezes, painted ceilings, Japanese motifs and a gorgeous mosaic fountain. It also has the best view in Bournemouth, overlooking the entire bay; the garden, containing some modern sculptures, is charming. It was from the cliff just below here that Eisenhower and Montgomery watched the rehearsals for the D-Day landings.

As for the collection, contemporary European painting didn't much interest the Russell-Coteses. They devoted their wealth to British artists such as Edwin Long, William Etty, Dante Gabriel Rossetti and Sir Lawrence Alma-Tadema. The result, reflecting that curious Victorian mixture of eroticism and sentimentality, is a plethora of biblical and pastoral scenes, Scottish glens and idealised women in various states of ecstasy and/or undress. Both grandiose and touchingly parochial, the sheer scale of the collection is impressive in itself. At first, Merton Russell-Cotes used it to decorate the Royal Bath Hotel; by 1891, the collection was valued at £300,000, a vast sum at the time.

But the Russell-Coteses didn't stop there. They were inveterate travellers (partly due to Merton's need for warmer climes for his bronchitis) and, sweeping through the Far East and Oceania, they returned with over a hundred cases containing everything from Japanese armour and furnishings to geological specimens, Maori artefacts and the odd stuffed bird. They were also avid admirers of Henry Irving and a collection of his memorabilia now fills one room of the museum. Other parts of the museum have been reserved for work by present-day artists.

The museum is very keen to entertain children: it supplies a fun guidebook specifically designed for them, and there's also a children's gallery in a brand-new annexe that also houses a modern café.

Russell-Cotes Museum & Art Gallery
East Cliff, Bournemouth (01202 451800/www.russell-cotes.bournemouth. gov.uk). **Open** 10am-5pm Tue-Sun. **Admission** free.

Bournemouth is not to be recommended. Poole Quay, dotted with nautical inns with tables outside, is much better. Shiver your timbers at the **Jolly Sailor** or the **Lord Nelson**. There's also an abundance of cheap eateries here of low to middle quality. Try the **Warehouse Brasserie** (01202 677238) for something a bit better and only marginally more expensive. Surfers may also like **Hot Rocks** (01202 555559), a large, American-style 'surf' restaurant and bar, opposite Bournemouth Pier. The decor – reed tables and a shark hanging from the ceiling – is fun.

Bistro on the Bridge

3-5 Bridge Street, Christchurch (01202 482522). **Food served** noon-2.30pm, 7-10.30pm Wed-Sun. **Set dinner** £16.95 3 courses. **Credit** AmEx, MC, V.
The famed Bistro on the Beach in Bournemouth (*see p132*) has spawned this cool, modern brasserie in Christchurch. The stress here is on dishes everyone knows, well prepared and presented. So, the set menu offers grilled fillet of herring on a warm potato salad with dill dressing followed by boeuf bourguignon; and the specials include skate with capers and beurre noir and rack of lamb with garlic and rosemary. The service is excellent and, compared to London, the prices for food of this quality are a steal.

Brasserie at the Haven Hotel

116 Banks Road, Sandbanks, Poole (01202 707333). **Food served** noon-2.30pm, 7-9pm daily. **Credit** AmEx, DC, MC, V.
The Brasserie is a long art deco room with fish tanks and a stunning sea view. The menu is simple; cooking and presentation, though, is more than decent. Starters include the likes moules marinière (£5) or brochette of scallops and king prawns with stir-fried veg (£8.20); mains might be calves' liver with herb mash (£12.50) or fried goujons of halibut with fries (a posh fish and chips, £11.50) – on a recent visit this was composed of tender fish with delicately flavoured breading. The hotel itself is an attractive 1920s building in a prime location. Marconi set up his aerials for his wireless experiments here in 1904.

Chine Hotel

25 Boscombe Spa Road, Bournemouth (01202 396234/www.chinehotel.co.uk). **Food served** 12.30-2pm, 7-8.30pm Mon-Fri, Sun; 7-8.30pm Sat. **Set lunch** £15.50 3 courses. **Set dinner** £19.75 3 courses. **Credit** AmEx, DC, MC, V.
Smart dress is required for this fine-dining restaurant overlooking the large hotel gardens (*see p131*). The cooking is artful, with traditional dishes given an ambitious and original twist. Starters could be shellfish bisque with rouille, or rillette of pork with caramelised apple wrapped in Parma ham; while braised guinea fowl with cabbage, pancetta and puy lentil broth, and grilled fillet of sea bass with lemongrass risotto and chive fondue have featured as recent main courses. Vegetarian options are creative, and include the likes of millefeuille of asparagus with orange-scented hollandaise. There's also a children's high tea served between 5pm and 5.30pm.

Coriander

22 Richmond Hill, Bournemouth (01202 552202/ www.coriander-restaurant.co.uk). **Food served** noon-10.30pm Mon-Thur, Sun; noon-11pm Fri, Sat. **Set lunch** £5.50 per person (1 platter to share). **Set dinners** £9.75, £11.25, both 2 courses. **Credit** AmEx, MC, V.
Friendly, family-style Mexican dining at rustic tables with crayons and paper for kids to design their own placemats, and plenty of more-ish cocktails to amuse the adults. Well-prepared and popular dishes include enchiladas, burritos and quesadillas with several choices of filling, and tortilla chips with an array of dips, as well as more ambitious dishes such as swordfish in a red wine sauce with olives.

Mansion House

7-11 Thames Street, Poole (01202 685666/ www.themansionhouse.co.uk). **Food served** noon-1.45pm, 7-9.15pm Mon-Sat; noon-1.45pm Sun. **Set lunch** (Mon-Fri) £17.55 3 courses; (Sun) £18.70 3 courses. **Set dinner** £19.75 2 courses. **Credit** AmEx, DC, MC, V.
As befits probably the smartest hotel in the town, if not the whole area, dining here is a fairly formal affair with a smart-casual dress code in the evenings, and for family lunch on Sundays. The menu is mouth-watering. Start, perhaps, with terrine of mackerel with pan-fried scallops and tomato chutney, or mussels cooked with Thai spices finished with coconut cream and coriander. Continue with roast guinea fowl with salsify and mushrooms or fillet of monkfish with prosciutto, broad beans and tomatoes. On Saturday nights, there is a roast of the day carved from the trolley. For a more relaxed atmosphere try the Bistro next door, serviced by the same kitchens. *See also p131.*

Salad Centre

667 Christchurch Road, Boscombe (01202 393673). **Food served** 11.30am-4.30pm Mon-Sat. **No credit cards.**
A little out of the way and tucked into an unprepossessing row of shops east of the town centre, this veggie wholefood caff is a blessing for visitors on a budget, serving a wide range of delicious salads, quiches and pies, a hot soup of the day and home-made breads. Leave some room for the large selection of cakes. It's extremely good value for money: expect to pay between £10 and £12 per person.

Salterns Restaurant at Salterns Hotel

38 Salterns Way, Lilliput, Poole (01202 707321/ www.salterns.co.uk/hotel). **Food served** noon-2pm, 7-9.30pm daily. **Credit** AmEx, DC, MC, V.
This upmarket hotel restaurant overlooks a large marina and has outside tables for summer eating. The view is great and food is excellent, though expensive. Starters could include Dorset air-dried ham with melon and lavender dressing (£5) or Poole Bay crab cakes with a sweet chilli and coriander, followed, perhaps, by turbot with a light curried mussel and leek nage (£16) or salt-crusted sea bass with a fennel medley and red capsicum sauce. Ingredients are of the highest available quality and preparation is admirably precise. The hotel also has a bistro for more informal eating.

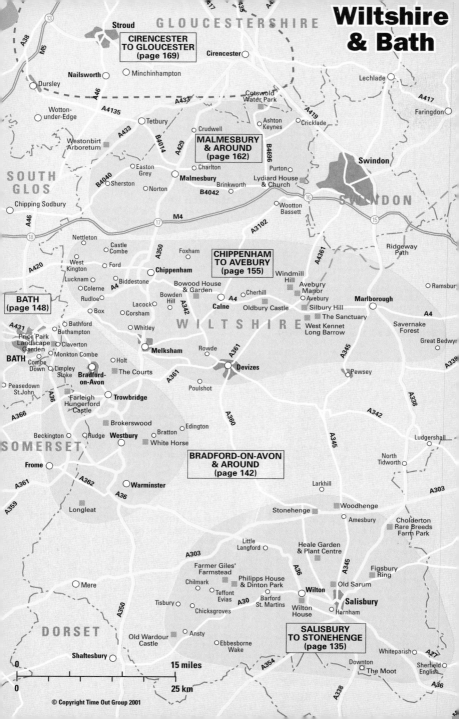

Salisbury & Stonehenge

From Stone Age to New Age.

What with pagans getting to work on Stonehenge as long as 5,000 years ago and Christians throwing up Salisbury Cathedral 4,000 years later, the West Country has long fostered its own independent spiritual traditions. Nowadays these traditions are stewarded by the opposing forces of the heritage industry and new-age hippies. But south Wiltshire isn't just about religious monuments. **Salisbury** can be explored for its illustrious history, narrow lanes, busy market and profusion of tearooms. On top of this, the West Country has a long tradition of pub-going and beer-brewing. Those that need excuses for imbibing can take walks through the picturesque rolling countryside from one village boozer to the next. Those that don't need any reason can simply roll up next to a red-faced local, drink the ale and chew the cud.

As far as the history of the town goes, **Salisbury** is a relocation of nearby Old Sarum. In the days before Sarum was 'Old', it was to this neck of the woods what 'new' Salisbury is now: the provincial capital. Then someone had the bright idea of moving the whole shooting match, lock, stock and masonry, about one mile

By train from London

Trains to **Salisbury** leave from **Waterloo** approximately every hour, passing through **Clapham Junction**; journey time is **1hr 30mins**. Info: www.swtrains.co.uk.

down the road. Salisbury therefore occupies a pretty little valley nailed to the landscape by the second highest steeple in Europe. Around the cathedral's steeple is the famous walled Close, home to Edward Heath and where motor cars give way to the human traffic of camera-laden tourists. So dominant is the stunning 13th-century Cathedral that the other items of interest in the town are necessarily eclipsed. However, this doesn't mean they don't exist and history anoraks in need of a fuller historical briefing can seek satisfaction at the **Salisbury & South Wiltshire Museum**, **Mompesson House**, the **Wardrobe**, the **Medieval Hall** and the Tourist Information Centre in the Guildhall on the main square. This is not to

Stonehenge – house of the rising sun.

mention the wealth of historical information to be found in the Cathedral and its **Chapter House**, which stores one of the few original copies of the Magna Carta of 1215 (*see p140* **Chapter and verse**). For those restless modern souls unmoved by history, who must shop to create meaning in their lives, the market on Saturday and Tuesday offers good-value local agricultural produce with both fish and fowl – the latter creatures' sacrifice to our dining tables being movingly commemorated by the stone stilted **Poultry Cross**. The **Market Square**, moreover, is an architecturally attractive space good for lounging about and fist-fighting on a Saturday night. The other thing that no market town can be without in this day and age is an annoying one-way system. Luckily, however, Salisbury is not only small enough to walk around, it is also small enough to walk out of altogether. One particularly popular walk takes you through the elegant **Queen Elizabeth Gardens**, across the water-meadows on the south side of the city where Constable parked his easel to paint his famous picture of the spire. Those who cannot live on architectural nostalgia alone can make the prettily located Old Mill pub and restaurant in **Harnham** their destination.

Outside Salisbury

Three miles west of Salisbury lies **Wilton**, the ancient capital of Wessex and home of Wilton carpets, the stately grandeur of **Wilton House**, and more antique shops than you can shake a Louis XIV brocaded stick at. This is classy idling country, with its startling Italianate church, ruined abbey and river walks along the Wylye. Further afield, six miles south of Salisbury, **Downton** is a chocolate-box, thatched village on the Avon, replete with village greens, Cuckoo Fair customs (first bank holiday Saturday in May), and the **Moot**. In the other direction, six miles north, next to the MOD's razor-wired expanses of Salisbury Plain, the quiet market town of **Amesbury** offers B&Bs and inns galore, but none of Salisbury's grander distractions.

Rock on

Unquestionably, the big attraction outside the Cathedral city is **Stonehenge** – perhaps the most famous pile of rocks on the planet. Picked out by the rising sun during the summer solstice, Stonehenge can be more conveniently located by following the New Age herd down the A303. The site is complemented by the prototype **Woodhenge** nearby, although the **Moot**, several miles south in Downton, is a lesser known, more stimulating ancient monument. It is a reputed Saxon parliament, but also has a medieval 'bailie' mound and amphitheatre set in grade I-listed 18th-century ornamental gardens.

What to see & do

Tourist Information Centres

Redworth House, Flower Lane, Amesbury, SP4 7HG (01980 622833/www.visitsalisbury.com). **Open** *June-Aug* 9am-5pm Mon-Sat. *Sept-May* 9am-5pm Mon-Fri.
Fish Row, Salisbury, SP1 1EJ (01722 334956/ www.visitsalisbury.com). **Open** *May* 9.30am-5pm Mon-Sat; 10.30am-4.30pm Sun. *June, Sept* 9.30am-6pm Mon-Sat; 10.30am-4.30pm Sun. *July, Aug* 9.30am-6pm Mon-Sat; 10.30am-5pm Sun. *Oct-Apr* 9.30am-5pm Mon-Sat.

Bike hire

Hayballs *26-30 Winchester Street, Salisbury (01722 411378).* **Open** 9am-5.30pm Mon-Sat.
A ten-minute walk from the station.

Cholderton Rare Breeds Farm Park

Amesbury Road, Cholderton (01980 629438/ www.rabbitworld.co.uk). **Open** *mid Mar-Oct* 10am-6pm daily. **Admission** £4.25; £2.75-£3.75 concessions.
Get a preview of genetic engineering in years to come: lop-eared bunnies, spotty percy pigs and seaweed-eating sheep! Tractor rides and pig-racing for parents, too.

Farmer Giles' Farmstead

Teffont Magna (01722 716338).
Open *Late Mar-early Nov* 10am-6pm daily.
Early Nov-late Mar 10am-dusk Sat, Sun.
Admission £3.95; £2.85-£3.50 concessions.
This 175-acre interactive dairy farm offers the chance to feed and groom the animals, and there's a restaurant and gift shop to keep the kids happy. The farm is ten miles west of Salisbury on the B3089.

Figsbury Ring

Just north of A30, 3 miles NE of Salisbury.
A ritual site? A settlement? Although commonly taken to be an Iron Age hill fort, there's no evidence to support this view. However, this vast circular earthwork with a deep inner quarry ditch does support a reasonable scenic view.

Heale Garden & Plant Centre

Middle Woodford (01722 782504).
Open 10am-5pm daily. Last entry 4.30pm.
Admission £3.25; £1.50 concessions; free under-5s.
The beautiful gardens of Heale House (not open to the public) feature a wide collection of roses, shrubs and plants amid clipped hedges and mellow stonework for wanderers and gardeners alike. Unusual plants for sale.

Medieval Hall

Cathedral Close, Salisbury (01722 324731/ www.salisburycathedral.org.uk). **Open** *Apr-Sept* 11am-6pm daily (presentations hourly). Last entry 5pm. **Admission** £1.50; £1 concessions.
Follow a 40-minute audiovisual presentation of the history of Salisbury in this beamed 13th-century hall.

Mompesson House

Cathedral Close, Salisbury (01722 335659/ www.nationaltrust.org.uk). **Open** *Apr-Oct* noon-5.30pm Mon-Wed, Sat, Sun. Last entry 5pm. **Admission** (NT) House £3.90; £1.95 concessions. *Gardens only* 80p.

Salisbury Cathedral – inspiring artists and pilgrims alike.

An elegant 18th-century Queen Anne house, which featured in the award-winning film version of *Sense and Sensibility*. Attractions include the Turnbull collection of glasses, period furniture and a walled garden.

Old Sarum Castle
Castle Road, Salisbury (01722 335398/www.english-heritage.org.uk). **Open** *Mar-June, Sept, Oct* 10am-6pm daily. *Nov-Feb* 10am-4pm daily. *Jul, Aug* 9am-6pm daily. **Admission** (EH) £2; £1-£1.50 concessions.
The knee-high remains of Old Salisbury, perched atop its atmospheric rise.

Old Wardour Castle
N of A30, near Tisbury (01747 870487/www.english-heritage.org.uk). **Open** 10am-6pm daily. **Admission** (EH) £2.50; £1.30-£1.90 concessions.
The unusual hexagonal ruins of this dreamy lakeside castle last saw violent action in 1643 – disputative picnickers aside. Landscaped grounds include an elaborate rockwork grotto.

Philipps House & Dinton Park
N side of B3089, Dinton (01985 843600/www.nationaltrust.org.uk). **Open** *Apr-Oct* 1-5pm Mon; 10am-1pm Sat. **Admission** (NT) £3.
A graceful neo-classical house surrounded by rolling parkland, nine miles west of Salisbury.

Salisbury Festival
Festival Office, 73 New Street, Salisbury, SP1 2PH (01722 332241/www.salisburyfestival.co.uk).
The annual international summer festival in May and June is dominated by classical music and attracts orchestras such as the London Philarmonic and major composers such as Philip Glass. Jazz, opera, theatre, films and dance also figure in an impressive line-up of events in venues including the Salisbury Playhouse, the Guildhall on Market Square, the Arts Centre on Bedwin Street and the Cathedral itself.

Salisbury Playhouse
Malthouse Lane, Salisbury (01722 320333/www.salisburyplayhouse.com). **Open** *Box office* 10am-6pm Mon-Sat. **Credit** AmEx, MC, V.
One of the powerhouses of British regional theatre, producing its own seasons and receiving major touring companies before they move on to perform in the West End in London. There is also a studio space designed for promoting and fostering new, alternative talent.

Salisbury & South Wiltshire Museum
Kings House, 65 The Close, Salisbury (01722 332151/www.salisburymuseum.org.uk). **Open** *July, Aug* 10am-5pm Mon-Sat; 2-5pm Sun. *Sept-June* 10am-5pm Mon-Sat. **Admission** £3.50; £1-£2.30 concessions.
This award-winning museum contains a Stonehenge gallery and a seminal archaeological collection (including the story of General Pitt-Rivers, founding father of modern archaeology). Also ceramics, costumes and surprise Turner watercolours.

Stonehenge
By junction of A303 and A360, W of Amesbury (info line 01980 624715). **Open** *mid Mar-May, Sept-mid Oct* 9.30am-6pm daily. *June-Aug* 9am-7pm daily. *Mid Oct-23 Oct* 9.30am-5pm daily. *24 Oct-mid Mar* 9.30am-4pm daily. **Admission** (EH and NT) £4.20; £2.20-£3.20 concessions.
Stonehenge has been fenced off and leased out to English Heritage, who in turn lease it back to the public, the very people who 'owned' it in the first place. So, under the guise of protecting them for posterity, you now have to pay £4.20 to see these big stones – and you still can't get close. There's also a money-spinning souvenir shop where you can even buy such neolithic memorabilia as Heritage Mustard. Impressive as the stones are, going to see them is a bit like renting your DVD player from the burglar who nicked it. On the summer solstice it hosts visits from druids and New Age followers, closely observed by the police.

The Wardrobe
58 Cathedral Close, Salisbury (01722 414536/www.thewardrobe.org.uk). **Open** *Feb, Mar, Nov* 10am-5pm Tue-Sun. *Apr-Oct* 10am-5pm daily. **Admission** £2.50; 50p-£1.90 concessions.
The local regimental museum is housed in a fine house dating from 1254, which was used by bishops in the 14th century to house clothing.

Wilton Carpet Factory
King Street, Wilton (01722 742733/www.wiltoncarpets.com). **Open** 9.30am-5.30pm Mon-Sat; 11am-5pm Sun. **Admission** £4; £2.50-£3.75 concessions.
Unravel the mysteries of Wilton and Axminster carpet-making, which dates back nearly 300 years. The Wilton factory outlet shop (plus fashion, textiles, sports equipment) is in the **Wilton Shopping Village** on Minster Street (01722 741211).

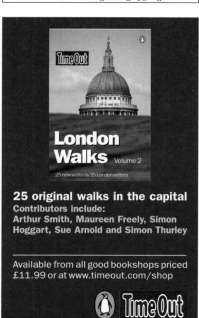

Waders in the Nadder at **Wilton House**.

Wilton House

Wilton (01722 746720/www.wiltonhouse.com).
Open *Easter-Oct* 10.30am-5.30pm daily. Last entry
4.30pm. **Admission** *House, exhibition & grounds*
£7.25; £4.50-£6.25 concessions. *Grounds only* £3.75;
£2.75 concessions; free under-5s.
Built by Inigo Jones, Wilton House contains a fabulous art
collection (including Van Dycks, Reynolds and a couple of
Brueghels). Now a family business, the house boasts a
Palladian bridge over the Nadder, 21 acres of landscaped
parkland, a Tudor kitchen, and an adventure playground.

Woodhenge

Off A345, just N of Amesbury.
Site of a covered wooden monument that predated
Stonehenge, discovered in 1925. Concrete posts now
mark the many excavated postholes. Enthusiasts only.

Where to stay

There's an abundance of classy farmhouse
B&Bs in south Wiltshire, while Salisbury
itself is known for its conference-quality hotels,
as well as decent guesthouses and inns with
rooms, such as the **King's Arms** (St Johns
Street; 01722 327629/www.oldenglish.co.uk).
See also p141 **Old Mill Hotel**.

Howard's House Hotel

Teffont Evias, Salisbury, SP3 5RJ (01722 716392/
fax 01722 716820/www.howardshousehotel.co.uk).
Rates £85 single occupancy; £95-£135 twin/double;
£155 four-poster; £135 plus £25 per child family
room. Special breaks. **Rooms** (all en suite) 1 twin;
6 double; 1 four-poster; 1 family.
Credit AmEx, DC, MC, V.
Seventeenth-century Howard's House sits in two acres
of prettily located classic English gardens, around ten
miles west of Salisbury. Smart, pastel-coloured comfort
and tranquillity are the bywords here. If you're around,
it's hard to resist a quality hotel with the tag-line 'children encouraged'. First-rate modern British cuisine from
head chef Boyd MacKintosh draws non-residents to the
restaurant, which is recognised by Michelin, among
others. Dogs welcome (£7 per night to stay in room).
A303 west; 8 miles after Stonehenge bypassing Wylye, turn
left (quarter of a mile after dual carriageway ends); after a
quarter of a mile turn left to Teffont Evias; turn right at
sharp bend in village; follow signs to hotel.

Little Langford Farmhouse

Little Langford, SP3 4NP (01722 790205/
fax 01722 790086). **Rates** £24-£26 per person.
Rooms 1 double; 1 double/twin (en suite); 1 twin.
No credit cards.
Set in the Earl of Pembroke's 1,400-acre estate eight
miles north-west of Salisbury, this imposing Victorian
farmhouse surrounded by smartly manicured lawns is
blessed with good-sized rooms and kitted out in the style
of a posh retirement home. When foot and mouth culls
aren't in progress, visitors can stroll round the farm and
watch the cows getting milked before they pour their
lactations over their breakfast cereal. A three-quarter-
sized billiard table is available for guests' use and the
whole building is no-smoking. Children welcome. Pets
by prior arrangement.
A36 from Salisbury to Bath; left at Stoford into Great
Wishford; keep church on left; turn right at Royal Oak pub;
after 2 miles follow sharp bend into Little Langford; house
on right.

Newton Farmhouse

Southampton Road, Whiteparish, SP5 2QL (tel/
fax 01794 884416/www.newtonfarmhouse.co.uk).
Rates £30 single occupancy; £40-£60 twin; £50-£60
double; additional person in double room £10
(5-12 yrs); £15 (12-18 yrs). **Rooms** (all en suite)
3 double; 3 double/twin; 1 family. **No credit cards**.
Salisbury is an eight-mile drive north of this 16th-
century listed farmhouse on the fringes of the New
Forest. Flagstoned floors downstairs contrast with carpeted comfort and four-poster beds in the assorted en
suite bedrooms, which are all decorated in a floral manner. A very warm and homely welcome is guaranteed
from the garrulous proprietress, who also makes bread
and jams for breakfast. There's an outdoor swimming
pool, too. Children welcome. No smoking throughout.
J2 M27; A36 past sign for Whiteparish; house is on left
after ½ mile, immediately before turning to Downton and
Redlinch.

Onion Store

Sherfield English, nr Romsey, SO51 6DU (tel/fax
01794 323227). **Rates** £52 per person. **Rooms** (all
en suite) 3 suites (each for 2 people). **No credit cards**.
A wildly romantic hideaway, with two suites in self-
contained out-houses plus one in the wing of the main
17th-century thatched cottage. These converted onion
stores offer both '70s hippy rustic chic and executive
luxury (they have their own private Jacuzzis). An indoor
swimming pool in the conservatory is open to guests
from spring to autumn, and the barbie facilities are also
a hit for summer dining. Not surprisingly, this warren
of indulgence is hugely popular and you'll need to book
months ahead. All suites are no-smoking.
Sherfield English is off A27, west of Romsey.

Red Lion

4 Milford Street, Salisbury, SP1 2AN (01722
323334/fax 01722 325756/www.the-redlion.co.uk).
Rates £84 single; £104 double/twin; £122 four-
poster/suite; £125 family. Breakfast £9.50 (Eng);
£7.50 (cont). Special breaks. **Rooms** (all en suite)
13 single; 18 double; 14 twin; 2 four-poster; 2 family;
2 suites. **Credit** AmEx, DC, MC, V.
Reputedly the oldest purpose-built hotel in the country,
the Red Lion has had since 1230 to develop its reputation.

Chapter and verse

Salisbury Cathedral is one of the most elegant and breathtakingly conceived pieces of architecture in the UK and, indeed, the world. Finished in 1258, it is an exceptional example of early Gothic architecture, miraculously put together in just 38 years. The body of the church is also distinguished by being built in a single style, its vaulted, fluted nave designed to raise the congregation's thoughts to heaven. It is a stunning achievement by any standards, but all the more incredible when you consider it was built without the aid of modern construction techniques.

The famous 404-foot spire was a later addition and the colossal weight of this gigantic spike required support from flying buttresses. But it was surely worth the effort for a sight that has inspired pilgrimages for centuries. It is also one of those quintessential symbols of Englishness that famously seduced the landscape painter John Constable.

Sadly, the cathedral has lost nearly all its medieval stained glass, which has been replaced by saccharine Edwardian and gruesome 20th-century alternatives. However, much of the interior is older: the bulk of the choir stalls are 13th century and the Chantry Chapel of Edmund Audley (Bishop 1502-24) is a prettily decorated hideaway that was partially vandalised during the Reformation. And, although Salisbury Cathedral was never monastic, it has the largest set of cloisters of any cathedral in the country.

The skeleton and organ clock and wattle-and-daub walls are just two of the talking points – along with the vivid, not to say loud, '80s decor. However, the creeper-clad courtyard is an oasis of peace just yards from the traffic of the city centre and the restaurant is good despite its rather outré suburban affectations. Children welcome. No-smoking rooms available.

White Hart
St John Street, Salisbury, SP1 2SD (0870 400 8125/ fax 01722 412761/www.heritage-hotels.com). **Rates** *Mon-Thur* £100 single; £140 double/twin; £155 deluxe double; £140 family; £155 four-poster/suite. *Fri-Sun* £58 per person single/ double; £68 per person four-poster/suite. **Rooms** (all en suite) 15 single; 20 double; 21 twin; 3 four-poster; 7 suites. **Credit** AmEx, MC, V.
Heritage Hotels have established a conference- and corporate-quality hotel in this smartly porticoed 17th-century building that looks like a town hall. Near the Cathedral Close in the centre of town, it has all the characteristics of 'traditional' English service and features such as open fires, tied-back curtains, tastefully framed prints and so on. As such it is both reliable, comfortable and well appointed with unostentatious, clean facilities. Downstairs, the carpeted vibe is hushed and personal, upstairs, in the bedrooms, facilities are standardised, smart and clean. Children welcome. Pets welcome; £10 per night. No-smoking rooms available.

Where to eat & drink

Drinking is one of the things they do best in these parts, and in Salisbury the **Moloko Bar** (5 Bridge Street) is a sleek and trendy diversion, offering a wide range of vodka. For contrast, try the **Wig & Quill** (1 New Street), a fine old Wadworth's boozer, serving up a range of robust real ales. Alternatively, the youth of today favour the **Cathedral Hotel** (a bland variation on All Bar One on Milford Street) or the lively music/comedy venue, **Chicago Rock Café** (30 Fisherton Street). Older folk may prefer the tranquillity of the many tearooms. **David Brown's** (31 Catherine Street) offers wholesome, reasonably priced snacks, while other top tearooms include **Michael Snell** (8 St Thomas Square) and **Bernieres Tea Room** and **Mompesson House** (*see p136*) – both located in the Close. Picnickers heading for the Close or further afield can stock up first at the **Good Food Shop** (50 Winchester Street) or **Reeve the Bakers** (2 Butcher Row).

If you're looking for an authentic country pub, best to drive out west, deeper into Hardy Country, and enjoy the rural boozing idylls of **Chilmark**, **Tisbury**, **Chicksgrove** and **Ansty** (with its very own maypole), or try the pretty **Horseshoe Inn** in Ebbesbourne Wake.

Courtyard peace at the **Red Lion**. *See p139.*

Wiltshire & Bath

The **Chapter House** off the cloisters is particularly striking. Built immediately after the main church, and originally set aside as a meeting place for the cathedral clergy, it features fine geometric tracery in its tall windows and long, thin columns of Purbeck marble. These are beautifully carved with foliage designs and the odd bird nesting in the branches. Beneath this, the medieval frieze girdling the structure tells stories from the early books of the Bible. Aside from an impressive collection of church silverware, the Chapter House also contains one of the four surviving original copies of the Magna Carta – the contract drawn up between King John and his not very merry Barons in 1215. Although clearly enshrining their feudal rights, it is a comparatively progressive document for the period, making provision that widows shouldn't be forced to remarry and that a 'free man' could not be imprisoned without trial. Those were the days.

Salisbury Cathedral

The Close, Salisbury (01722 555120/ www.salisburycathedral.org.uk). **Open** *June-Aug* 7.15am-8.15pm Mon-Sat; 7.15am-6.15pm Sun. *Sept-May* 7.15am-6.15pm daily. **Admission** free; £3.50 suggested donation.

Asia

90 Fisherton Street, Salisbury (01722 327628). **Food served** noon-3pm, 5.30-11.45pm Mon-Fri, Sun; noon-midnight Sat. **Set lunch** £5.95 3 courses. **Set dinner** £29.95 for 2, 3 courses. **Credit** AmEx, MC, V.
An unexpected array of Indian specialities straddling the subcontinent's north-south divide. Dishes go a little bit off the chicken tikka massala piste with the likes of naryal duck, an exotic southern treat suffused with coconut, or kurzee lamb, a whole roasted leg for two (with 24 hours notice). All the food here is cooked with real care, giving it the nod ahead over the nearby **Rajpoot** (140 Fisherton Street; 01722 334795).

Barford Inn

Barford St Martin (01722 742242/ www.barfordinn.co.uk). **Food served** noon-2.30pm, 7-9.30pm Mon-Sat; noon-2.15pm, 7-9pm Sun. **Set meal** (Mon) £8 3 courses. **Credit** MC, V.
A characterful 16th-century former coaching inn 'five miles from Salisbury, yet right in the middle of countryside'. Sup Badger brews under beamed ceilings and enjoy great, genuinely appetising and imaginative food courtesy of head chef Gino Babord. Friday night is barbecue night. Accommodation is also available in the inn's annexe (double room £50-£55).

Haunch of Venison

1-5 Minster Street, Salisbury (01722 322024). **Food served** noon-2.30pm, 6.30-9.30pm Mon-Thur; noon-2.30pm, 6.30-10pm Fri, Sat; noon-2.30pm Sun. **Set lunch** £9.95 3 courses. **Credit** AmEx, MC, V.
After a bit of a dip last year, the new chef at the Haunch is busy restoring its reputation with the likes of Haunch Cobbler (venison stew with red onion mash, £7.95), or venison steaks (£14.95), although the menu does offer a wider range of dishes (fish and chicken are regulars) than the restaurant's name suggests. It's an original, Dickensian chop-house, with black wooden walls and floors every bit as crooked as Fagin. Have a drink at one of Britain's two remaining pewter bars, or squeeze into the minute nobs' snug halfway up the cramped spiral staircase. Beware the mummified hand of a card sharp in a hole in the wall.

LX1X

67-71 New Street, Salisbury (01722 340000). **Food served** noon-2.30pm, 7-10.30pm Mon-Sat. **Set lunch** £12-£16 2 courses. **Credit** AmEx, DC, MC, V.
You'll need to book ahead to sample the food in what is easily the best modern British restaurant in Wiltshire. But don't be intimidated by the menu – chef Rupert Willcocks and front-of-house manager Andrew Grigg are as friendly as they are creative. The good news is that they've now started up a bistro (Après LX1X) next door offering variations on their coveted menu at more amenable prices. Expect to pay anything from £20 to £35 for a three-course meal.

Old Mill Hotel

Town Path, Harnham (01722 327517/ www.oldenglishinns.co.uk). **Food served** noon-2.30pm, 7-9pm Mon-Sat; noon-7pm Sun. **Set meals** £9.95 2 courses; £11.95 3 courses Sun. **Credit** AmEx, MC, V.
Yes, it's an actual old mill and your final destination on that summer stroll out of Salisbury over the water-meadows. Not only is there a pleasant weir view to go with your pint, but any kids you may have spawned can amuse themselves on the banks of the River Nadder by netting tiny fish. Simple pleasures are also available in the form of pub lunches, while the plush adjoining restaurant offers more gastronomic delights (swordfish, fillet steak, mushroom casserole – main courses between £8 and £18). There are 11 bedrooms (doubles £80) in case you can't face leaving.

Bradford-on-Avon & Around

A medieval town, a 19th-century canal and the lions of Longleat.

Characterised by the terraced weavers' cottages that line up in ragged succession along a steep river valley, **Bradford-on-Avon** combines dramatic topography, historical charm and appealing architecture. It is often considered the most southerly town in the Cotswolds, and shares the same honey-coloured limestone with its counterparts in northern Wiltshire and Gloucestershire. However, Bradford avoids the chocolate-box effect by clinging resolutely to reminders of its industrial past.

The town dates back to prehistoric times, having sprung up naturally around a handy crossing point along the River Avon. The Iron Age settlement was developed and expanded in turn by Roman and Saxon settlers, both of whom left their mark on the town. One of the town's historical highlights is the tiny and atmospheric Saxon **Church of St Laurence** on Church Street.

The 'broad ford' was spanned in the 13th century by a stone town bridge, which still forms the centre of the town today. During the next few centuries Bradford grew to become a powerful centre for the woollen and cloth industries, its prosperity reflected in the size of the 14th-century **Tithe Barn** (located half a mile south of the town bridge).

Bradford's affluence reached a peak in the 17th century, as evidenced by the number of generously appointed merchants' houses surviving from that time. Weavers' cottages were built on the steep hillside north of the river and remain a defining feature of the town's architecture and appearance – the best examples are along Tory, Middle Rank and Newtown. With the arrival of mechanisation, the wool trade moved from individual houses to large mills, which can still be seen (in various degrees of restoration or disrepair) in the centre of town. After a steady decline, the wool trade had collapsed entirely by the 1840s, but the town reinvented itself as a rubber manufacturer almost immediately afterwards, and the mills were retooled to this end. The famous Moulton bicycle was produced in the town for several decades.

Today, Bradford is a bustling small town of cramped medieval streets and 21st-century traffic. With Bath only 15 minutes away by train or car (*see p148*), it makes an excellent base from which to explore the attractions of the surrounding area.

Along the Kennet & Avon Canal

Bradford lies on the route of the **Kennet & Avon Canal**, which links Bristol with the Thames at Reading. Opened in 1810, it was one of the most ambitious waterway projects ever undertaken in Britain, but by the 1840s it was all but superseded by the Great Western Railway, which runs parallel to it, as though in open mockery. The canal remained neglected until the 1980s, when its recreational potential finally sparked a massive, still on-going restoration plan.

With no steep gradients – apart from a famed series of 22 locks at Devizes (*see p155*) – and with leisurely barges comprising the only motor traffic, the canal towpath makes a very pleasant walking route, threading through some delightful woodland, country parks and 19th-century architecture. On the way to Bath (about three hours' walk from Bradford), you will cross several splendid aqueducts at **Avoncliff** and **Dundas**, and pass a Victorian water-powered pumping station at **Claverton**, not to mention plenty of waterside watering holes at Avoncliff, **Limpley Stoke**, Claverton and **Bathampton**. The towpaths are also popular with anglers and cyclists (*see p143* **Bike hire**). Canoes and self-drive day boats are also available, and the nearby **Bradford-on-Avon Wharf** (01225 868683) runs 1½-hour narrowboat trips from April to October. And if you'd like to stay afloat for longer, **Sally Boats** at Bradford-on-Avon Marina (A363 south of the town centre; 01225 864923) hires out live-in barges.

Further afield

Heading out of Bradford, tucked away in the Mendip Hills and the valleys of the Avon and Frome rivers, is a profusion of stately homes, gardens, prehistoric monoliths, medieval

Bradford's 13th-century **town bridge**.

castles and picturesque villages. Close by are the attractive gardens of **Iford Manor** and **The Courts**, while half an hour's drive south is **Longleat**, the home of the Marquis of Bath and a menagerie of animals.

Go east from Longleat towards Salisbury Plain and carved into the side of a hill overlooking the town of **Westbury**, and visible on a clear day from Bradford-on-Avon, is one of the oldest and largest white horses in the country. **Westbury White Horse** possibly dates back to the ninth century but has been recut and concreted since. There are great views and hang-gliding from the top of the hill, if the urge should take you. In the early '90s the fields below were the site of some of Wiltshire's most elaborate crop circles (fake or otherwise). Nearby is the Iron Age hill fort of **Bratton Castle** and the fortified 14th-century mansion **Edington Priory** (01380 830374). Every August a festival of church music is held here.

The area around **Westbury** and **Warminster** is particularly pleasant

countryside for walking and cycling, and includes the privately owned (but publicly accessible) ancient forest of **Brokerswood**.

What to see & do

Tourist Information Centres

34 Silver Street, Bradford-on-Avon, BA15 1JX (01225 865797/www.bradfordonavon.org.uk). **Open** *Apr-Christmas* 10am-5pm daily. *Jan-Mar* 10am-4pm daily. *Central Car Park, Warminster, BA12 9BT (01985 218548).* **Open** *Apr-Oct* 9.30am-5.30pm Mon-Sat. *Nov-Mar* 9.30am-4.30pm Mon-Sat.

Bike hire

Lock Inn Cottage, Frome Road, Bradford-on-Avon (01225 868068).
A five- to ten-minute walk from the station.

Courts Garden

Holt, nr Bradford-on-Avon (01225 782340/ www.nationaltrust.org.uk). **Open** *Apr-Oct* 1-5.30pm Mon-Fri, Sun. Out of season by appointment only. **Admission** (NT) £3.50; £1.50 concessions.
Seven acres of authentic English country garden run by the National Trust. Well maintained, with water features, yew hedges and unusual topiary.

Farleigh Hungerford Castle

Farleigh Hungerford (01225 754026/www.english-heritage.org.uk). **Open** *Apr-Sept* 10am-6pm daily. *Oct* 10am-5pm daily. *Nov-Mar* 10am-4pm Wed-Sun. **Admission** (EH) £2.30; £1.20-£1.70 concessions.
This large, semi-ruined castle in the Frome valley was once home to the Hungerford Lords, whose colourful deeds during the Middle Ages are explained in a free audio tour. There are battle re-enactments throughout the year (phone for details).

Iford Manor Garden

off A36, 8 miles SE of Bath (01225 863146/ www.ifordmanor.co.uk). **Open** *Apr, Oct* 2-5pm Sun, Easter Mon. *May-Sept* 2-5pm Tue-Thur, Sat, Sun, bank hol Mon. Closed Oct-Mar. **Admission** £3; £2.50 concessions; free under-10s (weekdays only).
The residence of 19th-century architect Harold Peto is famed for its award-winning Italianate gardens. Peto plundered classical artefacts and design ideas from across Europe, combining plants and architectural features to

By train from London

There are roughly three direct trains a day that run from **Waterloo** to **Bradford-on-Avon** (via **Warminster**), with a journey time of just under **2hrs**. Trains also leave from **Paddington** half-hourly, but passengers must change at **Bath Spa** or **Westbury**, with a 15-30min wait for connections. Journey time is about **2hrs** and **2hr 30mins** respectively.
Info: www.great-western-trains.co.uk and www.walesandwest.co.uk.

create his vision of the perfect garden. The result is enchanting. There is a festival of classical music, jazz and opera every year, from mid-June to mid-August (call 01225 868124/www.ifordarts.co.uk for details). Children under ten are not allowed in the garden at weekends.

Longleat

nr Warminster (01985 844400/www.longleat.co.uk). **Open** *House* Easter-Sept 10am-5.30pm daily. Oct-Easter guided tours only 11am-4pm daily. *Safari Park* Mar-Oct 10am-4pm Mon-Fri; 10am-5pm daily school hols, bank hols. Closed Nov-Feb. *Attractions* Mar-Oct 11am-5.30pm daily. Closed Nov-Feb. **Admission** £14; £11 concessions. *Safari Park only £7; £5 concessions.*

Lord Bath's home has amassed an ever-expanding roll-call of attractions over the years: safari park, cosmic-themed hedge mazes, *Dr Who* exhibition, *Postman Pat* village. Oh yes, there's a house here, too – an exquisite Elizabethan manor stacked with art treasures, historic exhibits and general relics of the aristocracy. Where there are attractions there are crowds, however, and on a hot summer weekend you may find yourself wishing you'd gone elsewhere. The 'Lion-Link' bus service collects visitors from Warminster.

Westwood Manor

Westwood, Bradford-on-Avon (01225 863374/ www.nationaltrust.org.uk). **Open** *Apr-Sept* 2-5pm Tue, Wed, Sun; by appointment at other times. **Admission** (NT) £3.80.

Two miles from Bradford in the village of Westwood, this 15th-century manor house was built by the Horton family, the first residents of Iford Manor (*see p143*). The original building was altered in the 17th century to add late Gothic and Jacobean features and fine plasterwork.

Where to stay

For a touch of luxury, try **Babington House**, at Babington, north-west of Frome (01373 812266/www.babingtonhouse.co.uk; doubles from £190) or beautiful **Bishopstrow House**, near Warminster (*see p146*). Other, more down-to-earth options include the **Georgian Lodge** in Bradford-on-Avon (*see p146*) and the **Woolpack** in Beckington (*see p146*), or **Dundas Lock Cottage** (01225 723890) at the intersection of two canals just off the main road to Bath. For a different kind of break, consider **Center Parcs Village** (08705 200300/www.centerparcs.com), a purpose-built holiday complex located in Longleat Forest.

Bay Tree House

48 St Margaret's Street, Bradford-on-Avon, BA15 1DE (01225 867861). **Rates** £50-£70 single/double occupancy. **Rooms** (2 en suite, 1 with private bathroom) 3 double. **No credit cards.**

Slap bang in the centre of town but surprisingly quiet inside, this guesthouse will be a welcome relief for visitors who are trying to avoid the chintz-on-chintz look. Each of the three tastefully decorated bedrooms has its own individual design and colour scheme: warm ochres in the Mediterranean room; fresh greens in the English room and cool blues in the Scandinavian room. The two larger rooms have luxurious en suite facilities with underfloor heating, while the smaller Scandinavian room has private use of an adjacent bathroom. Downstairs, guests can hang out in the cosy living room and chow down on hearty breakfasts in the dining room. Children welcome. No smoking throughout.

Bradford Old Windmill

4 Masons Lane, Bradford-on-Avon, BA15 1QN (01225 866842/fax 01225 866648/ www.distinctlydifferent.co.uk). **Rates** £69-£89 single occupancy; £79-£109 double. **Rooms** (all en suite) 3 double. **Credit** AmEx, MC, V.

This converted mill perched on the hillside overlooking the town is eccentric, very popular (book two to three months ahead) and rather overpriced. Exposed beams, mill-related ornaments, ethnic knick-knacks and folkie décor predominate to create a cluttered but unique atmosphere. The three rooms all have a character of their own: the cheapest, Damsel, features a waterbed and high conical ceiling; Great Spur has its own bed and a hanging wicker chair; and Fantail has its own lounge, plus a minstrels' gallery with a box bed for kids. There's a spacious circular lounge on the ground floor, too. Well-travelled owners Priscilla and Peter Roberts provide ethnic vegetarian evening meals (and carnivore-friendly breakfasts). No smoking throughout.

A363 S towards Bradford-on-Avon town centre; shortly after Castle pub turn left into private drive; house is the round building immediately before first roadside house (no sign or number).

Eagle House

Church Street, Bathford, nr Bath, BA1 7RS (01225 859947/fax 01225 859430/www.eaglehouse.co.uk). **Rates** £39-£52 single/single occupancy; £52-£82 double/cottage rooms. Breakfast (Eng) £3.40. **Rooms** (all en suite) 2 single; 4 double; 2 cottage rooms. **Credit** MC, V.

For a quintessentially English break, consider this beautiful, refined Georgian house designed by Bath planner John Wood the Elder and located in a charming conservation village. The elegant but unstuffy interiors include a large octagonal drawing room with marble fireplace overlooking the terraced garden (with grass tennis court). The six rooms in the house itself vary in size, with good views of the surrounding countryside. Even better is the self-contained two-bedroom cottage in the adjoining walled garden, which has its own kitchen and sitting room. Children and dogs welcome. No-smoking rooms available. Recommended.

A4 NE from Bath; after 3 miles turn right on to A363; after 100 yards take left fork into Bathford Hill; after 300 yards, take first right into Church Street; house on right after 200 yards.

Great Barn Maplecroft

Leigh Road West, Bradford-on-Avon, BA15 2RB (tel/fax 01225 868790/www.gbarn.co.uk). **Rates** £30-£35 single occupancy; £50-£65 double; £65 family room (sleeps 5) plus £10 per child, £15 per adult. **Rooms** (en suite) 2 double; 1 family. **No credit cards.**

The Great Barn is one of a cluster of redeveloped residential buildings on the edge of Bradford-on-Avon with delicious views of the surrounding countryside. Three

Step back in time among the weavers' cottages and alleyways of **Bradford-on-Avon**.

simple, modern ground-floor guest rooms have been converted from the shell of a 14th-century barn, retaining the original exposed beams and rustic decor to create a plain, unfussy, soothing environment. The accommodation is completely self-contained: the owners live in a beautifully converted house next door. Breakfast is served in an adjoining conservatory, and on summer evenings guests are encouraged to sit outside and enjoy the sunset. Children welcome. No smoking throughout.
From Bradford-on-Avon town centre, take B3109 N towards Chippenham. At traffic lights turn left on B3105, going W; after about ¼ mile, turn into a private drive on the right. The Great Barn is signposted.

Grey Lodge
Summer Lane, Combe Down, nr Bath, BA2 7EU (01225 832069/fax 01225 830161). **Rates** £35-£40 single occupancy; £60-£70 double/twin; £75-£105 family suite. **Rooms** (all en suite) 2 double/twin; 1 family suite. **No credit cards.**
This 19th-century house with well-maintained gardens feels like it's in the middle of nowhere but it's actually less than ten minutes' drive from either Bath or Bradford-on-Avon. The house enjoys beautiful views across the valley from the steep garden and the two back bedrooms, one of which has a small adjoining room with an extra single bed. The third room overlooks the front garden and road but is just as quiet. All three rooms are very comfortable, tasteful and well equipped. Above all, the owners are genuinely warm and accommodating. Children welcome. No smoking throughout.
A36 S from Bath; after 4 miles turn right up hill at traffic lights by Viaduct Inn; take first left to Monkton Combe; ½ mile after village, first house on left.

Priory Steps
Newtown, Bradford-on-Avon, BA15 1NQ (01225 862230/fax 01225 866248/www.priorysteps.co.uk). **Rates** £60 single occupancy; £36-£40 double per person. **Rooms** (all en suite) 2 twin; 3 double. **Credit** MC, V.

This pretty, family-run guesthouse has been converted from a terrace of 17th-century weavers' cottages a few minutes from the centre of town. The individually styled rooms have private, modern bathrooms, well-chosen antique furnishings and fine views across town and beyond. Healthy three-course set dinners (£21) are served every evening in the intimate dining room (book in advance); there's also a library and sunny terraced garden. Part of the Wolsey Lodge group. All bedrooms are no-smoking. Children welcome.
From centre of Bradford-on-Avon, take A363 N towards Bath; then second turning on the left signed to Turleigh; Priory Steps is third house on the left on this road.

Woolley Grange
Woolley Green, Bradford-on-Avon, BA15 1TX (01225 864705/fax 01225 864059/ www.woolleygrange.com). **Rates** £125-£165 small double; £195-£210 double; £225-£230 large double; £265 suite; £305-£315 interconnecting rooms. 10% reduction for single occupancy. **Rooms** (all en suite) 17 double; 3 suites; 3 pairs of interconnecting rooms. **Credit** AmEx, DC, MC, V.
If you've money to spare, this is the place to come for a good pampering. Woolley Grange is a beautiful ivy-covered Jacobean mansion with stone balustrades, set in some 15 acres of garden, with a heated swimming pool, tennis court and croquet lawn. Inside, there's plenty of period detailing (oak panelling, parquet floors) alongside refurbished areas. The hotel is family run and family orientated; kids can stay free in parents' rooms, and have their own nursery and games rooms in an outlying building, with childminders (10am-6pm daily). Rooms vary in size and location (some are in outbuildings), but all are beautifully furnished, well equipped, and offer luxury extras such as fresh fruit, newspapers, and even in-room massages (for a fee). The hotel has a very good restaurant, too (*see p146*). Children and dogs welcome. Recommended.
Woolley Grange is on B3109 about 5 minutes out of Bradford-on-Avon town centre.

Where to eat & drink

For upmarket dining, head into Bath (*see p148*) or treat yourself to the mouth-watering cuisine at the Mulberry Restaurant in **Bishopstrow House** (*see below*). Bradford has a handful of decent eateries, and there are plenty of fine pubs in the area. For teas (nearly 30 different types), coffees and home-made cream cakes sagging with richness, don't miss the **Bridge Tea Rooms** at 24A Bridge Street in Bradford (01225 865537), where you can expect to be served by staff in period costume.

Bradford is also well supplied with pubs. In the town centre, locals flock to the **Bunch of Grapes** (14 Silver Street; 01225 863877) and the **Dandy Lion** (35 Market Street; 01225 863433) for food, drink and a convivial atmosphere. In summer, walk east along the canal towpath to the **Beehive** (253 Trowbridge Road; 01225 863620) for excellent home-made pub grub (try the cheese pie), served by the best publican in the area. A pleasant walk in the other direction will bring you to the **Cross Guns** at Avoncliff (01225 862335), a hostelry that is hugely popular (read hideously packed) due to its enviable position right beside the aqueduct. Further afield, try the **George Inn** at Bathampton (01225 425079), the **Hop Pole** in Limpley Stoke (01225 723134) or the **Full Moon** in Rudge (01373 830936) for the best of local flavour – cuisine, ales and people.

Bishopstrow House

off B3414, Warminster (01985 212312).
Food served 11am-9.30pm daily. **Set dinner** £38 3 courses. **Credit** AmEx, DC, MC, V.
This Georgian house represents one of the best eating and accommodation options in the area. It combines a classic country-house setting and extensive grounds with a casual, friendly atmosphere. Modern luxuries include a state-of-the-art spa and a heated swimming pool. The Mulberry Restaurant turns out some excellent rich and rural food, with a touch of Mediterranean thrown in. Toasted goat's cheese or perfectly cooked scallops are typical starters, with roasts and fish dishes given a twist here and there. Ornate desserts complete the picture. Starters are around £8, mains £19, desserts £5. Bishopstrow House sells accommodation in two-night packages, which include dinner and breakfast, for £133 per person per night.

Georgian Lodge Hotel & Restaurant

25 Bridge Street, Bradford-on-Avon (01225 862268). **Food served** 7pm-late Mon; noon-2pm, 7pm-late Tue-Sun. **Credit** AmEx, DC, MC, V.
This former coaching inn overlooking the bridge is one of the best places to eat in town. The lower half of the split-level dining room is bright and simple, while the upper level has a more traditional white-tablecloth ambience. The menu tends towards strong Mediterranean flavours, but also takes in the local and the exotic, all to a consistently high standard. You can also choose from

the good selection of daily specials. Starters are about £4, mains £15, desserts £5. Unremarkable rooms are also available here (double £70-£90).

Thai Barn

24 Bridge Street, Bradford-on-Avon (01225 866443). **Food served** noon-2.30pm, 6-10.30pm Tue-Sun. **Set dinner** £17.95 2 courses. **Credit** MC, V.
Authentic Thai cuisine at affordable prices. Curries are especially good, as the pastes are made on the premises from fresh herbs and chillies. The interior is a spacious converted barn with high ceilings and a split-level dining area. Mains won't cost you more than a tenner, and there's a takeaway service available, too. Recommended.

Tollgate Inn

Holt, nr Bradford-on-Avon (01225 782326). **Food served** noon-2pm, 7-9pm Tue-Sat; noon-2.30pm Sun. **Set lunch** £9.95 2 courses. **Set meal** (Tue-Thur) £11.95 3 courses. **Credit** MC, V.
For posh nosh in a roadside inn, head to Holt, three miles east of Bradford. Flowers, candles and sofas soften up the surroundings in the bar, while upstairs in the no-smoking dining room good food is served chummily and attentively. Highlights include sea bass and crab and a rosy loin of venison on a king-sized bed of bubble and squeak. Expect to pay about £40 a head including wine.

Woolley Grange Hotel Restaurant

Woolley Green, Bradford-on-Avon (01225 864705/ www.woolleygrange.com). **Food served** noon-2pm, 7-9.30pm daily. **Set lunch** £15.50 2 courses; £20 3 courses. **Set dinner** £34.50 3 courses. **Credit** AmEx, DC, MC, V.
The restaurant at Woolley Grange serves the best of country-house cooking in an appropriately grand setting. The internal dining area is split into two rooms, plus an adjoining conservatory with a more casual tone. All serve the same menu, consisting of dishes such as veal with ceps, oxtail dumplings and shallot and port sauce, or roasted guinea fowl with prunes, brandy and pancetta. Aside from the set meals, the place is unsurprisingly pricey, with main courses going on for £20. Ingredients are as local as possible (including vegetables from the hotel's own garden). The wine list is extensive and the selection of desserts (£4.50) and cheeses sumptuous. For hotel accommodation, *see p145*.

Woolpack

Warminster Road, Beckington, nr Bath (01373 831244). **Food served** noon-2.30pm, 6.30-9.30pm Mon-Sat; noon-2.30pm, 7-9pm Sun. **Credit** AmEx, MC, V.
While under private ownership this 16th-century coaching inn established a strong local reputation for excellent cooking and attentive service, and little has changed now it is part of the Old English Inns chain. The menu majors on freshly prepared local ingredients and includes the likes of home-made cod and salmon sausages (£12.95), alongside classic starters (smoked salmon, prawn gravadlax and fennel marmalade) and desserts (chocolate and liqueur mousse). The airy bar area with its flagstone floor and large open fireplace is a good place for lunch; in the evening try the more formal surroundings of the restaurant or the garden room. Bed and breakfast is also available in 11 pleasant en suite rooms (£80 twin/double; £95 four-poster bedroom).

Footing the hill

This two-mile circular walk will take you to the best of Bradford-on-Avon's historic sights, many of which would be easy to miss on a stroll around town. Note that the walk involves narrow steps, steep gradients and some potentially muddy footpaths. It starts and finishes in St Margaret's Street car park, off the A363 in the centre of town.

Turn left out of the car park towards the Norman **town bridge**, which was widened and redeveloped in the 17th century, but has retained two of its original Gothic arches. The 17th-century improvements also added a small chapel halfway across the bridge, topped by a weather vane depicting a gudgeon. The chapel was later used as a prison for drunks and troublemakers: those who were locked up here were said to be 'under the fish and over the water'. Ahead of you are the façades of several former mills, some converted into luxury retirement flats, others in a state of near-dereliction.

On the other side of the bridge, turn left into the **Shambles**, a charming, tiny pedestrian shopping street. Stop off at **Ex Libris** bookshop (01225 863595), an excellent source of books about the area, and don't miss the second-hand book barn at the back.

At the end of the Shambles, cross Market Street in front of the 15th-century **Swan Hotel** and continue down Church Street, passing Abbey Mill on your left, and fine Georgian houses on your right. A right-hand kink in the road beside the river will bring you to the Norman **Holy Trinity Church** and the delightful **Saxon Church of St Laurence**, considered one of the most exquisite surviving examples of Saxon architecture in the country. Hidden for years among other buildings, and used as both a school and a private residence, it is mentioned in a 12th-century document by William of Malmesbury. Look out for the original stone angels keeping watch high up in the nave.

Continue along Church Street past tiny picture-postcard cottages until the road becomes a footpath. Climb the shallow steps past Barton Orchard, and take a hidden left turn into a narrow, flower-choked alleyway where the **Lady Well** spring bubbles up through the limestone. Turn right at the end of the alley and walk along Newtown, a road of tall weavers' cottages.

Turn left up Conigre Hill opposite Priory Steps guesthouse (*see p145*) and follow the steep road up the hill, taking the left fork on to Tory as the path divides. The paved footpath follows the contours of the hill, flanked by weavers' cottages on one side and tiny gardens on the other. At the far end is the **Chapel of St Mary Tory**, constructed in the Middle Ages as a pilgrimage stop on the route to Glastonbury.

Pause to admire the beautiful view over the town – on a clear day you can see as far as **Westbury White Horse** – then take the flight of steep steps back down to Newtown. Rejoin the shallow steps that lead back to Church Street and turn right on to Barton Orchard. The path will take you past more stone cottages before dipping down towards the railway. Cross the tracks and follow the muddy path towards a 14th-century **packhorse bridge** over the Avon that leads to **Barton Farm Country Park**.

This tract of land between the river and the towpath of the **Kennet & Avon Canal** is thronged with families, cyclists and fishermen on summer weekends. From the bridge you will be able to see the roof of the 14th-century **Tithe Barn**. Used to collect taxes in the form of produce and livestock for the nunnery at Shaftesbury, the barn is a vast vaulted space with a cathedral-like aura. The restored stone roof, made up of a series of graded tiles, is one of the largest in Europe. Around the barn are the stone farmhouse, granary and other outhouses that made up the medieval **Barton Farm**; many have now been converted into craft workshops and tearooms. Stop for a cream tea before concluding your walk along a wooded path under the railway, which skirts the river back into the centre of town. Pass Bradford swimming pool (01225 862970) and the Riverside pub, before emerging into St Margaret's Street car park.

Wiltshire & Bath

Bath

Hot springs and hot flushes.

The Romans were the first people to properly tap the waters of Britain's only hot springs, building a bathhouse which formed the gushing heart of Aquae Sulis. The Roman Baths flourished until the fifth century AD, and were finally excavated some 1,400 years later, actually missing out on Bath's Georgian heyday, when the nearby Cross Bath and Hot Bath were in use (*see p153* **Taking the plunge**).

Between-times, Edgar, the first king of England, was crowned at a Saxon monastery on the site of Bath Abbey in 973; the city's medieval menfolk were terrorised by Geoffrey Chaucer's earthy 'Wife of Bath', and the city saw Queen Elizabeth I slip out of her farthingale on a visit to the trendy Tudor bathing spa in the 1570s. In the 18th century, John Wood (first the elder, then the younger) constructed many of the city's landmark buildings and honey-stone streets, while the dandyish 'Beau' Nash presided over a burgeoning social scene. The Pump Room adjoining the baths dates back to the Georgian era – when it was indisputably the place to be seen – as does the luxurious arc of the Royal Crescent, the Circus, the Cross Bath and Hot Bath, the Assembly Rooms and Pulteney Bridge over the River Avon, one of only three shop-lined bridges in the world.

Literary spa-ing

Among the artists, writers and musicians inspired by Bath were Dickens, Scott, Gainsborough and Handel. London resident Daniel Defoe once said of the city: 'Bath is a spot of ground which our countrymen ought to esteem as a particular favour of heaven.' The city's most famous literary resident, however, was Jane Austen. 'Oh, who can ever be tired of Bath?' sighed the heroine of *Northanger Abbey*, echoing the sentiment of many a social butterfly who flitted from the Pump Room to the new Theatre Royal, between the promenades, balls and assemblies that confirmed the city as high society's favourite watering hole in the 1800s.

By train from London

Trains leave **Paddington** for **Bath Spa** approximately every half hour, taking **1hr 25mins**. Info: www.great-western-trains.co.uk.

Bask under the fan vaulting at **Bath Abbey**.

It wasn't until the 1880s that the cellars of the Pump Room finally gave up their secret of the Great Roman Bath and temple to Minerva, providing yet more ungodliness for Good Queen Victoria to contend with: she is said to have snapped shut the curtains of her carriage when she was being driven through the city, for fear of clapping eyes on half-naked bathers.

For throughout its 18th- and 19th-century prime, Bath was synonymous with sex, or rather with an escape into subtle resort-town decadence. This must have been why playwright and essayist Oliver Goldsmith claimed that: 'Scandal must have fixed her throne in Bath, preferable to any other part of the kingdom.' Even now that sexual contact routinely extends to more than fluttering eyelashes and heaving bosoms, this costume-drama city still acts as something of a romantic magnet, where couples stroll hand in hand through the very fabric of a glamorous past.

A visit today is a journey back in time. Summon up 18th-century dandy, gambler and

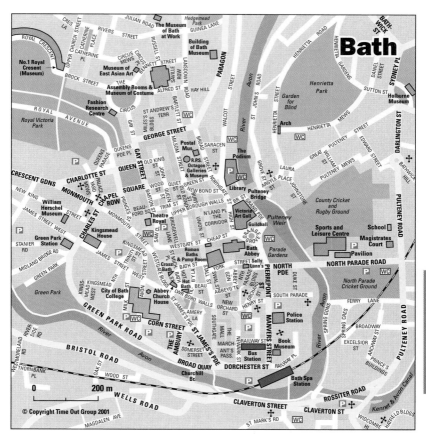

arbiter of fashion Richard 'Beau' Nash as your guide as you explore the Paragon. Window-shop for antiques and dusty tomes that mention your hotel. Try out the echo from the green in the middle of the Circus, and wonder at the throwaway fact that the constituent crescents have a diameter exactly matching that of Stonehenge. Gaze into the hypnotic horseshoe weir set before Robert Adam's Pulteney Bridge. Gourmandise. Quaff. Dip a toe into a splendid living museum. Immerse yourself in Bath.

Boredom is not likely to be a problem in Bath; the city is packed with museums (around 20), most of them excellent. And if the weather is fine, hire a boat at the Victorian **Bath Boating Station** (Forester Road; 01225 466407) or a bike.

Tourist Information Centre

Abbey Chambers, Abbey Churchyard (01225 477101/www.visitbath.co.uk). **Open** *Oct-Apr* 9.30am-5pm Mon-Sat; 10am-4pm Sun. *May-Sept* 9.30am-6pm Mon-Sat; 10am-4pm Sun.

Bike hire

Avon Valley Cyclery *behind Bath Spa Station (01225 446267).*
The Bristol and Bath railway path, part of the Avon cycleway, is a particularly pleasant way to enjoy a traffic-free day. Maps are available on request.

American Museum & Gardens

Claverton Manor (01225 460503/ www.americanmuseum.org). **Open** *Museum* Apr-July, Sept-mid Dec 2-5pm Tue-Sun. Aug 2-5pm daily. Closed 2wks Nov, mid Dec-Mar. *Gardens* Sept-July 1-6pm Tue-Fri; noon-6pm Sat, Sun. Aug 1-6pm Mon-Fri; noon-6pm Sat, Sun. **Admission** *Museum and gardens* £6; £3.50-£5.50 concessions.

Admire the curve of the **Royal Crescent**.

Taking you from 17th-century colonial times through to the beginning of the US Civil War in the 19th century, the reconstructed historical domestic interiors are fascinating, with exhibits including Shaker furniture and traditional quilts. The grounds include a colonial herb garden, a replica of George Washington's garden in Virginia, an arboretum and a teepee. The museum also hosts special events including wartime (Civil, French and American Indian) re-enactments and Independence Day celebrations. Bus 18 runs from Bath bus station to a bus stop at the Avenue, ten minutes' walk from the museum.

Bath Abbey
Abbey Churchyard (01225 422462/
www.bathabbey.org). **Open** *Easter-Oct* 9am-6pm Mon-Sat. *Nov-Easter* 9am-4.30pm Mon-Sat.
Admission free; donations appreciated.
Vaults £2; £1 concessions.
Above the great west door of the Abbey is a Latin inscription, which translates as: 'Behold, how good and pleasing it is.' How true. Bath Abbey dates back to the 15th century, although it incorporates parts of a once-massive Norman predecessor, and was the last Tudor church to be built prior to the Reformation. It suffered at the hands of Henry VIII, but Elizabeth I ensured its reconstruction and called it 'the Lantern of the West'. Enjoy the heavenly colours and spectacular fan vaulting, and explore the site's 1,600-year history in the 18th-century cellars.

Bath Boating Station
Forester Road (01225 466407). **Open** *Easter-Sept* 10am-6pm daily (weather permitting). Closed Oct-Easter. **Admission** £4.50 per person for 1st hour

(£1.50 per hour thereafter); £2.25 concessions (75p per hour thereafter); £6 all-day student ticket. Hire a punt, skiff or canoe from this unique Victorian boating station with tea gardens, ten minutes' walk from the city centre.

Bath Postal Museum
8 Broad Street (01225 460333/
www.bathpostalmuseum.org). **Open** 11am-5pm Mon-Sat. **Admission** £2.90; £1.50-£2.20 concessions; free under-5s.
The world's first stamp, the Penny Black, was posted here in 1840. The museum includes a re-created Victorian post office, kids' activity room, film room, tearoom and exhibits on the history of written communication from 2000 BC.

Building of Bath Museum
The Countess of Huntingdon's Chapel, the Vineyards (01225 333895/www.bath-preservation-trust.org.uk). **Open** *mid Feb-Nov* 10.30am-5pm Tue-Sun. Closed Dec-mid Feb. **Admission** £4; £1.50-£3 concessions.
Intelligent and witty, this exposition of how the World Heritage site of Bath came into being and how its buildings were designed and used has a spectacular model of the city as its centrepiece.

Holburne Museum of Art
Great Pulteney Street (01225 466669/
www.bath.ac.uk/holburne). **Open** *Feb-mid Dec* 10am-5pm Tue-Sat; 2.30-5.30pm Sun. Closed mid Dec-Jan. **Admission** £3.50; £1.50-£3 concessions.
Stunning displays of silverwork, porcelain and glass presented alongside paintings by the likes of Turner, Gainsborough and Stubbs. Jane Austen lived opposite, at 4 Sydney Place, between 1801 and 1804.

Museum of Bath at Work
Bath Industrial Heritage Centre, Julian Road (01225 318348). **Open** *Apr-Oct* 10am-5pm daily. *Nov-Mar* 10am-5pm Sat, Sun. **Admission** £3.50; £2.50 concessions.
This rechristened and expanded museum (it was formerly Mr Bowler's Business) has exhibits on 'work' themes including cabinet making and the story of Bath stone. One hundred years' worth of collected ephemera from a Bath bottled-water firm provides added insight and entertainment.

Museum of Costume & Assembly Rooms
Bennett Street (01225 477789/
www.museumofcostume.co.uk). **Open** 10am-5pm daily. Last entry 4.30pm. **Admission** £4.20; £3-£3.75 concessions.
Four hundred years of costume are presented in an eye-opening, benchmark collection of bustles, paniers and pantaloons. The earliest complete costume in the museum is a formal cream silk dress woven with silver thread from the 1660s – a very rare survival.

Museum of East Asian Art
12 Bennett Street (01225 464640/www.east-asian-art.co.uk). **Open** 10am-5pm Tue-Sat; noon-5pm Sun. **Admission** £3.50, £1-£3 concessions.

This extensive collection of oriental fine and applied art features treasures from China, Mongolia, Japan, Korea, Thailand and Tibet, dating from 5000 BC right up to the present day.

No.1 Royal Crescent

1 Royal Crescent (01225 428126/338727/ www.bath-preservation-trust.org.uk). **Open** *mid Feb-Oct* 10.30am-5pm Tue-Sun. *Nov* 10.30am-4pm Tue-Sun. Last entry 30mins before closing. Closed Dec-mid Feb. **Admission** £4; £3 concessions. The corner townhouse in John Wood's famous crescent, designated a World Heritage Building, is restored, redecorated and furnished to appear as it might have done when it was built in 1786.

Prior Park Landscape Garden

Ralph Allen Drive (01225 833422/info line 09001 335242/www.nationaltrust.org.uk). **Open** *Easter-Sept* 11am-5.30pm Mon, Wed-Sun. *Oct, Nov* noon-dusk Mon, Wed-Sun. *Feb-Easter* noon-5.30pm or dusk Mon, Wed-Sun. **Admission** (NT) £4; £2-£3 concessions. This hilltop 18th-century garden was built by one of Bath's founding fathers, Ralph Allen (with advice from 'Capability' Brown and poet Alexander Pope). There are lakes and a grand Palladian bridge, and excellent views over Bath and the area. No parking on the site.

Roman Baths

Abbey Church Yard (01225 477785/ www.romanbaths.co.uk). **Open** *Jan, Feb, Nov, Dec* 9.30am-5.30pm daily. *Mar-June, Sept, Oct* 9am-6pm daily. *July, Aug* 9am-10pm daily. **Admission** £7.50; £4.20-£6.50 concessions; free under-6s. An excellent handset-guided tour takes you around the steamy bowels of the Roman Baths. Apart from the photogenic Great Bath, there are surprising complexes of indoor baths, the Minerva temple and bubbling King's Bath source. Great collections of temple sculpture, jewellery, pottery, wishing-spa coins and curses. A must-see.

Sally Lunn's Refreshment House & Museum

4 North Parade Passage (01225 461634/ www.sallylunns.co.uk). **Open** *Restaurant* 10am-10pm Mon-Sat; 11am-10pm Sun. *Museum* 10am-6pm Mon-Sat; 11am-6pm Sun. **Admission** *Museum* 30p; free under-16s, OAPs, students. This is the oldest house in Bath, dating back to the 12th century, when it formed part of a large monastic estate, and it is said to be haunted by the ghost of a Benedictine monk who chants his prayers in the early hours of the morning. Sally Lunn baked her first Bath bun here in the 1680s, and they're still on sale today – along with an entire Lunn-related museum in the refreshment rooms.

Victoria Art Gallery

Bridge Street (01225 477233/www.victoriagal.org.uk). **Open** 10am-5.30pm Tue-Fri; 10am-5pm Sat; 2-5pm Sun. **Admission** free. Bath and North-East Somerset's excellent gallery houses a permanent collection of British and European art from the 15th century right up to the present day, plus temporary exhibitions.

William Herschel Museum

19 New King Street (01225 311342/www.bath-preservation-trust.org.uk). **Open** *Mar-Oct* 2-5pm daily. *Nov-Feb* 2-5pm Sat, Sun. **Admission** £3.50; £2 concessions. Here's the very house where the great astronomer discovered Uranus in 1781. No giggling at the back, thank you.

Where to stay

Unlike the other towns and cities in the region, there are no pubs offering a good standard of accommodation anywhere in the centre of Bath. The genteel evolution of the city has given rise to three options: a classy hotel near the centre,

There are exciting prospects for the **Bath Spa Project**.

an almost as classy guesthouse perched somewhere up on the rim of the bowl enveloping the golden city (try **Haydon House** 9 Bloomfield Park; 01225 44919/ www.haydonhouse.co.uk), or a genteel bed and breakfast a couple of miles out of town such as the **Eagle House** in Bathford (*see p144*), or its near neighbour the **Lodge** (*see below*). A fourth option is the **Bath Priory Hotel** (01225 331922/www.thebathpriory.co.uk), which, at £230-£320 a night, is a place you should really stay when the weather is so appalling that you can justify staying in the complimentary spa health club all day.

Apsley House Hotel

141 Newbridge Hill, BA1 3PT (01225 336966/ fax 01225 425462/www.apsley-house.co.uk). **Rates** £60-£85 single occupancy; £75-£98 double/twin; £85-£130 four-poster; £95-£130 triple/family room; £15 additional person. **Rooms** (all en suite) 8 double/twin; 1 four-poster. **Credit** AmEx, MC, V.
David and Annie Lanz's stunning country house was built for the Duke of Wellington in 1830 and is backed by beautiful gardens. Although it's located in a residential area 20 minutes' stroll from Bath centre, Newbridge Hill is a main throughfare, so you'd be wise to ask for a bedroom at the rear. Inside, many original period features remain and it is adorned with oil paintings and antiques, but the atmosphere is that of a family home rather than a hotel. Children over five welcome. No-smoking rooms available.
1½ miles west of city centre; on Newbridge Hill off Newbridge Road (A4).

Harington's Hotel

8-10 Queen Street, BA1 1HE (01225 461728/fax 01225 444804/www.haringtonshotel.co.uk). **Rates** £65-£88 single occupancy; £88-£108 double; £98-£118 twin; £118-£138 triple. **Rooms** (all en suite) 10 double; 2 twin; 1 triple. **Credit** AmEx, DC, MC, V.
Probably the best value of all the central hotels, Harington's really is smack in the middle of things – only 100 yards from the main shopping street and near a number of restaurants and bars. Unfortunately there is no adjacent parking space, so guests have to unload on the narrow, cobbled Queen Street, and then go around to Charlotte Street car park (£5 per 24 hours), five minutes' walk away. All rooms have a TV and kettle, but smokers are allowed to spark up only in the downstairs coffee lounge/bar. Children welcome.

Holly Lodge

8 Upper Oldfield Park, BA2 3JZ (01225 424042/ fax 01225 481138/www.hollylodge.co.uk). **Rates** £48-£55 single; £79-£97 double/twin; £87-£97 four-poster; £25 extra person. **Rooms** (all en suite) 1 single; 4 double/twin; 2 four-poster. **Credit** AmEx, DC, MC, V.
This Victorian townhouse is resplendent with glass chandeliers, swagged curtains and antique furniture. Owner George Hall, who totally revamped the place after taking it over in the late '80s, is only too pleased to help or just chat. Outside there is a floodlit gazebo and statue-strewn terraced garden to enjoy when weather permits. Breakfast is served in the conservatory. Ask

for a room with a view when booking here, as Holly Lodge is perched high above the city. Children welcome. No smoking throughout.
Take A367 Wells Road south of centre; up hill, first right into Upper Oldfield Park; 100 yards on right.

Lodge Hotel

Bathford Hill, Bathford, BA1 7SL (01225 858575/fax 01225 858172/ www.lodgehotelbath.co.uk). **Rates** £65 single occupancy; £65-£110 double/twin. **Rooms** (all en suite) 6 double/twin. **Credit** MC, V.
Just out of town to the east, Mary and Keith Johnson have a refreshingly down-to-earth approach to running their country hotel, including encouraging guests to help themselves to sherry in the small lounge. The six rooms are decked out in florals, with original shutters to ensure a sound night's sleep. A healthy as-much-as-you-can-eat breakfast is served in the ground-floor dining room, which is adorned with plenty of interesting conversation pieces. From May to October there is an open-air swimming pool in the three-acre garden. The Johnsons also offer a pick-up service from the airport or train station, and daily hire of the family narrowboat moored on the Kennet and Avon canal. Children are welcome and pets are admitted with prior permission.
Exit J18 from M4; follow A46 to end of dual carriageway; follow Chippenham signs; at island at end of dual carriageway come off at the right railway arch; from there you will see the Crown Inn; hotel is next door.

Queensberry Hotel

Russell Street, BA1 2QF (01225 447928/fax 01225 446065/www.bathqueensberry.com). **Rates** £100-£120 single occupancy; £120-£185 double/twin; £210 four-poster. Breakfast £9.50 (Eng). **Rooms** (all en suite) 28 double/twin; 1 four-poster. **Credit** MC, V.
If you really want to live it up when you come to Bath, there are few better ways to do it than to stay here. The Queensberry is laid out over four adjacent Regency townhouses, purchased gradually over the years by Stephen and Penny Ross. The grandest rooms are what were formerly drawing rooms at the front of the houses, while back rooms offer a view. Prices and ceiling heights descend the higher up the hotel you stay. The four-poster room offers a huge en suite to die for, with a free-standing cast-iron bath, handpainted with fish. The hotel's Olive Tree restaurant (*see p154*) is highly acclaimed, and the courtyard gardens at the rear are especially popular for drinks on summer evenings. Children welcome. All bedrooms no-smoking.

Royal Crescent

16 Royal Crescent, BA1 2LS (01225 823333/0800 980 0987/fax 01225 339401/0800 980 0876/ www.royalcrescent.co.uk). **Rates** £220 single occupancy/double/twin; £320 deluxe double/twin; £420-£560 four-poster suites; £800 Sir Percy Blakeney suite. Breakfast £17.50 (Eng); £14.50 (cont). **Rooms** (all en suite) 13 double/twin; 16 deluxe double/twin; 4 four-poster suites; 12 suites. **Credit** AmEx, DC, MC, V.
One should expect nothing but the best from the hotel with possibly the best address in Britain, slap bang in the centre of the 'world's finest crescent'. Take your aperitif as you knock about on the immaculate croquet lawns, or bliss out in the Roman-style Bath House.

Taking the plunge

Considering that bathing is the one activity that has brought visitors to Bath throughout the city's long, long history, it seems rather unfair that tourists have been denied the experience for more than 20 years. And, considering that Bath's natural spring waters have been used for healing purposes ever since Bladud, the city's founder, is said to have cured his leprosy in the waters here, it is especially ironic that public health concerns were the reason for the closure of the bathing facilities in the late 1970s.

During the 1980s and '90s, numerous attempts were made by the local council and businesses to reopen the baths, but costs proved prohibitive. Then, in 1997, the Millennium Commission agreed to pump a grant of £7.78 million into the project. The grant was given with the intention that Bath should set an example to Britain's other spa towns in reviving spa culture.

The grand opening of 'Europe's most remarkable new spa' is scheduled for 2002. The whole project has involved the refurbishment of five listed buildings as well as the construction of a contemporary four-storey spa complex.

Two of the restorations are the **Hot Bath** and the **Cross Bath**. The Hot Bath building, designed by John Wood in 1775, is adjacent to the new spa complex. It has been used as a modern art gallery for a number of years, but plans for its future include a restaurant and 12 treatment rooms plus an octagonal pool, making it the place to go for a massage or specialist water therapy.

Just across the road from this is the Cross Bath, whose oval pool and oval roof have been completely renovated. It is intended that it will function primarily as a swimming pool for Bath residents.

The grand new spa complex is being built on Beau Street in golden Bath stone, surrounded by glass and steel cladding. We are promised a steaming Turkish bath-style pool with huge columns rising out of it, towers and terraces, steam rooms and whirlpools, all culminating in a rooftop pool, giving views across the city skyline to the surrounding countryside.

What a shame the opening is planned for autumnal October.

The Bath Spa Project

9-10 Bath Street, BA1 1SN (01225 477710/www.bathspa.co.uk).

Alternatively take advantage of the unique hotel facility of a 1923 river launch and hot-air balloon. Obviously it will set you back a bit, but once you've come this far, who's counting? Children and dogs are welcome, and no-smoking rooms are available.

Where to eat & drink

Thought to have more restaurants per capita in the UK than any other city outside London, Bath offers plenty of choice between the premium, Georgian-housed award-winners and the less lavish. Some of the best are included below, but there are plenty of others worth a mention. If price is no object, head for the **Dower House Restaurant** at the Royal Crescent hotel (*see p152*) or the excellent **Bath Priory** hotel (Weston Road; 01225 331922). Otherwise, the wine bar/bistro **Moon & Sixpence** (6A Broad Street; 01225 460962) and the **Circus** (34 Brock Street; 01225 318918) are more moderate. For an authentic French experience, try **Le Clos** (1 Seven Dials, Saw Close; 01225 444450). The

vibrant **Fishworks** (6 Green Street; 01225 448707) serves up the fish caught fresh by its own Cornish boat.

Perhaps unexpectedly, Bath is a city that's fairly hot on Indian/Asian food: the **Rajpoot** (4 Argyle Street; 01225 466833) is a cut above, the **Eastern Eye** (8A Quiet Street; 01225 422323) is cartoon opulent beneath its Georgian ceiling, but good fun, while **Mai Thai** (6 Pierrepoint Street; 01225 445557) deserves its good reputation.

Pub-wise, you're spoilt for choice: for starters, check out the **Bell** at 103 Walcot Street, which has excellent live music and cracking real ales, the **Star** (23 Vineyards), the **Pig & Fiddle** (2 Saracen Street), and the **Cross Keys** (corner of Midford Road and Southstoke Road; 01225 832002 – garden and aviary, good for kids). A definite must is the tiny **Old Green Tree** (12 Green Street), whose hand-pumped RCH Pitchfork, Bath Spa and Brand Oak are all worth trying. For somewhere a little out of town visit the canalside **George Inn** in Mill Lane, Bathampton, or consult the Bradford-on-Avon chapter (*see p142*).

Demuths

2 North Parade Passage, off Abbey Green (01225 446059/www.demuths.co.uk). **Food served** 10am-5.30pm, 6-10pm Mon-Fri, Sun; 9am-5.30pm, 6-11pm Sat. **Credit** AmEx, MC, V.

The slogan 'positively vegetarian' should give you some idea what Demuths is about: no fish, flesh, fowl or genetically modified food, and a promise to cater to those with special diets or food allergies. Owners Rachel Demuth and Nicho Troupe travel the globe exploring new cooking techniques to bring home and apply creatively to their restaurant, cookery school and books. Exemplary main courses include yetakelt w'et (lunch £6.95), a spicy Ethiopian mixed vegetable platter with fruit and nut pilaf and basil yoghurt, and a delicious tempeh temptation wrap (lunch £5.95). There are also menus for children (pizza fingers, sandwiches and toasties), evening appetisers (nachos, boridas) and a breakfast menu served until 11.45am. Even if you only fancy a coffee, come here for a unique view of Georgian architect Ralph Allen's house through the rear window.

Hullaballoos

36 Broad Street (01225 443323/ www.hullaballoos.co.uk). **Food served** noon-2.15pm, 6-10.15pm Tue-Sat. **Set lunch** £7.99 2 courses; £10.99 3 courses. **Set dinner** £15 3 courses. **Credit** AmEx, DC, MC, V.

While its name suggests a young, boisterous establishment, Hullaballoos is actually pretty calm and relaxed. The menu is straightforward and prices are pretty reasonable – starters include wild mushroom risotto (£3.70) or deep-fried Camembert with orange and onion marmalade; main courses are the likes of braised lamb steak with tomato, olive and rosemary sauce (£12.95) or couscous with fried tomato, chickpea and halloumi cheese. Although the place has an alcohol licence, you can bring your own wine.

Jamuna

9-10 High Street (01225 464631). **Food served** noon-2.30pm, 6pm-midnight daily. **Set meals** £11.95, £16.50, £17.50 (all 4 courses). **Credit** AmEx, MC, V.

Less ostentatious than some local Indian restaurants, the ever-popular Jamuna is the pick of the bunch. Established restaurant favourites such as roghan josh, methi dopiaza or fish massala (each £5.75) or the delicately spiced king prawn masala (£10.95) are joined on the menu by more unusual dishes such as the Goan speciality xacutti lamb or chicken (£6.95) – cooked with peanuts, egg yolk, coconut and fearsome chillies. The restaurant's bright, crescent-shaped dining room is on the first floor, with views of the Abbey opposite.

Restaurant Lettonie

35 Kelston Road (01225 446676/www.lettonie.co.uk). **Food served** noon-2pm, 7-9pm Tue-Fri; noon-2pm, 7-9.30pm Sat. **Set lunch** £15 2 courses; £25 3 courses. **Set dinner** £47.50 3 courses. **Credit** AmEx, DC, MC, V.

With two Michelin stars, this restaurant is a confident, virtuoso affair. In a spacious Georgian house, head chef Martin Blunos creates the classiest of French dishes with distinctive Latvian touches. They include the likes of roast breast of Gressingham duck on spätzle with apples and a calvados cream sauce, or, for a supplement of £16 to the set menu, a starter of scrambled duck egg topped

Drink to the glory of the **Pump Room**.

with Beluga caviar served with blinis and a glass of vodka. If you're a strict vegetarian, you may find yourself stuck, but non-smokers will love the no-smoking dining room. The restaurant also has accommodation attached (doubles £95-£150).

Moody Goose

7A Kingsmead Square (01225 466688/www.moody-goose.com). **Food served** noon-2pm, 6-9.30pm Mon-Thur; noon-2pm, 6-10pm Fri, Sat. **Set lunch** £12 2 courses; £16 3 courses. **Set dinner** £23 3 courses. **Credit** AmEx, DC, MC, V.

A stone's throw from the Theatre Royal, the Moody Goose is held in high esteem by fans of modern British cuisine. Fresh, local ingredients are key here: we chose a rich cream of butterbean soup with Cheddar cheese gnocchi followed by pan-fried fillet of bream with roasted artichokes, shallots and thyme. Dessert was an impossibility, although the temptation of fresh rhubarb cheesecake was hard to resist. Eat in the airy basement restaurant or more intimately in the small, vaulted dining room. Main courses are around £18.

Olive Tree

Queensberry Hotel, Russell Street (01225 447928/ www.bathqueensberry.com). **Food served** noon-2pm, 7-10pm Mon-Thur; noon-2pm, 6.45-10pm Fri, Sat; 7-9pm Sun. **Set lunch** £13.50 2 courses; £15.50 3 courses. **Set dinner** £26 3 courses. **Credit** MC, V.

The Queensberry's restaurant is quite independent from the hotel (*see p152*), but has just as strong a reputation, as it continues to serve up the best of contemporary fare. Our choices were typical: a starter of rocket and cheddar gnocchi (£6.25) was perfectly light, leaving room enough for a tasty slow roast pavé of Glenarm salmon served with celeriac roulade and sauce verte (£16.75). In 1996 the *Times* declared this 'the best place to eat in Bath', and while the competition has certainly hotted up since then, the Olive Tree has moved with the times and still merits a place among the city's finest restaurants.

Pump Room

Abbey Church Yard (01225 444477/ www.milburn.co.uk). **Food served** *Jan-June, Sept-Nov* 9.30am-4.30pm daily. *July, Aug* 9.30am-4.30pm, 5.30-8.45pm daily. *Dec* 9.30am-4.30pm, 7-10.30pm daily. **Set lunch** £10.95 2 courses; £12.95 3 courses. **Credit** AmEx, MC, V.

Something of a Bath institution, the Pump Room is an obligatory stop for afternoon tea between a trip to the Abbey and the adjacent Roman Baths. There's also a morning menu consisting of continental breakfast, brunch or elevenses, and a slightly more substantial lunch menu ; we tried mouthwatering venison sausages with cider, apple and juniper sauce and parsnip purée (£8.75) and somewhat lighter salmon fishcakes with parsley sauce and celeriac gratin.

Chippenham to Avebury

Neolithic sites, villages in aspic – come to Marlborough country.

Odd circles crop up in **Wiltshire**.

Wiltshire & Bath

Marlborough is a natural stop within this region, and a good base from which to strike out west to explore the Marlborough Downs' unsurpassable trove of neolithic wonders, the area's market towns, historic houses and the deep Wiltshire countryside dotted with delicious limestone hamlets.

Built on the slopes of the River Kennet's valley, Marlborough has a wide, attractive high street lined with coaching inns and colonnaded Georgian buildings, now largely given over to establishments of the tweely named and touristy variety. Despite all claims to be a magickal celebrity gravesite ('Merlin's barrow'), the town in fact takes its name from the chalk mound ('marl'), which has lain neglected over the centuries, and now sits topped by a water tower in the grounds of Marlborough College.

Once upon a time...

To the west lies the gentle but often dramatic skein of the Marlborough Downs. From Hackpen Hill the A361 slices through the village and famous standing stones of **Avebury** circle. Other ancient-world stars are **Silbury Hill** (Bronze Age, 2700 BC), one of the largest man-made prehistoric mounds in

Europe, and **West Kennett Long Barrow**, one of Britain's largest neolithic burial tombs. This is the epicentre of neolithic Britain, a suggestively curvy and cleft landscape rich with temples to the fecundity of the earth itself. If any one of a hundred neolithic sites on the Downs were transported elsewhere in the country, they would be huge draws in their own right. Here, it's all too easy to succumb to barrow-, circle-, stone- and dolmen-fatigue, and take for granted the near-miracle of these landmarks' creation and survival (*see p159* **Pagan pastures**).

Heading west on the A4 towards Bath (*see p148*), the ancient gives way to the merely old – historic houses like **Dyrham Park**, **Corsham Court**, stunning **Bowood** and settlements

By train from London

Trains to **Chippenham** leave **Paddington** about every half an hour (journey time **1hr 13mins**), passing through **Reading** and **Swindon**. Info: www.greatwesterntrains.co.uk.

created by wool wealth in the 17th and 18th centuries. White horses, dating to the 19th century, abound: **Cherhill**, on the site of Oldbury Castle, an Iron Age hillfort, is a good example – its four-foot-wide eye was once filled with upturned bottles giving it a winking sparkle until souvenir hunters robbed it of its twinkle. This is pig-rearing country, centred around **Calne**, which had its day in 1864 when the former Harris bacon factory became the first to use the principle of bacon curing. Nearby **Chippenham** is a market town that holds more historical than contemporary interest – King Alfred sited his hunting lodge here, on a site that's now at the heart of a ring-road system. It's worth taking the time to penetrate it for a stroll round the market on Friday and Saturday mornings.

The western wedge of this area is the most attractive – all leafy, curvy, sexy, secret ups and downs. **Corsham**, founded on stone and cloth, is a historic treasure. Investigate the high street, with houses dating back to 1540, the finest almshouses in the country on Pound Pill, and the only shaft stone mine in the world to be open to the public. The Hare & Hounds was once the residence of Moses Pickwick, Dickens' inspiration for *The Pickwick Papers*.

Chocolate-box country

The village at **Castle Combe** is for many people the prettiest chocolate-box lid in the land. It certainly has all the right elements – tinkling riverside setting, turreted church and serried gorgeous cottages, but it can get very crowded with tourists. A palpable atmosphere of unreality surrounds this tiny toytown where every hedge is viciously clipped, every bridge half-remembered from the cover of *People's Friend*, every swan seemingly scrubbed whiter than white. Less famous, and hence less crowded villages such as **Nettleton**, **West Kington** and **Biddestone** (home of Starfall pottery) are also well worth a gander.

A short drive to the south, the abbey village of **Lacock** also finds itself strangely frozen in time: as coincidence would have it, it was here that Fox Talbot invented photography, and of course a museum exists to capture the moment perfectly. The influence of the abbey and old wool money very nearly prevented the 19th and 20th centuries happening in this grid of four superb sandstone and lichen streets. It's amazing to think that people actually live in this feudal village, and that they assume it's quite normal for second-storey windows to open virtually at eye-level; for 700-year-old barns to stand on street corners, and for bread and pastries to taste uniformly as good as the fare at the Lacock Bakery.

Twenty-nine and counting – **Caen Hill** locks.

Devizes

Dipping south again, the countryside irons itself out towards the Vale of Pewsey, the Kennet and Avon Canal and **Devizes**. There are 500 listed buildings in Devizes, and a healthy proportion of them are Wadworth pubs fuelled by the rambling Victorian brewery that looms over the western entrance to the semicircular Market Place. Presiding over the square from atop the (converted) Corn Exchange, Ceres, god of agriculture, looks down in bafflement as traffic pours into town for Friday night, heading for the pubs, the groovy restored art deco Palace cinema and the revamped Wharfside. The town also boasts crafty shops, a good little theatre, and a private Victorian folly that would like to be known as a castle. Just in case you visit the fine museum and hear about the time when the town boasted 'the finest castle in Europe', this isn't it. Just outside the town is the famous **Caen Hill** flight of 29 locks, the longest in the country. If you are completely smitten by the romance of the canal, you can 'adopt' a section of it (contact the Kennet & Avon Canal Trust; 01380 721279); but boat trips and canal holidays are perhaps the most relaxing way to take in this laid-back region (White Horse Boats, 8 Southgate Close, Pans Lane, Devizes; 01380 728504). Following the canal and the A365 west you come to **Melksham**, once a centre for the weaving trade, which also basks in past glory, with its smattering of 17th- and 18th-century merchants' houses.

By foot and by bike

Barging aside, there's good walking country all over the region, with many great pathways to latch on to, including the **Ridgeway**, the **Macmillan Way** and the **Cotswold Way**. The **Savernake Forest**, just east of Marlborough, is an ancient hunting forest more recently sculpted with superb beech-lined paths that emanate from a central hub. For bikers, the **Wiltshire Cycleways** have some fantastic routes, notably Corsham to Great Bedwyn (about 41 miles in total). If you don't fancy the exercise, take a lazy drive; there are plenty of lanes to explore: try around **Bowden Hill** from the A342 to **Lacock** (part of the old route taken by Pepys and others from London to Bath) and from the A4 at **Box**, taking in the divine village of **Colerne** and on up to **Ford**. Great hostelries pop up at every turn, and Wadworth beer is the norm in these parts. Paddle, pedal, hike or drive: most people will do anything for a pint of Wadworth's 6X.

What to see & do

Tourist Information Centres
George Lane car park, Marlborough, SN8 1EE (01672 513989). **Open** *Apr-Oct* 10am-5pm Mon-Sat; *Nov-Mar* 10am-4.30pm Mon-Sat.
United Reform Chapel, Green Street, Avebury (01672 539425). **Open** *Apr-Oct* 10am-5pm Mon-Sat. *Nov-Mar* 10am-5pm Wed-Sun.
The Citadel, Bath Road, Chippenham, SN15 2AA (01249 706333). **Open** 9.30am-5pm Mon-Sat.
Cromwell House, The Market Place, Devizes, SN10 1JG (01380 729408). **Open** *Apr-Oct* 9.30am-5pm Mon-Sat. *Nov-Mar* 9.30am-4.30pm Mon-Sat.
Also has a small exhibition focussing on the history of the castle, particularly its role in Stephen and Matilda's struggle for power in the 11th century.
32 Church Street, Melksham, SN12 6LS (01225 707424). **Open** *Apr-Oct* 9am-5pm Mon-Fri; 9.30am-4.30pm Sat. *Nov-Mar* 9.30am-4.30pm Mon-Fri; 10am-4pm Sat.

Bike hire
MJ Hiscock Cycles *59 Northgate Street, Devizes (01380 722236).*

Alexander Keiller Museum
High Street, Avebury (01672 539250).
Open *Apr-Oct* 10am-6pm daily. *Nov-Mar* 10am-4pm daily. **Admission** (NT) £3.50; £1.50 concessions; free under-5s.

Photography was born at **Lacock Abbey**.

Founded in the 1930s, this museum displays many of the thrilling bits and bobs from the great archaeologist's Stone Age excavations on Windmill Hill, north-west of Avebury. Note the curious curled remains of a child buried 5,000 years ago in a ditch below the hill.

Atwell Wilson Motor Museum Trust
Stockley Lane, Calne (01249 813119). **Open** *Apr-Oct* 11am-5pm Mon-Thur, Sun. *Nov-Mar* 11am-4pm Mon-Thur, Sun. **Admission** £2.50; £1 concessions.
Vintage classic cars and motorcycles from 1924 to 1983, lovingly restored and in perfect running order.

Avebury Manor
High Street, Avebury (01672 539250).
Open *Gardens* Apr-Oct 11am-5.30pm Tue, Wed, Sat, Sun, bank hols. *House* Apr-Oct 2-5.30pm Tue, Wed, Sun, bank hols. **Admission** (NT) *House & gardens* £3.50; £1.70 concessions; free under-5s. *Gardens only* £2.50; £1.20 concessions; free under-5s.
Dating from 1550, Avebury Manor was extended in the 17th century. Its grounds contain the formal Monk's Garden, topiary, fine borders, a wishing well and fountains. Charles II and Queen Anne stayed here.

Avebury Stones
Considered one of the greatest achievements in prehistoric Europe, there are now 27 stones remaining from what was once an inner and outer circle of 200 (many were destroyed to provide stone for the village). They're not cordoned off, so you can wander among them, or visit the Henge shop to unravel their significance.

Bowood House & Gardens
Off A4 at Derry Hill, between Calne and Chippenham (01249 812102/www.bowood-estate.co.uk). **Open** *Apr-Oct* 11am-6pm daily. **Admission** £5.90; £3.70-£4.90 concessions; free under-5s.
Home of the Earl and Countess of Shelburne, building began at Bowood in 1625. The house has two claims to fame: Dr Joseph Priestley discovered oxygen here in 1774, and Napoleon's death mask is on show. There are other attractions, however. 'Capability' Brown masterminded the gardens, with lawns running down to a long lake, and grottoes and cascades. And, in May and June, when the rhododendrons are in bloom, hordes of visitors come to Bowood for the astounding rhododendron walks. There's also a fabulous treehouse adventure playground, and lovely teas and lunches.

Broadleas Gardens Charitable Trust
Broadleas, Devizes (01380 722035).
Open *Apr-Oct* 2-6pm Wed, Thur, Sun. **Admission** £3; £1 concessions.
Lady Anne Cowdray's beautiful valley gardens feature a secret garden, a winter garden, a wood, a sunken rose garden and a silver border packed with tender plants rarely seen in the English open air.

Castle Combe Race Circuit
South of Castle Combe on the B4039 (01249 782417/www.castlecombecircuit.co.uk). **Open** phone for race meeting times/dates. **Admission** varies; phone to check.
The 'Prettiest Village in England' is also known for its racing circuit, the home of motor, biking and karting thrills for 50 years. Great fun for big kids of all ages.

It's a fairy tale retreat of French rustic charm at **Fosse Farmhouse** near Chippenham.

Corsham Court

Off Church Street, Corsham (01249 701610/ www.corsham-court.co.uk). **Open** *Jan-Mar, Oct, Nov* 2-4pm Sat, Sun. *Apr-Sept* 2-5pm Tue-Sun. **Admission** *House & garden* £5; £2.50-£4.50 concessions. *Garden only* £2; £1-£1.50 concessions. The site of a royal manor in Saxon times, the core of the present house is Elizabethan, dating back to 1582. It contains more than 140 paintings and statues; the Capability Brown-designed grounds contain a fine Gothic bathhouse. The house was the backdrop for the film *Remains of the Day*.

Dyrham Park

nr Chippenham (01179 372501/fax 01179 372501). **Open** noon-4.45pm Fri-Tue. **Admission** (NT) £7.80. Built around the turn of the 18th century for William III's 'Secretary at State and at War', this National Trust property is furnished with paintings, furniture and ceramics, reflecting the Dutch style. Recently restored Victorian domestic rooms include the kitchen, bakehouse, tenants' hall, delft-tiled dairy and larders.

Lacock Abbey & Grounds & Fox Talbot Museum

Lacock, nr Chippenham (01249 730459/ www.lacock.co.uk/fox-talbot). **Open** *Museum* Mar-Oct 11am-5.30pm daily. Nov-Feb 11am-4pm Sat, Sun. *Abbey* Apr-Oct 1-5.30pm Mon, Wed-Sun. Closed Nov-Mar. **Admission** *Museum & abbey* £6. *Museum only* £3.80. *Abbey only* £4.80. As an extension of your tour around the *Pride and Prejudice/Moll Flanders* set of Lacock, it's possible to visit the former Lacock Abbey and laze in the tranquil meadows of Snaylesmeade. Converted into a country house in 1539, the new owners added a brewery, the Great Hall and Gothic archway, retaining the cloisters running round its centre. William Fox Talbot made the Abbey his home in 1835 and invented photography here – his negative of the oriel windows is the oldest in existence. There's a museum devoted to his work.

Wiltshire Heritage Museum, Gallery & Library

41 Long Street, Devizes (01380 727369). **Open** 10am-5pm Mon-Sat; noon-4pm Sun. **Admission** £3; £2 concessions; free under-17s. Free Sun. Owned by the Wiltshire Archaeological and Natural History Society, the museum boasts one of the finest prehistoric collections in Europe.

Where to stay

Marlborough High Street is a good bet – check out the **Merlin** pub (01672 512151; doubles £60-£70), the **Ivy House Hotel** (01672 515333; doubles £65-£98) as well as the **Castle & Ball** (01672 515201; doubles £85). There are also plenty of options in Devizes: the **Bear Hotel** (01380 722444; doubles £88) and the **Black Swan** (01380 723259; doubles £75) are in the Market Place, the **Elm Tree Inn** (01380 723834; doubles £50) is at the end of Long Street. In Castle Combe, a night at the AA three-star **Castle Inn** (01249 783030; doubles £120-£165) will set you back considerably less than the **Manor House** (*see p159*), and you even get a whirlpool bath in your room. **Shurnold House** near Melksham (01225 790555; doubles £78-£88) offers a warm welcome in a delightful Jacobean House. There are plenty of delightful country B&Bs, too – try **Fosse Farmhouse** in Nettleton (01249 782286; doubles £85-£125).

At the Sign of the Angel

6 Church Street, Lacock, SN15 2LB (01249 730230/ fax 01249 730527/www.lacock.co.uk). **Rates** £68 single occupancy (Mon-Fri, Sun only); £99-£137.50 double/twin. **Rooms** (all en suite) 5 standard double; 3 superior double; 2 twin. **Credit** AmEx, DC, MC, V.

Red Lion in Avebury stone circle. *See p160.*

Pagan pastures

To the Mother Earth-worshippers of prehistoric times, the Marlborough Downs were the sacred navel of the world – centrally accessible, spectacularly fecund and (to those who knew what they were looking for) full of suggestively female rolling hills and clefts. This was a Stone Age mecca, with Avebury as its focal point – intensively maintained to present pilgrims with a distillation of their megalithic culture's mounds and stones – and surrounded by the lushest crops in the land.

At 130 feet, **Silbury Hill** is the largest Bronze Age man-made mound in Europe. Impressive today even though you're not suppose to climb it, imagine the apparition it must have presented when it was coated white with chalk, a beacon to pilgrims heading south along the Ridgeway. Just a little north is **Avebury** itself, where a massive circular earthwork and ditch enclose the amazing remains of the main stone circle, 500 yards across, with two lesser circles and half a village (largely constructed from felled stones) within. The West Kennett avenue of 27 (once there were 200)

paired lozenge (female) and phallus (you guessed) stones extends south-east toward the **Sanctuary** on Overton Hill, whose original stones were cleared for 18th-century agriculture. The **West Kennett Long Barrow** is the largest stone-chambered collective tomb in England and Wales, consisting of five chambers and upwards of 50 burials.

The views from Silbury, the Sanctuary and **Waden Hill** are spectacular. **Windmill Hill**, walkable to the north-west of Avebury, is scarred with three concentric ditches cut to different depths and distances, the largest earthwork of its type in Britain. A bowl barrow and a bell barrow show the site was a burial site, as well as a ceremonial meeting place. **Devil's Den** is a rare example of a dolmen in these parts, with one huge sarsen stone precariously balanced on two others, formerly part of a much greater barrow now scattered... And all of this is barely scraping the surface: buy a specialist guidebook if you're beginning to feel intrigued (Julian Cope's *The Modern Antiquarian* is published by Thorson's, £30).

George Hardy is the welcoming angel to this ship-like 15th-century hotel. Inside, it's Alice in Wonderland-goes-medieval, with roaring fires and wobbly beams contributing to the homely, oaky atmosphere. Four bedrooms are in the house, four in the cottage across the garden – comfy, cuddly, filled with antique furniture. One of the doubles is dominated by a vast carved bed, which once belonged to Isambard Kingdom Brunel. The interconnected dining rooms are a major draw in their own right, cooking up hearty, trad English fare. Dogs welcome (not in public areas). All bedrooms no-smoking.
M4 J17 to Chippenham and Warminster; village is 3 miles south of Chippenham on A350; hotel is at far end of village.

Castle Hotel
New Park Street, Devizes, SN10 1DS (01380 729300/fax 01380 729155/www.castledevizes.com). **Rates** £55 single occupancy; £75 double/twin; £80 family room. **Rooms** (all en suite) 5 single; 5 double. Special breaks. **Credit** MC, V.
A former coaching inn set on a busy corner within a minutes' walk from Market Square. Family run, it's somehow comforting to come down to your Full English Breakfast and find the entire staff sitting together around a table, eating theirs. Immediately welcoming – kids no problem, park in the old stables, what are you drinking? – the bar and noisy, first-class restaurant are recommended whether you're staying or just dropping by. Children welcome. No-smoking rooms available.

Chilvester Hill House
Calne, SN11 0LP (01249 813981/fax 01249 814217/www.chilvesterhillhouse.co.uk). **Rates** £45-55 single occupancy; £75-£85 double/twin. **Rooms** (all en suite) 3 double/twin. **Credit** AmEx, DC, MC, V.
Dr and Mrs Dilley welcome guests into their Victorian family home (now part of the Wolsey Lodge group). The three large bedrooms are blue, green and pink, and hugely flowery. The Dilleys do dinner from around £20; everyone eats together. When it comes to food, Jill (army daughter and well travelled) likes to mix traditional English with Middle Eastern. Her wicked breakfasts were given 11 out of ten by broadcaster Derek Cooper. No children under 12. No-smoking areas available.
Take A4 from Calne towards Chippenham; after 1 mile turn right towards Bremhill and Ratford, then immediately right into hotel driveway.

Manor House Hotel
Castle Combe, SN14 7HR (01249 782206/fax 01249 782159/www.exclusivehotels.co.uk). **Rates** £145-£350 single occupancy; £145-£350 double; £285-£350 four-poster. Breakfast £15 (Eng). **Rooms** (all en suite) 34 double; 12 four-poster. **Credit** MC, V.
The perfect place to play Lord of the Manor or a round of golf. This impressive 'heraldic' traditional hotel, dating back to the 14th century, is approached by a sweeping drive over a weir and the trout-stuffed Bybrook, and sits in 26 acres of grounds, including the romantic Italian

gardens. The luxurious rooms, named after fields in the Castle Combe parish, feature bathrooms fitted with tellies and phones. There's grand feasting in the barn-style restaurant, where non-residents are welcome to drop in for a spectacular Sunday lunch. The chef is fond of themed mini-tasters such as 'every which way to cook rhubarb and salmon'. Very accomplished and popular. Children welcome. No smoking throughout.
Castle Combe is off B4039.

Red Lion

High Street, Avebury, SN8 1RF (01672 539266/ fax 01672 539377). **Rates** £30 single occupancy; £60 double/twin. **Rooms** 1 single (en suite); 2 double; 1 twin (en suite). **Credit** MC, V.
Set right in the middle of the Avebury stone circle, this is the spot for any serious diviner of neolithic vibes. There's nowhere else in the world where you can snap open your curtains on a scene like this… and that's why the four bedrooms tend to be in major demand during the hectic tourist season. The sprawling pub and food options are understandably geared toward volume, but there's an agreeably pokey snug and an undeniable up-for-it atmosphere. There's a well in the main bar, for goodness sake, as well as three ghosts to keep you company just in case you do find a quiet corner. Bedrooms are no-smoking. As a suggested overspill, try the **New Inn** in Winterbourne Monkton (01672 539240; doubles £50), a tiny pub in a backwater village within a couple of minutes' drive from Avebury. No ghosts, plenty of friendly locals, and children are welcome. All bedrooms are no-smoking.

Red Lion

1 High Street, Lacock, SN15 2LQ (01249 730456/ fax 01249 730766). **Rates** £55 single occupancy; £75 double/twin. **Rooms** (all en suite) 1 twin; 4 double. **Credit** AmEx, MC, V.
The no-nonsense red-brick frontage belies the Red Lion's early 18th-century origins. The bar is an absolute joy, all flagged or scuffed wooden floors, rough beams and amber light courtesy of the Wadworth ales. Food is hearty home cooking, with daily-changing blackboard specials. Recently refurbished to a high, agreeably unfussy standard, bedrooms feature good old wooden furniture, and aren't as pricey as you might expect. Doused as it is in history and quality, the Red Lion will never lose sight of the fact that it's a pub at heart. Children welcome. All bedrooms are no-smoking.

Waverley Café – simple, honest retro fare.

Rudloe Hall Hotel [Offer]

Leafy Lane, Rudloe, SN13 0PA (01225 810555/ fax 01225 811412/www.rudloehall.co.uk). **Rates** £79-£99 single occupancy; £89-£209 double; £199-£209 four-poster. **Rooms** (all en suite) 11 double; 4 four-poster. Special breaks. **Credit** MC, V.
An exercise in Victorian kooky Gothic, John and May Lyndsey-Walker's target audience is 'the discerning romantic', and indeed the rooms are theatrically melodramatic – the grander variety have four-posters, bathing alcoves with baths on legs and screens to undress behind. Check out the relaxing gardens and spectacular vistas towards Bath (rooms 6, 7 and 9 have the best views). Dinner can be taken either in the twinkling/roaring candlelit dining room or in the privacy of your own room. No children under 14. Dogs welcome (£6.95 charge per night). No-smoking rooms available.
At the top of Box Hill on A4 between Box and Corsham (6 miles east of Bath).

Where to eat & drink

There are some cracking boozers in this part of Wiltshire, primarily because there are two fantastic local breweries, Moles at Melksham and Wadworth at Devizes. Gems include the **Rising Sun** near Lacock up Bowden Hill, the **Six Bells** in Colerne and the **White Horse** in Biddestone. Other musts include the **Quarryman's Arms** at Box (01225 743569) and the **Raven** at Poulshot (01380 828271), both with excellent restaurants, plus the **Bear** in the Market Place in Devizes. Try the **Ivy House** (High Street, Marlborough; 01672 515333), the **Castle Hotel** (*see p159*) and **Manor House Hotel** (*see p159*) for more upmarket eating. **Ye Olde Pie Shoppe** on Market Street, Devizes, is a good tip for a snack. For picnic goodies, try ham, bacon and Tracklements mustards and horseradish from **Michael Richards** on London Road in Calne or some smoked delights from **David Farquhar** at Foxham.

Posh high teas are available at **Lucknam Park** and the **Manor House Hotel** (*see p161 and p159*), or choose more down-to-earth but equally tasty ones at **Bowood House** (*see p157*), the **Stable Tea Rooms** at Lacock (they rustle up a mean beef, tomato and basil roll) or the **Lock Cottage Tea Rooms** at the top of Caen Hill. **Polly's** tearooms in Marlborough feature a cake selection rightly guarded like jewels under glass. Pride of the region for classic retro honesty is the **Waverley Café** at the top of Chippenham market place.

Circle Restaurant

off High Street, Avebury (01672 539514). **Food served** noon-3pm daily. **Credit** MC, V.
Run by the charming Mike Pitts, the no-frills decor of this vegetarian restaurant keeps the mind focused on the toothsome, home-made, mostly organic food – much of it grown in the restaurant garden, where you can also

You can travel any way you like at the **Lucknam Park Hotel** – but just resting is easier.

sit and eat. Hot lunches are served every day; for less than a tenner you can have a feast, choosing a spinach and cranberry sandwich, perhaps, or a roast pepper and spinach tart with a cracked wheat salad. Cakes and cream teas (£3.75) are also on the menu. Expect queues on Sundays and at summer solstice.

George Inn
4 West Street, Lacock (01249 730263). **Food served** noon-2pm, 6-9pm daily. **Credit** MC, V.
A buzzing and jolly 13th-century pub. John Glass, a natural-born landlord, loves to show you the old dogwheel that once turned a spit. Portions are huge and prices reasonable. The menu offers no elaborate explanations – there's the likes of swordfish steak with boozy mango sauce, Wiltshire ham salad and treacle sponge.

George & Dragon
High Street, Rowde (01380 723053). **Food served** noon-2pm, 7-10pm Tue-Sat. **Set lunch** £10 2 courses; £12.50 3 courses. **Credit** MC, V.
Helen and Tim Withers run a top-quality restaurant that is renowned for its fish. It looks like a pub but don't be put off – the food is the thing; the setting and decoration are nowt special. Fresh fish is delivered from the market in Cornwall at least twice a week, and cooked to create delicious dishes that do not overpower – crab and asparagus salad and lemon sole are excellent. The atmosphere can be quiet; everyone's too busy stuffing their faces to talk. The set lunches are very good value.

Lucknam Park Hotel
Colerne (01225 742777/fax 01225 743536). **Food served** 7.30-9.30pm Mon-Thur; 7-10pm Fri, Sat; 12.30-2.30pm, 7.30-9.30pm Sun. **Set lunch** £25 3 courses. **Set dinner** £45 3 courses. **Credit** AmEx, MC, V.
This Palladian Georgian pad is approached via a mile-long drive of majestic beech trees. The food served in the former ballroom is lavish and exquisite, with each course perfectly balanced down to the final petits fours – top marks to head chef Robin Zavou. Salad of new season crayfish with marinated new potatoes and sauted foie gras to start, followed by a succulent roasted loin of venison served with game chips, spiced poach pear and a red wine chocolate sauce. And if that isn't enough, finish off with a poached peach served in a puff pastry case, accompanied by a fondant glaze and a peach sorbet. There's also an impressive special veggie menu with six starters and six mains. Hotel amenities include an indoor swimming pool, whirlpool spa, gymnasium, tennis courts or equestrian centre to shed some pounds. Rooms are superb (doubles £195-£320).

Pear Tree
Top Lane, Whitley (01225 709131). **Food served** 12.30-2.30pm, 6.30-9.30pm Mon-Fri; 12.30-2.30pm, 6.30-10pm Sat; 12.30-2.30pm, 7-9pm Sun. **Set lunch** £9.95 2 courses; £12.25 3 courses. **Credit** MC, V.
Despite fears from villagers of losing their darts and skittles local, Martin and Debbie Stills have triumphed in turning the Pear Tree into a class-act restaurant at the back serving modern British fusion (Med and Far East) food, which won *The Publican*'s Catering Pub of the Year award 1999. Up front is the thriving pub. The interior is decorated with rustic curiosities and warm muted colours, and the tables are well spaced and intimate. The menu might include such dishes as roasted duck breast with an apple and celeriac mash, and Pimms cheesecake with a strawberry and mint compote. You can eat two courses with wine for around £50 for two. The set lunch represents excellent value.

Taste of Bengal
58 New Park Street, Devizes (01380 725649/ 727997). **Food served** noon-2pm, 5.30pm-midnight daily. **Credit** MC, V.
Comfortably the best of Devizes' three Indian restaurants, the Bengal looks at first sight little more than a takeaway. Down an inauspicious alleyway, however, is hidden a small, comfortable restaurant offering an extensive menu that runs rings around the culinary traditions of the entire subcontinent. Here we find thali, tandoori and balti dishes (most around £4.95) happily rubbing shoulders with 'calypso curry' (honey, coconut, almonds and marla liqueur: untested!). Self-styled 'Bangladeshi' dishes (with aubergines, egg and mushroom) are piquant and saucy, but the top recommendation has to be the sizzling shahee nawabi with mushrooms and fried curd cheese (£8.95). First class.

White Hart
Ford, nr Chippenham (01249 782213). **Food served** noon-2pm, 7-9.30pm Mon-Thur; noon-2pm, 7-10pm Fri, Sat; noon-2pm, 7-9pm Sun. **Credit** AmEx, MC, V.
This 16th-century inn has bags of individual charm and a lovely setting with trout stream, ducks and pretty gardens. Sample ten real ales and two ciders including the scary-sounding Black Rat, play pool on a revolving round table and eat superb food in the restaurant prepared by chef Tony Farmer. Dinner is around £25 and might include ham hock, pork knuckle and black pudding to start and rack of lamb for a main, or at lunchtime cold roast beef for a fiver. There is also very comfortable, reasonably priced (mostly four-poster) accommodation (double £84).

Wiltshire & Bath

Malmesbury & Around

Endless opportunities for a quiet and gentle laze.

Locals never tire of telling you that **Malmesbury** is the oldest borough in Britain, but few know what makes this fact so very significant. The best story about the town concerns the flying monk, St Elmer, who leapt from the 620-foot west tower of the Abbey in 1010 in a home-made glider. To his credit, he travelled more than a furlong before becoming 'agitated by the violence of the wind and awareness of his rashness'. He broke both legs on landing. However, he reportedly lived happily ever after, and turned his energies to astronomy instead.

With the exception of Elmer and certain other hedonistic monks in the Abbey's history, the people of Malmesbury have been a peaceable, undistinguished lot. The great exception is the philosopher Thomas Hobbes, who was born in **Charlton**, north-east of the town, in 1588. Anyone not believing there can be so little to this ancient borough should refer to Dr Bernulf Hodge's spirited pamphlet *A History of Malmesbury*, available from the tourist information centre in the Town Hall.

Malmesbury and the surrounding area is therefore the perfect destination for a non-touristy, lazy weekend for those content with not doing a great deal. The characteristic honey-coloured stone buildings are pretty, but this is not an area of outstanding architectural interest. Happily, the **Cotswold Water Park** towards Cirencester keeps most activity maniacs occupied in one location and leaves the rest of us to mooch about doing little more than eat, sleep and, most importantly, drink. If that is what you fancy, this is the place for you.

Walk on the mild side

There is good walking to be had here and major routes can be joined: the **Cotswold Way** – a 100-mile trek from Chipping Campden to Bath; the **Macmillan Way** – a 200-mile route from Rutland to Dorset; and **Monarchs Way** – 610 miles from Worcester to Shoreham. The Cotswold Water Park, apart from its 132 lakes, includes a nature reserve for those who would rather navigate terra firma. Malmesbury and Tetbury both have town trails and these walks are set out in leaflets available from the relevant tourist offices. **Westonbirt Arboretum**, the arboreal paradise, has 17 miles of marked trails through its 600 acres of landscaped countryside.

Westward bound

This area is divided east and west by the A429 and it is the west side, where Malmesbury and Tetbury are found, that is markedly more pastoral. In Malmesbury itself there is the largely ruined, partially used Abbey, an elaborately vaulted market cross of 1390 providing shelter from the rain and the Abbey House gardens with their 2,000 types of rose. **Tetbury** is a very attractive little town with fantastic antique shops (*see p167* **Going for a song**) and tempting tearooms (notably Tetbury Gallery Tea Room, 18 Market Place; 01666 503412). The area is also home to royalty – Prince Charles, Princess Anne and Prince and Princess Michael of Kent all own stately piles hereabouts.

However, a more permanent attraction of the town is the fixed central feature of the Market House, built on stilts in 1655 as a sheltered market. The Georgian Gothic church of St Mary the Virgin, with the fourth-highest spire in England (built 1777-81) is also worth a look.

What to see & do

Tourist Information Centres

Town Hall, Market Lane, Malmesbury, SN16 9BZ (01666 823748/www.malmesbury-towncouncil.org). **Open** *Easter-Sept* 9am-4.30pm Mon-Fri; 9am-4pm Sat. *Oct-Easter* 9am-4.30pm Mon-Fri.

33 Church Street, Tetbury, GL8 8JG (01666 503552/www.tetbury.com). **Open** *Mar-Oct* 9.30am-4.30pm Mon-Sat. *Nov-Feb* 11am-2pm Mon-Sat.

Bike hire

CH White & Son *51 High Street, Malmesbury (01666 822330/www.chwhite.btinternet.co.uk).* **Open** 9am-1pm, 2-6pm Mon-Wed, Fri, Sat; 9am-1pm Thur.

Abbey House Gardens

Market Cross, Malmesbury (01666 822212/www.abbeyhousegardens.co.uk). **Open** *end Mar-end Oct* 11am-6pm daily. **Admission** £4.50; £2-£4 concessions. **No credit cards.**

Sound advice on how to pace yourself is clearly labelled outside **Tetbury Market House.**

A horticultural Eden, with five acres of gardens around a late Tudor house next to the Abbey. Star attractions are the 2,000 varieties of roses and herbs.

Cotswold Water Park

Keynes Country Park, Spratsgate Lane, nr Somerford Keynes (01285 861459/ www.waterpark.org). **Open** 9am-9pm daily. **Admission** free; phone for details of activities.
No weekend would be complete without a spot of splashing about – and so they invented Britain's biggest water park. There is a ridiculous number of water-borne activities available on the 132 lakes fashioned out of gravel quarries: sailing, canoeing, windsurfing, water- and jet-skiing, sub-aqua diving, power boating, and coarse and fly fishing. Aquaphobes can go walking, cycling, play golf or tennis, go horse riding, settle down for wildlife- and bird-watching or visit the shop or fossil exhibition. Children get to frolic in their own beach and play area. The less energetic can sunbathe or simply spectate from the cafés and picnic sites. Activities should be booked well in advance.

Lydiard House & Church

Lydiard Park, Lydiard Tregoze, nr Swindon (01793 770401/www.swindon.gov.uk). **Open** *Mar-June* 10am-1pm, 2-5pm Mon-Sat. *July-Sept* 10am-5pm Mon-Sat; 2-5pm Sun. *Nov-Feb* 10am-1pm, 2-4pm Mon-Sat. **Admission** £1.40; 70p concessions; free under-5s.
Tucked away behind unlovely industrial estates and new-town closes is this impressive Georgian residence in elegant grounds. Beware: it is hard to find and there are only six restored rooms for your admission fee. Also, you must phone first to get the key to the church and the *St John Triptych* (a remarkable family portrait from 1615) can only be viewed by prior appointment.

Malmesbury Abbey

Malmesbury (01666 826666/824339). **Open** *Apr-Oct* 10am-5pm daily. *Nov-Mar* 10am-4pm daily. **Admission** (EH) free; £2 suggested donation.
Time has not been kind to the Abbey, founded in the seventh century as a Benedictine monastery by St Aldhelm. Three hundred years after its consecration in 1180, the spire fell in and, following years of neglect by libertine monks (one abbot was killed in a drunken brawl) and the Dissolution of the monasteries in 1539, the site was sold. It was then returned to the people of Malmesbury as a parish church and now also functions as a retired people's social club. The fabulously carved Norman arch and the gloriously illuminated Bible of 1407 make it worth a visit.

Westonbirt Arboretum

Westonbirt, nr Tetbury (01666 880220/ www.forestry.gov.uk/westonbirt). **Open** 10am-dusk daily. **Admission** £4.20; £1-£3.50 concessions; free under-5s.
This world-famous tree sanctuary (established in 1829) features some 18,000 varieties of trees and shrubs. It's particularly renowned for its huge banks of rhododendrons, azaleas and magnolias, as well as the Autumn

---

By train from London

There are no train stations at **Malmesbury, Tetbury** or **Wootton Bassett** – the nearest station is at **Swindon**; trains leave **Paddington** every 15mins, and take about **1hr.** Info: www.firstgreatwestern.co.uk.

Westonbirt Arboretum – famous for its Autumn Spectacular and its Enchanted Wood.

Spectacular – when the sanctuary is transformed by magnificent vistas of red, orange and gold from September until mid-October. There are occasional musical events and fireworks in the evenings, and a lovely walk along a mile-long illuminated stretch known as the Enchanted Wood.

Where to stay

1 Cove House

Ashton Keynes, SN6 6NS (tel/fax 01285 861226).
Rates £27-£32 per person. **Rooms** (both en suite) 1 double; 1 twin. **No credit cards**.
Valerie Threlfall's colourful personality is stamped all over this beautifully appointed and femininely decorated manor house crouching behind a thick beard of green ivy. Val has a passion for interior design with a colourfully floral spin that reaches its apotheosis in the cosy red dining room lined with William Morris wallpaper. She is extremely warm and friendly, but you can also seek out your own company in the sitting room or under the magnificent 250-year-old copper beech on the lawn. Children welcome. No smoking throughout.
A419 towards Cirencester; follow signs for Cotswold Water Park and Ashton Keynes; turn left at White Hart pub, then left into driveway behind stone wall.

Calcot Manor Hotel

Nr Tetbury, GL8 8YJ (01666 890391/fax 01666 890394/www.calcotmanor.co.uk). **Rates** £120 single occupancy; £135-£150 twin/double; £175 deluxe double/twin; £185 family suites (£15 extra per child under 12; £25 per child 12 and over).
Special breaks. **Rooms** (all en suite) 7 double/twin; 11 deluxe double/twin; 10 family suites. **Credit** AmEx, DC, MC, V.
'A better class of people' stay at Calcot Manor, confided the proprietor of a local guesthouse. Sure enough: a nobbier sort of person (many proudly sporting a royal blue rinse) was to be found milling around in the manor's halls. Its rooms are decently proportioned, smartly and prettily decorated (satisfying both corporate and private tastes) in soft colours, and some feature whirlpool baths for the more sybaritic. An excellent breakfast provides a good variation on the often all-too-full English breakfast. The grounds include a croquet lawn, swimming pool and tennis courts. Children are competently catered for in the hotel's playroom. *See also p165.*
A46 towards Stroud; after 12 miles turn right on to A4135 towards Tetbury; hotel is immediately on left.

Close Hotel

Long Street, Tetbury, GL8 8AQ (01666 502272/ fax 01666 504401/www.theclosehotel.co.uk).
Rates £75 single occupancy; £90-£120 double/ twin; £120-£150 four-poster. Special breaks.
Rooms (all ensuite) 12 double/twin; 3 four-poster.
Credit AmEx, MC, V.
A delightful 400-year-old former wool merchant's house right in the middle of Tetbury that is gentle, calm and affordable. The rooms are individually decorated and named (Rose, Turrett, Deco), and have little touches that lift the place above the typical chintzy country hotel. The lovely walled garden is another attraction, but

most guests come for the food. Note that the Close is a popular spot for weddings – so book early. Children are welcome (but not admitted to the restaurant in the evenings). All bedrooms are no-smoking.

From Malmesbury enter Tetbury and follow along the High Street, over a roundabout, and take the 1st left for Dursley, then 1st left again into Close Gardens. The hotel car park is at the end.

Manor Farmhouse

Crudwell, nr Malmesbury, SN16 9ER (01666 577375/fax 01666 823523). **Rates** £30 single occupancy; £25 per person (double/triple). **Rooms** 1 double (en suite); 1 triple (with own separate bathroom). **No credit cards.**

A good, clean, well-run, flagstone-floored B&B next to the manor house and church of the village. Owner Helen Carter runs a smart ship and avoids flouncy touches. Rooms have views of cows and the churchyard and gardens. Mrs Carter bakes her own bread in the Aga and grows her own organic vegetables, which are often used for dinner (a very reasonable £15; BYOB). There is a tennis court in the garden with a rough tarmac surface. Children welcome. No smoking throughout.

3 miles north of Malmesbury on A429; turn right at Plough Inn in Crudwell; immediate left after church; house is behind church.

Manor Hill House

Purton, nr Swindon, SN5 9EG (01793 772311/fax 01793 772396). **Rates** £35 single; £44 double/twin/four-poster. **Rooms** (all en suite) 2 single; 3 double; 1 twin; 1 four-poster. **No credit cards.**

An ivy-covered Victorian house in the countryside near Purton. Filled with Victoriana and pictures, its dark interiors is pierced by shafts of strong light from the windows. The brooding hallway with coloured tiles and an open fire leads to a reading room, dining room and TV room. The main feature, however, is the chunky farmhouse kitchen where breakfast is served. The rooms are smallish but bright and prettily decorated, each with varying en suite facilities and satellite TV. Children welcome. All bedrooms are no-smoking.

M4 J16 towards Wootton Bassett; take Hook to Purton Road 2nd exit; follow road to main roundabout; take 3rd exit to Hook; through village; right at T junction to Lydiard Millicent; follow road to mini roundabout; take turning to Purton; house is ½ mile on the right.

Old Bell Hotel

Abbey Row, Malmesbury, SN16 0AG (01666 822344/fax 01666 825145/www.luxury-family-hotels.co.uk). **Rates** £75 single; £100-£115 double; £135-£160 deluxe double; £190 suite. **Rooms** (all en suite) 3 single; 13 double; 15 deluxe double; 6 suite. **Credit** AmEx, DC, MC, V.

The most prestigious hotel in the district is set in a rambling old building situated plumb by the remains of the famous Malmesbury Abbey. In the main house, the hotel is filled with sturdy Victorian furnishings and illuminated by recessed mullioned windows. It features a comfortable lobby, a stately dining room and more cosy bistro bar. The Victorian solemnity of the main building contrasts with the coach house, where the proprietors have created a faux-Japanese extension – bedroom furnishings are consistent with these themes. Children are provided with Z-beds for no extra charge and there is a well-appointed indoor

playroom and playground, to the delight of children and parents, located at the rear of the main building. Dogs welcome. *See also p166.*

Old Rectory Country House Hotel & Restaurant

Crudwell, nr Malmesbury, SN16 9EP (01666 577194/fax 01666 577853/www.oldrectorycrudwell.co.uk). **Rates** £88-£98 double/twin; £110 superior double/twin; £120 suite. Special breaks. **Rooms** (all en suite) 12 double/twin; 7 deluxe; 2 suite. **Credit** AmEx, MC, V.

The new proprietors, chirpy, enthusiastic Derek and Karen Woods, came from Essex to reinvent the old Crudwell Court and are making their mark on this lovely 17th-century rectory. In a rabbit warren of corridors the rooms have been refurbished to a traditional/executive style that merely needs a little ageing. The hotel lounges are perfect for unwinding, and outside there's a charming walled garden. The dining room is also worth patronising (*see p166*), and the prettiness of the village is an added bonus. Children welcome. Pets allowed by arrangement. All bedrooms no-smoking.

J17 off M4; the Old Rectory is 3 miles N of Malmesbury on A429; next to church.

Where to eat & drink

Spit-and-sawdust pubs, gastropubs, nouveaux conservatory extensions – you can take your pick in this area. The **Three Crowns** at Brinkworth (01666 510366) is very popular, not least for their cheesy dumplings and bolder meat offerings of crocodile and ostrich. The **Rattlebone** at Sherston (01666 840871) is a classic olde worlde inn with good-value staples and a fine selection of real ales. The **Pear Tree** at Church End, Purton (01793 772100), offers accomplished modern European cooking in an airy, formal dining room. For a good-value Thai, try **Som's Thai Café** above a fitness centre at Stainsbridge Mill in Malmesbury (01666 822022).

Close Hotel

Long Street, Tetbury (01666 502272/www.theclosehotel.co.uk). **Food served** noon-2pm, 7-9pm daily. **Set lunch** £12 2 courses; £15.95 3 courses. **Set dinner** £32.50 3 courses. **Tasting menu** £54 7 courses. **Credit** AmEx, MC, V.

The Close lives up to its fine-dining billing and certainly deserves its three AA Rosettes. The setting is a calm, classic Adams-style dining room overlooking a walled garden; in summer months there's the option of dining outside on the terrace. The menu includes a selection of modern European fare such as honey roast tuna or roast Italian tomato soup to start and pan roast supreme of chicken or seared fillet of red mullet for a main course. Round the corner is the more informal option of the Close Brasserie, which offers a cappuccino-and-ciabatta style menu. *See also p164.*

Gumstool Inn

Calcot Manor, nr Tetbury (01666 890391). **Food served** noon-2pm, 7-9.30pm Mon-Fri; noon-9.30pm Sat, Sun. **Credit** AmEx, DC, MC, V.

Calcot Manor's (*see p164*) smart, bright conservatory and the rustic modern extension known as the Gumstool are among the area's more upmarket eateries. Both are fed by the same kitchen – the cooking is a little more rarefied in the conservatory, while the moderately priced Gumstool provides a fine spread that can be enjoyed out on the patio. Here, starters (£5-£6) include dishes such as Mary Quickes' cheese soufflé and smoked chicken and avocado salad. Mains (£8-£12) run from the likes of salmon steak to Calcot shepherd's pie. There is a good selection of classic wines and two real ales on tap, all very reasonably priced for this kind of chichi establishment. Note: it's busy at Sunday lunchtime.

Old Bell Hotel
Abbey Row, Malmesbury (01666 822344/ www.oldbellhotel.com). **Food served** 10am-10pm Mon-Sat. **Set lunch** £11.75 2 courses; £15 3 courses. **Set dinner** £21.75-£28 3 courses. **Credit** AmEx, DC, MC, V.

The Old Bell is considered by many locals to be *the* place to dine but, we were warned, service can be slow. The canny diner eats in the cheaper bar-side bistro, which serves the same modern English cooking as the formal and imposing main dining room. Chef Mike Benjamin can be over-elaborate but the simpler, more English food is very good. From the set dinner try roasted loin of Gloucester Old Spot pork with honey and spices, served with caramelised apples and truffle mashed potato, and finish with warm rice pudding with a poached red wine pear. For the perfect ending, enjoy coffee and petits fours by a roaring fire in one of the lounges. *See also p165.*

Old Rectory Country House Hotel & Restaurant
Crudwell, Malmesbury (01666 577194/ www.oldrectorycrudwell.co.uk). **Food served** noon-2.30pm, 7-9.30pm daily. **Set lunch** £14.50 2 courses; £17.95 3 courses. **Set dinner** £24.50 2 courses; £27.50 3 courses. **Credit** AmEx, MC, V.

There's sophisticated and inventive modern British food to be had in the mini-grand setting of the Old Rectory. There are two choices of dining room – formal panelled or conservatory, both overlooking the gardens. Try wild mushroom soup with seared scallop and white truffle oil followed by pan-fried breast of guinea fowl with bubble 'n' squeak, and end with a divine banoffi tart. Roasts are added to the menu on Sunday. *See also p165.*

Smoking Dog
62 High Street, Malmesbury (01666 825823). **Food served** noon-2pm, 7-9.30pm daily. **Set lunch** £12.50 2 courses Sun. **Credit** MC, V.

The people's choice in Malmesbury town, this is a good, simple, chatty pub with a pine-furnished restaurant to the rear. The menu enables you to mix light pastas and salads (both around £6-£7) or stuffed ciabattas (around £5) with main meals. Starters (including white Stilton torte with warm cherry tomatoes and baby onions) are around £5 and mains (including char-grilled yellow fin tuna steak with roast chillies) are £9-£14. Hard to resist for pudding is the dog's bo***cks, a rich baked chocolate torte with clotted cream at £4.25.

Trouble House Inn
Cirencester Road, Tetbury (01666 502206). **Food served** noon-2pm, 7-9.30pm Tue-Sun. **Credit** AmEx, DC, MC, V.

The Trouble House takes its name from its troubled past – ghosts and a previous owner found hanging outside are just some of the tales. But now that Sarah and Michael Bedford (ex-head chef at City Rhodes in London) have taken over, the only bother to be found here is deciding what to choose from the small, but first-rate and reasonably priced menu. Choices might include curried parsnip soup, followed by duck confit with white beans and lentils and apple croustade. Starters and puds are around £5 or less; mains are all under £12 and wines are around the £12 mark. A real find.

Vine Tree
Foxley Road, Norton, nr Malmesbury (01666 837654/www.thevinetree.co.uk). **Food served** noon-2pm, 7-9.30pm Mon-Sat; noon-9.30pm Sun. **Credit** MC, V.

Charles Walker and Tiggy Wood took over this unspoilt, flagstone-floored country pub and are building on its existing good reputation. There's an intimate, old, beamed no-smoking area, a traditional bar with real fires, a delightful walled garden and a small adventure playground. The wine list is impressive, and the food ranges from traditional pub snacks to more sophisticated dishes. The chef is hot on fish such as roasted fillet of cod (£12.50) or pan-fried squid stuffed with seafood risotto (£12.95). There are daily specials, a wine of the moment, a kid's menu, and Spanish nights – all in all, an easygoing, jolly place.

Old Bell – the locals' choice.

Going for a song

In the Middle Ages, **Tetbury**'s market gained a reputation as the best place to buy wool and yarn. Today, Tetbury's reputation is as a centre for antiques; a community of dealers continues to grow and prosper, creating a vibrant edge to this Cotswold market town. Many of their shops can be found in the oldest and most elegant buildings that dominate the main streets spreading out from the town's covered market. A stroll around the antique shops is as good a way as any to get a feel for the town, with the added bonus of possibly picking up a gem or two – there is something to suit all pockets and levels of interest here, from the browser to the first-timer or serious collector. Here is just a taster.

    Sieff is a groovy, new kind of antique shop that has mastered the combination of fine antiques and contemporary design; its stylish shop sets out 'pieces' as you would want to have them at home. **Artique** is brimming with an eclectic mix of carpets, artefacts and furniture from the nomadic cultures of Central Asia. George Bristow is the colourful owner, and he has oodles more stuff in a barn near Tetbury. You can also stay in his recently opened Persian suite above the shop, decorated with prize pieces. Dennis Leroy started off in London's Camden Passage, then moved to Bath and has now just opened the **Ark Angel**, selling country, folk and primitive artefacts. Should you hear the melodic sound of (recorded) birdsong, you must be passing the **Decorator Source**, where Colin Gee offers up a wild mix of French rustic and refined pieces in an elegant Queen Anne townhouse set out over three floors. Ann and Roger Day have a passion for early oak and country furniture and related items and run **Day Antiques**, which specialises in traditional English and Welsh pieces. **Morpheus** at Elgin House sells an amazing range of old and new beds. They have satellite shops on London's King's Road and in Harrogate.

    Finally, for a relaxed wander-about go to the **Antiques Emporium** in a converted chapel, home to 40 antique dealers, each with their own speciality. The

relaxed atmosphere is a welcome change from the stuffiness associated with some antique shops – in Tetbury everybody is made welcome.

Antiques Emporium
The Old Chapel, Long Street (01666 505281). **Open** 10am-5pm Mon-Sat; 1-5pm Sun.

Ark Angel
33 Long Street (01666 505820). **Open** 10am-5pm Mon-Sat.

Artique
Tallboys House, 17 Church Street (01666 503597/www.artique.uk.com). **Open** 10am-6pm Mon-Wed, Sat; 10am-8pm Thur, Fri; noon-4pm Sun.

Day Antiques
5 New Church Street (01666 502413). **Open** 10am-5pm Mon-Sat.

Decorator Source
39A Long Street (01666 505358). **Open** 10am-1pm, 2-5pm Mon-Sat.

Morpheus
1 New Church Street (01666 504068). **Open** 9am-5.30pm daily.

Sieff
49 Long Street (01666 504477). **Open** 10am-1pm, 2-5.30pm Mon-Sat.

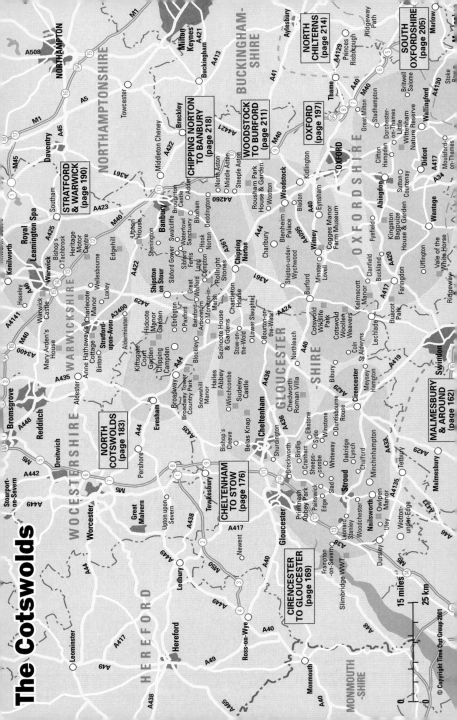

The Cotswolds

Cirencester
to Gloucester

Cotswolds confidential: the home of royalty.

For those who love the Cotswolds but hate the hordes of daytrippers who feel the same, this slice of glorious country balanced on the edge of the Gloucestershire Cotswold Hills is heaven. Between the Roman towns of Cirencester (Corinium) and Gloucester (Glevum) there's a fabulous spread of countryside, historic houses, ancient sites and good eating and drinking.

The area is anything but isolated: the M4 and M5 aren't far away, there are major towns in abundance and a significant rural population. Yet there's a beguiling intimacy to this historically key corner of the country, perched on the doorstep of Wales and the South-west. The Cotswold Way bisects the region, meandering along woodland-clad ridges overlooking sheltered valleys, which are at their most seductive, perhaps, in the area around **Painswick**. This gem of a town ('Queen of the Cotswolds'), tumbling down the side of the valley, is hardly undiscovered, yet has valiantly resisted the onslaught of the tearooms. The town centres on the Church of St Mary and its extraordinary churchyard, famed for its altar tombs and 99 yew trees (the oldest dating back to 1792); standing sentinel, they are trimmed into rather eerie shapes and, according to legend, are impossible to count (although that does beg a question…). Close by is Dennis French's wonderful shop Painswick Woodcrafts

(3 New Street; 01452 814195). Dennis has been working in wood for more than 50 years, and his expertise shows in beautiful domestic pieces such as bowls and cheeseboards. Another must-see is the unique **Painswick Rococo Garden**.

A tour of the easygoing neighbouring villages of **Edge**, **Sheepscombe** and **Slad** is rewarding. If you've heard of the latter, chances are it is through the childhood recollections of Laurie Lee's *Cider with Rosie*. Lee grew up in Slad and was a long-time regular at the Woolpack. It's still a likeable, down-to-earth (and tiny) pub, even though the current owners are making more of its Lee connections than previously. Lee is buried in Slad churchyard, a short stumble from the pub.

Prinknash Abbey Park, between here and Gloucester, offers the delights of birds, tame deer, fine walks and monk-made pottery.

Gloucester was described by Dickens as 'a wonderful and misleading city'. In some strange way, and despite what locals might say, it still is. It's actually a rather downmarket working town, but this is a refreshing contrast to the tweeness of nearby Cheltenham (*see p176*) and most of the Cotswolds. Much of the centre is blighted by utterly characterless modern development, and strolling the streets is hardly a joy. Yet there are gems to be uncovered – the most rewarding of which is the wonderful cathedral. The restored Victorian docks are also well worth a look. Within the buildings are the National Waterways Museum and the Gloucester Antiques Centre, home to 90 dealers. The Gloucester City Museum & Art Gallery is also worth a visit.

Cirencester and around

Around 20 miles south-east of Gloucester lies the agreeable small town of **Cirencester**. A considerable leap of imagination is required to picture this gentle local centre as the one-time capital city of the Dobunni tribe and then the strategically vital Roman town of Corinium, commanding the juncture of the Fosse Way, Ermine Street and Akeman Street. It was once the second-largest Roman city in the country after London; the population today is little more

By train from London

There are four direct trains a day from **Paddington** to **Gloucester** (journey time is **1hr 50mins**) and to **Stroud** (journey time **1hr 30mins**), although you can also take the hourly train to **Swindon** and change, which takes about **2hrs** (**1hr 40mins** to **Stroud**). Direct trains from **Paddington** (four a day) to **Kemble** take **1hr 10mins** to **1hr 30mins**; an hourly linking coach service (01242 522021) runs to **Cirencester**, four miles away. Info: www.firstgreatwestern.co.uk and www.stagecoachgroup.co.uk.

Pass by the lychgate at **Duntisbourne Abbots** and visit the yews at **St Mary's, Painswick**.

than 15,000, but there is plenty of evidence of Cirencester's heyday. The Corinium Museum is the best source of Roman relics. To the west of the town are the remains of the second-century BC Roman amphitheatre. The other main sight in town is the wonderful 'wool' Church of St John the Baptist on Market Place, with its elaborate Perpendicular-style porch (c1500).

Church lovers also shouldn't miss a tour of the **Dunt Valley**, just north-west of Cirencester off the A417, where there's a succession of superb small churches in villages such as **Elkstone**, **Winstone**, **Syde** and **Duntisbourne Rouse**.

West from Cirencester

From Cirencester heading towards Stroud, you pass through royal country (Prince Charles's Highgrove and Princess Anne's Gatcombe Park are nearby) down into the **Golden Valley** of the River Frome and Thames and Severn Canal. The grand project for a canal joining the Severn and the Thames was completed in 1789 and immodestly, but not inaccurately, described by its own PR as 'an elaborate and stupendous work of art'. Its high point (literally) is the Sapperton Tunnel, running more than two miles through the Cotswold limestone. Stop at **Chalford**: pick up the old towpath and walk east up a delightful wooded valley to the tunnel portal (just under four miles there and back). It's always been short of water, and the last boat went through in 1911, so don't expect much activity on what water remains, but there's plenty of wildlife and a pub at the halfway point.

Stroud is a working town, with a surprisingly large 'alternative' community into all things green and organic. The centre isn't

particularly picturesque, but it is largely pedestrianised and has a few good shops and cafés. There's a regular farmers' market and, on the High Street, Woodruffs Organic Café (01453 759195) and Bishopston Trading Company (01453 766355), which sells Indian-made fair-trade clothes.

The region to the south of the town is more densely populated than that to the north, but still well worth exploring. The huge wind-tossed expanse of Minchinhampton Common is a wonderful spot to fly a kite, and there's bags of history and culture to be discovered in these parts, from the remnants of an Iron Age hill fort at **Uley** and the nearby long barrow (the magnificently named **Hetty Pegler's Tump**; both off the B4066), through the Tudor **Owlpen Manor** to the spooky unfinished Victorian masterpiece of **Woodchester Mansion**. West of here the country flattens as it reaches the Severn – a perfect environment for a spot of twitching at the **Slimbridge Wildfowl & Wetlands Trust**.

What to see & do

Tourist Information Centres

Corn Hall, Market Place, Cirencester, GL7 2NW (01285 654180). **Open** *Apr-Oct* 9.30am-5.30pm Mon; 9.30am-5.30pm Tue-Sat. *Nov-Mar* 10am-5pm Mon; 9.30am-5pm Tue-Sat.

28 Southgate Street, Gloucester, GL1 2DP (01452 421188/www.visit-glos.org.uk). **Open** 10am-5pm Mon-Sat.

Subscription Rooms, George Street, Stroud, GL5 1AE (01453 760960/www.visitthecotswolds.org.uk). **Open** 10am-5pm Mon-Sat.

The Cotswolds

Corinium Museum

Park Street, Cirencester (01285 655611/
www.cotswold.gov.uk/museum). **Open**
10am-5pm Mon-Sat; 2-5pm Sun. **Admission**
£2.50; 75p-£2 concessions.
This award-winning museum, as you can guess from
its name, concentrates on the Roman history of
Cirencester. There are reconstructions of a butcher's
shop, dining room and kitchen, but the museum is particularly strong on mosaic floors. Children can have a
go at mosaic building; the museum is as much aimed
at kids as adults.

Gloucester Cathedral

College Green, Gloucester (01452 528095/
www.gloucestercathedral.uk.com). **Open** 7.30am-6pm
Mon-Fri; 7.30am-5pm Sat; 7.30am-4pm Sun.
Admission free; donations welcome.
While much of old Gloucester has gone, it's surprising and refreshing to find its magnificent cathedral in
such a fine state of preservation. A Saxon abbey stood
on this site, but the current building was started by
Benedictine monks in the 11th century. When
Gloucester agreed to take the body of the murdered
King Edward II (remember that red-hot poker?) in
1327, after Bristol and Malmesbury had refused, the
cathedral became a place of pilgrimage, financing the
14th- and 15th-century development of the building
into the greatest example of the Perpendicular style in
the country. The huge expanse of the Great East
Window (1350) is magnificent, as is the fan vaulting
in the cloisters (the first example of such vaulting in
Britain). A must-see.

Gloucester City Museum & Art Gallery

Brunswick Road, Gloucester (01452 524131).
Open *Oct-June* 10am-5pm Mon-Sat. *July-Sept*
10am-5pm Mon-Sat; 10am-4pm Sun.
Admission £2; £1 concessions; free children.
The entertaining and informative city museum focuses
on Gloucestershire's early history, and includes dinosaur
bones and the re-creation of the appearance of the 2,000-
year-old 'Birdlip Lady'. There's also some fine 18th-cen-
tury furniture, and paintings by the likes of Rembrandt,
Gainsborough and Turner, plus enough hands-on stuff
to keep the kids amused.

National Waterways Museum

Llanthony Warehouse, Gloucester Docks, Gloucester
(01452 318054/www.nwm.org.uk). **Open** 10am-5pm
daily. **Admission** £4.95; £3.95 concessions.
The museum tells the 200-year story of Britain's canals,
using plenty of working models, engines, archive film,
hands-on and interactive exhibits to bring it all to life.

Owlpen Manor

Uley, nr Dursley (01453 860261/www.owlpen.com).
Open *Apr-Sept* 2-5pm Tue-Sun. Closed Oct-Mar.
Admission £4.50; £2 concessions.
Gardens only £2.50.
Formal terraced yew gardens and bluebell woods surround this lovely Tudor manor (1450-1616), currently
home to the Mander family. The interior contains some
fine Arts and Crafts furniture and 17th-century wall
hangings. Teas are served in the Tithe Barn. The house

feels wonderfully remote – 'Owlpen – ah, what a dream
is there!' as Vita Sackville-West was moved to say.
There are some lovely holiday cottages scattered around
the house (www.owlpen.com/cottages.htm).

Painswick Rococo Garden

Painswick (01452 813204/www.rococogarden.co.uk).
Open *mid Jan-May, Oct, Nov* 11am-5pm Wed-Sun,
bank hols. *May-Sept* 11am-5pm daily. **Admission**
£3.30; £1.75-£3 concessions.
Charles Hyett built Painswick House in the 1730s and, in
the following decade, his son Benjamin created a flamboyant rococo garden. Over the years, the six-acre garden became overgrown, and it was only in the 1970s that
interest revived in what was the only surviving garden
from this period of English garden design (1720-60).
Restoration work started in 1984. The result is wonderful – a combination of the formal (geometric patterns,
long vistas, architectural features) and the informal
(winding paths, off-centre designs, woodland walks).

Prinknash Abbey Park

Cranham (shop 01452 812066/bird park 01452
812727/www.prinknashabbey.org.uk). **Open** *Park*
Apr-Sept 9am-5.30pm daily. Oct-Mar 9am-4.30pm
daily. *Bird park* 10am-5pm daily. **Admission** *Park*
free. *Bird park* £2.70; £1.75-£3 concessions.
The Benedictine Abbey of Prinknash (the 'k' is silent)
combines a (remarkably ugly) working abbey with a
pottery (where the monks' creations can be bought), a
bird park (packed with peacocks and waterfowl, most
of which will take food from your hand) and a deer park
(many of the deer can be petted and fed). There's also
the Tudor Wendy House, the Monks' Fish Pond, a lake,
tearoom, gift shop and the 13th-century Old Grange
building. A surefire hit for kids.

Slimbridge Wildfowl & Wetlands Trust

Slimbridge (01453 890333/www.wwt.org.uk). **Open**
Apr-Oct 9.30am-5pm daily. *Nov-Mar* 9.30am-4.30pm
daily. **Admission** £6; £3.60-£4.80 concessions.
The Wildfowl & Wetlands Trust was set up by artist
and naturalist Sir Peter Scott in 1946 to promote his central belief that the conservation message is best com-
municated by fostering the interaction of people and
wildlife. A wonderful range of birdlife can be seen,
including six types of flamingo and the world's largest
collection of ducks, geese and swans.

Woodchester Mansion

Nympsfield, Stonehouse (01453 750455/www.the-
mansion.co.uk). **Open** *Easter-June, Sept, Oct* 1st full
weekend of the month. *July, Aug* 11am-6pm Sat, Sun,
bank hols (last admission 4pm). **Admission** £4;
£2 concessions.
This extravagant exercise in Victorian Gothic is one of
the most unusual and enigmatic country houses in
Britain, not least because it was never finished. The
over-optimistic vision of Catholic zealot Edward Leigh,
it is a unique example of a Victorian work-in-progress,
and has been described as 'one of the great achievements
of 19th-century domestic architecture'. The only access
to the mansion is from a car park close to the Coaley
Peak picnic site and viewpoint on the B4066 Stroud to
Dursley road. From here it's a pleasant one-mile walk to
the mansion, or a trip in the shuttle bus.

The Cotswolds

Woodchester Mansion – completely extravagant but never completed.

Where to stay

In addition to the places below, the **Village Pub** in Barnsley has rooms (*see p175;* doubles £70-£125), as has the **Bathurst Arms** in North Cerney (*see p174;* doubles £65-£70) – both pubs serve notable food. There are also a couple of good B&Bs in Meysey Hampton, east of Cirencester – **Hampton Fields** (01285 850070; doubles £60-£68) and the **Old Rectory** (01285 851200; doubles £60-£70) – and rooms are also offered at the Georgian rectory of **Winstone Glebe** (01285 821451/www.wolsey-lodges.co.uk; doubles £33-£36) in Winstone, just off the A417.

It is also worth considering accommodation located in neighbouring areas. The **Bibury Court Hotel** (*see p214*), the **New Inn at Colne** (*see p215*) and the **Greenway** (*see p180*) are all particularly close by.

Cardynham House
The Cross, Painswick, GL6 6XX (01452 814006/fax 01452 812321/www.cardynham.co.uk). **Rates** single occupancy £43-£47; £60-£120 double/four-poster. **Rooms** (all en suite) 1 twin; 1 double; 7 four-poster. Special breaks. **Credit** MC, V.
A stunner. Californian Carol Keyes has decorated every room in this outstanding B&B with a level of style and

dash that most hotels can only envy. There are four-posters in every room bar one (and even that has a half-tester), and if you thought that theming was naff, just wait until you see Old Tuscany, Medieval Garden or Palm Springs. The huge room at the top of the house, Dovecote, is suitable for families, and, amazing as it seems, the Pool Room actually contains a small swimming pool. Warmer service would be nice, though. Book well in advance. Children and pets welcome.
A46 N of Stroud; once in Painswick pass churchyard on right; take first right into Victoria Street; turn left at end of road; house is next to March Hare restaurant.

Frampton Court
The Green, Frampton-on-Severn, GL2 7EU (01452 740267/fax 01452 740698). **Rates** £40-£45 per person. **Rooms** 2 single (1 en suite); 1 double/four-poster; 1 twin (en suite); 1 self-catering house. **No credit cards.**
The Clifford family have been living in Frampton since the 11th century and their phenomenal early 18th-century Grade I-listed mansion gives up four bedrooms for B&B and also lets out the orangery for self-caterers (sleeps eight; phone for details). The B&B rooms are large – the double is hung with a Flemish tapestry and equipped with a double-tester bed; the twin enjoys wonderful views and some lovely wooden panelling. Frampton itself is an intriguing village, very close to the Severn estuary. Children and dogs welcome (orangery only). All bedrooms no-smoking.
Take B4071 off A38; turn left and go through village green; house is on left (entrance between two large chestnut trees).

Grey Cottage

Bath Road, Leonard Stanley, GL10 3LU (tel/fax 01453 822515). **Rates** from £38 single; £52-£58 double; £55-£60 twin. **Rooms** 1 single (en suite); 1 double; 1 twin (en suite). **No credit cards**.

A warm welcome (and tea and scones) greets guests at Rosemary Reeves' Grey Cottage. The decor is clean, fresh and free of extraneous frills and flounces. Of the bedrooms, the twin is the nicest and largest, with a sizeable en suite shower room. Breakfast is outstanding – undyed haddock and poached eggs, full fry-up, smoked salmon with scrambled eggs, kedgeree, kippers – you name it. A first-rate no-choice dinner is also served by arrangement. Leonard Stanley itself isn't a particularly appealing village, being mainly strung out along a main road, but it's a perfect base for exploring the area. Children over 10 welcome. All bedrooms no-smoking.
A419 W of Stroud towards M5 (Edley bypass); after 1 mile follow filter to Leonard Stanley; go through King's Stanley; house is on left on bend just after Leonard Stanley Junior school.

Mason's Arms

28 High Street, Meysey Hampton, GL7 5JT (01285 850164). **Rates** £40 single occupancy; £60 double; £68 family. **Rooms** (en suite) 9 double/twin/family. **Credit** MC, V.

Meysey Hampton is an appealingly dozy little village, a few miles east of Cirencester. Its focal point is the 17th-century Masons Arms, a deservedly popular local pub, which offers a good range of rooms, some with beams and exposed brickwork. There's first-rate ales at the bar, and decent grub, too. Children and pets welcome.
A419 towards Cirencester; take the Fairford turning; then signs for Latton; turn right through Down Ampney; into Meysey Hampton, pub on village green.

Painswick Hotel

Kemps Lane, Painswick, GL6 6YB (01452 812160/ fax 01452 814059/www.painswickhotel.com). **Rates** £75-£135 single; £115-£180 double/twin; £180 four-poster; £125-£140 family. **Rooms** (all en suite) 2 single; 4 twin; 9 double; 2 four-poster; 2 family. **Credit** AmEx, MC, V.

Painswick's grandest accommodation option clings to the hillside just down from the town's wonderful yew-filled churchyard. It's a friendly place, with some beautiful views from many of the well-proportioned rooms (some with four-posters). Relaxing gardens and a good restaurant serving upmarket dishes or light lunches are further attractions. Children and pets welcome.
A46 N of Stroud; once in Painswick pass churchyard on right, and turn right into Victoria Street; right at March Hare; hotel is on right down hill.

Where to eat & drink

There aren't a huge number of bona fide restaurants in the area, but there is plenty of excellent dining to be had in the area's many great pubs. The **Crown of Crucis** in Ampney Crucis (east of Cirencester) is an ambitious pub/restaurant/hotel (01285 851806). South of Cirencester, the comfy **Wild Duck** in Ewen (01285 770310) does good grub, and the **Eliot Arms** in South Cerney (01285 860215) is another

popular locals' haunt. South of Stroud, there's excellent food, and bedrooms and working waterwheels, at the **Egypt Mill** in Nailsworth (01453 833449). Also try the **Black Horse** in Amberley for its great views. In Cranham, north-east of Painswick, the tiny 17th-century **Black Horse** (01452 812217) has above-average food and beer. The **New Inn at Coln** (*see p217*) serves excellent food in the Courtyard Bar, and also in its restaurant. **Waterman's Bar & Restaurant** in Nailsworth (01453 832808) is a good spot to enjoy contemporary cuisine in a relaxed atmosphere.

Ban Thai at the March Hare

The Cross, Painswick (01452 813452). **Food served** 7-10pm Tue-Sat. **Set dinner** £21.50 4 courses. **No credit cards**.

In the same building as Cardynham House B&B (*see p173*), this separately run Thai restaurant offers unusually good (though rather pricey) food, freshly prepared by the proprietor's Thai wife. There's no choice – but there are likely to be few complaints about the set meal, which consists of a plate of starters, followed by three well-balanced dishes – perhaps a curry, a noodle dish and veg, and then mango or lemon sorbet. The short wine list is reasonably priced. Charming service.

Bathurst Arms

North Cerney, nr Cirencester (01285 831281). **Food served** noon-2pm, 7-9pm Mon-Thur, Sun; noon-2pm, 7-9.30pm Fri; Sat. **Credit** MC, V.

A great, atmospheric pub for a drink, a snack or a full-blown meal. Expect the likes of chicken livers with salad (£4.50), steak and Guinness pie (£7.95) and chilli prawns with stir-fried noodles (£8.50). The beamed and panelled bar, with fireplaces at either end, is a cosy spot to hole up in cold weather. In summer, take your scoff outside on to one of the picnic tables on a grassy area leading down to a stream and the main road).

Butchers' Arms

Oakridge Lynch, nr Stroud (01285 760371). **Food served** *Bar* noon-2pm, 6.30-9.30pm Mon-Sat; noon-2pm Sun. *Restaurant* 7.30-9.30pm Wed-Sat; noon-4pm Sun. **Credit** MC, V.

A gem of a pub, with top-notch bar snacks as well as the Stable Room restaurant. It's not far off the A419 but feels utterly removed from urban civilisation. Internationally inspired dishes served with chunky deep-fried potato wedges are a speciality (£5.50-£6.95), as are excellent hot baguettes (£4.75). Fine selection of real ales.

Hare & Hounds

Fosse Cross, nr Chedworth (01285 720288). **Food served** noon-2.30pm, 7-9.30pm Mon-Sat; noon-3pm Sun. **Credit** MC, V.

Lovely, warm staff and unusual good food mark out this pub on the A429, close to Chedworth Roman Villa (*see p177*). The interior is minimally and sensitively modernised, with stripped floors, exposed brick and beams, but it's the food that really shines. Expect the likes of dressed Brixham crab with sweet and sour chutney (£5.50), smoked tuna loin with grape mustard (£5) and risotto with walnuts, goat's cheese and mixed salad (£9).

Royal Oak

Church Road, North Woodchester (01453 872735).
Food served 12.15-2.15pm, 6.15-9.15pm daily.
Credit MC, V.
This is a cracker of a dining pub – free of the affected-
ness that afflicts some country gastro-taverns, and with
an assured hand in the kitchen. It's a tiny place, with a
bar on one side and a small, plain dining room on the
other. Relaxed, and yet thoroughly professional staff dis-
pense well-crafted, no-nonsense dishes such as grilled
calf's liver, bacon and mash (£7.90) and fillet steak with
garlic butter (£12.50). The ales here are also notably fine.

Village Pub

High Street, Barnsley (01285 740421).
Food served noon-2.30pm, 7-9.30pm Mon-Thur;
noon-3pm, 7-10pm Fri, Sat; noon-3pm, 7-9.30pm Sun.
Credit MC, V.
The name may appear to lack imagination, but there
is nothing hackneyed about the superb contemporary
food served up at this extremely popular dining pub.
Typical dishes include crab cakes with spicy courgette
chutney (£6.50) and seared turbot, beurre rouge and
chives (£14). Note that the pub is entirely given over to
diners in the evenings.

Whiteway Colony

Were you to pass through the tiny hamlet
of Whiteway, a few miles north-east
of Stroud, the one thought you are
guaranteed *not* to have is: 'Gosh, if I'm
not mistaken, I appear to be in a century-
old Tolstoyan anarchist commune.'
Yet that is exactly where you would be.

In the dying years of the 19th century,
as Victorian capitalism boomed, many
people became increasingly appalled by
the inhuman conditions under which poor
people lived. Inspired by Tolstoy's ideal of
equality among all men, many formed what
were known as Brotherhood Churches to
discuss how to build a better society.

One idea was to form libertarian,
egalitarian model communities, living off
the land, in the hope of encouraging others
to abandon capitalism and follow suit.
In 1898, after an abortive attempt to set
up such a community in Essex, members
of the Croydon Brotherhood Church
bought some land at Whiteway (and
then symbolically burned the title deeds
– all land was to be held in common).

From the early days, colonists made
a point of having no written constitution.
Individualism was paramount. Residents
could think, do, dress as they pleased,
providing they didn't infringe on the
freedom of others. Restrictive Victorian
clothing was rejected in favour of
comfortable, practical smock dresses
for women, and loose shirts, shorts and
sandals for men (one early colonist was
fined ten shillings for indecency after
passing the local vicar wearing only
his shorts).

The evolution of the colony was
sometimes painful; some of the most
radical ideas (like refusing to use
money, and communal living) had to
be abandoned as impractical. But, over

the years, Whiteway acted as a refuge
and an inspiration for a huge range
of international visitors, from Russian
anarchists to refugees from the Spanish
Civil War to left-wing intelligentsia (Malcolm
Muggeridge was a regular visitor).

Locally, Whiteway has always been
an object of bemused (and sometimes
lurid) curiosity. There were wild tales of
nudism and free love, the great majority
of which were untrue (although free
union, the living together of unmarried
couples – shocking enough at the
time – was common). But that didn't
stop charabancs full of nosey outsiders
regularly driving up to Whiteway in the
hope of a cheap thrill.

The colony today is a less radical place
than in its early days. Vegetarianism isn't
universal, as it was initially. Plots of land
are now fenced, where once there were
no boundaries. The occupations of
today's colonists are unremarkable –
around half are self-employed, and there
are artists, a screen-printer, a garage
owner, a metal worker, a nurse, a
teacher, an accountant, builders and
civil servants. Yet the Whiteway spirit
remains. Land is still held in common.
There are still colony meetings, where
decisions affecting the village are made,
and community feeling and pride in the
colony's history and ideals are strong.

In many ways, Whiteway was ahead of
its time – who now doesn't wear shorts
and sandals in summer? And who now
is shocked by unmarried couples living
together? And with the current popularity
of vegetarianism, the organic movement,
environmentalism and anti-capitalist, anti-
globalisation sentiment, it seems that
many people, a hundred years down the
line, are finally catching up with Whiteway.

The Cotswolds

Cheltenham to Stow

Regency unrivalled.

For a dose of Regency town and regal country, a visit to self-confident Cheltenham and the bucolic expanses stretching westward towards Stow is a winner. Cheltenham was an ordinary small Cotswold town until the spa was discovered in 1716 and its healing properties promoted by various nobles and literary figures, among them the Duke of Wellington and Charles Dickens. The royal patronage of George III, who came to drink the waters in 1788, led to the town's rapid transformation into a fashionable spa resort, where the middle classes came to take the water and revive their spirits. In some ways, Cheltenham has changed little since. It still has an almost haughty complacency and a very conservative feel, which is tempered slightly when the **International Festival of Music** (July) and the **Festival of Literature** (October) come town, each for two weeks.

The Festival of Music, which began life in 1945, is an upmarket mixed bag. In past years it has attracted the likes of the BBC Philharmonic Orchestra, Julian Lloyd Webber, and opera and ballet music from Covent Garden's Royal Opera House orchestra. The Festival of Literature, which was established a few years later, is thought to be the longest-running literary festival in the world. It comprises an impressive 250 literary events, including writing, poetry and drama. Phone 01242 237377 for a brochure on the festivals, or 01242 227979 for the box office, or check out the website at www.cheltenhamfestivals.co.uk.

The town boasts some beautiful architecture and graceful parks, making it a perfect place to stroll around in fine weather. The Montpellier area, packed with upmarket shops, many selling antiques, is the most attractive part of Cheltenham. Heading north into the town centre you make your way along the Promenade – a handsome esplanade flanked with grand shops and parks. Behind this are some very ordinary streets of shops and two shopping malls, one of which, the Regent Arcade, is made less anonymous and uniform by the addition of the **Wishing Fish Clock**, a fantastical clock designed by Kit Williams,

By train from London

There are four trains a day that run directly from **Paddington** to **Cheltenham Spa**. Journey time is **2hrs 10mins**. Note that the station is about a mile from the town centre. Info: www.firstgreatwestern.co.uk.

author and illustrator of *Masquerade*. Children love to stand and gaze as the clock face regularly emits bubbles and small animals appear from hatches. While you're in town, it's worth popping into the **Cheltenham Art Gallery & Museum**. A real gem, it features an interesting mix of classic and contemporary work, with a significant collection of Arts and Crafts furniture.

Fans of horse racing will be familiar with the Cheltenham races; the racecourse, at the foot of Cleeve Hill, a ten-minute walk north of Pittville Park, is the focus of the National Hunt Festival in March. (*See p180* **The Hunt is on... off... on**).

A castle, abbey and two Slaughters

Tiny **Winchcombe**, to the north-east of Cheltenham, is a small, perfectly formed village best known for nearby **Sudeley Castle** and its nine stunning gardens. Winchcombe itself is pretty and pleasant to wander around. Other cultural draws in the area include the once-mighty Cistercian **Hailes Abbey** (to the north) and the wonderfully situated **Belas Knap** neolithic long barrow (to the south). It's a two-mile walk from Winchcombe to the long barrow – the most perfectly preserved burial chamber in England.

The distinctive pale yellow stone of the area gives the buildings and villages their warm, comfortable feel. Nowhere typifies this more than the disturbingly named but entirely unthreatening **Upper Slaughter** and **Lower Slaughter**, to the east of Cheltenham; Lower Slaughter, in particular, is stunning, with a small walled river winding through its heart and ducks and geese wandering lazily across the roads.

It's fantasy time – the **Wishing Fish Clock**.

The serenity of Stow

East of Cheltenham is **Stow-on-the-Wold**, meaning 'meeting place on the uplands', and, indeed, eight roads converge on the town. Thankfully, none of them disrupts the beautifully preserved town centre. Stow is a pretty market town of honey-coloured stone houses and cottages, with a fine central marketplace flanked on all sides by antique and bric-a-brac shops and teashops.

The town is peaceful – if you discount the hordes of daytrippers who swarm through it on summer days – but stay on into the evening and the pace settles down. Have a look at the attractive King's Arms Old Posting House on Market Square, which used to receive stagecoaches through its huge broad arch as they stopped on their way to Cheltenham. Soak up the ambience as you wander about, perhaps dropping in for a pint at the Queens Head; the more temperance-minded can enjoy a cup of tea at Edward's Café (both in Market Square).

Northleach, south of Bourton-on-the-Water, is another village well worth a visit – pretty and peaceful with a beautiful 15th-century church boasting a collection of brasses. The village also offers the unexpected delights of **Keith Harding's World of Mechanical Music** (The Oak House, High Street; 01451 860181) – the pianolas, music boxes and other mechanical instruments on show make this a fun place to

go with children. If you want to gain a fuller understanding of the area, then visit the Cotswold Heritage Centre (Fosse Way; 01451 860715; closed Nov-Mar). Housed in a renovated 18th-century prison, it traces the agricultural history of the region and includes a collection of antique farming equipment and tools.

What to see & do

Tourist Information Centres
77 Promenade, Cheltenham, GL50 1PP (01242 226554/www.visitcheltenham.gov.uk). **Open** 9.30am-5.15pm Mon-Sat.
Cotswold Visitor Information Centre, Hollis House, The Square, Stow-on-the-Wold, GL54 1AF (01451 831082). **Open** *Easter-Sept* 9.30am-5.30pm Mon-Sat; 10.30am-4pm Sun. *Oct-Easter* 9.30am-4.30pm Mon-Sat.

Bike hire
Compass Holidays *Cheltenham Spa rail station, Queens Road, Cheltenham (01242 250642/ www.compass-holidays.com).*

Birdland Park & Gardens
Bourton-on-the-Water (01451 820480). **Open** *Apr-Oct* 10am-6pm daily. *Nov-Mar* 10am-4pm daily (last admission 1hr before closing). **Admission** £4.50; £2.50-£3.50 concessions; free under-4s.
The place for ornithologists young and old. Seven acres of woodland, river and gardens are inhabited by more than 500 species of bird, including flamingos, penguins and cranes. There are also aviaries of parrots and toucans, and tropical, desert and temperate houses.

Chedworth Roman Villa
Yanworth, on A429 nr Northleach (01242 890256/ www.ntrustsevern.org.uk). **Open** *Late Feb-late Mar, late Oct-mid Nov* 11am-4pm Tue-Sun, bank holidays. *Late Mar-late Oct* 10am-5pm Tue-Sun, bank holidays. **Admission** (NT) £3.70; £1.90 concessions.
Discovered in 1864, this sizeable second-century AD house is one of the best-exposed Romano-British villa sites in the country. Set amid woodland with views across the countryside, it houses a water shrine, two bath houses and mosaics.

Cheltenham Art Gallery & Museum
Clarence Street, Cheltenham (01242 237431/ www.cheltenhammuseum.org.uk). **Open** 10am-5.20pm Mon-Sat; 2-4.20pm Sun. **Admission** free; donations welcome.
This outstanding collection comprises furniture and silver made by craftsmen from the Arts and Crafts movement, including William Morris, as well as oriental porcelain and English ceramics, and exhibits on the social history of Cheltenham.

Hailes Abbey
Off B4632 nr Winchcombe (01242 602398/ www.english-heritage.org.uk). **Open** *Apr-Sept* 10am-6pm daily. *Oct* 10am-5pm daily. *Nov-Mar* 10am-4pm Sat, Sun. **Admission** £2.60; £1.30-£2 concessions.
This Cistercian Abbey was founded in 1246 by Richard, Earl of Cornwall, younger brother of Henry

The Cotswolds

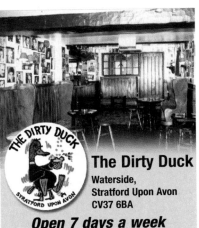

All hail, **Hailes Abbey**.

This ancient castle has quite a history: its banqueting hall dates from around 1450 and the chapel houses the tomb of Henry VIII's sixth wife, Katherine Parr. After Henry's death in 1547, Katherine married her former lover, Lord Seymour of Sudeley, but died in childbirth here only a year later. The castle was also Charles I's headquarters during the Civil War and was besieged in 1643 and again in 1644. Nowadays you can relax in its nine beautiful gardens, bounce against the 15-foot-high double yew hedges and admire the art collection, which includes works by Constable, Rubens and Turner.

Where to stay

The Cotswolds have always attracted a certain class and age of visitor and this is reflected in high hotel prices and the fact that many of the hotels don't wholeheartedly embrace families. That said, there is a good selection of pleasant places to stay, many of which offer special two-night deals. Note, also, that many hotels get booked up weeks in advance before the National Hunt horse racing in March. The Festival of Music (July) and the Festival of Literature (October) are other busy times.

In addition to **Lower Slaughter Manor** (*see p181*), the village boasts the equally luxurious *Lords of the Manor* (01451 820243/ www.lordsofthemanor.com; doubles £150-£300). In Stow, the upmarket choices are the flower-festooned **Unicorn Hotel** (Sheep Street; 01451 830257/www.cotswold-inns-hotels.co.uk; doubles £90-£110) and the lavish **Wyck Hill House** (on the A44 between Stow and Burford; 01451 831936/www.wyckhill.com; doubles £105-£155). In Cheltenham, the **Hotel Kandinsky** (Bayshill Road, Montpellier; 01242 527788/www.hotelkandinsky.com; doubles £85) is smart and lively and has its own nightclub.

III. In medieval times one of the relics it was said to house was some of Christ's blood, an object of reverence for pilgrims and mentioned in Chaucer's *Canterbury Tales*. The abbey fell into ruin after the dissolution of the monasteries in 1539, but its attractive woodland setting makes it worth a visit. There's a museum, too, with fine medieval sculpture and decorated floor tiles.

Holst Birthplace Museum
4 Clarence Road, Cheltenham (01242 524846/ www.holstmuseum.org.uk). **Open** 10am-4pm Tue-Sat. **Admission** £2.50; £1.25 concessions.
The composer of *The Planets* suite was born here in 1874 and the Regency terrace house is now home to a museum in his honour. As well as Holst's original piano and miscellaneous remnants illustrating his life story, the house offers an idea of how life would have been in Victorian and Edwardian Britain, with a working kitchen, children's nursery and elegant drawing room.

Model Village
High Street, Bourton-on-the-Water (01451 820467). **Open** *Apr-Oct* 9am-5.45pm daily. *Nov-Mar* 10am-4pm daily. **Admission** £2.75; £2 concessions.
Made entirely of Cotswold stone, this is a 1:9 scale model of the village of Bourton as it was in 1937, complete with rivers, miniature trees and a model of the model as well.

Sudeley Castle & Gardens
Winchcombe, nr Cheltenham (01242 602308/ www.stratford.co.uk/sudeley). **Open** *Gardens* Mar-Oct 10.30am-5.30pm daily. *Castle* Apr-Oct 11am-5pm daily. Last entry 4.30pm. **Admission** *Castle & gardens* £6.20; £3.20-£5.20 concessions. *Gardens only* £4.70; £2.50-£3.70 concessions.

Cleeve Hill Hotel
Cleeve Hill, Cheltenham, GL52 3PR (01242 672052/fax 01242 679969/ www.smoothhound.co.uk/hotels/cleeve.html). **Rates** £45 single; £70-£90 double/twin; £75-£110 family. **Rooms** (all en suite) 6 double; 2 twin; 1 family; 1 single. **Credit** MC, V.
Cleeve Hill is set up high on the eponymous hill ten minutes' drive to the north-east of Cheltenham and two miles from the National Hunt racecourse. All the bedrooms are of a respectable size with en suite bathrooms and tremendous views either across the valley to the Malvern Hills or to Cleeve Common. There's a bar in the lounge, and an ample breakfast is served in the airy conservatory. The proprietors uphold a strict no-smoking policy, no pets are allowed, nor children under eight years of age.

Dial House Hotel
The Chestnuts, High Street, Bourton-on-the-Water, GL54 2AN (01451 822244/fax 01451 810126/ www.dialhousehotel.com). **Rates** (per person) £57 single/double/twin; £69 four-poster. **Rooms** (all en suite) 14. **Credit** MC, V.

This Cotswold stone house was built in 1698 in the heart of tourist heavy Bourton-on-the-Water by local architect Andrew Paxford. And it is nothing if not authentic: both its weathered exterior and interior decor reflect the age of the house. Most of the rooms are furnished with characteristic antique pieces, and current owners Jane Howard and Adrian Campbell have made it a welcoming place and are always on hand to help out. Imaginative food is served in the ground-floor restaurant (see p182). Rooms in the extension are more modern and less charming than those in the main house. No-smoking rooms are available. No children under 12.

Off A429, 4 miles SW of Stow-on-the-Wold.

The Greenway

Shurdington, nr Cheltenham, GL51 5UG (01242 862352/fax 01242 862780). **Rates** £79-£139 single occupancy; £165 double; £230 four-poster. **Rooms** (all en suite) 1 single; 20 double/twin; 1 four-poster. **Credit** AmEx, DC, MC, V.

A 16th-century manor house hotel covered in creeper, the Greenway is welcoming and luxurious and manages to avoid too much formality. Rooms are clean, comfortable and spacious, and look out over the hotel's formal gardens and croquet lawn and beyond to the beautiful surrounding countryside. The hotel is only a few minutes' drive from Cheltenham. The food in the restaurant is as elaborate and well executed as you'd expect. Children over seven are welcome. No-smoking rooms available.

On A46 2 miles SW of Cheltenham.

Hotel on the Park

38 Evesham Road, Cheltenham, GL52 2AH (01242 518898/fax 01242 511526/ www.hotelonthepark.co.uk). **Rates** £79.50 single occupancy; £99.50-£119.50 double/twin; £159.50 four-poster; £129.50 suite. Breakfast £8.50 (English); £6.25 (continental). **Rooms** (all en suite) 10 double/twin; 1 four-poster; 1 suite. **Credit** AmEx, DC, MC, V.

Not far from the heart of Cheltenham, this very well-preserved Regency townhouse is a pretty classy base for a weekend. You can take the air across the road in Pittville Park, or alternatively, a 15-minute stroll will take you into the hustle and bustle of Cheltenham town centre. All the rooms are exquisitely furnished in keeping with the Regency style and offer plenty of home comforts. Overlooking the park from the ground floor, the bacchanalian restaurant offers a modern British menu. No children under eight. No-smoking rooms available.

The Hunt is on... off... on...

Cheltenham is almost synonymous with horse racing: little wonder since the town's 15 days of races usually draw around 275,000 visitors annually – more than the total number of people who visit the town throughout the rest of the year.

In 2001, however, the outbreak of foot and mouth disease had a devastating effect on the caterers of Cheltenham and its immediate environs. The **National Hunt Festival** was first postponed from March to April, and then cancelled altogether. It was the first time since World War II that the festival had not taken place and, naturally, visitor numbers plummeted.

There has been racing in Cheltenham since 1815, when the first meet was held on Nottingham Hill, above Bishop's Cleeve. The first version of the Cheltenham Gold Cup was not inaugurated until four years later, with a prize of 100 guineas offered to the winner of the three-mile, weight-for-age flat race on Cleeve Hill. By the mid-1820s the Cheltenham races had become as prestigious as Ascot or Goodwood.

It wasn't long, however, before the betting and boisterous merrymaking surrounding the races came to the attention of a preacher called Francis Close, who roused likeminded puritanical killjoys to demonstrate against all the fun on the racecourse in 1829. One year later the grandstand was burned down. That was all it took to discourage people from turning up, and by 1855 flat racing had died out altogether at Cheltenham.

Meetings were still going on elsewhere, however, and in April 1834 the first Grand Annual Steeplechase (so named because it was run between two church steeples) took place in Andoversford, where it has been run every year since. Nowadays the country's most prestigious steeplechase event is the Cheltenham Gold Cup, which dates back to 1924, when the first Gold Cup Steeplechase took place at Prestbury Park. In those days the prize money was £685. If the race had gone ahead in 2001 the winner of the Tote Cheltenham Gold Cup would have taken away a prize worth an estimated total of £300,000.

Cheltenham Racecourse

Prestbury Park, Cheltenham GL50 4SH (01242 513014/ www.cheltenham.co.uk). **Open** *Hall of fame* 10am-4.30pm Mon-Fri. **Admission** free.

Art deco and **The Daffodil**. *See p182.*

Lower Slaughter Manor

Lower Slaughter, GL54 2HP (01451 820456/ fax 01451 822150/www.lowerslaughter.co.uk). **Rates** £175 single occupancy; £200 double; £260-£325 deluxe double/twin; £350 four-poster; £350-£400 suite. **Rooms** (all en suite) 2 double; 9 deluxe double/twin; 2 four-posters; 3 suites. **Credit** AmEx, DC, MC, V.

If money is no object, this is the place to come. A manor house has stood on this site, dominating the famously beautiful village of Lower Slaughter, for more than 1,000 years, but the current building dates from 1658. From the smell of an open fire at reception, the choice of newspaper with your morning drink, to the huge piles of towels by the side of the indoor swimming pool and the pleasant private grounds, your every whim will be attended to here. Smart casual dress is required if you wish to dine in the hotel restaurant, otherwise opt for room service and slob out in your towelling bathrobe. No children under 12.

A429 S of Stow-on-the-Wold; after 1½ miles turn right after Esso garage towards the Slaughters; manor is on right.

Wesley House

High Street, Winchcombe, GL54 5LJ (01242 602366/fax 01242 602405/www.wesleyhouse.com). **Rates** £40-£55 single; £37.50-£40 per person double/twin. **Rooms** (all en suite) 1 single; 2 twin; 3 doubles. **Credit** AmEx, MC, V.

In the middle of Winchcombe, a half-timbered building dating from around 1435 houses Wesley House restaurant (*see p182*) and B&B. Most of the smallish bedrooms are directly above the restaurant and are reached via a rickety little staircase, while a single room is tucked away in the attic. The place is clean, crisp and very pleasant, with good attention to detail – biscuits and fresh milk for tea and coffee await you in the rooms, and a generous breakfast is served. The en suite bathrooms are furnished with showers rather than baths because of the limited space, but don't let that put you off – this is a lovely place to stay. Children welcome. All bedrooms are non-smoking.

B4632 E of Cheltenham; Winchcombe is signposted to the right. The hotel is on the right in the High Street.

Where to eat & drink

Cheltenham can now pride itself on a good number of fine eating establishments that offer menus to suit every size of wallet. However, the town is not overly endowed with hearty, traditional pubs. Unless you opt for the studenty **Whole Hog Ale House** or the All Bar One-ish **Circus Bar** on the Promenade, you're going to find yourself in a gentrified bar. Out of town there is no shortage of country boozers. In Stow, try the **Royalist Hotel** in Digbeth Street (01451 830670) for reliable modern European dishes, or the **Eagle & Child** (same number), their sister outlet next door, for tradional pub-grub with a touch of flair. Just east of Stow, the **Horse & Groom** (01451 830584) in Upper Oddington, has a sizeable, recently redesigned garden and also offers accommodation, while in Lower Oddington the **Fox** (01451 870555) is a good gastropub. Further south are the **King's Head** in Birdlip (01452 862299), known for its excellent food and wines, and the **Hare & Hounds** at Fosscross near Chedworth (01285 720288). Racing enthusiasts should try the **Hollow Bottom** in Guiting Power, between Bourton and Winchcombe, or the **Plough** in Ford; nearby are the cute **Halfway House** in Kineton, and the cheery **Black Horse** in Naunton.

Belgian Monk

47 Clarence Street, Cheltenham (01242 511717). **Food served** noon-3pm, 5.30-10pm Mon-Thur; noon-10pm Fri, Sat; noon-9pm Sun. **Credit** MC, V.

As the name suggests, this is the Cheltenham equivalent of Belgo, serving up Trappist beers and moules frites. Close to the town centre and offering a good choice of beers with a reasonably priced menu, it is a popular venue with a lively, relaxed atmosphere. Sausages of all kinds are served up with mashed potato and gravy but it goes almost without saying that the moules and frites are the best reason to eat here.

Le Champignon Sauvage

24-26 Suffolk Road, Cheltenham (01242 573449/fax 01242 254365). **Food served** 12.30-1.30pm, 7.30-9.15pm Tue-Sat. **Set lunch** £16.50 2 courses; £19.95 3 courses. **Set dinner** £19 du jour; £33 2 courses; £39 3 courses; £46 4 courses. **Credit** AmEx, DC, MC, V.

Since they opened Le Champignon Sauvage 15 years ago, husband and wife team David and Helen Everitt-Matthias have gone from strength to strength, winning a string of prestigious awards, including two Michelin stars. This is just reward for their well-thought-out dishes, home-made breads and attentive service. Now one of Cheltenham's most celebrated restaurants, it remains surprisingly inexpensive, with set-price menus offered at both lunch and dinner. Choose from main courses such as fillet of red mullet, black olive purée and yellow pepper compote, or breast of guinea fowl with a light foie gras mousse. The wine list is not as startlingly pricey as you might expect either; Le Champignon's most recent accolade was the *Decanter*'s Restaurant of the Year 2000 award.

The Cotswolds

The colourful and lively **Orange Tree**.

Choirs

5-6 Well Walk, Cheltenham (01242 235578).
Food served noon-1.30pm, 7-9pm Tue-Sat.
Set meals *dinner* £14.50 2 courses; £17.50
3 courses. **Credit** MC, V.

Choirs is a typically provincial French-style restaurant that offers consistently good food (all free from genetically modified soya and maize) at a reasonable price. Baguettes, sandwiches and omelettes are a good choice at lunchtime, while the evening set menu on our visit featured twice-baked smoked Applewood Cheddar soufflé with grape and walnut dressing to start, followed by roasted chicken marinated in Chinese spices with coconut rice and sweet chilli sauce, and a rhubarb and mascarpone tart to finish.

The Daffodil

18-20 Suffolk Parade, Cheltenham (01242 700055).
Food served noon-2.30pm, 6.30-10.30pm Mon-Sat.
Credit AmEx, MC, V.

Some might say it's a shame that this remarkable art deco building had to relinquish its cinema in order to make way for an eating establishment, but at least this restaurant is deserving of its setting. Sophie Grigson once described it as 'Cheltenham's hottest restaurant', and it is a wonderfully lively place. Cuisine is modern and refreshingly simple, relying on the flavour of good ingredients rather than too much fanciness. You can eat in the relaxing ground-floor restaurant or the bar area upstairs, reached by a pair of sweeping staircases. Starters are around the £6 mark and include the likes of asparagus spears topped with a poached egg and chive dressing, or smoked Seychelles marlin with melon and lime dressing. Main courses might be goat's cheese and potato flan or a fillet steak. Save some space for the marbled passion fruit cheesecake with summer fruits.

Dial House Hotel

The Chestnuts, High Street, Bourton-on-the-Water (01451 822244/www.dialhousehotel.com). **Food served** noon-2pm, 7-9pm daily. **Credit** MC, V.
Awards from both the AA and Egon Ronay have been slapped on the Dial House restaurant and new head chef Jonathan Lane-Robinson maintains standards with a

well-thought-out menu and good food. The dark oak beams, inglenook fireplace and well-stocked bar score highly in the cosy dining room stakes. Choose from a fair range of fish, meat and vegetarian options – try truffled French bean salad (£5.95) for starters, and move on to pan-roasted scallops, roast rack of lamb served with gratin dauphinois and crushed minted peas (both £16), or wild mushroom timbale and Madeira sauce (£14). Puddings are worth a viewing, too. *See also p179.*

Orange Tree

317 High Street, Cheltenham (01242 234232/ www.theorangetreeuk.co.uk). **Food served** 10am-9pm Mon-Thur; 10am-10pm Fri, Sat; 11.30am-3pm Sun. **Credit** MC, V.
Vegetarian restaurants are few and far between in Cotswold country, so what a relief to find such a good one. His eaterie may be in a less-frequented part of town, but manager Shai Patel has made it into a popular and welcome retreat decked out with wood furnishings and coloured paper lanterns. The diverse menu has something for any time of day or night, whether you fancy a late breakfast, falafel and pitta bread washed down with organic wine or beer, mascarpone cheesecake or apple strudel (all around £3) with coffee, or something from the huge and daily-changing meal menu. Weekend lunchtimes can be very busy. Gluten-free and dairy-free diets catered for.

Le Petit Blanc

The Promenade, Cheltenham (01242 266800/ www.petit-blanc.co.uk). **Food served** noon-3pm, 6-10.30pm Mon-Sat; noon-3pm, 6-10pm Sun. **Set meals** (noon-3pm, 6-7pm) £12.50 2 courses, £15 3 courses. **Credit** AmEx, DC, MC, V.
One of Raymond Blanc's ever-expanding family of restaurants, Le Petit Blanc was something of a culinary groundbreaker when it opened in Cheltenham. Current head chef Tim Cook still provides a menu that caters to diners on a budget as well as those for whom money is no object. The bright, modern interior manages to be both relaxed and smart, with plate glass windows affording views of the grand Promenade. Food is excellent, with well-cooked and flavourful versions of both British and French classics; as is the wine list, which starts at just £10.65 a bottle. Children are made more than welcome with their own, reasonably priced menu.

Wesley House

High Street, Winchcombe (01242 602366/ www.wesleyhouse.com). **Food served** noon-2pm, 6.45-9.30pm Mon-Sat; noon-2pm Sun. **Set dinner** £26 2 courses; £31 3 courses. **Credit** AmEx, MC, V.
This is the place that locals choose to come to when they want to celebrate in style. Food could be described as French with a modern twist, with such dishes as smoked haddock and spinach soufflé with a chive fish cream on the starter list, and main courses such as loin of lamb stuffed with spinach and caramelised shallots on ratatouille. However, as with many French-inspired restaurants, vegetarians don't get much of a look-in. They can take full advantage of the puddings, of course, which run along the lines of warm chocolate tart with chocolate sauce and Chantilly cream. The wine list is broadminded, drawing on a number of New World countries as well as France. On Saturday nights diners are charged for a minimum of three courses.

North Cotswolds

Golden villages, country paths and sweet garden air.

The even, chocolate-box beauty of this part of the Cotswolds results from the honeyed tones in the stone from which most of its buildings were created. The handsome churches, fine mansions and rows of pretty almshouses grew out of the vast fortunes of beneficent wool merchants. Ironically, the later decline of the wool industry is responsible for the area's attractive appearance today – the terrible hardship suffered by local people meant that little was built here after the 18th century and the harmonious vernacular prevails.

The area's pleasures are not a well-kept secret. Its accessibility and immense popularity mean that at peak times during the summer months you could, without careful planning, end up sharing your rural escape shoulder-to-shoulder with thousands of camcorder-wielding tourists. It's also worth pointing out that most of the discreet bourgeois charms of this area are adult-oriented: village-hopping, walking, visiting gardens, antiques browsing, eating and drinking; there are few attractions specifically aimed at energetic younger children, and it is always worth checking if smaller hotels and B&Bs are happy to cater for kids.

But when the sun is shining and the road is clear, the north Cotswolds are gloriously seductive: slow-paced, sensuous and visually stunning. When they are at their best, even the most hardcore urbanite will struggle to suppress subversive *Good Life* fantasies about giving it all up and moving here to while away summer evenings tending their cottage garden. Whether idling through the architecturally distinctive towns and villages, strolling along country footpaths or grazing in the area's many top-class pubs and restaurants, the north Cotswolds offer a tonic for weary metropolitan senses.

A traveller's rest

The lively market town of **Moreton-in-Marsh** – its wide main street lined with 17th- and 18th-century coaching inns and pubs – has for

centuries been a stop-off point for Londoners arriving in this part of the Cotswolds (it is on the old London-Worcester road, now the A44). It is worth a stroll down the main drag (a section of the Roman Fosse Way) to admire the buildings, some of which claim diverting historical trivia of the 'King Charles I sheltered here during the Civil War' variety. You can restock your hamper and wallet here (cashpoints are thin on the ground elsewhere). Weekenders will miss the vast market held in the town centre on Tuesdays.

On Broadway

Broadway, another former staging post on the road from Worcester to London, is allegedly the Cotswolds' most-visited village. Broadway's role as a coaching stop has bequeathed it an array of inns and hotels, pubs and tearooms. These are accompanied by numerous shops of varying degrees of frivolity and tweeness

The Jacobean gatehouse at **Stanway House**.

By train from London

Trains from **Paddington** to **Moreton-in-Marsh** leave half-hourly. Journey time is between **1hr 20mins** and **1hr 50mins**. Info: www.thamestrains.co.uk.

(enthusiastically hyped in the brochures as the 'Bond Street of the Cotswolds'). Here you will find purveyors of all manner of souvenirs and handicrafts – some ghastly, some desirable, all overpriced. A five-minute walk up the main street to the east takes you away from the madding crowds, however, and reminds you why the village was a magnet for William Morris and the Pre-Raphaelite artists. Serenely gorgeous limestone cottages abound, bedecked with wisteria, clematis and climbing roses.

South of Broadway are the idyllic villages of **Stanton** and **Stanway**. The 17th-century **Stanway House** (Stanway; 01386 584469) is open to the public and boasts an elaborate gatehouse where Stanway beer is still brewed in copper vats over log fires. Also worth seeing is the thatched cricket pavilion, perched on staddle stones to keep out the damp. Stanton is arguably the loveliest and most unspoiled Cotswolds village of all, the warm golden stone appearing sundrenched year round.

Chipping crafts
Chipping Campden, just east of Broadway, centres on its gently curving high street and 17th-century market hall. Wealthy wool merchants bankrolled the towering church of St James; brasses on the floor of the church pay tribute to their wisdom and munificence. Sadly the church, like so many in this area, was 'restored' in the 19th century – in other words medieval wall paintings were whitewashed and ornately carved pews with candelabras at either end were torn out – but it still repays a visit with wonderful stained glass windows, marble effigies of local benefactors and 15th-century altar hangings. The town's fortunes declined when the wool trade crashed, rising again when CR Ashbee made it the base for his bold Guild of Handicraft experiment in 1902, moving here from the East End of London with a group of cockney craftsmen intent on protecting and promoting traditional craft skills against the mass production techniques of modern industry. Although his Arts and Crafts project ultimately failed (mass production rivals imitated the Guild's goods and sold them more cheaply), the town has remained a centre for silversmiths, jewellers, wood carvers, cabinet makers and enamellers, as well as a mecca for Arts and Crafts movement devotees from all over the world. The town's rustic, unspoiled ambience is ironically the product of rigidly enforced modern planning strictures. The Campden Trust, formed by craftsmen and architects in 1929, restored many of the town's old buildings and set exacting conservation standards. Telegraph wires and power cables are buried underground or tucked away out

of sight, while shops, pubs and restaurants are forced to maintain a discreet presence.

Chipping Campden is a convenient base for ramblers: the 100-mile **Cotswold Way** starts here en route to Bath, and there are countless local walks. A strenuous one-mile hike up Dover's Hill to the north of the town repays with impressive views over the Vale of Evesham.

A number of delightful villages lie within a five-mile radius of Chipping Campden, not to mention magnificent gardens and stately homes. Immediately south lies **Broad Campden**, where you can catch a glimpse of CR Ashbee's old house, a converted Norman chapel. **Blockley**, with its gently flowing brook, was the thriving centre of the silk industry in the 18th and 19th centuries. You can walk by the old silk mills, now converted into sumptuous houses. You may be lucky enough to catch a languorous afternoon's village cricket match at **Ebrington**, with its dinky pitch in the shadow of a fine old church. Look out, too, for the clever millennium sundial on the diminutive village green.

What to see & do

Tourist Information Centres
1 Cotswold Court, Broadway, WR12 7AA (01386 852937). **Open** 10am-1pm, 2-5pm Mon-Sat.
High Street, Chipping Campden, GL55 6AL (01386 841206/www.chippingcampden.co.uk). **Open** 10am-5.30pm daily.
Cotswold District Council Offices, High Street, Moreton-in-Marsh, GL56 0AZ (01608 650881/ www.cotswold.gov.uk). **Open** 8.45am-4pm Mon; 8.45am-5.15pm Tue, Wed; 8.45am-7.30pm Thur; 8.45am-4.45pm Fri; 9.30am-1pm Sat.

Bike hire
The Toy Shop *High Street, Moreton-in-Marsh (01608 650756).*
Cotswold Country Cycles *London Farm Cottage, Longlands, Chipping Campden (01386 438706).*

Broadway Teddy Bear Museum
76 High Street, Broadway (01386 858323/ www.jks.org/broadwaybearsanddolls). **Open** 10am-4pm Wed-Sun. **Admission** £1.50; £1 concessions.
Kids will adore this charming pint-sized museum with buttons to press, and teddies from around the world. Adults, meanwhile, can moon nostalgically over Big Ted. There's also a hospital for ailing bears and dolls.

Broadway Tower Country Park
Just off A44, Broadway (01386 852390). **Open** *Tower* Apr-Oct 10.30am-6pm daily. Last entry 5pm. Nov-Mar 10am-dusk Sat, Sun. *Park* Apr-Oct 10am-4.30pm daily. Closed Nov-Mar. **Admission** *Tower & park* £4; £2.30-£3.50 concessions.
The tower is an 18th-century folly, housing exhibitions on its one-time occupant, William Morris. There's an adventure playground, deer enclosure, picnic sites, and magnificent walks with views over 12 counties.

The Cotswolds

Moreton-in-Marsh (*above*) and **Stanton** (*below*) – a market town and a sleepy village.

Cotswold Falconry Centre & Batsford Arboretum

Batsford Park, off A44, nr Moreton-in-Marsh (01386 701043/www.cotswold-falconry.co.uk). **Open** *mid Feb-mid Nov* 10.30am-5.30pm daily. Last admission (Nov) 3.30pm. **Admission** £4; £2-£3 concessions.

Hour-long demonstrations of the art of falconry with eagles, falcons, owls and kites are held four times daily (phone for details). The arboretum next door contains over 1,500 species of tree and shrub, many of them rare. Particularly colourful in the spring and autumn.

Gloucester Warwickshire Steam Railway

Toddington Station (info line and timetable 01242 621405). **Fares** £7; £4 concessions; free under-5s. Take a 13-mile round trip to Gretton, with great views over the Cotswold hills, on a steam train.

Hidcote Manor Garden

Hidcote Bartrim, nr Chipping Campden (01684 855370/www.nationaltrust.org.uk). **Open** *Apr, May* 11am-6pm Mon, Wed, Thur, Sat, Sun. *June, July* 10.30am-6.30pm Mon-Thur, Sat, Sun. *Aug-Oct* 10.30am-5.30pm Mon, Wed, Thur, Sat, Sun. Last admission 1hr before closing/dusk. **Admission** (NT) £5.70; £2.80 concessions.

Magnificent, highly influential formal gardens designed by Major Lawrence Johnston in the early 20th century. He travelled the globe to find specimens for the different garden 'rooms', separated by walls and hedges. Liable to serious overcrowding on Sundays and bank holidays.

Kiftsgate Court Gardens

Nr Hidcote, 4 miles NE of Chipping Campden (01386 438777/www.kiftsgate.co.uk). **Open** *Apr, May, Aug, Sept* 2-6pm Wed, Thur, Sun. *June, July* noon-6pm Wed, Thur, Sat, Sun. **Admission** £4; £1 concessions.

A few minutes from Hidcote lies this magical garden designed by three generations of women. Set on the edge of the Cotswold escarpment, with heart-stopping views over the Vale of Evesham, this is a space to treasure. Look out for the splendid swimming pool, the famous Kiftsgate Rose, which grows up to 60ft (18m) high, and a recently added water garden.

Sezincote House & Gardens

2 miles SW of Moreton-in-Marsh, off A44 (no phone). **Open** *House* May-July, Sept 2.30-5.30pm Thur, Fri. *Garden* Jan-Nov 2-6pm/dusk Thur, Fri, bank hols. **Admission** £5; £2 concessions.

An extraordinarily exotic place, with Asian influences everywhere, from the Hindu statues hidden among the bamboo and Japanese maples to the house itself, which was inspired by Indian temples and fortresses, and was the model for Brighton Pavilion. Note: children under 16 are not allowed in the house.

Snowshill Manor

Snowshill, nr Broadway (01684 852410/www.nationaltrust.org.uk). **Open** *House* Apr-Oct noon-5pm Wed-Sun, bank hol Mon. *Grounds* Apr-Oct 11am-5.30pm Wed-Sun, bank hol Mon. **Admission** (NT) £6; £2.50 concessions.

Eccentric owner Charles Wade was forced to live in a simple cottage in the lovely terraced gardens of this 15th- and 16th-century manor after he had filled its rooms with breathtaking collections of toys, clocks (including some fascinating Japanese examples), musical instruments, spinning wheels, bicycles and more. The *samurai* armour is particularly memorable. The small, pretty garden and Wade's cottage are also worth a visit, if for no other reason than to try to learn more about this strange man. Expect big crowds at weekends.

Where to stay

This area has a phenomenal range of accommodation options – for all wallets. It is essential to book in advance, however, and don't even think of trying for a room during Cheltenham National Hunt Festival in March, and expect a similar rush for accommodation during the music and literature festivals in July and October respectively (*see 176*). The following are just a sample; the tourist information offices (*see p184*) can provide lists of more basic B&Bs at prices as low as £20 per room per night.

Cotswold House Hotel

The Square, Chipping Campden, GL55 6AN (01386 840330/fax 01386 840310/www.cotswoldhouse.com). **Rates** (B&B) £85 single; £130-£190 double/twin; £200 four-poster. Special breaks. **Rooms** (all en suite) 1 single; 7 double; 4 twin; 1 four-poster. **Credit** AmEx, MC, V.

For a room overlooking the 'most beautiful street in England', try this stately hotel, its solid handsome façade belying a light, airy interior. Rooms are decorated with vague 'themes' in mind – feminine, colonial and so on – with quieter rooms (Room 10 is a good choice) overlooking the terrace and long garden at the back. There are two restaurants serving expertly prepared and delicious food – the rather formal pastel-hued Garden Restaurant, complete with pianist; and Hicks' Brasserie (*see p188*). Lavish, superb breakfasts make lunch inconceivable. Children and pets welcome. All bedrooms no-smoking.

A44 W of Moreton-in-Marsh; hotel is in square on main street in Chipping Campden, on B4081.

Evesham Hotel

Coopers Lane, off Waterside, Evesham, WR11 6DA (01386 765566/fax 01386 765443/www.eveshamhotel.com). **Rates** £65 single; £103 double/twin; £152 family suite. **Rooms** 5 single; 21 double; 2 family. **Credit** AmEx, DC.

Alton Towers meets Fawlty Towers in this rambling hotel; on our visit the affable but eccentric owner yelled at someone for using a mobile in the bar ('so vulgar') while a regular – a spitter for the Major – nodded approvingly. Large rooms are a bit shabby but contain everything you need from irons to rubber ducks, and some of the themed rooms are wonderful. Our favourite was the Alice in Wonderland family suite with Mad Hatter's tea party and crazy mirrors, but the tropical room with fishtank under the sink is also fun. There's an indoor swimming pool, table football, toys every-

where, and even a C5 for driving around the huge garden. It's all relentlessly jokey – if the hotel had a motto it would be 'You don't have to be mad to stay here, but it helps' – and even the room-key fobs are teddy bears. You'll either love it or hate it; your kids will definitely love it. Children welcome. No-smoking rooms available.
Off M40 at exit 8/9, follow A40 round Oxford to Burford, follow A424 to Stow-on-the-Wold, follow A44 to Broadway/ Evesham. In Evesham at first proper traffic lights turn left, do not go straight over bridge.

Holly House
Ebrington, nr Chipping Campden, GL55 6NL (01386 593213/fax 01386 593181). **Rates** £22-£24 per person. **Rooms** (all en suite) 1 single; 3 double/twin/family. **No credit cards.**
The rooms here are nothing ritzy, but they are clean and private, having separate, exterior entrances. Breakfast is served in a bright and cheerfully furnished modern family house, and there is a garden room for the use of guests. Without, perhaps, the character of some its more expensive rivals, it is perfectly situated within walking distance of Hidcote, Kiftsgate and Chipping Campden while being far enough away to escape the crowds. Children welcome. No smoking throughout.
B4035 E from Chipping Campden; after half a mile follow signs to Ebrington on left; house is in village centre after Ebrington Arms pub.

Lower Brook House
Lower Street, Blockley, GL56 9DS (tel/fax 01386 700286). **Rates** £65-£75 single occupancy; £80-£96 double; £145 four-poster; £50 per person per apartment. **Rooms** (all en suite) 5 double; 2 four-poster; 1 apartment (sleeps 6). **Credit** MC, V.
The character and fortunes of this hotel centre upon the expansive personality of its welcoming owner, Marie Mosedale-Cooper. Personal touches are everywhere, from the family photos and bric-a-brac downstairs to the books, magazines and flowers in the rather small and self-consciously cottage-like rooms. Not for the shy, the intimate restaurant encourages conversation between guests over imaginative meals. Breakfast, too, is excellent. Children welcome. Dogs allowed in the apartment only. All bedrooms no-smoking.
Off A44 between Moreton-in-Marsh and Broadway; at Bourton-on-the-Hill take turning to Blockley; head down into valley, which takes you straight into hotel drive.

Lygon Arms Hotel
High Street, Broadway, WR12 7DU (01386 852255/ fax 01386 858611/www.savoy-group.co.uk). **Rates** £135-£149 single occupancy; £180-£255 double; £329-£359 four-poster; £370-£625 suite. Breakfast £16.50 (Eng); £10.50 (cont). **Rooms** (all en suite) 52 double/twin; 11 four-poster/suites.
Credit AmEx, DC, MC, V.
Those whose ships have come in will want the oak-panelled Charles I room (£600), complete with log fire, four-poster and antiques dating from the period when the doomed monarch stayed here. Only marginally more affordable are the other atmospheric rooms at the front of this handsome 16th-century coaching inn. Rooms in the ugly '60s extension at the back are perfectly nice, but removed from the historic splendour of the maze of staircases and wood-panelled sitting rooms of the old part. There is an indoor swimming pool, fitness centre, two restaurants (*see p188*), and plenty of snug firelit corners in which to take afternoon tea. Children and dogs welcome. No-smoking rooms available.
Off A44 between Moreton-in-Marsh and Evesham; on High Street in Broadway village centre.

Malt House Hotel
Broad Campden, nr Chipping Campden, GL55 6UU (01386 840295/fax 01386 841334/www.malt-house.co.uk). **Rates** £59.50-£89.50 single occupancy; £79.50-£118.50 double; £112.50-£137.50 suite/family room. **Rooms** (all en suite) 6 double/twin; 2 double; 3 suites/family. **Credit** AmEx, DC, MC, V.
Leaded and mullioned windows look out from this long, low house over a large garden and orchard; a blaze of colour in summer and a blizzard of snowdrops

At the **Malt House Hotel** the rooms overlook a garden, orchard, brook and summerhouse.

in winter. Rooms are traditionally decorated havens of tranquillity – particularly those with their own entrances. An extraordinary rose-coloured cat greets you in a cosy beamed sitting room with firelight reflecting off the gold-leaf walls. Genial owner Nick Brown is justifiably proud of his breakfasts. Children and dogs welcome. All bedrooms no-smoking.

A44 towards Evesham; take B4081 towards Chipping Campden; follow signs to Broad Campden; hotel is in centre of village.

Where to eat & drink

Beams, log fires, real ale and, increasingly, decent food come as standard in most of the village pubs hereabouts. One worth making a special trip for is the 15th-century NT-owned **Fleece** at Bretforton, with three cosy firelit rooms around a bar serving home-made wines (rhubarb, dandelion) and oddly named ales (Morris Dancer, Pig's Ear), and a large garden with an aviary and playground. Otherwise, you can't go wrong with the friendly **Baker's Arms** in Broad Campden, the lovely old **Snowshill Arms** in Snowshill, the **Plough** at Stretton, the **Coach & Horses** in Longborough (there are two – ask for 'Top Coach') or the **Farrier's Arms** in Todenham. The **Horse & Groom** at Bourton-on-the-Hill is all lemon and green sofas and parlour palms, but the food lacks the verve of the decor. The **Eight Bells** in Chipping Campden (01386 840371) does good food, as does the **Howard Arms** in Ilmington (01608 682226), the nearby **Fox & Goose** at Armscote (01608 682293), and the **Churchill Arms** at Paxford (*see below*).

Thanks to planning restrictions, there is a dearth of interesting dining choices in Broadway, although **Oliver's Brasserie**, (Lygon Arms Hotel, High Street; 01386 854418) is worth trying, but Chipping Campden's options more than compensate. As well as **Hicks'** (see below), there is a lively Greek restaurant, **Alexiou's Tavern** (High Street; 01386 840826), serving Olympian portions, and a reliably good Italian, **Caminetto** (High Street, Chipping Campden; 01386 840934). In Moreton, in addition to the **Marsh Goose** (see below), there is **Annie's** (3 Oxford Street; 01608 651981), for delicious French-influenced food.

Churchill Arms

Paxford, nr Chipping Campden (01386 594000/ www.thechurchillarms.com). **Food served** noon-2pm, 7-9pm daily. **Credit** MC, V.

The scrum to order and pay at the bar, the infuriating no bookings policy and the frequently grumpy bar staff are all forgotten when the artistry of the kitchen becomes apparent. Starters of squid stuffed with basil risotto (£6.25) or marinated mushrooms with poached egg salad (£4.75) were over all too quickly; roast grey mullet came on a bed of mussels and baked garlic

(£10.95) and was near perfect, and the venison with sweet potato purée (£13) was beautifully cooked with a rich juniper jus. Puddings (£4) included a wonderfully gooey toffee pudding and a creamy passion fruit mousse which had us aching to lick the plate. The wine list is excellent value – several well-selected, mainly New World, house wines are £9.75. Upstairs, you can sleep off the excess in one of four comfortable en suite rooms (doubles £70).

Hicks' Brasserie Bar

The Square, Chipping Campden (01386 840330/ www.cotswoldhouse.com). **Food served** 12-2.30pm, 6-9.45pm daily. **Set lunches** £10.95 2 courses; £14.45 3 courses. **Credit** AmEx, MC, V.

This relaxed, modern brasserie is a real find in chintzy Chipping Campden, and the understated menu barely hints at the sophistication of the kitchen. A perfect battered hake and chips (£9.50) came with a piquant home-made tartare sauce, packed with capers, and a minted pea purée; while tuna loin with couscous arrived via Le Corbusier – geometrically stacked and surrounded by colourful swirls of sweet pepper sauce, chilli jam and topped with a spinach tempura. This attention to aesthetic detail is not to the detriment of flavours, however – chef Alan Dann's tutelage under Michel Roux at the Waterside Inn in Bray is much in evidence.

Lygon Arms Hotel (Great Hall)

High Street, Broadway (01386 852255/ www.savoygroup.co.uk). **Food served** 7.30-9.15pm Mon-Fri; 12.30-2pm, 7.30-9.15pm Sat, Sun. **Set lunch** £25 3 courses. **Set dinner** (Mon-Thur, Sun) £39.50 3 courses. (Fri, Sat) £42.50 3 courses. **Credit** AmEx, DC, MC, V.

This stately oak-panelled hall, complete with a roaring log fire, heraldic friezes and a 17th-century minstrels' gallery, is home to a restaurant with a truly excellent reputation. This was not entirely borne out on our visit, however. The set menu was very much the poor relation of the sample advertised, and à la carte starters of squab pigeon, russet apple and celeriac (£14) and scallops with lobster risotto and saffron froth (£15) left us slightly cold, as did mains of turbot braised in a red wine fumet (£25) and breast of Goosnargh duck infused with vanilla and five spice (£26). While the flavours of the meat and fish were well developed, accompanying vegetables and sauces veered between bland and salty. For such a formal setting, service was curiously inattentive – food arrived before wine, and dirty plates hung around for a little too long. Nevertheless, in terms of atmosphere, it's unbeatable. *See also p187.*

Marsh Goose

High Street, Moreton-in-Marsh (01608 653500/ www.marshgoose.com). **Food served** 7.30-9pm Tue; 12.30-2pm, 7.30-9pm Wed-Sat; 12.30-2pm Sun. **Set lunch** £18.50 3 courses. **Credit** AmEx, DC, MC, V.

Much-fêted chef Sonya Kidney now divides her time between this light, elegant restaurant and her other venture, the Churchill Arms (*see above*), but if starters of chicken liver and butternut ravioli with lime cream sauce (£8.50) and mains of pavé of lamb with lemon couscous (£15) are anything to go by, standards have remained consistently high. For a taster of such delights, try the Marsh Goose café next door, or the extremely good-value lunch menu.

The Campden Races

Anyone supposing that the special gift of the English for hooliganism only developed in the 20th century is very much mistaken; this noble heritage dates back at least to the Cotswold Olympicks, started in 1612 by Robert Dover.

Held over two days every Whitsun, the games involved a variety of activities including beating one's opponent over the head with sticks, shin kicking (competitors would apparently train for weeks by beating their shins with pieces of wood), and even, some say, dwarf throwing – though evidence of this appears to have disappeared in the mists of time. These high jinks continued unhindered for many years, with the approval of King James I, and were immortalised in print by Shakespeare and Ben Jonson.

However, in the mid 19th century, horse-racing was introduced, drawing railway navvies and crowds of hoi polloi from the industrialised Midlands. With them they brought drunkenness, rioting and vandalism to add to what was already a heady mix of sanctioned braining and ritual humiliation. It was at this point that the good burghers of Chipping Campden decided enough was enough and Parliament passed a bill to prohibit the games in 1853.

Just under 100 years later, a rather tamer version of the games was reintroduced and still takes place every May on what came to be known as Dover's Hill. At the 'Scuttlebrook Wake', a modern-day Robert Dover, appropriately dressed and on horseback, opens the proceedings, and the marching bands begin. Hounds sweep across the field, accompanied by a trumpeter, and cannons fire. There is morris dancing, tugs of war, wrestling and what are quaintly termed 'rustic activities'. As dusk falls, a huge bonfire is lit and fireworks set off, after which a torchlit procession moves down the hill into the town, where the singing, dancing and carousing carries on well into the night.

Tapestries Restaurant at Dormy House Hotel

Willersey Hill, Broadway (01386 852711/ www.dormyhouse.co.uk). **Food served** 7.30-10am, 12.30-2pm, 7-9.30pm Mon-Fri; 7.30-10am, 7-9.30pm Sat; noon-2pm, 7-9pm Sun. **Set lunch** (Sun) £19.95 3 courses. **Set dinner** (Mon-Sat) £32.50 3 courses. **Credit** AmEx, DC, MC, V.

Fresh, high-quality ingredients and inspired attention to detail are what make the food here special. Starters (around £9 à la carte) might include seared Scottish salmon open ravioli or smoked haddock risotto topped with a poached egg and hollandaise sauce. Typical main courses (around £20) include venison with a quenelle of parsnip mash with deep-fried leek on a green pepper-corn sauce, or Cornish halibut with mixed spice and gaz-pacho. The wine list is as considered as it is extensive. As with so many hotel restaurants, however, the atmos-phere can be rather leaden – hushed tones and smart dress are advised. Book a table near the window for stunning views over the Vale of Evesham.

Stratford & Warwick

Shakespeare may be the draw, but there are also castles, canals and creative cuisine to keep you entertained.

Avon calling.

South Warwickshire is known as the Heart of England, both for its central location and by virtue of the prominent role it has played in English history. This importance is largely the result of the River Avon and its tributaries, which have been major trade and travel routes from prehistory until modern times. The availability of ample water also created fertile farmland, which makes for glorious driving country with stunning views. Nevertheless, the area's place in history has been overshadowed by its association with William Shakespeare, and, as a result, much of the richness of the county's story has been subsumed by the ubiquitous marketing of 'Shakespeare Country' and tourists are never far away.

Much ado about William

Stratford-upon-Avon and the surrounding area is one of England's biggest tourist draws outside of London – and all because of one man. An otherwise unremarkable town, Stratford is inundated with visitors year round, most of whom come to pay homage to the world's most famous playwright. They follow the Shakespeare trail from the theatres to his birthplace on Henley Street, and then on to his grave at Holy Trinity Church in the Old Town (*see p194* **Bard news**).

Stratford's cutesy half-timbered architecture, cobbled mews and teashop culture aren't everyone's cup of char. Local proprietors aren't shy when it comes to milking Shakespeare's connection with the town – look out for names such as Thespian's (a restaurant) and Much Ado About Toys. Sheep Street, in particular, has fallen prey to pricey boutiques and restaurants, and ghastly souvenir shops. Yet it is all worth braving if you're a genuine Shakespeare junkie (and there is very pleasant walking along the canal, though avoid the heinous Cox's Yard, a grim mix of a boisterous pub and deeply naff shops). And make sure you have an escape route at the end of the day. For this reason, it may be better to stay in one of the farms or guesthouses in the surrounding villages rather than in the town itself.

Smooth runs the water
The Stratford-upon-Avon Canal meets the River Avon at the Bancroft Basin and lock in front of the Royal Shakespeare Theatre. This stretch of waterway is one of Stratford's greatest attractions, providing visitors with the chance to cruise, row, canoe, punt or just stroll and laze under willows on the grassy banks.

The **Countess of Evesham** (01789 293477/ www.countessofevesham.mistral.co.uk) offers lunch and dinner cruises along the River Avon. Alternatively, there's **Prince Regent II** (01608 662216), a luxury cruising restaurant. For a regular hour-long cruise, head for **Stratford Marina** (01789 269669). And for something totally different, try **Roses Boathouse** (01789 267073), which rents out an Edwardian craft or genuine Venetian gondola for short cruises, along with more standard rowing boats, punts and canoes. The long-established **Avon Boating** (01789 267073/www.avon-boating.co.uk) also provides punts, rowing boats, Canadian canoes and passenger boats along the river. For further information on activities including hire boat companies, leaflets, walks and education packs, phone or send an SAE to British Waterways, Brome Hall Lane, Lapworth, Solihull, B94 5RB (01564 784634/www.britishwaterways.co.uk).

Warwick
The county town of **Warwick**, an appealingly small and low-key place, is famed for its magnificent castle. The town grew from an eighth-century market – 'Werburgh's trading place' – and a produce market is still held in the town's square on Saturdays. In 1694, fire destroyed a large proportion of the original town. Extensive rebuilding gave the town centre its Georgian character, although some of the older buildings on the outskirts have survived to this day. The **Lord Leycester Hospital**, built in the 14th century and established as a hospital for war veterans in 1571, is one of the best examples of medieval architecture in the country. Those interested in the area's local history can visit the **Warwickshire Museum** (Market Place, Warwick; 01926 412500).

Spa from the madding crowd
Warwick has its castle; Stratford has its bard; the town of **Royal Leamington Spa** (more commonly known as Leamington) has its shops. The attractive Parade and award-winning

By train from London
Trains to **Warwick** and **Stratford-upon-Avon** leave **Paddington** every 2hrs. Journey time to Warwick is **1hr 50mins**; it is an additional **25mins** to Stratford. Trains to **Royal Leamington Spa** leave **Marylebone** half-hourly; the journey time is **1hr 40mins**.
Info: www.thamestrains.co.uk and www.chilternrailways.co.uk.

Royal Priors shopping centre have a good selection of high-street and speciality shops. And there's no fear of getting lost as the town is built on a grid, in a combination of grand Regency and Victorian architecture, with wide tree-lined avenues and elegant squares. Leamington was a favourite with Queen Victoria (hence the royal prefix), and the town was a playground for the rich and famous during its heyday as a fashionable spa resort. The supposed healing properties of the spa waters attracted thousands of credulous people over the years, among them Charles Darwin and Florence Nightingale.

Exit stage left
If these tourist-heavy towns get too much, take heart in the fact that there are many lesser-known (and hence generally less crowded) places of interest that are well worth seeing. Visit **Charlecote House**, with its gardens landscaped by 'Capability' Brown, or the old watermill at **Wellesbourne** (01789 470237/ www.wellesbournemill.co.uk; phone for opening times); alternatively, take a brisk walk up **Edgehill**, site of the first battle in the Civil War, in 1642, for fantastic views of Warwickshire with the Cotswolds on the horizon. There are dozens more places to visit – too many to include here, so contact the local tourist offices for brochures and leaflets before your trip.

What to see & do

Tourist Information Centres
Royal Pump Rooms, The Parade, Royal Leamington Spa, CV32 4AB (01926 742762/www.shakespeare-country.co.uk). **Open** *Easter-Oct* 9.30am-5pm Mon-Sat; 11am-4pm Sun. *Nov-Easter* 9.30am-5pm Mon-Sat; noon-4pm Sun.

Bridgefoot, Stratford-upon-Avon, CV37 6GW (01789 293127/www.shakespeare-country.co.uk). **Open** *Easter-Oct* 9am-6pm Mon-Sat; 11am-5pm Sun. *Nov-Easter* 9am-5pm Mon-Sat; 11am-4pm Sun.

The Court House, Jury Street, Warwick, CV34 4EW (01926 492212/www.warwick-uk.co.uk). **Open** 9.30am-4.30pm daily.

The Cotswolds

Charlecote Park

Charlecote, 5 miles E of Stratford-upon-Avon (01789 470277/www.nationaltrust.org.uk). **Open** *House* Easter-Oct noon-5pm Mon-Wed, Fri-Sun. Closed Nov-Easter. *Grounds* Easter-Oct 11am-6pm Mon-Wed, Fri-Sun. Closed Nov-Easter. **Admission** (NT) £5.60; £2.80 concessions; free under-5s.

Though the present house dates from the mid 16th century, the interior is early Victorian. Shakespeare is said to have been caught poaching in the fine deer park, which was later landscaped by 'Capability' Brown.

Heritage Motor Centre

Banbury Road, Gaydon, 10 miles SE of Warwick (01926 641188/www.heritage.org.uk). **Open** 10am-5pm daily. **Admission** £8; £6-£7 concessions; free under-5s.

Holding the largest collection of historic British cars in the world, the Heritage Motor Centre offers demonstrations and activities in its 63 acres of grounds.

Kenilworth Castle

Kenilworth (01926 852078/www.english-heritage.org.uk). **Open** *Apr-Sept* 10am-6pm daily. *Oct* 10am-5pm daily. *Nov-Mar* 10am-4pm daily. **Admission** (EH) £4; £2-£3 concessions; free under-5s.

The impressive red sandstone ruins are what is left of 12th-century Kenilworth Castle. Visitors can see the Norman keep, great hall and the wonderful reconstructed Tudor gardens. Audiotape tours available.

Lord Leycester Hospital

High Street, Warwick (01926 491422). **Open** *Hospital* 10am-4pm Tue-Sun. *Garden* Easter-Sept 10am-5pm Tue-Sun, bank hols. Closed Oct-Easter. **Admission** *Hospital* £2.75; £1.50-£2 concessions. *Garden* £1; children free.

Built in the 14th century, the hospital was acquired by Robert Dudley, Earl of Leicester in 1571. The chapel, great hall, guildhall, galleried courtyard and restored garden (nearly 600 years old) are all open to the public.

Royal Pump Rooms

Royal Leamington Spa (01926 742762/www.royal-pump-rooms.co.uk). **Open** 9.30am-5pm Mon-Sat; noon-4pm Sun. **Admission** free.

Next to Jephson Gardens, the Pump Rooms are where people once came to take the healthful Leamington waters. A major restoration programme has created a complex containing the Assembly Room, the Royal Pump Rooms, an art gallery/museum, library, tourist information centre and café.

Royal Shakespeare Company

Waterside, Stratford-upon-Avon (box office 01789 403403/tours 01789 403405/ www.rsc.org.uk). **Backstage tours** times vary; phone to check. **Tickets** £4; £3 concessions.

See a production of one of Shakespeare's plays or take a backstage tour. Booking is essential.

St John's House Museum

St John's, Warwick (01926 412132). **Open** *May-Sept* 10am-5.30pm Tue-Sat; 2.30-5pm Sun. *Oct-Apr* 10am-5.30pm Tue-Sat. **Admission** free; donations welcome.

This beautiful Jacobean mansion contains displays relating to the social history of Warwickshire, including costumes and a 19th-century kitchen, parlour and schoolroom. It also houses the **Royal Warwickshire Regimental Museum**.

Warwick Castle

Warwick (01926 406600/www.warwick-castle.co.uk). **Open** *Apr-Oct* 10am-6pm daily. *Nov-Mar* 10am-5pm daily. **Admission** *Summer* £11.50; £6.75-£8.20 concessions. *Winter* £10.25; £6.25-£7.35 concessions; free under-4s.

Warwick Castle began life in 914, when the mound of earth upon which it sits was claimed by Ethelfleda. The motte and bailey were further fortified by William the Conqueror. Among the highlights of the present-day building are the Ghost Tower – said to be haunted by the ghost of Sir Fulke Greville, who owned the castle in the 17th century – the great hall, restored to its former glory after a devastating fire in 1871, the elegant state rooms and the 17th-century chapel. The castle is impressive enough, but if you're expecting to be educated, you'll be disappointed. Visitors are shuffled from one room to the next, and there's little in the way of explanations about the exhibits. Phone for details of special events.

Where to stay

In Warwick, try the **Aylesford Hotel** (1 High Street; 01926 492799; doubles £75), a short walk from the castle and town centre.

Caterham House Hotel

58-59 Rother Street, Stratford-upon-Avon, CV37 6LT (01789 267309/fax 01789 414836). **Rates** £70 single occupancy; £80-£85 double/twin. **Rooms** (all en suite) 10 double/twin. **Credit** MC, V.

Just ten minutes' walk from the Royal Shakespeare Theatre, this small private hotel is popular with both the actors and audience. Run for over 20 years by Anglo-French couple Dominique and Olive Maury, it boasts a friendly but unobtrusive atmosphere. All the rooms are beautifully decorated: each has an individual character; some have half-tester beds. Note that when the main house is completely full, guests stay in the house next door (where rooms are decidedly less characterful). Children and dogs are welcome.

Gravelside Barn

Binton, nr Stratford-upon-Avon, CV37 9TU (tel/fax 01789 750502). **Rates** £40-£50 single occupancy; £60 double/twin. **Rooms** (all en suite) 2 double; 1 twin. **Credit** MC, V.

If the word 'barn' conjures up images of poky farm outhouses, think again. This huge self-contained building, part of the property owned Guy and Diane Belchambers since 1975, contains three comfy bedrooms plus a cosy lounge/dining room where guests tuck into a cooked breakfast in the morning. The barn is set high on a hill, and the views are spectacular, with the Malverns and Cotswolds on the horizon, and farmland, woodland and villages closer in. Two-night minimum stay at weekends. Children over 12 welcome. No smoking throughout. *A46 from Stratford towards Evesham; after 4 miles turn left towards Binton; turn left at Blue Boar pub; house 400 yards down hill on right; turn into drive; house is on left.*

Exploring the ramparts at **Warwick Castle**.

Leamington Hotel & Bistro

*64 Upper Holly Walk, Leamington CV32 4JL
(01926 883777/fax 01926 330467).* **Rates**
£37.50 single; £55 double/twin; £70 four-poster.
Breakfast £6.75 (Eng). **Rooms** (all en suite) 1
single; 27 double/twin; 2 four-poster.
Credit AmEx, DC, MC, V.

Blending in well with the rest of Leamington's grand
architecture, the Leamington Hotel & Bistro does a
roaring trade. Though it's big, and now owned by the
Best Western chain, the staff have managed to keep a
personal, down-to-earth feel to the place. Rooms vary in
size and decor, but furnishings are all good quality, if
a little corporate. Weekend break rates are excellent,
starting at just £32 per person per night. The Bistro
menu won't win any awards for adventurousness
but prices are good for the quality. Children welcome.
No-smoking rooms available.

Loxley Farm

*Loxley, Warwick, CV35 9JN (01789 840265/
fax 01789 840645).* **Rates** £64 suite (sleeps 2-3).
Rooms (both en suite) 2 suites. **No credit cards.**

If you'd prefer to spend the night away from the big
towns, the pretty village of Loxley is a good choice.
Guests at Loxley Farm stay in a converted 17th-
century barn, the Shieling (meaning 'shelter in the
hills'), overlooking a well-kept English garden. The
bedrooms are charming; one boasts a private conservatory, while the other has its own kitchen and lounge
area. Combining the rooms would make this a good
option for a family or two couples. English breakfast
is served in the late 13th-century thatched cottage,
where King Charles I is said to have stayed after
his defeat at Edgehill. Children and dogs welcome.
Both bedrooms no-smoking.
*A422 SE of Stratford; go through Loxley village to the
bottom of the hill; turn left (towards Stratford); Loxley farm
is the 3rd house on the right.*

Mallory Court

*Harbury Lane, Bishop's Tachbrook, CV33
9QB (01926 330214/fax 01926 451714/
www.mallory.co.uk).* **Rates** £165-£225 single
occupancy; £185-£320 double/twin. Breakfast
£10 (Eng). Special breaks. **Rooms** 18 double/twin
(16 en suite). **Credit** MC, V.

Allan Holland and Jeremy Mort have created an oasis of
calm in their manor house hotel. In 2001 it celebrated its
25th anniversary, which coincided with the addition of
a new wing of eight additional suites that are expertly
blended into the rest of the building. Personal touches
are evident throughout, and bedrooms are beautifully and
individually furnished. In warmer weather guests can sit
out on the terrace overlooking the manicured gardens and
outdoor swimming pool. Absolute luxury. Children over
nine welcome. No-smoking rooms available.
S of Leamington Spa off B4087.

Shrewley Pools Farm

*Parish of Haseley, nr Warwick, CV35 7HB (01926
484315/www.bbgl.co.uk/lodgings).* **Rates** £45-£50
double/twin/family; £10 per child supplement.
Rooms (both en suite) 1 twin; 1 double/family.
No credit cards.

If it's a farm experience you're after, you've come to the
right place: be careful not to run over a chicken or goose
– or Terry the dog – as you pull into the drive. This 17th-
century farmhouse has many of its original features –
exposed beams, uneven floors, leaded windows and
mind-your-head doorways. The Rooms are comfy, and
owner Cathy Dodd is very friendly. Guests are welcome
to stroll around the rambling garden, with its rhododendrons and herbaceous borders. Children welcome.
No smoking throughout.
*A4117 NW of Warwick towards Solihull; go through
Hatton; at large roundabout take 1st exit into Five Ways
Road signposted Shrewley and Claverdon; farm is ½ mile on
left, opposite Farm Gate Poultry.*

The Cotswolds

Bard news

Nearly 400 years after his death, you might think we know all there was to know about William Shakespeare. Then along comes a major new discovery. Since the 18th century it was thought that Mary Arden, Will's mum, lived in the property known imaginatively as Mary Arden's House, in the village of Wilmcote. However, in November 2000 new research suggested that Mary Arden had not, in fact, lived in that building but in the rather more downmarket one next door, hitherto known as Glebe Farm. As a result, Glebe Farm has now been renamed Mary Arden's House, and the building previously known as Mary Arden's House is now called Palmer's Farm, after Adam Palmer, its 16th-century owner and builder.

In order to back up the written evidence, an architectural survey and tree-ring dating analysis was carried out, which corroborated the facts by showing that Glebe Farm dates mainly from 1514, before Mary Arden was born. Modernisation was carried out in the 17th century, when a large chimney was inserted into the hall and a dairy was added behind the kitchen, and it was in more or less continuous occupation until the 1970s.

Because of the difficulty involved in returning the house to its 16th-century

All dressed up at **Mary Arden's House**.

condition, it has been decided to keep it much as it was when its last occupant died in 1978. Thus, the eclectic collection of Edwardian furnishings will remain in place. Upstairs will be used as an education centre.

Also on the site is a complex of farm buildings, including a dovecote, an open-fronted cowshed and small barn with cider press, and a stable and large barn now housing a display of farming equipment. These, along with more farm buildings to the west, comprise the Shakespeare Countryside Museum.

All in all, the property makes for a fascinating trip. Guides in both Palmer's Farm and Mary Arden's House set the buildings in a wider historical context. There's also a country walk from the site. And don't miss the beautiful birds of prey (falconry courses for children are offered).

Victoria Spa Lodge

Bishopton Lane, Bishopton, CV37 9QY (01789 267985/fax 01789 204728/www.stratford-upon-avon.co.uk/victoriaspa.htm). **Rates** £65 double/twin; £80-£100 family. **Rooms** (all en suite) 3 double; 1 twin; 3 family (sleeps 5). **Credit** MC, V.
Just minutes from Stratford, Victoria Spa Lodge has the feel of a grand country house. Paul and Dreen Tozer have lent the Georgian property a personal touch, with a characterful dining room and floral decor in the rooms. Princess Victoria stayed here before ascending the throne in 1837, and her coat of arms is built into the gables. Children welcome. No smoking throughout.
A46 S; at A46 and A3400 intersection take 2nd exit (Bishopton Lane); 1st house on right, just before bridge.

Where to eat & drink

Most Stratford restaurants open early and close late, and offer good value pre- and post-theatre meals. If you're after a quick bite rather than a

lengthy gastronomic experience, try the **Black Swan** (Stratford Way; 01789 297312), more commonly known as the Dirty Duck, where you may find yourself brushing shoulders with members of the RSC. For a snack in Stratford town centre check out the Light Bites menu at the **Vintner** (4-5 Sheep Street; 01789 297259), the **Deli Café** (13-14 Meer Street; 01789 295705); alternatively, get into the spirit of the place with a dollop of clotted cream, jam and a scone to balance it on, washed down with a cuppa. **Hathaways Tea Rooms** (19 High Street; 01789 292404) set in the eaves above its own bakery, serves a good cream tea. If you want a more elegant and luxurious setting, take high tea on the terraces of **Mallory Court** (*see p193*). **No.1 Pimlico's** (Pimlico Lane, Alveston; 01789 295510) opened in summer 2001 – too late to review for this guide – sounds promising. Set in a 7,000 square-foot

Stratford and the surrounding area are packed with other Shakespeare-related sights (see also www.shakespeare.org.uk). We list Mary Arden's house, and other main locations, below.

Anne Hathaway's Cottage
Cottage Lane, Shottery, 2 miles W of Stratford-upon-Avon (01789 292100). **Open** *Apr-Oct* 9am-5pm Mon-Sat; 9.30am-5pm Sun. *Nov-Mar* 9.30am-4pm Mon-Sat; 10am-4pm Sun. **Admission** £4.50; £2-£4 concessions; free under-5s.
The thatched cottage belonging to Shakespeare's wife is surrounded by beautiful gardens. There are many pleasant walks leading from the property.

Hall's Croft
Old Town, Stratford-upon-Avon (01789 292107). **Open** *Apr-Oct* 9.30am-5pm Mon-Sat; 10am-5pm Sun. *Nov-Mar* 10am-4pm Mon-Sat; 10.30am-4pm Sun. **Admission** £3.50; £1.70-£3 concessions. This 16th-century house was the home of John Hall, the doctor husband of Shakespeare's eldest daughter, Susanna. Appropriately, it contains an exhibition on medicine.

Holy Trinity Church
Old Town, Stratford-upon-Avon (01789 266316). **Open** 8.30am-6pm Mon-Sat; 2-5pm Sun. **Admission** £1; 50p concessions; free under-5s.
Set on the banks of the River Avon, this beautiful parish church is the site

of Shakespeare's grave, and keeps records of the playwright's baptism and death exhibited in a case.

Mary Arden's House & Shakespeare Countryside Museum
Wilmcote, 4 miles NW of Stratford-upon-Avon (01789 293455). **Open** *Mid Mar-mid Oct* 9.30am-5pm Mon-Sat; 10am-5pm Sun. *Mid Oct-mid Mar* 10am-4pm Mon-Sat; 10.30am-4pm Sun. **Admission** £5.50; £2.50-£5 concessions; free under-5s.

Nash's House & New Place
22 Chapel Street, Stratford-upon-Avon (01789 292325). **Open** *Apr-Oct* 9.30am-5pm Mon-Sat; 10am-5pm Sun. *Nov-Mar* 10am-4pm Mon-Sat; 10.30am-4pm Sun. **Admission** £3.50; £1.70-£3 concessions; free under-5s.
This house was once owned by Thomas Nash, who married Shakespeare's granddaughter. Outside is the site of Shakespeare's final home, New Place, and his Elizabethan-style garden.

Shakespeare's Birthplace
Henley Street, Stratford-upon-Avon (01789 204016). **Open** *Apr-Oct* 9am-5pm Mon-Sat; 9.30am-5pm Sun. *Nov-Mar* 9.30am-4pm Mon-Sat; 10am-4pm Sun. **Admission** £6; £2.50-£5.50 concessions; free under-5s.
This half-timbered house has an exhibition about Shakespeare's life.

The Cotswolds

split-level space in landscaped gardens, the restaurant serves interesting modern European food and boasts a wide-reaching wine list.

There are plenty of good country boozers in the area. The **King's Head** at Aston Cantlow (01789 488242) is well worth a visit for its quality Italian and Mediterranean food. For good basic pub grub and a smooth pint of ale, try the **Fox** at Loxley (01789 840991), the **Bell** at Shottery (Bell Lane; 01789 269645), or watch the world go by at the **Tilted Wig** in Warwick's Market Place (01926 410466). For something posher, try the highly rated **Restaurant Bosquet** in Kenilworth (97A Warwick Road; 01926 852463) for the rich cooking of south-west France.

Desport's Restaurant
13-14 Meer Street, Stratford-upon-Avon (01789 269304/www.desports.co.uk). **Food served** noon-2pm, 6-10pm Tue-Sat. **Credit** AmEx, DC, MC, V.

Set above the deli of the same name, Desport's is run by husband and wife team Paul and Julie Desport. The original features of the 16th-century building, including the wooden beams, are effectively combined with contemporary bright colours. The menu is short and divided into rather twee categories such as 'from the earth' (vegetarian dishes) and 'from heaven' (desserts). But although eclectic, the dishes stop short of being overelaborate, and the quality of the cooking is indisputably good. Likewise, the standards of presentation are high, as in the grilled red mullet on roasted aubergine, zucchini and sweet pepper salad with gazpacho potatoes (£15.95). Be sure to save room for dessert, which might include warm coconut and rum tart with mango ice-cream (£5.50). Service is friendly, but it can also be slow.

Findon's
7 Old Square, Warwick (01926 411755/www.findons-restaurant.co.uk). **Food served** noon-2pm, 7-9.30pm Mon-Fri; 7-9.30pm Sat. **Set dinner** £15.95 2 courses. **Credit** AmEx, DC, MC, V.

The **Howard Arms**. Great food in a real pub.

Occupying an early Georgian townhouse and serving rich French-influenced food, Findon's attracts a clientele that includes Germaine Greer and Stan Collymore (presumably not together). The interior, with its swish curtains and chandeliers, might not be to everyone's taste, but there's no denying the pedigree of the modern cooking. Main courses might include shank of lamb cooked with red wine, tomatoes, rosemary and garlic (£16.95); if meat isn't your thing then go for one of the imaginative vegetarian dishes, such as warm salad of goat's cheese, portobello mushrooms, rocket, basil and walnut pesto with spiced polenta cake (£12.95). Prices are high at Findon's, but they reflect the standard of cooking; if you're strapped for cash, the set menu is less hard on the wallet.

Fox & Goose Inn

Armscote, off A3400 Stratford-upon-Avon –Shipston-on-Stour (01608 682293/ www.foxandgoose.co.uk). **Food served** noon-2.30pm, 7-9.30pm daily. **Credit** AmEx, MC, V.
This pub has undergone a couple of name changes over the years, but has gained the most attention since it opened as the Fox & Goose in April 2000. The interior is inviting and rather sumptuous – dark red walls and velvet cushions – and the owners are keen. The inventive food from the frequently changing menu (with dishes such as a starter of warm salad of black pudding, bacon, chorizo, sausage and sesame; £4.95) is one of its major attractions. But then so are the drinks – champagnes by the glass, excellent wines, and beers and ales including the pub's own Fox & Goose Bitter by Brakespeare. The self-described 'slightly eccentric' bedrooms are true to their name, but are nonetheless luxurious (doubles £80). Diners can sit out on the deck in the lovely garden (where barbecues are held in summer).

Howard Arms

Lower Green, Ilmington (01608 682226/ www.howardarms.com). **Food served** noon-2pm, 7-9pm Mon-Thur; noon-2pm, 7-9.30pm Fri, Sat; 12.30-2.30pm, 6.30-8.30pm Sun. **Set lunch** £15.50 3 courses Sun. **Credit** MC, V.
The Howard Arms was named the *Good Pub Guide* Warwickshire Dining Pub of the Year 2001 and it's easy to see why. The vibe is definitely pub – although there's a separate dining room, you choose from the chalked-up menu and order from the bar. The weekly changing menu incorporates seasonal produce, and dishes are imaginative but not overfussy – a starter of char-grilled beef satay with lime yoghurt dressing (£5), perhaps, and a main of marinated corn-fed chicken breast, hoi sin plum sauce and crisp noodles (£9.50). As it's a freehouse, there's a good choice of well-kept cask ales and keg beers, including Everard's Tiger and North Cotswold Brewery's Genesis. If you've overdone it, repair to one of the cosy bedrooms upstairs (doubles £74-£84), look out onto the village green and dream of moving to the country. Highly recommended.

Opposition Restaurant

13 Sheep Street, Stratford-upon-Avon (01789 269980). **Food served** noon-2pm, 5.30-10.30pm Mon-Sat; noon-2pm, 6-10pm Sun. **Credit** MC, V.
Another of Stratford's highly rated restaurants, the Opposition is right next to its sister restaurant, Lamb's. The bare brick walls, low-beamed ceilings and candlelit tables are all in keeping with the 16th-century building. The seasonally changing menu draws on a number of cuisines, with dishes such as whole lemon sole with tartare sauce, green beans and new potatoes (£11.75), and grilled goat's cheese salad with a basil oil dressing (£8.50). In summer there are tables outdoors in a courtyard. Book well in advance.

Russon's

8 Church Street, Stratford-upon-Avon (01789 268822). **Food served** 11.30am-1.45pm, 5.30-9.45pm Tue-Sat. **Credit** AmEx, MC, V.
Russon's is often fully booked – for a reason. Fish is the forte; even classics are given a makeover – try the haddock in beer batter with chips and pea mint purée, (£7.95). But carnivores and vegetarians also get a good look-in, with dishes like hot spinach and feta cheese filo pastry pie (£9.95). Prices are so reasonable (main course pasta dishes start at £6.95) that there's no pre-theatre menu. The wine list, too, generally stops short of the £25 mark.

Simpson's Restaurant

101-103 Warwick Road, Kenilworth (01926 864567/ www.simpsons-restaurant.co.uk). **Food served** 12.30-2pm, 7-10pm Mon-Fri; 7-10pm Sat. **Set lunch** £15 2 courses; £20 3 courses. **Set dinners** £26 2 courses; £34 3 courses. £49.95 6-course tasting menu. **Credit** AmEx, DC, MC, V.
Contrasting starkly with its less-than-glamorous location on the traffic-heavy Warwick Road, Simpson's is an arresting sight – perfectly manicured miniature trees outside, blonde wood and crisp linen tablecloths inside. Typical starters include terrine of ham hock, foie gras with mustard lentils and parsley vinaigrette (£8.75); main courses might be roast Gressingham duck with celeriac purée, pak choi, poached pear and rich red wine sauce (£19.50). It's pricey – this is one for a splurge.

Oxford

Colleges and factories, academics and mechanics – a city for all souls.

Perfect punting at **Cherwell Boathouse**.

When a city has the irresistible twin draws of possibly the world's most famous university, and probably the best-loved and grumpiest detective on TV, Inspector Morse, it's no surprise that the locals sometimes feel under siege. Of Oxford's 118,000 inhabitants, some 15 per cent are reckoned to be the transient university population, and in addition the streets throb all year round with tourists and rucksacked European school parties. The city centre is dominated by the university and its colleges, although there are other parts of town – notably Jericho and Summertown to the north, and Headington and Cowley to the east – with their own distinct identities and considerably fewer sightseers and students. There is also a wealth of museums, from the quirky Pitt Rivers to the all-embracing Ashmolean (*see p203* **Ashmolean Museum**).

There is a certain perversity to place names in Oxford, ranging from downright mispronunciation (Magdalen is 'Maudlin', the River Cherwell is 'Charwell') to renaming (the Thames is known as the Isis here). Then there is the strange predilection for dropping the 'street' part of road names (the High, the Turl, the Broad). In this latter category are a number of streets named after obscure saints (St Aldate's, St Ebbe's, St Giles').

Oxford arose as a Saxon burg built to defend Wessex from the dastardly Danes – the 11th-century St Michael's Tower in Cornmarket Street is the only surviving building of this period. Its position at the confluence of the Cherwell and Isis was easy to defend, helped by the city wall built by the Normans (Charles I agreed, as he made the city his Royalist HQ during the Civil War).

The gown vs the people

By the 12th century, Oxford saw its status as a market town becoming eclipsed by the nascent monastic colleges, which by the 13th century had developed into the university. The presence of this institution inevitably led to a degree of disharmony between town and gown.

This antipathy has often been fierce, and never more so than in the St Scholastica's Day Massacre of February 1355. An affray in the Swindlestock Tavern (now the Abbey National at Carfax crossroads) erupted into a bloody riot, which left 60 students dead. The city's representatives were forced to attend a yearly penitential mass for nigh-on five centuries to rub their collective nose in their underdog status.

Today, the separation of town and gown is still apparent – witness the Cowley Road around 5pm, as students cycle to their digs passing Cowley workers returning home.

Motor city

The city finally got out from under the university's gown-tails thanks to the motor magnate William Morris, who graduated from a city-centre bicycle shop at the turn of the

> ### By train from London
>
> Direct trains to **Oxford** leave **Paddington** about every half an hour; the journey time is approximately **1hr**. Info: www.thamestrains.co.uk and www.virgintrains.co.uk.

The Cotswolds

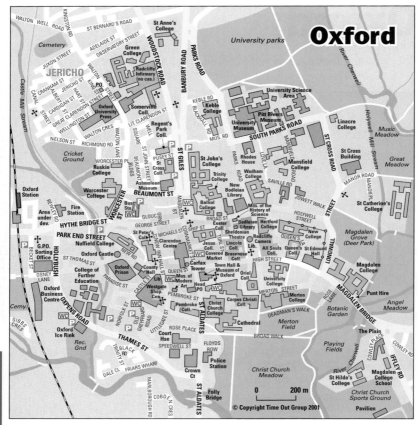

century to making 41 per cent of Britain's cars in his Cowley plant by the mid-1920s. (His original garage can be seen on Longwall Street.) The Mini, Morris Minor and (no surprises here) Morris Oxford all came out of Cowley. The plant, now owned by Rover, has suffered an uncomfortable number of redundancies over the past decade, but it remains one of the area's major employers.

Oddly, for a city with such close links to the motor industry, Oxford's council is vehemently anti-car. A medieval streetplan and one of the most tortuous one-way systems in the civilised world have recently been compounded by a programme of pedestrianisation that has entirely sealed off Cornmarket Street and half of Broad Street to traffic, and restricted access to the High Street between 7.30am and 6.30pm (only buses are allowed). The clear message is

that you should leave the car at home: fortunately, bus services are good (there's a Park & Ride service from car parks on the outskirts) and bicycling students and residents are a familiar sight in the city. Both the Oxford Tube and the CityLink run fast and frequent coaches to London.

Green spaces

Finally, it is worth noting the large open spaces in this yellow-stone town. Every college has some green, whether it is closely clipped lawns in the quads, or more natural expanses such as Worcester College's lake and gardens or Christ Church meadow. Venture further afield to the university parks to witness some first-class cricket (and occasionally touring international teams), or go beyond Jericho to Port Meadow, one of the largest expanses of common land left in the country, where wild horses roam and houseboats moor. A walk across this flat expanse of land makes for a picturesque approach to the Perch or Trout pubs (for both, *see p204*).

What to see & do

Beware of the city's exploitative tourist honeypots, and of the open-top tour buses claiming to offer unsurpassed views of the colleges, since large sections of the city centre are inaccessible to them.

Tourist Information Centre

The Old School, Gloucester Green, OX1 2DA (01865 726871/www.visitoxford.org). **Open** *Easter-Oct* 9.30am-5pm Mon-Sat; 10am-3.30pm Sun. *Nov-Easter* 9.30am-5pm Mon-Sat.

Bike hire

Warlands *63 Botley Road (01865 241336).* Not far from the station.

Bodleian Library

Broad Street (01865 277000/www.bodley.ox.ac.uk). **Open** *Apr-Dec* 10am-4pm Mon-Fri; 10am-12.30pm Sat. *Jan-Mar* Sat only (phone for details). **Tours** *Apr-Oct* 10.30am, 11.30am, 2pm, 3pm Mon-Fri; 10.30am, 11.30am Sat. *Nov-Mar* 10.30am, 11.30am Mon-Fri; 10.30am, 11.30am Sat. **Admission** *tour* £3.50.

The university's huge, reference-only library incorporates some of the most spectacular architecture in Oxford. Its earliest part is the 15th-century Divinity School, with a lierne vaulted ceiling; the Duke Humfrey's Library (1488), replete with wooden beams and resident deathwatch beetle, was home to the founder's collection of manuscripts. Post-printing press, the library was re-founded by Thomas Bodley in 1602, which led to the construction of the Jacobean Old Schools Quadrangle, and later James Gibbs's reading rotunda, the Radcliffe Camera (1749). The library is entitled to a copy of every book published in Britain, and over six million of them are housed in its stacks – miles of underground shelving. Note that children under 14 are not allowed. The guided tour lasts an hour.

Carfax Tower

Carfax (01865 792653). **Open** *Apr-Oct* 10am-5.15pm daily. *Nov-Mar* 10am-3.30pm daily. **Admission** £1.20; 60p concessions.

The walk up the 99 steps of this 13th-century tower – the only surviving remnant of St Martin's Church, demolished to make room for traffic in 1896 – is hard on the calves, but rewarding on the eyes with a panoramic view of the city and the hills beyond.

Colleges of Oxford University

The university, which has been in existence since at least the 12th century, is undoubtedly the city's major draw. Over the years the colleges have seen to the education of vast numbers of the great and the good, as well as every British prime minister of the 20th century except James Callaghan and John Major. If, however, you are motivated by more than a rubberneck

Jacobsen's Modernist lines at **St Catherine's**.

desire to see where Rupert Murdoch, say, went to college (Worcester, if you are that interested), then the principal attraction has to be the architecture – the 'dreaming spires' of tourist-board cliché. The majority of the city's 41 colleges are open to the public, usually in the afternoon (details are displayed at the porter's lodges; some colleges charge a fee for admission).

The largest of the Oxford colleges is **Christ Church** (founded 1525), whose Tom Tower – a Gothic space-rocket designed by Wren – dominates the St Aldate's skyline. The college has its own gallery, full of old masters, and its chapel also serves as the city's cathedral. **Magdalen** (1458) has large gardens and a deer park, and choristers sing madrigals atop its tower at dawn on May Morning (1 May). The famous Bridge of Sighs can be found connecting the two parts of **Hertford** (1283), which also has an impressively quirky spiral staircase giving on to the main quad. The largely Hawksmoor-designed **All Souls** (1438) is reserved solely for Fellows; **Trinity** (1555) has extensive, beautiful gardens, **Merton** (1264) a stunning medieval chapel, **Oriel** (1324) an impressive Jacobean quad; and **New College** (1379) harbours a stunning garden, atmospheric cloisters and a most beautiful chapel (including an Epstein sculpture and El Greco painting). If you weary of seeing yet more Gothic buildings in that same yellowy stone, try the 18th-century classicism of **Queen's** (founded 1341), the almost industrial Victorian brickwork of **Keble** (1868), or the clean Modernist lines at **St Catherine's** (1964) – entirely designed by Arne Jacobsen, even down to the cutlery.

The Cotswolds

Martyrs' Memorial

St Giles'.

George Gilbert Scott's 1841 Gothic spire commemorates the Protestant martyrs Cranmer, Latimer and Ridley, who Queen Mary burned around the corner in Broad Street in 1555-6 (a cross marks the spot). Now foreign language students gather on its steps.

Museum of the History of Science

Broad Street (01865 277280/www.mhs.ox.ac.uk). **Open** noon-4pm Tue-Sat. **Admission** free; donations welcome.

The original premises of the Ashmolean, this 17th-century building is now crammed with a fascinating collection of timepieces, astrolabes, microscopes and other scientific ephemera, including Einstein's blackboard, on which the great man diligently shows all his working.

Museum of Modern Art

30 Pembroke Street (01865 722733/ www.moma.org.uk). **Open** 11am-6pm Tue, Wed, Fri-Sun; 11am-9pm Thur. **Admission** £2.50; £1.50 concessions; free under-16s.

A converted brewery with no permanent collection, the award-winning Museum of Modern Art shows various temporary exhibitions of modern art, ranging from the pioneering to the pretentious.

Museum of Oxford

St Aldate's (01865 252761). **Open** 10am-4pm Tue-Fri; 10am-5pm Sat; noon-4pm Sun. **Admission** £2; 50p-£1.50 concessions.

A relatively informative journey through the history of the city, and of the land on which it stands. The story begins in prehistoric times, and a number of the exhibits are showing their age, too.

The Oxford Story

6 Broad Street (01865 790055/ www.oxfordstory.co.uk). **Open** *Apr-June, Sept, Oct* 9.30am-5pm daily. *July, Aug* 9am-5.30pm daily. *Nov-Mar* 10am-4.30pm Mon-Sat; 11am-4.30pm Sun. **Admission** £6.10; £4.90 concessions.

The Oxford Story is pretty much restricted to the story of the university. Visitors sit behind mobile desks and trundle through its history, with a presentation illustrated by a series of mannequins and audio commentary – in other words, it's a tourist trap. There are better ways of spending an hour.

Oxford University Botanic Garden

Rose Lane (01865 286690). **Open** *Apr-Sept* 9am-5pm daily. *Oct-Mar* 9am-4.30pm daily. **Admission** *Apr-Aug* £2; free under-12s. *Sept-Mar* donation; free under-12s.

A typical house and the extraordinary **Oxford University Botanic Garden**.

Founded in 1621 to grow medicinal plants for university research, the Botanic Garden is the oldest in Britain. Look out for the century plant (*Agave americana*), which flowers only once in ten to 30 years.

Pitt Rivers Museum

Parks Road (01865 270927/ www.prm.ox.ac.uk). **Open** 1-4.30pm Mon-Sat; 2-4.30pm Sun. **Admission** free; donations welcomed.
The Pitt Rivers Museum is the anthropological annexe to the University Museum (*see below*). Its dark corners and glass cabinets are chock-a-block with such arcane delights as voodoo dolls, shrunken heads, peace pipes and a totem pole, all marked with tiny, handwritten labels. Pull open the drawers to find more ethnological delights under glass. Quite spectacular in a donnish kind of way, and it's a winner with children.

Punting

The quintessential Oxbridge pastime, punting has developed from a form of freight transportation to a lazy summer pursuit – the punter propels the boat with a long pole from the hollow of the stern. There are two principal departure points for punting on the River Cherwell: **Magdalen Bridge Boathouse** (01865 761586; punt hire £10 per hour, plus £30 deposit; bring identification) or the **Cherwell Boathouse** in Bardwell Road (01865 515978; £8-£10 per hour, plus £40-£50 deposit).

Sheldonian Theatre

Broad Street (01865 277299/www.sheldon.ox.ac.uk). **Open** *mid Feb-mid Nov* 10am-12.30pm, 2-4.30pm Mon-Sat. *Mid Nov-mid Feb* 10am-12.30pm, 2-3.30pm Mon-Sat. **Admission** £1.50; £1 concessions.
This Restoration theatre was built – by Christopher Wren, then professor of astronomy at the university – for university degree ceremonies, although these days the grimacing cherubs painted on the ceiling also look down on concerts. The hirsute busts outside, sometimes referred to as emperors, are actually stylised versions of non-specific, off-the-shelf Romans.

University Museum

Parks Road (01865 272950/www.oum.ox.ac.uk). **Open** noon-5pm daily. **Admission** free; donations welcome.
A taxidermist's dream, this natural history museum is stuffed with numerous beasties and dinosaurs. The museum is also worth visiting purely for its Victorian Gothic architecture and the vaulted glass-and-iron roof. Hidden at the back is the Pitt Rivers Museum (*see above*), which is packed full of anthropological treats – the two are a sure-fire hit with children.

Where to stay

This isn't a town packed with stylish places to stay, so pitch your expectations accordingly. Accommodation is split down the middle: hotels in the city centre tend to be expensive, whereas all the best B&Bs are a considerable distance out of town, near the ring road.

Bath Place Hotel

4 & 5 Bath Place, OX1 3SU (01865 791812/fax 01865 791834/www.bathplace.co.uk). **Rates** £90-£125 single occupancy; £95-£150 double; £105-£120 twin; £140-£145 four-poster; £125-£155 cottage suite. **Rooms** (all en suite) 8 double; 2 twin; 2 four-poster; 2 suites. **Credit** AmEx, DC, MC, V.
Converted from Jacobean weavers' cottages built on the outer side of the city wall (sections of it are still visible in the restaurant and beside the neighbouring Turf Tavern), Bath Place has all the appropriate idiosyncrasies – heavy wooden beams, whitewashed walls and the uneven floors. The hotel is family-run (by the Fawsitts) and is no-smoking (except in the bar). Children welcome. Pets admitted by arrangement.

Burlington House

374 Banbury Road, OX2 7PP (01865 513513/fax 01865 311785/www.burlington-house.co.uk). **Rates** £35-£50 single; £70-£75 double. **Rooms** (all en suite) 5 double, 4 single. **Credit** MC, V.
Royd Laidlow and Tony Gedel have given this Victorian house a modern, fresh look and created a very stylish small hotel with B&B prices. It's all in the details, from excellent power showers to top-quality breakfasts. The latter are a particular treat, a fact that has been recognised by the AA, which has awarded Burlington House its prestigious three eggcups. Try the home-made granola and the excellent Gruyère omelette. The hotel has an arrangement with the Esporta health club, with pool, a short walk away – hotel guests can get a day pass for just £5. No smoking throughout.

The Cotswolds

Gables Guesthouse

6 Cumnor Hill, OX2 9HA (01865 862153/fax 01865 864054/www.oxfordcity.co.uk/accom/gables). **Rates** £30 single; £50 double/twin. **Rooms** (all en suite) 2 single; 4 double/twin. **Credit** MC, V.

Sally and Tony Tompkins' friendly, competitively priced B&B is quite a long way down the Botley Road (where it turns into Cumnor Hill), but well worth the journey. Sally's motto would seem to be that you don't get anywhere in this business by standing still: she is continually redecorating the rooms to keep them fresh and creating impressive floral displays in the huge garden, as well as arranging special deals with the local video shop so guests can hire films for the combined TV/video in every room. A scrapbook of her previous accolades ('Landlady of the Year', 'Britain in Bloom' et al) in the conservatory testifies to this. Children welcome. No smoking throughout.

Galaxie Hotel

180 Banbury Road, OX2 7BT (01865 515688/ fax 01865 556824/www.galaxie.co.uk). **Rates** £44-£55 single; £80 double; £70-£80 twin; £104 four-poster; £89-£95 family room. **Rooms** 6 single (4 en suite); 14 double (13 en suite); 7 twin (6 en suite); 1 four-poster (en suite); 4 family (all en suite). **Credit** MC, V.

A large, ivy-clad building in Summertown that caters mainly to a business crowd, the Galaxie strikes a midpoint in both price and location between the city-centre hotels and the peripheral B&Bs. The rooms are decorated in restrained pastels; and, despite the ashtrays, they are all no-smoking. Check into the honeymoon room and you will find a four-poster bed, marble bathroom and a fabulously gimmicky pair of remote-controlled curtains. Breakfast is taken in a spacious conservatory, and the garden even has a pool of placid koi carp. Children and dogs welcome.

Old Bank Hotel

92-94 High Street, OX1 4BN (01865 799599/fax 01865 799598/www.oldbank-hotel.co.uk). **Rates** £135 single occupancy; £155-£225 double/twin; £255-£300 suites. Breakfast £11 (Eng); £8 (cont). **Rooms** (all en suite) 4 single, 36 double/twin. **Credit** AmEx, DC, MC, V.

This is a hip hotel indeed. Sleek and modernist, the rooms are individually decorated; try to get ones with the best views of the 'dreaming spires'. Each has two phone lines, TV, bedside radio and a digital CD player. Every wall is hung with exceptional art – check out the Stanley Spencer drawings. Service is attentive and discreet. The funky Quod Bar & Grill is influenced by Italian cooking, with lots of char-grilling and pasta dishes, and is a great place to hang out. At £8.75, the two-course express lunch is a bargain. There's also a south-facing wooden decked terrace for al fresco dining on those hot days and nights. Oh, and the location's great, right in the heart of the city. Children welcome. No-smoking rooms available.

Old Parsonage Hotel

1 Banbury Road, OX2 6NN (01865 310210/fax 01865 311262/www.oxford-hotels-restaurants.co.uk). **Rates** £130 single occupancy; £155-£200 double; £170-£200 twin. **Rooms** (all en suite) 30 double/twin. **Credit** AmEx, DC, MC, V.

Over the years, the Old Parsonage has been inhabited by nuns, a wigmaker, two mayors and the undergraduate Oscar Wilde. Since 1989, however, it has been easily one of the classiest hotels in Oxford; its rooms have a traditional, countryish air, with authentically creaky floorboards but also luxurious marble bathrooms. The small Parsonage Bar is crammed with prints and paintings and offers a high-quality modern menu; food and drink are also available via 24-hour room service. They'll even arrange private guided tours of the colleges for you. The owner, Jeremy Mogford, is also responsible for Gee's restaurant (*see p204*) – meals there can be charged to your hotel account – and the new Old Bank Hotel. Children welcome.

The Randolph

Beaumont Street, OX1 2LN (0870 400 8200/ fax 01865 791678/www.heritage-hotels.com). **Rates** £140 single; £170 double/twin; £190 deluxe double/twin; £230 four-poster; £250-£400 suite. Breakfast £13.95 (Eng/cont). **Rooms** (all en suite) 32 single; 54 double; 16 twin; 7 deluxe double; 2 four-poster; 9 suites. **Credit** AmEx, DC, MC, V.

Oxford's most famous hotel is inevitably pricey, but gives you a big dollop of grandeur for your money. The rooms are individually decorated in a self-consciously grand style, with William Morris (the designer, not the car magnate) wallpaper and heavy drapes; those converted from staff quarters on the top floor are more restrained. The clientele tends towards the corporate – but *Inspector Morse* creator Colin Dexter can also be found propping up one of the hotel's bars on occasion. At the time of writing, major renovations were in the pipeline. Plans include a new restaurant with a champagne and oyster bar attached due to open in October 2001. Children and dogs are welcome, there's 24-hour room service, and no-smoking rooms available.

Where to eat & drink

While Oxford has a lot of good-quality restaurants, there are not that many in the city centre. The centre does better with cafés: there is the **Grand Café** (84 High Street; 01865 204463) on the site of the first coffee house in England (1641) and the **Rosie Lee Café** (51 High Street; 01865 244429), which does traditional English breakfasts and classic cream teas. Little Clarendon Street, at the northern end of St Giles', has a number of chain restaurants (**Café Rouge**, **Pierre Victoire**), as well as the superior brasserie **Browns** (1-5 Woodstock Road; 01865 311415). Jericho is the increasingly groovy place to hang out and eat. **Freud Arts Café** (119 Walton Street; 01865 311171) is a café in a neo-classical former church, serving pizzas, coffee and cocktails. **Loch Fyne** at 55 Walton Street (01865 292510) serves wonderful fish and seafood. **Rosamund the Fair** is a charming boat restaurant at Castlemill Boatyard, Cadigan Street, in Jericho (01865 553370). It serves modern British food; booking is essential. Further north is **Gousse**

Ashmolean Museum

A perfectly formed, perfectly sized gem of a museum, the **Ashmolean** was founded by Oxford lawyer Elias Ashmole in 1683 and is home to the university's collection of arts and antiquities. Ashmole donated his own collection of coins, books and manuscripts, along with some inherited curiosities from the traveller John Tradescant. Over subsequent centuries, treasures have been added through bequests, gifts and significant purchases.

For a museum outside London it boasts a striking array of collections, ranging from Greek coins to exquisite works by the world's finest painters, including Uccello, Michelangelo, Picasso and Van Gogh. Other popular draws include a lantern used by Guy Fawkes and a mantle belonging to the father of Pocahontas. Made of deerskin and decorated with shells, this is from the original Tradescant Collection. New acquisitions include Titian's *Portrait of Giacomo Doria*, bought for a cool £2.5 million.

More recent works have not been neglected as the museum expands. The newest addition to the building houses the Early Twentieth Century Gallery, which brings together some exciting names from painting and sculpture, including Ben Nicholson and Henry Moore. Another new gallery has been built to house the museum's collection of 20th-century Chinese art.

The Ashmolean offers an impressive range of activities along with special exhibitions. Object of the Month is a new initiative designed to attract visitors, and there are highlight tours every Saturday morning. However, the audacious art thieves who broke into the museum on New Year's Day 2000 – removing Cézanne's *Auvers-sur-Oise* – probably did the most to push up visitor numbers. Following the theft, large crowds converged on the museum to take a look at the crime scene.

Ashmolean Museum

Beaumont Street (01865 278000/ www.ashmol.ox.ac.uk). **Open** *Jan-May, Sept-Dec* 10am-5pm Tue-Sat; 2-5pm Sun. *June-Aug* 10am-5pm Tue, Wed, Fri, Sat; 10am-7pm Thur; 2-5pm Sun. Highlight tours 11am Sat. **Admission** free; donations welcome.

d'Ail (268 Woodstock Road; 01865 311936), a well-known restaurant where the grand set menu is preferable to the otherwise expensive haute cuisine experience.

Down the vaguely bohemian Cowley Road are a large number of curry houses and Chinese takeaways, as well as **Mario & Mario** (103 Cowley Road; 01865 722955), an excellent pizzeria, and the **Hi-Lo Jamaican Eating House** (70 Cowley Road; 01865 725984), a Caribbean restaurant with a menu that changes daily. **Kazbar** (25-27 Cowley Road; 01865 202920) offers Spanish and North African tapas-style food in a Moorish-style interior. **Aziz Indian Cuisine** (228-230 Cowley Road; 01865 794945) is good Indian food in a smart and light restaurant.

Oxford pubs are plentiful, but not cheap or quiet. Among the more studenty choices are the **King's Arms** at the corner of Holywell Street, the **Bear** on Blue Boar Street (low ceilings and a 'fascinating' collection of ties) and the **Turf Tavern** between Hertford and New Colleges (equally low-slung and Oxford's oldest inn). The **White House** behind the station is a gastro-pub with live trad-jazz at Sunday lunchtime, while the part-thatched **Perch** on Binsey Lane has a big garden and a children's play area. The **Trout Inn** at Lower Wolvercote (01865 302071) is beside a weir and serves good pub food but can get packed.

Al-Shami

25 Walton Crescent (01865 310066). **Food served** noon-midnight daily. **Set meal** £15 2 courses. **Credit** MC, V.

It's probably most fun to visit this restaurant in a large group and concoct a meal to share from a selection of meze dishes. The usual Lebanese line-up is all present and correct. It includes meaty hors-d'oeuvres such as Armenian spiced sausages, or, for the more adventurous, fried sweetbreads with lemon juice or even lamb's brain salad, in addition to the usual tabouleh and houmous. As is often the case in Lebanese restaurants, the main courses are on the ordinary side, but the mixed grill of lamb, lamb kofta and chicken is good value at £7.40.

Branca Bar Italian Brasserie

111 Walton Street (01865 556111). **Food served** noon-11pm Mon-Thur, Sun; noon-11.30pm Fri, Sat. **Set meal** (noon-6.30pm Mon-Fri) £5 2 items from à la carte menu. **Credit** AmEx, MC, V.

A very groovy newcomer to Jericho, this Italian brasserie has a busy and buzzy bar area at the front (cocktails a speciality) and a popular restaurant area with banquette seating behind. Authentically rustic dishes such as white bean and roast garlic soup join the likes of crab risotto with chilli gremolata, roast hake (£12.45) and hard-to-resist puds such as chocolate nemesis with raspberry sorbet on the menu. Wines are sourced exclusively from Italy.

Cherwell Boathouse Restaurant

Bardwell Road (01865 552746/ www.cherwellboathouse.co.uk). **Food served** noon-2pm, 6.30-10pm daily. **Set lunch** £18.50 3 courses. **Set dinner** £20.50 3 courses. **Credit** AmEx, DC, MC, V.

Based at one of the city's major punting termini, the Cherwell Boathouse Restaurant is hidden in an inconspicuous pavilion down a north Oxford backstreet, where it is actually possible to see real-live chaps sporting *Three Men in a Boat* candy-striped blazers. The set menu lists starters such as pan-fried pigeon breast with crispy bacon salad; mains might include grilled fillet of salmon with mustard and basil butter; and you can finish your meal with a good old-fashioned chocolate mousse.

Gee's

61 Banbury Road (01865 553540). **Food served** noon-2.30pm, 6-11pm Mon-Sat; noon-11pm Sun. **Set lunch** (Mon-Sat) £9.50 2 courses. **Credit** AmEx, MC, V.

Formerly a florist's shop, Gee's Victorian conservatory dining room is light and airy with some leafy, green plants. It is a popular venue with a consistently good modern European menu. Starter choices (around £5-£6) could include grilled marinated aubergine with goat's cheese or freshly steamed mussels; mains (mostly £10-£15) could be sweet shallot and plum tomato tatin with rocket pesto or char-grilled rare tuna steak. Some puddings go the retro route: we loved the steamed marmalade sponge with vanilla sauce. The wine list is comprehensive and knowledgeable.

Le Petit Blanc

71-72 Walton Street (01865 510999/www.petit-blanc.com). **Food served** noon-10.30pm Mon-Fri; 11am-10.45pm Sat, Sun. **Set meals** (noon-7pm Mon-Fri) £12.50 2 courses; £15 3 courses. **Credit** AmEx, DC, MC, V.

Depending on which part of Raymond Blanc's Jericho brasserie you are sitting in, you can look either at a bright mural of Oxford landmarks or the aluminium canteen hatch where the food is prepared. Starters such as carpaccio of tuna with a chilli and coriander dressing (£5.50) or quenelle of polenta and Gruyère (£4.75) are followed by mains that run from the robust (poussin with pearl barley and vegetable broth, £12.25) to the more delicate (sea bass in red wine jus with fennel, £13.50). It's all outstanding value for money. Children are actively welcomed, have their own menu and – to the joy of many parents – can be looked after in a partitioned part of the restaurant on Saturday and Sunday.

Restaurant Elizabeth

82 St Aldate's (01865 242230/www.restaurant-elizabeth.com). **Food served** 12.30-2.30pm, 6.30-11pm Tue-Sat; 12.30-2.30pm, 7-10.30pm Sun. **Set lunch** £17 3 courses. **Credit** AmEx, DC, MC, V.

With escargots à la bourguignonne (£6.50) among the starters, and main courses such as suprême de canard à l'orange (£18.25) and filet de boeuf maison (£18.75), Restaurant Elizabeth is the top spot in Oxford for no-nonsense, traditional French dishes. The place is decorated with wonderfully witty variations on original *Alice in Wonderland* illustrations, such as Humpty Dumpty offering Alice a glass of wine and Tweedledum and Dee agreeing to have a bottle rather than a battle.

South Oxfordshire

Historic market towns on the Thames overlooked by the Chilterns and the Downs.

The abbey at **Dorchester-on-Thames** was a 12th-century replacement for a Saxon church.

The area south of Oxford is a gentle, unspectacular landscape, well cultivated (and populated) and packed with carefully groomed commuter villages and rich farmland. The River Thames cuts a swathe through its eastern flank, wending its way northwards through the university town and then west towards its source in Gloucestershire. To the south, the ancient Ridgeway path crosses the Berkshire Downs. And, lending a pagan dash of the primitive, the impressionistic slash of the chalk White Horse fuels countless local legends and gives its name to the adjacent valley.

Abingdon, painted by Turner and admired by Ruskin, is the oldest continuously occupied town in England and the largest in the Vale of the White Horse. Sadly choked by traffic at the weekends, but with a good Thames-side setting and pleasant river walks, it contains an abbey that was founded in the late seventh century, a row of 15th-century almshouses still in use (the Long Alley Almshouses) and the magnificent English Baroque County Hall (now a museum), built by a protégé of Christopher Wren. It also boasts the area's only (and usually packed) branch of Pizza Express, along with plenty of tea and sandwich shops. River trips to Oxford by steamer leave from Nags Head Island between May and September (Salter Brothers, 01865 243421/www.salterbros.co.uk) and there are boats and bicycles for hire to help you explore the surrounding countryside (enquire at the Tourist Information Centre on Bridge Street, or *see p207* **Bike hire**).

The other main towns in the area are **Faringdon**, to the west off the A420, which was besieged by Cromwell's troops during the Civil War and is now famous for Lord Berners'

By train from London

Trains for **Didcot Parkway** leave **Paddington** up to five times an hour (twice an hour on Sundays). The journey takes between **45mins** and **1hr 20mins**. Info: www.greatwesterntrains.co.uk or www.thamestrains.co.uk.

The Faringdon Collection at Buscot Park

It may be an imposing 18th-century monument to the lucrative rewards of City finance and Empire trade, but Buscot House, north-west of Faringdon, has a fascinating role in mid-20th century left-wing politics and cultural life. Under the second Lord Faringdon, the flamboyant socialist Gavin Henderson, Buscot fairly epitomised the peculiarly 1930s intermingling of aestheticism, connoisseurship, radical politics and country-house decadence.

Strolling through the parkland past the astonishing Peto water garden, or admiring the lakes, the walled garden, the fabulous open-air swimming pool and dramatic woodland avenues, it's strange to think that the place served as a glorified weekend conference centre for Fabians, pacifists, poets and artists. This was principally Henderson's doing. A dapper bachelor (and one of the Bright Young Things of the 1920s immortalised in the novels of Evelyn Waugh), he was serious enough about politics to serve as a London councillor, but not, it appears, to the exclusion of parties, art and life's finer things.

The house itself reflects this duality: a mural on the pavilion by the pool depicts Henderson as a heroic young man addressing a political rally; inside, an eclectic (if minor) collection of art and furniture owes practically nothing to socialist realism. Some of the paintings were collected by Henderson's father, an austere-sounding financier of equally catholic artistic tastes: Rembrandt rubs shoulders with Rubens, Rossetti and Edward Burne-Jones's vast Pre-Raphaelite mural, the *Legend of the Briar Rose*.

Owned by the National Trust since the mid 1950s, Buscot is a gem. Its opening hours are maddeningly illiberal but it is well worth seeking out.

Buscot Park

Faringdon (01367 240786/ www.nationaltrust.org.uk). **Open** *House & grounds* Apr-Sept 2-6pm Wed, Thur, Fri; 2-6pm 2nd and 4th full weekend of the month. Closed Oct-Mar. *Grounds only* Apr-Sept 2-6pm Mon-Fri; 2-6pm 2nd & 4th full weekend of the month. Closed Oct-Mar. **Admission** (NT) *House & grounds* £4.40; £2.20 concessions. *Grounds only* £3.30; £1.65 concessions.

140-foot tall brick folly, built in the 1930s. Further south and east, the town of **Wantage** was the birthplace, in 848, of Alfred the Great, warrior, statesman and educational pioneer. His statue is the centrepiece of the town square, which is also the site of a twice-weekly market (Wednesdays and Saturdays) and several small shops including a good baker and the India Shop (5 Hilliers Yard; 01672 851155) packed with Asian knick-knacks. At **Wallingford**, a town that strategically straddles the Thames to the east, there are the disappointing remains of Wallingford Castle (one of the largest in the country until dismantled by Oliver Cromwell), Saxon earthworks and a fine medieval bridge, as well as antiques shops galore.

Among the many pretty villages in the area is the thatched and half-timbered **Blewbury**, off the A417 south of Didcot, and **Buscot** (off the A417 beyond Faringdon to the west), whose church of St Mary's contains a superb set of stained-glass windows by Edward Burne-Jones

manufactured by Morris and Company. The chancel dates from around 1200. The splendid abbey at **Dorchester-on-Thames**, on the site of a Saxon cathedral, has been a centre of Christianity for nearly 14 centuries. The present building was begun during the 12th century and still contains a Norman font, medieval floor tiles and the 13th-century effigy of an unknown knight in the act of drawing his sword, said to have influenced Henry Moore. Take a wander round the village along the (Roman) Watling Lane and past the grand antiques shops. Sleepy **Ewelme**, a few miles south-east of Dorchester and on the edge of the Chiltern Hills, boasts a picturesque 15th-century church with almshouses and school (founded by Alice Chaucer, granddaughter of the poet Geoffrey Chaucer). The church is in demand as a location for TV dramas; the school is now a state primary. A brook (Ewelme means 'spring source' in old English) runs the length of the village, alongside the main street.

Ewelme School – founded by Alice Chaucer.

Literary links

South Oxfordshire boasts countless associations with literature and literary figures. The churchyard at **Sutton Courtenay** contains the grave of one Eric Arthur Blair, better known as George Orwell (there's also a monument to the pre-World War I prime minister Lord Asquith). The stretch of the River Thames occupied by the Beetle & Wedge Hotel (*see p208*) was immortalised by Kenneth Graham in *The Wind in the Willows* (the author lived in Blewbury between 1910 and 1924) and by Jerome K Jerome. The hotel is one of several that claim Jerome was in residence when he wrote *Three Men in a Boat*. Meanwhile, his hapless fictional trio stopped off at the Barley Mow in **Clifton Hampden** and the Anchor Inn at Abingdon Wharf. Jerome is buried in the churchyard at Ewelme. The Craven in **Uffington** (*see p.?208*) enjoys a walk-on part as 'a low-lying wayside inn' in *Tom Brown's Schooldays* – its author, Thomas Hughes, lived nearby. The poet John Betjeman also lived in the village during the 1930s.

What to see & do

Tourist Information Centres

25 Bridge Street, Abingdon, OX14 3HN (01235 522711). **Open** *Apr-Oct* 10am-5pm Mon-Sat; 1.30-4.15pm Sun. *Nov-Mar* 10am-4pm Mon-Fri; 9.30am-2.30pm Sat.
7A Market Place, Faringdon, SN7 7HL (01367 242191). **Open** *Apr-Oct* 10am-5pm Mon-Fri; 10am-1pm Sat. *Nov-Mar* 10am-1pm Mon-Sat.

Bike hire

H & N Bragg *2 High Street, Abingdon (01235 520034).*
If you're coming from Oxford, you'll need to catch a bus or taxi to Abingdon as there's no train station here.

Didcot Rail Centre

Entrance through Didcot Parkway station, Didcot (01235 817200/www.didcotrailwaycentre.org.uk). **Open** *Apr-Sept* 10am-5pm daily. *Oct-Mar* 10am-4pm Sat, Sun. **Admission** £4; £6.50 (steam days); £3-£3.50 concessions.
A homage to Isambard Kingdom Brunel's Great Western Railway and a trainspotters' paradise. It contains a collection of steam locomotives, either lovingly restored or in the process of being renovated, and a variety of GWR passenger coaches and freight wagons. There's a level crossing and signalbox, a travelling post office and mail exchange, and, for the really besotted, special Railway Experience Days when punters can drive a steam engine.

Kingston Bagpuize House & Garden

Kingston Bagpuize, nr Abingdon (01865 820259/ www.kingstonbagpuizehouse.org.uk). **Open** *House & garden* Feb-Nov selected dates only; phone for details. Closed Dec, Jan. **Admission** *House & garden* £4; £3.50 concessions. *Garden only* £2; free under-5s.
A handsome red-brick and wood-panelled baroque house set in mature parkland containing an early Georgian gazebo. There's also a tearoom.

Little Wittenham Nature Reserve

Information 01865 407792/ www.northmoortrust.co.uk.
The reserve incorporates Little Wittenham Wood and Wittenham Clumps. Comfrey and teasel grow along the woodland paths and over 30 different species of butterfly have been spotted in an area that combines woodland, grassland and riverside areas with scenic views (climb to the top of Round Hill for views over Oxfordshire, the Cotswolds and the Chilterns). On Castle Hill is the site of an Iron Age hill fort. A riverside walk from here leads to Dorchester Abbey.

Wellplace Zoo

Ipsden (01491 680473/www.wellplacezoo.fsnet.co.uk). **Open** *Oct-Mar* 10am-5pm Sat, Sun. *Apr-Sept* 10am-5pm daily. **Admission** £2; £1 concessions.
A modest, idiosyncratic collection of real farmyard animals, exotic and domestic birds, and life-size replica dinosaurs. There's a rather ramshackle air about the place, but the animals seem spirited and fairly happy. No surprises, but great fun for younger kids, who can feed the goats and donkeys, and attempt to converse with the talking parrot.

Keep the red rose flying – **Orwell's grave**.

The Cotswolds

It's a short step from the water to the wine at the **Beetle & Wedge Hotel** in Moulsford.

White Horse & Ridgeway

The oldest and possibly most famous of the 17 white horses in England, this one isn't etched into the hillside like the others, but made from several 10-foot wide, chalk-filled trenches that have to be weeded and refilled from time to time – a service performed by locals for generations, but now carried out by the National Trust. The figure has been dated back nearly 3,000 years to the late Bronze or early Iron Age, and may have acted as a banner for the inhabitants of Uffington Castle, the hill fort whose remains lie nearby. The distinctive, flat-topped hill below the horse is Dragon Hill, where St George reputedly slew the beast. And about a mile to the west along the ancient Ridgeway path (which runs for 85 miles from near Avebury in Wiltshire to Ivinghoe Beacon in Hertfordshire) is the prehistoric chambered tomb known as **Wayland's Smithy**, where legend has it that horses left overnight would be shod by Wayland, the Anglo-Saxon smith god. The White Horse and Ridgeway path beyond are accessible up a narrow path leading off the B4507; although the approach is spectacular, the horse is best seen from a distance, near Fernham (south of Faringdon) or from the Highworth to Shrivenham road. The Ridgeway is popular with horse-riders and cyclists as well as walkers, and can get extremely muddy.

Where to stay

There is no shortage of unremarkable wayside inns, basic B&Bs or rooms above pubs in the area, though their proximity to London and Oxford tends to be reflected in their prices. Here are a few of the more noteworthy options. The **Lamb Inn** in Buckland also has rooms (see p210, £42.50-£59.50 doubles).

Beetle & Wedge Hotel

Ferry Lane, Moulsford-on-Thames, OX10 9JF (01491 651381/fax 01491 651376). **Rates** £95-£125 single occupancy; £150-£165 double/twin. Extra bed for child £25. Special breaks. **Rooms** (all en suite) 10 double/twin. **Credit** AmEx, DC, MC, V.
You'll pay good money to stay in this splendid hotel overlooking the Thames, but, with fabulous views and beautiful gardens unfolding down to the riverbank, it's probably worth it. The rooms are generally spacious and comfortable, and it's worth paying extra for one with a clear river view. There are two restaurants: a formal dining room and the more relaxed Boathouse restaurant, but the river is the star, and the prospect of a cool glass of wine by the water's edge on a sunny summer's afternoon is what it's all about. Understandably popular with weddings and Henley Regatta goers; the owners suggest booking at least three months ahead for the summer. Children welcome. All bedrooms no-smoking.
From M4, take J12 towards Reading; take A4 S; at second roundabout take A340 towards Pangbourne; then A329 towards Streatley and Moulsford; turn down Ferry Lane in the village; hotel is at end of lane.

The Craven

Fernham Road, Uffington, SN7 7RD (01367 820449/www.thecraven.co.uk). **Rates** £28-£40 per person. **Rooms** 1 single; 1 double; 2 double (en suite, half-testers); 2 four-poster (en suite). **Credit** AmEx, MC, V.
A recent refurbishment has enhanced the charms of this idyllic, 300-year-old thatched cottage in pretty Uffington village, near the White Horse and the Ridgeway. There's now a fourth en suite room, and a new thatched roof. Carol Wadsworth treats her guests as part of the family (indeed, you half expect to be told to eat up your greens or to help with the washing up) and breakfast is shared by guests at a large table in the crimson-painted

kitchen, with french windows opening onto the terrace. One of the best rooms, the Elizabethan double, with chintz-hung four-poster and en-suite bathroom, is on the ground floor; the others are up the crooked stairs and down winding passageways stocked with faded family photos and back copies of *Horse & Hound*. Children welcome by arrangement. No smoking throughout.
Turn off the B4057 for Kingston Lisle. Go through Kingston Lisle; after about 2 miles you are in Uffington; take first right out of village after the church; after about ⅓ mile the Craven is on the left hand side.

Crazy Bear Hotel

Bear Lane, Stadhampton, OX44 7UR (01865 890714/fax 01865 400481). **Rates** £60-£100 single occupancy; £80-£120 double; £100 four-poster; £150-£190 suite; £240-£280 cottage.
Rooms (all en suite) 3 double; 1 four-poster; 5 suites; 2 cottages (sleep 5 or 6). **Credit** AmEx, MC, V.
A 16th-century building refurbished in the mid 1990s, the privately owned Crazy Bear pursues a robustly individual approach based on the simple but sound proposition that a hotel experience should be nothing like home, as opposed to home-from-home. Hence, zebra-print carpets, bright colours, and 'daring' iron work in the original rooms; the 'themed' rooms added last year sport a sleek limestone-tiles-and-chrome look, with a luxury bath at the foot of the bed. Crazy, yes, but fun, and infused with a passionate, idiosyncratic spirit. There are two excellent restaurants, a garden terrace, and a cosy bar offering champagne on draught. The bear itself, incidentally, is a stuffed, full-size grizzly suspended in an alcove over the bar. Children welcome.
J7 off M40 towards Birmingham; left at end of slip road; follow A329 for 4 miles; straight across mini-roundabout; immediately left after petrol station; turn sharp left down Bear Lane.

Fords Farm

Ewelme, Wallingford OX10 6HU (01491 839272/www.country-accom.co.uk). **Rates** £35 single; £48-50 double. **Rooms** 1 double; 2 twin.
No credit cards.
This handsome 15th-century farmhouse B&B (with a working sheep farm attached) has views of the village church on one side and open countryside to the other. It offers unpretentious, good-value accommodation. Bedrooms are spacious, and comfortable (although none

have en suite bathrooms), and the cooked breakfasts are good. Ewelme itself is utterly charming, with an historic church and exquisite alms houses, so this is an ideal base for exploring south-east Oxfordshire.
Turn off the B4009 for Ewelme. On entering the village, turn left at the T-junction beside a pond. Fords Farm is on the right after about 100 yards, opposite the 15th-century school building.

George Hotel

High Street, Dorchester-on-Thames, OX10 7HH (01865 340404/fax 01865 341620). **Rates** £65 single; £75 single occupancy; £85 double/twin; £97 four-poster; £100 family. Breakfast £3.50 (Eng). Special breaks. **Rooms** (all en suite) 2 single; 13 double/twin; 2 four-poster; 1 family.
Credit AmEx, MC, V.
This 15th-century whitewashed coaching inn is a useful stopover, rather than a charming place to lay one's head for the night. The en suite rooms in the main building (there are modern rooms in the courtyard annexe) are large and low-beamed, if a little grimy and gloomy, and there's a pleasant bar downstairs. Dorchester Abbey and the town's antique shops are seconds away – Hallidays (Old College; 01865 340068) is particularly worth a browse, although prices are steep. The tariff rather stingily includes continental breakfast but not the full English version, for which a £3.50 premium is demanded. Children and pets welcome (guests' bedrooms only). No-smoking rooms available.

Le Manoir aux Quat' Saisons Relais Château

Church Road, Great Milton, OX44 7PD (01844 278881/fax 01844 278847/www.manoir.com). **Rates** £245-£395 double/twin; £245-£395 four-poster; £525-£575 suite; £650-£750 executive suite. Breakfast £10 (Eng). Special breaks. Min 2-night stay if incl a Sat, May-Sept. **Rooms** (all en suite) 6 double/twin (4 four-poster); 13 suites (2 four-poster).
Credit AmEx, DC, MC, V.
The delights of chef Raymond Blanc's famous two-Michelin-starred restaurant need no introduction. But Le Manoir also offers serious luxury as a hotel – not to mention being 'a hymn to contemporary style', according to Sir Terence Conran. Clearly, prices aren't what one would call 'competitive', so it's a good idea to preview the rooms on the hotel website before booking; each is individually and extravagantly themed, and you wouldn't want to choose the wrong one. The pretty gardens are fine for a light stroll. Children and pets welcome (there are kennels on the grounds). No-smoking rooms available.
In Great Milton village centre, past the church.

Where to eat & drink

The area is peppered with good pubs. Among those recommended for eating as well as drinking are the **Red Lion** in Chalgrove (115 High Street; 01865 890625), which has been owned by the local church for several hundred years, Pot Boy's bar in the **George** at Dorchester (*see above*), and the roadside **Chequers Inn** at Burcot (01865 407771), where

Le Manoir – high-quality food and rest.

The Cotswolds

salad and herbs for the kitchen are grown in a garden at the back. The **Plough** (01865 407811) and the **Barley Mow** (01865 407847) are both in Clifton Hampden, the latter newly refurbished, with a good garden. It's an ideal place to refuel after a Thameside walk (although the grub is pretty standard fare). The **Bear & Ragged Staff** in Cumnor has roaring log fires in winter and sofas to slump in; further south, the **Boar's Head** is in the pretty village of Arlington. The **Harrow** at West Ilsley is popular with walkers taking a break from the nearby Ridgeway and overlooks its own well-kept cricket pitch. The **Beetle & Wedge Hotel** (*see p208*) offers notable classic country cooking in two different restaurants and the **Manoir aux Quat' Saisons** (*see p209*) offers an award-winning gourmet experience in a league of its own (count on spending £100 a head if you're eating à la carte, although there's a set-price lunch menu at £45).

Crooked Billet
Newlands Lane, Stoke Row (01491 681048/ www.crookedbillet.co.uk). **Food served** noon-2.30pm, 7-10pm Mon-Sat; noon-10pm Sun. **Set lunch** £11.95 2 courses; £14.95 3 courses. **Credit** MC, V.
An endearing pub in a picturesque setting, offering reliable modern cooking at restaurant prices. This is the spot where Kate Winslet and Jim Threapleton tied the knot, favouring bangers and mash for their wedding breakfast. You don't have to follow suit: pan-fried pigeon breasts with haggis, baby spinach and roast figs, Irish rock oysters, and local game pie with spring vegetables have all found their way on to recent menus. Main courses on the bar menu are around the £15 mark; otherwise there is a choice of two set meals. Evenings occasionally feature jazz (with a cover charge).

The Goose
Britwell Salome (01491 612304). **Food served** 12.30-2.30pm, 7-9.30pm Tue-Sat; 12.30-2.30pm Sun. **Set lunch** (Tue-Sat) £10 3 courses. **Set dinner** £21 2 courses; £26 3 courses. **Credit** MC, V.
From the outside it's an unpromising old pub by the side of the main road. Inside it's a spirited, if slightly cramped, take on the modern gastropub: warm, bright, and individualistically modernised, with sage green walls, and Pollock-esque toilet wall painting. Chef Chris Barber has 11 years under his belt as personal chef to Prince Charles at Highgrove; his menu draws heavily on game, fish and local produce, simply cooked but not stuffy. You are not overburdened with choice (the set dinners have three main-course options – none of them suitable for vegetarians on our visit). Gratin of scallops Florentine was saucy and succulent; cream of leek and potato soup was fresh and, well, creamy. For mains, the bloody and rich roast saddle of venison was offset by subtle creamed leeks, crushed new potatoes, apple and bacon. The fillet of halibut (with ragout of vegetables) was tender and subtle. The optional afters continue the British flavour: rhubarb cake and rhubarb ice-cream; or a selection of English (and French) cheeses. The 51-bottle wine list runs from £11.50 to £59.

The Greyhound
Gallowstree Road, Rotherfield Peppard (0118 9722227). **Food served** noon-3pm, 7-9.45pm Tue-Sat; 12.30-4pm Sun. **Credit** MC, V.
This old timber-brick pub extends from the low-ceilinged bar into a roomy dining room. The food is excellent: on a recent visit, simple but well-cooked dishes included a starter of crisp grilled goat's cheese salad with apple walnut dressing (£4.25) and a creamy haddock fillet with spinach (£9.50). Service is relaxed and friendly, but professional. There's a pretty garden out front, with a pond seething with carp and goldfish.

Lamb Inn
Lamb Lane, Buckland (01367 870484). **Food served** noon-2pm Mon-Thur; noon-2pm, 7-9pm Fri, Sat; noon-3pm, 7-9pm Sun. **Set lunch** (Sun) £20.95 3 courses. **Credit** AmEx, MC, V.
Not one for laid-back pub-crawlers, the rather sedate Lamb lies in the heart of a village filled with quaint thatched and clematis-covered cottages. You can grab a ploughman's here, or roast beef and Yorkshire pudding, but the menu also offers more ambitious options: roast Gressingham duck with rhubarb and ginger sauce, or escalope of veal in masala sauce. Bread is crusty and own-made and service is attentive. You can eat in the bar, the restaurant or on a small terrace at the back. The inn also has four rooms, all with bath or shower and TV (doubles £42.50-£59.50).

Leatherne Bottel
Goring-on-Thames (01491 872667/ www.leathernebottel.co.uk). **Food served** noon-2pm, 7-9pm Mon-Thur; noon-2pm, 7-9.30pm Fri; noon-2.30pm, 7-9.30pm Sat; noon-3.30pm Sun. **Set dinner** (Mon-Fri) £19.50 3 courses. **Credit** AmEx, MC, V.
The very essence of picture-postcard tranquillity, the Leatherne Bottel has the advantage of a Thames-side terrace that seats 25. Inside, the two small dining rooms are stuffed to the gills with flowers and candlesticks, books and baskets and gilt-framed mirrors. The shortish, rather expensive menu lists the likes of wok-seared tuna loin and tatsoi with lemongrass, chilli, basil and roasted pine nuts (£8.50); squid with tabouleh and crispy seaweed; and lambs' tongues and sweetbreads pan-fried with crisp belly pork, with sage and onion mashed potato and crisp sage leaves (£16.95). For those with less of a hearty appetite, there are soups and salads for a lighter meal. The wine list is impressive but expensive.

White Hart
Main Road, Fyfield (01865 390585). **Food served** noon-2pm, 7-10pm daily. **Credit** AmEx, MC, V.
Don't be fooled by the unimpressive exterior: inside the medieval White Hart lie several rambling rooms and a high-ceilinged, beamed main hall filled with refectory tables, benches and candles, and a galleried seating area above. There's an extensive blackboard bar menu, mainly listing old favourites (garlic chicken wings, £4.50; steak, mushroom and Guinness pie, £7.95; poached salmon, £10.95), but also some vegetarian options, along with children's meals of the fish fingers and chicken nugget variety. The garden at the back is ideal for lazy summer lunches and there's even a better-than-average children's play area. With a range of ales on tap (Theakstons Old Peculier and Hook Norton Best, for instance) this is a pub that should please everyone.

Woodstock to Burford

The epicentre of rural prettiness.

The word picturesque was invented for the Cotswolds. Clusters of fairytale stone cottages with thatched or lichened roofs and smoking chimneys give each village a beauty that's very civilised and terribly, terribly English. Pheasants waddle through glowing fields of rape, rabbits leap in hedgerows, birds sing and blossom falls: the Cotswolds exemplify rural England. It's all fecundity, fresh air and four-wheel-drives.

Not surprisingly, the Cotswolds is now officially designated an Area of Outstanding Beauty. Visitors long to spend their twilight years surrounded by such all-out prettiness, and consequently the area functions as the ultimate free-range retirement home. It's a sedate beauty that attracts an older crowd, so anticipate fresh air and pub meals rather than a rave-up.

The Romans are ultimately responsible for the area's wealth; they introduced the long-woolled breed of sheep, the 'Cotswold Lion', to these parts. Cotswold wool quickly gained an international reputation, flourishing between 1300 and 1500, and the wealth it brought to the area paid for the churches and grand houses that still dominate the villages. In the Middle Ages, grazing sheep took priority over human residents, occupying great tracts of land; in some cases, villagers were even evacuated from villages to give the sheep more room.

Nowadays, the Cotswolds' main industry is tourism, a fact that's reflected in some steep

A cottage garden in **Burford**.

prices. Yet the main attractions are free. Planted deep in the rich countryside are ancient ruins and historical country piles. It's not surprising that some serious – and not-so-serious – creative types have been inspired to live here, from Chaucer, William Morris and Laurie Lee (*see p169*) to Jilly Cooper. There are attractive walks between most of the small villages – and pubs en route to ease the effort.

Eight miles north of Oxford, on the southern edge of the Cotswold Hills, lies the historic market town of **Woodstock**, centred around the country seat of the Dukes of Marlborough, **Blenheim Palace**. The birthplace of Sir Winston Churchill (who was buried in nearby Bladon), Blenheim is one of the most extraordinary buildings in the country: its sheer size will stop first-time visitors in their tracks, while the luxury and splendour of Sir John Vanbrugh's design is simply breathtaking.

By train from London

The nearest station to **Woodstock** is **Hanborough**, 2½ miles away. The journey from **Paddington** takes **1hr 20mins** and trains run every 2hrs. Buses from **Hanborough** to **Woodstock** are scarce, so you're better off getting a taxi (Pejay Taxis 01993 881103). For Burford, your best bet is to get a train to **Oxford** (*see p197*), then get a bus to **Burford**. Info: www.thamestrains.co.uk.

The Cotswolds

Woodstock itself was known for many centuries for two main crafts – glove-making and decorative steel work – and supplied royalty with both. The town has certainly entertained its fair share of blue blood: legend has it that King Alfred stayed in the town in 890, while Henry II frolicked here with his mistress during the 12th century. One bizarre ritual continues from the 18th century: the Mock Mayor Elections, which hark back to the time when inhabitants, fed up with their pompous mayor, decided to hold their own elections. The people would elect a mayor and corporation for Old Woodstock with 'mock formality' and then throw him into the River Glyme. Modern Woodstock is, in general, a more sophisticated place, with a good market and antique shops. A few miles north is **Rousham House**, a rather stern-looking Tudor Gothic pile with exquisite landscaped gardens designed by William Kent, 'the father of modern gardening'.

Heading west towards Burford, **Minster Lovell** is well worth a stop and a stroll. One of the quietest and most unspoilt villages in the area, it boasts not only a gorgeous 15th-century church but also the dramatic ruins of Minster Lovell Hall. Dating from the 1440s, the Hall and its well-restored medieval dovecote make an imposing sight on the banks of the River Windrush. The stunning thatched cottages are some of the prettiest around.

Burford, an elegant and historic coaching town by the Windrush, makes a good, if pricey, base from which to explore the surrounding area. The much-photographed main street comprises a welter of pretty cottages clinging to a steeply sloping hill, and is smattered with antique shops, tearooms, an inordinate number of stripy shirt and jumper shops, and a massive garden centre. For much of the year, the entire village is chockful of traffic; aim to visit in early spring or winter.

Burford's Norman church, remodelled in the 1400s, is proud of its graffiti, inflicted during the 17th century by some of the 400 Leveller mutineers imprisoned here by Cromwell (*see p217* **Levellers' Day**). There are plenty of good riverside walks nearby; try the path to Taynton via the Barringtons or to nearby Swinbrook, where writer Nancy Mitford is buried. To the north, there are paintings and

Man-made and natural beauty: **Burford** church and **Blenheim** butterfly house.

The Cotswolds

fragments of Roman mosaics in the tiny church at Widford. A few miles north of Burford, the petite village of **Shipton-under-Wychwood** boasts a pretty church, which has a stained-glass window designed by the William Morris company and some Pre-Raphaelite archangels. Taynton is a similarly picturesque, peaceful village with exquisite houses.

England's prettiest village?

It's worth continuing about ten miles to the west of Burford to see the village described by William Morris as the most beautiful in England. It seems that the rest of England flocks to **Bibury** each year to check the truth of this statement – it oozes tourists. Based around a wildfowl reserve, the Rack Isle, and the trout-filled River Windrush, Bibury has a certain tweeness but is undeniably pretty. Indeed, when Henry Ford visited it in the 1920s he liked it so much he tried to take part of it back to the States with him. Fortunately, he was stopped. The part in question, Arlington Row, is a crooked row of cottages that was originally a medieval agricultural building, and converted into cottages in the 17th century to house the weavers who made cloth for the nearby mill (mentioned in the Domesday Book and now a museum). Try to hook your supper at the **Bibury Trout Farm** (open daily; 01285 740215), or buy a licence to fish for half a day from the Swan Hotel (£20). Off the main drag, the Saxon church of St Mary's, rebuilt by the Normans in 1156, is awesomely peaceful. There's a lovely walk from Bibury along the River Coln to Coln St Aldwyns.

What to see & do

Blenheim Palace is the big one, and is well worth a visit purely on the grounds of, well, the grounds. A more quirky place to go is **Glass Heritage** (113 High Street, Burford; 01993 822290), a 16th-century building housing a stained-glass studio, which runs weekend courses for beginners and some one-day workshops. Diehard shopaholics, on the other hand, might be more interested in **Bicester Village** (01869 323200), a big discount shopping outlet a few miles east of Woodstock.

Tourist information centres

The Brewery, Sheep Street, Burford, OX18 4LP (01993 823558/www.oxfordshirecotswolds.com). **Open** *Mar-Oct* 9.30am-5.30pm Mon-Sat; 10am-3pm Sun. *Nov-Feb* 10am-4.30pm Mon-Sat.
The Oxfordshire Museum, Fletcher's House, Park Street, Woodstock, OX20 1SN (01993 813276/ www.oxfordshirecotswolds.com). **Open** *Apr-Oct* 9.30am-5.30pm Mon-Sat; 1-5pm Sun. *Nov-Mar* 10am-5pm Mon-Sat; 1-5pm Sun.

Bike hire

Burford Bike Hire *Woollands, Barns Lane, Burford (01993 823326/07713 444519).* Phone ahead to book, Monday to Friday. The shop is a one-minute walk from the bus stop.

Blenheim Palace

Woodstock (24hr recorded info 01993 811325/ www.blenheimpalace.com). **Open** *Palace, Park & Gardens* mid Mar-Oct 10.30am-4.45pm daily. Closed Nov-mid Mar. *Park* 9am-4.45pm daily. **Admission** *Palace, Park and Gardens* £9.50; £4.80-£7.30 concessions. *Park only* £5-£6 per car and occupants; £1-£2 per person; 50p-£1 per person concessions.
After defeating the French at the Battle of Blenheim in 1704, John Churchill, first Duke of Marlborough, was so handsomely rewarded by Queen Anne that he could afford to build this fabulous palace. Designed by Sir John Vanbrugh and set in 2,100 acres of grounds landscaped by Capability Brown, Blenheim is the only non-royal residence in the country that's grand enough to be given the title 'palace'. Even if you decide not to tour the palace itself – with its remarkable long library, gilded state rooms and Churchiliana exhibition (Sir Winston was born here, and buried at nearby Bladon) – there's plenty to keep you occupied in the grounds, including a butterfly house, miniature railway, boating and fishing on the lake, and the Marlborough Maze, the world's biggest symbolic hedge maze.

Cogges Manor Farm Museum

Church Lane, Cogges, Witney (01993 772602). **Open** *late Mar-Oct* 10.30am-5.30pm Tue-Fri; noon-5.30pm Sat, Sun. Closed Nov-late Mar. **Admission** £3.70; £1.60-£2.15 concessions.
Featuring costumed guides and a working farm, this charming museum aims to recreate rural Oxfordshire in Victorian times. Covering 20 acres, the farm is stocked with traditional Victorian breeds of livestock, and has displays of traditional farm implements and machinery. In the historic manor house, which has recently been restored, you can chat to the maids in the kitchen about the history of the house, sample fresh baking from the range, and explore a variety of period displays including a Victorian bedroom and nursery. Special events, such as falconry displays, take place throughout the year.

Cotswold Wildlife Park

Burford (01993 823006/ www.cotswoldwildlifepark.co.uk). **Open** *Apr-Oct* 10am-5pm daily. *Nov-Mar* 10am-4pm daily. **Admission** £6.50; £4 concessions.
Set in 160 acres of gardens and parkland around a listed Victorian manor house, the Cotswold Wildlife Park is one of the Oxfordshire Cotswolds' most popular attractions. Every year over 300,000 people come to the park to see the likes of rhinos, zebras, lions and ostriches roaming in spacious paddocks. Among the many endangered species that the park helps to conserve are red pandas and giant tortoises. Penguins, tropical birds, monkeys, meerkats and otters live in the walled gardens, and there are houses for insects and reptiles and an aquarium. There are also some 200 fruit bats. A mini-railway runs between April and October, and there's a children's farmyard and adventure playground for younger visitors.

The Cotswolds

Cotswold Woollen Weavers

Filkins, nr Lechlade (01367 860491). **Open** 10am-6pm Mon-Sat; 2-6pm Sun. **Admission** free.

Though the importance of the Cotswold wool industry has diminished since wealthy merchants built the famous 'wool churches' such as those at Burford and Northleach in the 15th century, it's still a fascinating part of the region's history. At this working woollen mill you can discover more about the history of the wool trade and watch fleece being woven into woollen fabric using age-old skills. The museum shop has a wide range of knitwear, rugs and accessories and there's also a coffee shop, free parking, and a picnic area.

Kelmscott Manor

Kelmscott, nr Lechlade (01367 252486/ www.kelmscottmanor.co.uk). **Open** *Apr-June, Sept* 11am-1pm, 2-5pm, Wed; 2-5pm 3rd Sat of month. *July, Aug* 11am-1pm, 2-5pm Wed; 2-5pm 1st, 3rd Sat of month. Last entry 30mins before closing. Closed Oct-Mar. **Admission** £7; £3.50 concessions; free under-8s.

Kelmscott Manor was the country home of the poet, artist, craftsman, printer and leader of the Arts and Crafts movement, William Morris, from 1871 until his death in 1896. Today it contains a wonderful collection of his possessions and works, including furniture, textiles and ceramics, and is an unmissable element of any break in the Oxfordshire Cotswolds. The Morris Cottage nearby, built by Jane Morris in 1902 in memory of her husband, and the village church, are also worth a look.

Rousham Park House & Garden

Nr Steeple Aston (01869 347110/www.rousham.org). **Open** *House* Apr-Sept 2-4.30pm Wed, Sun, bank hol Mon. Closed Oct-Mar. *Garden* 10am-4.30pm daily. **Admission** *House* £3. *Garden* £3.

This rather gloomy, imposing Jacobean mansion was remodelled in Tudor Gothic style by William Kent, a predecessor of Capability Brown, in the 18th century. He also designed the outstanding gardens, inspired by Italian landscape painting, with grouped trees, winding paths, glades and waterfalls dotted with statues and temples. Rousham is determinedly uncommercialised, with no shop or tearoom; you're encouraged to bring a picnic and stay for the day wandering the grounds. Children under 15 and dogs are not invited, however, as numerous signs point out.

Where to stay

Bay Tree Hotel

Sheep Street, Burford, OX18 4LW (01993 822791/ fax 01993 823008/www.cotswold-inns-hotels.co.uk). **Rates** £119 single occupancy; £135 double/twin; £145 garden double; £185 junior suite; £210 master suite. **Rooms** (all en suite) 10 double; 4 garden double; 4 junior suites; 4 master suites. **Credit** AmEx, MC, V.

Set back from Burford's main thoroughfare on pretty Sheep Street, the Bay Tree Hotel has been welcoming visitors since 1565. Unsurprisingly, it's become something of an institution over the years, but it's to the management's credit that, despite it's lofty reputation, the hotel remains friendly and the atmosphere is never snooty. Its 21 spacious rooms are decorated with old-fashioned,

wooden beds, heavy floral upholstery and attractive prints of local landscapes – the look is upmarket and staunchly traditional, but never lapses into the twee. The award-winning restaurant offers high-quality modern British cuisine in a pleasant, candlelit dining room overlooking the beautiful, split-level herb garden. Children and pets welcome. No-smoking rooms available.

Bibury Court Hotel

Bibury, Cirencester, GL7 5NT (01285 740337/fax 01285 740660/www.biburycourthotel.co.uk). **Rates** £100 single occupancy; £115-£130 double/twin; £130-£150 four-poster; £180 suite. Breakfast £6.95 (Eng). Special breaks. **Rooms** 8 double/twin (all en suite); 6 four-poster (5 en suite); 1 suite. **Credit** AmEx, DC, MC, V.

A stunning 17th-century mansion, Bibury Court is beautifully located in six acres of land next to the River Coln. Although the building's stunning Cotswold stone façade smacks of genuine luxury, once inside, you'll find that the decor is more eccentric than opulent, and the atmosphere relaxed and informal. Many of the spacious rooms are panelled and filled with heavy antique furniture, while the small, comfy bar and impressive drawing room have been decorated in grand, period style. Trout fishing is available for residents. Bibury itself is a typically lovely Cotswolds village. Children and dogs are welcome.
A40 W of Oxford; take left on to B4425 to Bibury; hotel in village centre in front of church.

Burford House Hotel

99 High Street, Burford, OX18 4QA (01993 823151/fax 01993 823240/www.burford-house.co.uk). **Rates** £75 single occupancy; £95-£125 double/twin/four-poster. **Rooms** (all en suite) 3 double; 2 twin; 2 four-poster. **Credit** AmEx, DC, MC, V.

A friendly, family atmosphere pervades this charming hotel, situated on Burford's busy, sloping High Street. There are wonderful, homely touches such as the 'honour bar', which offers a selection of fine spirits and liqueurs, and relies on the honour of the guests to add any drinks consumed to their own bills. The rooms are smartly decorated in typical English country style, while several of the spacious, en suite bathrooms feature beautiful, free-standing Victorian baths. There are sitting rooms with log fires and a courtyard for warmer days. No evening meals are served, but an exemplary English breakfast is available in the bright dining room overlooking the High Street. Children welcome. All bedrooms are no-smoking.

Feathers Hotel

Market Street, Woodstock, OX20 1SX (01993 812291/fax 10993 813158/www.feathers.co.uk). **Rates** £99-£140 single occupancy; £135-£185 double/twin; £240-£290 suite. Breakfast £14.95 (Eng). **Rooms** (all en suite) 17 double/twin; 5 suites. **Credit** AmEx, DC, MC, V.

Second only to Blenheim Palace in the Woodstock pecking order, the Feathers is a grand old institution comprising four 17th-century townhouses seamlessly joined together. It is characterised by its elegance and restraint: the smart yet homely rooms are adorned with stylish floral prints, antiques and original paintings, while the communal areas, such as the cosy bar and large, first floor drawing room, are formal, but never intimidating. To the rear of the hotel, the charming courtyard garden is perfect for pre-dinner drinks on

William Morris's **Kelmscott Manor**.

summer evenings. The new wing has five rooms including a family suite with private patio and lounge. Book at least four weeks ahead in summer. Children and dogs welcome. *See also p216.*

King's Arms Hotel

19 Market Street, Woodstock, OX20 1SU (01993 813636/fax 01993 813737). **Rates** £50 single occupancy; £55-£80 twin; £55-£85 double; £90 deluxe double. **Rooms** (all en suite) 1 single; 6 double; 2 twin. **Credit** AmEx, MC, V.

Directly opposite the historic Feathers Hotel (*see p214*), the King's Arms offers an altogether more modern experience. Owners David and Sara Sykes have refused to bow to convention and have decorated their 18th-century townhouse in stylish and contemporary colours, with sprawling indoor plants and modern art. The light, airy restaurant offers basic, but well-executed Mediterranean-style food. Comfortable and hospitable, the King's Arms offers a great alternative to the stereotypical quaintness of so many Cotswold hotels. Children welcome. Pets by prior arrangement. All bedrooms no-smoking.

Manor Farmhouse

9 Manor Road, Bladon, nr Woodstock (tel/fax 01993 812168/www.oxlink.co.uk/woodstock/manor-farmhouse/). **Rates** £58 double; £48 twin. **Rooms** 1 twin; 1 double (both sharing shower room). **No credit cards**.

Hidden away on a backstreet in sleepy Bladon, this stylishly renovated Grade II-listed house is ideal for a peaceful, restful stay. The owner, Mrs Stevenson, offers two guest rooms, both with tea-making facilities and colour TV: the larger double has a restrained Laura Ashley bedspread and furnishings and a white wrought-iron bed. The Manor is always a quiet spot, but on Sundays the only sounds are church bells (Churchill is buried in the churchyard) and woodpigeons. Just one word of warning: beware the pale carpets in muddy boots. Children welcome. Pets by arrangement. No smoking throughout.

A44 NW of Oxford; take A4095 left after Begbroke; take last turn left in Bladon village into Manor Road; house has iron railings and is on second bend.

Mill & Old Swan Inn

Minster Lovell, OX29 0RN (01993 774441/fax 01993 702002/www.millandoldswan-isc.co.uk). **Rates** *Swan* £50-£70 per person. *Mill* £30-£50 per person. Special breaks. **Rooms** (all en suite) *Swan* 2 single; 11 double/twin; 3 four-poster. *Mill* 2 single; 45 double/twin. **Credit** AmEx, DC, MC, V.

The Mill & Old Swan is housed in two separate buildings situated on either side of the narrow B road that winds through the blissfully quiet village of Minster Lovell. Though the Mill itself dates back to the 16th century, most of its rooms are housed in a modern extension and are decorated in contemporary Scandinavian style with good spacious bathrooms. The river rooms have private patios by the picturesque River Windrush. The Swan, meanwhile, dates back to the 11th century and offers more characterful accommodation: many of the rooms feature exposed beams, several have four-posters, and one even has its own ghost. Shared facilities include a tennis court, fishing path, croquet lawn, putting green, mountain bikes and a gym with a sauna. The romantic ruins of 15th-century Minster Lovell Hall are just ten minutes' walk away. Children and small dogs welcome.

A40 W of Oxford; after 14 miles take the sliproad on right signposted 'Carterton, Minster Lovell'; right at junction; through Minster Lovell; right at T-junction; immediate left into valley; left over stone bridge; hotel reception is on left.

New Inn at Coln

Coln St Aldwyns, GL7 5AN (01285 750651/ www.new-inn.co.uk). **Rates** £72 single; £99-£125 double. **Rooms** (all en suite) 1 single; 9 double; 3 twin. **Credit** AmEx, MC, V.

Very well known in the area, the creeper-clad New Inn offers pub, restaurant (*see p217*) and hotel in one slick, well-run package. The smart, individually decorated bedrooms are divided between the main building and the Dovecote, and feature notably comfy beds and plenty of chintz and floral motifs. No children under ten. Pets welcome. No smoking throughout.

A40 W towards Cheltenham; turn left on to B4425 towards Bibury 1 mile after passing Burford; continue for 5 miles; turn left shortly after Oldsworth; take signs to Coln St Aldwyns; pub is on the main street.

The Cotswolds

Shaven Crown Hotel

High Street, Shipton-under-Wychwood, OX7 6BA
(01993 830330/fax 01993 832136). **Rates** £55
single occupancy; £85-£95 double; £95 twin; £120
four-poster. **Rooms** (all en suite) 8 double/twin;
1 four-poster. **Credit** AmEx, MC, V.

This fabulously historic hotel, dating back to the 14th
century, is one of the ten oldest licensed premises in
the UK, and derives its rather unusual name from the
fact that it once housed a monk's hospice. Today, the
Shaven Crown offers excellent value for a quirky stay.
The galleried medieval hall, which is now the lounge,
has a vaulted ceiling and roaring fire, and there is also
a beamed dining room (it's worth staying in for
dinner). The rooms are comfortable, if not exactly
plush, and are decorated in that generic, and slightly
dated, English country house style. The hotel has
the use of two tennis courts and a bowling green.
Children and dogs welcome.

A40 W of Oxford past Witney; turn right at Burford on
to A361 to Shipton-under-Wychwood; hotel faces church
and village green.

Where to eat & drink

In general, the area cashes in on its appeal to
tourists and prices are high. It will come as
no surprise, then, that many recommended
restaurants are within pricey hotels. Book
well ahead for most restaurants, or you may
be disappointed. A good starting point might
be the brasserie **Off the Square** (4 Lombard
Street, Eynsham; 01865 881888), once a local
favourite called Baker's, and still with Stuart
Baker as chef. On Burford High Street, the
Golden Pheasant (01993 823223) and
the **Old Bull** (01993 822220) both serve
reasonable food at reasonable prices.
Meanwhile, away from the Burford hordes,
the **Swan Inn** (01844 822165) in Swinbrook
is an unspoilt, down-to-earth old bar by the
river serving food. In Bibury, **Jankowski's**
offers reasonably priced snacks and lunches
in a courtyard. In Woodstock, **Vickers**
(01993 811212) serves unexceptional but
affordable food in pleasant, candlelit
surroundings, and there's also the highly
regarded Chinese, **Chef Imperial** (22 High
Street; 01993 813591). The **Queen's Own**
(59 Oxford Street; 01993 813582) is a good
hideaway pub for a quiet pint.

Feathers Hotel

Market Street, Woodstock (01993 812291/
www.feathers.co.uk). **Food served** 12.30-2pm,
7-9pm daily. **Set lunches** £15.50 2 courses; £19.50
3 courses. **Credit** AmEx, DC, MC, V.

In keeping with the luxurious accommodation of the
hotel, the award-winning restaurant at the Feathers is a
seriously swanky affair. Dinner in the beautiful oak-
panelled dining room (no smoking) includes starters
such as risotto of wild mushrooms and duck confit (£13),
generous mains such as roast fillet of sea bass with

crushed potatoes, sauce vierge and caviar aubergine
(£22), and luxurious desserts such as hazelnut parfait
with fresh strawberries and red fruits. The lunch menu
includes the likes of risotto of foie gras with truffle oil,
and nage of seafood, Jerusalem artichokes and rocket.
A more informal menu is available in the hotel bar. Non-
residents can enjoy lunch, tea or a drink in the pretty
garden. *See also p214.*

King's Head Inn & Restaurant

Chapel Hill, Wootton, nr Woodstock (01993 811340/
www.kings-head.co.uk). **Food served** noon-2pm,
7-9pm Mon-Sat; noon-2pm Sun. **Credit** MC, V.

A big hit with local foodies, Tony Fay's King's Head
Inn is housed in a beautiful 17th-century Cotswold
stone house, with a cosy, salmon-pink bar, log fires and
large sofas. The candlelit restaurant serves superb
modern menus based on European cuisine: there are starters
such as mousseline of duck liver with red berry essence
and freshly baked brioche (£5.95); mains could include
a tower of Orkney fillet steak with potato rosti, wild
mushrooms and a smooth black pepper dressing
(£15.95). Desserts, all around a fiver, could include
caramelised citrus tart and vanilla bean, yoghurt and
mascarpone terrine. Comfortable accommodation is
also available (doubles £75-£95).

Lamb Inn

Sheep Street, Burford (01993 823155). **Food
served** 7-9pm Mon-Sat; 12.30-1.45pm, 7-9pm
Sun. **Set lunch** £20 3 courses. **Set dinner** (Mon-
Thur, Sun) £22 2 courses. (Fri, Sat) £27 3 courses.
Credit MC, V.

No visit to the Oxfordshire Cotswolds would be complete without a meal at the famous Lamb Inn. Widely
regarded as the place to eat in Burford, the Lamb's
gorgeously traditional bar and lounges, and light, plant-
filled dining room are constantly buzzing with
enthusiastic diners. The lunchtime bar menu might
include duck leg confit with creamed potato, vegetables
and peppercorn sauce (£9), while the more extravagant
three-course dinner menu offers traditional mains such
as grilled whole sole with roast baby fennel, rosemary
and lemon butter and indulgent desserts like a dark
chocolate torte with raspberries and double cream. This
place is popular with both tourists and locals, and booking is essential at weekends. The Lamb also has accommodation (doubles £110-£120).

Lamb Inn

Shipton-under-Wychwood (01993 830465). **Food
served** noon-2pm, 7-9.30pm daily. **Credit** AmEx,
DC, MC, V.

A delightful, family-run pub,restaurant and B&B, the
Lamb offers that winning combination of good food,
relaxed surroundings and excellent service. A great-
value lunchtime buffet (from £6.95) includes robust
dishes such as Cotswold pie – crammed full of beef,
venison and ham – and stilton and leek quiche, plus an
abundance of salad and hot vegetables. Dinner, meanwhile, may be taken in the no-smoking dining room or
the more lively bar, and might include magret of duck
with cranberry and ginger (£11.95) and cassoulet of
pork belly, duck, lamb and sausage (£10.95). If you
don't feel like moving too far after your dinner, an
overnight stay costs £75 for a double room, or £90
for a room with a four-poster bed.

New Inn at Coln

Coln St Aldwyns, nr Cirencester (01285 750651/www.new-inn.co.uk). **Food served** noon-2pm, 7-9pm Mon-Thur; noon-2pm, 7-9.30pm Fri, Sat; noon-2.30pm, 7-9pm Sun. **Set lunch** (Sun) £17.50 3 courses. **Set dinners** £23.50 2 courses; £27.50 3 courses. **Credit** AmEx, DC, MC, V.

Lunch offers high-quality, traditional dishes in the bar (£5.25-£9.50), or well-priced set meals in the restaurant, but it's the dinner menu that really excels. Served in cosy, candlelit dining rooms, expertly prepared and beautifully presented dishes might include starters such as pan-fried fois gras with rocket salad and sherry vinegar reduction, mains like seared pink sea bream with coriander, noodles and shitake mushrooms, and sumptuous desserts such as iced tiramisu with coffee anglaise. Regularly filled to overflowing, the New Inn represents both quality and decent value. *See also p215.*

Swan at Southrop

Nr Lechlade (01367 850205). **Food served** noon-2pm, 7-9.30pm Mon-Sat; noon-2.30pm Sun. **Credit** MC, V.

After a change of management and a £250,000 refurbishment, the new Swan is basically a rather more splendid version of its former self. The look of this 16th-century inn remains largely traditional and countrified, with log fires and plenty of exposed stone, although there's certainly a touch more sparkle about the furniture, accessories and upholstery. Starters (around £4-£6) could include salmon and smoked haddock fish cakes with lemon butter sauce, and asparagus and soft poached eggs with butter and chive sauce. Mains might be skate wing cooked in burnt butter with a herb salad and salsa verdi (£15) or a pea and mint risotto with lemon and parsley butter (£10). The Swan represents the best value in the area.

Levellers' Day

Visit Burford in mid May and you may find a number of rather unusual characters hanging around. Every year, on the nearest Saturday to the 17th, an eclectic band – comprising politicians, musicians, political radicals and even the odd 17th-century soldier – congregates in the ancient market town to commemorate a highly significant, and yet little-known, historical event: the brutal crushing, by Oliver Cromwell and Sir Thomas Fairfax, of the last significant uprising of the political adjutants, the Levellers.

Led by John Lilburne, the Levellers existed as an organised group between around 1645 and 1649. The principal beliefs of the movement were rooted in liberty and equality: they campaigned for universal suffrage, demanded elected representatives in parliament and tried to promote religious tolerance.

Towards the end of the English Civil War, the group was gathering a good deal of support from the ranks of Cromwell's parliamentarian army, who had become embroiled in disputes over non-payment of wages, lack of indemnity for wartime acts and proposed drafting to Ireland.

In May 1649, one such dispute led to full-scale mutinies by three Leveller regiments: those of Colonels Scrope and Ireton at Salisbury, and Captain William Thompson at Banbury. In an attempt to placate the mutineers, Cromwell recognised the troops' financial grievances and pledged £10,000 towards payment of arrears; he also promised

that the soldiers' other complaints would be heard, and that no force would be used against them.

However, on 13 May, when Thompson's regiment were camped outside Burford on their way to a rendezvous with their fellow Levellers at Salisbury, Cromwell ordered a surprise attack. Several mutineers were killed in the skirmish and the rest were imprisoned in the town's Norman church. Cromwell had shamelessly abandoned his promise of non-aggression, but the worst was still to come: four days later, three of the rebel 'ringleaders' were led out of the church and executed in the graveyard outside.

The Levellers had been totally betrayed and three of their number brutally murdered to serve as an example to future mutineers. The movement never really recovered from the blow and on 25 May 1649, Cromwell triumphantly announced the successful suppression of the Levellers in the army.

The physical marks of these inglorious events – bullet holes and graffiti left by the imprisoned Levellers in the parish church of St John the Baptist – can still be found in Burford today, but the social legacy is just as important. The continued celebration of 'Levellers' Day' (contact Mrs Jones; 01865 249336) – when free citizens meet to commemorate the past and debate the present – seems like a perfect tribute to one of this country's first truly democratic political groups.

Chipping Norton to Banbury

A battlefield, a castle, prehistoric stones and Cotswold villages – an intriguing mix.

The ultimate rural idyll: **Bleddington** village green.

It's tempting to bypass an area with as wistful a soubriquet as the 'Gateway to the Cotswolds'; it smacks of hopeful councillors and falling property prices. True, this part of the country doesn't have quite the number of honeypot villages that you'll find out west, but the area's charms should not be underestimated – and nor should the relief of escaping the tourist masses found less than an hour's drive away in Gloucestershire, Stratford or Oxford.

The landscape is a mix of cow-parsley lanes, undulating cornfields, meadows, wooded hills and rivers, all peppered with villages that haven't changed very much in centuries. There's little modern building in the area, and because stone has always been cheap around here, builders used glorious red-brown ironstone – now speckled with orange lichen – or rich, sun-soaking, golden Cotswolds limestone. Medieval wool money paid for many handsome churches, with local stone-cutting skills evident in fine tracery and other detailing. The medieval vocabulary of mullioned windows and gables is also much in evidence in the striking Jacobean cottages, farmhouses and manor houses around every turn.

Antique crafts of Chipping

Chipping Norton itself is a small market town, pretty but not overwhelmingly touristy. There are lots of traditional teashops, inns and pubs, but all are peopled with locals, and the place has an affluent, relaxed feel.

Terraced into the hillside, it's the highest town in Oxfordshire, and you get glimpses of rolling countryside between the rooftops, as well as the bizarre and now defunct Bliss Tweed Mill, designed to resemble a great stately home with a giant chimney rising from the centre, and now turned into luxury flats. In addition to a small museum, there are lots of antiques shops in Chipping Norton, with far keener pricing than those of the northern Cotswolds. The **Station Mill Antique Centre** (Station Road; 01608 644563) is a great place to browse for an hour or so, and has a small café.

Also worth a visit, if only to see the Graham Rush murals in the bar and wonderful theatrical cartoons in the lavatories, is the highly regarded **Chipping Norton Theatre** on Spring Street. Just down from there, on Church Lane, are pretty 17th-century almshouses and the imposing wool church of St Mary, which has one of the finest 15th-century interiors in the county.

Rolling back the years

North and north-west of Chipping Norton are the pretty villages of **Little Rollright** – an unspoilt hamlet set among meadows – and **Great Rollright** – little grey stone cottages on a breezy hillside. Between them lie the Rollright Stones (see p221 **Like a Rollright Stone**), a group of prehistoric stones said to be third in the stone-circle pecking order after Stonehenge and Avebury. There are beautiful walks to be had around this area, and it's not far to **Hook Norton**, a large ironstone village where the most wonderful beer of the same name – known locally as 'Hooky' – is brewed. West of Chipping Norton, the A44 takes you further into the Cotswolds and to **Chastleton House**, one of the best-preserved Jacobean houses in the country, set in a cosy hillside nook. Continue on the A44 and you'll get to Moreton-in-Marsh (see p183); taking the A436 will take you to Stow-on-the-Wold (see p176).

The sleepy villages roll on; high on the hilltops above Hook Norton are **Sibford Gower** and **Sibford Ferris**; **Shenington**; **Swalcliffe**; and across the border into Warwickshire, **Brailes** and **Compton Wynyates**, an elegant Tudor country house no longer open to the public but surrounded by lovely walks. From the nearby village of **Tysoe**, there's great hillwalking along **Edgehill**, and spectacular views across to

An invented England made real.

Stratford-upon-Avon (see p190). Nearby is the 17th-century **Upton House**, with a staggering art collection and beautiful gardens descending to pools in the valley below.

Crossing Banbury

The north-east of this area is bounded by Banbury, a market town known for its cakes and its cross, immortalised in the nursery rhyme 'Ride a Cock-horse to Banbury Cross'. Since the demise of its world-famous cattle market there is little to attract the visitor in Banbury, but just south-west of the town is the romantic **Broughton Castle** and three pretty villages known for their imposing church spires: '**Bloxham**, for length, **Adderbury** for strength, **Kings Sutton** for beauty' – as the local saying goes.

Further south, down the A4260, there's the historic market town of **Deddington**, now a centre for antiques. Then, on the banks of the winding Cherwell river, the **Astons**: **North**, **Middle** and **Steeple**, with more fine walking and some excellent pubs. The Arcadian landscape of wooded hills and small villages continues from here back to Chipping Norton, by way of the Bartons, Kiddington, the Enstones, Glympton and the Tews.

The jewel in the crown is the fabulously picturesque **Great Tew**, a village with perfect thatched cottages nestling in a lushly wooded dell. The way it looks is no accident:

By train from London

Trains from **Marylebone** to **Banbury** leave every half-hour (journey time approximately **1hr 20mins**). There is no station for Chipping Norton – the nearest is at **Kingham**, five miles away. Trains leave **Paddington** every 2hrs; journey time is **1hr 32mins**. Info: www.chilternrailways.co.uk and www.thamestrains.co.uk.

The Cotswolds

Standing guard through the centuries at **Broughton Castle**.

in Victorian times, the village's owners planned this effect carefully, planting great clumps of trees and adding Gothic porches to all the cottages, so the village would complement the rest of their estate.

What to see & do

This area is best for gentle meandering on foot, by bicycle or by car. The fantastically helpful Tourist Information Centre in Chipping Norton (*see below*) has leaflets outlining circular walks and bike rides throughout the area. In general, Oxfordshire's paths and bridleways seem to be particularly well signposted.

Tourist Information Centre

The Guildhall, Chipping Norton, OX7 5NJ (tel/fax 01608 644379). **Open** *Mar-Oct* 9.30am-5.30pm Mon-Sat. *Nov-Feb* 10am-3pm Mon-Sat.

Broughton Castle

SW of Banbury (01295 262624/ www.broughtoncastle.demon.co.uk). **Open** *Mid May-mid Sept* 2-5pm Wed, Sun, bank hols. *July, Aug* 2-5pm Wed, Thur, Sun, bank hols. Closed Oct-mid May. **Admission** £4.50; £2-£4 concessions.
More of a moated manor house, really, Broughton Castle is best known as the location for *Shakespeare in Love*. Bought by William of Wykeham in the 14th century, it has been in the same family ever since. Their surname changed to Fiennes in the 15th century, and Ralph, Joseph and Ranulph are all cousins of the present owner, Nathaniel. The house has some impressive plasterwork ceilings and atmospheric vaulted passages, as well as heirlooms connected with the many colourful episodes in the family's history – not least as a hotbed of anti-monarchical intrigue during the Civil War.

Chastleton House

Chastleton, off A44 NW of Chipping Norton (01608 674355/www.nationaltrust.org.uk/ thameschilterns). **Open** *Apr-Sept* 1-5pm Wed-Sat. *Oct* 1-4pm Wed-Sat. Closed Nov-Mar. **Admission** (NT) £5.20; £2.60 concessions.
A Jacobean manor house with a dramatic five-gabled front. Inside there is a great collection of original panelling, furniture, tapestries and embroideries. The gardens display some fine and imaginative topiary. It's now in the National Trust's care and, unfortunately, you have to pre-book to visit.

Hook Norton Brewery

Brewery Lane, Hook Norton (01608 737210/ www.hook-norton-brewery.co.uk). **Open** *Museum* 10am-4pm Mon-Fri. *Shop* 9am-4.30pm Mon-Fri. **Admission** *Museum* £2; £1 concessions. *Tours* phone for details.
Tours of this, one of the last tower breweries in the country, are hugely popular; you'll need to book a long way in advance. In September 1999, a museum and visitor's centre was opened.

Upton House

off A422 S of Edgehill, nr Banbury (01295 670266/ www.ntrustsevern.org.uk). **Open** *Apr-Oct* 1-5pm Mon-Wed, Sat, Sun. Last admission 4.30pm. Closed Nov-Mar. **Admission** (NT) £5.50. Garden only £2.70.
A late 17th-century house famous for its extensive art collections, which include work by Stubbs, Canaletto, Hogarth, El Greco and more, as well as Sèvres porcelain, Brussels tapestries and 18th-century furniture. The gardens are spectacular, too, with ornamental pools and all kinds of colourful surprises.

Water Fowl Sanctuary & Children's Farm

Wiggington Heath, nr Hook Norton (01608 730252). **Open** 10.30am-5.30pm/dusk daily. **Admission** £3; £2 concessions.

The Cotswolds

The unlikely home of ostriches, emus, parrots, chipmunks and a glorious snowy white peacock. An eccentric place, with all the usual farmyard friends and an inordinate number of ducks in a series of ponds crisscrossed by pathways. Kids will love the petting room, where they can pick up fluffy little rabbits, chicks and ducklings. Wellies advisable.

Where to stay

Castle Inn
Edgehill, nr Banbury, OX15 6DJ (01295 670255/fax 01295 670521/www.our-web-site.com/the-castle-inn).
Rates £35 single occupancy; £55 double; £65 four-poster. **Rooms** (all en suite) 1 double; 1 twin; 1 four-poster. **Credit** AmEx, DC, MC, V.
Built on the summit of Edgehill in the 18th century, this extraordinary folly marks the spot where Charles I's

army gathered before the first major battle of the Civil War. There are two towers, each containing two bedrooms – those in the main tower are the ones to go for, with sweeping views over the battlefield below. Decor is not especially imaginative, but the rooms are comfortable, and the pub downstairs has decent food and a large garden with an Aunt Sally. Children welcome. All bedrooms are no-smoking.

College Farmhouse
Kings Sutton, nr Banbury, OX17 3PS (01295 811473/fax 01295 812505/ www.banburytown.co.uk/accom/collegefarm).
Rates £36 single occupancy; £58 double/twin. **Rooms** (all en suite) 3 double/twin. **Credit** MC, V.
A smart, elegant, but wonderfully relaxed 18th-century house on the outskirts of Kings Sutton. The place has its own beautiful, secluded garden with a tennis court, and even has its own lake, too. Inside, there's a large,

Like a Rollright Stone

These prehistoric stone monuments are shrouded in legends. Many legends. Rather as you will never – allegedly – count the same number of the **Rollright Stones** twice, it sometimes feels you will never hear the same version of how they came to be here. The basic plot, subject to hundreds of variations, is reflected in the names of the stones: the circle of 70 or so is known as the King's Men; the five upright stones standing at a distance the Whispering Knights; and the tall solitary stone, the King Stone (pictured).

A king and his men were crossing the area, it is said, with the intention of conquering England. A local witch, hip to their tricks, appeared and set out the following challenge: 'Seven long strides shalt thou take/ If Long Compton thou canst see/ King of England shalt thou be.' The crest of the hill was just seconds away and the king confidently accepted. On taking his final stride, however, he found his view blocked by a hillock and he and his circle of men were turned to stone, as were five traitors (the Whispering Knights) who had sneaked off to plot the king's downfall. The witch turned herself into an elder tree – clumps of elder still grow on the site – although quite what she gained from this has escaped historical memory.

The stories do not end there. Locals tell how a farmer tried to drag one of the stones from his land – he and his team of horses struggled all day to drag it just a few feet. Giving in to superstition, he

decided to return the stone to its original place: this took one horse no time at all. Another tale tells of the baker who tried to count the stones by placing a loaf on each one, but as he rounded the circle he found the first loaves had disappeared. Or was it cakes?

Rollright Stones
S of A3400 NW of Chipping Norton (PO Box 333, Banbury OX16 4XA/tel/fax 01295 277244/ www.rollright.demon.co.uk). **Open** sunrise-sunset daily. **Admission** 20p-50p.

The Cotswolds

beamed sitting room with an inglenook fireplace over-looking the lawns; a long, airy kitchen/family room; cosy, peaceful bedrooms that feel more like a friend's rather nice spare rooms, and piles of books everywhere – in the rooms, in the corridors – all very obviously for visitors to peruse. You're very much a guest in a family house – and delicious organic breakfasts, with home-made bread, are taken *en famille*. However, if you really want to be alone, you could always consider the larger Barn Room, which is in a separate outbuilding, with its own little kitchen. Dinner costs £18 (three courses) and is served by arrangement only. Children welcome. All bedrooms no-smoking.
B4100 towards Adderbury; after 5 miles take right turn to Kings Sutton; at crossroads in centre of village turn right down Astrop Road; after 500 yards take last turning right before leaving village down a lane leading towards College Farmhouse.

Crown & Cushion Hotel
High Street, Chipping Norton, OX7 5AD (01608 642533/fax 01608 642926/ www.thecrownandcushion.com). **Rates** £59-£75 single occupancy; £75-£110 double; £90-£110 four-poster. Special breaks. **Rooms** (all en suite) 5 single; 10 double; 12 four-poster. **Credit** MC, V.
The rambling layout, dusty beams and laid-back members of staff keep this *soi-disant* 'conference and leisure centre' from feeling too much like a business hotel, as does the spirit of its former owner – none other than Keith Moon. The rooms in this 15th-century former coaching inn are nothing fancy, but they are all comfortable, with good-sized bathrooms (which come in two styles: floral or blue and white, the latter infinitely preferable). The rooms overlooking the High Street are particularly good value for money. The cosy bar, a big favourite with locals as well as guests, is the real hub of the hotel, but hidden away at the back is a small fitness centre and indoor pool. Some dirt-cheap deals are to be had if you choose to eat from the surprisingly extensive menu in the hotel's country-cottage-style dining room. Children and pets welcome. No-smoking rooms available.

Falkland Arms
Great Tew, nr Chipping Norton, OX7 4DB (01608 683653/www.banbury-cross.co.uk/falklandarms). **Rates** £40 single; £65-£80 double; £75 four-poster. **Rooms** (all en suite) 3 double; 1 single, 2 four-poster. **Credit** AmEx, MC, V.
How this pub retains its olde worlde feel while thronged with mooning Londoners is something of a mystery, but policies such as a ban on mobile phones certainly help. Old mugs, jugs, pipes and snuffboxes line every inch of shelf and beam, a fire blazes in an inglenook, and outside a large garden looks out over rolling hills. The same view can be had from the attic room, which is worth paying a bit extra for; the other rooms are a little cramped and chintzy. Location is what you're paying for here – not just the great pub downstairs, but one of the most beautiful villages in the country. Lunch and dinner are available, but booking is essential, even for guests. Children under 14 are not allowed. All bedrooms no-smoking.
A361 SW from Banbury; follow signs to Great Tew; on outskirts of the village, bear right towards the post office; Falkland Arms is three houses down from the post office.

Thatched roofs at **Great Tew**.

King's Head
The Green, Bledington, nr Kingham, OX7 6XQ (01608 658365/fax 01608 658902/ www.kingsheadinn.net). **Rates** £45 single occupancy (Sun-Thur only); £60-75 double/twin; £90 four-poster. **Credit** AmEx, MC, V.
Overlooking a picture-book village green – complete with ducks known locally by name – and within walking distance of Kingham station, the King's Head is very popular, and deservedly so. The charming young couple who recently took it over have ripped out the chintz and decorated the bedrooms with understated elegance, and are making every effort to uphold the restaurant's reputation for excellent food. Tom Waits and Van Morrison provide the soundtrack in the low-beamed bar with inglenook fireplace, but this is no cynical bid to woo weekending Londoners; locals are carefully looked after with guest beers and their own room to escape the visiting masses. Rooms above the 15th-century inn are supposedly haunted; for a guaranteed peaceful night's sleep, head for the modern rooms around a courtyard at the back – the room with half-tester has a good view. Children and pets welcome. No-smoking rooms available.
B4450 from Chipping Norton towards Stow; turn off left for Bledington; the King's Head is on the Green.

La Madonette
North Newington, nr Banbury, OX15 6AA (01295 730212/fax 01295 730363/ www.lamadonette.co.uk). **Rates** £42 single occupancy; £62 double; £85 four-poster; £75 family room. **Rooms** (all en suite) 2 double/twin; 1 four-poster; 2 family. **Credit** DC, MC, V.
A 17th-century converted Jacobean millhouse, La Madonette is quite idyllically situated in a beautifully tended garden with a stream running through it and stunning views. A swimming pool is tucked neatly out of sight for use in the summer months. Inside, the guest rooms are low-ceilinged and beamed and, to be absolutely honest, could use a paintbrush. Fading floral patterns mocked by perky china wheelbarrows of dried flowers seems to be the prevailing scheme, the notable exception being the lovely four-poster room, with a huge bathroom and modern decor. To enjoy great views, ask for a room at the front of the house (those with baths rather than showers are bigger and nicer, and, as we've said, they have baths)

and throw open the windows. Friendly staff serve excellent breakfasts in a pretty dining room. Children welcome. All bedrooms no-smoking.
B4035 SW of Banbury; follow signs to North Newington, house is on right before village.

Where to eat & drink

There are surprisingly few top-notch restaurants for such a well-heeled area – Chavignol in Chipping Norton was the best known, but was in the process of relocating to the Old Mill Hotel in Shipston at the time of writing, having caused the demise of its closest rivals. Aside from those included here, there are a handful of pubs serving good food: the tiny **Swan** in Wiggington (01993 830345), the **White Horse** at Kings Sutton (01295 810843), and the thatched **Stag's Head** at Swalcliffe (01295 780232).

Other cosy hostelries serving good ales and decent food include the **Blue Boar** in Chipping Norton (01608 643525); the **King's Head** in Bledington (*see p222*); the friendly **Blinking Owl** in North Newington (01295 730650) or the nearby **North Arms** in Wroxton (01295 730318); or, further afield, the **White Bear** in Shipston on Stour (01608 662612). The **Falkland Arms** (*see p222*) has an extensive range of real ales, English country wines and real cider; it also serves decent lunches in the garden. For out and out drinking, the **Pear Tree** or the **Sun** in Hook Norton are both popular, as is the **Cherington Arms** in Cherington, where there's a lovely garden with a river at its end.

'Chav' Brasserie
7 Horsefair, Chipping Norton (01608 645968).
Food served 6.30-10pm Mon; 12.30-2pm, 6.30-10pm Tue-Sat. **Credit** MC, V.
Michelin-starred Chavignol upped sticks and moved to Shipston (but had not yet opened by the time this guide went to press), bequeathing this more informal brasserie to the town. Regrettably the exacting standards of cuisine and service appear not have been part of the legacy. A starter of gruyère and chive gnocchi (£5), and main course of smoked haddock risotto (£12.50) were both slightly sludgy and without much bite or flavour, while another starter of prawn samosas was so badly burned it had to be sent back. Huge Thai fish cakes served with satay sauce (£12.50), however, were bursting with robust oriental flavours, and braised oxtail faggot (£13) was a skilfully prepared high point. Service was over-attentive and yet strangely ineffectual, but profuse apologies were forthcoming and things look set to improve once the new kitchen finds its feet.

Dexter's
Market Place, Deddington (01869 338813). **Food served** noon-2pm, 7-9pm Tue-Sat. **Set meals** £18.50 2 courses; £23.50 3 courses. **Credit** MC, V.

Dexter's serves modern European fare in minimalist surroundings. Starters range from carrot and coriander soup (£4.50) to seared king scallops on couscous (£7.50), while main courses include smart modern dishes such as fricassé of artichokes, mushrooms, basil and crème fraîche on linguini (£11), or lemon sole with olive tapenade (£12.50). While the food is competently handled, prices for extras can push the bill up considerably; new potatoes are £4, and veg another £2.50. If you can stretch to a pudding, we can recommend the tarte tatin.

Fox & Hounds Inn
Great Wolford (01608 674220).
Food served noon-2.30pm, 7-9.15pm Tue-Sat; noon-2.30pm Sun. **No credit cards.**
The charms of this 16th-century pub are no secret, and it pays to book. The look is low beams, dim lighting, stuffed animals, candles on tables and bunches of hops, with classical music barely audible over the din of happy eaters. The food tends towards the hearty. A standard pub grub menu is bolstered by a blackboard offering ribeye of beef (£8.95), lamb shank with garlic mash (£11.95) and poached cod with fennel confit (£10.50). To complement all this is an outstanding range of ales and whiskies. In summer there are tables outside.

Mason's Arms
Banbury Road, Swerford, Chipping Norton OX7 4AP (01608 683212/www.masonsarmsswerford.co.uk).
Food served noon-2pm, 6-9.30pm Mon-Sat; noon-9.30pm Sun. **Set meals** £24.95 4 courses.
Credit MC, V.
What used to be a rather unlovely pub squatting on the side of a main road has undergone a complete transformation, inside and out. The back of the building has been opened up and the garden made public so that diners can enjoy the wonderful view over the valley, and the interior redecorated in fresh modern colours and seagrass matting. Food is a delight; starters of pigeon in a port and juniper berry reduction (£5.95) and gateau of Mediterranean vegetables with goat's cheese (£3.95) were tasty and well presented, as was a main course of Gloucester sausages on apple and parsnip mash with red onion gravy (£8.95). The real showstealer, however, was the rich and buttery *babotie* of monkfish, cod, mussels, prawns and scallops with saffron rice at a mere £11.95. A word of warning; portions are enormous – resist the lure of the home-made bread.

Red Lion
Steeple Aston (01869 340225).
Food served noon-2pm (bar snacks), 7.30-9pm Tue-Sat. **Credit** AmEx, MC, V.
A cosy pub, with beams, pewter mugs, a fireplace and books, popular with a firmly middle-class, middle-aged crowd. You can sit out on the hanging basket-laden patio area for lunch in summer and eat bar snacks and sandwiches. On Friday and Saturday evenings, the tiny, old-fashioned, pub-style dining room is opened, serving classy dishes made with fresh ingredients. Starters typically include Arbroath smokies or moules marinières; while venison, duck and a lamb dish generally feature among the mains. The proprietors are very friendly and three courses with coffee will set you back around £23-£26. Book well in advance. range of ales and whiskies. The low ceilings mean it can get terribly smoky at times, but in summer there are tables outside on the terrace.

The Cotswolds

Windsor & Around

'Sweet Thames! run softly, till I end my song.'

Londoners escaping west into this region tend to cluster around the twin draws of Royal Windsor and the Thames in 'Royal' Berkshire. That said, the region's country houses, countryside walks, pubs and restaurants are hardly off the beaten track, and seem to carry on very nicely even if they don't bask in the glory of an ancient kingly thumbs-up. The ultimate seal of royal approval was bestowed on the area much more recently, in World War I, when the Saxe-Coburg-Gothas decided they liked Windsor so much that they started to pretend it was their own name.

At home with the Windsors

Strategically placed at the top of the town by William the Conqueror just a few years after the Battle of Hastings, **Windsor Castle** has survived countless rambling extensions and the occasional mishap, such as the devastating 1992 fire allegedly caused by the Queen Mother's casually discarded cigarette (a worker's blowlamp is the official version of the story). Now completely restored, the looming castle is the focal point of any trip to the town,

By train from London

Direct trains from **Waterloo** to **Windsor & Eton Riverside** depart every half hour, and take **50mins**. Trains to **Henley-on-Thames** leave hourly from **Paddington**; with a change at **Twyford**, the journey takes just under **1hr**. Hourly trains to **Marlow** leave from **Paddington** (change at **Maidenhead**); journey time is about **1hr**. Info: www.thamestrains.co.uk and www.southwesttrains.co.uk

and once within its walls there's no limit to the time it's possible to spend exploring. The cobbled precinct around the castle is known as Guildhall Island, named after the Guildhall that stands within it, which was built by Windsor resident Sir Christopher Wren in the late 17th century. Today you can take tea in the curious, lopsided timber building, imaginatively called the **Crooked House Tea Rooms** (01753 857534): inside, you'll notice that the

The pedestrian bridge that crosses the Thames links **Windsor** to a reluctant Eton.

pillars don't quite reach the ceiling – this was Wren's way of cocking a snook at the town planners, who insisted that there be columns inside the building in the interest of safety. Pizza Hut, Pizza Express, Burger King, McDonalds and Haagen-Dazs are all at the food of the castle walls.

Those bloody playing fields

Joined with Windsor by a pedestrian bridge over the river at the foot of Thames Street, **Eton** likes to consider itself quite separate from its merely royal neighbour. Eton's unique identity is centred, of course, on its famous school (that's 'The King's College of Our Lady of Eton Beside Windsor' to you), which sits at the end of a high street lined with antique shops, Edwardian uniform outfitters, 'heritage' pubs and the Cockpit restaurant, which still has the original cock-fighting area from the 17th century. Eton College was founded in 1440 by Henry VI for just 70 pupils; the roll call probably takes slightly longer these days, with around 1,300 boys on the books. Arrange a guided tour to see more of the College, its Perpendicular chapel and the playing fields where the slaughters of World War I were reputedly played out by future generals.

If you're pining for some greenery after all these historic buildings, there are several parks and gardens within easy reach of Windsor, chief among them the ancient Windsor Great Park (*p229*) **Windsor Great Park**). Fresh air fans and monument spotters might also like to visit nearby **Runnymede**, where King John sealed the Magna Carta in 1215; here you can see the memorial erected by the American Bar Association in 1957 to commemorate it, and, on the nearby hillside, a memorial to JFK. On a clear day, you can see forever – and count the continuous stream of jumbo jets zeroing in on Heathrow.

One seasonal attraction of the area is the relatively low-key spectacle of Swan Upping, the marking of the Queen's swans by none other than the official Monarch's Swan Marker, accompanied by brave members of the Royal Vintners and Dyers livery companies in suitably medieval attire. The small flotilla of rowing skiffs sets out from Windsor in the third week of July, embarking on a five-day journey upstream. If you take to the river, be sure and have a gander at the midstream attractions of **Temple Island** (with Georgian folly) and Eton College's **Queen's Eyot**.

Sit down to Bray

Bray was the setting of John Donne's poem *The Vicar of Bray*, about turncoat vicar Simon Alwyn, who changed his politics repeatedly during the reigns of four monarchs to keep his job. With its high street of timbered cottages, the village is certainly picturesque, but the main reason for coming here is to sample the culinary delights of its cluster of acclaimed restaurants (*see p231*).

Just north of Bray, off the A4094, is **Cookham**, a riverside village thought to have been inhabited since Roman times. It is best known as the birthplace of one of Britain's most famous – not to mention eccentric – artists, Sir Stanley Spencer (1891-1959). Spencer had the habit of painting biblical scenes featuring Christ set in and around his beloved Cookham, which he called, rather optimistically, 'a village in heaven'. The artist was born in the house called Fernlea on the high street, and the nearby village chapel has been converted into a museum showing his works, among them the sign that warned drop-in visitors to leave him alone while he was hard at it. **Cookham Dean**, a short distance uphill, boasts several commendable pubs. A trip to the area wouldn't be complete without seeing the splendour of **Cliveden**, set high on the hills. The stunning building – now a luxury hotel – began life as a hunting lodge in 1666, though the present central mansion dates from 1850, when it was rebuilt by Charles Barry, architect of the Houses of Parliament.

Marlow, a few miles west on the A4155, has long been associated with its literary inhabitants, among them Jerome K Jerome. He is said to have penned much of *Three Men in a Boat* in the town's best pub, the Two Brewers, on St Peter's Street. Albion House on West Street was home to the Shelleys during the period when Mary wrote *Frankenstein*; TS Eliot lived at No.31 just down the road. Like its neighbour Henley, Marlow gets packed out in the summer with tourists eager to get close to the river, but it's still far less hectic – despite the introduction of its very own mini one-day regatta held in mid June. With all due respect to William Tierney Clark and his supension bridge, Marlow has few proper sights, and even fewer pubs of any standing. The country to the north-west of Marlow, however, is an area of outstanding beauty, enough to bring out the walker in anyone. Villages of particular note include **Frieth**, with two fine country pubs and a recommended B&B, and **Turville**, where *The Vicar of Dibley* is filmed, and which is home to the excellent modern cooking of the **Bull & Butcher** (01491 638283).

Row, row, row your boat

Thanks to its prestigious annual **Royal Regatta**, which spans five days at the end of June and the beginning of July, Henley is synonymous with the sport of rowing. Ever since the Regatta's inauguration in the 19th century, upper-class revellers have descended on the town in droves to spill champagne on each other, noisily. Rowing doesn't lose its grip when the Regatta is over, however: on a summer stroll along the towpath, crews from local rowing clubs provide a rhythmic megaphoned backbeat. There's also a new **River and Rowing Museum** of a strikingly modern design.

Oenophiles might like to extend their interest to include – dare we say it – English wines: try one of the informative wine tastings at the **Thames Valley Vineyards** (just off the B3018 at Stanlake Park, Twyford; 01189 340176), or try before you buy at **Old Luxters** (off the A4155 from Henley to Marlow past Hambleden; after two and a half miles take the road to the left before Skirmett; 01491 638330). If you're into walking, the area provides ample opportunities to get close to nature. Good places for starting walks include **Remenham, Burnham Beeches** and **Boulter's Lock**.

Cliveden – where John met Christine.

What to see & do

Tourist Information Centres
King's Arms Barn, Kings Road, Henley-on-Thames, RG9 2DG (01491 578034/fax 01491 411766/ www.henley-on-thames.org.uk). **Open** *Apr-Sept* 9.30am-6pm daily. *Oct-Mar* 9.30am-4pm daily.
24 High Street, Windsor, SL4 1LH (01753 743900/ accommodation line 01753 743907/fax 01753 743904/www.windsor.gov.uk). **Open** *mid Apr-June* 10am-4pm Mon-Fri; 10am-5.30pm Sat; 10am-4.30pm Sun. *July-Aug* 10am-6pm daily. *Sept-mid Apr* 10am-4pm daily.

Bike hire
Windsor Roller Rink & Cycle Hire *Alexandra Gardens, Alma Road, Windsor (01753 830220).* Just outside the train station, inside the coach park.

Ascot Racecourse
Ascot SL5 7JN (01344 876876/www.ascot.co.uk). Racing highlights include Royal Ascot in June, De Beers Diamond Day (July), the Shergar Cup (August), and the Ascot Festival (September).

Cliveden
Off B476, Taplow, nr Maidenhead (01628 605069/hotel 01628 668561/ www.nationaltrust.org.uk). **Open** *Grounds* Mar-Oct 11am-6pm daily. Nov-Dec 11am-4pm daily. Closed Jan, Feb. *House & Octagon Temple* Apr-Oct 3-6pm Thur, Sun. Closed Nov-Mar. **Admission** (NT) *Grounds* £5; £2.50 concessions. *House, Octagon Temple & grounds* £6 extra; £3 concessions.
Set high on chalk cliffs overlooking the Thames and surrounded by 375 acres of gardens and parkland, this stunning 19th-century Italianate mansion is a National Trust property. Construction here began in the 17th century, and the house has been home to various earls, princes and the Astors – it seems fitting that it is now one of the country's most luxurious hotels (and site of the notorious Profumo/Keeler swimming pool incident). Mere plebs can wander the fabulous gardens, which feature roses, topiary, water gardens, exquisite statuary and sweeping views over the cliffs. The mosaic interior of the Octagon Temple (Chapel) and three rooms in the house are also sometimes open to non-residents. If you fancy staying here, a double will set you back from £345.

Dorney Court
Dorney, Windsor (01628 604638/fax 01628 665772/ www.dorneycourt.co.uk). **Open** *May* 1.30-4.30pm bank hols and preceding Sun. *Aug* 1.30-4.30pm Mon-Fri, Sun. **Admission** £5; £3 concessions.
One of England's finest examples of a many-gabled Tudor manor house, nestling with its attendant church in ancient woodland near Windsor. Built in 1440, the house witnessed the first ever pineapple to be grown in England (presented to Charles II in 1661).

Eton College
Eton High Street, Eton (01753 671177/ www.etoncollege.com). **Open** *Term-time* 2-4.30pm daily. *Holidays* 10.30am-4.30pm daily. *Guided tours* Apr-Sept 2.15pm, 3.15pm daily. **Admission** £3; £2 concessions. *Guided tour* £4; £3 concessions.
Have a wander round or book a guided tour to get the full low-down on the 15th-century College, which has educated 18 British prime ministers.

Fawley Court
Off A4155 N of Henley (01491 574917). **Open** *May-Oct* (except Easter and Whitsun weekends) 2-5pm Wed, Thur, Sun. Closed Nov-Apr. **Admission** £4; £1.50-£3 concessions.
Worth visiting for a gander at the elaborate ceiling by Grinling Gibbons and the landscaped grounds by 'Capability' Brown that lead down to the river. Bed and breakfast also available (phone for rates).

Make your weekends count...

Nestled alongside the graceful River Thames, the Runnymede is the only hotel with 2 restaurants, a 9000 square foot health spa, 5 tennis courts and river frontage, within 5 miles of historic Windsor, Legoland and Thorpe Park. Spend some quality time together at the Runnymede, and make your next weekend count.

Runnymede
Hotel & Spa
★ ★ ★ ★

The Best Riverside Address in the Thames Valley

Windsor Road, Egham, Surrey TW20 0AG
www.runnymedehotel.com
e-mail: info@runnymedehotel.com

For details of special weekend
offers please call
01784 220 980
quoting ref RWB004

There's much more to life at
the Runnymede

Frogmore House

Home Park, Windsor (01753 869898/
www.royalresidences.com). **Open** *May* dates
vary; usually weekend in mid May. *Aug* bank hol
weekend. **Admission** £5.20; £3.20-4.20 concessions.
No children under 8 admitted.

This property dates from 1680, although it wasn't
until 1792 that George III snapped it up for Queen
Charlotte, who proceeded to plant many unusual
botanical specimens in the garden. Queen Victoria is
buried alongside her beloved Prince Albert in the
Royal Mausoleum next to the house.

Legoland Windsor

Winkfield Road, Windsor (01753 626111/
www.legoland.co.uk). **Open** *mid Mar-July, Sept,*
Oct 10am-6pm daily. *July, Aug* 10am-7pm daily.
Closed Nov-mid Mar. **Admission** £19;
£13-£16 concessions.

This award-winning theme park certainly does the
business with families (at a considerable price).
Favourite areas include Miniland, a tour of Europe made
from over 20 million Lego bricks, Duplo Gardens, and
the Lego Traffic area, where the little terrors can get
their own driving licence (2-12 years).

Windsor Great Park

This 5,000-acre hunting-cum-picnic
ground dates back to the 13th century,
with Windsor Castle records of 1365
showing it in something like its present
form. The current Ranger, the Duke of
Edinburgh, restored the deer herds to
the park after the World War II, and then
somehow held back from hunting them.

The Park starts with the Long Walk
at the gates of Windsor Castle, and
stretches as far as the artificial lake and
associated curios of Virginia Water, via
the statue of the Copper Horse on Snow
Hill, the Queen Mum's country gaff, the
35-acre Savill Garden and an excess of
grass, woodland and fresh air.

It's one of those unquestioned
eccentricities of history, so common
about these royal parts, that noone
seems to know the exact length of the
Long Walk. Everywhere you look, it's
estimated at somewhere around two or
three miles. Suffice to say it's a very
Long Walk indeed, starting out from the
castle along an unerringly straight tree-
lined way, where the constant uphill
perspective gives rise to a distinct
impression that you'll never arrive.

The legendary status of the park has
been boosted over the past 1000 years
by the recurrent apparition of a ghostly
Herne the Hunter, purportedly warning
of times of trouble ahead. Wearing the
antlers of a stag, he rides a phantom
black stallion at the head of a pack of
black hounds. If you see him, you know
you're in trouble.

The manned gateway near Bishop's
Gate is the entrance to the Royal Lodge,
the Queen Mother's Windsor residence.
It's hardly a secret that she lives here,
but the hiding away of so much private
land within the park boundaries adds to

its mystery. And it's not just Royal
Lodge – elsewhere within its 14-mile
circumference the park shelters
Cumberland Lodge college, Smiths Lawn
(home of the Guards Polo Club), a village
for the people who work here, and even
a school for their children.

Savill Garden was created in 1932,
by Deputy Warden Eric Savill, who
modestly dubbed it 'the Bog Garden'.
It's now recognised as one of the finest
landscaped woodland gardens in
temperate climes, providing breathtaking
displays year-round: rhododendrons,
azaleas, camellias and magnolias
in spring; roses during summer; rich
autumnal colours; and misty lakeside
vistas in winter.

Virginia Water (*pictured*), the Georgian
artificial lake at the south end of the park,
is surrounded with yet more strangeness.
The Valley Gardens, on the northern
shores of the two-mile-long lake, are very
nearly in the Savill class. As for the 100ft,
12-ton North American totem pole, the
artificial waterfall and grotto, the obelisk
raised by George II, and the Roman ruins
imported from Tripoli and erected here
by the Prince Regent... they're quite
clearly in a class of their own.

The Chilterns to York

River & Rowing Museum

Mill Meadows, Henley-on-Thames (01491 415600/ www.rrm.co.uk). **Open** *May-Aug* 10am-5.30pm daily. *Sept-Apr* 10am-5pm daily. **Admission** £4.95; £3.75 concessions.

A history of the regatta and life on the river from source to sea. Everything from Saxon log-boat to speedy state-of-art racers.

River trips/boats for hire

Rivertime
Whitegates House, Berries Road, Cookham (01628 530600/www.rivertime.com).
Push off from various points between Windsor and Oxford, self-manned or skippered.

French Brothers
Clewer Boathouse, Clewer Court Road, Windsor (01753 851900/www.boat-trips.co.uk).
Trips run all year round, weather permitting

Kris Cruisers
Southlea Road, Datchet, nr Windsor (01753 543930/ www.kriscruisers.co.uk).
Family-run company hires out a range of rowing boats and other self-drive boats.

Royal Windsor Horse Show

Royal Mews, Windsor Castle, Windsor, SL4 1NG (01753 860633/www.royal-windsor-horse-show.co.uk).
Four days in mid May given over to international showjumping, dressage and other horsey events.

Royal Windsor Racecourse

Maidenhead Rd, Windsor SL4 5JJ (01753 498400/www.windsor-racecourse.co.uk).
A regular programme of race days throughout the year.

Stanley Spencer Gallery

King's Hall, High Street, Cookham (01628 471885/ www.stanleyspencer.org). **Open** *Easter-Oct* 10.30am-5.30pm daily. *Nov-Easter* 11am-5pm Sat, Sun, bank hols. **Admission** £1; 50p concessions.
Works on display include *The Last Supper* (1920) and *Christ Preaching at Cookham Regatta* (1953-9), which the artist was working on when he died. Phone for details of specialist talks.

Windsor Castle

Windsor (01753 868286 ext 2549/24hr recorded info 01753 831118/www.the-royal-collection.org.uk). **Open** *Mar-Oct* 9.45am-4pm (last entry) daily. *Nov-Feb* 9.45am-3pm (last entry) daily. *Changing of the Guard* (weather permitting) Apr-June 11am daily. July-Mar check information line. **Admission** £11; £5.50-£9 concessions.
Admission to Windsor Castle normally includes entry to the state apartments, St George's Chapel, Queen Mary's Doll's House, the Albert Memorial Chapel, the castle precincts and the gallery. The state rooms, destroyed by the 1992 fire, have now been fully restored and are open to the public: they include the opulent Waterloo Chamber, which was built to celebrate the famous victory over the French in 1815. The gorgeous 15th-century St George's Chapel is the burial place of ten monarchs, including Henry VIII (note that the chapel is closed to visitors on Sunday,

though worshippers are welcome). Edward Lutyens' amazing doll's house (complete with flushing loos and electricity) involved the work of 1,500 men and took three years to complete.

Where to stay

There are accommodation options aplenty in the area but, with a couple of notable exceptions listed below, there are few hotels of real character in the towns, although the **Aurora** in Windsor (Bolton Avenue; 01753 868686; doubles £100-£115) is pleasant and comfortable. Seekers of something special might do best heading for one of the countless riverside hotels or country B&Bs. The **Waterside Inn** (*see p232*) and the **Walnut Tree** (*see p231*) both offer accommodation. **Holmwood** in Binfield Heath (01189 478747; doubles £60) is a charmingly atypical B&B in a wonderful Georgian building; the **Red Lion** (Hart Street, 01491 572161; doubles £145) is the grandest accommodation in Henley, while **Martens House** (Willow Lane, 0118 940 3707; doubles £50) is a tranquil Thames-side base in Wargrave. Lottery winners, meanwhile, might be interested in staying at **Cliveden** (*see p227*).

Inn on the Green

The Old Cricket Common, Cookham Dean, SL6 9NZ (01628 482638/fax 01628 487474/ www.theinnonthegreen.com). **Rates** £100-£110 single occupancy; £120-£130 double/twin; £130 four-poster. **Rooms** (all en suite) 8 double; 2 twin; 1 four-poster. **Credit** AmEx, MC, V.
If nearby Cliveden is beyond your budget, then try the award-winning Inn on the Green. The rooms have a real country feel: most have exposed beams, and the black slate in the stunning bathrooms contrasts starkly with the white fittings. The four-poster room, decked out in exotic oranges and dark greens, is known as the Kama Sutra room. Head chef Derek Moran, previously of Cliveden, serves up the finest modern French/English fare – you can eat in the courtyard in summer. Three-course set menu dinner costs £17.95. Children and pets welcome.
A404 towards Marlow; follow signs from Marlow to Cookham Dean; turn left at war memorial after the Jolly Farmer pub.

Monkey Island Hotel – a fantasy come true.

Little Parmoor

Frieth, RG9 6NL (01494 881447/fax 01494 883012). **Rates** £26-£28 per person. **Rooms** (all en suite) 1 single; 2 double/twin. **No credit cards.**
Hosts Wynard and Julia Wallace go out of their way to make you feel at home in their wonderful Georgian house, set in farmland in the Chilterns. Rooms, decked out in floral bedspreads and wallpaper, are large and extremely comfortable, and guests are welcome to use the lovely panelled drawing room. There's a garden and vine-covered terrace, where visitors can breakfast in the summer. One-night bookings are sometimes refused at weekends. Children over five welcome; dinner by arrangement. No smoking throughout.
Head through Frieth in direction of Henley and Hambleden and follow road round to left. House is after ¾ miles on right.

Monkey Island Hotel

Old Mill Lane, Bray-On-Thames, SL6 2EE (01628 623400/fax 01628 784732/www.methotels.com). **Rates** £130 single; £190-£205 double/twin; £235-£295 suite. **Rooms** (all en suite) 2 single; 10 double; 2 suites. **Credit** AmEx, DC, MC, V.
If your dream is to have the run of your own private island – especially one with a name straight out of the Famous Five – then Monkey Island and its eponymous hotel will lend your weekend break an unmistakable air of romance. There's a footbridge over to this groovy white stucco mid-Thames hideaway, but far better to splash about by boat. The five acres of grounds are practically a nature reserve (though, alas, there are no monkeys). If fishing, boating or visiting the gym sound too ambitious, maybe you could stretch to a game of croquet on the lawn. Children welcome. No-smoking rooms available.

Oakley Court Hotel

Windsor Road, Water Oakley, SL4 5UR (01753 609988/fax 01628 637011/www.moathousehotels.com). **Rates** £165-£192 single occupancy; £140-£229 double/twin; £165-£269 family; £200-£320 four-poster/suite. Breakfast £14.95 (Eng/cont). **Rooms** 35 twin; 51 double; 12 four-poster/suite; 20 family. **Credit** AmEx, DC, MC, V.
A vast Gothic Victorian mansion set atop a grand sweep of summery lawn sloping down to the Thames, dotted with parasols and weeping willows. Some 200 films were shot around the Court's 35-acre estate, including the St Trinian's series, *The Rocky Horror Picture Show* and sundry Hammer Horrors. It now boasts 108 bedrooms, an award-winning restaurant, tennis courts, an indoor swimming pool, gym, sauna and spa. At least drop by for a (reassuringly expensive) coffee or beer on the lawn. Children welcome. No-smoking rooms available.
M25 W; come off at J6 on to A332 towards Windsor; turn off onto A308 signposted Maidenhead; hotel is 2½ miles past Windsor racecourse on the right.

Sir Christopher Wren's House Hotel

Thames Street, Windsor, SL4 1PX (01753 861354/fax 01753 860172/www.wrensgroup.com). **Rates** (breakfast incl weekend only) £99-£145 single; £135-£185 double/twin; £165-£225 deluxe double/twin/four-poster; £150-£200 triple; £195-£250 suite. Breakfast (Mon-Fri) £10.50 (Eng); £8.50 (cont). **Rooms** (all en suite) 11 single; 24 double; 8 twin; 16 deluxe double; 2 deluxe twin; 3 four-poster; 1 triple; 5 suites. **Credit** AmEx, DC, MC, V.

As the name suggests, the hotel was once the home of Wren himself (the house has been significantly extended over the centuries); indeed, Room 2, with its beautiful wooden panelling, was once the architect's bedroom, and is said to be haunted by his ghost (as is Room 1). The hotel occupies several buildings on both sides of the street: the main building and, opposite, a champagne and oyster bar and two apartments for longer stays. The rooms are of a high standard; many are decorated with antiques, marble bathrooms and fireplaces. Strok's Riverside Restaurant overlooks the Thames and Eton Bridge, and serves award-winning modern European cuisine. Children welcome. No-smoking rooms available.

<h2 style="background:black;color:white">Where to eat & drink</h2>

You'll trudge a long and lonely road in this high-growth, high-price region before you find a pub that has turned its back on the London tripper market to turn out ploughman's lunches to the locals. Surprisingly, while some villages, such as Frieth and Shiplake Row have three or more decent pubs apiece (in the latter, the lovely **White Hart**, 01189 403673, also serves good food), in towns such as Henley, you'll be hard-pushed to find one. Bray, on the other hand, seems to have an abundance, with at least five notable pubs and restaurants; in addition to the places mentioned below, the **Fish** (Old Mill Lane; 01628 781111) and the **Crown** on the High Street (01628 621936) are also worth a visit. And be sure and check out **Oakley Court Hotel** (*see above*) at Dracula's Thameside castle. Another favourite is the **Walnut Tree** at Fawley (01491 638360), which serves traditional British food with the occasional twist.

Beer lovers should note that Henley is the home of Brakspear bitter, so you're likely to come across it in most pubs in the area. As well as the pubs and restaurants that we list below, the restaurants in the **Sir Christopher Wren's House Hotel** (*see above*) and the **Inn on the Green** (*see p230*) are highly recommended, as is the Michelin-starred **Waldo's** at Cliveden (*see p227*). If you fancy a decent Chinese or Indian, both can be found in Cookham. The **Peking Inn** (49 High Street; 01628 520900) serves high-quality Chinese food in swish surroundings. Alternatively, the **Cookham Tandoori** (High Street; 01628 522584) is in a refurbished pub, with food a cut above that served in your average high-street Indian restaurant.

Al Fassia

27 St Leonard's Road, Windsor (01753 855370). **Food served** noon-2.30pm, 6.30-11pm Mon-Sat. **Set lunches** £13.50 2 courses; £17.50 3 courses. **Set dinners** £16.95-£19.95 3 courses. **Credit** AmEx, DC, MC, V.

Hookahs, a camel saddle, Moroccan lanterns and hanging carpets impart an authentically cosy feel to this corner of Berks that shall be forever North Africa. Listen to the friendly waiters and sample a starter selection of briwats (savoury pastries filled with seafood, lamb or veg) and bastilla (ditto, filled with chicken, almonds and cinammon). Djaj belbarkouk is a mighty fine chicken and sweet prune tagine served with couscous.

Alfonso's
19-21 Station Hill Parade, Cookham (01628 525775). **Food served** 12.30-2pm, 7-10pm Mon-Thur; 12.30-2pm, 7-11pm Fri; 7-11pm Sat. **Credit** AmEx, DC, MC, V.
Despite its less-than-glamorous setting (in a parade of shops near the train station), Alfonso's continues to attract plaudits for its inventive cooking. Starters could include creamed crab risotto delicately infused with white truffle oil; a main dish might be fillets of sole baked with red onions and cider, flamed with calvados; summer bottled cherry tart with a cool crème anglaise is a typical dessert.

Bottle & Glass
Harpsden Road, Binfield Heath (01491 575755). **Food served** noon-1.45pm, 7-9.30pm Mon-Sat; noon-1.45pm Sun. **Credit** AmEx, MC, V.
Parts of this cosy black-and-white-timbered pub date back to the 15th century. There's a low, beamed bar, a huge open fireplace and, for a real sense of history, you can peruse the family records of earlier landlords etched into the windows. Food is traditional pub fare with a modern twist – a main course could be beef Oxford, for example, akin to steak casserole, with apricots and red wine. Desserts could include raspberry roulade or chocolate and orange cheesecake.

Fat Duck
High Street, Bray (01628 580333). **Food served** noon-2pm, 7-9.30pm Tue-Fri; noon-2pm, 7-10pm Sat; noon-3pm Sun. **Set lunch** (Tue-Sat) £25.75 3 courses. **Credit** AmEx, DC, MC, V.
You can enjoy something like ten or more courses at the Fat Duck. Example: lime and green tea sorbet to cleanse the palate, then a whole mustard ice-cream with red cabbage gazpacho pre-starter before ballatine of foie gras, smoked eel and jasmine with mead jelly and Sichuan peppercorn. Main dishes are but one float in a carnival procession of flavours: the saddle of lamb was hardly recognisable as such (it was better); mullet will never be mullet again unless artfully accompanied by a velouté of borlotti beans with rosemary and vanilla. As to pudding – Fat Duck's bay leaf and almond foam is beyond words. Fantastic, and unforgettable.

House on the Bridge
Windsor Bridge, Eton, SL4 6AA (01753 860914/fax 01753 790198/www.house-on-the-bridge.co.uk). **Food served** noon-2.30pm, 6-10.30pm daily. **Set lunches** £19.95-£21.95 3 courses. **Set dinner** £29.95 3 courses. **Credit** MC, V.
Score a window table looking out on to the Thames, the cast-iron Windsor Bridge and the ramparts of the castle beyond, and you'll feel you're luxuriating on the lid of a chocolate box, just downstream from the playing fields and old boathouses of Eton College. Thankfully, head chef Etienne Emo doesn't rely solely on location

Riverside at the **House on the Bridge**.

for his reputation. Amid the array of veal, duckling and lamb dishes, vegetarian options were creditably plentiful and imaginative, including a marvellously fresh, rich tortellini with saffron butter, spinach and roasted red peppers. Trout Bretonne (£16.95) was also excellent. A dessert of crêpes with cognac and chocolate sauce (for two, £15.95) was moreish, to say the least.

Waterside Inn
Ferry Road, Bray (01628 620691/www.waterside-inn.co.uk). **Food served** noon-2pm, 7-10pm Tue-Sun. **Credit** AmEx, DC, MC, V.
Not cheap, needless to say. But what do you expect with Michel Roux at the helm, with three Michelin stars under his belt? Food is distinctly Gallic: delicacies such as pan-fried lobster medallions with a white port and ginger sauce (£37.50), and roast Challandais duck served with stuffed cabbage and a spiced port jus (for two, £64.50). It's worth breaking any diet (or budget) for food like this. You could always go the whole hog and book a room for the night (doubles £135). Closed for five weeks from Boxing Day.

Yew Tree
Frieth (01494 882330). **Food served** noon-3pm, 6-10.30pm Mon-Sat; noon-3pm, 7-10pm Sun. **Credit** AmEx, MC, V.
The Yew Tree is the sort of time-warp country pub once so common, but rarely found nowadays – a warm, timbered room decorated with assorted trinkets, and complete with (friendly) old geezer drinking at the bar. The menu is classic '70s (mixed grill garni; beef Wellington; chocolate fudge cake) though at thoroughly '90s prices. It's obviously good enough for the local Aston Martin club, whose members meet here once a month.

The Chilterns to York

North Chilterns

Walk the paths, cruise the canals, cycle the tracks.

A woodland patch on the **Ridgeway**, an 85-mile ancient path that runs as far as Wiltshire.

With the Grand Union Canal to the north, the River Thames to the south, and the Chiltern Hundreds draped across the middle, it's little wonder that these undulating fields and beech and bluebell woods are dotted with the stately homes and parks of so many nobles and notables, and of their modern equivalents – bankers, industrialists and pop stars.

Waddesdon Manor, a Renaissance-style château built in the 1870s for Baron Ferdinand de Rothschild, has a stunning collection of 18th-century French decorative arts, and is well worth a visit. Another of the area's fine houses is **Hughenden Manor**, former home of Queen Victoria's favourite prime minister, Benjamin Disraeli. **Hartwell House**, once home to the exiled King Louis XVIII, also has a fascinating history; and in the pretty village of Chenies, the Manor House was the residence of the Earls of Bedford, and both Henry VIII and Elizabeth I were entertained here. It has beautiful gardens.

Take the Chiltern Way

In 1965, the Chiltern Hills were designated as an Area of Outstanding Natural Beauty, recognising that the countryside is among the finest in England. Twice the national average of footpaths cross the Chilterns area, all studded with characterful pubs. The Chiltern Society celebrated the millennium by launching a new 134-mile walk called the **Chiltern Way**, which takes in four counties, ten districts and 60 parishes.

The picturesque village of **Aldbury**, with its pond, stocks and whipping post, lies east of Tring at the foot of a Chiltern ridge. **Tring** itself is a good starting point for some splendid walks alongside the Grand Union Canal and the Ridgeway Path to Ivinghoe Beacon, the spectacular finale of the Chilterns. The ancient **Ridgeway Path** starts here and ambles 85

By train from London

Direct trains from **Marylebone** to **Aylesbury** leave about every 20mins and take just under **1hr**. Some services stop at **Wendover**, **Great Missenden** and **Amersham**. There are three trains an hour from **Marylebone** to **High Wycombe**, which take between **30mins** and **40mins**; some stop at **Beaconsfield**. Info: www.chilterntrains.co.uk.

Discover Disraeli at **Hughenden Manor**.

Cathedral (and includes memorials to Geoffrey Dormer who, with two wives, had no less than 25 children). Pop in to Quirky's Courtyard (12A High Street; 01844 218860) for a snack of home-baked focaccia, or tea with home-made marmalade and preserves. For something a little more substantial, visit the Old Trout (*see p237*). A couple of miles away, just off the A329, is the gorgeous little 15th-century **Rycote Chapel**.

Heading north-west from Thame is the village of **Brill**, which has superb views and ruins dating from neolithic times. Nearby Ludgershall Church is where in 1378 John Wycliffe began his translation of the scriptures into the English language.

The village of **Lacey Green** lies along the top of another Chiltern ridge, above the main Princes Risborough to High Wycombe road. Its windmill is the oldest surviving smock mill in the country, originally built in Chesham in 1650 but dismantled and moved to its current spot in 1821 (it's open to visitors on Sundays and bank holiday afternoons from May to September). Two miles south-east of Lacey Green is the village of **Speen**, embraced on three sides by the arms of an Iron Age earthwork, Grims Ditch, giving rise to the theory that the village might mark the site of an ancient settlement. A circular walk around the area could be rewarded at the acclaimed Old Plow (*see p238*).

Twin peaks

Amersham is a town of two halves. The 'Old Town' (referred to as 'Elmodesham' in the Domesday survey of 1086) nestles in the Misbourne valley and has buildings dating back to the 16th century. The Norman church of St Mary's dates back to the 12th century, while much of the magnificent stained glass is 300 years old. The new town, known as Amersham-on-the-Hill, is a more recent affair, owing its presence to the arrival of the railway in 1862; sadly many of the buildings from that era have disappeared. However, **Chenies Manor House** is nearby, as are **Bekonscot Model Village** and **Odds Farm Park**.

Great Missenden, at the head of the Misbourne valley, was home to Robert Louis Stevenson and Roald Dahl. The long, curving high street has a number of half-timbered and Georgian shops; there's also a 14th-century church, and a good French restaurant, La Petite Auberge (*see p238*).

miles into Wiltshire; for much of its route it follows the Icknield Way, which, at 3,000 years old, also lays claim to being the oldest pathway in the country. A scenic steam train journey can be taken along the Icknield Way from Chinnor to Princes Risborough.

The **Vale of Aylesbury** provides the perfect location for cyclists as it's at the heart of the new National Cycle Network. You can choose between quiet country lanes through gently hilly countryside, or rougher trails that allow you to explore the woodland environment at close quarters. For those seeking a real challenge, Wendover Woods has a specially designated mountain bike course at **Aston Hill**. For the less energetic, the lovely canal path from Wharf Road in the centre of **Wendover** winds along the water's edge towards **Weston Turville** and beyond, giving wonderful views to the Chilterns.

Thame for tea

If you're looking for a break from walking or cycling the Chilterns, pick up a leaflet from the Tourist Office and follow the route around the pretty and historic town of **Thame**. Sites of interest include a 13th-century parish church dedicated to St Mary the Virgin, the interior of which is said to be a miniature Lincoln

What to see & do

Tourist Information Centres

8 Bourbon Street, Aylesbury, HP20 2RR (01296 330559/www.aylesburyvale.net). **Open** *Apr-Oct* 9.30am-5pm Mon-Sat. *Nov-Mar* 10am-4.30pm Mon-Sat.

Market House, North Street, Thame, OX9 3HH
(01844 212834). **Open** 9.30am-5pm Mon-Fri;
10am-4pm Sat.
The Clock Tower, High Street, Wendover, HP22
6DU (01296 696759/www.chilternweb.co.uk/
wendover). **Open** 10am-4pm Mon-Sat.
Paul's Row, High Wycombe HP11 2HQ
(01494 421892/ www.wycombe.gov.uk).
Open 9.30am-5pm Mon-Thur; 9.30am-4.30pm Fri;
9.30am-4pm Sat.

Bekonscot Model Village

Warwick Road, Beaconsfield (01494 672919/
www.bekonscot.org.uk). **Open** mid Feb-Oct 10am-5pm
daily. **Admission** £4.50; £2.75-£3.50 concessions.
Children will love the oldest model village in the world
(opened in 1929), which allows them to be giants in a
nostalgic portrayal of rural England. There are, in fact,
six villages plus many moving models, including a
Gauge 1 model railway. Refreshments are available, and
there are picnic areas, too.

Paradise regained

Perhaps it's a romantic notion to believe
that it was John Milton's deeply anti-
establishment stance that ensured
that the site of his birthplace at Bunhill
Fields, along with many of the houses
he occupied during his lifetime, remain
curiously unmarked; even his burial-
place was left unmarked for 116 years.
All of which makes the little cottage in
the Chilterns where he spent a mere
11 months all the more poignant.

In 1665, as the plague raged in
London, Milton asked his friend and
secretary, Thomas Ellwood, to search
for lodgings in the country; he found
this 'pretty box' in the little village
of 'Giles Chalfont'. It was here,
according to legend (and Ellwood's
autobiography), that Milton completed
Paradise Lost, and the idea of writing
Paradise Regained was born.

As well as being England's
greatest epic poet, Milton wrote
at length on freedom of speech and
freedom of the press, and published
papers on the education system,
divorce laws (introducing the notion of
'incompatibility'), and the 'Irish question'.
He spoke seven languages, was an
expert swordsman and an excellent
organist. He was also a renowned
political activist and staunch anti-royalist.
Two of the many papers and books he
published (Eikonoclastes and Defence
of the English People) were recalled and
burnt, and he became a wanted man,
forced to live in hiding.

His efforts to see England made
a republic (he was Latin Secretary to
Oliver Cromwell) eventually caused him
to curtail his writings and throw all his
energies into the Parliamentary cause.
However, the restoration of King Charles
II in 1660, following the short-lived
commonwealth, left him a disillusioned
man. Half-blind at this stage, and with
many of his friends either in exile or
prison (including Ellwood), Milton's time
spent at the cottage may well have been
lonely, but it did allow him to finish
his epic poem – begun back in 1642.

The cottage itself dates back to the
16th century, and the museum exhibits
one of the finest collections of Milton's
works, published during or shortly after
his lifetime. The well-stocked cottage
garden also features many of the plants
mentioned in Milton's poetry. These,
together with curator Edward Dawson's
obvious love and unbridled enthusiasm
for the man whose writings and thoughts
have had such a powerful influence and
impact on our culture, make Milton's
Cottage a treasure.

Milton's Cottage

Deanway, Chalfont St Giles, HP8 4JH
(01494 872313). **Open** Mar-Oct
10am-1pm, 2pm-6pm Tue-Sun, bank
hols. Closed Nov-Mar. **Admission**
£2.50; £1 concessions.

The Chilterns to York

Chenies Manor House

Chenies (01494 762888). **Open** *Apr-Oct* 2-5pm
Wed, Thur, bank hols. Closed Nov-Mar.
Admission *House & gardens* £5; £3
concessions. *Gardens only* £3; £1.50 concessions.
Built by Sir John Cheyne around 1460, this was the
first Earl of Bedford's principal residence. The house
contains contemporary furniture and tapestries, plus
a medieval well, various underground passages, a
reconstructed penitential maze and a reputed priest's
hole. The grounds contain several beautiful gardens,
including a physic garden.

Chiltern Brewery

*Nash Lee Road (on B4009), Terrick, nr Aylesbury
(01296 613647/www.chilternbrewery.co.uk).*
Open *Museum* 9am-5pm Mon-Sat. *Guided tours*
phone for details. **Admission** *Museum* free.
Guided tours £3.50; £3 concessions.
Buckinghamshire's oldest working brewery produces
five award-winning beers and many others. If you take
a tour (ring to arrange), your guide will explain the brewing processes and there will be opportunities for sampling. The premises also house England's first
'Breweriana' Museum.

Chiltern Open Air Museum

*Newlands Park, Gorelands Lane, Chalfont St Giles
(01494 871117/24hr info 01494 872163/
www.coam.org.uk).* **Open** *Apr-Oct* 10am-5pm daily.
Admission £5.50; £3-£4.50 concessions.
Over 30 historic buildings have been rescued from
demolition and re-erected in 45 acres of countryside.
They include barns, granaries, stables, a toll house and
a 1940s prefab. There is even a reconstruction of an Iron
Age house. A Victorian farm complete with farm animals offers horse and cart rides.

Hughenden Manor

*Valley Road, High Wycombe (01494 755573/
infoline 01494 755565/www.nationaltrust.org.uk).*
Open *House* Mar 1-5pm Sat, Sun. Apr-Oct 1-5pm
Wed-Sun. Closed Nov-Feb. *Garden* Mar 1-5pm Sat,
Sun. Apr-Oct noon-5pm Wed-Sat. Closed Nov-Feb.
Admission (NT) *House* £4.20; £2.20 concessions.
Garden £1.50; 75p concessions.
The home of Victorian prime minister and statesman
Benjamin Disraeli from 1848 until his death in 1881.
Many of his pictures, furniture and books remain here.
There are beautiful walks to be enjoyed in the garden,
which have been re-created according to designs by
Disraeli's wife Mary Anne.

Odds Farm Park

*Wooburn Common, nr Beaconsfield (01628 520188/
www.oddsfarm.co.uk).* **Open** *mid Feb-Oct* 10am-5pm
daily. *Nov-mid-Feb* 10am-4pm Thur-Sun.
Admission £4.25; £3.25-£3.55 concessions.
Activities include sheep-shearing, lambing, sheep dog
demonstrations, tractor and trailer rides, as well as the
opportunity to meet and even feed some rare and not so
rare farm animals.

Rycote Chapel

off the A329, nr Thame (01844 290176). **Open**
Apr-Sept 2-6pm Fri-Sun, bank hols. Closed Oct-Mar.
Admission (EH) £1.70; £1.30-90p concessions.

Bearing up – **Rothschild Zoological Museum**.

A stunning little 15th-century chapel with a painted
ceiling and intricate wood carving. There are also
roofed pews and a musicians' gallery.

Steam trains

(talking timetable/info line 01844 353535).
Tickets £5; £3-£4 concessions.
Trains depart from Chinnor station and travel through
scenic countryside to Princes Risborough; some have
cream teas aboard. Services are at weekends; phone to
check departure times. Children will particularly enjoy
a trip on the Thomas Special.

Waddesdon Manor

*Waddesdon, nr Aylesbury (01296 653226/
www.waddesdon.org.uk).* **Open** *House (including
wine cellars)* Apr-Oct 11am-4pm Wed-Sun, bank hols.
Closed Nov-Mar. *Grounds* Mar-Dec 10am-5pm
Wed-Sun, bank hols. Closed Jan, Feb. **Admission**
(NT) *House & grounds* £10; £7.50 concessions.
Grounds only £3; £1.50 concessions.
Baron Ferdinand de Rothschild's magnificent French
Renaissance-style château was built in the 1870s and
now houses some of the world's foremost collections of
18th-century French decorative art, along with some
important English paintings. The garden is famous
for its specimen trees, seasonal bedding displays and
rococo-style aviary of exotic birds. Check the website
for seasonal events, including wine tastings, and talks
on paintings and textiles.

Walter Rothschild
Zoological Museum

*Akeman Street, Tring (7942 6171/
www.nhm.ac.uk/museum/tring).* **Open** 10am-5pm
Mon-Sat; 2-5pm Sun. **Admission** £3.75; £2.10
concessions; free OAPs, under-16s.
Part of the Natural History Museum, this lovely zoological museum houses the private collection of Lord
Rothschild and features over 4,000 species of animals
within its Victorian gentleman collector's setting. It's a
delightfully quirky place, and has the finest collection
of stuffed mammals, birds, reptiles and insects in the
country, including a full-sized gorilla, a huge anaconda
and a now-extinct giant moa.

West Wycombe Caves

*West Wycombe Park Office, West Wycombe
(01494 533739).* **Open** *Mar-Oct* 11am-5.30pm
daily. *Nov-Feb* 11am-5.30pm Sat, Sun. **Admission**
£3.50; £2-£2.50 concessions.

The West Wycombe caves have a unique and fascinating history. They were excavated on the site of an ancient quarry in the 1750s under the auspices of a responsible landowner, Sir Francis Dashwood, as a means of occupation for unemployed farm workers following a succession of harvest failures. Dashwood also founded the Hellfire Club, members of which dressed up in white monks' habits and held black masses, assisted by mock nuns recruited from the ranks of London's ladies of the night. It's hardly surprising that rumours abounded of unspeakable orgies taking place in the caves. They are approached through an impressive flint forecourt that from a distance resembles a Gothic church.

Wycombe Museum

Priory Avenue, High Wycombe (01494 421895/ www.wycombe.gov.uk/museum). **Open** 10am-5pm Mon-Sat; 2-5pm Sun. **Admission** free.

High Wycombe has a long history of furniture-making, and this 18th-century museum focuses (with the aid of interactive displays) on the 200-year history of the trade and its role in the town's development. From mid November 2001 until January 2002, the museum will be holding an exhibition on the history of High Wycombe furniture manufacturer Ercol.

Where to stay

There's a wealth of places to lay your head in the Chilterns. If the ones we list are full, try the **Five Arrows** in Aylesbury (01296 651727/ www.waddesdon.org.uk; doubles £80-£90),

Expect material comforts at the **Old Trout**.

Bennett End in Radnage (01494 483273; doubles £55), the **Old Vicarage** in Mentmore (01296 661243; doubles £55), the **King's Arms** in Stokenchurch (01494 609090; doubles £89-£129) or **Holmdale** in Little Chalfont (01494 762527; doubles £65). If money's no object, head to the luxury of **Champneys**, the posh health resort at Wigginton near Tring (01442 291000/ www.champneys.com; doubles £400 per person per night for a minimum two-night stay).

George & Dragon

High Street, West Wycombe, HP14 3AB (01494 464414/fax 01494 462432/www.george-and-dragon.co.uk). **Rates** £70 double/twin; £70 family room (sleeps 3; £10 for extra person); £74 four-poster. **Rooms** (all en suite) 6 double; 1 twin; 1 family room; 2 four-poster. **Credit** AmEx, DC, MC, V.

This old coaching inn dates back to the 17th century and is situated in a little street in the National Trust-preserved village of West Wycombe. Two of the rooms have four-poster beds, one overlooks the inn's courtyard, and all have uneven floorboards; front rooms in the 'modern' extension (1720) are taller and brighter. The well-worn bar serves well-kept ales and the menu includes many home-made specialities such as beef Wellington, Louisiana gumbo, and a range of grills, all generously portioned and reasonably priced (£5.35-£12.95). Children and pets welcome.
Off A40 SE of Stokenchurch.

Hartwell House

Oxford Road, nr Aylesbury, HP17 8NL (01296 747444/fax 01296 747450). **Rates** £140-£175 single; £225-£345 double/twin; £385-£395 four-poster; £400-£700 suites. Breakfast £17.50 (Eng); £13.50 (cont). **Rooms** (all en suite) 7 single; 22 double/twin; 5 four-poster; 12 suites. **Credit** AmEx, MC, V.

Exquisitely restored by Historic House Hotels (who are also responsible for Middlethorpe Hall in York; *see p263*), Hartwell House stands in 90 acres of landscaped parkland. The house has a history stretching back 1,000 years: it was home to the son of William the Conqueror, and was also leased to the exiled King Louis XVIII. Beautiful antiques and paintings furnish all the rooms, and service is distinguished. Spa facilities are available and there's also a 50ft swimming pool. Children over eight welcome. No-smoking rooms available.
A418 NE towards Aylesbury; hotel is signposted after Thame.

Old Trout

29-30 Lower High Street, Thame, OX9 2AA (01844 212146/fax 01844 212614/ www.theoldtrouthotel.co.uk). **Rates** £60 single; £85 double/four-poster. **Rooms** (all en suite) 2 single; 1 double; 4 four-poster. **Credit** MC, V.

The Old Trout is one of Thame's most historic buildings, dating back over 500 years. The beamed rooms are creaking and comfortable; some of them have prettily canopied four-poster beds (avoid the one over reception, though – it can get noisy). The popular restaurant has a crackling log fire in winter and serves interesting, well-prepared food. A good breakfast is guaranteed. Children welcome. All bedrooms no-smoking.
Hotel is at lower end of Thame High Street, 200 yards before church and opposite courthouse.

Poletrees Farm

*Ludgershall Road, Brill, nr Aylesbury, HP18 9TZ
(tel/fax 01844 238276).* **Rates** £25-£35 per person.
Rooms 2 double/twin (1 en suite); 1 family room.
No credit cards.
Set in the heart of the countryside but only eight miles
from Oxford, this 150-acre mixed farm started life
as a 16th-century coaching inn on the old Oxford to
Buckingham Roman road. The owners produce generous English breakfasts using farm produce, and evening
meals are also available by arrangement. Children
welcome by arrangement. No smoking throughout.
*B4011 NW of Thame; follow signs to Brill on right; house is
before railway bridge on sharp bend.*

Where to eat & drink

In addition to the hotels mentioned above, all
of which serve reliable if not outstanding food,
there's a wealth of good pubs in the area, many
offering excellent grub. Among the best are the
Angel Restaurant in Long Crendon (Bicester
Road; 01844 208268), the **Rising Sun** at Little
Hampden (The Rignall; 01494 488393) and the
Mole & Chicken in Easington (01844 208387).
In Amersham there's no shortage of places to
eat: the **King's Arms** (30 High Street; 01494
726333), where Arthur Machen, the Welsh
novelist, used to meet with his good friend,
songwriter John Ireland; **Gilbeys** (1 Market
Square; 01494 727242), **La Zucca** (18 High
Street; 01494 728667); and the **Famous Fish
Company** (11 Market Square; 01494 728665).
Good drinking pubs include the **Seven Stars**
in Dinton, the **Dinton Hermit** in Ford,
the **Pheasant** in Brill, the **Crown** in Little
Missenden, the **Polecat** in Prestwood, the
George & Dragon in West Wycombe and
the **Lions of Bledlow** in Bledlow.

La Chouette

*Westlington Green, Dinton, Aylesbury (01296
747422).* **Food served** noon-2pm, 7-9pm Mon-Fri;
7-9pm Sat. **Set lunch** £11 3 courses. **Set dinners**
£29 4 courses; £36 5 courses. **Credit** MC, V.
Allow an extra ten minutes to find La Chouette (signposted 'Westlington only' and down a dead end). Belgian
Frédéric Desmette cooks and serves virtually single-
handedly but has passion enough for a roomful of staff.
The olde worlde restaurant specialises in delights
such as Belgian shrimp salad (£11) and fillet of salmon
with bacon (£13.60). Ingredients are top quality, and
eating from the carte is not cheap: starters cost £10-£15,
mains £13.60-£16.50. Belgian beers are also available
from the bar.

Green Dragon

*8 Churchway, Haddenham, Aylesbury
(01844 291403/www.eatatthedragon.co.uk).*
Food served noon-2pm, 7-9.30pm Mon-Sat;
noon-2pm Sun. **Credit** AmEx, MC, V.
Originally a 12th-century coaching inn, this attractive
dining pub in the picturesque village of Haddenham is
decorated in blues and yellows, with a log fire adding to

its warm appeal in winter. Fresh ingredients are key
here; a meal could consist of home-made soup (£3.75)
followed by seared Cornish sea bass resting on braised
fennel with orange and juniper berries (£12.95). Puddings (all £4.25) include warm soft chocolate cake with
marscapone and passion fruit coulis, and treacle tart
with clotted cream.

Old Plow Bistro & Restaurant

Flowers Bottom Lane, Speen (01494 488300).
Food served noon-2pm, 7-9pm Tue-Fri; 7-9pm Sat;
noon-2pm Sun. **Set lunch** £9.95 1 course;
£14.95-£21.95 2 courses); £25.95 (3 courses).
Set dinners £25.95 2 courses; £29.95 3 courses.
Credit AmEx, MC, V.
It reputedly opened in the year 1610, and one of the
inn's early customers is said to have been diarist
Samuel Pepys. More recently, it attracted fame in the
1930s when the daughter of Ramsay MacDonald, then
prime minister, became its hostess. Today it's owned
by the Cowans who run a 'starched linen' restaurant
in one half of the establishment, and a bistro in the
other, both expertly provided for by the skilled chef
and polite front-of-house staff. Encouragingly, seafood
only appears if maritime weather conditions are
favourable and might be warm scallop salad with oriental dressing. On a recent visit, meat dishes of grilled
loin of English lamb with apricot, mango and fresh
mint preserve, and char-grilled veal with mushroom
sauce, were sumptuously rich and full of flavour.
Desserts feature the likes of cappuccino ice-cream and
toffee sauce and blackcurrant mousse cake – made
in-house, of course. A meal in the bistro (à la carte
only) is about £20 a head; eating from the carte in the
restaurant costs around £30.

La Petite Auberge

107 High Street, Great Missenden (01494 865370).
Food served 7.30-10.30pm Mon-Sat. **Credit** MC, V.
It's worth wandering through a few side streets on the
way to this tudor-beamed restaurant that nestles in the
woods of Great Missenden. It serves accomplished, classic food – typical starters include foie gras (£9.80) or
aubergine terrine with lemon dressing (£5.60), with
mains of escalope of turbot with anchovy and caper
sauce (£15.60) or free range guinea fowl stuffed with
oyster mushrooms (£14.90). Desserts could be iced
nougat with chocolate sauce or crème brûlée.

Sir Charles Napier

Spriggs Alley, nr Chinnor (01494 483011).
Food served noon-2pm, 7-9.30pm Tue-Sat;
noon-2pm Sun. **Credit** AmEx, MC, V.
This brick and flint hostelry is the place to head
for seriously fine cooking, although the views and
walks hereabouts aren't too bad either. The warm
and welcoming atmosphere is boosted by the fact that
you're never far from a crackling log fire in winter
(there are two of them). A typical starter might be
risotto nero with pan-fried squid (£6.75), while mains
could include monkfish with winter vegetables
(£15.50), or halibut with a herb crust and rouille sauce
(£18.50). The experienced wine waiter can help guide
you through the 14-page wine list. Then trip off to
dessert heaven with chestnut parfait in a pistachio
sauce, or sample the fine, predominantly British and
Irish cheeses. You'll be glad you came.

Hertfordshire

A mix of the old and the new, and the always has been.

White horse as seen from the **Green Man**.

Less than 20 minutes from King's Cross, Hertfordshire is dotted with golfing greens, rolling hills and out-of-the-way watering-holes. Indeed if golf is your bag then a visit to Herts is a must: St Albans-born Samuel Ryder founded the eponymous Cup, and the county is home to both the English Open and British Masters. The rolling hills and green pastures of Hertfordshire are a perfect setting for the sport and, between courses, there's many a fine house or park to enjoy.

Don't be mistaken; it's not all rural idyll: Letchworth Garden City (the first in the country) and Welwyn Garden City are not quite as fecund as their names might suggest, unless, of course, you're counting outcrops of concrete. Bushey, on the other hand, does live up to its name with plenty of fields, a golf course, an animal encounter centre and riding stables. Even Watford is smartening up its act with a fresh batch of chill-out bars and smart cafés. The area is served by several motorways (A1, M25 and M1) and speedy train services, so it's possible to be in the thick of meadows, glistening fairways and leafy lanes within 20 minutes of leaving London.

Bushey tales

The deep south of Herts is made up of small villages which have expanded to such an extent that the boundaries between them are unclear. **Bushey** lies cheek by jowl with Oxhey, which

in turn is within walking distance of Watford. To further confuse the issue Bushey station (17 minutes from Euston) is actually in Oxhey village and Bushey village is up the hill towards Bushey Heath and Harrow. Bushey (apart from being home to George Michael) is also famous for the Herkomer School of Art which flourished from 1883-1912. Sadly all that's left of the school is the rose garden and small park area over the road from Bushey Golf Course. Nearby on Melbourne Road, stands one of Europe's oldest remaining daylight film studios. The founder of the school and the studio, Sir Hubert von Herkomer, also had his home on Melbourne Road, called 'Lululaund'. Only the frontage remains, cunningly reworked into the porch of the British Legion Club. The home of another famous former resident, painter Lucy Kemp-Welch, is here, too: 'Kingsley', at No.20 High Street.

Following the canal (and train route) westwards you come to **Berkhamsted**. Just

By train from London

Probably the only Hertfordshire town with enough to do to warrant a visit by train is **St Albans**. It is a mere **19mins** from **King's Cross Thameslink** by the quarter-hourly fast trains.
Info: www.thameslink.co.uk.

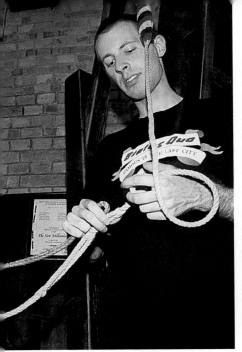

Campanologists get busy in **Bushey**.

behind the train station are the remains of the Norman castle. In fine weather, the very helpful resident guide will present an impromptu re-enactment of Norman life for you (call Mr Stevens on 01442 871737). The castle looks quite spectacular after a torrent, too, when the moat fills and cuts the whole place off like an island. The town centre is off to the right, sporting the usual Café Rouge and Pizza Express, plus an utterly brilliant health food emporium. Behind these shops is the canal which has fine views and is a good place for a leisurely walk.

A Roman first

Due east is the market town of **St Albans**. In AD 43 the first Roman fort was built to the north-east of the Belgic settlement of Verlamion. All that remains of this important stage in the history of St Albans are sections of the city walls and hypocaust in Verulamium Park and the famous thoroughfare of Watling Street. On Wednesdays and Saturdays, St Albans market still bustles on St Peter's Street, offering a curious mix of wares, from bargain goods to local cheeses. Continue on past the town hall and the clock tower (pausing only briefly to ponder the notice on the small door at the side of the tower that reads 'commit no nuisance'), before arriving at the junction with

Chequer Street and High Street. Off to the right, past the upmarket designerwear shops on George Street, is the cathedral, with its magnificent 13th-century wall paintings. Follow the road down to where it becomes Fishpool Street to find coaching houses, and a mixture of Elizabethan, Georgian and medieval architectural styles vying for attention.

Not a hitch

Due north is the hip and happening and yet ultra-quaint little town of **Hitchin**. Vintage '50s garb and furniture can be had on the outskirts of town at Red, 93A Walsworth Road. In the heartland you can take a tour of the historic buildings, from St Mary's Church, built in 792, to the Skynners' Almshouses, dating from 1670. Pick up a tour leaflet from Hitchin Library (01438 737333). The Market Place is a good place to start for refreshments and shopping. Then head for Bridge Street, off Sun Street, for bookshop browsing, fine art, beauty treatments and then dinner.

What to see & do

Tourist Information Centres

Dacorum Information Centre, The Marlowes, Hemel Hempstead, HP1 1DT (01442 234222/ www.dacorum.gov.uk). **Open** 9.30am-5pm Mon-Fri; 9.30am-4pm Sat.

Town Hall, Market Place, St Albans, AL3 5DJ (01727 864511/www.stalbans.gov.uk). **Open** *Easter-mid July* 9.30am-5.30pm Mon-Sat. *Mid July-mid Sept* 9.30am-5.30pm Mon-Sat; 10am-4pm Sun. *Mid Sept-Easter* 10am-4pm Mon-Sat.

Ashridge Estate

Ringshall, Berkhamsted (01442 851227/recorded info 01494 755557/www.nationaltrust.org.uk). **Open** *Monument* noon-5pm Sat, Sun, bank hols. *Estate* free access daily. *Visitors centre* 2-5pm Mon-Thur, Sat, Sun **Admission** (NT) *Monument* £1; 50p concessions; free under 5s.
Situated on the Bucks/Herts border, this estate affords great opportunities to spot local flora and fauna along the ridge of the Chiltern Hills. It has bluebell woods and verdant commons, and even a monument erected to the Duke of Bridgewater in 1832. It's a touch ironic considering the duke's contribution to Britain's industrial development.

Hatfield House

Just off A1, Hatfield (01707 287010/www.hatfield-house.co.uk). **Open** *House* Easter-Sept noon-4pm daily. Guided tours noon-4pm Mon-Fri. *West Gardens* Easter-Sept 11am-5.30pm daily. *East Gardens* Easter-Sept 11am-5.30pm Fri. *All* Closed Oct-Easter. **Admission** *House, park & gardens* £7; £3.50 concessions. *Park & gardens* £4.50; £3.50 concessions. *Park only* £2; £1 concessions.
Built by Robert Cecil, Earl of Salisbury, in 1611, this superb Jacobean mansion oozes history. In the grounds stands the remaining wing of the Royal Palace of Hatfield, the childhood home of Queen Elizabeth I, where

in 1558 she held her first Council of State. The 42 acres of gardens include herb terraces, orchards and fountains restored to their former glory by the present marchioness.

Knebworth House & Gardens

Knebworth, nr Stevenage (01438 812661/ www.knebworthhouse.com). **Open** *House* Mid Apr-Aug noon-5pm daily. Sept-mid Apr noon-4.30pm Sat, Sun, bank hols. *Park* Mid Apr-Aug 11am-5.30pm daily. Sept-mid Apr 11am-5.30pm Sat, Sun, bank hols. **Admission** £7; £6.50 concessions; free under-4s.

Home to the Lyttons since 1490, this Gothically embellished Tudor mansion house is still the family residence. The 250-acre parkland also houses the formal gardens and woodland, the maze, 'Fort Knebworth' adventure playground and a miniature railway. Major rock concerts have added to the attractions since 1974 (with Led Zeppelin's legendary appearance in '79 and Oasis in '96). Car shows, craft fairs, flower festivals and classical concerts have since replaced the grinding guitars and metal posturing. Knebworth also opens daily during school holidays outside the summer season; phone to check.

Water world

The Grand Junction Canal arrived at Berkhamsted in 1798, as part of Britain's burgeoning canal system that carried goods from the manufacturing towns of the Midlands to London.

Now called the Grand Union Canal, the waterway has swapped its heavy-duty working barges for decorative narrowboats that are fully equipped for holidaymakers to take a leisurely tour through the Chilterns.

Bridgewater Boats is housed in a beautiful old wharf building decked out with trailing hanging baskets; all its vessels are named after TS Eliot's cats. Opposite is the Crystal Palace pub, which originally had a glass front inspired by the Great Exhibition of 1851, and now has tables outside for waterside refreshments; nearby is a Canadian totem pole presented to a local timber merchant.

When you're ready to cast off from Bridgewater, staff will navigate you through your first lock. In a weekend afloat you can take in the picturesque Marsworth village and the bird sanctuary at Tring. Alternatively, you can follow the canal south to Little Venice and enjoy the sights of London from your floating home. Berkhamsted has a Waitrose and the enterprising Cook's Delight wholefood emporium (01442 863584/www.organiccooksdelight.co.uk) stocks everything you could need for a healthy break; phone first in summer to make sure its open. Bon voyage!

Bridgewater Boats

Castle Wharf, Berkhamsted, HP4 2EB (01442 863615/fax 01442 863619/www.bridgewater-boats.co.uk). Minimum two-day breaks, with prices from £200 including all mooring fees and fuel.

The Chilterns to York

Museum of St Albans

Hatfield Road, St Albans (01727 819340/
www.stalbansmuseums.org.uk). **Open** 10am-5pm
Mon-Sat, bank hols; 2-5pm Sun. **Admission** free.
Impressive display of local history with plenty of
medieval and Roman artefacts. Downstairs there's a fine
collection of tools created in carpentry and agriculture, plus
a gallery to the rear on two levels.

Paradise Wildlife Park

White Stubbs Lane, Broxbourne (01992
468001/www.pwpark.com). **Open** 9.30am-6pm daily.
Admission £8; £6 concessions.
On the road to Ware, this is a good family stop-off point,
with an adventure play area and indoor under-fives
playroom, children's rides, walk-through farmyard,
reptile encounter, plus monkeys, big cats, camels and
birds of prey. Refreshments for visitors and feed for the
animals are available.

Redbournebury Watermill

Redbournebury Lane, Redbourne Road, St Albans
(01582 792874). **Open** *April-Oct* 2.30-5pm Sun;
bank hols, open days (phone for details). Closed Nov-
Mar. **Admission** £1.50; 80p concessions. Free Sun.
This 18th-century working watermill is open for demonstrations throughout the year. Displays of local crafts
accompany the events. Cream teas are served 2.30-5pm
on Sundays.

Scott's Grotto

Scott's Road, Ware (01920 464131/www.scotts-
grotto.org). **Open** *Apr-Sept* 2-4.30pm Sat, bank hols
(other times by appointment). Closed Oct-Mar.
Admission by donation.
A series of quirky subterranean passages built by John
Scott of Amwell House (now part of Ware College).
Dating back to around 1760, and fronted by a flint-
encrusted portico, the tunnels extend 67ft into the hillside with seven chambers decorated with shells from
around the world, plus local flints and minerals. Visitors
are requested to bring a torch with them.

Shaw's Corner

Ayot St Lawrence, nr Welwyn (01438
820307/ recorded info 01494 755567/
www.nationaltrust.org.uk). **Open** *Apr-Oct* 1-5pm
Wed-Sun, bank hols. Last admission 4.30pm.
Admission (NT) £3.50; £1.75 concessions;
free under-5s.
This was the home of George Bernard Shaw from 1906
to 1950. A sizeable brick dwelling with many rooms as
the great man left them, including his restored revolving
writing hut. Works undertaken by Shaw here include
Pygmalion and *St Joan*. Plays are performed in the
grounds in summer.

Verulamium Museum

St Michael's Manor, St Albans (01727 751810/
www.stalbansmuseums.org.uk). **Open** 10am-5.30pm
Mon-Sat; 11am-5.30pm Sun. Last admission 5pm.
Admission £3.10; £1.85 concessions; free under-5s.
Featuring everything you ever wanted to know about
the Romans and a little bit more, with reconstructions,
mosaics, statuary and audio-visual presentations,
conveniently close to the Roman ruins in Verulamium
Park. The museum is much improved by extension

work, which allows for some Iron Age scene-setting in
the new gallery, as well as the splendid airy entrance,
shops and display areas. The Legion XIV are on guard
roughly once a month.

Victorian Chemist Shop & Physic Garden

Hitchin Museum, Paynes Park, Hitchin (01462
434476/www.nhdc.gov.uk). **Open** 10am-5pm Mon,
Tue, Thur-Sat. **Admission** free.
Joseph Lister's medical memorabilia and pharmaceutical
artefacts are on display, as well as local historical information. The physic garden reveals the importance of
medicinal herbs, both historically and in modern times.

Where to stay

Hertfordshire has plenty of grand hotels,
converted from illustrious but ill-fated
country estates, plus some unique and remote
guesthouses, and pub accommodation in most
major towns. The **Watford Hilton** (01923
235881/fax 01923 220836/www.hilton.com) is
the largest hotel in the Bushey area. Some of
the choicest places to stay are listed below.

Brocket Hall

Welwyn, AL8 7XG (01707 335241/fax 01707
375166/www.brocket-hall.co.uk). **Rates** (Melbourne
Hall) £150 single; £170 double. Special breaks.
Rooms (all en suite) 4 single; 12 double. **Credit**
AmEx, DC, MC, V.
Brocket Hall was home to the cuckolded first Lord
Melbourne, whose spouse cavorted with George IV,
while the second Lord Melbourne married Lady Caroline
Lamb, whose love for Lord Byron was anything but
discreet. The house proper is mainly used for conferences and parties. Melbourne Lodge, although a golf
buggy's journey away from the hall, manages to maintain an air of opulence and, indeed, genuine romance
with lashings of taffeta drapery and brocade, and wooded vistas. Since much of the parkland is given over to
the golf course there are few places to take a stroll without fear of flying balls. Clay pigeon shooting, coarse and
game fishing, croquet, tennis and archery are also available. Note that jeans, trainers and baseball caps are
banned. Children welcome. No-smoking rooms available.
A1 J4; follow signs to Wheathampstead and B653; once on
Brocket Road, turn into entrance to golf club and restaurant
for Melbourne Lodge.

Hitchin Priory

Tilehouse Street, Hitchin, SG5 2DL
(01462 420500/ fax 01462 422101/
www.hitchinpriory.co.uk). **Rates** £85 single;
£100 double/twin. **Rooms** (all en suite) 15 single;
45 double; 1 twin. **Credit** AmEx, DC, MC, V.
Not to be confused with that other, more famous place
where the rich and famous go to dry out, this beautiful
hotel is situated in the stunning grounds of an early
14th-century Carmelite friary. The current façade is
17th century, but some cloisters have been incorporated
into the design. The hotel has 61 rooms and offers
superior B&B accommodation. Children welcome. Pets
by arrangement. No-smoking rooms available.

The **Lord Lister Hotel** has a curious history.

Homewood

Old Knebworth, SG3 6PP (01438 812105/fax 01438 812572/www.homewood-bb.co.uk). **Rates** £45 single occupancy; £70 double (£15 supplement per child). **Rooms** (all en suite) 1 double; 1 family/suite. **No credit cards.**

'A bit of friendly, gracious living', says the brochure of this Edwardian English country house designed by Edwin Lutyens. Certainly, the informality of Homewood does its name justice. The grounds are spacious and include part of the nearby wood, and breakfast can be taken on the beautiful flowery terrace. The rooms are light and airy, accessed off an intriguing landing decorated with old maps of London. The owners request that potential visitors phone for a map, which gives detailed directions to Homewood. Children welcome. Dogs by arrangement. No-smoking throughout.
B197 into Knebworth; turn into Station Road (which becomes Park Lane), 300 yards after crossing motorway bridge, left into public footpath; after 300 yards bear left through lodge gates, house is at end.

Lord Lister Hotel

1 Park Street, Hitchin, SG4 9AH (01462 432712/459451/fax 01462 438506). **Rates** £60 single; £70 double/twin; £75 four-poster; £70 family. **Rooms** (all en suite) 4 single; 15 double/family; 3 twin; 1 four-poster. **Credit** AmEx, DC, MC, V.

Very friendly family-run hotel (you'll run into a few of the owners' offspring in the lounge) with a creaky winding staircase and immaculately clean rooms. There's a small bar downstairs, a TV lounge and a large, bright breakfast room. The history of the hotel is quite intriguing. It was once a Quaker school, where the young Joseph Lister (father of antiseptics) obtained his formative education. During the late 1800s the building was reopened as a home for 'weak-minded and deficient girls'. Children and pets welcome. No-smoking rooms available.

St Michael's Manor

Fishpool Street, St Albans, AL3 4RY (01727 864444/fax 01727 848909/www.stmichaelsmanor.com). **Rates** £120-£160 single; £155-£200 double/twin; £185 four-poster single; £250 four-poster double; £240 single suite, £295 double suite. Special breaks. **Rooms** (all en suite) 3 single; 3 twin; 17 double; 1 double four-poster; 1 suite. **Credit** AmEx, DC, MC, V.

No two rooms are alike in this lovely independently owned hotel, which is only a minute's walk from the cathedral and Verulamium Park, yet it's remarkably peaceful. Pampering is so complete visitors hardly need to bring any luggage – almost everything is provided. The higher up the creaky staircase you go the more quirky the rooms are, with sunken baths, and shower cubicles built in under the roof beams. If your budget can stand it, opt for the suite with a balcony for a fine view of the garden. There are trays of strawberries and nuts in the lobby and lounges, and the grounds are beautifully designed with fountains and wildfowl in abundance. Saturdays are popular for weddings. Children welcome. No-smoking rooms available.

Where to eat & drink

In Bushey, the **Swan** (Park Road; 020 8950 2256) is a lovely real ale pub. Rolls and toasties are available at lunchtimes and there's a sizeable garden to the rear. It was Watford and District Pub of the Year for 2000. The **Three Crowns** (020 8950 2851) in Bushey Heath does a mean Sunday lunch and has a variety of good wines on offer.

Watford has a new lease of life courtesy of a couple of new bars on the block – the delightfully laid-back **Aura** with its waitress service and comfy sofas, and **Øl Bier Grill** (9 Market Street; 01923 256601), a Danish establishment with an elegant steak restaurant below. The **Green Man** in Great Offley (01462 768256) is a good bet if you're heading north towards Letchworth and Hitchin; it offers a fantastic range of high quality dishes, good beers and has brilliant views over the countryside. In Hitchin itself, the **Sun Hotel** (Sun Street; 01462 436411) was the most important coaching inn of its day. The **Rose & Crown** in Hemel Hempstead (19A Old High Street; 01442 395054) is a popular pub that is very accommodating to children, and has a fine Thai restaurant.

There are numerous real ale pubs in St Albans, including the oldest, the **Lower Red Lion** on Fishpool Street (01727 855669), which serves cask bitter, country wines and cheap eats such as toasties like brie and almond for £2. It also offers accommodation (doubles from £45). For entertainment, the **Horn** (01727 853143) on Victoria Street has jazz every Sunday lunchtime. In Watton at Stone, the **George & Dragon** (01920 830285), has

The Chilterns to York

A flower for Scotland – **Café Ecosse**.

good local food; the **White Lion** in Walkern (just east of Stevenage) is ideal for children, with an excellent play area, as is the **Brocket** at Ayot St Lawrence, which boasts a great garden and an amusingly taciturn landlord. The **Sow of Pigs** at Thundridge (01920 463281) is also good for families, with a spacious garden and large rustic tables in the dining area.

If you feel like dressing up and splashing out, the **Zodiac** in Hanbury Manor, Ware (01920 487722) is grand indeed; its sister establishment, **Vardon's**, is more relaxed and family-friendly.

Auberge du Lac
Brocket Hall, Welwyn (01707 368888/www.brocket-hall.co.uk). **Food served** noon-2.15pm, 7-10.30pm Tue-Sat; noon-2.15pm Sun. **Set lunches** (Tue-Sat) £25 3 courses; (Sun) £30 3 courses. **Credit** AmEx, DC, MC, V.
Superior, value-for-money dining, adjacent to a lovely lake and overlooking Brocket Hall (*see p242*). The à la carte menu is a blend of modern French and Asian influences. Starters could be carpaccio of yellowfin tuna with avocado and kumquat chutney, or chilled tomato soup with vanilla pod and crab meat; mains are the likes of black sea bass with braised vegetable barigoule with white wine and olive oil emulsion, or perhaps English lamb, courgette flowers and provençale lavender jus. It doesn't come cheap, but then food this good often doesn't.

Bar Meze
35 Bucklerbury, Hitchin (01462 455566). **Food served** 6.30-10pm Mon; 11.30am-2pm, 6.30-10pm Tue-Sat. **Set meal** £13.95 4 courses. **Credit** MC, V.
There seems to be a bit of a craze for meze in this neck of the woods and this long restaurant is very, very popular. Dishes include chunky charcoal-grilled mushrooms, marinated pork sausage, meat and vegetable skewers, stuffed vine leaves and meatballs. Greek wines and desserts are available, too.

Café Ecosse
12-13 Bridge Street, Hitchin (01462 431661). **Food served** noon-3pm, 6.30-11pm Tue-Sat; noon-4pm Sun. **Credit** MC, V.
'A fusion of Scottish and European food' reads the notice over the door, and this intimate restaurant sure does deliver what it sets out to provide. The 'Scottish' side is taken care of with the likes of Arbroath smokies (£5.95). There's 'fusion' with dishes such as Angus beef with mustard mash and a Mediterranean mix of pan-fried vegetables (£9.95). Then the 'European' element is taken care of with dishes such as sweet potato fritatta and penne pasta. Most eateries in Hitchin are very popular at weekends and Café Ecosse is no exception – book first or you'll find yourself going home disappointed.

Café Mezze
144 Lower High Street, Watford (01923 211500/ www.cafemezze.co.uk). **Food served** noon-10.30pm daily. **Credit** AmEx, DC, MC, V.
A stylish and friendly meze specialist with a good range of meat, fish and vegetarian options: the mixed meze plate is a great starter to share, and the seafood platter is popular, too. It's worth working up an appetite for the puddings – Lebanese pastries, or cheesecakes and flans – though if you really can't manage one the owners are happy to give you a goody bag so you can snack later. Lebanese beers and wines.

The Conservatory
St Michael's Manor, Fishpool Street, St Albans (01727 864444/www.stmichaelsmanor.com). **Food served** 12.30-2pm, 7-9pm daily. **Set lunch** £17.50 2 courses; £21 3 courses. **Set dinner** £35 3 courses. **Credit** AmEx, MC, V.
A pleasant, airy conservatory, which overlooks a lawn and lake, and has a buzzing atmosphere on Sunday lunchtimes. Starters include the likes of avocado salad with white crab claw meat and pink grapefruit or chicken liver and foie gras with toasted 'grand rustique' bread. British and Modern European choices for main courses could include roast sirloin of Aberdeen Angus with Yorkshire pudding, crispy potatoes and honey roast parsnips, perhaps, or roast leg of English lamb studded with rosemary and thyme, served with château potatoes and sauce soubise; apricot and sage stuffed loin of pork with crispy crackling and a bramley compote is another possible choice. Desserts could be panna cotta with strawberries and basil syrup, or chocolate and walnut roulade with raspberries and mascarpone.

St James Restaurant
30 High Street, Bushey (020 8950 2480). **Food served** noon-2pm, 6.30-9.30pm Mon-Sat. **Credit** AmEx, MC, V.
A well-kept secret in Bushey village, this fine dining restaurant is just a few doors away from artist Lucy Kemp-Welch's former home. Starters (£4-£8) range from garlic tiger prawns to warm potato and vegetable terrine. Mains (£15-£18) include medallions of beef with mash and a Bordeaux jus, grilled halibut with sautéed asparagus and Parma ham, and calf's liver with a potato and onion cake, crispy pancetta and a red onion jus. Wine tasting evenings take place once a month, on Monday evenings.

Rutland

Small and perfectly formed.

Rutland's reputation often precedes it.
However, it's a reputation that bears little
resemblance to reality. TV comedy fans of a
certain age usually recall Eric Idle's short-lived
spoof *Rutland Weekend Television*, itself best
remembered for bringing the world the greatest
band that never were, Neil Innes's Beatles-
pastiching Rutles. Everyone else conjures
up images of irascible Farmer Giles types
campaigning relentlessly for their independence
from Leicestershire. Less Little Englanders,
more Little Rutlanders.

The truth is different. Sure, this is a small
county – easily the smallest in England, at 150
square miles and with a population of a mere
34,000 – and its residents are fiercely proud of
their locality. But their pride is understandable
when you visit: aside from the clutches of bland
modern houses that ring a few of its larger
settlements, Rutland is largely unspoilt by
the late 20th century, and better for it. Driving,
cycling or walking through the countryside is
like stepping back 50 years in English history,
an impression that is hardly shattered when
civilisation is encountered. Quiet roads
threading through still-life honey-stone villages
could have been dreamed up by Enid Blyton or
Agatha Christie. In case you weaken and grow
twitchy away from the capital, the medieval
town of Stamford, lying on Rutland's doorstep
in Lincolnshire, can up the excitement level a
notch. But no more than a notch.

Otherwise, you're never more than 15
minutes from its centrepiece, the calming, still
waters of Empingham Reservoir, aka **Rutland
Water**. Only the odd truncated B-road leading
off into the shallows, and the disappearance
of the prefix 'Upper' from the village of
Hambleton, serve as a reminder that the area
was only dammed and flooded in the early '70s;

Rutland Water – graveyard
of Lower Hambleton.

somewhere beneath the bobbing boats lies
Lower Hambleton. **Rutland Belle Cruises**
(01572 787630/www.rutlandwatercruises.com)
offer trips around the reservoir; the more
energetic might like to hire a bike from
Rutland Water Cycling (01780 460705/
www.rutlandcycling.co.uk), located at
Whitwell and Normanton car parks.

Three towns in the country

Rutland's county town is **Oakham**, just to
the north-west of Rutland Water. Its picture-
book quality is a little broken down by nominal
progress, but it's still jumbled with some
delightful Victorian streets, Georgian villas and
older jewels. The 16th-century public school
nestles between the site of the castle and a cute
market square (market days Wednesday and
Saturday), centred around the octagonal Butter
Cross and its old public stocks.

South of here is **Uppingham**, a tiny market
town (market day Friday) dominated by
another 16th-century public school (tours June

By train from London

Trains for **Stamford** and **Oakham**
leave **King's Cross** hourly. There is
a change at **Peterborough**; total
journey time is between **1hr** and **1hr
30mins**. Oakham is the stop 12mins
after Stamford. Info: www.gner.co.uk
and www.centraltrains.co.uk.

The Chilterns to York

Burghley House – Elizabethan splendour.

to September, but call to confirm 01572 822216, as tours didn't run in 2001). Its clock tower, cupolas and lawns are hidden away behind a towering stone façade better suited to a castle, or maybe a prison. Shopping here is dominated, a little oddly, by the second-hand book trade. The three shops, all open on Sundays, sit within steps of each other: the three-storey Rutland Bookshop is just 12 feet square but three storeys high; the Tardis-like Forest Books a few doors down on the high street offers a nice range of sheet music among its stock; and Goldmark Books, over on Orange Street, is the biggest and also contains a large gallery space.

Stamford's stock has risen sharply since it starred in the BBC's *Middlemarch* series. Barely a single building fails to conform to the symphony of weathered-yellow Lincolnshire stone, which still clings to a medieval street pattern on the Welland. Historically a wealthy textile town and staging point, Stamford was home to William Cecil, chief minister of Elizabeth I, who built his splendid **Burghley House** close by. Sadly, the Stamford bull run and race meeting are now history, although the rumbustious town-centre funfair is still held in the week following Mothering Sunday. North-east is **Tallington Lakes** (01778 347000/ www.tallington.com), a watersports centre featuring 160 acres of natural spring-fed water split between eight lakes.

Away from the towns, Rutland is a noted centre for cycling, sailing, bird-watching and walking through the unspoiled pastures where deer were once hunted, and foxes still are. The **Viking Way** (marked by a Viking Helmet) passes through on its journey from the Humber to Oakham, while the **Jurassic Way** (look for the shell sign) runs between Stamford and Banbury. There are Forestry Commission woodlands at **Clipsham** (including the half-mile avenue of sculpted 150-year-old yew trees), **Southey Wood** (between Upton and Ufford), **Fineshade** (off the A43 east of King's Cliffe) and nearby **Wakerley Great Wood**.

Elsewhere, the churchyard at **Braunston-in-Rutland** features a stone carving of a pagan goddess; an 82-arch viaduct sits near **Seaton**; **Wing** boasts a tiny medieval turf maze (*see p249* **Maybe I'm a maze**); and John Betjeman's favourite church lies in **Brooke**. Visit the picturesque hamlet of **Teigh**, or step into the church porch at **Stoke Dry**, where the Gunpowder Plot is said to have been hatched. Go fishing on the nearby **Eyebrook Reservoir**. See the stocks on the green at **Market Overton**, where Sir Isaac Newton played as a child. Explore the lime kiln at **Pickworth**. But whatever you do, take it easy. It's what Rutland's all about.

What to see & do

Tourist Information Centres

The Arts Centre, 27 St Mary's Street, Stamford, PE9 2DL (01780 755611/www.skdc.com). **Open** *Easter-Oct* 9.30am-5pm Mon-Sat; 11am-4pm Sun, bank hols. *Nov-Easter* 9.30am-5pm Mon-Fri; 9.30am-4pm Sat; 11am-4pm bank hols.

Flore's House, 34 High Street, Oakham, LE15 6AL (01572 724329/www.rutnet.co.uk). **Open** *Apr-Sept* 9.30am-5pm Mon-Sat; 10am-3pm Sun. *Oct-Mar* 10am-4pm Mon, Wed, Fri, Sat; 10am-3pm Sun.
Because Stamford is actually just outside Rutland, there's very little in the way of Rutland information there. For that, head to this helpful Oakham operation.

Bike hire
See p245 **Rutland Water Cycling**.

Barnsdale Gardens

The Avenue, Exton (01572 813200/ www.barnsdalegardens.co.uk). **Open** *Mar-Oct* 10am-5pm daily. *Nov-Feb* 10am-4pm Sat, Sun. Last entry 90mins before closing. **Admission** £5; free under-16s.
Barnsdale Gardens were the creation of *Gardeners' World* presenter Geoff Hamilton. Since his death in 1996, the beautiful gardens have been open to the public by way of tribute. Coffee shop and an excellent nursery.

Burghley House

1 mile E of Stamford on B1443 (01780 752451/www.burghley.co.uk). **Open** *Apr-Oct* 11am-5pm daily. Closed Nov-Mar. **Admission** £6.80; £3.30-£6.30 concessions; free 5-12s (one per full-paying adult).
Burghley is one of the grandest Elizabethan houses in England. Commissioned by William Cecil, the first Lord Burghley, it was constructed from finely carved local

limestone on the remains of a 12th-century monastery. The house was later used as a Royalist refuge in the Civil War and laid under siege by Cromwell, who luckily never carried out his threat to raze it to the ground. Of the 18 magnificent state rooms, those decorated with Antonio Verrio's lavish 17th-century frescos are the most famous. The art, sculpture and porcelain on display comprise one of the most important private collections in the world. There's also an extensive deer park, a 1932 Olympic silver medal courtesy of Lord 'Chariots of Fire' Burghley, annual horse trials every September, and Queen Victoria's hard, lumpy bed.

Lyddington Bede House
Blue Coat Lane, Lyddington (01572 8224380/ www.english-heritage.co.uk). **Open** *Apr-Sept* 10am-6pm daily. *Oct* 10am-5pm daily. Closed Nov-Mar. **Admission** (EH) £2.75; £1.40-£2.10 concessions.
This medieval palace, built for the sporting Bishops of Lincoln, was converted into almshouses for the poor after the Reformation. The 16th-century interiors are lovely, and there are events throughout the summer.

Normanton Church Museum
Nr Edith Weston, off A606 (01572 6530267). **Open** *Easter-Sept* 11am-4pm Mon-Fri; 11am-5pm Sat, Sun, bank hols. *Oct-Easter* 10am-4pm daily; phone to check. **Admission** 80p; 50p concessions.
Rutland's best-known landmark, the Italianate Georgian church from the submerged Normanton estate, now stands on a promontory on the edge of the reservoir and houses a display dedicated to the history of the Anglian Water reservoir and surrounding area.

Oakham Castle
Off Market Place, Oakham (01572 723654/ www.rutnet.co.uk). **Open** *Apr-Oct* 10am-1pm, 1.30-5pm Tue-Sat; 1-5pm Sun. *Nov-Mar* 10am-1pm, 1.30-4pm Tue-Sat; 1-4pm Sun. **Admission** free; donations welcome.
'Castle?' Not any more: all that remains from the 12th-century construction is the Great Hall. However, it's a lovely building, highlighted in odd fashion by the 200-plus decorative horseshoes hanging on the wall: tradition dictates that a peer of the realm must forfeit one to the lord of the manor on his or her first visit to Oakham.

Rutland County Museum
Catmos Street, Oakham (01572 723654/ www.rutnet.co.uk). **Open** *Apr-Oct* 10am-5pm Mon-Sat; 2-5pm Sun. *Nov-Mar* 10am-5pm Mon-Sat; 2-4pm Sun. **Admission** free; donations appreciated.
Housed in the 200-year-old former Rutland Cavalry riding school, this museum opened in 1969 and offers information about the rural life and agriculture of Rutland. Among the exhibits is a rare 1917 Sanderson tractor.

Rutland Open-Air Theatre
Tolethorpe Hall, Little Casterton (01780 756133). Plays *June-Aug* (phone for details). Closed Sept-May. **Tickets** £10-£13; £9-£12 concessions.
Only Stamford Shakespeare Company actors need pray for fine weather at this 600-seat auditorium in an idyllic woodland setting: while they perform on an uncovered stage, the audience is entirely sheltered. There's a bar, a picnic area and a restaurant. Amateur dramatics at their loveliest.

Rutland Railway Museum
Ashwell Road, Cottesmore (01572 813203). **Open** *May-mid Sept* 11am-5pm Wed-Sun. *Mid Sept-Apr* 11am-5pm Sat, Sun. **Admission** free.
Located at the southern end of a train track built to serve the now-defunct local ironstone collieries, this rather chaotic collection of old trains is tended by enthusiastic volunteers. Steam train rides are offered around 12 times a year: call for details.

Rutland Water Butterfly Farm & Aquatic Centre
Sykes Lane car park, North Shore, Rutland Water (01780 460515). **Open** *Apr-Oct* 10.30am-5pm daily. Last entry 4.30pm. Closed Nov-Mar. **Admission** £3.50; £2.50-£3 concessions.
One of the best freshwater aquaria in the country, packed with waterfalls, and river and reservoir displays. There's also a heated exotic 'free flight' butterfly house, complete with parrots, carp, terrapins and iguanas in the undergrowth, and a creepy-crawly- and reptile-dominated exhibit.

Rutland Water Nature Reserve
Egleton Reserve, 1 mile S of Oakham; Lyndon Reserve, 1 mile E of Manton on S shore (01572 770651). **Open** *Apr-Oct* 9am-5pm daily. *Nov-Mar* 9am-4pm. **Admission** £4; £2-£3 concessions.
Both of Rutland Water's informative and helpful visitors' centres contain well-stocked shops, and sell day permits. They also arrange wildlife and arts and crafts courses, and assorted walks with or without wardens.

Stamford Museum
Broad Street, Stamford (01780 766317). **Open** *Apr-Sept* 10am-5pm Mon-Sat; 2-5pm Sun. *Oct-Mar* 10am-5pm Mon-Sat. **Admission** free; donations welcome.
A standard local museum laid out over two floors, and highlighted by side-by-side grotesque models of 52-stone Daniel Lambert, who died in town while visiting the races, and 3ft 4in tall General Charles Stratton, who visited it several years later.

Where to stay

There's an abundance of reinvented coaching inns and village pubs (all offering food, most with rooms) plus good farmhouse B&Bs scattered throughout Rutland and south-west Lincolnshire. Among them are the **Finch's Arms** (doubles £65; *see p249*) and the **King's Arms Inn** (doubles £75; *see p249*).

Barnsdale Lodge Hotel
The Avenue, Rutland Water North Shore, nr Oakham, LE15 8AH (01572 724678/fax 01572 724961). **Rates** £69 single; £89 double/twin; £109.50 deluxe double/twin/four-poster/suite; £89 family room (plus £15 per child; max 2 children). **Rooms** (all en suite) 8 single; 23 double/twin; 5 deluxe double/twin; 2 four-poster; 5 suites; 2 family. **Credit** AmEx, DC, MC, V.
This 17th-century farmhouse made a switch when its land disappeared under the waves of Rutland Water. Now extended and expanded with the addition of bedrooms

A fanfare for the farrier at **Oakham Castle**.

around a brightly planted courtyard, the stone walls and flagged floors of the old building retain great character amid a cornucopia of Edwardian-chic decor. The restaurant is recommended; there are also lighter meals and superb views from the conservatory. Children and dogs welcome. No-smoking rooms available.

A1 N to A606 towards Oakham; through Empingham and Whitwell; hotel is on right.

The George
St Martins, Stamford, PE9 2LB (01780 750750/ fax 01780 750701/www.georgehotelofstamford.com). **Rates** £78 single; £105-£115 double/twin; £155 deluxe double; £145-£175 four-poster/suite. Special breaks. **Rooms** (all en suite) 11 single; 23 double/twin; 2 deluxe double; 4 four-poster; 7 suites. **Credit** AmEx, DC, MC, V.

This Stamford landmark boasts of being 'perhaps England's greatest coaching inn', and on first impressions – a cobbled, ivy-clad courtyard where Crusaders stopped for mead, rooms royally slumbered in by King Charles I and William III – it's hard to argue. The famous gallows sign spanning the road outside stands as a warning to highwaymen not to flout the ancient jacket-and-tie law (which still applies in the restaurant). Decor in the 50-plus individually decorated rooms ranges from tasteful to vile, so keep your fingers crossed. Children and dogs welcome. No-smoking rooms available.

A1 N; follow signs at roundabout to Stamford (right); hotel is on left down hill.

Hambleton Hall
Ketton Road, Hambleton, Oakham, LE15 8TH (01572 756991/fax 01572 724721/ www.hambletonhall.com). **Rates** £175-£335 single occupancy; £200 double/twin; £235-£335 deluxe double/twin; £235 four-poster; £500-£700 suite (sleeps 4). Breakfast £12 (Eng). **Rooms** (all en suite) 10 double/twin; 4 deluxe double/twin; 1 four-poster; 1 suite. **Credit** AmEx, DC, MC, V.

'Do as you please' is emblazoned over the entrance of this imperious country manor, converted into a 15-room hotel in 1979 by owners Tim and Stefa Hart. Stefa is responsible for the proudly old-fashioned English decor: all rooms are individually themed and stocked with elegant antique furniture, and most have views over Rutland Water. The priciest lodgings come in the two-bedroom croquet pavilion, added by the Harts relatively recently. The hotel scores highly with its Michelin-starred restaurant, and though the à la carte menu ain't cheap, the set lunch menu (£16.50 two courses, £21.50 three courses) offers better value. Children and dogs welcome. No-smoking rooms available.

A1 N to A606 off A1; 10 miles towards Oakham; hotel is on peninsula of Rutland Water.

Lake Isle
High Street East, Uppingham, LE15 9PZ (tel/fax 01572 822951). **Rates** £45-£52 single; £65-£69 double/twin; £80 cottage suite. Special breaks. **Rooms** (all en suite) 1 single; 12 double/twin; 2 cottage suites. **Credit** AmEx, DC, MC, V.

This cosy operation (fronted by a restaurant, the hotel entrance is actually around the back) compares well to the grander, seen-better-days Falcon opposite, both in terms of its unpretentious food and its homey, individually decorated rooms (and rest assured: the good-value cottage suites are nicer inside than out). The details are all looked after, from the fresh biscuits, iced water and sherry waiting in every room to the quality of the breakfasts. Children and dogs welcome.

A1 to A47 towards Peterborough; follow signs W to Uppingham; hotel is in Uppingham town centre.

Whipper-Inn Hotel
Market Place, Oakham, LE15 6DT (01572 756971). **Rates** £69 single; £79 double/twin; £94 executive/four-poster. Special breaks. **Rooms** 3 single (all en suite); 15 double/twin (14 en suite, 1 private bathroom); 6 executive/four-poster (all en suite). **Credit** AmEx, DC, MC, V.

This stuccoed 17th-century coaching inn is an excellent operation, both food-wise and as a hotel. The individual bedrooms are olde worlde, but charmingly so: most are capacious, with beams accenting many of them. Service is pleasingly unobtrusive yet efficient, and the morning breakfasts are worth getting up for. The two restaurants offer contrasting menus and atmospheres: the George is the more traditional, while No.5 offers more inventive cuisine (pan-fried ostrich steak is £12.95). One of the area's more appealing accommodation options.

Where to eat & drink

Rutland's pub culture is one of its greatest assets, not least because many village boozers offer excellent food alongside well-kept ales. For foodie pubs, try the friendly **Old Plough** at Braunston-in-Rutland (01572 722714), the **Black Bull** in Market Overton (01572 767677), the **Cuckoo**, just down from the King's Arms (*see p249*) in Wing (01572 737340); the **Olive Branch** in Clipsham (01780 410355); and the **Ram Jam Inn** at Stretton on the Great North Road (01780 410776).

Maybe I'm a maze

Play a game of word association on the word 'maze', and the chances are you'll immediately think of vast rows of hedges, huge eight-foot shrubs hemming you in as you try, fruitlessly and for hours on end, to reach the centre. Specifically, you may be thinking of the maze at Hampton Court Palace that fits this description fairly well. But it's highly unlikely you're thinking of the maze in the Rutland village of **Wing**.

Wing's maze contains no vast hedges, no huge shrubs, and no tourists struggling to get out. Rather, the teensy-weensy 50-foot maze is made of turf cut from the ground in what's known as a 'Chartres' design (named after Chartres Cathedral in France, whose nave boasts a pavement maze in the same style). Wing's turf maze

was cut into the ground during medieval times, although its origins remain a little hazy; as, indeed, does its original purpose. Though a few people believe that the maze formed a game popular at village fairs, it's more commonly thought to have been part of a religious rite: penitent sinners began in the middle and had to find their way out on their hands and knees, praying as they went.

The turf maze at Wing is one of only eight such mazes in England, and is well signposted from the main road: it's just past the excellent Cuckoo pub on the right if you're driving west to east through the village. Hampton Court it ain't, of course. But charmingly esoteric it most certainly is.

More 'pubby' pubs include the **Hole in the Wall** (good for ales), up Cheyne Lane in Stamford; the **Waggon & Horses** (High Street East, Uppingham); the **White Horse** in Empingham; the **Millstone Inn** (Millstone Lane, Barnack, Lincolnshire); and the **Grainstore** on Station Road in Oakham, notable for the fine beers brewed on site. Try, too, to take a tour of the wonderful **Melbourn Bros' Brewery** (All Saints Street, Stamford; 01780 752186; tours by appointment Mon-Fri), drinking some apricot beer while you're there.

If you're in search of a curry, the **Voujon Balti Hut** in Oakham (4 Burley Corner, High Street; 01572 723043) is your best bet. But the area's best food comes from the old-fashioned restaurant and modern brasserie at the **Whipper-Inn Hotel** (*see p248*). Alternatively, more moneyed diners can head out of Oakham to the Michelin-starred (and with mains starting at £27.50 and desserts around £12, it should be) restaurant at **Hambleton Hall** (*see p248*).

Finch's Arms

Upper Hambleton (01572 756575). **Food served** noon-2.30pm, 7-9.30pm daily. **Credit** MC, V.
A textbook example of how to maintain an old pub while moving seamlessly into the 21st century. The Finch's Arms is a pub, though in name alone: the decor is a tasteful, slyly modish set-up with a restaurant attached at the back with views over Rutland Water (you can also eat from the same menu in the not-especially-pubby pub bit). Beers come from the Grainstore pub, and the food from an inventive chef: grilled mackerel with stir-fried vegetables (£8.95), shark steak with sushi rice (£11.95), or a divine chicken breast salad (£9.25). The welcome is warm and the ambience a delight. A winning enterprise.

King's Arms Inn

Top Street, Wing (01572 737634). **Food served** noon-2pm, 7-9pm Mon-Fri; noon-2pm, 6.30-9.30pm Sat; noon-2pm, 7-8.30pm Sun.
Credit AmEx, DC, MC, V.
Dating to 1649, this is another sprawling old village local offering real ales, superior pub nosh and reliable accommodation. The King's Bar is the oldest part of the inn, with flagstone floors, low beams, nooks and crannies and two open log fires for a totally cosy overkill outside the summer months. Local herb sausages, local trout and Rutland cheese feature on the perfect pub menu. Mains will set you back anything from £6.95 to £12.75.

King's Cliffe House

31 West Street, King's Cliffe (01780 470172).
Food served 7-9.30pm Wed-Sat. **No credit cards.**
Despite being on the fringes of Rutland, King's Cliffe is well worth a spin south. Hidden away off the crooked village street, Emma Jessop and Andrew Wilshaw restrict themselves to polite opening hours on only four nights a week, spending the rest of their time collecting fresh ingredients and preparing their immaculate country menu. Prices are high-ish, with starters about £5.50, mains about £14, and desserts about £5.

Loch Fyne

11 All Saints Place, Stamford (01780 761370).
Food served 9am-10.30pm daily. **Credit** AmEx, MC, V.
This piscine chain recently opened a branch in Stamford, and the locals seem to have taken to it like fish to water. Anyone familiar with Loch Fyne's other restaurants (they have branches in Oxford, Henley and Crouch End, among others) will know what to expect. Those that aren't should look forward to starters that include Loch Fyne kippers (£4.95) and haddock chowder, and mains such as baked sea bass (£12.95) and pan-fried salmon. Happily, the restaurant promises that all its products come from sustainable resources.

The Chilterns to York

Lincoln

A city of two halves.

Founded by the Romans in AD 48, Lincoln was one of Europe's most important cities right up to the 17th century, a status that leaves it with a treasure trove of Roman and medieval architecture to equal York or Canterbury. However, after its glory years Lincoln drifted off into relative obscurity (it doesn't even have a direct train link with London), and has only recently woken up to its tourism possibilities, making it a far more relaxing place to visit than any of its more popular competitors on the British heritage trail.

Uphill...

The city is dominated by the magnificent cathedral, a towering Gothic precipice perched on the only hill for miles around. At night it is

The once-splendid **Bishop's Palace**.

spectacularly floodlit and if you arrive by train or car across the region's flat plains, it looks beautifully other-worldly. Its companion is the medieval castle, which was built just after the Norman Conquest.

Surrounding the cathedral and castle is the uphill area; crammed with cobbled streets and ancient houses, it's largely car-free and has plenty of quirky and traditional shops (including an old-fashioned sweet shop, several second-hand bookshops, crafts and pottery outlets and a lovely florist's) and many a pub in which to refuel. It's in this area that you'll find most of the city's visitor attractions.

... and down

The residential bulk of the city is downhill, including a busy pedestrianised High Street with extensive – if predictable – shopping possibilities and a vibrant covered market (there's also a Farmers' Market on the first Friday of every month). Here you'll also find the **Brayford Pool**, an expanse of water around which the original Celtic inhabitants settled when they came to the area. It became an important inland harbour for the Romans, and later, by the 18th century, when grain was brought in for the breweries that lined the Brayford's banks and local wool was taken away for export, this was the fourth busiest port in the whole of Britain. Nowadays it is a pleasant marina, with the new University of Lincoln taking up much of the land on its southern banks.

Life story

Lincoln started life as a Roman garrison, growing into a thriving community as legionaries retired and settled here. There are plenty of remnants of the Roman era, including Newport Arch, the only surviving Roman arch in Britain that still has traffic driving through it. After the Romans left around AD 500, Lincoln became part of the Anglo-Saxon community of Lindsey, and later one of the principal 'burghs' of the Danelaw established by the invading Vikings. The city received its charter in 1071 from William the Conqueror, who ordered the building of both the castle and the cathedral. By 1086 it was a walled metropolis of 5,000 people.

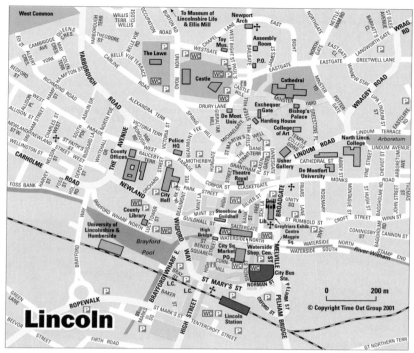

Lincoln

Medieval Lincoln can be seen best on the aptly named **Steep Hill**, the picturesque link between uphill and down. Here you'll see such ancient dwellings as the **Norman House** and the **Jews House**. The latter dates back to the 1170s and is Britain's oldest continuously occupied domestic building. Other later examples include the half-timbered houses on **High Bridge** – the nation's oldest bridge to have buildings over it – and the three surviving city gates, at Pottergate, Minster Yard and the Stonebow.

By train from London

There are, alas, no direct trains from London to Lincoln, but the service from **King's Cross** to **Newark Northgate** (one train every 30mins to 1hr) takes just under **1hr 30mins**; from there a connecting service to **Lincoln Central** takes just under **30mins**. Info: www.gner.co.uk and www.centraltrains.co.uk.

Lincoln's later prosperity was based on the fertile agricultural region surrounding the city, and it was actually agriculture that led it to become a centre of heavy industry. From the manufacture of steam tractors and threshing machines grew a series of foundries and engineering works, producing everything from earth-moving equipment to monumental gas turbines for power stations.

Revitalised but still unspoilt

In 1996 Lincoln became a university town, and it plays its new academic role to the full. The rapidly growing campus now fills the wasteland left by the city's industrial past, bringing new life to the area around the Brayford Pool, and energising the city with an influx of young people. Lincoln is looking increasingly towards tourism for its income, and its annual one million visitors are well-catered for, with a wealth of places to stay and a growing number of good restaurants. However, there is, as yet, mercifully little of the intensive coach-party tourism and sightseeing-by-numbers you'll find in many similar British cities. Make the most of it while you can.

What to see & do

Think of Lincoln in two parts, uphill and down, so you minimise the number of times you have to walk up Steep Hill. That one obstacle apart, it's a very walkable city, with the major attractions very close to each other. However, there's a useful hop-on-hop-off sightseeing bus, **Guide Friday**, that covers all the major sights and runs from mid April to mid September.

If you fancy a trip along the local waterways (the River Witham and the Roman Foss Dyke Canal), there are boat services from the William IV pub by the Brayford and from the Waterside shopping centre. You get a nice view of Lincoln and (on some journeys) a trip to the Pyewipe Inn, an above-average riverside pub just outside the city.

Tourist Information Centres

21 The Cornhill (High Street), LN5 7HB (01522 873256/www.lincoln-info.org.uk). **Open** 9.30am-5.30pm Mon-Thur; 9.30am-5pm Fri; 10am-5pm Sat.

9 Castle Hill (Castle Square), LN1 3AA (01522 873213/www.lincoln-info.org.uk). **Open** 9.30am-5.30pm Mon-Thur; 9.30am-5pm Fri; 10am-5pm Sat, Sun.

Ask about guided tours (£2 adults, £1 children) – they start outside the Castle Square office. Ghost walks (no need to book) also start from here every Wednesday, Friday and Saturday – for more information phone 01522 874056.

Bishop's Palace

Minster Yard (01522 527468/www.english-heritage. org.uk). **Open** *Apr-Sept* 10am-6pm daily. *Oct* 10am-5pm daily. *Nov, Jan-Mar* 10am-4pm Sat, Sun. *Dec* 10am-4pm Sat, Sun, Christmas market days. **Admission** (EH) £2.50; £1.30-£1.90 concessions.

Said to have once been Britain's most luxurious residence, with banqueting halls, apartments and offices, the Bishop's Palace was an important building though not much of the original splendour survives except the restored Alnwick Tower. However, displays here show just how well the medieval bishops lived as they entertained monarchs and ran much of the city. The ruins are very atmospheric, the site is pretty, the views are splendid and there's even a small vineyard clinging to the side of the hill.

Christmas Market

Castle Square.

Lincoln is twinned with Neustadt an der Weinstrasse, a German wine-producing town, which provided the inspiration for a Christmas market in the late 1980s. More then ten years on, the market is a mix of food and drink (mulled wine and roast chestnuts through to sausages and chips), fairground rides (the more sedate kind), and a mass of stalls (some tacky, some charming). It's a very popular event, and also very festive – not least because of the dramatic location, against the backdrop of the castle and cathedral. The forthcoming markets are planned for 6-9 December in 2001, and 5-8 December in 2002.

Ellis Mill

Mill Road (01522 523870/528448). **Open** *May-Sept* 2-6pm Sat, Sun. *Oct-Apr* 2pm-dusk Sun. **Admission** 70p; 30p concessions.

In days gone by the long ridge on which Lincoln is built was peppered with windmills. Now there's just one, built in 1798 and restored in 1981. If the wind's blowing and they're grinding corn, it's a fascinating place to visit; fresh stoneground flour is for sale, too.

Greyfriars Exhibition Centre

Broadgate (01522 530401). **Open** 2-4pm Tue; 10am-1pm, 2-4pm Wed-Sat. **Admission** free.

Housed in a 13th-century building, this centre is a good starting point for a tour of Lincoln's long history. Its changing displays are drawn from the collection of the old City and County museum; they cover aspects of Lincoln from its prehistory to around 1750, and include many objects retrieved from local archaeological excavations. Items range from the sublime to the ridiculous: we saw an albino hedgehog (chosen from a large

Lincoln Cathedral: medieval architecture doesn't get much finer than this.

The West Front

For the first time since 1984, the magnificent entrance to the cathedral is on full view to visitors. The West Front, which had been hidden by scaffolding, was unveiled in March 2001. A 17-year restoration project has seen the stone cleaned and conserved, and eight panels of the Romanesque frieze re-carved (the fragile originals have been removed and it is hoped that at some stage a special gallery will be built).

The sculpted frieze was created in the mid 12th century and depicts the following stark images: 'Punishment for Lust', 'Punishment for Sodomy', 'Punishment for Avarice', 'The Harrowing of Hell', 'The Elect in Heaven', 'Abraham's Bosom', 'Feast of Dives' and 'Death of Lazarus and Dives in Hell'.

Today we're used to seeing the cathedral as a building and tourist attraction, as well as a place of worship, but these carvings give a powerful glimpse of the world as it was seen by medieval England. Restoration of the cathedral is an ongoing task – next in line for the treatment are the southern panels.

collection of albino animals), some exquisite Roman jewellery and the oddly affecting tombstone of Claudia Chrysis (at 90 years, the oldest known woman to have lived in Roman Britain). People from the Past – an exhibition on interpreting evidence from history – runs until 27 April 2002.

Incredibly Fantastic Old Toy Show

26 Westgate (01522 520534). **Open** *Easter-Sept* 11am-5pm Thur-Sat; noon-4pm Sun, bank hols. *Oct-Dec* 11am-5pm Sat; noon-4pm Sun. Closed Jan-Easter. **Admission** £2.20; £1.20-£1.80 concessions.
The slightly garish exterior hides a charming collection of vintage toys. The dolls, teddies, trucks, puppets and models are displayed thematically, plus there's old film footage. There are also plenty of funfair mirrors and coin-operated mechanical attractions (for which you buy old pennies). Every age group should enjoy this one.

Lincoln Castle

Castle Hill (01522 511068/www.lincolnshire.gov.uk). **Open** *Apr-Oct* 9.30am-5.30pm Mon-Sat; 11am-5.30pm Sun. *Nov-Mar* 9.30am-4pm Mon-Sat; 11am-4pm Sun. **Admission** £2.50; £1-£1.50 concessions; free under-5s.
On a cobbled square, facing the cathedral, is the entrance to Lincoln Castle. Built immediately after the Norman Conquest, this was a key defence for an important and wealthy town. It saw action in the 1140s during the Battle of Lincoln between King Stephen and the invading Matilda, when it was besieged several times, and then in 1644 when Cromwell's Parliamentary soldiers stormed it in less than an hour and booted the king's soldiers out of the city. In more peaceful times the castle has been the site of a Victorian prison and a Crown Court, which is still in operation. These days, its grounds are the site of a busy programme of events throughout the year, from plays, classical concerts and brass bands, to re-enactments, medieval jousting and archery, and a vintage car rally. There's a coffee shop here, too.

Walk around the perimeter walls for some great views of the city and surrounding countryside (especially from the Observatory Tower). Round to the east, Cobb Tower contains some grisly dungeons, complete with manacles and prisoners' 13th-century carved graffiti. In the southern part of the grounds, the prison is worth a look, too, not least for its chapel, the only surviving example of the 'Pentonville separate system', a maze of interlocking doors, which kept prisoners completely isolated even while they were sitting next to each other.

Also housed in the prison building is the Magna Carta, the foundation of the nation's civil liberties and rule of law. This is one of the four surviving original documents that King John signed in 1215. It has been kept in Lincoln ever since.

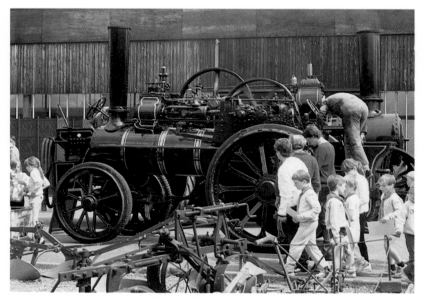

Transport is just one facet of local history covered at the **Museum of Lincolnshire Life**.

Lincoln Cathedral

Minster Yard (01522 544544/
www.lincolncathedral.com). **Open** *June-Aug* 7.15am-
8pm Mon-Sat; 7.15am-6pm Sun. *Sept-May* 7.15am-
6pm Mon-Sat; 7.15am-5pm Sun. **Admission** £3.50;
£3 concessions; free under-14s.

For several centuries, when its three Gothic towers were
capped by enormous spires, Lincoln Cathedral was (at
540ft) the tallest building in the world. Today it remains
among the most beautiful, described by John Ruskin as
'out and out the most precious piece of architecture in the
British Isles'. It is visible from almost anywhere in the city
and now that much of the exterior restoration is complete,
its imposing west front is free of the scaffolding that
obscured it for a decade *(see p252* **The West Front**).
The diocese of Lincoln once stretched from the Thames
to the Humber, the largest in the country, so it was only
appropriate that such a grand cathedral should be here.
Most of what stands today was built by St Hugh, a
French monk who became Bishop of Lincoln in 1186.
Hugh brought to the building an elegant continental
style previously unknown in England, and this style
was followed throughout the four centuries of the building's construction, although the lower parts of the west
front are the remnants of a much earlier cathedral, a
1072 Norman structure built by Remigius, the first
Bishop of Lincoln. The rest of this structure was
destroyed by an earthquake in 1141.

Lincoln Cathedral's most recent claim to fame was as
the setting for some Trollope-esque ecclesiastical
intrigue resulting from a long-running stand-off between
the Dean and the Bishop over a tour of Australia to
show off the cathedral's original of the Magna Carta

(now kept in the castle). Intervention by Mrs Thatcher
and a 'randy vicar' sex scandal added fuel to the fire
and the Church now refers to 'Lincoln' as one of its more
embarrassing moments.

None of this affected the beautiful building, however,
and a visit is a must, as the 900-year-old cathedral
boasts some of the finest medieval architecture and
craftsmanship to be found anywhere. There's the beautiful Early English Angel Choir, where you'll find the
Lincoln Imp, the city's devilish mascot; the fine wood
carving (especially the hidden designs under the
Bishops' perches), the fine stained glass throughout,
and the library, designed by Sir Christopher Wren. In
the cathedral garden stands a huge statue of Tennyson
by George Frederick Watts.

Museum of Lincolnshire Life

Burton Road (01522 528448). **Open** *May-Sept*
10am-5.30pm daily. *Oct-Apr* 10am-5.30pm Mon-Sat;
2-5.30pm Sun. **Admission** £2; 60p concessions.

A gem of a museum if you like a little bit of everything.
All aspects of Lincolnshire's social and economic
history are represented here. Period interiors (a printer's,
a wheelwright's, a chemist shop, a school room), weird
agricultural implements, period costumes, and scores
of beautifully restored traction engines and horse-
drawn carriages all vie for attention. Modern Lincoln
was built on heavy engineering, so there are plenty of
iron giants here, including the world's first tank (built
in the city's foundries). The museum hosts frequent
talks and other events: we saw a great collection of US
military vehicles; other weekend activities include
motorcycle shows, stamp fairs, brass bands and a
Victorian Day Christmas Celebration.

The Stonebow & Guildhall

Saltergate (01522 881188/www.lincoln-info.org.uk).
Open *Guided tours* 10.30am, 1.30pm Fri, 1st Sat of
month. **Admission** free.

In the 15th and 16th centuries the Stonebow – a limestone archway that spans the pedestrianised High Street
– was the southern gateway into the walled city, a
replacement for one that the Romans erected (its companion gates exist in Pottergate and in Minster Yard
between castle and cathedral). Nowadays it's mostly a
landmark for rendezvous under its clock. Inside is the
council chamber and a room displaying a wealth of civic
insignia: swords, seals and mayoral chains.

Usher Gallery

Lindum Road (01522 527980). **Open** 10am-5.30pm
Tue-Sat, bank hols; 2.30pm-5pm Sun. Last entry
4.30pm. **Admission** £2; 50p concessions. Free Fri.

A handsome provincial art gallery housing an
acclaimed collection of coins, jewellery and timepieces,
in keeping with the profession of its founder, James
Ward Usher, a local jeweller. There are also watercolours by Turner, and a collection of work by Peter de
Wint, as well as paintings by LS Lowry, John Piper and
Walter Sickert and Ruskin Spear. Much of the work has
a local theme or subject matter and there's a fine
collection of memorabilia relating to the Lincolnshire-
born Alfred Lord Tennyson. There is a programme of
temporary exhibitions, workshops and talks. The café
is a pleasant, sun-filled spot.

Where to stay

Lincoln lacks much truly characterful
accommodation, but is teeming with B&Bs,
especially in the 'West End' area of the city
(try along Yarborough Road or West Parade).
Most hotels are part of a chain; the ones listed
below are chosen for reasons of location,
style and price – and not every one has all
three attributes.

Courtyard by Marriott

*Brayford Wharf North, LN1 1YW (01522 544244/
fax 01522 560805/www.marriott.com).* **Rates** £51-
£79 single; £64-£80 double/twin. **Rooms** (all en
suite) 49 single; 20 double; 20 twin. **Credit** AmEx,
DC, MC, V.

Part of an American hotel chain, this hotel was a major
part of the regeneration of Lincoln's Brayford Pool area.
It's built in a vaguely wharf-style design: the rooms are
clean, efficient, predictable and air-conditioned; the
bathrooms all boast power-showers and underfloor
heating. The location is handy for the central High
Street shopping area (it's a 15-minute walk uphill to
the cathedral). The place has a businesslike air, but
families are made very welcome. Children welcome.
No-smoking rooms available.

D'Isney Place Hotel

*Eastgate, LN2 4AA (01522 538881/fax 01522
511321/www.disneyplacehotel.co.uk).* **Rates** £53.50-
£73.50 single occupancy; £83 double/twin; £93
family room; £93-£103 deluxe double. **Rooms** (all
en suite) 1 single; 13 double/twin; 3 deluxe double;
2 family. **Credit** AmEx, DC, MC, V.

There are no public rooms in this charming red-brick
Georgian townhouse, but the guest rooms are all very
pleasant (and the larger ones positively luxurious – one
even has a jacuzzi). As well as being close to the historic
side of the city, there's a piece of it in the delightfully
secluded garden: a 700-year-old tower, part of the old
wall that once surrounded the cathedral. Breakfast is
served in your room. Children welcome. Smoking and
pets allowed by arrangement.

Edward King House

*The Old Palace, Minster Yard, LN2 1PU (01522
528778/fax 01522 527308).* **Rates** £19 single;
£37 twin; £56 family room. Breakfast £2 (Eng).
Rooms 5 single; 11 twin; 1 family. **Credit** MC, V.

The former official residence of the Bishop of Lincoln,
this large guest house is still run by the Church. It has
one of the best (and most peaceful) locations in the city,
being close to the cathedral while overlooking the ruins
of the medieval Bishop's Palace. There are no en suite
rooms, but the bathrooms are spotlessly clean and for
the price, Edward King House is hard to beat, especially as the atmosphere is relaxed, too. Children welcome.
No smoking throughout. Pets by arrangement.

Posthouse

*Eastgate, LN2 1PN (enquiries 0870 400 9052/
bookings 0345 404040/www.posthousehotels.com).*
Rates £46-66 single occupancy; £92
double/twin; £92 family room (under-16s free
if sharing parents' room). Special breaks.
Rooms (all en suite) 3 single; 51 double/twin;
7 family. **Credit** AmEx, DC, MC, V.

This rather brutal-looking modern hotel makes a startling contrast with the cathedral across the road, but
has the twin attributes of great location and value for
money. The place could do with a refurb, but the staff
are friendly, the rooms a decent size, and it makes a good
uphill alternative for those allergic to B&Bs. It even has
a few Roman remains in the grounds. Children and pets
welcome. No-smoking rooms available.

St Clements Lodge

21 Langworth Gate, LN2 4AD (01522 521532).
Rates £35 single occupancy; £47-£52 double/twin;
£68-£80 family. **Rooms** (all en suite) 3
double/twin/family. **No credit cards.**

A small but immaculately presented B&B close to all
the uphill attractions. The rooms are large and comfortable; the owners are welcoming. The kind of place
that gets a lot of repeat bookings. Children welcome. All
bedrooms no-smoking.

White Hart Hotel

*Bailgate, LN1 3AR (01522 526222/fax 01522
531798/www.heritagehotels.com).* **Rates** £95 single;
£105 double/twin; £115 deluxe double/twin; £135
four-poster; £135 suite. Special breaks. **Rooms** (all en
suite) 6 single; 26 double/twin; 4 deluxe double/ twin;
1 four-poster; 11 suites. **Credit** AmEx, DC, MC, V.

A historic coaching inn that dates back to the 1400s, the
White Hart is part of Forte's Heritage Hotels chain and
is situated smack in between castle and cathedral. All
the rooms (some of which feel a bit cramped) have been
recently renovated to a high standard and the hotel is
filled with antique porcelain, paintings and furnishings.
Children welcome. No-smoking rooms available.

The Chilterns to York

Where to eat & drink

Lincoln is not over-endowed with fine restaurants, but there's enough choice to keep most people happy for a weekend. Hotel restaurants are generally dependable, especially the **White Hart** (*see p255*), as are many of the pubs – try the **Duke William Hotel** (44 Bailgate; 01522 533351). **The Victoria** (6 Union Road; 01522 536048) has Lincoln's best range of real ales and no music. Both the **Bombay Restaurant** (The Strait; 01522 523264) and the **Raj Douth Tandoori** (Eastgate; 01522 548377) serve decent Indian meals, while **Hari Kumar's** (80 Bailgate; 01522 537000) is Lincoln's only fusion restaurant. Reliable chains include **Pizza Express** (269 High Street; 01522 544701); **Costa Coffee** (in Ottakar's bookshop, High Street) and **Starbucks** (313 High Street). **Café Society** (262 High Street; 01522 514772) makes a good pitstop between up and down town, and serves coffee, cakes, all-day breakfasts and light meals; almost opposite is **Puccino's** (285 High Street; 01522 519268), a cosy hangout offering a great range of coffees, plus paninis and pastries, pizzas, pastas and grills. The best budget option is often fish and chips – the city is well served by Grimsby's daily catch. Try the **Newport Fish Bar** (20 Newport; 01522 528553) – haddock and chips costs £2.95.

Good food and real ales at the **Wig & Mitre**.

Brown's Pie Shop
33 Steep Hill (01522 527330). **Food served** noon-10pm daily. **Credit** AmEx, MC, V.
Traditional British food, in the form of pies and puddings, sets the tone at Brown's. It's a quaint Dickensian restaurant, serving hearty, old-fashioned meals at reasonable prices. Start with Yorkshire pudding with spiced onion gravy, or potted prawns, and move on to steak and kidney pie or Cumberland sausages with mash and gravy. Starters are £3.50-£6.50, mains £7.95-£15.95 (for fillet steak).

Jews House
15 The Strait (01522 524851). **Food served** noon-2pm, 6.30-9.30pm Mon-Sat; 11.30-4pm Sun. **Set dinners** £27.50 2 courses; £32.50 3 courses. **Credit** DC, MC, V.
The city's most upmarket restaurant serves modern European food in what is possibly the oldest inhabited house in the country (it dates back to 1190). The small but comfortable interior makes a pleasant setting for top-notch meals: a typical lunch or dinner might be smoked salmon salad with cucumber and tarragon followed by monkfish brochette with olive and caper dressing. Staff are young and pleasant.

Stokes High Bridge Café
207 High Street (01522 513825). **Food served** 9am-4.30pm Mon-Sat. **No credit cards**.
A quaint-looking café on the first and second floors of a half-timbered house, overlooking a scenic part of the river. Motherly waitresses serve nostalgia trips in the form of sausage baps, teacakes, crumpets and scones, roast of the day and knickerboker glory. Coffee and tea are specialities (sold from the shop on the ground floor): espresso costs £1.25, a cafetiere is £3.25. Great comfort food and a nice atmosphere.

Wig & Mitre
30 Steep Hill (01522 535190). **Food served** 8am-11pm daily. **Set meals** (noon-6pm daily) £9 2 courses; £12 3 courses. **Credit** AmEx, DC, MC, V.
Although it's a pub/restaurant spread across a number of rooms, the Wig is the closest Lincoln has to a brasserie. Real ales, a lengthy wine list, and unfussy but first-rate food are served in a relaxed, music-free ambience. Prices are slightly high for Lincoln, but it's worth it, whether you're having breakfast (including a very creamy porridge), a snack (sandwiches, a bowl of chilli – £6) or a full meal (mains, such as pork and herb pattie with onion gravy, creamed potatoes and veg, £8.95-£16.95). Very civilised.

Zucchini's
47 Silver Street (01522 530760). **Food served** noon-2.30pm, 5.30-10.30pm Mon-Fri, Sun; noon-10.30pm Sat. **Credit** MC, V.
This jolly Italian restaurant and pizzeria (decorated in a vibrant orange) is a good bet for families. Prices are cheaper at lunch (mozzarella, tomato and basil salad costs £2.95 at lunch, £4.95 in the evening) and the staff are good-natured and tolerant. Pizzas run from margharita to seafood, and there are plenty of pasta and steak dishes, too. At dinner a livelier crowd takes over. Uphill, Gino's (7 Gordon Road; 01522 513770) performs a similar role.

York

An embarrassment of riches.

York makes for an ideal urban weekend break. The city that for much of the past 2,000 years was second in importance only to London is now less than two hours from the capital by train (beleaguered rail service permitting). And the fact that it was largely bypassed by the Industrial Revolution means that York's compact core has remained remarkably intact. It's the perfect walking city. Unusually for the UK, a large portion of its heart is pedestrianised (a ring road and park-and-ride schemes keep most traffic at a distance) and cycle lanes proliferate.

Large tracts of medieval wall ring a wealth of listed buildings – medieval, Tudor, Georgian – and some fine museums and other attractions, the list topped by the magnificent **Minster**. The inevitable downside is that York is no secret. With a population of roughly 200,000 and annual visitor numbers in the region of four million, the place can seem like a tourist-choked open-air heritage theme park in peak season. The city's at its best on a bright, crisp winter's day.

Romans, Saxons and Vikings

As with London, York is fundamentally a Roman creation. There may have been an Iron Age settlement in the area but it was the arrival of the legions in AD 71 and their setting up of a camp on the land between the Ouse and Foss rivers that marked the foundation of the city. Eboracum, as the fort was known (meaning 'place of the yew trees') soon grew into a permanent settlement and was subsequently taken over by the Saxons. The first church in York dates from the seventh century and the town, by now the capital of the kingdom of Northumbria, soon became established as second only to Canterbury in the church hierarchy, a position it retains today.

In the middle of the ninth century the Vikings raided and then settled the entire north of the country. Saxon Eoforwic became Norse Jorvik. Although the Viking period lasted less than a century, their street and place names have proved more permanent. No town in Britain has more thoroughfares suffixed with '-gate' (meaning 'street'). Some of the street names may refer to individuals (Goodramgate, for instance), and many refer to the trades

carried out there (Coppergate was home to the carpenters, Skeldergate to the shield-makers).

The shape of the city changed little in medieval times. Narrow ginnels (alleys) still criss-cross the centre, providing countless short cuts (see p261 **Exploring the ginnels and the snickelways**). Coffee Yard, the covered passageway linking Stonegate with Grape Lane, is only five foot ten inches high in places. And Grape Lane itself was, of course, the haunt of York's vintners. Well, not exactly. Those down-to-earth medieval folk were even more literal than that. 'Grap' meant 'grope', and when you know that this was the city's red-light district you can guess the rest. The crazily teetering houses on York's best-known street, The Shambles, were once home to the city's butchers; reputedly, they were built with overhanging storeys to keep direct sunlight off the meat. Now the overhanging eaves cool overexcited tourists searching for ceramic teddy bears and spurious coats of arms. There's no little irony that what was once York's most foul-smelling, pestilential street is now its most twee. At its southern end is the city's most delightfully and bafflingly named street, Whip-ma-whop-ma-gate.

The daily city

York isn't all teashops and tour groups. The university, just to the south-east of the centre in Heslington, a big influx of business and industry (particularly bioscience) and the continuing presence of chocolate companies (one plant nearby is devoted solely to the production of the ever-popular Kit-Kat) means that this town is no historical fossil.

And there are plenty of shopping opportunities if you get tired of visiting the historic sites. Coney Street has all the high-street names, while Swinegate and Daveygate contain more upmarket boutiques along with some designer fashion outlets. There's also an

By train from London

Two to three trains an hour go to **York** direct from **King's Cross**. The journey time is between **1hr 50mins** and just over **2hrs**. Info: www.gner.co.uk.

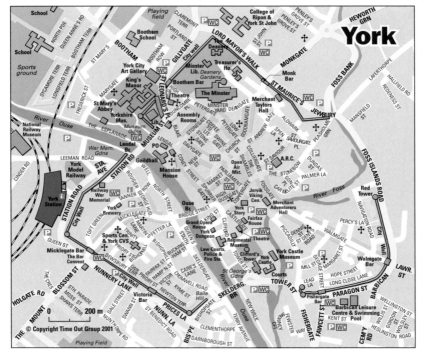

ugly purpose-built shopping centre on Coppergate, not far from the Castle Museum and Clifford's Tower. The open-air Newgate Market is the place to head for local produce, from herbs and fresh fish to batteries or bars of soap. Lawries deli on the corner of the market is good for local cheeses and sandwiches made to order.

First Stop York by Train

If you visit York by train you can take advantage of the 'First Stop York by Train' scheme that entitles rail travellers to half-price admission to all the major sights plus discounts at a number of restaurants and the York Theatre Royal. In addition, special rates are available at 30 of the city's hotels and guesthouses. Phone York Tourist Information Centre (see below) for more information.

What to see & do

York is packed with museums and other visitor attractions, although some of them are rather insubstantial and unashamedly aimed squarely at the tourist market. We list the

best sights below; head to the Tourist Information Centre for information on many more. The main sights tend to be clustered either to the north of the centre of town around the Minster, or, alternatively, to the south around the castle area.

Tourist Information Centre

De Grey Rooms, Exhibition Square, YO10 7HB (01904 621756/www.york.gov.uk). **Open** 9am-6pm Mon-Sat; 10am-4pm Sun.
There's also a branch inside York railway station and at 20 George Hudson Street.

Bike hire

Bob Trotter's *13 Lord Mayor's Walk (01904 622868).*
A ten-minute walk from the train station.

ARC

St Saviourgate (01904 654324/ www.yorkarchaeology.co.uk). **Open** *School holidays only* 10am-5pm Mon-Sat. Last entry 3pm.
Admission £4.50; £4 concessions.
The Archaeological Resource Centre, located within the old church of St Saviour, is an admirable attempt to make archaeology accessible. Its hands-on exhibits, mainly aimed at children, illuminate York's history.

Barley Hall
*2 Coffee Yard, off Stonegate (01904 610275/
www.barleyhall.org.uk).* **Open** *Mar-Oct* 10am-4pm
Tue-Sun. *Nov-Feb* 11am-3.30pm Wed-Fri; 10am-4pm
Sat, Sun. **Admission** £3.50; £2.50 concessions.
A splendid medieval townhouse that has been lovingly
restored by the Archaeological Trust to something resem-
bling its former glory. An amusing and informative audio
tour is provided by Judi Dench and Robert Hardy.

Castle Museum
off Tower Street (01904 613161/www.york.gov.uk).
Open *Apr-Oct* 9.30am-5pm daily. *Nov-Mar* 9.30am-
4.30pm daily. **Admission** £5.75; £3.50 concessions.
Undoubtedly York's best museum, this inspired collection of everyday objects from the past 300 years was
started by Dr John Kirk, who wanted to preserve
evidence of a vanishing way of life. There are carefully
reconstructed period rooms, a plethora of vintage
domestic appliances, tons of old toys and extensive
re-created Victorian and Edwardian streets and shops.
Kids love it, particularly the informative and entertaining section on chocolate. Among the more mundane
exhibits representing everyday life in the 19th and 20th
centuries is one ancient gem: an Anglo-Saxon helmet,
the oldest to have been found in Britain.

City Walls
Strolling the extensive surviving sections of York's
medieval (13th- and 14th-century) walls is one of the
greatest pleasures of a visit to the city. Stretching for
three miles, they are punctuated by four bars (gates) –
Micklegate Bar (on the original road to London),
Bootham Bar, Monk Bar and Walmgate Bar (unique in
the UK in still retaining its defensive barbican). There's
a small museum in Micklegate Bar and an exhibition on
Richard III in Monk Bar.

Clifford's Tower
*Tower Street (01904 646940/www.english-
heritage.org.uk).* **Open** *Apr-July, Sept* 10am-6pm
daily. *Aug* 9.30am-7pm daily. *Oct* 10am-5pm daily.
Nov-Mar 10am-4pm daily. **Admission** (EH) £2;
£1-£1.50 concessions.
One of York's most immediately recognisable landmarks, the bluff white-stone tower sits on a mound
raised by William the Conqueror to allow him to keep
an eye on the troublesome citizens. The original Norman
keep was destroyed by the same locals in 1109 when the
city's Jews sheltered from a mob inside and committed
suicide rather than face the rabble. The current structure dates from 1245. There's nothing much more than
a shell here, but it's an evocative shell, and there are good
views from the walls.

Fairfax House
Castlegate (01904 655543/www.fairfaxhouse.co.uk).
Open *late Feb-early Jan* 11am-4.30pm Mon-Thur,
Sat; 1.30-4.30pm Sun. Guided tours only 11am, 2pm
Fri. Closed early Jan-late Feb. **Admission** £4;
£1.50-£3.50 concessions.
This fine Georgian house was designed by John Carr for
the ninth Viscount Fairfax of Emley in 1750. It was
rescued from obscurity as an office and cinema and
meticulously restored during the 1980s and is now home
to the splendid Noel Terry (of chocolate fame) collection
of Georgian furniture.

The **Theatre Royal** hosts excellent productions, including kids' shows.

Guildhall

St Helen's Square (01904 613161/
www.york.gov.uk). **Open** *May-Oct* 9am-5pm
Mon-Fri; 10am-5pm Sat; 2-5pm Sun. *Nov-Apr*
9am-5pm Mon-Fri. **Admission** free.

The one-time administrative centre of the city is best
viewed from the south side of Lendal Bridge. The
medieval riverside building, standing on the site of
the first Roman bridge across the Ouse, was all but
obliterated by German bombs during World War II.
However, it has been beautifully restored, and the
interior can be toured.

Jorvik Viking Centre

Coppergate (information line 01904 643211/advance
booking 01904 543403/www.vikingjorvik.com). **Open**
Apr-Oct 9am-5.30pm daily. *Nov-Mar* 9am-3.40pm
daily. **Admission** £6.95; £4.95-£5.95 concessions.

York's number one tourist draw has recently undergone a £5 million facelift and confidently expects to
pull in around 500,000 punters a year. When it opened
in the 1980s, it was a pioneer of the time-car-ride-
through-history type of visitor attraction. The idea is
that time has stopped one October day in 948, and you
are able to pass through the sights, sounds and smells
of Viking York, before disembarking in the 21st
century and examining some of the actual finds that
were excavated from Coppergate between 1976 and
1981. Be prepared to queue.

Merchant Adventurers' Hall

Fossgate (01904 654818/www.theyorkcompany.
sagenet.co.uk). **Open** *Easter-Sept* 9am-5pm Mon-Sat;
noon-4pm Sun. *Oct-Easter* 9am-3.30pm Mon-Sat.
Admission (EH) £2; 70p-£1.70 concessions.

One-time home to the city's most powerful guild, this
massive medieval building (completed in 1362) is in a
wonderful state of preservation.

National Railway Museum

Leeman Road (01904 621261/www.nmsi.ac.uk/nrm).
Open 10am-6pm daily. **Admission** £7.50; £5
concessions; free OAPs, under-16s.

The two huge halls that make up the NRM are heavily
geared towards children (rides on Thomas the Tank
Engine, stories from the Fat Controller) and railway
junkies. The whole history of the railway is here, including such locomotive icons as Stephenson's stumpy 1829
Rocket and the undeniably beautiful *Mallard*. There are
engines galore, plus pots of memorabilia, but not a lot
to convert the unconvinced into a rail fanatic.

St William's College

College Street, opposite Minster (01904 557233/
www.yorkminster.org). **Open** 9am-5pm daily.
Admission 60p; 30p concessions.

Built around 1475, this fine half-timbered building was
once home to 23 priests and a provost. The modest
restaurant within the building spills out into the lovely
interior courtyard in summer. Some of the medieval
rooms can be viewed.

Treasurer's House

Chapter House Street (01904 624247/
www.nationaltrust.org.uk). **Open** *Apr-Oct* 11am-5pm
daily. Last admission 4.30pm. Closed Nov-Mar.
Admission (NT) £3.70; £2 concessions.

One of the architectural gems of York, built on the site
of the 11th-century house of the Treasurer of York
Minster, this beautiful late 16th- and early 17th-century
building contains some fine furniture and collections
of china and glass.

York Brewery

12 Toft Green (01904 621162/www.yorkbrew.co.uk).
Guided tours 12.30pm, 2pm, 3.30pm, 5pm Mon-Sat.
Admission £4.25; £3-£3.80; free under-14s.

This tiny independent brewery has only been operational since 1996, bringing brewing back within the city
walls for the first time in 40 years. Sample a half of its
Stonewall bitter before an entertaining and informative
half-hour tour that's capped with a half of the admirably
sharp Yorkshire Terrier.

York City Art Gallery

Exhibition Square (01904 551861/
www.york.gov.uk). **Open** 10am-5pm
daily. **Admission** £2; £1.50 concessions.

This easily digestible municipal collection spans 600
years (though large swathes of that are only covered very
sketchily) and is a little too heavy on workaday British
19th-century paintings. It is notable, however, for a large
number of works by York-born William Etty, and for its
good-quality and imaginative temporary exhibitions.

York Minster

Deangate (01904 557216/www.yorkminster.org).
Open *Jan-Mar, Nov, Dec* 7am-6pm daily. *Apr*
7am-6.30pm daily. *May* 7am-7.30pm daily. *June-Aug*
7am-8.30pm daily. *Sept* 7am-8pm daily. *Oct* 7am-7pm
daily. **Admission** *Tower* £3; £1 concessions.
Chapterhouse £1; 80p concessions. *Foundations,*
treasury & crypt £3; £1-£2.60 concessions.

York's chief glory is its Minster. The sheer scale of the
honey-coloured stone building – it's the largest Gothic
church north of the Alps – is testament to the city's
prominent role in medieval England. Begun in the 1220s
by Archbishop Walter de Grey, the building took 250
years to complete, employing a variety of architectural
styles. Broadly speaking, the transepts are in Early
English style (1220-60), the nave is Decorated Gothic
(1280-1350) and the chancel is Perpendicular (1361-1472).
The nave is the widest of its type in Europe, but it is,
perhaps, the proliferation of wonderful medieval stained
glass that impresses most. The Great West Window
(1338), with its curvaceous flamboyant tracery, is known
as the 'Heart of Yorkshire'; the Great East Window
(1405-8) at the far end of the chancel contains the world's
largest surviving piece of medieval stained glass, while
the Five Sisters' Window in the north transept is the
oldest complete window in the Minster (1260).

Entrance to the Minster is free, but there are
individual charges to climb the tower, see the chapter
house, crypt, treasury and foundations. The harmonious chapter house is a gem. Built in the 1270s and
1280s, it is unusual in having no central supporting
pillar. Less compelling is the crypt, which contains a
variety of architectural fragments. The (decidedly
tough) climb to the top of the tower is rewarded by fine
views (although, strangely, York looks more impressive from ground level than above). If you're short of
time (or money), though, make the foundations your
priority. In the late 1960s, excavation work to secure
the foundations of the central tower (which was

Exploring the ginnels and the snickelways

The best way to explore the city is undoubtedly on foot. And if you want to escape the crowds and the traffic, and uncover a slice of the city's past at the same time, then plunge into its ancient system of secluded passageways.

This network of age-old shortcuts known as snickelways – sometimes dim and dank alleyways, sometimes bustling sunlit passages – honeycombs the city from the Minster to the castle, between the rivers and the city walls. Names such as Hornby's Passage, Pope's Head Alley, Queen's Path, Simons' Yat or Mad Alice Lane conjure up a colourful past and offer unexpected views of the city, leading you into quiet residential streets or through churchyards at one moment, and on to busy shopping precincts the next.

For the full story, buy a copy of Mark Jones's excellent *A Walk Around the Snickelways of York* (£4.99, available at the Tourist Office), which contains details and maps of dozens of snickelway walks, ranging from those which allow you to glimpse the major sights but avoid the tourists, to one particularly recommended for exploration during foul weather.

threatening to collapse) uncovered not just parts of the Norman cathedral but also an Anglo-Saxon and Anglo-Scandinavian cemetery and evidence of the original Roman basilica. It was within this building that, in all probability, Constantine the Great was proclaimed Roman Emperor by his troops on the death of his father in AD 306. It's a tremendously evocative display.

York Model Railway
York station (01904 630169). **Open** *Apr-Oct* 9.30am-6pm daily. *Nov-Mar* 10am-5.30pm daily. **Admission** £2.95; £1.95-£2.65 concessions.
One for little boys of all ages. The scale of the display (incorporating 600 buildings, 1,000 vehicles and 2,500 tiny people) certainly impresses.

Yorkshire Museum
Museum Gardens (01904 551800/ www.york.gov.uk). **Open** 10am-5pm daily. **Admission** £4.50; £2.95 concessions.
Well worth a visit for its enlightening displays on the history of the city and region from Roman times. There's a welter of facts, but they're imaginatively presented, with displays on the daily life of monks and some of the oddities of Roman cuisine ensuring that kids don't get bored. The reconstructed vestibule of the chapter house of the Abbey of St Mary (the ruins of which can be seen outside the museum in Museum Gardens), complete with monkish chanting, is particularly well done and very atmospheric. Another of the museum's prize exhibits is the tiny but exquisite 15th-century pendant known as the Middleham Jewel. A good place to escape the city crowds.

Dairy Guesthouse: a laid-back B&B.

Where to stay

York may have a surfeit of splendid sights and no end of teashops, but it's surprisingly lacking in noteworthy accommodation. There are few hotels or B&Bs within the city walls (we've included the **Dean Court Hotel** as the best of the bunch); however, most places to stay are located on busy main roads leading into the city. However, with the exception of **Middlethorpe Hall**, none of the hotels mentioned below is more than a 15-minute walk from the city centre.

Bishops Hotel
135 Holgate Road, YO24 4DF (01904 628000/ www.bishopshotel.co.uk). **Rates** (per person) £35-£40 single/double/twin; £40 four-poster/canopy. **Rooms** (all en suite) 2 single; 5 double/twin; 1 four-poster; 2 canopy. **Credit** MC, V.
Run by Denise Magson and her sister Gill, Bishops is a small and friendly hotel about ten minutes' walk from the station. The rooms are spick and span, painted with a glaringly bright but fresh colour scheme, and the bathrooms sparkle. The breakfast room overlooks a small garden. The hotel is very child-friendly, with the right facilities, services and attitudes: family rooms, toys, kids' menus, high chairs and cots, and, most important of all, a thoroughly relaxed and tolerant attitude. It's a bit of a hike to the city centre, however. No smoking throughout.

Dairy Guesthouse
3 Scarcroft Road, YO23 1ND (01904 639367/ www.dairyguesthouse.freeserve.co.uk). **Rates** £32-£42 single occupancy; £20-£25 per person double; £22.50 per person four-poster; £67.50 family. **Rooms** 4 double/family (2 en suite); 1 four-poster. **No credit cards.**
This former dairy on the southern edge of town is one of the most laid-back B&Bs around. The owners live in a house at the back of a small flower-filled courtyard, allowing their guests free rein in the five-bedroomed Victorian terrace at the front. There's a well-stocked kitchen where guests are encouraged to help themselves to snacks from the fridge or share their takeaways, and the rather garishly decorated rooms are equally well equipped. Next door to Melton's (*see p264*) and about a ten-minute walk from the Minster, the Dairy has a loyal clientele, so book well in advance. Children welcome (pets by arrangement). No smoking throughout.

Dean Court Hotel
Duncombe Place, YO1 7EF (01904 625082/ fax 01904 620305/www.deancourt-york.co.uk). **Rates** £82.50 single; £130 double/twin; £160 deluxe double; £175 four-poster; £145-£160 family room. **Special breaks. Rooms** (all en suite) 7 single; 13 double; 3 deluxe double; 1 four-poster; 4 family rooms. **Credit** MC, V.
The 1850 red brick hotel in York with the best location turns out to be run by the Best Western chain. But don't let that put you off. The so-called 'country house' decoration is maintained to a good standard throughout and the setting – right opposite the Minster – is worth

paying a bit extra for. Bathrooms come complete with fluffy white bath towels, the deluxe rooms have four-posters and double-glazing to muffle the tolling of the Minster bells, and the hotel includes a formal restaurant and a conservatory café. Popular with business travellers, as well as American and Japanese tourists. Children welcome. No-smoking rooms available.

Easton's
90 Bishopthorpe Road, YO23 1JS (01904 626646).
Rates £32-£62 single occupancy; £41-£69 double/twin; £65-£78 family. Special breaks. **No credit cards**. **Rooms** (all en suite) 10 double/twin/family.
A good few notches better than your average B&B, not only does Easton's offer swathes of rich William Morris wallpapers and fabrics, a lovely sitting room and good-sized bedrooms, but a breakfast menu that includes such scandalously forgotten Victorian gems as kedgeree and devilled kidneys. There's a minimum stay of two nights at the weekend, and three over bank holidays. Children over five welcome. No smoking throughout.

Grange Hotel
1 Clifton, YO30 6AA (01904 644744/fax 01904 612453/www.grangehotel.co.uk). **Rates** £100-£165 single occupancy; £100-£220 double; £175 deluxe double/twin; £190 four-poster; £220 suite. **Rooms** (all en suite) 3 single (with shower); 7 double/twin; 16 deluxe double/twin; 2 four-poster; 1 suite. **Credit** AmEx, DC, MC, V.
On a street of handsome red-brick Georgian terraced houses, a few doors up from WH Auden's birthplace, this grand 30-room hotel is set in a Regency town house. It has an impressive entrance and luxurious bedrooms, with plenty of four-posters, antiques and chintz. All rooms have en suite bathrooms and satellite TV. There are three popular eateries, worth visiting even if you're not staying here: the more expensive and formal Ivy, serving French and modern British dishes, the basement Brasserie and the Dom Ruinart Seafood Bar. Children and pets welcome. No-smoking rooms available.

Holmwood House
114 Holgate Road, YO24 4BB (01904 626183/fax 01904 670899/www.holmwoodhousehotel.co.uk). **Rates** £45-£65 single occupancy; £55-£85 double; £65-£80 twin; £80-£105 four-poster; £75 triple; £130-£140 family suite. **Rooms** (all en suite) 11 double/twin/family suites; 2 four-poster (1 with spa bath); 1 triple. **Credit** AmEx, MC, V.
A bit of a trek from the centre of town, but handy for the railway station, Bill Pitts' and Rosie Blanksby's B&B is spread over two Victorian terraced houses on a main road. The floral-decorated rooms are all slightly different, mostly embracing Victoriana. The plushest room has a four-poster bed and twin spa bath. Breakfast – including kippers or croissants – is served in a basement restaurant. Children welcome. No smoking throughout.

Middlethorpe Hall
Bishopthorpe Road, YO23 2GB (01904 641241/fax 01904 620176/www.middlethorpe.com). **Rates** £109 single; £140 single occupancy; £160 double/twin; £200 deluxe double/twin; £250 four-poster; £220-£325 suite. Special breaks. **Breakfast** £14.50 (Eng); £11.50 (cont). **Rooms** (all en suite) 4 single; 12 double/twin; 6 deluxe double/twin; 2 four-poster; 7 suites. **Credit** MC, V.

The place to splurge in York, Middlethorpe Hall lies a couple of miles south of the city opposite the racecourse. The fabulous William III building, set in 26 acres of grounds, has been restored to its full country house splendour by Historic House Hotels. Rooms vary greatly in size and decor, but all are in keeping with the overall classically restrained mood of the house. Some are in a courtyard block. The formal wood-panelled restaurant offers classical French-based cuisine (*see p265*) and there's a popular new health spa with an indoor swimming pool and whirlpool, steam room, sauna, solarium and beauty treatment rooms (book treatments well in advance). The tranquillity of the beautiful, extensive park and gardens is, alas, marred by the streaming traffic on the adjacent A-road. Children over eight welcome. No-smoking rooms available.

Mount Royale Hotel
119-121 The Mount, YO24 1GU (01904 628856/fax 01904 611171/www.mountroyale.co.uk). **Rates** £85-£105 single occupancy; £95 double/twin; £105 deluxe double/twin; £105 four-poster; suite £140. Special breaks. **Rooms** (all en suite) 9 double/twin; 5 deluxe double/twin; 3 four-poster; 6 suites. **Credit** AmEx, MC, V.
The horsey memorabilia is a reminder that the once grand Mount Royale is close to the racecourse. It's also only about a 15-minute walk from the city centre. The eccentric surroundings are gloriously mismatched, including a carpeted semi-tropical garden corridor, kidney-shaped (outdoor) swimming pool, and a cosy bar for late-night post mortems of the day's racing events. Rooms are large, and ours boasted a sunken bath (actually, an ordinary bathtub buried to an unexpected depth in the floor). Staff are charming and the breakfasts huge. Children and pets welcome.

York Backpackers
Micklegate House, 88-90 Micklegate, YO1 6JX (01904 627720/fax 01904 339350/www.yorkbackpackers.co.uk). **Rates** £9-£15 per person. Breakfast £3 (Eng); £2 (cont). **Rooms** (140 beds) 1 double; 7 dorm (sleeps 8-20); 3 family (sleeps 4-6). **Credit** MC, V.
Located in a beautiful listed Georgian mansion on the main road leading into town, this brightly decorated hostel maintains a jolly atmosphere. Accommodation (there are 140 beds) is in dormitories, double or family rooms, and there's a bar, café, TV, laundry room and pool table, as well as Internet facilities. Popular with large groups, including stag and hen parties.

Where to eat & drink

York has plenty of places to eat, but not many of real quality. The **Grange** (*see p263*) has a restaurant, brasserie and seafood bar worth patronising even if you're staying elsewhere; the restaurant at **Middlethorpe Hall** is also excellent; **Melton's** is an understandably popular local in a residential area offering sophisticated cooking at very reasonable prices.

For something less formal, there's a **Pizza Express** at 17 Museum Street (01904 672904) and, even more casual, **Petergate Fisheries**

The Chilterns to York

(97 Low Petergate; 01904 624788) for the best takeaway fish and chips in town.

For a lunchtime snack or coffee and a cake, try the airy **Spurriergate Centre** in the former church of St Michael on Spurriergate (01904 629393), or the admirable **Blake Head Bookshop & Café** at 104 Micklegate (01904 623767) for warming veggie fare and bargain-priced books. **Alley Cat's Café Bar** (3 Coffee Yard, off Stonegate, 01904 643307) is a bare-boards, half-timbered sort of place offering breakfasts and a good range of snacks (wraps, pasta dishes, jacket potatoes, steak sandwiches and beers or wines by the glass). An all-day place, with excellent home-made cakes and puddings and a jazz soundtrack, is **Café Concerto** at 21 High Petergate (01904 610478) opposite the Minster. And an excellent new juice bar, the **Juice House**, has opened at 28 the Shambles (01904 674684).

The nostalgic **Betty's** teashop in St Helen's Square (01904 659142) belongs to an era when waitresses wore frilly caps and is something of a tourist institution; it's at its best on a Sunday morning. There's a branch and small shop at 46 Stonegate (**Little Betty's**, 01904 622865). More rewarding, perhaps, are the plethora of old-style bakeries that churn out the sort of retro buns most of us thought were extinct – including the excellent local pastry of choice, the curd tart. Try one from **Thomas the Baker** (corner of Church Street and King's Square).

Happily, the city is well provided with characterful taverns and good beer, though pub food is generally poor. Among the best boozers are the **Blue Bell** (53 Fossgate), a tiny Edwardian drinkers' pub; the **Olde Starre** (Stonegate), the oldest licensed pub in the city and popular with tourists; the medieval, timber-framed **Black Swan** (23 Peaseholme Green) also famed for its ghosts; the **Spread Eagle** (98 Walmgate), has good beer and a lively atmosphere); and the **Swan** (16 Bishopsgate Street) is a charming and unspoilt Edwardian local close to Melton's restaurant.

19 Grape Lane

19 Grape Lane (01904 636366/ www.19grapelane.com). **Food served** noon-2pm, 6-10pm Tue-Sat. **Credit** MC, V.
The modern British menu prepared by proprietor Kenny Robertson at this popular and central restaurant might feature goat's cheese with black olive and basil vinaigrette, and rabbit with garlic and balsamic cream and honey-roasted parsnips. A low, beamed ceiling, inoffensive cottagey decor and an intriguing New World-biased wine list are further attractions.

Blue Bicycle

34 Fossgate (01904 673990). **Food served** noon-2.30pm, 6-10pm daily. **Credit** AmEx, DC, MC, V.

One of the most popular names on the York restaurant scene, the BB concentrates on the broadly French and fishy in an informal, thoroughly agreeable atmosphere. Mains might be halibut marinated in red wine served with celeriac and creamy mash (£15) or Cajun-spiced white fish stew (£14.50), followed by rib-sticking desserts such as sticky toffee pudding or creamed rice with roasted fruit (£4.50).

Ha Ha Bar & Canteen

13-17 New Street (01904 655868/ www.hahaonline.co.uk). **Food served** noon-10pm Mon-Sat; noon-9.30pm Sun. **Credit** MC, V.
A slick bar/canteen in the All Bar One mould, but with a better, more innovative menu. A young crowd packs the pale wood and aluminium interior, which has a long bar down one side and an open kitchen at the back. The range of pasta and grills or chips with dips is keenly priced. Try a plateful of grilled halloumi with pistachios, onion bread and salad, or some tagliatelle with asparagus, mushrooms and Parmesan (both £6), with a generous side order of broad beans with pancetta (£3). Wines come by the glass, and there is a range of beers on tap. A welcome injection of modern style in a traditional town.

Kites Restaurant & Wine Bar

13 Grape Lane (01904 641750). **Food served** noon-2pm, 6.30-10.30pm Mon-Sat. **Set lunches** £5 2 courses; £7.50 3 courses. **Set dinners** £10 2 courses; £12.50 3 courses. **Credit** AmEx, DC, MC, V.
Just a few doors down from 19 Grape Lane (*see above*), Kites presents a more modern face of York dining, with shockingly red walls, wooden floors and internationally influenced dishes such as bang bang chicken or seared tuna with spiced lentil salsa. The restaurant is on the top floor, and there's a new wine bar on the ground floor.

Melton's Restaurant

7 Scarcroft Road (01904 634341/ www.meltonsrestaurant.co.uk). **Food served** 5.30-10pm Mon; noon-2pm, 5.30-10pm Tue-Sat; noon-2pm Sun. **Set lunch & early dinner** (order by 6.15pm, leave by 7.45pm) £16.50 3 courses. **Credit** MC, V.
An intimate shopfront restaurant in a quiet residential street south of the city centre, Melton's is run by husband and wife team Michael and Lucy Hjort. Inside the atmosphere is hushed, the murals depicting happy-looking diners mirroring the satisfied customers seated on banquettes below, tucking into the excellent

Ha Ha Bar – an injection of modern style.

On the town

Although a night out still mostly revolves around the pub, there are plenty of other evening and daytime activities to keep you entertained in York.

The massive dual nighclubs **Ikon & Diva** opened just outside town in 1999. The independent **City Screen** cinema shows a good range of arthouse and mainstream movies, has a Saturday morning Kids' Club, changing displays of art, a riverside bar and an Internet café. There's also an **Odeon** cinema near the railway station. The **Grand Opera House** may have seen better days, but you might be able to catch a night of the Reduced Shakespeare Company in between performances of *The Meatloaf Story* or productions of *Grease*. And the **Theatre Royal** hosts invariably excellent productions and includes an increasing number of shows for kids in its repertoire.

Classical music buffs can track down the BBC Philharmonic or the Northern Sinfonia at the university's **Central Hall & Sir Jack Lyons Concert Hall**, or investigate a recital at **National Centre for Early Music**. And for those with literary leanings, York's sizeable **Borders** bookshop hosts a series of literary events, ranging from creative writing groups and poetry readings to local ghost story tellings or Saturday night live music events.

And, of course, York is also a big horseracing town. **York Racecourse**, ust south of the city centre, hosts major flat race meetings between May and October, the biggest being the Ebor Meeting in August.

For more details of these, and other seasonal events in York, contact the Tourist Information Office.

Borders
1-5 Davygate (01904 653300/ www.borders.com). **Open** 9am-9pm Mon-Sat; 11am-6pm Sun.

Central Hall & Sir Jack Lyons Concert Hall
University of York, Heslington (01904 432439).

City Screen
Coney Street (01904 612940/ www.picturehouse-cinemas.co.uk).

Grand Opera House
Cumberland Street (01904 671818/ www.york-operahouse.co.uk).

Ikon & Diva
Stirling Way, Clifton Moor Retail Park (01904 693999/www.ikondiva.co.uk).

National Centre for Early Music
St Margaret's Church, Walmgate (information 01904 632220/ www.ncem.co.uk).

Odeon
Blossom Street (01904 623287/ 01426 954742/www.odeon.co.uk).

Theatre Royal
St Leonard's Place (01904 623568/ www.theatre-royal-york.co.uk).

York Racecourse
Tadcaster Road (01904 620911/ www.yorkracecourse.co.uk).

roster of modern European dishes. The menu changes every couple of months and offers half a dozen or so choices in each course. There might be a buckwheat blini served with beetroot and crème fraîche (£4.60) or canneloni of crab with fresh herbs (£6.70) among the starters, to be followed by calf's liver with a herb crust, Parma ham, vegetable purée and kale (£15.80) or chicory and onion tart tatin with a warm French bean salad (£12.50). Puddings are a treat: try the parfait of white chocolate with rhubarb (£4.60) or the soufflé of pannetone and Marsala with orange and honey cream (£5.80). The wine list deserves some serious attention and the mark-ups are kept to a sensible size. Even better, bottled water, filter coffee and service are all included in the price. Melton's is deservedly popular, so book in advance.

Middlethorpe Hall
Bishopthorpe Road (01904 641241/ www.middlethorpe.com). **Food served** 12.30-1.45pm, 7-9.45pm daily. **Set lunches** £14.50-£16 2 courses; £16.50-£19 3 courses. **Set dinner** £36 3 courses. **Credit** AmEx, MC, V.
If you fancy a bit of starched linen, creaking floors, classically rich cuisine and wood-panelled formality, then Middlethorpe supplies it in spades. For the set dinner you get three courses (plus canapés): perhaps including seared scallops with samphire, Sevruga caviar and thyme or terrine of foie gras with toasted brioche, followed by roast sea bass with pak choy and mussels or braised oxtail with morels and mash. Relax afterwards in the stunning drawing room. Good value, considering the quality of food and peerless setting.

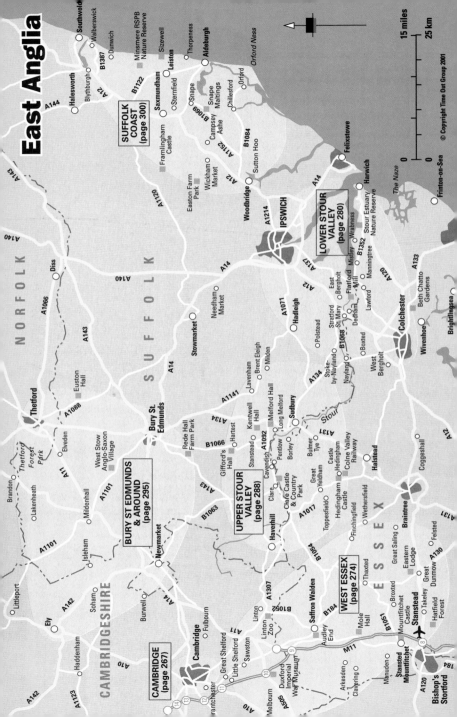

East Anglia

© Copyright Time Out Group 2001

15 miles
25 km

SUFFOLK COAST (page 300)

LOWER STOUR VALLEY (page 280)

BURY ST EDMUNDS & AROUND (page 295)

UPPER STOUR VALLEY (page 288)

WEST ESSEX (page 274)

CAMBRIDGE (page 267)

NORFOLK

SUFFOLK

CAMBRIDGESHIRE

ESSEX

The Naze

Southwold
Walberswick
Dunwich
Minsmere RSPB Nature Reserve
Sizewell
Thorpeness
Aldeburgh
Orford Ness
Leiston
Snape
Snape Maltings
Chillesford
Orford
Saxmundham
Sternfield
Campsey Ashe
Framlingham Castle
Wickham Market
Easton Farm Park
Sutton Hoo
Woodbridge
Felixstowe
Harwich
Ipswich
Stour Estuary Nature Reserve
Mistley
Wrabness
Manningtree
East Bergholt
Flatford Mill
Dedham
Lawford
Colchester
Beth Chatto Gardens
Wivenhoe
Brightlingsea
Frinton-on-Sea
Diss
Needham Market
Hadleigh
Polstead
Stratford St Mary
Boxted
West Bergholt
Stoke-by-Nayland
Nayland
Stowmarket
Lavenham
Brent Eleigh
Milden
Sudbury
Long Melford
Melford Hall
Kentwell Hall
Hartest
Bulmer Tye
Castle Hedingham
Colne Valley Railway
Halstead
Coggeshall
Thetford
Euston Hall
West Stow Anglo-Saxon Village
Elveden
Bury St Edmunds
Rede Hall Farm Park
Gifford's Hall
Stansted
Cavendish
Pentlow
Borley
Clare
Clare Castle & Country Park
Great Yeldham
Toppesfield
Finchingfield
Wethersfield
Braintree
Great Saling
Eastern Lodge
Felsted
Thetford Forest Park
Brandon
Lakenheath
Mildenhall
Newmarket
Havenhill
Hedingham Castle
Great Dunmow
Littleport
Isleham
Burwell
Soham
Ely
Haddenham
Saffron Walden
Audley End
Thaxted
Broxted
Takeley
Hatfield Forest
Stansted
Stansted Mountfitchet
Mountfitchet Castle
Bishop's Stortford
Cambridge
Fulbourn
Great Shelford
Little Shelford
Sawston
Linton
Linton Zoo
Melbourn
Arkesden
Clavering
Manuden
Grantchester
Duxford Imperial War Museum
Mole Hall
Great Saling
A11 A14 A140 A143 A134 A1088 A11 A1101 A142 A1123 A10 A141 A134 A1141 A1092 B1066 B1063 A143 A1307 A1017 B1057 B1052 B184 A1301 A505 M11 A120 A130 A131 A133 A12 A120 A137 A14 A1214 B1084 B1069 B1122 B1387 A144 A140 A1120 A1071 B1068 B1352 A131 A134

Cambridge

Colleges, commons and pastures green – a punter's paradise.

King's College and bikes – quintessential Cambridge.

There is a casual air to Cambridge that lingers in the stonework of the old town centre, that drifts in the breeze above the rippling waters of the River Cam and permeates the grassy glades that edge the town to the south and west and encroach upon parts of the centre that should, by rights, be built up with houses and roads and multi-storey car parks. This is a green and pleasant town, with a character that intermingles the lofty and distracted mind of academia (the kind that sits around waiting for an apple to drop) and the mildly more industrious life of a market town.

Cambridge stretches out across its grass commons and pastures, but the historic centre of town (where the majority of the sights are situated) is compact and easily walkable. Indeed, much of the central area is semi-pedestrianised, the red-brick roads encouraging the unwary to wander with carefree abandon. This, however, is just what the cyclists are waiting for, and with a stealthy silence they will mow you down with an equally free abandon, chiming their little bells in celebration.

Many of these bell-ringing free-wheelers are students of the university, and it is the college buildings that draw in the majority of visitors who throng here. Cambridge became a centre of learning in the 13th century, when some sort of fracas at Oxford – apparently involving a dead woman, an arrow and a scholar holding a bow – led to some of the learned minds bidding a hasty farewell to Oxford and a hearty hello to Cambridge. Cambridge was chosen because of its ecclesiastical connections – there were several orders of monks in the town and they were looked to for the provision of teachers. The first college, Peterhouse, was established in 1284 and the most recent, Robinson, was built in 1977 – a reminder that Cambridge isn't all history and is very much a thriving centre of academic (and particularly scientific) research.

By train from London

Trains run direct from **King's Cross** to **Cambridge** about four times an hour and take about **50mins**. Note that the railway station is a good mile's walk from the city centre. Info: www.wagn.co.uk.

East Anglia

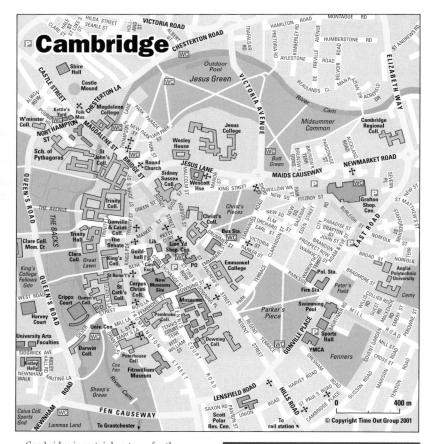

Cambridge is certainly a town for those who love architecture, and the legacy in stone includes the Saxon St Bene't Church, the late Gothic magnificence of King's College Chapel, the classicism of Christopher Wren (the Wren Library and Emmanuel College) and James Gibbs (King's College) and the modern-day polychromatic excesses of John Outram (Judge Institute of Management Studies). These buildings probably won't hold the same attraction for kids, but then, so long as the weather is fine, strolling The Backs (the cattle-grazed grasslands behind the colleges bordering the Cam), splashing about in boats and picnicking in Grantchester Meadows offer simpler and timeless pleasures.

Alternatively, if you want to pretend you're a student, hire a bike (see p269 **Bike hire**).

What to see & do

Cambridge is essentially a small, semi-rural town in a beautiful setting. There are plenty of specific sights, but it's also very pleasant to just wander around, imbibing the centuries of history and that deep-scented ambience of academia. The daily market (fruit, veg, clothes and more) is worth a nose and, unsurprisingly, there are some impressive bookshops, both second-hand and new; **Heffers** (20 Trinity Street) leads the pack. A walk along The Backs will give a sense of the pastoral side of Cambridge, and a stroll across Coe Fen from Mill Lane will take you in the direction of the Fitzwilliam Museum. For information on what's on during your visit, pick up a copy of the free weekly magazine *Ad Hoc* or visit its website, www.adhoc.co.uk/cambridge.

Tourist Information Centre

The Old Library, Wheeler Street, CB2 3QB (01223 322640/www.tourismcambridge.com). **Open** *Apr-Oct* 10am-6pm Mon, Wed-Fri; 10am-6.30pm Tue; 10am-5pm Sat; 11am-4pm Sun. *Nov-Mar* 10am-5.30pm Mon-Fri; 10am-5pm Sat.

Morning and afternoon guided walking tours (two hours, £7) usually include King's College and Chapel. The schedule and number of tours available varies depending on the time of year; ring for details.

Bike hire

Geoff's Bike Hire *65 Devonshire Road (01223 365629).*

Located near the train station (walk through the station car park, under the bridge and turn left), Geoff's has over 900 bikes for hire, mostly of the sit-up-and-beg variety, perfectly adequate for Cambridge's flat streets.

Botanic Gardens

Corey Lodge, Bateman Street (01223 336265/ www.botanic.cam.ac.uk). **Open** *Apr-Sept* 10am-6pm daily. *Nov-Mar* 10am-4pm daily. **Admission** £2; £1.50 concessions; free under-5s.

Cam punting.

Festival fever

If you visit Cambridge during term-time, you get a much better feel for that special blend of gown and town. In summer, when the students have gone, you may miss out on the hustle and bustle of university life, but there are compensations – the streets are quieter, a serenity descends on the colleges' lawns and halls – and it's festival season. Bands play and assorted shindigs happen at weekends thoughout the summer on Cambridge's green spaces, mainly Parker's Piece and Jesus Green, but the three big culture fests are the main attractions.

The most famous is the **Cambridge Folk Festival**, held for four days at the end of July. Now in its 37th year, it has a deserved reputation as Europe's leading folk festival, presenting the best of British and foreign musicians whose work falls into the multifaceted definition of folk. This year's line-up ranged from Suzanne Vega and Richard Thompson to the unmissable Peatbog Faeries. It's very popular and often sells out, so book early.

If your image of folk music is bearded hippy types shaking tambourines, then maybe you'd prefer the **Cambridge Shakespeare Festival**. Every year during July and August, six plays – mainly comedies, but with the occasional tragedy thrown in – are performed in the gardens of various colleges. The acting may not always be Oscar-quality, but if it's a warm evening, the pastoral setting and historic buildings provide a perfect backdrop to the bard's tales of romance and intrigue.

Also held in July, the ten-day **Cambridge Film Festival** – launched in 1977 – made a welcome return in 2001 after a gap of five years. Aimed at audiences rather than critics, it's an eclectic and independently minded mix of premieres, new features, revivals, documentaries and shorts, with a strong international element. Most films are shown at the recently revived three-screen Arts Picture House on St Andrews Street.

Cambridge Film Festival
Bookings 01223 504444/ www.cambridgefilmfestival.org.uk.

Cambridge Folk Festival
Information 01223 457245/booking 01223 357851/www.cam-folkfest.co.uk.

Cambridge Shakespeare Festival
64 Girton Road, Cambridge, CB3 0LN (Information 01223 511139/ bookings 01223 357851/ www.cambridgeshakespeare.com).

East Anglia

A wander around the collection at the **Fitzwilliam Museum** is sure to prove rewarding.

The Botanic Gardens belong to the university and was established in the early 19th century. The layout is quite formal for an English garden, with a broad avenue leading up to a fountain and terrace garden. The low rumble of traffic is never far away, however, so if you simply want to escape the rigours of city life, a walk along the towpath to the meadows is a better option. If you're into botany, however, the alkaline soil here supports plants of a contrasting nature to those at Kew and Edinburgh.

Colleges of Cambridge University

Each of the 31 colleges is independently run and the cost and times for being allowed to wander through the hallowed halls and around the green courtyards vary from college to college. What you can expect for your money also varies greatly, from the splendour of **Trinity** (one of the largest), the elegance of Wren's **Emmanuel College** and the magnificent gatehouse of St John's to the dreary **Clare College**. There are many restrictions imposed upon visitors (which parts of the colleges are accessible, and so on), and during exam time (May and early June) most colleges are closed to the public while students get their heads down. So don't go expecting to see more than a veneer of university life. However, the colleges have a palpable sense of history and tradition, and it's fun to conjure up the great names of the past who would have passed this way – a young Lord Byron bathing in the fountain at Trinity with his pet bear (regulations forbade the keeping of a dog); Wittgenstein reclining in his deckchair; Wordsworth skipping lectures at St John's; and Newton, sitting on the grass outside the gate of Trinity, still waiting for that apple to drop. Check out the colleges' website at www.cam.ac.uk.

Fitzwilliam Museum

Trumpington Street (01223 332900/ www.fitzmuseum.cam.ac.uk). **Open** 10am-5pm Tue-Sat; 2.15-5pm Sun. **Admission** free; donations welcome.

This is a wonderfully diverse and much under-visited museum. There's something for everyone, including painting, sculpture, antiquities from Egypt, Greece and Rome, furniture, armour, textiles, fans and a fantastic ceramics collection. The Egyptian collection is a highlight; besides some great funerary gear, it includes surprising smaller finds, such as a broken section of frieze depicting a jackal attacking a duck's nest and the blue-glazed snout of a hippopotamus. Among the great paintings in the collection are a portable altarpiece by Fra Filippo Lippi, some Rubens oil sketches and Joos van Cleve's *Virgin and Child*. From January 2002, only the main building will be open as construction begins on the Courtyard Development to provide more gallery space and a new shop and café. Work is expected to last 18 months.

Kettle's Yard

Castle Street (01223 352124/www.kettlesyard.co.uk). **Open** *House* Apr-Sept 1.30-4.30pm Tue-Sun, bank hols. Oct-Mar 2-4pm Tue-Sun. *Gallery* 11.30am-5pm Tue-Sun, bank hols. **Admission** free.
Located to the north of the town centre, just a short stroll over Magdalene Bridge, Kettle's Yard was founded in 1957 as 'a refuge of peace and order, of the visual arts and of music'. It comprises a house with a collection of 20th-century artworks, among them works by Ben and Winifred Nicholson, Brancusi, Miró and Hepworth, and an art gallery with a changing programme of contemporary and modern art. Phone for details of chamber music concerts held in the house.

King's College Chapel

King's Parade (01223 331250/ www.kings.cam.ac.uk). **Open** *Term-time* 9.30am-3.30pm Mon-Sat; 1.15-2.15 Sun. *Holidays* 9.30am-4.30pm Mon-Sat; 10am-5pm Sun. **Services** (term-time) 5.30pm Mon-Sat; 10.30am, 3.30pm or 6pm Sun. **Admission** £3.50; £2 concessions; free under-12s. Services free.

Cambridge's most famous building, this long, thin chapel was funded by not one king but many, including Henry VIII, who was responsible for the ornate Tudor decoration of the ante-chapel and the magnificent stained glass. His initials (and those of his then wife, Anne Boleyn) are carved into the dark oak screen that divides the building in two. The narrowness of the chapel emphasises its height to great effect, as do the slender, linear columns that stretch up to an explosion of fan vaulting – a Perpendicular Gothic extravagance that has no equal in Britain. Rubens' *Adoration of the Magi* (1634) stands next to the altar. If you visit in term-time, be sure to attend a service, when the choirboys' otherworldly voices provide a sublime counterpoint to the beauty of the building.

Punting on the Cam

This slow-paced means of transport is ideal for casting a leisurely eye over the colleges, their manicured gardens and the bridges that link the town to the country. In fact, in May and June, when the colleges are closed to the public, it's the only way to see The Backs properly. It's not as easy as it looks, of course, and to avoid the embarrassment of taking an unexpected dip, you can hire a chauffeured punt. This is quite a good idea (though costlier) as chauffeurs double as guides to the colleges and bridges, such as the Bridge of Sighs (a copy of the Venetian original) and the Mathematical Bridge (now in its third incarnation since it was first built in the mid 18th century). You can also punt to the tiny village of Grantchester, two miles upriver, famous for its association with Rupert Brooke and his poem about the Old Vicarage (now the home of disgraced Tory lord and novelist Jeffrey Archer). Punts are available (April to October daily, November to April weekends only) at various points along the river, though most are hired from Granta Place at the end of Mill Lane. Self-hire punts cost around £10 per hour; rates for chauffered punts are higher and depend on the number of passengers.

Round Church (Church of the Holy Sepulchre)

Bridge Street (01223 311602/
www.christianheritageuk.org.uk).
Open 10am-5pm daily. **Admission** free.
A 12th-century medieval church, although its Norman appearance is a style given to it much later (in the 19th century) by some overzealous restorers. Its circular format is very rare in Britain and was based upon the Church of the Holy Sepulchre in Jerusalem.

St Bene't Church

Bene't Street (01223 353903).
Open 8.30am-6pm daily. **Admission** free.
With its Saxon tower, St Bene't (a contraction of St Benedict) is the oldest surviving building in Cambridge. It was the original chapel of Corpus Christi College and is handily located just opposite the Eagle pub and the Bath Ale House.

Where to stay

Cambridge is notoriously lacking in classy accommodation in all price brackets. The arrival of the **Meadowcroft Hotel** (*see p272*) has improved the pricier options, but many of

the B&Bs are functional and rather dull. We've tried to pick out the best in all categories, but it still doesn't pay to have too high expectations here. Despite this, beds are often in short supply, so book ahead. The Tourist Information Centre runs an accommodation booking service (for a fee), but you need to give them five days notice if you're not there in person.

46 Panton Street

46 Panton Street, CB2 1HS (01223 365285/
fax 01223 461142). **Rates** £69 double/twin.
Rooms 1 double (en suite); 1 twin. **Credit** MC, V.
This small and pretty 19th-century terraced house is on a quiet street just around the corner from the Botanic Gardens. There's a pleasant-looking pub with a garden across the road and the town centre is no more than a ten-minute walk away. The proprietor, Alice Percival, is clearly proud of her elegant and well-maintained rooms, and this is very much a place for a quiet and sedate stay. There are only two rooms, which obviously makes for an intimate atmosphere, and there are no communal areas, so guests are asked to vacate the property during the day. Book well ahead, especially for weekends, as it's very popular. No smoking throughout.

Arundel House Hotel

53 Chesterton Road, CB4 3AN (01223 367701/fax
01223 367721). **Rates** £57.50-£82.50 single; £72.50-
£105 double/twin; £98-£120 family. Breakfast free
(cont); £5.95 (Eng). **Rooms** (all en suite) 40 single;
65 double/twin; 6 family. **Credit** AmEx, DC, MC, V.

Fan vaulting in **King's College Chapel**.

Arundel House receives a lot of recommendations, but this must be more for its proximity to the centre of town (five minutes' walk) and views from the north bank of the River Cam over Jesus Green than for the bedrooms, which feature uninspiring expanses of magnolia porridge paper. Also, staff can be a bit offhand and the prices are on the steep side. An old coaching inn at the back of the building contains 22 bedrooms and conference facilities; the rooms are a little fresher than those in the main building. Children welcome. All bedrooms no smoking.

Crowne Plaza

Downing Street, CB2 3DT (01223 464466/fax 01223 464440). **Rates** £122-£157 single occupancy; £149 double/twin; £156-£164 deluxe double/twin; £174-£187 suite. Breakfast £11.95 (cont/Eng). **Rooms** (all en suite) 141 double/twin; 18 deluxe double/twin; 6 suites. **Credit** AmEx, DC, MC, V.
The façade of this large hotel, plumb in the centre of town, is a mild-mannered piece of 1980s neo-classicism, which more or less sets the tone for what you find inside – an atmosphere that, like Switzerland, is keen to maintain its neutrality. Formerly a Holiday Inn, the hotel has been upgraded and completely refurbished and redecorated. Its size – 165 rooms – precludes intimacy; its principal attractions are location and the guarantee of a certain standard, including pristine air-conditioned rooms. There is, of course, a restaurant and a (well-patronised) bar. Most rooms are no-smoking; some are fully equipped for disabled drivers. Children welcome.

Meadowcroft Hotel

16 Trumpington Road, CB2 2EX (01223 346120/fax 01223 346138/ www.meadowcrofthotel.co.uk). **Rates** £95 single; £130-£150 double/twin (weekend rate £110 per night, 2 nights min); £150 family. **Rooms** (all en suite) 9 doubles; 3 twins. **Credit** AmEx, MC, V.
Opened in July 2000, this attractive red-brick hotel is a welcome – and much-needed – addition to Cambridge's accommodation scene. In fact, its elegant rooms, spacious lounge and bar, original Victorian features and Brackenhurst Restaurant (open to non-guests for lunch and dinner) put it head and shoulders above the competition. The 12 rooms are all decorated differently, with the emphasis on bold florals, and vary in size: the biggest are Bengal and Mayfield, which also have four-poster beds. Three other rooms have tester beds. Bonuses include the huge garden at the back and plenty of parking at the front. It's further out than some hotels – about a mile from the city centre – but it's a pleasant walk. Children welcome. Pets by arrangement. No smoking throughout.

Sleeperz Hotel

Station Road, CB1 2TZ (01223 304050/fax 01223 357286/www.sleeperz.com). **Rates** £30-£35 single; £45 twin; £55 double; £65 triple. **Rooms** (all en suite) 4 double; 20 twin; 1 triple. **Credit** MC, V.
Formerly a granary, this newish hotel, bang next to the station, has made remarkable use of space, creating simple modern cells influenced in equal measure by Scandinavia and Japan. Each tiny room, in which the swing of a cat would result in a swift call from the RSPCA, has an en suite shower, small portable TV and phone. Twin rooms make use of space-saving bunks,

Beds are made for **Sleeperz**.

while doubles have futon bases with more substantial mattresses. Sleeperz is ideal for youngish or just youthful visitors who don't have much luggage and will be out and about for most of the day and evening. It offers excellent value for money. Children and pets welcome. No-smoking throughout.

Suffolk House

69 Milton Road, CB4 1XA (01223 352016/fax 01223 566816). **Rates** £65-£80 double/twin; £75-£90 family. **Rooms** (all en suite) 2 double; 2 twin; 4 family. **Credit** AmEx, MC, V.
Suffolk House is one of many undistinguished B&Bs on roads towards the edge of the town centre. Milton Road is to the north and the guesthouse is equidistant from the Grafton Shopping Centre and the heart of Cambridge (about a 15-minute walk to each). The rooms are clean and tidy with floral print wallpaper and a few prints of the Cambridge colleges dotted around. The breakfast room looks out over a surprisingly large and attractive garden. All rooms have TVs. Children over 10 welcome. No smoking throughout.

Where to eat & drink

Surprisingly for a town with so much wealth splashing around, there are few really good restaurants in Cambridge. In fact, if the weather is fine, a picnic assembled from the various delis, bakeries and wine merchants in the centre of town and taken to The Backs or Grantchester Meadows is the ideal way to enjoy a leisurely lunch or early evening meal. That said, there are of course exceptions to the rule, **Midsummer House Restaurant** (*see p273*), with its pleasant location alongside the Cam, being the most notable. If you want your spending to be rather more modest, it's worth knowing that there's a **Café Rouge** on Bridge Street opposite St John's College (01223 364961), and a **Dôme** right next to the Varsity (*see p273*) on St Andrew's Street (01223 313818). A branch of **Chez Gerard** (01223 448620) opened in summer 2001 next door to Café Rouge, and the French menu at the brand-new **Brackenhurst Restaurant** (inside the Meadowcroft Hotel, *see above*) looks promising.

Alternatively, if you just want something basic to eat, perhaps accompanied by some of the rather good Suffolk ales that are served hereabouts, then it is as well to stick to a pub. You can usually get a meal for about a fiver in various creaky old inns with uneven floorboards and scalp-scraping beams. The **Eagle** on Bene't Street (01223 505020) is the one that usually receives all the plaudits, but in truth there are many of equal merit, including the **Pickerel Inn** at 30 Magdalene Street just to the north of the bridge (01223 355068), **Fort St George** by the river on Midsummer Common (01223 354327), the **Mill** (01223 357026) and the **Anchor** (01223 353554), which are practically next door to each other on the river between Granta Place and Silver Street, and **Bath Ale House**, opposite the Saxon church back on Bene't Street (01223 350969).

22 Chesterton Road

22 Chesterton Road (01223 351880/ www.restaurant22.co.uk). **Food served** 7-9.45pm Tue-Sat. **Set dinner** £24.50 4 courses. **Credit** AmEx, DC, MC, V.
This tiny, candlelit restaurant close to the Cam offers an adventurous, globally influenced menu. Not everything comes off, but there are more hits than misses, and a very good wine list. Examples of mains include roast skate wings with pancetta, capers and herbs, and broad bean, pea and celery risotto; desserts can include pavlova with summer berries. The menu changes monthly.

Copper Kettle

4 King's Parade (01223 365068). **Food served** 11.30am-2.30pm Mon-Sat; 9am-5.30pm Sun. **No credit cards.**
This slightly shabby, old-fashioned place just beyond the shadow of King's College Chapel is not actually a restaurant, but it's a good place for tea and cakes. The view from the glass-fronted room takes in the fanciful gateway to the courtyard of King's College and the James Gibbs neo-classical building beyond.

Dojo Noodle Bar

1-2 Miller's Yard, Mill Lane (01223 363471/ www.dojonoodlebar.co.uk). **Food served** noon-2.30pm, 5.30-11pm Mon-Thur; noon-4pm, 5.30-11pm Fri-Sun. **Credit** MC, V.
Essentially a Japanese restaurant with the emphasis on noodles, the menu at Dojo extends around the Pacific Rim to take in a smattering of Chinese fry-ups and one or two Thai-style dishes. Portions are generous and the fresh and tasty noodle soups are particularly good. The small interior is simple and geometric, with shared bench seating, Wagamama-style, plus some tables in the courtyard outside. A starter, main course and an Asahi shouldn't set you back more than £12.

Loch Fyne Oyster Restaurant

37 Trumpington Street (01223 362433/www.loch-fyne.com). **Food served** 9am-10pm Mon-Fri; 9am-10.30pm Sat; 10am-9.30pm Sun. **Set lunch** £9.95 2 courses. **Credit** AmEx, MC, V.
Handily located opposite the Fitzwilliam Museum, this is one of a (steadily growing) handful of offshoots of the Loch Fyne Oyster Bar in western Scotland – which is where the smokehouse and oyster beds for this and the other restaurants are situated. It's an informal place, with pale wood dominating the capacious beamed interior, and you are welcome to pick and mix your dishes

from across the menu. As well as Loch Fyne's own oysters (£1 each) and plenty of salmon, there are rustic soups and sumptuous, if slightly daunting, shellfish platters served on ice (£21.95). The lunch specials are an especially good deal.

Michel's

21-24 Northampton Street (01223 353110). **Food served** noon-2.30pm, 6-10pm daily. **Set lunch** £6.95 2 courses; £8.45 3 courses. **Credit** AmEx, DC, MC, V.
This is a bright and breezy restaurant, just to the north of Magdalene Bridge and, therefore, outside the throng of the town centre. It has two pleasant rooms at the front, one at the back and a wine bar upstairs (usually open on weekend evenings).The modern European menu has a hankering for Italy, with a predominance of healthy foods such as fish, pasta and chicken. The lunchtime set meals are a bargain.

Midsummer House Restaurant

Midsummer Common (01223 369299/ www.midsummerhouse.co.uk). **Food served** noon-2pm, 7-10pm Tue-Sat. **Set lunches** £15 2 courses; £20 3 courses. **Set dinner** £42 4 courses. **Credit** AmEx, MC, V.
Midsummer House is a great restaurant by any standards, and in Cambridge it stands out a mile, enticingly sited on the northern edge of Midsummer Common by the banks of the Cam. Bright and modern in design, there's seating in the original house, the large, light conservatory and a garden. The inventive menu offers a short selection of mainly French-influenced dishes; the wine list is extensive, and the choice of house wines (six red, six white) starts at £12. Service is formal but friendly, and a passion for food is evident (waiters are keen to explain the nuances of every dish). Vegetarian meals are cooked on request, but it's a good idea to call ahead of time to ensure a decent choice.

Rainbow Café

9A King's Parade (01223 321551/ www.rainbowcafe.co.uk). **Food served** 11am-10.30pm Mon-Sat. **Credit** MC, V.
A small, pink-walled vegetarian café, tucked away in a basement down an alley opposite King's College. As well as the usual soups, salads and baked potatoes, there are more substantial mains (all £6.75) such as a hearty Moroccan-style tagine and Latvian potato bake. All dishes are vegetarian, some are vegan, and there are also gluten-free cakes (£2.95), soy ice-cream and organic wine, beer and cider.

Varsity

35 St Andrew's Street (01223 356060). **Food served** noon-2.30pm, 5.30-10.45pm daily. **Credit** AmEx, DC, MC, V.
This friendly Cypriot restaurant, located south from the town centre on the road to the station, has been on the same site and in the same family since 1954 – so they know what they're doing. The set vegetable meze (£10.95, minimum two people) gives vegetarians a fair number of options, and there's plenty of chicken, steak and kebabs for the more carnivorous. The decor is simple, with plenty of exposed wood and plain white walls and a scattering of mirrors and glass to add an illusion of space.

West Essex

Utterly endearing Uttlesford.

This part of Essex (sometimes known as 'Uttlesford') runs along a north–south axis that takes in the area's three principal towns – Saffron Walden, Thaxted and Great Dunmow. Take virtually any road out of these towns and you will pass through a series of picturesque little villages, each exhibiting the classic elements of our assumed past: thatched wooden cottages; windmills; winding lanes; and obscure, not to say eccentric, traditions. By the 18th century fortunes were ultimately tied to agriculture, and the Industrial Revolution passed the area by almost completely, ensuring that a rustic tranquillity can still be found in this corner of East Anglia.

Saffron Walden was something of a boom town in the Middle Ages, benefiting from its proximity to Roman trade routes and its agricultural resources. And, with additional wealth from ephemeral moneyspinners such as saffron and cutlery, there was extra cash to throw around. Evidence of those medieval good times is still plentiful today, in the form of orderly market towns, sprawling manor houses and extravagantly well-appointed churches, and the largely intact patchwork of rolling countryside and ancient forests. It's not brimming with things to do as such (theme parks and shopping complexes are thankfully absent), but with innumerable public footpaths, quiet roads and large tracts of common land, it's ideal country for walking, cycling or even horse riding.

The town that saffron built

Saffron Walden dates back to pre-Roman times, and received its name and much of its wealth from the saffron crocus (the town was originally called Chipping Walden), which was prized for its colouring, flavouring and medicinal applications. Uttlesford was the national saffron centre between the 15th and 18th centuries, until explorers discovered it could be obtained abroad for a fraction of the price. Now a Conservation Area, Saffron Walden's compact centre hasn't changed much since those times, consisting of a central Market Square (there's still a market on Tuesdays and Saturdays) surrounded by narrow lanes (now dominated by antiques shops, as much of the region seems to be) and thinning out to generous townhouses towards the outskirts.

Some 400 wobbly, oak-framed and wattle-and-daubed buildings survive, displaying characteristics you'll find throughout the region such as overhanging upper storeys and pastel-coloured plasterwork with ornate patterns known as pargeting (*see p277* **Parget practice**). There's also late Georgian and Victorian architecture, particularly the Italianate Corn Exchange (now the library) in Market Square. East of the square, on the ancient common, is an even older relic – the turf maze, said to be the largest in the country and to date back more than 800 years. It's more than a mile long in total, and not as easy to master as it looks, nor as dramatic a sight as one might hope. St Mary's church is worth a visit; as with many of the towns round here, it's large and imposing, and has the town's history written in its stones and interior decoration. There's also a Victorian hedge maze, modelled on Hampton Court's, in the attractive Bridge End Gardens, though an appointment is required (contact the Tourist Information Centre, *see p276*).

Essex crop tops.

Audley End House and guests.

Music and morris dancing

Ten minutes down the B184, **Thaxted** has a similar history and make-up to Saffron Walden, but fewer 20th-century interventions like high street stores and banks. It has been consistently praised over the years as one of the most charming villages in the country; John Betjeman admired its 'beauty, compactness and juxtaposition of medieval and Georgian architecture', composer Gustav Holst completed *The Planets* here (the music festival he originated still takes place here in June and July; 01371 831421), and many London émigrés have decamped to Thaxted, adding a cosmopolitan edge to its friendly, everyone-knows-everyone atmosphere. A precarious three-storey Guildhall is the town's centrepiece, and one of the best surviving examples in the country, although its widely touted connection with the Cutlers' Guild is disputed by some historians. On the hill behind it, near to John Webb's windmill (not open, but worth the glimpse), the magnificent 14th-century church is another source of local pride (the finest in England, they'll tell you), with a white-painted perpendicular-arched interior and intricately carved ceiling. The light is uplifting, and even the graveyard is pretty. The vicar in the 1920s, Conrad Noel, is remembered for running up the communist and Sinn Fein flags and slashing the tyres of incensed protesters. Noel's wife, however, was instrumental in turning the village into a morris-dancing mecca – dancers still strut their stuff in the town every bank holiday Monday, although the chief festival is a 'Morris Weekend' on the first weekend after the Spring Bank Holiday.

Bacon rituals

Carry on south down the same road and you'll reach **Great Dunmow**, another ancient market town, similar to Saffron Walden and Thaxted, although lacking their cosy beauty. Great Dunmow's claim to fame is the Flitch Trials, in which a flitch (side) of bacon is awarded to couples who manage not to 'quarrel, differ or dispute' for a year and a day after their marriage. They are then paraded through town on the 'bacon chair', which sits in Little Dunmow parish church. The none-too-serious custom dates back to the 12th century and was revived this century, taking place every leap year.

Once you have savoured the town's delights, it is well worth striking out into the countryside east and west of the B184. There are innumerable stereotypically lovely villages hereabouts, most notably **Clavering**, **Manuden** and **Hazel End**, along the Stort Valley to the west of the M11, and **Linton** and **Melbourn**, just south of Cambridge. East of Thaxted, complete with duck pond, river, windmill and village green, **Finchingfield** is commonly labelled 'the most photogenic village in Essex', if not necessarily the most peaceful. The area is popular with motorcyclists, who like to congregate in the village after speeding through these otherwise serene country roads of a weekend, much to the retired villagers' consternation.

By train from London

The nearest station to **Saffron Walden** is **Audley End**, two miles away; about four trains an hour go there direct from **Liverpool Street**. The journey takes between **50mins** and **1hr**. Info: www.wagn.co.uk.

East Anglia

Duxford Imperial War Museum – plain joy.

you all you need to know. Phone to book a guided tour (October only). Opposite, there's a miniature railway through Lord Braybrooke's estate woodland (separate admission; 01799 541354).

Duxford Imperial War Museum
Duxford Airfield, Duxford (01223 835000/ www.iwm.org.uk). **Open** *Apr-Oct* 10am-6pm daily. *Nov-Mar* 10am-4pm daily. **Admission** £7.70; £3.70-£5.40 concessions; free under-16s.
Aviation heaven, with over 150 historic aircraft from biplanes to Spitfires to Concorde. Norman Foster designed an award-winning building here to house the American Air Force collection, including a B52. Air shows throughout the summer.

Flitch Way
A good route for walking, cycling or riding, along 15 miles of disused railway line from Hatfield Forest through Great Dunmow to Braintree. Wild flowers and animals as well as Victorian railway architecture. Get the tourist office at Great Dunmow (*see above*) to send you a leaflet.

Fry Art Gallery
Off Castle Street, Saffron Walden (01799 513779/ www.uttlesford.gov.uk). **Open** *Easter-July, Oct* 2.30-5.30pm Sat, Sun. *Aug, Sept* 2.30-5.30pm Tue, Sat, Sun, bank hols. Closed Nov-Easter. **Admission** free.
Paintings, prints, and ceramics by local artists including Eric Ravilious, Edward Bawden and Michael Rothstein.

Gardens of Easton Lodge
Little Easton, Great Dunmow, CM6 2BB (01371 876979/www.eastonlodge.co.uk). **Open** *Easter-Oct* noon-6pm Fri-Sun, bank hols; or by appointment. *Feb, Mar* times vary; phone to check. Closed Nov-Jan. **Admission** £3.80; £1. 50-£3.50 concessions; free under-3s.
Since the 1970s, the Creaseys have been restoring the gardens originally laid out at the beginning of the 20th century by Harold Peto. There was once a royal hunting lodge here, but both the Elizabethan and Jacobean wings have been largely lost to fires. Now, it's more the gardens that you come to see. There's a dovecote, a tree-house, an Italian garden and a glade, and of course, cream teas. The place also opens up for the snowdrops in February and March – phone for details.

Hatfield Forest
Takeley, off A120 (01279 870678/ www.nationaltrust.org.uk). **Open** *Forest* free access throughout the year. *Car park* Easter-Oct 10am-5pm daily. Closed Nov-Easter. **Admission** (NT) *Car park* £3 per car.
A former medieval royal hunting forest, now a pleasant woodland and nature reserve with plenty of 400-year-old pollarded trees and ornamental lakes. Unfortunately the 18th-century Shell House is closed as it is undergoing a long renovation project.

Linton Zoo
Hadstock Road, Linton (01223 891308). **Open** *Apr-Oct* 10am-6pm daily. *Nov-Mar* 10am-dusk daily. **Admission** £5.50; £4.50-£5 concessions.
Conservation-oriented zoo with an emphasis on breeding. There are big cats, including white tigers and snow leopards, and other exotic creatures.

What to see & do

Tourist Information Centres
District Council Offices, 46 High Street, Great Dunmow, CM6 1AN (01799 510490). **Open** 8.30am-5pm Mon-Thur; 8.30am-4.30pm Fri.
1 Market Place, Saffron Walden, CB10 1HR (01799 510444/www.uttlesford.gov.uk). **Open** *Apr-Oct* 9.30am-5.30pm Mon-Sat. *Nov-Mar* 10am-5pm Mon-Sat.

Audley End House & Gardens
Saffron Walden (01799 522399/www.english-heritage.org.uk). **Open** *House* Apr-Sept noon-4pm Wed-Sun, bank hol Mon. Oct guided tours only 10am-3pm Wed-Sun. Closed Nov-Mar. *Gardens* Apr-Sept 11am-5pm Wed-Sun, bank hols. Closed Oct-Mar. **Admission** (EH) *House & gardens* £6.75; £3.40-£5.10 concessions. *Gardens only* £4; £2-£3 concessions; free under-5s.
An unmissable Jacobean house on the grandest of scales, Audley End is brimming with the accumulated wealth of successive aristocratic owners. Opulent furnishings, priceless books and artworks (Holbein, Lely and Canaletto are among the featured artists) and a monumental collection of stuffed birds and animals fill the rooms, while other highlights include an elegant suite of rooms designed by Robert Adam and a magical chapel above the Great Hall. The grounds were landscaped by 'Capability' Brown around the River Cam, which runs along the bottom of the front lawn. There are no dry information labels; a guide in each room tells

Mole Hall Wildlife Park

*Widdington, nr Newport, Saffron Walden
(01799 540400/www.molehall.co.uk).* **Open** *Apr-Oct*
10.30am-6pm daily. *Nov-Mar* 10.30am-dusk daily.
Admission £5; £3.50-£4 concessions; free under-3s.
Kid-friendly, family-run wildlife park in 20 acres of
grounds surrounding a moated manor house. Among
the species present are small monkeys, deer, otters,
reptiles and the Butterfly Pavilion (closed in winter).

Mountfitchet Castle & House on the Hill Toy Museum

*Stansted Mountfitchet (01279 813237/
www.gold.enta.net).* **Open** *Castle* mid Mar-mid Nov
10am-5pm daily. Closed mid Nov-mid Mar.
Museum 10am-5pm daily. **Admission** *Castle*
£4.80; £3.80-£4 concessions. *Museum* £3.80;
£2.80-£3.50 concessions.
Award-winning reconstructed Norman motte and bailey castle and village built on an original site, complete
with siege weapons and retro farm animals. The adjacent toy museum has over 50,000 exhibits, including a
museum of slot machines.

Saffron Walden Museum

Museum Street, Saffron Walden (01799 510333).
Open *Mar-Oct* 10am-5pm Mon-Sat; 2-5pm Sun. *Nov-
Feb* 10am-4.30pm Mon-Sat; 2-4.30pm Sun, bank hols.
Admission £1; 50p concessions; free under-16s.
Good local history from the year dot onwards, plus
anthropological, geological and costume exhibitions.
Adjacent to the remains of the Norman castle keep.

Where to stay

In this area, large hotels are uncommon, and
even B&Bs are relatively thin on the ground
and consequently fill up rapidly during the
summer. Furthermore, many establishments
prefer the weekday business market, and
reclaim their privacy at the weekends. Below
are some that are amenable to weekend guests.

In Saffron Walden there's the slightly ageing
Saffron Hotel (10-12 High Street; 01799
522676; doubles £80), or if you just want a bed,

Parget practice

Today we have pebble-dash and fake
brick cladding to beautify our properties.
But a brief wander past the rendered
street fronts of the historic townhouses
in this neck of the woods will reveal
a more ancient art, more
pleasing to the eye and
infinitely more varied.
Pargeting can be seen
everywhere, but particularly
fine examples can be found
on the houses lining Watling
Street in Thaxted, and on
the Sun Inn in Church
Street, Saffron Walden.

The carved, moulded and
stamped designs on the
plasterwork façades of
these towns' timber-framed
buildings are for the most
part the work of 16th- and
17th-century pargetors,
skilled craftsmen employed by the
wealthy wool merchants of the time to
decorate their homes. Some patterns are
combed, some are wood-block stamped;
in some cases you'll find initials, friezes,
herringbone patterns or cartouches;
some are just plainer stippling and
spiralling, all gashes and curls. Often
sections of pargeting are framed,
creating a series of panels to decorate
the space between windows and timbers.

The most respected pargetors worked
freehand, reinforcing their plaster mix
with anything from wood scrapings to
beer or cheese to help shape and hold
the design. Styles varied partly according
to the status of the house
and its owner. On the more
formal town buildings
moulded friezes depicting
oak leafs, vines or
honeysuckle reflect the
influence of continental
styles, while some of the
more low-key markings
suggest either a pargetor
of average skill, and/or a
homeowner of more
mediocre means.

Origins of the word are
not certain. It may have
come from the old French
par jeter, to throw over a
surface; or from the Italian noun *parge*,
a plaster mix of cow-dung, horse-hair,
lime, mud and sand.

As this ancient form of house
decoration begins to gather renewed
interest in Uttlesford, the local council
is keen to dissuade amateurs from
experimenting, explaining that modern
materials are less suited to the art.
'Don't try this at home', seems to
be the message.

East Anglia

try the wonderful 14th-century building now run by the **Youth Hostel Association** (1 Middleton Place; 01799 523117; ring for details). If you don't smoke, they'll welcome you warmly at **Purlins** (12 High Street, Little Shelford; 01223 842643; doubles £46), a modern house with a large garden; and in Great Dunmow, the **Starr Inn** (*see p279*) is a safe if slightly pricey option.

Archway Guest House

Church Street, Saffron Walden, CB10 1JW (01799 501500/fax 01799 506003). **Rates** £30 single; £50 double/twin; £65-£75 suite/family. **Rooms** 1 single; 5 double/twin; 1 suite/family. **No credit cards.**

This Georgian-fronted building is a quirky B&B opposite St Mary's church. There's a friendly and eccentric atmosphere here, not least because it's decorated from top to bottom by rock memorabilia and antique toys. It's almost as if you're stepping over them, which you may have to do if you choose to play the original '60s jukebox. The rooms are more discreet, (they aren't snowed under with memorabilia), but they remain bright and lively nevertheless, and the position in Saffron Walden is perfect. Book early. Children are welcome, but not pets. No smoking throughout.

Crossways Guest House

32 Town Street, Thaxted, CM6 2LA (01371 830348). **Rates** £35 single occupancy; £53 double/twin. **Rooms** (all en suite) 2 double; 1 double/twin. **No credit cards.**

The real attraction of this 16th-century townhouse is that it is centrally located just opposite the Guildhall in beautiful old wool-town of Thaxted. Proprietors Michael and Pepe have been in the business for 20 years, and have their presentation and unpretentious cooking down to a T. There are two double rooms upstairs overlooking the high street – smart and clean, but not especially large – and an adjoining lodge in the back garden with a twin/double, all with decor that stops just short of kitsch. It's nothing spectacular, but it's a perfect base from which to explore the area. There's also a pleasant and popular tearoom at the front. Children welcome. All bedrooms no-smoking.

Homelye Farm

off Braintree Road, Great Dunmow, CM6 3AW (01371 872127/fax 01371 876428/ www.homelyefarm.com). **Rates** £30 single; £50 double/twin; £85 family. **Rooms** (all en suite) 3 single; 3 double; 2 twin; 1 family. **Credit** MC, V.

This matter-of-fact B&B stands in an exposed and isolated working farmstead on the crown of a hill just off the A120, although it is only ten minutes from Stansted Airport. The simple, clean and relatively spacious rooms are in a converted stable block next to the house, so you can easily come and go as you please. The wholesome English breakfast is served in the farmhouse itself, although in summer guests can eat al fresco in a small meadow looking over the rolling fields. There's no traffic (the farm is at the end of a lane), so it's good for children, and the Pickford family will happily provide a tour of the farm. Children welcome. No smoking throughout.

1 mile E of Great Dunmow off A120; turn into lane opposite water tower; farm is at bottom of lane.

Wander and wonder in **Thaxted**'s lanes.

Springfield

16 Horn Lane, Linton, CB1 6HT (01223 891383/ fax 01223 890335/www.smoothhound.co.uk/ hotels/springf2.html). **Rates** £20-£25 per person. **Rooms** 2 double (1 en suite). **No credit cards.**

This welcoming and relaxed B&B is in an elegant converted Victorian schoolhouse in a quiet corner of a historic village. It isn't plush, but the house has a charming lived-in feel, and the grounds are homely. Two airy double bedrooms (another twin is available at a push) look out on to a pretty river at the bottom of extensive gardens. Guests also have their own dining room (in a plant-filled conservatory) and lounge downstairs, and there's a grass tennis court in the garden. Serene proprietor Judith Rossiter lives here with dog and children, and can arrange horse riding on the nearby Ickield Way. Meals other than breakfast are not provided, but there is decent food available at the Crown Inn around the corner. Children welcome. No smoking throughout.

Approaching Linton along A1307 SW of Cambridge; left into High Street then first right after the Crown pub into Horn Lane; house on right next to chapel.

Whitehall Hotel

Church End, Broxted, CM6 2BZ (01279 850603/fax 01279 850385/www.whitehallhotel.co.uk). **Rates** £98 single; £125 double/twin; £150 deluxe double; £195-£220 suite. Breakfast £11 (Eng); £7 (cont). Special breaks. **Rooms** (all en suite) 5 twin; 14 double; 6 deluxe double; 1 suite. **Credit** AmEx, DC, MC, V.

This sprawling Elizabethan manor house provides some of the most luxurious accommodation in the area. Rooms are individually named; those in the original house are more pleasant than those in the new extension (exposed beams and oak panelling, and a stone fireplace in the Garden Room), although they are all spacious with good views over the well-maintained gardens. The restaurant, bar and lounge areas are similarly well appointed, especially the double-height banquet hall with its exposed studwork. Special weekend food-and-board packages are a good option if you've just come to put your feet up and relax. It is close to a flight path to Stanstead, and your stay might clash with a wedding, but the comfort level is high. Children welcome.

Take A120 E of Stansted Airport; follow signs for Broxted.

Where to eat & drink

You won't need to drive far in this area to find a decent country pub, though you might have trouble finding a specific destination in this maze of country lanes. Fine dining, as you'd expect, is thinner on the ground, but not altogether absent.

In addition to the places below, there's good grub at the 16th-century **Cricketers** in Clavering (01799 550442) and good drinking at the **Flitch of Bacon** in Little Dunmow, and the **Eight Bells** in Saffron Walden. The **Bell** in Wendens Ambo has a large garden and good animal-petting opportunities. The **Sheene Mill** (Melbourn; 01763 261393), owned by TV chef Steven Saunders, is 12 or so miles southwest of Cambridge and is a local destination dining spot.

Axe & Compasses

Arkesden (01799 550272). **Food served** noon-2pm, 6.45-9.30pm daily. **Set lunch** (Sun) £15 3 courses. **Credit** MC, V.

Situated in an attractive corner of the middle of nowhere, the Axe is local favourite, renowned for both its relaxed atmosphere and exceptional food. It's a thatched 17th-century building, divided into several spaces, with dark beams, polished brasses, horse paraphernalia and open fireplaces. You can eat in either the restaurant or the bar, choosing from the carte or blackboard menus. The range is extensive. Starters (£3-£3.50) run from breaded brie to home-made chicken liver pâté; mains (£7.95-£15.50) in the restaurant could include wild Barbary duck, tournedos rossini, or prawns in cream cheese sauce. The steak and kidney pudding is excellent.

Dicken's Brasserie

The Green, Wethersfield (01371 850723). **Food served** noon-2pm, 6.30-9.30pm daily. **Credit** MC, V.

This friendly restaurant beside a village green feels like a private house. John Dicken has added his personal touch to the olde-worlde charm of the interior – it's bright and cheery, with gastronomic quotations written along the walls. Food is traditional-based with Mediterranean accents: wholesome soups (fish is a favourite); game dishes that manage to be sumptuous without requiring a health warning; simple desserts and a respectable wine list. Good value for money. Mains start at £10.75.

Pink Geranium

Station Road, Melbourn (01763 260215/ www.pinkgeranium.co.uk). **Food served** noon-2pm, 7-9.30pm Tue-Sat; noon-2pm Sun. **Set lunch** £19.50 3 courses. **Credit** AmEx, MC, V.

Set on the edge of the sizeable village of Melbourn, the Pink Geranium is a converted cottage harbouring a charming dining room and a lounge with a roaring log fire. Service is extremely attentive – you order from the lounge, and are called through to your table after your aperitif. The menu matches the care and attention of the service: typical dishes include a steamed canon of lamb wrapped in leeks with tomato and tarragon jus; sautéed tranche of sea bass on boulangere potatoes; or ragout of wild mushrooms and asparagus with a truffle sauce. It's one of the best in the area, so expect to pay £35-£45 per head if you eat à la carte.

The Restaurant

2 Church Street, Saffron Walden (01799 526444/ www.the-restaurantweb.com). **Food served** 7.30-10pm Tue-Sat; 12.30-3pm Sun. **Set dinners** (Tue-Thur) £9.95 2 courses, £13.95 3 courses. **Credit** MC, V.

This basement space is one of the best eating options in Saffron Walden. It's divided into smoking and no-smoking rooms, with bare brick walls framed by clean colours and lines. The minimalist decor is matched by a refreshingly concise menu (about six starters and mains), which includes dishes such as roast duck breast served with port and cranberry sauce, parsnip purée and garlic roasted potatoes (£14.95), or the inventive fresh cod fillet with green curry, served with fragrant rice and 'cucumber spaghetti' (12.95). Produce is organic wherever possible, the wine cellar is well stocked and reasonably priced, and service is polite but casual. Main courses start from £8.95 and go up to £15.95.

The Starr

Market Place, Great Dunmow (01371 874321/ www.zynet.co.uk/menu/starr). **Food served** noon-1.30pm, 7-9.30pm Mon-Sat; noon-1.30pm Sun. **Set lunch** £11.50-£20 2 courses; £25 3 courses. **Set dinner** £23 2 courses; £33 3 courses. **Credit** AmEx, DC, MC, V.

The 500-year-old interior of this restaurant has been kept up to date with light furnishings and modern lighting, aided by a spacious conservatory at the back. Similarly, on the food front there's a combination of country standards and modern global cuisine. Start with roast pigeon on creamed leeks with baby onions and chestnuts, and move on to roasted cod with salsa verde served with lentils as a main. It's not cutting edge, but – thankfully – it's not over-ambitious either. A good place for Sunday lunch.

White Hart

The Street, Great Saling, Braintree (01371 850341). **Food served** noon-3pm, 7-9.30pm daily. **Credit** AmEx, MC, V.

Another local landmark, partly due to its connection with the *Lovejoy* television series. It was in the bakehouse here that the 'huffer' was created, a traditional, triangular sandwich of soft white bread with a choice of fillings. It's more of a snack, really, but they also do a wide range of dishes, from steak or Indian curries, to the more continental offerings of ciabattas and lasagne (mains about £7-£13).

Lower Stour Valley

Where Constable brought the countryside to the world.

It was John Constable who immortalised it, but the Lower Stour Valley would stand its ground as a place of inspiring beauty without artistic representation. The pieces that make up the Constable picture – locks and mill-ponds, spreading oaks and willows, tumbledown cottages and giant brick waterside mills – are all part and parcel of the painter's home patch of Dedham Vale.

Some of the elements that add most to this area's rural charm – especially the massive mills, built for cleaning wool and grinding corn – are left over from the area's earlier prominence as one of the economic hubs of the medieval wool trade. Such wealth means that nearly all the villages have grand, near cathedral-scale 15th-century churches with emphatic towers and spires, paid for by the local wool merchants of the time.

The Stour Valley stretches roughly from Nayland to Cattawade, along the border between Essex and Suffolk. The Industrial Revolution seemed to bypass this area and the valley landscapes of the Stour still fit Constable's description, written in 1830: 'The beauty of the surrounding scenery, the gentle declivities, the luxuriant meadow flats sprinkled with flocks and herds, and well cultivated uplands, the woods and rivers, the numerous scattered villages and churches, with farmyard and picturesque cottages, all impart to their particular spot an amenity and elegance hardly anywhere else to be found.'

Rowing down the Stour from **Dedham** to **Flatford Mill** you see Jersey cows, buttercups and poppies and the square church of St Mary's at Dedham through the lush banks and overhanging willows. It's a soft, mellow landscape with a happy mixture of greenery and water – of dipping valleys and hills, with wide skyscapes and the luminescent light that East Anglia is renowned for. Verdant roads roll up, down and around villages with little apparent order, making cycle rides a journey of discovery. There is no natural stone in Essex so the villages are made up of Georgian brick houses and bulging-walled half-timbered cottages, gaily painted in white, pinks and yellows. This is above all an ideal area for relaxed, unstressed walking. Everywhere there are excellent footpaths and the **Essex Way**, devised by pupils from Chelmsford Technical High School, runs for 81 miles from Epping to Harwich, with plenty of pubs and B&Bs in timbered old coaching inns along the way.

Dedham

As a child, Constable used to walk from his birthplace in East Bergholt to the grammar school in **Dedham**, a town made rich by the medieval wool trade. Its source of wealth is still apparent in some of the town's buildings – the timber-framed Marlborough Head pub was formerly the wool exchange, the Flemish Cottages were once a medieval cloth factory. The high street boasts many elegant Georgian houses, and next to the school is the grand St Mary's church with the square flint tower that featured in so many of Constable's paintings. Inside there is a tablet to a woman who died aged 35 in 1748 'in consequence of having accidentally swallow'd a pin'. A newly acquired Constable, *The Ascension*, faces you as you enter the side door, but unfortunately it is a passionless commission.

Upmarket crafts are housed in an old church and in the low, beamed cottages on the high street you'll find antiques, gift shops and bookshops for maps and guides. As Pevsner wrote: 'There is nothing in Dedham to hurt the eye', and even to this day there are no street lights to compromise the beauty of its architecture. The home and studio of the once-fashionable painter Sir Alfred Munning, in Castle House (01206 322127), has been kept as it was in the artist's heyday. The son of a Suffolk miller, Munning was president of the Royal Academy from 1944 to 1949. Alongside his famous depictions of horses and horse-racing there are sculptures and East Anglian landscapes on display.

> ## By train from London
>
> Eight trains an hour leave **Liverpool Street** for **Colchester** and **Ipswich**. Journey time to Colchester is **55mins**. Ipswich is a further **20mins**. For **Harwich Town**, change at Manningtree. Total journey time is around **1hr 30mins**. Info: www.gner.co.uk and www.angliarailways.co.uk.

Catch a glimpse of the extraordinary **Erwarton Manor**, or visit the church at **East Bergholt**.

East Bergholt

The house where Constable was born in this peaceful village has long since gone, but you can still see his studio, a cream cottage with pantiled roof. His early painting tutor John Dunthorne lived across the road in what is now a hairdresser's. The village church has a tower that has been in ruins for centuries. A planned new spire was never built because of the Reformation; ever since, the church's bells have been housed in the unique bell cage at ground level. From the tower you can walk down the hill to **Flatford** and see the pretty riverside cottage of Willy Lott, foreman to Constable's father, Golding (*see p287* **Constable's country**). Constable made sketches of the Vale from Gun Hill and the top of St Mary's Church

tower in Langham. **Stratford St Mary** is a pretty riverside village walkable from Flatford with the Priest's House, a beautiful white and dark-timbered cottage, overhanging the main road. In **Nayland**, a large village with a striking main street, the church houses Constable's altarpiece *Christ Blessing the Bread and Wine*, which his aunt paid him to paint in 1809. Nearby, **Stoke-by-Nayland** offers spectacular views and a beautiful old Maltings and Guildhall. Constable painted the church, with its 120-foot-tall square flint and brick tower. **Hadleigh** is a likeable old market town with a long high street down which sheep were once driven. Among the mix of architecture you'll find a Tudor chip shop and the Suffolk County Council offices based in the Corn Exchange.

East Anglia

From cows to swans

Heading east towards Felixstowe, dip into the Shotley Peninsula, where undulating arable fields run down to the water's edge. St Mary's church at **Erwarton** has a generous view from the tombstones. Inside there are carved monuments to families who have owned the extraordinary Erwarton Manor. The house is not open to the public but it's worth looking over the wall to glimpse this red-brick Tudor house. In **Shotley Gate** marina fluttering yachts tack down the Stour and run up the Orwell or head out into the open sea, while across the bay you can glimpse the massive cargo containers that line the docks at Felixstowe.

Taking the south side of the estuary towards **Harwich** leads you past estuary views and through once busy ports. **Manningtree** was a thriving port in Constable's day, but is now a small, sleepy backwater. It was the home of Matthew Hopkins, the 'Witchfinder General', who 'persuaded' 400 local women to confess that they were witches and then condemned them to death. He is said to have been buried in the now-demolished St Mary's Church in **Mistley**. The oddest buildings nearby are the twin Mistley Towers on the Manningtree Road, all that remain of a neo-classical Roman temple built by Robert Adam in 1776. At Mistley Quay, cargo such as coal and timber could be transferred to barges and taken up the Stour to Sudbury or into Thames sailing barges for the sea journey into London. Grain, bricks, chalk and flour, and hay for cab horses were in turn brought downriver from Sudbury, headed for London. There is also a secret concrete bunker at Mistley (Shrubland Road; 01206 392271/ www.essexsecretbunker.com; open daily Mar-Oct, at weekends Nov-Feb), which was used as a Cold War operations centre.

Further along the estuary, **Wrabness** is a perfect starting point for marshy walks, with the Stour Estuary Nature Reserve providing a habitat for waterfowl and woodland birds. The ferry-port town of **Harwich** flourished in the reign of Elizabeth I, and if you head for the quay you'll find a mixture of Tudor, duckboard and brick houses in the narrow streets of the old town. You can enjoy a film in Edwardian splendour at the 1912 Electric Cinema or imagine two men walking inside the twin wooden treadmills of the Treadwheel Crane. The site of the 19th-century Ha'penny Pier was the departure point for the *Mayflower* when it set sail for the Americas in 1611.

Celts and Saxons

If you need a break from village life, you can explore Colchester and Ipswich. Colchester was the capital of Roman Britain before being burned to the ground by Boudicca. It was later invaded by the Normans and besieged during the Civil War. Fragments of the walls, a Roman road and a great gate to the West remain; the Norman keep is also worth a visit. Despite the alarming spread of shopping centres, many old and quirky buildings remain.

Ipswich's streets still follow the line of those of its Saxon past, and its compact historic centre, centuries-old dock area and a string of medieval churches make it worth a visit. Particularly noteworthy is the magnificent Ancient House, with its lavishly carved façade, and the fine art collection at **Christchurch Mansion**.

What to see & do

The best way to appreciate the Stour Valley is, naturally, to walk it. For non-strenuous strolling, one easy but enjoyable route is the path from Dedham to Flatford and back (the round trip takes around one to two hours). Another is the path between Dedham and East Bergholt – walked by Constable every day on his way to school – which features in *The Cornfield*. Walking maps and guides, including the handy illustrated booklet *The Essex Way* (£3), are on sale at Tourist Information Centres, bookshops in Dedham and the post office in East Bergholt. For less obvious walks along the marshes near Mistley and Wrabness, get hold of the free *Tendring Trails* booklet. For cyclists, *Cycle South Suffolk* and *Cycling Round the Shotley Peninsula* show the signed bike routes.

Tourist Information Centres

All of the centres have accommodation details and you can make ferry bookings for the contintent from Harwich. For information on the Shotley Peninsula you need to contact the Sudbury office in Suffolk.

1 Queen Street, Colchester, CO1 2PG (01206 282920/www.colchester.gov.uk). **Open** 9.30am-6pm Mon, Tue, Thur-Sat; 10am-6pm Wed; 10am-5pm Sun.

Flatford Lane, Flatford, East Bergholt, CO7 6UL (01206 299460/www.babergh-south-suffolk.gov.uk). **Open** *Easter-June, Oct* 10am-5pm daily. *July-Sept* 10am-5.30pm daily. Closed Oct-Easter.

Iconfield Park, Parkston, Harwich, CO12 4EN (01255 506139/www.essexcc.gov.uk). **Open** *Apr-Sept* 9am-7pm daily. *Oct-Mar* 9am-5.30pm Mon-Fri; 9am-4pm Sat.

Town Hall, Market Hill, Sudbury, CO10 1TL (01787 881320/www.babergh-south-suffolk.gov.uk). **Open** 9am-5pm Mon-Fri; 10am-4.45pm Sat.

Bike hire

Street Life *Sudbury Bus Station (01787 310940).*
Action Bikes *24 Crouch Street, Colchester (01206 541744).*
One mile from the train station.

Flatford Mill: Constable's home patch.

Alton Water Sports Centre

Holbrook Road, Stutton (01473 328408).
Open 10am-8pm Mon-Fri; 10am-6pm Sat, Sun.
Casual day users are welcome to windsurf, canoe and
sail on Ipswich's drinking water. The centre uses 25
acres of the inland reservoir to let people loose in
Wayfarers (£12 an hour or £48 a day), canoes (£5 and
£30) and windsurfers (£8 and £30). Private tuition for
a minimum of three hours can be booked in advance and
a one-day windsurfing course costs £50.

Beth Chatto Gardens

Elmstead Market, nr Colchester (01206 822007/
www.bethchatto.co.uk). **Open** *Mar-Oct* 9am-5pm
Mon-Sat. *Nov-Feb* 9am-4pm Mon-Fri. **Admission**
£3; free under-14s.
Before 1960 this large site was an overgrown wasteland.
Over the years Beth Chatto has turned the car park into
a gravel garden with stunning shell-pink poppies,
dammed a ditch to create ponds surrounded by lush
plants and nurtured shade-loving plants under a huge
oak tree. There is a nursery adjoining, so if you fancy
some of the unusual perennials or herbs in your garden
you may well be able to buy them. Picnickers are
welcome and there is also a tearoom.

Blue Baker Yachts

Woolverstone Marina, Woolverstone, Ipswich
(01473 780008/www.bluebakeryachts.com).
Open 9am-5pm Mon-Fri; 10am-3pm Sat; by
arrangement Sun. **Credit** MC, V.
If you are a novice and feel like splashing out, Suffolk
Yacht Charters, in conjunction with the Pier Hotel, will
take you out on a day cruise in the backwaters of the
estuaries or out into the North Sea. Competent skippers
take the helm of a classic sloop or an 1860s fishing smack.
For this treat you pay from £160 for one day's sailing,
with dinner and accommodation at the Pier included.

Boat hire on the Stour

Dedham Boatyard *01206 323153.*
It costs £9 per hour (maximum five hours), to hire a var-
nished wooden row boat; it takes around 45 minutes to
row along the river under weeping willows to Flatford.
Tickets are on sale in the ship-shape boatyard café.
The Stour Trust *01206 393680.*
A dinky electric river cruiser from Flatford that costs
£2.50 (£1.50 concessions) for a half-hour ride.
Baines Backwater Boats *07970 115382.*
Cruises from the Ha'penny Pier in Harwich. The con-
verted lifeboat *City of Glasgow II* takes adults (£10) and
children (£5) round the harbour and up the rivers.

Christchurch Mansion & Wolsey Art Gallery

Christchurch Park, Ipswich (01473 433554/433500).
Open *Mar-Oct* 10am-5pm Tue-Sat, bank hols; 2.30-
4.30pm Sun. *Nov-Feb* 10am-4pm/dusk Tue-Sat;
2.30pm-4pm/dusk Sun. **Admission** free.
This Tudor house was originally built as a priory for
Augustinian monks. As well as chests and chairs in
period rooms, you can also admire the work of Ipswich
resident Thomas Gainsborough (1727-88). Among his
early formal portraits of the local elite is the wooden
portrait of the headmaster of Ipswich School, the Rev

East Anglia

Robert Hingeston, and a lively later portrait of a relaxed William Woolaston playing the flute. Constable came to Ipswich to learn from Gainsborough and if you've been trailing Constable you'll be excited by the paintings *The Flower Garden* and *The Millstream*.

Colchester Castle Museum

Castle Park, Colchester (01206 282931/ www.colchestermuseums.org.uk). **Open** 10am-5pm Mon-Sat; 11am-5pm Sun. **Admission** £3.90; £2.60 concessions; free under-5s.

Since the 16th century this castle has been a ruin, a library and a jail for witches. It has the largest keep built by the Normans and stands on the site of a Roman Temple of Claudius. Today it's a museum that tells the story of Boudicca's devastation of Colchester, life under siege during the Civil War and life in Roman Britain. As well as looking at an inventive display that includes a bronze statue of Mercury and the Colchester Sphinx, kids can try on Roman armour and togas and handle pottery.

Flatford

Bridge Cottage, Flatford (01206 298260/ www.nationaltrust.org.uk). **Open** *Bridge Cottage* Jan, Feb 11am-3pm Sat, Sun. Mar, Apr, Oct 11am-5.30pm Wed-Sun. May-Sept 10am-5.30pm daily. Nov, Dec 11am-3.30pm Wed-Sun. **Tours** *Apr-Oct* 11am, 1pm, 2.30pm daily. **Admission** *Bridge Cottage* (NT) free. *Tours* £1.80.

Most of the tiny clutch of buildings at Flatford, the subject of Constable's most famous paintings, are now in the hands of the National Trust. You can see the flat ford and the mill foreman's late-medieval house which feature in Constable's *The Haywain*, and there's a copy of the painting in the small exhibition in Bridge Cottage, which also houses a café and a shop. You can only admire the Georgian Flatford Mill from the outside unless you pre-book a tour for a party of ten. One-day and residential courses in arts and the environment (about £118 for a weekend) are held in Flatford Mill, Willy Lott's house and Valley Farm, a beautiful white and timber-framed medieval farmhouse once owned by Golding Constable. There's also a Granary Museum, with eclectic rural bygones, and a dry dock where barges were built and repaired. The privately owned car park costs £1.50.

Stour Estuary Nature Reserve

Ramsey, nr Harwich (01255 886043/ www.rspb.org.uk). **Open** free access. **Admission** free; donations welcome.

Stour Estuary is one of the most important estuaries in Britain for wading birds. From the reserve's three hides you may see redshanks and dunlins in the saltmarsh; from late July, black-tailed godwits from Iceland appear. Grey plovers, pintails, brent geese and shelducks also feed here. Wear your wellies.

There are plenty of B&Bs scattered around the Stour Valley villages. If those listed below are full, others worth considering include **May's Barn Farm** in Dedham (01206 323191; doubles £44), **Gladwins Farm** in Nayland (01206 262261; doubles from £60), **Ryegate House** in

Stoke by Nayland (01206 263679; doubles £60 for one night, £95 for two) and **Highfield** at Holbrook on the Shotley Peninsula (01473 328250; doubles £39-£46).

Angel Inn

Polstead Street, Stoke by Nayland, CO6 4SA (01206 263245/fax 01206 263373). **Rates** £50 single occupancy; £65 double/twin. **Rooms** (all en suite) 5 double, 1 twin. **Credit** MC, V.

The Angel has been functioning as an inn in one of the most attractive Dedham Vale villages since the 16th century. Downstairs there's a dining room and lounge with a brick fireplace (great for nestling beside with a nightcap). The rooms are smart and comfortable – your only worry as you head for bed will be not hitting your head on the low ceiling beams. All bedrooms are non-smoking. *From Colchester, take 1st exit on right as you come into Nayland; over the bridge, go past Anchor pub, and bear right at junction; the Angel Inn is on crossroads as you approach the village.*

Dedham Hall

Brook Street, Dedham, CO7 6AD (01206 323027/ fax 01206 323293/www.dedhamhall.demon.co.uk). **Rates** £45 single occupancy; £75 double/twin; £85-£95 family. **Rooms** (all en suite) 1 single; 4 double/ twin; 1 family. **Credit** MC, V.

Guests at Dedham Hall are treated partly as members of the family and partly as pampered house guests. The open kitchen, with its orange Aga and gleaming pots, is at the heart of things: wholesome food is provided here for guests on painting courses. The hotel also has an upmarket restaurant, the Fountain House (*see p286*). Bedrooms are snug and light, and there is a cosy, low-ceilinged residents' lounge with wood panelling and a bar with leather armchairs. A short walk by the river brings you to Flatford. Children welcome. *Off A12, at the far end of Dedham High Street on the left.*

Edge Hall Hotel

2 High Street, Hadleigh, IP7 5AP (01473 822458/ fax 01473 827751/www.edgehall-hotel.co.uk). **Rates** £30-£45 single; £50-£75 double/twin; £70-£75 four-poster; £65-£85 family room. **Rooms** (all en suite) 2 single; 5 double/twin; 1 four-poster; 2 family. **No credit cards.**

A bright pink Georgian townhouse with a walled garden and croquet lawn. Decor and furnishings are in keeping with the building's architecture – you can stay in an elegant four-poster in the main house or in the lodge overlooking the garden. It's a family-run establishment; the restaurant serves traditional home-cooked food from a set menu (£21) using veg grown in the garden. Children welcome. Pets allowed by arrangment. No smoking throughout.

Maison Talbooth

Stratford Road, Dedham, CO7 6HN (01206 322367/ fax 01206 322752/www.talbooth.com). **Rates** £120-£150 single occupancy; £155-£210 double/twin; £210 suite. Breakfast free (cont); £7.50 (Eng). Special breaks. **Rooms** (all en suite) 8 double; 10 suites. **Credit** AmEx, DC, MC, V.

This hotel was set up so that diners at Le Talbooth (*see p286*) would have somewhere to stay after dinner. It's a cosy pink-washed Victorian rectory decorated in grand

style with chintzes in the bedrooms, a large piano in the drawing room and french windows leading outdoors to a giant chess set. Rooms are luxurious – the Keats suite, for example, has a Jacuzzi. There is no dining room in the hotel so breakfast is served in your room or on the balcony; a courtesy car takes you to and from Le Talbooth restaurant. The hotel has beautiful views of Dedham Vale. Children welcome.
From Dedham High Street, with church on left-hand side, drive out of the village; take 1st turning on the right after a row of houses; Maison Talbooth is 200 yards up on the left.

Milsoms

Stratford Road, Dedham, Colchester, CO7 6HW (01206 322795/fax 01206 323689/ www.talbooth.com). **Rates** £67.50-£87.50 single occupancy; £80-£120 double/twin. Breakfast £10 (Eng); £5 (cont). **Rooms** (all en suite) 14 double/twin. **Credit** AmEx, DC, MC, V.
The Milsom dynasty of hoteliers sold this hotel in 1993 when it was the Dedham Vale Hotel, and now they've bought it back. (They also own Le Talbooth, Maison Talbooth and the Pier at Harwich). Inside, Geraldine Milsom has applied her makeover techniques to create 14 en suite bedrooms that are fresh and stylish – a deluxe room, Wheeler, has no view but is comfortable and light with a square leather table, hessian carpet and a blue lion design on the upholstery. The atmosphere downstairs is relaxed and excellent modern European food is available all day (*see p286*). Children welcome.
Come off A12 following signs for Dedham; cross over bridge and take first turning on left after bridge.

Old Vicarage

Higham, nr Colchester, CO7 6JY (01206 337248). **Rates** £35 single occupancy; £58 double; £70 triple occupancy. **Rooms** (all en suite or with private bathroom) 3 double/triple. **No credit cards.**
Sprightly Mrs Parker treats you to afternoon tea with cake when you arrive at this 16th-century vicarage – if you can first find the bell hiding in a creeper. Meadows, cows, the River Stour and the square church tower combine to create a stunning view from the garden or elegant drawing room. The garden and river are littered with facilities such as tennis courts, a trampoline, a punt and a canoe – all of which are for guests' use. Children (£10 per child extra) and dogs are welcome.
On A12 between Colchester and Ipswich. From Stratford St Mary, take the Higham Road; the Old Vicarage is about a mile along on left.

Pier at Harwich Hotel

The Quay, Harwich, CO12 3HH (01255 241212/ fax 01255 551922/www.pieratharwich.com). **Rates** £62.50-£75 single occupancy; £80-£100 double/twin*;* £80-£150 suite. Breakfast £5.75 (Eng). **Rooms** (all en suite) 14 double/twin; 5 suites. **Credit** AmEx, DC, MC, V.
Gerald and Paul Milsom bought this square-shaped Victorian hotel for Harwich-to-Holland travellers in 1978, which means you can get a weekend break deal with the Maison Talbooth (*see p284*) and a delicious lobster in the Harbourside Restaurant (*see p286*) as well. Rooms are decorated with a modern seaside look of weatherboarding, seashells, rope and hessian floors, and five of them overlook the harbour. The former Angel Inn next door has been converted to provide more accom-

modation, including the luxurious Mayflower Suite. The hotel is ideal for an overnight stop on the way to the continent, or if you need a break after a hard day's yachting. Children welcome.

Round Hill House

Parsonage Hill, Boxted, nr Colchester, CO4 5ST (tel/fax 01206 272392). **Rates** £35 single occupancy; £50 double/twin; £50 family room (plus extra £5 for cot, £10 for child's bed). **Rooms** 1 double; 1 twin (en suite); 1 family (en suite). **No credit cards.**
The modern hilltop house may not be historic but the views of Dedham Vale are gorgeous and because there is a ha-ha at the end of the lawn it looks as though the cows are actually in the garden. The rooms are comfortable and Mrs Carter's hefty breakfasts are served in an attractive dining room with a log fire, or outside if it's warm. The house has its own tennis court, coarse fishing stream, expansive living room with baby grand piano and memorabilia from Colonel Carter's military career. Evening meals (£22.50) can be booked, and you can invite your friends along, too. Children and dogs are welcome (please warn in advance).
From Colchester, take A134; turn right down Boxted Church Road; Round Hill House on the left after 2 miles.

Where to eat & drink

You can tumble upon pub after pub along the old coaching routes around Dedham Vale. Many of them, such as the **Angel** and the **White Horse**, listed below, serve restaurant meals worthy of a journey from London. For pub grub in Dedham the **Sun** (01206 323351) offers all-day meals and has a grassy beer garden and a restaurant. The **Cock Inn** in Polstead (01206 263150) offers upmarket food in a venerable old village pub. Formerly the Wool Exchange, the friendly **Marlborough Head** in Denham (01206 323124) is a cosy and convivial timber-beamed pub with Adnams, bar food and a restaurant.

In East Bergholt (where the locals conduct an annual pub-crawling pram race round its six pubs), the **Red Lion** (01206 298332) is an unpretentious local with a pool table and pleasant garden. The **Swan** in Stratford St Mary was built in 1520 and at its height had stabling for 200 horses. The tiny timber-beamed bars are cosy in the winter and there is a river garden across the road for the summer. There is another **Swan** in Chappell (01787 222353), which has a garden on the River Colne.

There are fewer pubs along the Stour Estuary but the **Crown Hotel** in Manningtree (01206 396333) and the **Thorn Hotel** on the quay at Mistley (01206 392821) offer good views. On the Shotley Peninsula there is a beautiful view of the Orwell from the **Butt and Oyster** at Pin Mill (01473 780764). It's so close to the water that it's said that yachts used to sail up to the hatch and be served drinks. Nowadays you can savour your Adnams while watching the barge race at the end of June. For fine fishy food try the **Queen's Head** (01473 787550) at Erwarton.

Angel Inn

Stoke-by-Nayland (01206 263245). **Food served** noon-2pm, 6-9.30pm daily. **Credit** MC, V.
You can eat in the Well Room (with its 52ft well) or at a table for two on a lovebird balcony looking down on the barn-like room. Fresh seafood is the treat here: langoustine (£6.75), Mediterranean prawns (£6.95), and monkfish with cheese risotto and fresh vegetables are typical choices. Alternatively, you can eat pub fare in a number of timbered rooms, or, in summer, home-made celery soup and fine meat and game outdoors in a lovely bricked courtyard. This delightful Tudor inn has some mellow lanes nearby a pre-dinner stroll. *See also p284.*

Fountain House

Dedham Hall, Brook Street, Dedham (01206 323027/www.dedhamhall.demon.co.uk). **Food served** 7-9.30pm Tue-Sat. **Set dinner** £23 3 courses. **Credit** MC, V.
In the comfortable surroundings of a 15th-century farmhouse you can watch owner and chef Wendy Sarton prepare her upmarket version of home cooking. The fixed-price dinnner menu offers a choice of eight starters such as watercress salad with bacon and croutons or cullen skink and tiger prawns in filo pastry. Main course meats cover beef, chicken, steak, pork and roasted duck breast in orange; vegetarian dishes are also available.

Milsoms

Stratford Road, Dedham, Colchester (01206 322795). **Food served** noon-2.15pm, 6-9.30pm Mon-Thur, Sun; noon-2.15pm, 6-10pm Fri, Sat. **Credit** AmEx, DC, MC, V.
The former Dedham Vale Hotel has undergone a new and super-groovy makeover. You can hang out drinking cups of tea (£1.20) and reading the papers, or relax from noon until 6pm snacking on oysters (£8.50), in the light and airy stripped pine bar. A more formal menu with the likes of chicken livers, mushroom risotto, braised lamb shank (£8.95) and the extremely popular shepherd's pie (£7.50) is served at lunch and in the evening. Walls are pale yellow, the ceilings are high (unless you're on the no-smoking upper balcony), and there are tables outside by the red-brick well and square pond. On Sunday nights from May to September a jazz or steel band accompanies the barbecue. The Milsoms' directive 'eat, drink, stay' is hard to disobey. *See also p285.*

Ha'penny Bistro & Harbourside Restaurant

The Pier at Harwich Hotel, The Quay, Harwich (01255 241212/www.pieratharwich.com). **Food served** noon-2pm, 6-9.30pm daily. **Set lunches** (Harbourside Restaurant, Mon-Sat) £15 2 courses; £17.50 3 courses. **Set dinner** (Harbourside Restaurant) £19.50 3 courses. **Credit** AmEx, DC, MC, V.
Children are welcome in the jolly Ha' penny Bistro. This light downstairs restaurant has a harbour view and is decorated with blue chequered tablecloths, nautical murals of old clippers rolling along the ocean waves and posters of crabs and fish. Bosomy ships' prows hang over you as you tuck into local cod, chips and peas, hot pot mussels and mushrooms, dressed local crab, mushy peas or prawns by the half pint. Upstairs in the Harbourside Restaurant both the view and the food are superior – fresh fish and seafood includes Dover sole (£17.50), grilled lobster (£24.95) and rock oysters (£1.25 each). The way is barred by a large dark wooden ship's wheel. Booking is essential. *See also p285.*

Stour Bay Café

39-43 High Street, Manningtree (01206 396687). **Food served** noon-2pm, 7-9.30pm Wed-Sat; noon-4pm Sun. **Set lunches** £10 2 courses; £11.50 3 courses. **Set dinners** (Wed) £17.50 3 courses; (Thur) £23.50 5 courses. **Credit** AmEx, MC, V.
This café is green on the outside with square brown bay windows, and orange, timbered and bricked within. Diners can eat sausages, Thai fish cakes and sticky toffee pudding at tables set with crisp white tablecloths for lunch. At dinner the fare is more fancy, with the likes of provençal fish soup, red mullet risotto, wood pigeon, sea bass, and roast salmon featuring on the carte; food is complemented by a fine choice of New World and French wines.

Le Talbooth

Gun Hill, Dedham (01206 323150/www.talbooth.com). **Food served** noon-2pm, 7-9pm daily. **Set lunch** £21 3 courses. **Set dinner** £28.50 3 courses. **Credit** AmEx, DC, MC, V.
The place really used to be a tollbooth for horse-drawn traffic. The 16th-century timber-framed house was also a weaver's cottage, but for the past 50 years it's been one of East Anglia's finest restaurants. You can have a gin and tonic beside the riverbank (although the A12 is to your right, it must be said) to work up an appetite for the delights of twice-baked cheese soufflé, monkfish on saffron paella, breast of Norfolk duck with butternut squash and cumin purée, and blackberry and yoghurt crumble soufflé. If your budget is tighter, there are summer barbecues with a jazz or steel band for £26 a head.

White Hart Inn

11 High Street, Nayland, nr Colchester (01206 263382/www.whitehart-nayland.co.uk). **Food served** noon-2pm, 6.30-9.30pm Mon-Sat; noon-2.30pm, 6.30-9pm Sun. **Set lunches** £11 2 courses; £13.50 3 courses. **Set dinners** (Tue-Fri) £16.50 2 courses; £21 3 courses. **Credit** AmEx, DC, MC, V.
Like the horse-drawn coaches trundling from London to Harwich in the 18th century, you, too, will have to seek out this beautiful timbered inn through the darkness – Nayland has no street lighting. Inside, the heritage interest has been developed into olde worlde chic to provide an atmospheric restaurant with an inventive menu and some fine wines. Walls have been removed to make the whole of the former pub area into a restaurant and small bar. Service is impeccable and friendly, even if some of the dishes didn't quite come off on a recent visit: a roquefort sauce threatened to steal the taste from the gratinated mussels set on a bed of spinach; and pan-seared slices of salmon were rather bland in their red wine sauce. All the food is beautifully presented, however, and the home-made vanilla ice-cream was very special indeed. Book well in advance if you fancy a convivial, memorable night in the country – the White Hart also has accommodation (doubles £71.50).

Constable's country

Constable loved where he lived, and it shows in his work. It was his deep attachment to his environment that moved him to develop his painting in the way that he did. He wrote: 'The sound of water escaping from mill dams... willows, old rotten banks, slimy posts, and brickwork. I love such things... As long as I do paint I shall never cease to paint such places. They have always been my delight... Painting is but another word for feeling. I associate my "careless boyhood" with all that lies on the banks of the Stour. They made me a painter, and I am grateful, that is, I had often thought of pictures of them before I had ever touched a pencil.'

He painted what he saw – mills, locks, farms, winding sunken lanes. The figures in his paintings were the farmhands and workers who had helped create his father's wealth. Willy Lott's cottage was the subject of many sketches and paintings, which culminated in *The Haywain* in 1821.

Even when Constable moved to London, painting portraits for a living, he returned to Dedham Vale whenever he could and sketched oil roughs that he then painted on to huge canvasses in his London studio in Charlotte Street.

In painting the real world as he saw it, Constable was an innovator. His fresh, unconventional approach meant he was initially spurned by the English art establishment. He was first recognised by the French, receiving a gold medal at the Paris Salon in 1824. He was finally admitted to the Royal Academy in 1829, and presented it with *The Lock*.

By this time he was a well-known artist, but Constable remained a modest man. In 1832 he wrote to his engraver: 'In the coach yesterday coming from Suffolk were two gentlemen and myself, all strangers to each other. One of them remarked to me – on my saying it was beautiful – "Yes Sir – this is Constable's country!" I then told him who I was lest he should spoil it.' *See also p284.*

East Anglia

Upper Stour Valley

A place that is forever England.

'Sleepy Suffolk' is less apt a turn of phrase than it once was. Droves of commuters have burst across the banks of the River Stour (which roughly rhymes with 'brewer') in their Mondeos and Beamers in search of their own personal *Lebensraum*, making some villages (such as Long Melford) seem more like Dorking than once ever seemed possible. Accusations of it being a place where nothing happens need quickly be dismissed as not being accusations at all. So what? The upper Stour Valley indulges life's simpler pleasures of sleeping and eating well, drinking fine beer and walking in some of the most lovely countryside and villages in the land. There's not the high drama of the North Yorkshire Moors or of the north coast of Cornwall, but its gentle undulation, whispering villages and crooked Suffolk-pink cottages are equally affecting. And the people, who some claim speak from the corner of a barely opened mouth because of the bitter winds that sweep in off the North Sea, walk a reasonable line between being helpful and welcoming and getting on with their own business, thank you very much.

The Stour Valley is a 60-mile stretch that flows from south of Newmarket, past Haverhill and then west to east, forming the Essex/Suffolk border, through the lovely Suffolk-pinked villages of Clare, Cavendish and Long Melford, past Dedham and Flatford Mill to its estuary in the east at the Cattawade Marshes. This break concentrates on the river's upper reaches, from Haverhill to Sudbury and up to Lavenham. (For the **Lower Stour Valley**, *see p280*.)

Historical landscapes

A fire swept through Haverhill (pronounced 'Ave-rill) in 1665, and there has been little of interest in this unlovely former wool town since. But to the east and north, the cluster of villages within a ten-mile radius around Sudbury represents some of the best that Suffolk has to offer. There is the grand medieval architecture of unmissable **Lavenham**, a village that grew rich on the wool trade; the thriving market town of Sudbury itself; and the idyllic English scene set by **Cavendish**. Much of Suffolk's beauty is in the detail: look for cottages covered with decorated plasterwork known as pargeting

The green and pleasant land near **Cavendish**.

(a house beside **Clare** churchyard offers a fine example; *see also p277* **Parget practice**). Many of the villages – especially Cavendish, with its village green and thatched cottages – have entered a kind of folk memory as the image of what an English village should look like. Indeed, it was the East Anglian understated undulations and villages that caused Cambridge-based poet Rupert Brooke to go so misty-eyed over England. It is also an area that wears its history in its place names: Latin, Saxon, Scandinavian and, finally, Norman French tongues inform whole clusters of village names. Similarly in the architecture: the Romans, who made their capital 30 miles to the south-east at Colchester, have left their mark in roads and numerous archaeological sites along the routes; the Saxon, and especially Norman, influence can be seen clearly in their ruined castles and churches. The splendour of Elizabethan England is evident in such great manor houses as **Melford Hall** (Elizabeth I stayed there) and **Kentwell Hall**, both in

By train from London

Trains depart from **Liverpool Street** about once every hour (changing at **Marks Tey**) to **Sudbury**. The total journey takes about **1hr 10mins**. Info: www.ger.co.uk.

Long Melford. Many of the region's churches are chronicles of the region's fortunes as well as each period's religious and architectural preferences (*see p293* **Profits of the flock**). That the area was once rich and powerful is not in any doubt: the Domesday Book of 1086 recounts numerous manors and holdings in Suffolk; and – in the days when ecclesiastical and state office and money were inextricably linked – Simon Theobald, also known as Simon of Sudbury, became Archbishop of Canterbury and Chancellor to the court of Richard II. He suffered a bloody end at the hands of rioters during the Peasants' Revolt of 1381, but his head finally found its way back to the theological college he had founded at St Gregory's in Sudbury, where it became the object of pilgrimages. His teeth were stolen as relics, and the head is now held in a little wall cupboard (if you want to see it, contact a church official; 01787 372611).

You will find, too, that history has left a trace on the landscape itself. At **Great Yeldham**, a 1,000-year-old oak still stands, even if it is girt with iron bands; and at Clare there is a huge man-made mound topped with a few ruins, which are all that remains of a Norman castle. (Incidentally, during the Hundred Years' War, the Lord of Clare was presented with lands in France, and the local wine – claret – still bears his name).

Long Melford – so called because it is a 'ribbon' village of about two miles in length – shows an insatiable appetite for expansion. The village, now closing in on the town boundaries of Sudbury itself, contains a wonderful church, two noble halls and close to a surely excessive 40 antique shops. Too-Long Melford might be closer to the mark. In the unlikely event that the shops don't have the item you're after, the old village school (situated by the bridge and more or less opposite a house once owned by World War I poet Edmund Blunden) hosts very popular antique fairs every bank holiday.

A few miles from Melford, lies the village of **Borley**, famous in the earlier part of this century for its extravagant ghosts. Once known as the 'most haunted house in Britain', the Rectory – built on the site of an old convent – apparently had the lot: ghostly nuns, carriages drawn by coal-black horses, wailings and all

kinds of nasty noises, until a careless poltergeist burnt the place down in 1939. Or at least, that's the story. Even now, spookologists stake out Borley church trying to capture a glimpse of something that goes bump in the night. The site of the former rectory is now private land and thus unvisitable, unless of course you're returning from the dead.

Situated in a loop in the River Stour, the ancient town of **Sudbury** is still, more than 1,000 years after its foundation, a thriving market town. Every Thursday and Saturday, a lively market takes place in the town square, just at the foot of painter Thomas Gainsborough's statue (which was clad in scaffolding at last inspection but will shortly be reappearing in even finer fettle). Author Dodie Smith uses this statue as a meeting place for the dogs in *The Starlight Barking*, her sequel to *101 Dalmatians*. Dickens modelled the rotten borough of Eatanswill in *The Pickwick Papers* on Sudbury; this fiction is commemorated on Boxing Day, when a stagecoach travels from Haverhill to Sudbury, via Cavendish and Long Melford. It's a fine town in which to spend a few hours: you can go rowing (the boathouse is at Ballingdon Hill); take in an exhibition at Gainsborough's House, the birthplace of the distinguished artist; and then eat lunch at the Red Onion (*see p294*).

One last point. Ipswich Town Football Club isn't the only East Anglian institution on the up and up. Its two celebrated brewers, Adnam's and Greene King, are finally appearing on pub taps across the UK. But they're still best savoured near to home and the hundreds of fantastic pubs in the area provide the perfect setting to sample them.

What to see & do

See also the Essex and Suffolk County Council websites (www.essexcc.gov.uk and www.suffolkcc.gov.uk respectively) for information and full local transport timetables.

Tourist Information Centres

Lady Street, Lavenham, CO10 9RA (01787 248207/www.babergh-south-suffolk.gov.uk). **Open** *Easter-June, Sept, Oct* 10am-4.45pm daily. *July, Aug* 10am-4.45pm Mon-Thur, Sun; 10am-5.45pm Fri, Sat. *Nov-Dec, Mar* 10am-3pm Sat, Sun.

Town Hall, Market Hill, Sudbury, CO10 1TL (01787 881320/www.babergh-south-suffolk.gov.uk). **Open** *Easter-Oct* 10am-4.45pm Mon-Sat. *Nov-Easter* 10am-2.45pm Mon-Sat.

Bike hire

Street Life Bus Station *Hamilton Road, Sudbury (01787 310940).* Close to the train station.

East Anglia

Clare Castle & Country Park

Maltings Lane, Clare (rangers 01787 277491).
Open *Park* free access. **Visitors' centre** *May-Sept* 10am-6pm daily. *Apr-Oct* 10am-6pm Sat, Sun, bank hols. **Admission** free.

Don't let the name fool you: all that is left of Richard de Bienfait's 11th-century castle is a motte, encircled by a spiralling path, and the ruins of the old walls that once protected the inner bailey. The view from the motte's top is pleasant enough, but there really is little to see of the castle. There's also a nature trail, but this is no more than a short walk though the woods. Also within the park borders are two old platforms, the remnants of the old Clare railway station – they make a perfect picnic spot. In Clare itself, the splendid parish church of St Peter and St Paul (built 1450) is worth a visit, too.

Colne Valley Railway

Yeldham Road, Castle Hedingham (01787 461174/ www.cvr.org.uk). **Open** *Mar-Oct* 10am-5pm daily. *Dec* varies; phone for timetable. Closed Jan, Feb, Nov. **Admission** *Railway complex only* £3; £1.50 concessions. **Tickets** *Steam trains* £6; £3-£5 concessions. *Heritage diesel trains* £5; £2.50-£4 concessions.

Run by the Colne Valley Railway Preservation Society, the restored Pullman carriages of this working steam and diesel railway will shunt you into the past. Now in its 27th year, the railway complex has been built up lovingly by enthusiasts. The railway offers various diversions: train-driving courses, Sunday lunches aboard the Pullman as it travels its private line (departing 12.45pm; booking essential) and various Agatha Christie-inspired murder mystery evenings. Entrance to the complex also gives admittance to the 30 acres of the **Colne Valley Farm Park**, where sheep, cattle and goats graze in the water meadows. Steam or diesel train tickets allow you to have as many rides as you like during the day.

Gainsborough's House

46 Gainsborough Street, Sudbury (01787 372958/ www.gainsborough.org). **Open** *Apr-Oct* 10am-5pm Tue-Sat; 2-5pm Sun. *Nov-Mar* 10am-4pm Tue-Sat; 2-4pm Sun. **Admission** £3; £1.50-£2.50 concessions.

Part museum, part gallery, the birthplace of painter Thomas Gainsborough (1727-88) is unusual in that it manages to combine both roles well. The house, older than its Georgian façade suggests, is a roomy, winding affair and each room highlights a different aspect of the artist's work: there are etchings, a bronze of a horse (the only known sculpture by him) and more paintings from throughout his career than anywhere else in the world, including *A Wooded Landscape With Cattle by a Pool* (1782). There are also regular visiting exhibitions of contemporary art and crafts, and a print workshop in the old coach house offers courses to the public. The lavender walk and a mulberry tree in the garden provide the ideal breather from the gallery.

Gifford's Hall

Hartest (01284 830464/www.giffordshall.co.uk). **Open** *Apr-Oct* 11am-6pm daily. Closed Nov-Mar. **Admission** £3.50; £3 concessions; free under-16s.

The good life made flesh? This 33-acre smallholding, centred on a Georgian homestead, is a self-sufficient farm with gardens, vineyards, meadows filled with wild flowers and animals ranging from a flock of St Kilda sheep to a posse of Rhode Island Red hens. Bees from the Hall's ten hives buzz about the sweet peas and the fruits of their labours can be bought at the farm shop. Gifford's Hall also has tearooms and offers bed and breakfast (doubles from £42).

Hedingham Castle

Castle Hedingham (01787 460261/www.english-heritage.org.uk). **Open** *Easter-Oct* 10am-5pm daily. Closed Nov-Easter. **Admission** (EH) £4; £3-£3.50 concessions.

This solid Norman castle, rising 110ft, was built by the Earl of Oxford, Aubrey de Vere, in 1140. It was besieged by King John, and Henry VII, Henry VIII and Elizabeth I all paid it a visit. Local builders plundering for stone proved to be the downfall of nearby Clare Castle but fortunately they didn't get their mitts on Hedingham. A Tudor bridge over the dry moat is a (relatively) recent addition to the castle. Inside, the great arched banqueting hall with minstrel's gallery and dormitory are simply presented and highly evocative of a lifestyle so removed from ours. The view offers a sweeping vista of the area's rolling hills. On bank holidays and other festive occasions, jousting tournaments are organised with mounted knights in full gear. Leave time to wander the impossibly picturesque village as well.

Kentwell Hall

Long Melford (01787 310207/www.kentwell.co.uk). **Open** *Apr-mid June, mid Sept-Oct* noon-5pm Sun. *Mid July-mid Sept* noon-5pm daily. Closed mid June-mid July, Nov-Mar. **Admission** £5.70; £3.40-£4.90 concessions.

A taste of a Tudor kitchen at **Kentwell Hall**.

Twenty-five years ago, this magnificent brick Tudor mansion, once seat to the Clopton family, was a ramble of neglect and decrepitude. Slowly, Kentwell's new owners – barrister Patrick Phillips and his family – have brought about the hall's resurrection. It is not a stately home in the mould of neighbouring Melford Hall (*see below*): this is a working house where Elizabethan kitchens, gardens and animals are still maintained. The Hall regularly holds historical re-creations ('public days'), which are immensely popular with visitors (mainly hordes of school children hyper on the sugar of history) and out-of-work actors who hey-nonny-nonny from morning 'till night. Phone to check when these events are taking place. If you prefer to overlook the artifice of all this (and it's not easy), then the rose garden maze, open-air Shakespearean theatre (July only) and various outhouses – brewery, dairy and stables, with heavy Suffolk Punch horses – are fun to walk around.

Lavenham

The village of Lavenham is the jewel in Suffolk's crown. It first got a market charter in 1257 and for four centuries grew rich on the wool trade – it was the 14th wealthiest town in the 17th century, with 33 cloth-making businesses. Since 1930, Lavenham has been without a cloth factory but its appearance and nature are still defined by the wealth the industry brought. Many of its timbered buildings and halls date from the 14th and 15th centuries and its most famous building, the Guildhall, was built in 1529. The church, while lacking some of the charisma of smaller village churches nearby (*see p293* **Profits of the flock**), is a magnificent, imposing and martial-looking structure, that rises up black and grey against the fields behind. Walking down the hill into the town it's possible to meander through the streets wondering at its remarkably untouched exposed beams and crooked angles. David Dymond's excellent *A Walk Around Lavenham* (£1.50) is worth getting from the Tourist Information Centre on Lady Street, as are many of the informative free pamphlets. Head to the Market Place to look round the **Guildhall of Corpus Christi** (01787 247646; open Apr-Oct 11am-5pm daily) and **Little Hall** (01787 247179; open Apr-Oct 2-5.30pm Wed, Thur, Sat, Sun). The former is celebrated by architects as one of the finest medieval buildings in England, but anyone and everyone should be swooning. The neighbouring Little Hall, another delightfully timbered building with gardens attached, offers further insight into the impact of wool money.

Melford Hall

Long Melford (01787 880286/ www.nationaltrust.org.uk). **Open** *Apr, Oct 2-5.30pm Sat, Sun. May-Sept 2-5.30pm Wed-Sun, bank hols. Closed Nov-Mar.* **Admission** (NT) £4.30; £2.15 concessions.
This turreted Tudor mansion is a well-maintained and mannered example of Suffolk's stately homes. Home to the Hyde Parker family since 1786, Melford Hall offers many set pieces: its original panelled banqueting hall; an 18th-century drawing room and a Regency library. Furniture and Chinese porcelain, captured from a Spanish galleon (the Hyde Parkers produced a number of admirals) are on display, while outside the gardens have a wonderful air of tranquillity; the walled garden is especially beautiful. A country fair is held in the

More Tudor magnificence at **Melford Hall**.

grounds each June; in November, it is also the venue for a vast conflagration in honour of Guy Fawkes' night. While you're in Melford, visit Holy Trinity church, just up the lane by the 16th-century almshouse, founded in 1573 for 12 poor men and two women. The battlemented church, with flint panelling known as flushwork, has a fine Lady Chapel. (*See p293* **Profits of the flock**).

Sue Ryder Museum

Cavendish (01787 282591). **Open** 10am-5.30pm daily. **Admission** 80p; 40p concessions.
Situated behind the duck pond and to the side of the Ryder Foundation's lovely Tudor house is a tiny amateur museum that makes up for in heart what it lacks in a rigorous taxonomy. At the end of World War II, its eponymous founder was a FANY (no sniggering at the back: the Female Auxiliary Nursing Yeomanry were a top-notch outfit) who saw at first hand the horror of the concentration camps, particularly in Poland. Sue Ryder converted her Cavendish premises into a refugee home and built a lasting link with Poland as a consequence. The museum has various uniforms, some rather ropey tableaux showing improvised hospitals, plus artefacts from the concentration camps, including – in somewhat dubious taste – a tin of Zyklon B.

Where to stay

Note that many pubs and restaurants in the area double up as B&Bs. The recently renovated **Black Lion Inn** (The Green, Long Melford; 01787 312 356; doubles from £93) has also improved upon its previous guise as the Countrymen (*see p294*).

The Bull

High Street, Long Melford, CO10 9JG (01787 378494/fax 01787 880307). **Rates** £65 single; £100 double/twin; £130 suite; £110 family room. **Rooms** (all en suite) 3 single; 17 double/twin; 3 family; 2 suites. **Credit** AmEx, DC, MC, V.
A well-established hotel and pub situated just past Melford Hall in this historic village. If beam-overload is possible then you're likely to be afflicted here as both the exterior and interior heavily feature both oak and

East Anglia

Wander through the village of **Lavenham** and swoon at the wealth of timber-framed homes.

acorn beams. It's Trusthouse Forte (something we sensed before being told); however, rooms have a period charm (the two suites have separate lounge areas and king-size beds with canopies), the bar has the dynamic duo of Adnam's and Directors and the menu tends towards the roast beef of olde England variety (*see p294*). The hotel is set for a refurbishment in September 2001 although, we were promised, the essence of the hotel would not be changed. Children and dogs welcome. No-smoking rooms available.

Bulmer Tye House

Bulmer Tye, nr Sudbury, CO10 7ED (tel/fax 01787 269315). **Rates** £20 single; £40 double. **Rooms** 2 single (1 en suite); 2 double. **No credit cards.**
Two miles south of Sudbury is this welcoming B&B set in a handsome Victorian house. It's teeming with books, clavichords, doll's houses and wooden cabinets, and owners Peter and Noël Owen are happy to talk you through the stories behind them. The grounds, which include a grass tennis court in a glade of trees, are also great fun to explore. In the village, there is a famous brickworks, which uses old methods to replicate the Tudor bricks needed for restoring the old homes of England and other countries. Children and dogs welcome. No smoking throughout.

Lavenham Priory

Water Street, Lavenham, CO10 9RW (01787 247404/fax 01787 248472/ www.lavenhampriory.co.uk). **Rates** £50-£60 single occupancy; £78-£110 double/four-poster; £78 twin. **Rooms** (all en suite) 4 double; 1 twin; 3 four-poster. **Credit** MC, V.
This 13th-century house was once home to a Benedictine order, before passing into the De Vere family (of Shakespearian fame) and then being sold to cloth merchants. It is to the Elizabethan period of these salesmen that the present owners have restored this breathtaking building. In the context of one of England's most idyllic towns, it still astounds. Each of the luxurious bedrooms has oak floors, usually sloping. Slipper baths and vast

beds (each bespoke for the respective rooms) add to the meeting of comfort and beauty. The three-acre gardens (with a separate walled herb garden) are as pretty as one could imagine. For weekends (you can't reserve Saturdays only), you need to book up to three months in advance. Make the effort. No smoking throughout.

Oliver's Farm

Toppesfield, CO9 4LS (01787 237642/fax 01787 237602). **Rates** £50-£55 double/twin. **Rooms** 2 double/twin (1 en suite). **No credit cards.**
Adjacent to a working farm, and set in two acres of landscaped gardens, Oliver's Farm is a 1650 house set in the heart of the countryside. The two bedrooms are comfortable and downstairs there's a dining room, sitting room and terrace. Mrs Blackie's full English breakfasts – including home-made bread and jams and bacon smoked locally in Sudbury – are sufficiently fortifying to rule out anything other than a light lunch. Historians among you may be interested to know that the house was built by the Symonds family, whose son emigrated to the US and became pals with John Winthrop, first governor of Massachusetts. No smoking throughout. *A120 towards Dunmow and Braintree; follow signs to Sudbury until you get to High Garrett; straight on until Sible Hedingham; A1017 to Great Yeldham; after White Hart pub turn left at Toppesfield signpost; last proper driveway on left before you get to Toppesfield T-junction.*

Red House

29 Bolton Street, Lavenham, CO10 9RG (01787 248074/www.lavenham.demon.co.uk/accommodation /redhouse). **Rates** £45 double. **Rooms** (all en suite) 3 double. **No credit cards.**
A homely and personable bed and breakfast service is offered in this elegantly proportioned Victorian house by Diana Schofield. The three double rooms all feature subtly colour-co-ordinated furnishings and the garden's ideal for a sundowner or a morning coffee. Dinners can be ordered by prior arrangement (£15 for three courses; BYOB). Children and dogs welcome. No smoking throughout.

Swan Hotel

*High Street, Lavenham, CO10 9QA (01787
247477/fax 01787 248286/www.heritage-hotels.com).*
Rates £95-£105 single; £115-£145 double/twin;
£120-£155 deluxe double/twin; £125-£160 four-
poster; £155-£175 suite. Special breaks. Breakfast
£14.95 (Eng/cont). **Rooms** (all en suite) 7 single; 22
double/twin; 4 twin; 7 deluxe double; 1 deluxe twin;
3 four-poster; 2 suites. **Credit** AmEx, DC, MC, V.
This sizeable 14th-century hotel holds court in the centre of Lavenham. A recent £2 million refurbishment has
been carefully handled, both in the bedrooms and in the
modern use of natural light in the reception area. The

Swan has been a hotel since at least 1667, and we felt
the years of experience with convivial and efficient service from the moment we walked through the door.
Several rooms boast four-poster beds and fireplaces big
enough to set up your own spit. Each room has a CD
player, TV and mini bar. Two bars and a restaurant add
to the appeal. Children and dogs welcome. No-smoking
rooms available.

Western House

*High Street, Cavendish, CO10 8AR (01787
280550).* **Rates** £32 double/twin. **Rooms** 1 double;
2 twin. **No credit cards**.

Profits of the flock

In early modern England there was no
way better to assert your wealth and
prosperity than to spend money on your
local church. As East Anglia's economy
began to boom on the back of the wool
trade in the 14th century, the towns and
the villages became home to wealthy
men, many of whom sought to give
to their church. There followed three
centuries of investment. This, together
with the fact that the upper Stour's
churches were overlooked by the
Victorians, with their dubious penchant
for 'restoration', is why the area can
claim some of the most fascinating
and beautiful churches in England.

This welcome neglect by Victorian
restorers is apparent in the church of St
Mary in **Brent Eleigh**, which dates back
to the 'decorated' style of the late 12th
and early 13th centuries. It still has its
exquisite 14th-century wall paintings of
Jesus flanked by his mother and St John.
(**Milden** church also has wall paintings.)
The carved wood Chantry Chapel, almost
certainly built with the money of the
Shelton family (of Shelton, south
Norfolk), is a classic example of how
monied families consolidated their
position within the Church and so within
the community. As the Sheltons had a
chapel, so other families had enclosed
pews (which are beautifully maintained,
some adorned with coats of arms).

Long Melford's church (pictured), too,
which was completed in 1484, bears
witness to its patrons – the Clopton
Chapel was built in honour of the Clopton
family; the recessed tomb of the father
of the chapel's sponsor, Sir William
Clopton, is on the north wall and there
are several brasses of the family on the

floor of the Kentwell Aisle. Indeed,
the door by the tomb was used by the
Cloptons when they travelled from their
home at Kentwell Hall – clearly, after the
journey, making it round to the other
side of the church was too much. Family
affairs aside, the church's Chinese-style
clock at the back of the Lady Chapel is
reputedly a 'Parliamentary clock', so-
called because when parliament taxed
watches and clocks in 1879 people
started to rely on church clocks.

Clare and **Lavenham** both boast
impressive Gothic wool churches,
although the latter may not be the
most rewarding to visit. Its exterior is
certainly impressive, but some of the
tat that's peddled inside takes the
edge off its impact.

The true pleasure of Suffolk's churches
is that they are so numerous, varied and
well-preserved: the church at **Monks
Eleigh**, with its wonderful view across the
Suffolk flats, **Chelsworth**'s Devil's Door
(so evil spirits could leave by the back
door), and the unique medieval stone
spire at **Polstead** are all worthy of
mention, but there are so many others.
They're an integral part of our heritage –
we have to make sure they're never lost.

During the 18th century Western House, whose foundations date back to the 11th, was a stop-off for carriages travelling along the Roman Way from Colchester to Bristol. Now, owners Peter and Jean Marshall have made the book-lined house, which sits just inside the Suffolk border, and its mature one-acre organic garden, into the most gentle and welcoming of B&Bs. Jean is a singing teacher so you may well be serenaded by pupils, and Peter runs a charming tiny health food store at the back. The dried banana chips and liquorice sticks are highly recommended. All the rooms are light and inviting, and the full breakfasts (home-made bread is a feature) are vegetarian. Children welcome.

Where to eat & drink

Note that many of the places listed below also provide B&B. Additionally, good eating and drinking can also be found at the cheery **Bell** in Castle Hedingham (01787 460350) and the hilltop **Plough** in Hundon (01440 786789). **Chimneys** in Long Melford (Hall Street; 01787 379806) serves up appealing if not very inventive fare, while the **White Hart** in Great Yeldham (Poole Street; 01787 237250) does both bar snacks and grander meals.

The Angel
Market Place, Lavenham (01787 247388/ www.lavenham.co.uk/angel). **Food served** noon-2.15pm, 6.45-9.15pm daily. **Credit** AmEx, MC, V.
Licensed premises since 1420, the Angel offers solid, rural food – game terrine and cumberland sauce; steak and ale pie; pan-fried sirloin steak or tomato and mozzarella tart – that aims itself squarely at the upper end of the pub grub spectrum. Eat in the beamed pub, all atmosphere and charm, or repair to a quieter dining room. Be sure to have an aperitif beforehand outside on Market Square, and watch the world pass slowly by. A meal without drinks comes to around £15 per person. The eight bedrooms (all en suite) make the best of this crooked, winding building (doubles from £69).

Black Lion
Church Walk, Long Melford (01787 312356/ www.ravenwoodhall.co.uk). **Food served** *Wine bar* noon-2pm, 7-9.30pm daily. *Restaurant* 7-9.30pm daily. **Set meals** £22.95 2 courses; £26.95 3 courses. **Credit** AmEx, MC, V.
Once called the Countrymen, this hotel has reclaimed its original name, but continues to provide modern British dishes with a splash of invention: the herbed chicken breast comes with aubergine chips, the marinated tuna steaks with an avocado cream quenelle and parmesan potato cakes, and the fillet of cod with curried coriander pesto. Bistro food is served in the wine bar. The B&B side of things is also comfortable (doubles from £65).

The Bull
High Street, Cavendish (01787 280245). **Food served** noon-2pm, 6.30-9pm Tue-Sat; noon-2pm, 7-9pm Sun. **Credit** MC, V.
You can certainly sample weighty ploughman's lunches at the Bull, but this busy country pub has made a name for itself with its other food, too: fresh fish is delivered daily, and the menu reflects this. Skate, dressed crab (£8.95), cod, plaice, haddock are all likely to be available on the daily changing menu. Vegetarians are well catered for, and dishes such as lamb tavas (braised lamb with Greek spices, wine and tomatoes, £9.95) hint at Mediterranean influences. It's a period inn, with exposed beams stripped of their lathe and plasterwork, enabling one to peep through from the bar area into a dining section set slightly to one side. Children are welcome; booking is essential on Sundays and bank holidays. The only downside is the lack of a decent beer garden (there's a small marquee over a patio).

Great House
Market Place, Lavenham (01787 247431/ www.greathouse.co.uk). **Food served** noon-2.30pm, 7-9.30pm Tue-Sat; noon-2.30pm Sun. **Set lunch** £9.95 2 courses; £15.95 3 courses. **Set dinner** £19.95 3 courses. **Credit** AmEx, MC, V.
This was once Stephen Spender's house; now it's an elegantly formal yet relaxed French restaurant and B&B run with Gallic verve and precision by Régis and Martine Crépy. The menu, undoubtedly one of the best and most fairly priced in Suffolk, derives its strength from its careful use of subtle flavours – the sensational crème d'asperges lunch starter being a case in point. Excellent à la carte lunch and dinner menus offer such dishes as pan-fried escalope of salmon with a wild mushroom sauce, and baked boneless and stuffed quail with foie gras and brandy sauce (exquisite on a recent visit). Meat and fish dishes are favoured and, while vegetarians are catered for, the chef asks for some advance warning. Home-made chocolates add the final flourish to a perfect meal. Children are welcome, particularly for Sunday lunch. Double rooms (from £70) are also available – ask for Room One which has a lovely view over Market Square and a gargantuan four-poster.

Red Onion
57 Ballingdon Street, Sudbury (01787 376777). **Food served** noon-2pm, 6.30-9.30pm Mon-Sat. **Set lunches** £7.50 2 courses; £9.50 3 courses. **Set dinners** £9.50 2 courses; £12.50 3 courses. **Credit** MC, V.
The Red Onion's conversion from an old motor factory shop into a bistro is so successful that diners would never believe that in the 1980s the kitchen may have been knee-deep in sump oil. With around 12 tables, the Red Onion is a bright, cheerful place, offering a short but first-class menu, with many vegetarian and fish options, at very reasonable prices. Filling soups and wonderfully stodgy puddings top and tail the menu.

Scutcher's Bistro
Westgate Street, Long Melford (01787 310200). **Food served** noon-2pm, 7-9.30pm Tue-Sat. **Credit** AmEx, MC, V.
Bought by its current owners in 1991, this Grade-II listed Georgian building has been completely refurbished and offers a menu and an atmosphere totally at odds with its past. The food steers a tasty course through fish and meat, but vegetarians won't fare too well – fillet of turbot lightly roasted with asparagus and a lemon hollandaise (£14.90), or roasted fillet of lamb on buttered spinach with a roast garlic sauce (£13.90) set the tone. A large wine list with over 200 choices features nine marques of champagne and four dessert wines.

Bury St Edmunds & Around

Stay busy in Bury.

Huge skies and flat lands in the **Fens** near Ely.

Dickens was a regular visitor to Bury St Edmunds, describing it in *The Pickwick Papers* as 'a handsome little town of thriving and cleanly appearance'. Back then, in the early 19th century, Bury made its money from textiles. Now sugar and beer are the dominant industries, but there's still a sense in which it resembles a Victorian burgher – solid, upright and intolerant of decadence and disorder. The streets positively gleam, and the presence of 'save our pound' demonstrations and the like seem to confirm Bury – the third most prosperous town in the UK, according to a recent survey – as a High Tory haven of snobbish insularity. Yet in all other respects, Bury is remarkably welcoming, with a helpful tourist information office and a sedate, intelligent take on its past, which extends to the obvious efforts made to keep monuments just-so and stop modernity from encroaching on the town in too brash and inappropriate a manner.

Bury grew up around the Benedictine Abbey of St Edmund – England's patron saint until George unseated him – in medieval times and was for centuries a place of pilgrimage. Bury's motto is 'Shrine of a king, cradle of the law', a reference to the legend that in 1214 the barons of England met in the Abbey church and swore an oath to force King John to accept demands that became enshrined in the Magna Carta. In 1539, however, the monastery was dissolved by Henry VIII and fell into ruin.

Bury has long been a busy market town. Until 1871, when the market was disbanded after complaints of 'rowdyism', it stretched all the way across Angel Hill, the gentle slope – now an enormous car park – which runs parallel to the Abbey gardens, overlooked on one side by the ivy-festooned Angel Hotel and at the far end by the Athenaeum assembly rooms. The modern market, the largest of its kind in East Anglia, now takes place on Wednesdays and Saturdays in the area around Cornhill and the Butter Market, best reached via Abbeygate Street, the main shopping thoroughfare.

Around Bury

Though there's enough in Bury to keep you busy for a weekend, it's worth remembering its proximity to **Newmarket** racecourse

By train from London

There are about eight trains a day to **Bury St Edmunds**, leaving from **King's Cross**. Journey time (including a change at Peterborough) is just under **2hrs**. **Liverpool Street** trains leave between every 10mins and 2hrs (change at Ely or Stowmarket) and take approximately **2hrs** in total. Info: www.ger.co.uk and www.angliarailways.co.uk.

(see p298 **A day at the races**), **Ely** and
Cambridge (see p267). Ely is worth the visit
for its majestic cathedral alone, although **Ely
Museum**, and Oliver Cromwell's House (also
the tourist information centre; 01353 662062)
offer interesting side attractions. Another
worthwhile excursion is 12 miles north to
Thetford. This handsome town, with plenty
of gardens and riverside walks, was once seat
of the kings and bishops of East Anglia and
more recently spawned 18th-century radical
Thomas Paine. Born in White Hart Street, he is
represented in the **Ancient House Museum**
in the same street. The tourist office is here,
too. Those wanting a country house experience
could view **Euston Hall** (01842 766366), near
Thetford, just off the A1088.

The dominating feature of this sparsely
populated area is the massive **Thetford Forest**,
planted in drearily regular rows by the Forestry
Commission in the 1920s. The **High Lodge
Forest Centre** (off the B1107 east of Brandon;
01842 815434) has details of forest walks.

Ely Cathedral – by far the handsomest.

What to see & do

Tourist Information Centres
*6 Angel Hill, Bury St Edmunds, IP33 1UZ (01284
764667/www.stedmundsbury.gov.uk).* **Open**
*Easter-Oct 9.30am-5.30pm Mon-Sat; 10am-3pm Sun.
Nov-Easter 10am-4pm Mon-Fri; 10am-1pm Sat.*

*Ancient House Museum, White Hart Street,
Thetford, IP24 1AA (01842 752599/
www.norfolk.gov.uk/tourism/museums/thetford.htm).*
Open *June-Aug 10am-12.30pm, 1-5pm Mon-Sat;
2-5pm Sun. Sept-May 10am-12.30pm, 1-5pm Mon-Sat.*
Admission *Museum July, Aug £1; 60p concessions.*

Bike hire
Mick's Cycles *68-69 St John's Street,
Bury St Edmunds (01284 753946).*
About 10-15 minutes' walk from the station.

Abbey ruins & gardens
*Angel Hill, Bury St Edmunds (01284 764667/
www.stedmundsbury.gov.uk).* **Open** *7.30am-dusk
Mon-Sat; 9am-dusk Sun.* **Guided tours** *2.30pm
Mon-Fri, Sun.* **Admission** *free. Guided tours £2.50;
£1 concessions.*
The Benedictine Abbey of St Edmund was destroyed
in the Dissolution of the Monasteries in 1539, and its
remains provide the focal point for Bury's tourist
industry. The gardens that now surround them, with
their roses, yew hedges and carefully tended beds of
forget-me-nots, are great for a peaceful stroll, with the
Alwyne House Tea House offering sustenance and fine
Sunday lunches. For some context, make for the
Abbey Visitors Centre in Samson's Tower, where you
can pick up the necessary gear for an audio tour: you
can be shown around by one Brother Jocelin de
Brakelond, who lived in Bury in the 12th century.
Alternatively, call the tourist information centre to
arrange a guided tour.

Ely Cathedral
*Chapter House, The College, Ely (01353 667735/
www.cathedral.ely.anglican.org).* **Open** *May-Oct 7am-
7pm daily. Nov-Apr 7.30am-6pm Mon-Sat; 7.30am-
5pm Sun.* **Admission** *£4; £3.30-£3.50 concessions.*
Bury may have some fine abbey ruins, better restaurants and accommodation, and a bigger market; but in
the cathedral stakes, Ely wins hands down. Founded as
a monastery in 673 by Saxon princess Etheldreda, a
shrine to whom sits in front of the High Altar, the cathedral, which dates from 1081, towers over the local landscape in a dauntingly imposing fashion. The inside is
no less impressive; the centrepiece is the 14th-century
Octagon, a stunning construction made up of eight
pillars that support 200 tons of timber, glass and lead.
Through the south door is a collection of medieval
monastic buildings still in use today; to the north a large
and lovely Lady Chapel. In addition, the South Triforium
holds a **Stained Glass Museum** (01353 660347),
which charges £2.50-£3.50 admission.

Ely Museum
*The Old Gaol, Market Street, Ely (01353
666655).* **Open** *Mar-Oct 10.30am-5.30pm daily.
Nov-Feb 10.30am-4.30pm daily.* **Admission** *£2;
£1 concessions.*
Situated in the town's former prison – the museum contains some unintentionally goofy re-creations of the
building's past on its first floor – the capacious Ely
Museum delivers a neat summation of the town's history. Take time out and watch the entertaining archive
documentary about the local eel-catchers, on permanent
repeat in one of the museum's several galleries.

Greene King Brewery
*Westgate Brewery, Westgate Street, Bury St Edmunds
(01284 714297).* **Open** *Tours 10am, 2pm Mon-Thur.*
Admission *Museum only £2; £1 concessions. Brewery
tours (includes museum) £5 (no under-18s).*
The first recorded mention of brewing in Bury came
in the Domesday Book of 1086, which mentioned the
Abbey's 'cerevisiarii', or ale brewers. Greene King

East Anglia

arrived on Westgate Street just over 700 years later, a fact commemorated and celebrated at the brewery's surprisingly informative if occasionally self-aggrandising new museum. As a counterpart to these displays, Greene King also offers tours of the brewhouse and fermenting room twice daily during the week; pre-booking is essential.

Manor House Museum

5 Honey Hill, Bury St Edmunds (01284 757072). **Open** 10am-5pm Tue, Wed, Sat, Sun. **Admission** £3; £2 concessions.

Built by John Hervey, the first Earl of Bristol, this Georgian mansion has been converted into an offbeat museum full of paintings, furniture, costumes, objets d'art and lots and lots of clocks. One can, you'll rapidly discover, have too many clocks, though the touch-sensitive computer screens in each room make fact-gleaning easy. The museum is also displaying some of the highlights of the Moyse's Hall Museum while the latter is closed for renovations (*see below*).

Moyse's Hall Museum

Cornhill, Bury St Edmunds (01284 757488/www.stedmundsbury.gov.uk/moyses.htm). **Open** 10am-5pm Mon-Sat; 2-5pm Sun. **Admission** phone for details; museum closed until early 2002.

Moyse's Hall has been many things in its 800-year history, including a tavern, a synagogue and a prison. Now it's a museum of local history and archaeology that numbers among its more ghoulish exhibits a lock of Mary Tudor's hair and a book covered in the skin of William Corder, the man convicted of the notorious Red Barn murder in 1827, as well as his flayed scalp. This latter exhibit is among the goodies temporarily transplanted to the Manor House Museum (*see above*) while Moyse's Hall gets a facelift. When it reopens – an event scheduled for early 2002, though call to check before visiting – it'll contain an education room, new gallery space and better visitor facilities.

Rede Hall Park Farm

Rede, Bury St Edmunds (01284 850695). **Open** *Apr-Sept* 10am-5pm daily. Closed Nov-Mar. **Admission** £2.50-£4.

A working farm, utilising machinery and methods from an era when genetically modified vegetables had not even been dreamt of. The wagons and 1930s tractors introduce an altogether slower pace to life, with cart rides, pets' corners and a farming museum among the attractions.

Relive the past in the **Anglo-Saxon Village**.

St Edmundsbury Cathedral

Angel Hill, Bury St Edmunds (01284 754933/www.stedscathedral.co.uk). **Open** *June-Aug* 8am-7pm daily. *Sept-May* 8am-6pm daily. **Admission** free; suggested donation £2.

More than 1,100 years old and still incomplete, St Edmundsbury was only granted cathedral status in 1914, and even then it was a toss-up between it and nearby St Mary's Church (also worth a peek) as to which one would get it. The cloisters and the crossing chapel are only partly built, but the most distinctive aspect of the otherwise slyly grand building is its lack of a tower. The cathedral is most of the way towards finding the £10.5 million it needs for completion by 2004. For guided tours, call the cathedral visitor officer on the above number. The Cathedral Refectory is popular for morning coffee and light snacks, while the Landing Gallery upstairs hosts temporary art exhibitions. The cathedral also hosts occasional classical concerts.

Theatre Royal

Westgate Street, Bury St Edmunds (01284 769505/www.TheatreRoyal.org). **Guided tours** *Apr-Oct* 11am-1pm, 2-4pm Mon, Wed; 11am-1pm Sat. Closed (for tours) Nov-Mar. **Admission** (NT) £2.50; £2 concessions.

Owned by Greene King, who once used it to store hops (it's opposite the brewery, *see p296*), the Theatre Royal is leased to the National Trust and is one of the smallest and oldest working theatres in the country.

West Stow Anglo-Saxon Village

Icklingham Road, West Stow (01284 728718/www.stedmundsbury.gov.uk/weststow.htm). **Open** 10am-5pm daily. Last entry 4pm. **Admission** £3.50-£4.50.

This replica village, a short drive from Bury on the A1101, is built on the site of an actual Anglo-Saxon dwelling excavated between 1965 and 1972. Hire an audio guide and wander from the Weaving House to the Living House to the Sunken House, learning about life in fifth-century East Anglia. Pigs and hens and crops add to the 'realism'. There's also a 125-acre country park (admission is free), with nature and wildfowl reserves and two visitors' centres.

Where to stay

Abbey Hotel

35 Southgate Street, Bury St Edmunds, IP33 2AZ (01284 762020/fax 01284 724770). **Rates** £55 single occupancy; £60-£68 double/twin; £75-£85 family; £75 suite. St Botolph's Cottage (sleeps 4) £75 as double, then £7.50 per person. **Rooms** (all en suite) 12 double/twin; 2 family; 1 suite. **Credit** AmEx, MC, V.

The endearingly chaotic assemblage of buildings that make up this hotel include a Tudor hostelry, a recent extension set up on stilts (apparently to make room for the requisite number of parking spots) and a character-packed converted stable and hayloft. Rooms vary considerably in size – and height, so mind your heads – but all are comfortable at the very least. The hotel is ten minutes' walk from the town centre. Children welcome. No-smoking rooms available.

East Anglia

A day at the races

The words 'racing' and 'Newmarket' go together about as well as 'Lester Piggott' and 'tax evasion'. The town exists almost entirely for the benefit of the racing industry, which employs a disproportionate number of the local population. Aside from the racecourses, which stage their first meeting of the year around Easter and their last in early November, Newmarket is home to Tattersalls, Europe's largest bloodstock auctioneers, and the town is ringed by a great many studs and stables.

Get up early enough and you'll be able to catch a great many nags out on the town's dewy gallops: the horses scything through the dawn mists makes for a majestic sight. But if you're not a morning person, worry not: there are enough days of racing here to fill the horse-shaped hole in most people's lives, with the Guineas Festival (May) and the Champions Meeting (October) the two biggest draws.

Even on non-race days, horses provide the main diversions. Easily the biggest is **National Horseracing Museum**, whose displays illuminate the story of the industry effectively enough. The museum also arranges tours to studs and racecourses (£16.50; advance booking is essential). The **National Stud** also offers tours of its premises; it's at the junction of the A14 and A11.

Out of the racing season, Newmarket is remarkably unremarkable. Time your visit right, though – wrapping it up with a dinner at the **Star Inn** (*see p299*) – and it'll be fun. Assuming, that is, you don't lose your shirt in the process.

National Horseracing Museum
99 High Street, Newmarket (01638 667333/www.nhrm.co.uk). **Open** *Sept, Oct; Easter-July* 10am-5pm Tue-Sun. *Aug* 10am-5pm daily. Closed Nov-Easter. **Admission** £4.50; £2.50-£3.50 concessions.

National Stud
01638 666789/www.nationalstud.co.uk. **Guided tours** Mar-Sept 11.15am, 2.30pm Mon-Sat; 2.30pm Sun. **Admission** £4.50; £3.50 concessions.

Newmarket Racecourses
01638 675500/ www.newmarketracecourses.co.uk.

Angel Hotel
3 Angel Hill, Bury St Edmunds, IP33 1LT (01284 753926/fax 01284 714001/www.theangel.co.uk). **Rates** £81 single; £111 double/twin; £159 four-poster; £189 family. Special breaks. **Rooms** (all en suite) 8 single; 8 twin; 43 double; 4 four-poster; 2 suites; 1 family. **Credit** AmEx, DC, MC, V.
The Angel is easily Bury's best-known hotel, thanks to the regular visits it received from one Charles Dickens (he wrote part of *The Pickwick Papers* here – you can still stay in his preferred room). A new wing has added 24 rooms, although the faintly naff decor will not be to everyone's taste. Eating options come via the respected Abbeygate Restaurant and its sibling, the Vaults brasserie. Children and pets welcome. No-smoking rooms available.

Chantry Hotel
8 Sparhawk Street, Bury St Edmunds, IP33 1RY (01284 767427/fax 01284 760946). **Rates** £49.50-£65 single; £69 standard double/twin; £79 superior double/suite. **Rooms** (all en suite) 3 single; 2 twin; 10 double; 1 suite. **Credit** AmEx, DC, MC, V.
Bob and Christine Pitt offer a friendly welcome in their hotel, one of the largest in central Bury. Made up of two buildings – one a Grade II-listed Georgian building, the other a 400-plus-year-old Tudor house – it stands on the site of a 12th-century chantry chapel, within a tankard's toss or two of the Greene King Brewery. The cosy bar/lounge makes for a nice start to any evening, and breakfasts are outstanding. Children and pets welcome by prior arrangement. No-smoking rooms available.

Northgate House
8 Northgate Street, Bury St Edmunds, IP33 1HQ (01284 760469/fax 01284 724008). **Rates** £55-£60 single occupancy; £95-£100 double. **Rooms** (all en suite) 3 double. **Credit** AmEx, DC, MC, V.
Astonishingly, this grand property remained derelict for 15 years after the death of its former owner, author Norah Lofts, in 1983. Joy and Gerard Fiennes have since

done it up wonderfully, and now let out a handful of the rooms – all en suite, and all furnished in an agreeably countrified style – as B&B. The warmth of their welcome is made complete by the decanters of Madeira left in each room, close to the pile of literature that contains some of Lofts' novels and a helpful, honest critique of the local restaurants. All bedrooms are no-smoking.

Old Egremont House
31 Egremont Street, Ely, CB6 1AE (tel/fax 01353 663118). **Rates** £41 single occupancy; £48 double/twin. **Rooms** 1 twin (en suite); 1 double (private bathroom). **No credit cards**.
This cosy B&B, run to a high standard by Sheila Friend-Smith, has a great view of the cathedral from the garden. Breakfasts use fresh local produce. Children welcome by arrangement. No smoking throughout.

Ounce House
Northgate Street, Bury St Edmunds, IP33 1HP (01284 761779/fax 01284 768315/www.ouncehouse.co.uk). **Rates** £60-£70 single occupancy; £85-£95 double/twin; £100 family. Special breaks. **Rooms** (all en suite) 1 twin; 2 double. **Credit** AmEx, MC, V.
Like Northgate House just down the road (*see p298*), this former Victorian merchant's house has a large garden at the back, along with spacious rooms and hand-picked antiques and paintings. All contribute to an air of solid bourgeois gentility, though to take advantage of it, be sure to book well ahead. The friendly owners, Simon and Jenny Pott, are key figures in the local community, and an excellent source of tips and gossip. Children welcome. No smoking throughout.

Where to eat & drink

The choice of restaurants in Bury has, thankfully, improved in recent years, and there are now enough respectable options with which to fill a weekend. However, be sure to book in advance.

Pubs-wise, Greene King boozers dominate the town. If you can't fit into the tiny **Nutshell Pub** on Skinner Street – at 16ft by 7.5ft, it's said to be the smallest pub in Britain – then try the **Masons Arms** (14 Whiting Street; 01284 753955) and **Rose & Crown** (48 Whiting Street) both pour a fine pint of the local ale, with the former also offering decent pub lunches. A couple of newcomers also catch the eye. **No. 3** (3 Risbygate Street) is more bar than pub, with serviceable cocktails and funky decor, while the splendid **Old Cannon Brewery** (86 Cannon Street; 01284 768769) puts up some competition to Greene King. Of the beers brewed on site here, Gunners Daughter is particularly fine, and the food's also worth sampling.

19 Angel Hill
19-21 Angel Hill, Bury St Edmunds (01284 704870). **Food served** noon-2pm, 7-9pm Tue-Fri; 7-9.30pm Sat. **Set dinner** (Wed) £15 3 courses. **Credit** AmEx, MC, V.
After an apprenticeship at the Savoy, and jobs in other top-notch kitchens in London and abroad, Peter and

Joanne Hewett moved out here to open their own restaurant. Judging by the lack of free tables on the Saturday we visited, the citizens of Bury have welcomed their classical yet inventive brand of cooking with open arms. Most mains cost between £10 and £15.

Harriet's Café Tearooms
57 Cornhill Buildings, Bury St Edmunds (01284 756256). **Food served** 9am-6.30pm Mon-Sat; 10am-6pm Sun. **Credit** MC, V.
Offering welcome solace from the hectic Saturday market, Harriet's aims to offer its visitors 'a truly English experience'. While comments such as this on the menu mark it immediately as a little touristy, the range of teas and cakes puts it back in credit again.

Leaping Hare
Wyken Hall, Stanton (01359 250287). **Food served** 10am-6pm Mon-Thur; 10am-6pm, 7-9.30pm Fri, Sat. **Credit** MC, V.
Housed in a 400-year-old barn next to the Elizabethan manor house Wyken Hall, the Leaping Hare is ten minutes' drive from Bury. The food manages to be Olde English and modern Mediterranean at the same time, with wine from Wyken Vineyards. Three courses with wine should work out at just over £20 per head.

Maison Bleue at Mortimer's
30-31 Churchgate Street, Bury St Edmunds (01284 760623/www.maisonbleue.co.uk). **Food served** noon-2.30pm, 7-9.30pm Tue-Sat. **Set lunches** £9.95-£12.95 2 courses; £14.95 3 courses. **Set dinner** £19.95 3 courses. **Credit** AmEx, MC, V.
All the fish served at this restaurant, one of the finest in Bury, is locally caught; try the sea bass fillet in a grapefruit butter sauce. That said, meat-lovers should find enough variety on the menu. Eating à la carte costs around £30 per head at dinner.

Somewhere Else
1 Langton Place, Hatter Street, Bury St Edmunds (01284 760750). **Food served** 10.30am-2.30pm, 6.30-10.30pm Wed-Sat. **Credit** AmEx, MC, V.
This is the perfect lunchtime stop if you're pub-lunched out, with a menu that takes in all manner of toasted and open sandwiches. In the evenings, it offers such tempting dishes as smoked haddock risotto at extremely reasonable prices in its small, cosy space.

Star Inn
The Street, Lidgate (01638 500275). **Food served** noon-2pm, 7-10pm Mon-Sat; noon-2.30pm Sun. **Set lunch** (Sun) £14.50 3 courses. **Credit** AmEx, MC, V.
A 15-minute drive south of Newmarket on the B1063, this delightful country pub – with a bar billiards table – has garnered quite a reputation for its impressive Catalan cooking. That said, while there's nothing wrong with the Sunday lunches, they don't merit the £14.50 price-tag.

La Vita é Bella
34 Abbeygate Street, Bury St Edmunds (01284 706004). **Food served** 6-10.30pm Tue; noon-2pm, 6-10.30pm Wed-Sun. **Credit** AmEx, MC, V.
The food at this airy restaurant is, if not outstanding, then certainly fine enough. But what distinguishes La Vita é Bella from its competitors is the warmth of the welcome offered by the Italian family that runs it. You'll pay around £15 for three courses, excluding drinks.

East Anglia

Suffolk Coast

The discreet charm of the Suffolk seaside.

Very odd, Suffolk. And it's not easy to say why. Perhaps it's because the county is not really on the way to anywhere (apart from Norfolk, and the sea) that it has managed to maintain its own distinct identity and a subtle otherness. Nowhere in the county is this more true than along the coast. The more sensitive visitor will revel in the marginally uneasy juxtaposition of the cosy and the bleak, the cultivated and the wild. It's perfect Barbara Vine territory, and it's no wonder that Ruth Rendell's darker alter ego has set several of her claustrophobic novels in the county (including *No Night is Too Long*, which makes use of Orford and Aldeburgh). This frisson is probably at its least noticeable during the height of the summer when crowds frolic on Southwold's shingle, and classical music-lovers attend the Proms season at Snape Maltings. But if you ever happen to be in, say, Orford, on a biting winter's day, walking in the shadow of the grim castle keep, past the fulminating fug of the blackened smokehouse, and down to the quayside as the mist rolls slowly and silently in from the River Alde, you'll know you're somewhere pretty special.

Being there

There's not a lot specifically to *do* along the coast (and beaches are predominantly pebbly, the sea icy) – in fact, locals rather look down their noses at 'attractions'. You come here to *be* rather than to *do*. **Woodbridge**, a few miles north-east of Ipswich, may be inland now, but this lively one-time Elizabethan shipbuilding port makes an agreeable introduction to the area. Stretching back up a hill from the River Deben, you'll find a scattering of minor sights (Woodbridge Tide Mill, the Suffolk Horse Museum, Woodbridge Museum), antiques shops, and the odd good pub and restaurant. Near the town is the site of probably the most celebrated archaeological find made in Britain, **Sutton Hoo** – the fabulous treasure-stuffed ship of a seventh-century East Anglian king.

Between Woodbridge and the coast, the wind-whipped Rendlesham and Tunstall forests provide a barrier that only adds to the invigorating feeling of isolation in little **Orford**. Overlooked by its 12th-century keep, it offers little to do but walking, eating and drinking, and contemplating the immense

Aldeburgh – the seafront that was never meant to be.

expanse of **Orford Ness** (*see p305* **Testing times**). In the 12th century the then-nascent shingle spit provided a sheltered harbour for Orford. Unfortunately, it wouldn't stop growing and, expanding by around 53 feet a year, it now all but cuts the village off from the sea. Boat trips run from the quay. Pick up picnic goodies from Richardson's Smokehouse, and take a quick look at the Norman church of St Bartholomew – there's a fine font inside and a huge rosemary bush in the churchyard.

Great Britten

The next major settlement on the coast heading north is **Aldeburgh**. It's a classy place and knows it (so pronounce it 'orl-brer' if you want to create the right impression) – a lot of London money has been sending property prices into the stratosphere in recent years. There are deliberately few concessions to the tourist industry along the long, wide High Street that runs parallel to the sea, but it's a relaxed spot to hang out nonetheless. At No.84 you'll find the **Aldeburgh Cookery School** (01728 454039/ www.aldeburghcookeryschool.com), which runs popular day and weekend courses.

Constant erosion of the coastline means that the current seafront is something of a jumble – it was never meant to face the ocean. The oldest building in town is here – the 16th-century moot hall – as is a shiny modern lifeboat station. If you don't fancy eating out at one of the town's surprising number of excellent restaurants, then join the often considerable High Street queues at the Aldeburgh Fish & Chip Shop and the Golden Galleon and then take your booty on to the pebbly beach.

Few people are more associated with their native region than **Benjamin Britten** is with the Suffolk Coast. Born in Lowestoft in 1913, he lived most of his life in the area. In 1947 Britten moved with the celebrated tenor (and his lifelong partner) Peter Pears to Crag House on Crabbe Street in Aldeburgh. Together with the producer and librettist Eric Crozier they came up with the idea of starting a modest musical festival. Today, the **Aldeburgh Festival** (now held a few miles inland at Snape Maltings) is one of the world's premier classical music and opera festivals. Many of Britten's works are set in Suffolk; fans should get hold of the 'Britten Trail' leaflet available at the tourist office.

Snape Maltings, a large collection of Victorian malthouses and granaries on the banks of the Alde, has been developed as far more than just a concert venue. It now encompasses a music school and a 'unique shopping experience', consisting of a music shop, gallery, kitchen shop, crafts shop, 'period home centre', clothes store, a pub and tearoom.

By train from London

Direct trains to **Woodbridge** are infrequent; services run about every two hours from **Liverpool Street**, with a change at **Ipswich**. The entire journey takes **1hr 35mins** to **1hr 45mins**. Info: www.angliarailways.co.uk.

Frankly, it's all rather unreal and overpriced. More appealing is the range of painting, craft and decorative arts courses run from here (01728 688305/www.snapemaltings.co.uk) and the regular river trips.

The powers that B

Thorpeness, a couple of miles north of Aldeburgh, is a surreal little place. With its rows of black-boarded and faux half-timbered houses, it has the air of a Tudor theme village. It's hardly a surprise when you learn that the entire settlement was dreamed up as a fashionable resort by GS Ogilvie when he bought the Sizewell estate in 1910. Go for a row on the Meare, dug by hand by navvies, and sprinkled with 20 islands named after characters in *Peter Pan* in honour of Ogilvie's friend JM Barrie. He also created a well and used a windmill to pump water to a tank on top of an 87-foot tower, which he disguised as an overgrown house, known as the 'House in the Clouds'. The windmill can be visited, and the Dolphin Inn is good for a spot of refreshment.

A little further up the coast is the area's most controversial presence: **Sizewell** twin nuclear power stations. Apart from the legion of pylons striding purposefully across the coastal flats, the power stations are a low-key presence. The huge dome of Sizewell B, the UK's only pressurised water reactor, is the most distinctive feature and an inescapable sight along this coast. There's a moderately popular beach by the power station for the truly blithe.

Dunwich and dusted

Unlikely as it seems, **Dunwich** (the 'w' is silent), a diminutive village with a good pub (the Ship), a few remaining beach-launched fishing boats and a seaside café serving up possibly the freshest fish and chips in the country, was a major port in the early Middle Ages. Up to 5,000 people lived within its walls, trading with the Baltic, Iceland, France and the Low Countries. Monasteries, over a dozen churches, hospitals, palaces and even a mint reflected the town's role as a busy trading port and one of England's major shipbuilding towns. Continual coastal erosion, however, exacerbated by a three-day storm in 1286, meant that by the

East Anglia

Beach huts line the coast.

16th century trade had dried up (the harbour had also silted up), and medieval houses and churches dropped slowly but surely over the crumbling cliffs. Little evidence now remains beyond the sparse ruins of Greyfriars Abbey and the salvaged remains of All Saints church and leper chapel in the churchyard of St James's. Don't miss the superb **Dunwich Museum**, which tells the remarkable story of this unique place.

Southwold to Walberswick

The northern extent of this break is marked by **Southwold**. It's the biggest 'resort' on this stretch of coast, yet in Suffolk all this means is that (in season) you get a lot of lobster-hued holidaymakers picnicking outside the brightly painted beach huts that stretch along the entire promenade (plus one tiny amusement arcade on the pier, which is currently being rebuilt), while the town up on the cliffs gets on with its own life. When you consider that one of Southwold's premier attractions is 'the only purpose-built museum dedicated to the story and history of amber' you get an idea of the sort of place it is. Low-key.

The most dominant force in Southwold life is the estimable Adnams Brewery, which owns the town's best two hotels (the Crown and the Swan, behind which it is situated). There are few greater Southwold pleasures than supping an Adnams brew on one of the many greens that speckle the town.

Another must is the 20-minute walk along the seafront or cross-country to the rowing-boat ferry over the River Blyth to **Walberswick**.

This somnolent little village was once home to painter Philip Wilson Steer and, in addition to the excellent Bell Inn, boasts a curious church-within-a-church. In the Middle Ages, Walberswick was a sizeable port, and the original 15th-century St Andrew's was to be a mighty church to reflect the status of the town. But its fortunes declined before the church was finished and much of it was dismantled to build the much smaller current church within the older building's ruins. Another notable church close by is at **Blythburgh**. The huge Holy Trinity, known as the 'Cathedral of the Marshes' has a wonderfully ornate exterior and is filled with light inside.

What to see & do

Tourist Information Centres

152 High Street, Aldeburgh, IP15 5AQ (01728 453637/www.suffolkcoastal.gov.uk). **Open** 9am-5.30pm daily.
69 High Street, Southwold, IP18 6DS (01502 724729/www.visit-southwold.co.uk). **Open** *Apr-Sept* 10am-5pm Mon-Fri; 10am-5.30pm Sat; 11am-4pm Sun. *Oct-Mar* 11am-3.30pm Mon, Tue, Thur, Fri; 11am-3pm Wed; 11am-4.30pm Sat.
Station Buildings, Woodbridge, IP12 4AJ (01394 382240/www.suffolkcoastal.gov.uk). **Open** *Easter-Sept* 9am-5.30pm Mon-Fri; 9.30am-5pm Sat, Sun. *Oct-Easter* 9am-5.30pm Mon-Fri; 10am-4pm Sat; 10am-1pm Sun.

Aldeburgh Festival/ Snape Maltings

Snape Maltings Concert Hall, Snape, IP17 1SP (01728 453543/www.aldeburgh.co.uk). **Tickets** vary; phone to check.
Founded by Benjamin Britten, Peter Pears and Eric Crozier in 1948, the famed annual Aldeburgh Festival (in June) is actually only the highlight of a busy musical year at Snape. The Britten-Pears School, based at the Maltings, puts on events throughout the year, but the big ones are the main festival in June and the Snape Proms in August. In addition, there's the annual Early Music Festival at Easter (featuring mainly baroque music), and, in October, a festival of music by Benjamin Britten. For all these events, you should check the dates with the local tourist information office (*see above*) and book well in advance (particularly for accommodation). There's also a major poetry festival here in November. In addition, the Maltings are home to a number of rather chichi and pricey shops, plus a pub and a teashop.

Dunwich Museum

St James Street, Dunwich (01728 648796). **Open** *Apr-Sept* 11.30am-4.30pm daily. *Oct* noon-4pm daily. Closed Nov-Mar. **Admission** free.
The extraordinary story of how the apparently unremarkable hamlet of Dunwich was once one of the region's major settlements is told with great verve in this excellent museum. At its peak in the early Middle Ages, between 4,000 and 5,000 people lived

within its walls, but inexorable erosion (and the occasional major storm) washed most of Dunwich into the North Sea by the 16th century.

Easton Farm Park

Easton, nr Wickham Market (01728 746475/ www.eastonfarmpark.co.uk). **Open** *Apr-June, Sept* 10.30am-6pm Tue-Sun, bank hols. *July, Aug* 10.30am-6pm daily. Closed Oct-Mar. **Admission** £4.75; £3.25-£4.25 concessions; free under-3s.

There's petting aplenty to be had in the beautifully situated 35 acres of the award-winning Easton Farm Park. Highlights include the Victorian dairy in full milking action, pony rides, feeding the fauna and the adventure playground. There are farmers' markets here one Saturday a month.

Framlingham Castle

Framlingham (01728 724189/www.english-heritage.org.uk). **Open** *Apr-Sept* 10am-6pm daily. *Oct* 10am-5pm daily. *Nov-Mar* 10am-4.30pm/dusk daily. **Admission** (EH) £3.70; £1.90-£2.80 concessions.

While Orford Castle (*see below*) has its keep but no curtain walls, Framlingham has its walls but no keep. The current keep – stronghold of the rebellious Bigod family – dates from the late 12th century. Edward VI gave it to his sister Mary, who was proclaimed queen here in 1553. Accompanied by an audio tour, visitors are taken along the battlements, punctuated by 13 towers.

Minsmere RSPB Nature Reserve

nr Westleton (01728 648281/www.rspb.org.uk). **Open** 9am-9pm/dusk Mon, Wed-Sun. **Admission** £5; £1.50-£3 concessions.

Follow the signs from the A12 or Westleton to reach Minsmere, one of eastern England's most important reserves for wading birds. Upwards of 200 species of bird have been recorded here in a year, including marsh harriers and bitterns. Minsmere's biggest success story is the avocet (symbol of the RSPB) – more than 100 pairs nest here each year. There's a shop, tearoom, nature trails, hides and frequent guided walks and events.

Orford Castle

Orford (01394 450472/www.english-heritage.org.uk). **Open** *Apr-Sept* 10am-6pm daily. *Oct* 10am-5pm/dusk daily. *Nov-Mar* 10am-4pm Wed-Sun. **Admission** (EH) £2.60; £1.30-£2 concessions.

Henry II built Orford Castle in 1165-73 in order to counter the considerable local power of uppity Hugh Bigod, who was based at nearby Framlingham Castle (*see above*). The castle's impressive curtain walls are long gone, but the impressive keep – one of the best preserved in Britain – remains. There's not much to see inside, but the views from the top over Orford Ness are lovely.

Sizewell

Sizewell Road, nr Leiston (01728 653890/ tour bookings 0800 376 0676/www.british-energy.com). **Open** *Easter-Oct* 10am-4pm daily. Closed Nov-Easter. **Guided tours** 11am.
Admission free.

Places on the 11am guided tours are limited, so call the freephone number above to book a place. The visitors' centre is now closed, and the times the power station is open to the public may change; phone to check.

Sutton Hoo

nr Woodbridge (tourist information 01394 382240). **Guided tours** *Easter-Oct* 2pm, 3pm Sat, Sun, bank hols. Closed Nov-Easter. **Tickets** £2; £1 concessions; free under-10s.

Anyone with any archaeological interest will be familiar with Sutton Hoo. From the 20 grave mounds set high on a hillside by the River Deben the richest archaeological treasure ever found in Britain was excavated (in 1938). The centrepiece was a 90ft-long ship, the likely last resting place of the Anglo-Saxon king of East Anglia, Raedwald. The magnificent cache of treasure found here can now been seen in the British Museum. There are 45-minute guided tours of the site (no need to book), which is only accessible by foot from the B1083. Opposite the turning to Hollesley, take the footpath signposted to Sutton Hoo; it's a 20-minute walk. If in doubt, ask at Woodbridge Tourist Information Office.

Where to stay

Book as far in advance as possible. Demand for accommodation outstrips supply on the Suffolk Coast. If the places reviewed below are full, try the **Uplands Hotel** in Aldeburgh (Victoria Road; 01728 452420; doubles £75), **Ferry House** in Walberswick (01502 723384; doubles £42-£45), or the **Crown Inn** in Snape (Bridge Road; 01728 688324; doubles £65). If you want to stay in Orford, there are rooms at the **King's Head** (Front Street; 01394 450271; doubles £55) and, near the quay, the **Jolly Sailor** (Quay Street; 01394 450243; doubles £40). In Dunwich, the **Ship Inn** (St James Street; 01728 648219; doubles £55) has three rooms.

Acton Lodge

18 South Green, Southwold, IP18 6HB (01502 723217). **Rates** £25-£40 single occupancy; £50-£70 double/twin. **Rooms** 2 double; 1 twin (2 en suite, 1 with private bathroom). **No credit cards.**

Enjoying a fantastic location close to the sea on one of Southwold's characterful greens, this weighty Victorian guesthouse is packed with original features and has been furnished in an appropriately antiquey style. Bedrooms are smart and have TVs, hairdryers and tea- and coffee-making facilities. Breakfasts are above average. Children welcome. No smoking throughout.

The fine **Bell Inn** at Walberswick. *See p304.*

Bell Inn

Ferry Road, Walberswick, IP18 6TN (01502 723109/ fax 01502 722728/www.blythweb.co.uk/ bellinn).
Rates £40-£70 single occupancy; £70 double/twin; £90-£130 family. Special breaks. **Rooms** (all en suite) 4 double; 1 twin; 1 family. **Credit** MC, V.

On the light-suffused apex of Walberswick's estuary and rivermouth, with views of both, this pleasingly plain 600-year-old pub has old stone floors eroded to a polish, wooden settles, fires and good fish dinners – and ceilings to suit the height of a 14th-century population. The six rooms have contemporary flourishes – en suite bathrooms, tea- and coffee-making facilities – but nothing (fortunately) can be done about their basically medieval character. Great garden. All bedrooms no-smoking. Children and dogs welcome.

A12 N; take B1387 E to Walberswick; inn is signposted in village; follow signs up track; hotel is on right.

Crown & Castle

Orford, Woodbridge, IP12 2LJ (01394 450205/ www.crownandcastlehotel.co.uk). **Rates** £65-£110 single occupancy; £80 double/twin; £95 family room. **Rooms** (all en suite) 9 double; 8 twin, 1 family. Special breaks. **Credit** MC, V.

David and (food writer) Ruth Watson took over the moribund Crown and Castle pub in late 1999 and have been slowly modernising its tired rooms ever since – to stunning effect. Those on the first floor of the main building are kitted out in cool, light paints and fabrics, with big comfy beds and funky tiles and massive-headed power showers in the bathrooms. The Trinity restaurant (see *p306*) is a winner, too – go for the great-value dinner, bed-and-breakfast deal (£120-£150 per couple per night). And be sure to pay the extra for a new room. Children and pets welcome. No-smoking rooms available.

Follow signs for Orford Castle from the Melton roundabout on A12; hotel is next to castle.

Crown Hotel

90 High Street, Southwold, IP18 6DP (01502 722275/fax 01502 727263). **Rates** £57 single; £82 double/twin; £107-£117 family. **Rooms** 2 single (en suite); 5 double (4 en suite, 1 private bath); 4 twin (3 en suite, 1 with private bath). **Credit** AmEx, DC, MC, V.

The number-two Adnams-owned hotel in Southwold is considerably smaller and cheaper than the nearby Swan (*see below*). Bedrooms tend towards the diminutive and are simply decorated, but the hotel's great plus is its snug marine-inspired Back Bar and a buzzing front barbrasserie – the best place to eat and drink in Southwold (*see p306*). Behind the Crown is the HQ and kitchen shop of Adnams Wine Merchants. Children welcome. Adnams also owns the Randolph, just outside town in Reydon (01502 723603; doubles £65-£70).

Dunburgh Guest House

28 North Parade, Southwold, IP18 6LT (01502 723253/www.southwold.ws/dunburgh). **Rates** £30-£40 single; £50-£65 twin/double; £55-£70 superior double. **Rooms** (all en suite) 1 single; 2 double/twin; 1 superior double. **No credit cards.**

This is the pick of the guesthouses along Southwold's North Parade, overlooking the sea. Karen Keable's friendly and immaculately kept place enjoys a fantastic location (close to the pier) and so, to make the most of it,

don't stint on the few extra quid needed for the superior or double room with balcony – the view will make your stay. Children welcome. All bedrooms no-smoking.

Ocean House

25 Crag Path, Aldeburgh, IP15 5BS (01728 452094). **Rates** £35-£55 single occupancy; £50-£65 double/twin. **Rooms** 1 single; 2 double/ twin. **No credit cards.**

Wonderfully situated overlooking Aldeburgh's pebbly beach, Ocean House is a mid-Victorian monolith that's been sensitively restored to its original condition by the welcoming Phil and Juliet Brereton. The bedrooms have views out over the beach and the icy North Sea, and there's a games room in the basement. Be sure to ask for one of the first-floor rooms at the front – they are by far the nicest. There's plenty of choice for breakfast – don't miss the smoked haddock with poached eggs. Be warned: you'll need to book months in advance to secure a spring or summer weekend. No smoking throughout.

Old Rectory

Campsea Ashe, IP13 0PU (tel/fax 01728 746524). **Rates** £45 single; £60-£65 double/twin; £75 four-poster. **Rooms** (all en suite) 1 single; 2 twin; 5 double; 2 four-poster. **Credit** AmEx, DC, MC, V.

It's not on the coast, but the Old Rectory (a Wolsey Lodge), situated in a small, tranquil village near Woodbridge, is a quirky, fun place to stay. Owner/chef Stewart Bassett creates an informal atmosphere in the sizeable Georgian house. There's a range of bedrooms, from the four-poster room overlooking the garden to the cosy attic room. An excellent no-choice dinner (three courses for £18.50) is served (compulsory if staying a Saturday night). Children and dogs welcome. No smoking throughout.

A12 N; take B1078 E to Campsea Ashe; go through village; over bridge; house is on right next to church.

Swan Hotel

Market Place, Southwold, IP18 6EG (01502 722186/ fax 01502 724800). **Rates** £65-£70 single; £100 double/twin; £125 deluxe double/twin; £180 four-poster; £170-£180 suite. **Rooms** 4 single (2 en suite shower, 2 en suite bath); 28 double/twin (26 en suite, 2 with private bath); 8 deluxe double/twin (all en suite); 1 four-poster (en suite); 1 twin suite (en suite). **Credit** AmEx, DC, MC, V.

The jewel in the Adnams hotel crown, the Swan has long been the most prestigious inn in Southwold. The most characterful parts of the building (such as the stone-flagged lobby) date from the 17th century. The portrait-hung lounge and leathery bar are great places to chill out and the stately restaurant is well worth trying (see *p306*). There are 25 bedrooms in the main hotel and a further 18 around what was once a bowling green (stay in the former if possible); decor is unobtrusive and bathrooms are bright and shiny. Breakfast is outstanding. But what impress most are the breezy friendliness and efficiency of the staff. A hotel very much at ease with itself. Children welcome. No-smoking rooms available.

Wentworth Hotel

Wentworth Road, Aldeburgh, IP15 5BD (01728 452312/01728 454343/www.wentworth-aldeburgh. com). **Rates** £67-£73 single; £107-£130 twin/double; £10 each additional child in parents' room. **Rooms** 6 single (4 en suite, 2 with private bath); 31 double/ twin (all en suite). **Credit** AmEx, DC, MC, V.

Owned by the Pritt family since 1920, this agreeably traditional hotel enjoys a fine seafront location. The bedrooms vary in size, but are all prettily decorated, and most have en suite bathrooms and sea views. There is a garden terrace, bar and restaurant, and there are open fires in the antique- and book-filled lounges. Children welcome. Dogs welcome (£2 per night). All bedrooms no-smoking.

Where to eat & drink

The best pubs in Southwold are those that allow al fresco spillover in fine weather. Try the **Lord Nelson**, between Market Hill and the sea (you can take your pint of Adnams to the seafront; the pub does a mean prawn sandwich) or the **Red Lion**, where drinkers chill out on the lovely South Green. Another food option besides those listed below is **Drifters Bistro** (36 East Street; 01502 714806).

In Woodbridge, the best pub is the **King's Head** on the High Street (01502 724517), which offers a wide range of good food, or you can try the Thai-Malaysian dishes at **Spice Bar Restaurant & Café** (17 The Thoroughfare; 01394 382557). In Aldeburgh, the **Regatta** (171 High Street; 01728 452011) offers reliable global

Testing times

Probably the most desolate spot in East Anglia, the ten-mile expanse of Orford Ness is the largest vegetated shingle spit in Europe, and a unique habitat for plants and birds. But it was not always so peaceful. The strangely shaped buildings peppering its wind-whipped bleakness provide clues to the spit's hush-hush past, for it served as the site of secret MOD research facilities for much of the 20th century.

During World War I an airfield was established here, and Number 37 Squadron, Royal Flying Corps was formed at Orford as an experimental unit (testing, among other things, early versions of the parachute and aerial photography techniques). In the 1920s the Ness was extensively used for armaments testing – the Black Beacon, south of the lighthouse, built to contain a navigation beacon, dates from that time.

Research was stepped up considerably in the 1930s, the most important period being '35-37 when Robert Watson-Watt and his team founded the 'Ionospheric Research Station', a cover for the R&D of the aerial defence system later to be known as radar.

The site was used by the Atomic Weapons Research Establishment from 1953 until '76. In 1968, work began on a top-secret Anglo-American System radar project, code-named 'Cobra Mist'. It was intended to fulfil a number of functions, including the detection and tracking of aircraft, but is best known for its alleged associations with UFOs. Following a number of problems, the project was abandoned in 1973. BBC

World Service transmitters can now be found in one of its buildings.

Orford Ness then narrowly missed becoming the home to a nuclear power station (Sizewell, just up the coast, was eventually favoured), before being taken over by the National Trust in the early 1990s, and finally returning to nature.

Today, you can find such rare botanical treats as the yellow horned poppy and the purple flowering sea pea, and, on neighbouring Havergate Island, a major nesting site for avocets. The only access to the spit is from Orford Quay, and it is deliberately limited to preserve the fragile ecostructure. There are monthly guided walks with the **National Trust Warden** (01394 450900; book in advance).

Orford Ness
(access info & ferry crossings 01394 450057/www.nationaltrust.org.uk).
Ferries *Mid Apr-June, Oct* 10am-2pm Sat (last return ferry leaves Orford Ness at 5pm). *July-Sept* 10am-2pm Tue-Sat. Closed Oct-mid Apr. **Tickets** £5.60; £2.80-£3.20 concessions; free under-3s.

dishes, and if you fancy a snack, the excellent café and sandwich shop **Scandelicious** (165 High Street) specialises in Nordic goodies.

Other pubs worth a visit are the **Crown Inn** (good for nosh; 01728 688324), and the **Golden Key** (01728 688510), both in Snape, and the fish-oriented **Froize Inn** (01394 450282) in Chillesford, not far from Orford. In Aldeburgh, you can try the **White Lion** (Market Cross Place), the **Mill** (Market Cross Place) or the flower-festooned **Cross Keys** (Crab Street), but the pick is the tiny, friendly, locals-packed **White Hart** on the High Street. Many folk grab fish and chips from the shop next door and devour them outside the pub, pint in hand.

Swan Hotel – one of Southwold's finest.

152

152 High Street, Aldeburgh (01728 454152/ www.lawsons152.co.uk). **Food served** *July-Sept* noon-2.30pm, 6-9.30pm Wed-Sun. *Oct-June* noon-2.30pm, 6-9pm Wed-Sun. **Credit** MC, V.
Warm terracotta paint and candlelight combine to provide a soothing backdrop for equally warming Med-influenced dishes. Regular favourites include a superb risotto nero with griddled squid (£5 as a starter) and simple treatment of local fish (such as grilled cod smothered in herby butter, £7.50). Grilled duck breast with cassoulet and spinach (£12.75) was particularly memorable, and service was friendly and efficient. A class act. Advance booking recommended.

Butley Orford Oysterage

Market Hill, Orford (01394 450277). **Food served** *Apr-Oct* noon-2.15pm, 7-9pm Mon-Fri; noon-2.15pm, 6-9pm Sat; noon-2.15pm, 6.30-9pm Sun. *Nov-Mar* noon-2.15pm Mon-Thur, Sun; noon-2.15pm, 6.30-9pm Fri; noon-2.15pm, 6-9pm Sat. **Credit** MC, V.
This long-standing Orford favourite is a top spot for quality local seafood. It's fairly spartan inside, so there's little to detract from the keenly priced and feisty-fresh fish – perhaps simple griddled squid (£6.50) or baked sea bass (£12.50). Advance booking recommended.

Captain's Table

3 Quay Street, Woodbridge (01394 383145/ www.captainstable.co.uk). **Food served** noon-2pm, 6.30-9.30pm Tue-Thur; noon-2pm, 6.30-10pm Fri, Sat; noon-3pm Sun. **Credit** MC, V.
The name isn't particularly promising, but, while there's plenty of fish on the regular and specials menus, the lack of nautical decorative theming in the three interconnecting dining rooms gives a clue that this pub/restaurant is of a superior breed. Expect the likes of sea bass with pernod and dill cream sauce (£10), squid ink risotto (£8.95) and skate with black butter and capers (£9.95).

Crown Hotel

90 High Street, Southwold (01502 722275). **Food served** 12.30-1.30pm, 7.30-9.30pm daily. **Set lunches** £16.50 2 courses; £19.50 3 courses. **Set dinners** £22 2 courses; £27 3 courses. **Credit** AmEx, DC, MC, V.
Probably the premier dining spot in Southwold, such is the Crown's popularity that tables can spill across the entrance hall from the lively bar-brasserie to the more sedate Parlour. The set-price lunch menu offers the likes of warm chicken salad with strawberries, followed by confit of duck leg with aubergine and herb-crushed potatoes, or curried parsnip soup, then sweet potato and Emmental pie with pearl barley broth. As Adnams Wine Merchants is based behind the Crown, you'd expect a varied and interesting wine list – and that is exactly what you get. Advance booking recommended.

The Lighthouse

77 High Street, Aldeburgh (01728 453377). **Food served** noon-2.30pm, 7-10pm daily. **Set meals** £13.75 2 courses; £16.50 3 courses. **Credit** MC, V.
Café and deli by day, the versatile Lighthouse shines brightest in the evening when its excellent value fixed-priced menu delivers such goodies as celery and roquefort soup, and roast Aldeburgh cod on steamed spinach with sun-dried tomato oil, or potted shrimps and duck breast with fennel and orange sauce. Boozy banana pancake is a classy way to finish. The wine list is notable – both for its range, quality and the very reasonable prices. Advance booking recommended.

Swan Hotel

Market Place, Southwold (01502 722186/ www.adnams.co.uk). **Food served** noon-1.30pm, 7-9.30pm daily. **Set lunches** £18 2 courses; £20 3 courses. **Set dinner** £26.50 3 courses. **Credit** AmEx, DC, MC, V.
The salmon-pink restaurant at the famous Swan can't quite shake off that hotel dining-room feel, but don't let that put you off. The napery may be starched but the service isn't, and the lunch menu promises the likes of pot roast of rabbit leg stuffed with Puy lentils wrapped in bacon with braised leeks (£8.90) and seared calf's liver, bacon and black pudding with red wine jus. All dishes are cooked with flair. *See also p304.*

The Trinity

Crown & Castle, Orford (01394 450205/ www.crownandcastlehotel.co.uk). **Food served** noon-2.30pm, 6.30-9.30pm daily. **Credit** MC, V.
The reputation of the Crown and Castle hotel in Orford (*see p304*) has improved around since it was taken over a couple of years ago. Its restaurant has established itself as one of the local gastronomic beacons, thanks to chef Brendan Ansbro's assured and inspired melding of the local and far-flung – classic dishes such as sirloin steak with béarnaise butter and (wonderful) hand-cut chips (£14) sit comfortably alongside oriental stunners such as Asian-style squid and crisp pork belly salad (£11). Effortlessly classy, thoroughly relaxed: a gem of a place.

East Anglia

The best for...

In addition to the standard index (*see p311*) we have compiled the following list of attractions by type, so that, say, the Roman-obsessed motoring enthusiast with kids to placate and a partner who's into beer and East Asian art can find the break with the maximum number of attractions to suit them.

Advertisers' Index

**Please refer to relevant sections for
addresses / telephone numbers**

Index

Exton, Rutland 246
Eyebrook Reservoir 246